W9-ABG-203

LITERATURE AND AMERICAN LIFE

FOR STUDENTS OF AMERICAN LITERATURE

By PERCY H. BOYNTON

GINN AND COMPANY

BOSTON · NEW YORK · CHICAGO · LONDON · ATLANTA

DALLAS · COLUMBUS · SAN FRANCISCO

436.3

The Athenæum Press
GINN AND COMPANY · PRO-
PRIETORS · BOSTON · U.S.A.

TO

THE STUDENTS AND SCHOLARS

THE CRITICS AND LIBRARIANS

TO WHOM

I AM IN DEBT

PREFACE

FAMOUS books and authors are data in the history of national ideas. The course of thought in America can be traced through its relation, near or remote, to religious and ethical controls. It is a line that passes through the dominance of religious faith and ethical precept in the seventeenth century, the challenge to the altar by the shop till and the flag in the eighteenth century, the challenge of the nineteenth century to the flag by the treasure vault and the machines it served, the twentieth-century breakdown of the money-changers after their capture of flag and machine and altar. And according to the weight of present evidence, as I see it, among both populace and intellectual leaders, something invincibly American is making fresh estimates as to the things that are desirable and praiseworthy and is facing the future perhaps with less confidence but with unshaken hope.

In following this line of thought I have tried to deal scrupulously with the writers and writings passed in review and to avoid forcing a thesis. I am sure that there are many other factors in American literature, many other illuminating approaches; and I have tried to indicate their places and proportions. Fortunately for the readers of literary history the chief documents are easily available to anyone who will stop running long enough to read.

It is impossible to make due and explicit acknowledgment to all who have helped toward this formulation. I have thanked them one by one, and I thank them together on the dedicatory page.

PERCY H. BOYNTON

ACKNOWLEDGMENTS

GRATEFUL acknowledgment is made to the following publishers, authors, and their representatives for permission to use selections held under copyright:

COWARD-MCCANN, INC.: "Our Singing Strength," by ALFRED KREYMBORG, reprinted by permission of Coward-McCann, Inc.

DODD, MEAD & COMPANY, INC.: "Along the Trail," by RICHARD HOVEY; and "Marching Men," by SHERWOOD ANDERSON, used by permission of Dodd, Mead & Company, Inc.

DOUBLEDAY, DORAN AND COMPANY, INC.: "The Pit," by FRANK NORRIS, copyright, 1903, by Doubleday, Doran and Company, Inc.

HARCOURT, BRACE AND COMPANY, INC.: "Main Street," by SINCLAIR LEWIS; and "Criticism in America," by H. L. MENCKEN, used by permission of Harcourt, Brace and Company, Inc.

HARPER & BROTHERS: "Life on the Mississippi," by MARK TWAIN; "Expression in America," by LUDWIG LEWISOHN; and "American Drama from the Civil War to the Present," by A. H. QUINN, used by permission of Harper & Brothers.

HENRY HOLT AND COMPANY: "Chicago Poems" and "Cornhuskers," by CARL SANDBURG; and "New Hampshire," "Mountain Interval," and "A Boy's Will," by ROBERT FROST, used by permission of Henry Holt and Company.

HOUGHTON MIFFLIN COMPANY: The extracts from "Poems and Poetic Dramas," by WILLIAM VAUGHN MOODY; "Education of Henry Adams," by HENRY ADAMS; "The Writings of Lafcadio Hearn"; "The Gentle Reader," by S. M. CROTHERS; "Life of Sill," by W. D. PARKER; and "Before the Altar," and "Chopin," by AMY LOWELL, used by permission of, and arrangement with, Houghton Mifflin Company.

MISS MILDRED HOWELLS: "Traveler from Altruria" (copyright, 1894, by Harper & Brothers; copyright, 1921, by Mildred Howells and John Mead Howells) and "Literary Friends and Acquaintances" (copyright, 1900, by Harper & Brothers; copyright, 1928, by Mildred Howells and John Mead Howells), by WILLIAM DEAN HOWELLS.

ALFRED A. KNOPF, INC.: The extracts from "A Man Said to the Universe," by STEPHEN CRANE; "The Mauve Decade," by THOMAS BEER; and "A Book of Prefaces," by H. L. MENCKEN. Reprinted by permission of, and special arrangement with, Alfred A. Knopf, Inc., authorized publishers.

J. B. LIPPINCOTT COMPANY: "An Hour of American Drama," by BARRETT CLARK, used by permission of J. B. Lippincott Company.

LITTLE, BROWN AND COMPANY: "The Poems of Emily Dickinson," Centenary Edition, edited by MARTHA DICKINSON BIANCHI and ALFRED LEETE HAMPSON.

LIVERIGHT PUBLISHING CORPORATION: "Collected Poems of Hart Crane," copyright, 1933, Liveright Publishing Corporation.

ROBERT M. MCBRIDE & COMPANY: "Beyond Life," "The Cream of the Jest," "The Cords of Vanity," and "The Rivet in Grandfather's Neck," by JAMES BRANCH CABELL, used by permission of Robert M. McBride & Company.

THE MACMILLAN COMPANY: "In Our Town," by WILLIAM ALLEN WHITE; "Peace in Friendship Village," by ZONA GALE; "The Village," by ERNEST POOLE; "The Medieval Mind," by HENRY OSBORN TAYLOR; "The Degradation of the Democratic Dogma," by HENRY ADAMS; and "Collected Poems" of EDWIN ARLINGTON ROBINSON, used by permission of The Macmillan Company.

CHARLES SCRIBNER'S SONS: "Partial Portraits," by HENRY JAMES; and "The Literary Mind," by MAX EASTMAN, used by permission of Charles Scribner's Sons.

SIMON AND SCHUSTER, INC.: "Hey-Rub-a-Dub-Dub," by THEODORE DREISER, used by permission of Simon and Schuster.

THE SOUTHWEST PRESS: "Vaquero of the Brush Country," by J. FRANK DOBIE, used by permission of The Southwest Press.

THE UNIVERSITY OF NORTH CAROLINA PRESS: "Joel Chandler Harris: Editor and Essayist," used by permission of The University of North Carolina Press.

THE VIKING PRESS, INC.: "Horses and Men," by SHERWOOD ANDERSON. Copyright, 1923, by B. W. Huebsch, Inc. Published by The Viking Press, Inc., New York.

HARR WAGNER PUBLISHING CO.: "Joaquin Miller's Poems," Bear Edition, six volumes, used by permission of the Harr Wagner Publishing Co.

CONTENTS

Part I · *The Early Period*

CHAPTER I

CHAPTER II

CHAPTER III

CHAPTER IV

CHAPTER V

CHAPTER VI

CONTENTS

Part II · *The Middle Years*

CHAPTER VII

CHAPTER VIII

CHAPTER IX

CHAPTER X

CHAPTER XI

PART III · *The Recent Past*

CHAPTER XII

CHAPTER XIII

PART I

The Early Period

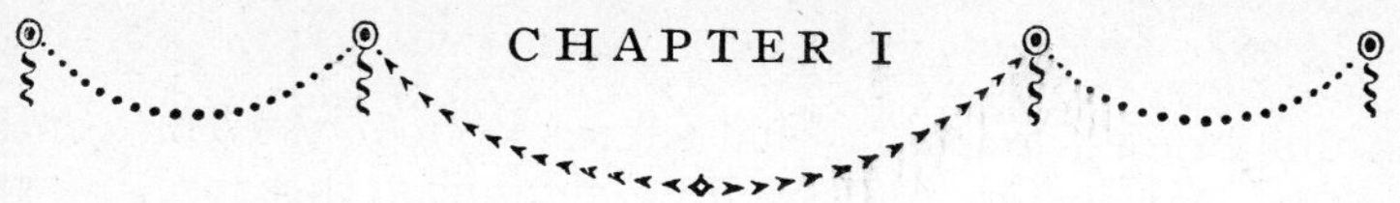

CHAPTER I

Colonial Backgrounds

The Legacy from the Middle Ages

THE first of the thirteen American colonies were English in parentage, western European in heritage, Mediterranean in remoter ancestry; and it was characteristic of these colonies, as of America to the present time, that they were oblivious to any civilization west of the British Isles or east of the Holy Land, — beyond the experience, as it were, of the crusading Richard of the Lion Heart. To confine the question of their descent to the narrow limits of western Europe and the countries from Italy to Palestine is to think of them as deriving from the Saxons and the Celts of the Gaul invaded by Caesar and from the Greco-Roman culture which he represented. They traced their early lineage, therefore, to a pagan barbarism and a pagan civilization. They could look back over the period when the pagan civilization was Christianized and when the missionary monk followed the conquering soldier. We of the present can see in the ten centuries bridged between the founding of the first monastery in western Europe and the settlement of the first colony in North America the long interplay and final fusing of those racial stocks and cultural traditions into the Elizabethan Englishmen who became forefathers of the dominant strain in modern North America.

One of the soundest historians of the Middle Ages[1] has

[1] Henry Osborn Taylor, "The Mediaeval Mind." 2 vols. See Chapter I, "Genesis of the Mediaeval Genius," p. 13, and, thereafter, Chapter III, "Greek Antecedents," pp. 50, 52–54, 58–60; Chapter IV, "The Patristic Mind," pp. 70, 74; Chapter IX, "The Conversion of the North," pp. 170, 195; Chapter XII, "The Eleventh Century; France," pp. 302, 306, 307; Chapter XXV, "Methods of Scholasticism," pp. 317, 324; Chapter XXVI, "Stages of Evolution," p. 359; Chapter XXXVIII, "The New Knowledge," p. 409.

put in briefest terms a characterization of the thirteenth-century European. It is doubly significant because he was probably unaware of how relevant it was to the seventeenth-century colonist on the Atlantic seaboard:

> The Latin Christianity of the Fathers and the antique fund of sentiment and knowledge, through their self-conserving strength, affected men in constant ways. Under their action the peoples of western Europe . . . passed through a homogeneous growth, and evolved . . . a spirit which stood in awe before its monitors divine and human, and deemed that knowledge was to be drawn from the storehouse of the past; which seemed to rely on everything except its sin-crushed self, and trusted everything except its senses; which in the actual looked for the ideal, in the concrete saw the symbol, in the earthly Church beheld the heavenly, and in fleshly joys discerned the devil's lures; which lived in the unreconciled opposition between the lust and vainglory of earth and the attainment of salvation; which felt life's terror and its pitifulness, and its eternal hope; around which waved concrete infinitudes, and over which flamed the terror of darkness and the Judgment Day.[1]

This description of two sets of men four centuries and three thousand miles apart is the more striking because of the steps that lead from one to the other. They trace the story of an invasion of a pagan world by a Christian dogma and, as the invasion progressed, of a struggle in which was fought the issue between enjoying the life of the present and saving the soul for the enjoyment of an afterlife. This in turn was resolvable into a series of conflicts between theory and practice; between an established faith and an increasing and opposing body of fact. And these conflicts led the lords of the invading civilization to the necessity of controlling or interpreting or even inventing facts to fit the patterns stamped in the forge of dogma.

The success of Christianity in coming to terms with pagan superstition, myth, and legend is a commonplace in intellectual history. It converted healing springs into places of baptism, heathen places of worship into church sites, bar-

---

[1] Taylor, op. cit. Vol. I, p. 13.

baric festivals into church days. It was the way of least resistance to pagan traditions that could not be stamped out. Thus in the fourth century — though the leaders of the Christians were superior in mind to the pagan priests and philosophers, and though intellectually the pagan cause was a lost and uninspiring cause — the Christian doctors could only assimilate and rechristen what they could not dismiss from the pagan mind; for though the transformation was often only a thin disguise, the pagan belief in magic, in the need for placating hostile spirits, in devils, angels, and supernatural interventions, had to be adopted and justified in the writings of the priesthood. This was not a weak concession: it was a basis of strength. The Fathers started from the assumption that the fundamentals of the Christian faith were beyond proof or disproof; and in their literal acceptance of divine revelation, the virgin birth, and the doctrine of the risen Christ, they subscribed to the acceptance of the miraculous on principle. The very incredibility of their premises made them the more credible to a world which was used to such beliefs, and attuned their own minds to the minds of those whom they wished to convert.

Moreover, this primitive approach to the mysteries of life, death, and the hereafter did not make the Christian formula acceptable only to the populace. It was reinforced by the likeness between the Christian concept of the salvation of man through the mediation of the Saviour and the doctrines of the newest school of philosophy. For the Neoplatonists were also intent on finding a system of mediation between man and the absolute First Principle. And the likeness did not disappear even when the Neoplatonists became divided; for, just as in Christian theology, the more elevated form was based on an ecstatic vision, a revelation not unlike that of the resurrection, atonement, and salvation, and the more popular form relied on "a principle of credulity more and more agape for fascinating or helpful miracles." [1] Thus, after the desire

[1] Taylor, op. cit. Vol. I, p. 58.

for salvation led men to become Christians and the God-man proved to be the sufficient mediator between man and God, a whole machinery of mediation was adopted that was closely parallel to the mediatorial persons, acts, and things of paganism. "The mediatorial persons were the Virgin and the saints; the sacraments were the magic mediatorial acts; the relic was the magic mediatorial thing."[1] Over all was the revelation of the Intercessor and the God to whom he was the approach. Below, as in all pagan thought, were the "conduits of credulity" to the superrational heights.

In the course of the Middle Ages, as Rome became the seat of increasing power, secular and religious, the Church of Rome became increasingly on guard against anything that menaced it; in consequence of which it subjected every branch of human inquiry and intellectual interest to its own ends. The theological bias of the Church Fathers closed their minds to many historical and natural facts and set them to making special interpretations of the rest. Knowledge of mankind or of nature could not be sought in the mood of open inquiry, for the conclusions of inquiry were predetermined. And throughout the Middle Ages the influence of the Vatican limited the substance of approved knowledge, and the task of the scholar was confined to apprehending, adopting, reexpressing, and reinterpreting. As the generations passed, a masterly technique was developed and an enormous momentum was gained.

So it followed that when the Church of Rome sent its emissaries to the northern countries they offered the unschooled peoples greater supernatural aid, a more impressive body of knowledge, and a more orderly theory of creation and fate than anything they had evolved for themselves. The authority with which the churchmen spoke was convincing enough to enlist the new converts and hold the allegiance of the generations to follow. The receivers of the gospel stood ignorant before the learned, and docile before

[1] Taylor, op. cit. Vol. I, p. 60.

intellectual and spiritual dictators. Yet each new northern region, however receptive of the new dogma, supplied its own quota of folklore and superstition, its own magic and miracle, which had to be incorporated into the religion imposed upon it. And the assimilation regularly took place. Again let us note that this was not true of the ignorant alone. "Even the Alexandria of the Ptolemies, with all the pedantry of its learned litterateurs and their minute study of the past, has nothing to offer like the . . . mediaeval University, which sought to set upon one throne the antique philosophy and the Christian revelation, that it might with one and the same genuflection bow down before them both."[1]

This temper of mind, a composite of elements native to western Europe, invaded and evangelized by centuries of emissaries from the shores of the Mediterranean, included the common factors in the lands that are now Germany, France, and Great Britain. It would be natural to infer that with the incursion of the New Learning the old partnership between mystical religion and popular superstition would be dissolved; but, as a matter of fact, the dissolution of partnership has been in process ever since. What was true of Christianized paganism under the Church of Rome continued to be true of the intellectual nature of Protestant Christianity, whether Continental or Anglican. What was true of the Anglican priesthood gained rather than lost at the hands of the nonconformists. Striking changes are recordable in terms of church polity, but in terms of fundamental belief all the churchmen deferred to the authority of the Scriptures; practically all accepted the secondary authority of traditional interpretations; the majority felt that any discord between the fruits of inquiry and the tenets of revealed truth must be accounted for by the feebleness of the human mind in its attempts to fathom the ways of God; and not even the most erudite questioned that a wonder-working Providence, ready to intervene at every moment and in every least event, was

[1] Taylor, op. cit. Vol. II, p. 409.

nevertheless actively and effectively opposed by the wiles of the devil. What the historian has declared of the intellectual equipment of the Christian Fathers was destined to be hardly less true of John Cotton, of the Mathers, of Michael Wigglesworth, and of the generations before whom they stood. For two hundred years the average Protestant communicant in America still stood in awe before his monitors, divine and human; seemed to rely on everything except his sin-crushed self; "in the earthly Church beheld the heavenly, in fleshly joys discerned the devil's lures"; and lived in the terror of darkness and the Judgment Day. Whatever he may have thought on questions of state, — and he thought much, — the determinative influence of what he accepted without thinking stamped the seventeenth-century colonist in America as an heir to the Middle Ages with the marks of his ancestry upon him.

His heritage did not stop here, of course; but the influences from classical days all came to him sifted through this medium. The colonist inherited the youthfulness of Greece,[1] the zest for life, the elevation of spirit. The period of the New Learning had reawakened him to it as if by the finding of a long-mislaid document, and the thrills it aroused were his to enjoy. If it had not been for this the march of exploration would not have brought him to the New World, would not have emboldened shipload after shipload to make the venture in face of the disasters to those who had preceded them. Greek learning had itself been supplanted at many a point, but Greek art had not; and the Greek spirit had communicated itself across the millenniums so that in the seventeenth century, just as two thousand years before, there was a fresh exhilaration in the air, a sense of walking in new paths and of dawning hopes and untried possibilities, a confidence that all things could be won if only men tried hard enough. Yet between the youthfulness and the exhila-

---

[1] Gilbert Murray, "The Value of Greece to the Future of the World," in "The Legacy of Greece," edited by R. W. Livingstone.

ration of the age of Pericles and the same eager traits in the age of Shakespeare the Middle Ages had intervened; and their centuries, in terms of intellectual experience, had been elderly and laborious, managing to preserve their standard customs but ever and again lapsing into recessive ways in spite of new impulses or, on the other hand, responding to new impulses yet halted by chains of antique workmanship whose links had been wrought in the reaches of the past. The free spirits of Elizabethan days had to fight clear of medieval theologians in their response to a happier paganism. The Elizabethan generation was still held fast in churchly shackles — whether Anglican or dissenter the bondage was close; and the dissenters, less susceptible to the charms of the New Learning, were more clearly medieval in their mental habits. Thus it befell that the brash Argonauts of the Western world who came to Jamestown came with the echoes of a theological strife ringing in their ears; and the Pilgrims and Puritans of Plymouth and Massachusetts Bay, though they were fighting in a great cause, cited no authorities from Hellas, relied on the authority of the Scriptures, accepted in all literalness the stories of Abraham and the burning bush, of Moses and the revelation on the mountain top, of Saul and the blinding light, and among the spiritual leaders were content to rest their cases with Luther and with Calvin. The colonist's legacy from Greece had suffered vital restrictions on its way down to him through the Middle Ages.

So also had the Roman spirit of conquest, love of order, sense of law. For the common law of England was in reality a native Germanic growth which at most adopted various features from the Roman code. It was a thousand years removed from its forerunner, and had been modified in its essential meaning by a thousand years of Christian ethics and of rising churchly domination. Turn, therefore, to the absorbing problem of subject and sovereign, earthly or heavenly, and the formulas are very much the same for Church and for State. The Biblical concepts of the King of Kings and the Prince of Peace were secular in their source and phrasing;

but they prevailed the better through the Middle Ages as the Pope held his own against the emperors. The most insistent interpreter of American thought in terms of political theory[1] comes no further than his first page before he acknowledges that the seventeenth-century colonial picture must be viewed through a lens of medieval making: "And it was the interweaving of the aims and purposes of these acquisitive yeomen and gentry . . . with the ideal of a theocracy and the inhibitions of a Puritan dogma, that constitutes the pattern of life to be dealt with here."[2]

Possibly the British, more isolated than their Continental neighbors, retained their medieval traits in heightened degree. Certainly the Saxon, no less animistic or primitive than the Celt, seems to have been a fallower subject for sober ethical controls. From the Norman Conquest on, the "blond beasts," described by their Celtic critic, conceded with the passing centuries something of the ravenous lust for food and drink, something of the lusty love of the fight, and gained something in the enjoyment of beauty. Chivalry adorned, redeemed, subdued, their barbarity; Christianity, their paganism.[3] Yet up to the sixteenth century the populace were still emerging from serfdom, and the rulers from the influence of a Romish Church and a Frankish court culture, though neither of these was assimilated, neither destined to dominate that strangely irresistible Saxon nature which in the end seems always to have overcome its conquerors as well as its subjects. Up to this time, too, it had gone far toward evolving its own literature and preserving its own evolving language.

Then into this stream, established in its deepening channel, came the fresh tributary stream from the south and the past; and the combination of the two, in the brief period almost compassed by Shakespeare's lifetime, was accompanied by one of the great outbursts of the English heart and mind.

---

[1] V. L. Parrington, "The Colonial Mind."

[2] Ibid. p. 3.

[3] H. A. Taine, "History of English Literature," Book I.

Something memorable happened which liberated English life, set old energies at work, awakened new dreams, and did not subside until England had set at naught its most dreaded enemy, had started on its imperial career, had freed itself from Rome, had in its fine frenzy emancipated itself for a while from kingship, and had spent itself at last in civil war and revolution.

The English Heritage

In one sense it may be said that there is no danger of overstating the wide and deep effects on the English nature of the Reformation and the Renaissance. In another sense there is every danger of implying, or inferring, that the old was swept away by the new. The old is never eliminated at a stroke; and in the colonial mind the survivals of pre-Elizabethan traits showed extraordinary vitality. The story of Elizabethan England is the story of medieval Europe in reverse. In the earlier story primitive paganism was overwhelmed by Christianity — cabined, cribbed, and confined by it. By the time the church had attained the ascendancy, when theology had beclouded religion, ritual had replaced worship, and external discipline had shouldered out self-control, the pendulum swing was due for reform within the church and reaction against it. The story of the Renaissance in England is the story — unchurchly, nontheological — of the reassertion of the pagan spirit. In an absorption in the nature of the world and of man, in the study of himself and his surroundings, in the early excursions of modern science, man found the whole realm of fact opened up as a territory that he could enter as an intelligent inquirer, relatively free — in theory utterly free — to accept the answers to his questions regardless of creed or dogma. It amounted to a counter-attack of cultural paganism on Christian culture. It brought in its train not only the beginnings of a new understanding of the facts of life but also a new zest for it. It was the spirit that could break through Hamlet's melancholy and cause him to exclaim on "this goodly frame, the earth . . . this most excellent canopy, the air . . . this brave o'erhanging firmament, this majestical roof, fretted with golden fire," and to continue with, "What a piece of work is man! how noble in reason! how infinite in faculty! in form and moving, how express and admirable! in action, how like an angel! in apprehension, how like a god! the beauty of the world! the paragon of animals!" It dealt a hard blow to the theory of asceticism that still survives in the Orient, and it set in motion the Occidental concept that it is good for the community to enjoy common wealth, common comfort, a high standard of living, a multiplication and satisfaction of needs. The building of chimneys and the building of theaters find their common source with the rise of poetry and science, a buoyant nationalism, and a lust for exploration.

But it must be remembered that this same period brought about the exclusion of the theaters from London City while the drama was at its height, that the drama had fallen under the disapproval of the dominant church as soon as it had passed beyond its precincts and control, and that the children of Elizabeth's subjects succeeded in closing the theaters as a prelude to the decapitation of their gay and worldly monarch. The England of Elizabeth may have been worldly and merry; but in these qualities there was a conscious defiance or a conscious defense against a somber censoriousness that is one aspect of Platonism, that Arnold dubbed Hebraism, and that this latter day has loosely rechristened Puritanism. And it is certainly more than a straw in the moralistic wind that in the years when Shakespeare and Jonson and Marlowe were coming into their own "The Schoole of Abuse" had launched its "plesaunt invective against Poets, Pipers, Plaiers, Jesters and such like Catterpillers of a Commonwelth"; that Lodge had offered his "Defence" to Gosson; and that the preëminent document in literary criticism was Sidney's "Apologie for Poetrie."[1]

[1] For this controversy see "Elizabethan Critical Essays" (edited by Gregory Smith), Vol. I, Introduction, pp. xi–xxxi; Lodge's "Defence of Poetry," with bibliography, pp. 61–86; Sidney's "Apologie for Poetrie," pp. 148–207.

The domination of a dour-eyed ethics over Sidney's merry England is nowhere better attested than in the rhetorical procedure of his threefold defense. He started with a somewhat faint-hearted offensive: that poetry was the best of teachers. He continued with replies to the four main clauses in the indictment: that other kinds of knowledge were fruitful, that poetry was the parent of lies, that poetry was the nurse of abuse, and that Plato had condemned it. On this rare point at which the New Learning could be cited in support of the discipline of the church he was most deliberate and respectful, not flouting the theologian in his adversary but appealing to his scholarship by citing the counter authorities of Socrates and Aristotle. It was not until he had thus screwed his courage to the sticking point that he ventured first to estimate the values of certain English writers and at last to be merry in his gaily brilliant peroration. England was still a school of morals; and though it may have had its truants and evidently admired them, it was still evidently living as in its great Taskmaster's eye.

The Colonial Problem

For these reasons the assertion has often been made that if you scratch the Cavalier you will find the Puritan beneath. Yet in spite of this epigram it has been the habit of literary historians to stress the great differences between the settlers at Jamestown and those at Plymouth, and to declare of them all that they were offspring of a dual England without recognition of their complex lengthening ancestry. At the risk of wearisome insistence two statements must be repeated: first, that the seventeenth-century American colonist, whether English or Continental, was a descendant from the Middle Ages; second, that the colonists of New England were peculiarly the heirs of the Middle Ages because the religious ideals of the Puritans and the separatists were narrow and inadequate, exclusive and pharisaical, and, in their exclusiveness, disregarded or distrusted the liberating influences of art and literature and science. They were protestants alike from the Church of Rome and from the school of the New Learning. Exceptions may be cited, of course; but the generalization holds good.

Only against the background of such a remoter heritage can one safely project the colonists' legacies from a nearer past. After all, and in spite of all the European origins of colonial life, English became the common language of the settlers, and old England contributed their dominant cultural traits. It is true that the earliest utterances from the South, before that section lapsed into comparative silence, reflected in little flashes the literary and scholastic enthusiasms of Shakespeare's England. The social life along the Maine coast, in the days when this district nominally belonged to the Massachusetts colony, was Elizabethan in so far as that word denotes an expansive and tolerant enjoyment of life.[1] But the so-called Puritan strain was the most assertive in both deed and word. It was a product of Reformation rather than Renaissance; but between the Reformation and the migration to America there had intervened a long struggle in England which marked the breakdown of feudalism and the upspringing of capitalism; and in the realignment of the relations of the citizen-communicant to state and church there followed an early assertion of what was one day to be called the doctrine of the natural rights of man. Thus the New England of the seventeenth century was in one sense a haven for the disaffected element in the old country; but it was also a battleground on which the issues of liberalism were being refought. For the broad victory was far from won with the landing at Plymouth or the settlement at Boston.

The word "Puritan," unhappily, has been used for three centuries in both a general and a particular sense. In popular parlance, both in its own day and at present, it sounds a

[1] Dane Yorke, "Shakespeare's New England," in the *American Mercury* (January, 1931), pp. 63–70; and, passim, Whittier's "Leaves from Margaret Smith's Journal," 1847.

note of derision at people who hold to strict standards of conduct and incline to impose them on others. "All good behaviour," wrote John Burgess in 1631,[1] "is scorned of many, as a matter of *Puritanisme,* and so tearmed." The scorn was still active in 1931. Yet as early as 1588 John Udall, in his "Demonstration," had offered a fair definition when he wrote,[2] "I mean them, that are not contented with the state, but mislike the gouernment of the Church, and would haue a new forme of gouernment." In this technical sense the Puritans stood between the Anglicans, who were content with the existing Church of England in itself and in its relations to the state, and the separatists, who were for repudiating the church rather than for capturing control and reforming it. Speaking in terms of religious sects the Anglicans are self-defined, the Puritans were at first advocates of the Presbyterian church polity, and the separatists approved the looser federation and the greater freedom of Congregationalism. Or, again, in political terms the Anglicans may be likened to Conservatives, the Puritans to Liberals, and the separatists to the more nearly radical element in politics for which each generation has its own abusive name.

In his essay on Milton, Macaulay wrote that "the Puritans were men whose minds had derived a peculiar quality from the daily contemplation of superior beings and eternal interests." It is immensely suggestive in connection with men of whom it is true; but it was equally true of the leading Puritans, and rather more urgently true, that their minds were affected by the depth to which they were involved in practical controversy. They began their long campaign with a resolve to purify the church from within, and with the insistent declaration that though they were bent on regulating their own church they were not less bent on rendering unto kingship all that was its due. What was due, however, turned out in their interpretation to be a little less than the

[1] Quoted by Perry Miller, "Orthodoxy in Massachusetts." The next several paragraphs are indebted to this work.

[2] Ibid.

supremacy that the Stuarts demanded. As a consequence the Puritans found themselves in a trying dilemma, fighting for a freedom and asserting a loyalty that could not be reconciled. They denied that they were separatists, but they could not win their way within the church. For a while it seemed that they could compromise the point by setting up their church so far from England that separatism could be actual without being acknowledged in theory. And in New England they sought first, last, and always for the churchly control to which they had always in theory subscribed.

To accomplish this they had first to organize a church according to the "due form" which they felt was acceptable to God, and to keep complete mastery over it; and, second, to maintain a state which ruled in harmony with the church. They were able to regulate the church by refusing to legalize groups of worshipers who did not commend themselves and by rejecting individual applicants for membership; they developed a discipline based on the Scriptures and a method for preserving uniformity. They were as completely in control of their own ecclesiastical organization as the Anglicans had been of the organization they had failed to capture in old England. But the task of harmonizing church and state was not so simple a one. The state "could hardly rule in accordance with Puritan ideals until it had first demonstrated it could rule at all";[1] and it faced the double need of shaking off English interference and controlling its own populace.

In political activities the Puritans demonstrated as practical an efficiency as they did in commerce and banking. It was in one mood that they prostrated themselves before their Maker, and in quite another that they set their feet upon the neck of a king. Even when they called for divine assistance they did not neglect the values of human aid, frustrating a hostile move at court, as Winthrop put it, "through the Lord's good providence, and the care of our friends in England."[2] On the whole they were successful in

---

[1] Miller, op. cit. p. 212.

[2] Ibid. p. 216.

the early days in winning local freedom. England was too far off; New England was too inconsiderable to make expensive interference justifiable. But the churchmen were less successful in holding the mastery at home. The rebel at the moment of his rebellion invokes principles that prove awkward when he has climbed to the seats of the mighty. The Puritans had appealed to rights against the crown that seemed highly debatable when adduced against the governor and magistrates of Massachusetts. So there was resumed almost at once the struggle of the commoner with the government that had been long in progress across the seas. At once the leaders were involved in the punishment of the insurgent and the banishment of the unwelcome. Their tactics with Thomas Morton provoked one of the earliest American classics in his satire on the Puritan autocrats.[1] Their difficulties with the dissenters stirred Nathaniel Ward to his peppery and memorable assault on the doctrine of toleration of divers beliefs.[2] Committed to their narrow orthodoxy and convinced of the divine sanction behind it, they were nevertheless forced into the devious ways of the casuist in defense of their position. The Presbyterians, advocates of a limited democracy in the rule of the elders, were hard pushed by the more liberal. The elected representatives of the people were soon too genuinely representative in their conflicts with the magistrates and the governor. John Cotton before long was appealing to scriptural authority for monarchy and aristocracy, and feebly exclaiming: "Democracy, I do not conceyve that ever God did ordeyne as a fitt government eyther for church or commonwealth. If the people be governors, who shall be governed?"[3] The unceasing controversy between rival theories of the state, and between rival theories as to the relation of church and state, was

[1] Thomas Morton, "The New English Canaan," Book III; in "Force Tracts," Vol. II (1838), No. 5.

[2] Nathaniel Ward (pseud. Theodore de la Guard), "The Simple Cobler of Aggawam in America."

[3] Thomas Hutchinson, "The History of the Colony of Massachusetts-Bay," Vol. I, p. 497.

being redefined in terms of local conditions and colonial policies. The colonists were indeed products of a multiplex tradition; but they were lodged in a new environment which "taught them a new way of looking at the destiny of the common man, trained them in adaptation to the conditions of the New World." Slowly in terms of these new conditions, not the least of which was the intermingling of old national stocks in surroundings new to all of them, the new nation was prepared for. It is worth while, therefore, to conjure up a portrait of the typical leader of these earliest days.

The Puritan Type

He had been bred in a family circle where his earliest memories were filled with the echoes of Biblical speech; twice each day he had heard it in family worship, in reading and prayer, and at least four times on Sundays. As soon as he had passed his elementary schooling he had been headed for college and a further education that should further equip him to "foil the ould deluder, Satan."[1] In this advanced academy he had followed with minor modifications the pursuit of the seven liberal arts — grammar, logic, rhetoric, arithmetic, geometry, astronomy, music. Grammar, logic, and rhetoric meant the study of these subjects in Latin. The whole program was now intended to promote and reinforce the local Protestant orthodoxy. Under a college president recruited from the pulpit, "moral philosophy" was taught him in senior year. "Natural" philosophy was glanced at; but natural and biological science were never allowed to conflict with the Biblical story of creation, literally interpreted, or with the so-called Biblical chronology which dated the creation of man in the year 4004 B.C. "Speculative" philosophy — the secular fields of metaphysics, ontology, teleology, and so on — was regarded as dangerous if not sacrilegious. Of the world in which he lived, of his own body and mind, of the social order in its social behavior, of

[1] Massachusetts Bay Colony Statutes, 1647.

any art except oratory, of any literature as literature, he learned nothing in college. And the highest honor the college could confer on him was the privilege of delivering in Latin a series of platitudes in the commencement program.

With his memory thus meagerly stocked from the storehouse of the past, with no formal introduction to social theory, in a complete technical ignorance of his material surroundings, and accustomed with all his generation to accept from folklore the explanations that science failed to supply, the young collegian was launched on his career. And, being educated, he was almost committed to become a professional man — in the pulpit, in the classroom, in the courtroom, or in the service of the state.

Fortunately, however, he was still free to pursue his "adult education," and there is plenty of evidence to show that among the early settlers in Massachusetts and Connecticut he might be one of the noteworthy proportion of gentlemen and scholars during the first hundred years.[1] He had his private library. He was forever buying, borrowing, and corresponding about books; and these books were invariably classifiable into theological, scientific, and military works. (If no modern librarian would accept such a system, for it is in truth complexly overlapping, it has at least equal merits with the first Harvard catalogues, in which the books were listed as Folios, Quartos, Octavos, etc., and Supplementary.) Miles Standish's collection has been too often cited; a note from dealer to purchaser in 1634 is quite as typical and briefer: "I hau here alsoe sent you a few others, which if you like not, I pray send them againe, or any of them.

Mercurius Rediuiuus per Norton
The Rarities of Cochin China
Wingates Logarithmes
An English Grammer
The Gunners Dialogue
Bedwells Messolabium[2]

[1] Thomas Goddard Wright, "Literary Culture in Early New England, 1620–1730," p. 34.

[2] Ibid.

It was only a natural consequence of the requirement that students at Harvard must recite and converse in Latin for the reading of it to continue in every kind of learned work; so that in a library of 1686 it is not surprising that out of two hundred and eighteen books on mathematics, astronomy, and history one hundred and sixty were in Latin. But it is not quite so easy to rejoice in the list of books supplied to William Adams by his reverend father when the boy set out for Yale in 1726. Out of thirty-three (supplemented by "some of his father's sermons"), after fifteen Greek and Latin texts, a couple in English, and a singing book or two, come Bibles or Testaments in three tongues, a catechism, and four tracts culminating with "A Call to Backsliders" and "The Penitent Prodigal." William was amply forewarned and forearmed, and his father would justify some of the harsher strictures of the anti-Puritans if he had been a prevailing type. Speaking broadly, however, the outstanding feature of this early library was the presence of so many works in Latin and so few works of contemporary English literature.

This typical Puritan gentleman and scholar could thus enjoy relations with the reading men of the old country. Many of the first sojourners ended their lives back at home; those who remained here continued old friendships. During the Commonwealth, New England contributed soldiers and preachers to the Cromwell regime; there was an actual exchange of students between the universities and the one college; friendly services were done for Harvard by men of such different types as Sir Kenelm Digby, genial dilettante, Thomas Hollis, scholarly patron, and Bishop Berkeley, churchman. And, most significant of all, there was a slender but unbroken succession of members and contributors to the researches of the Royal Society.

As the years advance one can see two strong cultural tendencies continually suggested in the colonial book lists. One is the steady incursions of unorthodoxy which gave rise to such racy writing as Thomas Morton's "New English

Canaan" and Nathaniel Ward's "Simple Cobler of Aggawam"; and the other is the mellowing invasion of the Puritan precincts by secular, not to say ungodly, literature, as in the case of Bishop Berkeley's gift to Yale of over a thousand volumes, "including the best of English literature from Shakespeare and Bacon to Pope, Gay and Swift, with several volumes of plays — even Wycherley"; or as in the case of Robert Boulter's shipment of eight hundred books on consignment, which included, toward the end of the list,

12 dr Faustus	6 fortunatus
12 Joviall Garland	6 royall arbours
12 Crown Garland	8 Soggins jests
6 Garland of delight	4 Mandevills travells

4 pack cards[1]

Thus schooled, if he were a typical product of Puritan culture, the colonial leader was a religious man who thought of life on earth as a preparation for an afterlife, who took on his fear-ridden shoulders the burden of man's first sin and the vengeance of an angry God, who hoped for salvation but lived in dread of the eternal torment which was the just punishment for his natural depravity. As a citizen, however, he believed that in his relation to his fellow sinners he was endowed with natural rights of which he might not be despoiled, even though the rulers of both church and state held their powers under a divine sanction. As a citizen again he was satisfied that he belonged to the group who were born and bred to govern. He would grant a voice in public affairs to the commoner only under local limitations and with respect to the problems of the neighborhood. He knew that he was of the politically elect, and he was certain that power should be kept in the hands of the elect.

As a churchman he hoped for a like assurance. He yearned to be of the elect who were assured of salvation. He was resolved to exclude from the church all whose behavior debarred them and all whose views disqualified them. He was

[1] Wright, op. cit. p. 121.

resolved to prevent those of alien views from worshiping together in his community. He had his legal machinery at hand for the punishment of offenders, and if the worst came to the worst he was ready to banish them into the wilderness. He was a cruel man, living in a cruel age in the fear of a cruel God. He had no qualms about subjecting other men to the rigors of the bilboes or the whipping post, to the tortures of branding and maiming, to treating women of unruly tongue to a swing on the ducking stool or a taste of the gag or the cleft stick, and to humiliating both men and women in the stocks or the pillory, with public rebuke in church or the stigma of the scarlet letter.

Yet, with all his severities, he could not hold his community in line. In the earliest days every town was a port, and no kind of town is harder to control. For generations most inland towns were trading posts, and a trading post is a port on the shore of the wilderness instead of the seashore. Trade brought the ribald and unorthodox to town, and their presence roused the latent unorthodoxy and ribaldry already in secret residence. And the attempt to make each town a fortress of conservatism was a challenge to the potential invader. The town could not be so walled in that

> No one would covet it or think it worth
> The pains of conquering to force change on.[1]

So this typical Puritan leader was confronted with an unconscious and unholy alliance between the wanton and ungodly and the crusaders for religious liberty. He was driven to the always defeated excesses of the oppressor by the aggressiveness of "divers opinions" and the prevalence of sins of the flesh. Though the elements in the two situations vary, Puritan New England in the seventeenth century and Soviet Russia in the twentieth offer obvious comparisons in the passionate conviction of the dominant group that their plan was a plan of salvation, that it must be made to succeed at

---

[1] Robert Frost, "North of Boston," p. 55.

all costs, and that it must be ruthlessly imposed on those perverse enough to resist it.

Furthermore, the Puritan has left abundant record that he had plenty of trouble and plenty of failure in the problems of self-control. Whatever the reasons for it, whether or no they are related to the experience of the would-be autocrat and the would-be ascetic, he seems to have been quick to wrath. He could vent his temper on the offender if an offender was at hand, but he could and did quarrel openly and noisily with other pillars of the church and state. He was a feaster as well as a faster, and the accountings of his religious festivals reveal large expenditures for spirituous liquors. He was a master of slaves, — Indian, Negro, and indentured white, — and he was none too easy a master; but he was also a slave trader, and he handled his victims in shipment as no intelligent livestock trader does or could do today.

In short, he was the normally complex personality in whom the observer may find about what he is seeking. Hawthorne decries his personal austerities and accepts the austerity of his moralism. Emerson applauds his integrity of character and flouts the narrowness of his dogma. He was in truth carnal, acquisitive, avid for power. If it be true that the Cavalier was a Puritan below the surface (and there is abundant evidence for this), it is no less true that beneath the distinguishing marks of his Puritanism the Puritan was the seventeenth-century Englishman or European, heir to a thousand years of cultural evolution, who perfectly corresponds to the portrait painted of his ancestor,[1] that medieval Christian who "in the earthly Church beheld the heavenly,

---

[1] See, for example, J. G. Whittier on "New England Supernaturalism," *Democratic Review*, Vol. XIII, pp. 279, 280:

"The careful observer will . . . discover . . . no infrequent traces of the Invisible World, in which our Puritan ancestry had united the wild extravagances of Indian tradition with the familiar and common fantasies of their native land; and that gloomy, indefinite awe of an agency of Evil which their peculiar interpretations of the Sacred Volume had inspired; — a theory which drew a veil of mystery over the plainest passages of the great laws of the universe — agitating their entire community with signs, and wonders, and dark marvels — poisoning the fountains of education, and constituting a part of their religion."

and in fleshly joys discerned the devil's lures; [who] lived in the unreconciled opposition between the lust and vainglory of earth and the attainment of salvation; [who] felt life's terror and its pitifulness, and its eternal hope; around [whom] waved concrete infinitudes, and over [whom] flamed the terror of darkness and the Judgment Day."

Until the turn of the twentieth century these traits continue to be determinants in the American character. They account for so much in the American point of view that the literature which is an index to this cannot be fairly appraised in its commissions and its omissions, in what it stresses and what it suppresses, unless medieval Christianity, English Puritanism, and colonial evolution are all retained in the reckoning.

Book List

ADAMS, BROOKS. The Emancipation of Massachusetts (rev. ed.). 1919.

ADAMS, CHARLES FRANCIS. Three Episodes of Massachusetts History. 1891.

ADAMS, JAMES TRUSLOW. The Epic of America, pp. 25–71. 1931.

ADAMS, JAMES TRUSLOW. The Founding of New England. 1927.

ADAMS, JAMES TRUSLOW. Provincial Society, 1690–1763. Volume III of A History of American Life, edited by Schlesinger and Fox. 1927.

ANDREWS, CHARLES MCLEAN. The Colonial Period. 1912.

ANDREWS, CHARLES MCLEAN. The Colonial Period of American History, Vol. I. 1934.

ARBER, EDWARD. The Story of the Pilgrim Fathers. 1897.

BEARD, CHARLES A. and MARY R. The Rise of American Civilization, Chaps. I–IV. 1930.

BECKER, CARL L. Beginnings of the American People. 1915.

BELL, MRS. M. S. Pathways of the Puritans. Compiled for the Massachusetts Bay Colony Tercentenary Commission. 1930.

BEST, MARY AGNES. Rebel Saints. 1925.

BOLTON, HERBERT E., and MARSHALL, THOMAS M. The Colonization of North America, 1492–1783. 1920.

CANBY, HENRY SEIDEL. "Quakers and Puritans," *Saturday Review of Literature*, Vol. II, pp. 457–459.

COBB, SANFORD H. The Rise of Religious Liberty in America. 1902.

EGGLESTON, EDWARD. The Transit of Civilization. 1901.

FISKE, JOHN. The Beginnings of New England (new ed.). 1930.

HALL, THOMAS C. The Religious Background of American Culture. 1930.

JERNEGAN, MARCUS W. The American Colonies, 1492–1750, Chaps. I, II, V, VI, VII. 1930.

MACY, JOHN. "A Glance at the Real Puritans," *Harper's*, Vol. CLIV, pp. 742–750.

MILLER, PERRY. Orthodoxy in Massachusetts. 1933.

MORISON, SAMUEL E. Builders of the Bay Colony. 1930.

MURRAY, GILBERT. "The Value of Greece to the Future of the World." The Legacy of Greece. 1921.

PARRINGTON, VERNON L. The Colonial Mind, Chaps. I, II. 1927.

RILEY, I. WOODBRIDGE. American Thought from Puritanism to Pragmatism. 1915.

SCHNEIDER, HERBERT W. The Puritan Mind, Chap. I. 1930.

SMITH, PRESERVED. The Age of the Reformation. 1920.

TAINE, HIPPOLYTE A. History of English Literature. Last edition by Henry Van Laun. 1925.

TAYLOR, HENRY OSBORN. The Mediaeval Mind, Chaps. I, III, IV, IX, XII, XXV–XXVII. 1911.

WALKER, WILLISTON. A History of the Congregational Churches in the United States. 1894.

WERTENBAKER, THOMAS J. The First Americans, 1607–1690. Volume II of A History of American Life (edited by Schlesinger and Fox), Chaps. I, III, IV, VII–XIII. 1927.

WERTENBAKER, THOMAS J. The Planters of Colonial Virginia. 1922.

WRIGHT, THOMAS G. Literary Culture in Early New England, 1620–1730. 1920.

CHAPTER II

The Seventeenth Century

Southern Settlers

ALTHOUGH the general characteristics of the English colonial settlers are definable, they are no sooner defined than inner distinctions arise. Throughout the hundred years before the first successful English settlements were established in America, the seeds of internal controversy had been taking root in England; and when Elizabeth was followed on the throne by the vain and unregal James I the crop turned out to be a harvest of dragons' teeth, Puritan democrats and Cavalier royalists fighting over the prostrate and helpless body of Britannia. What followed was the rise of Puritan power, culminating with the execution of Charles I and the establishment of the Commonwealth under the Cromwells from 1649 to 1660, and the peaceful restoration of monarchy at the latter date. It was during the midstages of this development that the English colonial wedge between the Spaniards to the south and west and the French to the east and north was first driven into the Atlantic coast line of North America, and both factions of contending Englishmen participated: the Puritans, technical nonconformists in religious terminology; the pioneer Royalists, simply nonconformists of another type who preferred taking chances on the frontier to living conventional lives at home.

The Royalists, who were to settle Virginia and the neighboring colonies, set out, like other travelers and explorers of their day, to settle new English territory as a landed aristocracy. They were a mixed lot, but not on the whole an irreligious lot. They believed in the established church as they did in the established government, and they persecuted with a good will those who tried to pursue other forms of worship than their own. They were, however, primarily fortune hunters, like the men who surged out to California in 1849 or those who went to Alaska fifty years later — and literally gold-seekers too at first. They hoped to make their money in the West and spend it in the East, as their successors did, and, except for a few rare wandering scholars, they took no thought of literature either as something to enjoy or as something to create.

When they wrote they did so from the motives that impel all pioneers: for one reason or another to keep in touch with the people in the home country. They depended on national support to back up their claims to land tenure; they depended on financial backers for their money, and were kept busy explaining why quick returns were not coming to the investors; they depended on further colonization for indispensable labor; and they emphasized climate and natural resources as encouragement to immigrants just as they emphasized the hardships of settlement to explain their nonproductiveness. Furthermore, they wrote familiar letters with no motive except to inform friends and relatives. In the South there was no interest in general education; rather a distrust of it on the aristocratic theory that too much knowledge would be dangerous incitement to discontent among the working element. Some few individuals wrote accounts and descriptions that are of interest to other than students of history, but these were not representative. They were Englishmen away from home, living temporarily in *Virginia* (province of the virgin queen), in *James*-town, in the *Carolinas* (from the Latin for Charles), as also in *Charles*-ton, in *Mary*-land, in *Charlotte* and *Charlottes*-ville, and, even as late as 1722, in *George*-ia.

The nonconformists whom adverse winds drove to the North thirteen years later than the date of the first Southern settlement were different in being predominantly out of tune with the Anglican regime. Many of the leaders were products of Cambridge University who had gone into the

Church of England only to be driven out because of their unorthodox preaching — leaders with courage enough to risk comfort and safety for opinion's sake. They came to America to try their fortunes, as the Southerners did, but also in order, as Mrs. Hemans put it, to have "freedom to worship God," though not to grant this freedom to other dissenters. They settled in compact towns where they could believe and worship together; they put up "meetinghouses" where they listened to the preacher on the Lord's Day and transacted public business at the town meeting, very likely with the same man as "moderator." He was the preëminent man — "pastor," or shepherd, and "dominie," or master, of the parish. And when the meetinghouses were completed, the settlers opened schoolhouses where children might learn to read the Scriptures. In 1647 the first American compulsory-education ordinance was passed in Massachusetts.

From the start the Pilgrims and the Puritans, unlike the Southern Cavaliers, came over with the intention to live and die in America. Their place names were Indian — Massachusetts, Agawam, Connecticut, Niantic; or derived from English towns rather than from English royalty — Boston, Plymouth, Falmouth, New London; or quaintly scriptural, like Martha's Vineyard, Providence, Salem, Hebron. They wrote for the same social and business reasons that the Virginians did; but they also wrote much on the overlapping themes of church and state, compiled the "Bay Psalm Book," published sermons and tracts, and recorded their foredoomed struggles to keep their region free from the invasion of "divers opinions." At first all the colonial writings were sent to England or the Continent for publication; but by 1639 the colonists had their own printing press, and the things they printed were not so much the sayings of individuals as the sentiments of the community.

The history of the migrations to the North and South during the seventeenth century is one with the history of the civil war in England. Up to 1640 colonization was slow and consistent in both sections. From 1640 to 1660 it increased rapidly in the South and declined in the North; for in England the Puritans were in the saddle and glad to remain there, and the Royalists were many of them glad for a haven of refuge. From 1660 on, with the return of the Royalists to power, Puritan migration was once more started to New England, and the home country was again secure for the followers of the king. The characters of the two districts were well established. Fundamentally English in spite of all international contributions, the America of today is still a compound of the qualities inherited from the oldest traditions passed on by aristocratic Virginia and the oldest traits of democratic and Puritan Massachusetts.

Every young community peopled from an older society passes through a first stage of temporary sojourners to a period when it is mainly peopled by permanent settlers and thence to the time when the native-born predominate. It happens that the soldier of fortune, John Smith, is the outstanding example for both South and North of the early descriptive writer, though his actual residence was in the former region. Subject of more or less controversy, he seems in the sober judgment of the less prejudiced to have been an amazing adventurer, a born leader, a competent observer, and, for the most part, a verifiable chronicler. He has supplied many a document for the historian. To literature he is the source of our first legendary story,[1] though the legend is grounded in fact. The story of the Indian girl-princess Pocahontas, her intercession for Smith in a moment of peril, her marriage to John Rolfe, and her subsequent residence in London are matters of romantic history. More important, though a little less picturesque, is the fact that her friendliness toward the whole group in the first months of hardship

---

[1] "Travels and Works of Captain John Smith," edited by Edward Arber. See also the story as treated in drama: J. N. Barker, "The Indian Princess, or La Belle Sauvage," 1808; G. W. P. Custer, "Pocahontas, or The Settlers of Virginia," 1830; R. D. Owen, "Pocahontas," 1837; C. M. S. Barnes, "The Forest Princess," 1848; John Brougham, "Pocahontas, or The Gentle Savage" (burlesque), 1855; and in fiction: David Garnett, "Pocahontas: or The Nonparell of Virginia," a novel, 1933.

brought them invaluable aid when the whole colony was on the verge of starvation. So much emphasis is laid on the religious motivation of the settlers at Plymouth and Boston that it is worth noting that in the foreword to his "True Relation" Smith writes no less devoutly of his efforts

> to the erecting of true religion among Infidells, to the ouerthrow of superstition and idolatrie, to the winning of many thousands of wandring sheepe, vnto Christs fold, who now, and till now, have strayed in the vnknowne paths of Paganisme, Idolatrie, and superstition.[1]

The same sort of religious locution is advanced by John Rolfe in his appeal for official sanction of his marriage with Pocahontas. Maybe the writers were expressing a genuine religious consecration; more probably they were simply falling into the manner of speech they felt the occasion demanded, as Presidents and governors not distinguished for religious zeal have conventionally done in proclamations; but it is evident that the formula was substantially the same for Jamestown as for Plymouth.

It was natural also for John Smith to make the somewhat conventional acknowledgment of nature's abundance: the "plentie of swannes, cranes, geese, duckes and mallards and diuers sorts of fowles," the "fish in great plenty," the "plaine fertile planted ground," the unsurpassable town site.[2] And it was more natural still for this man of multifarious adventure to tell not only of his haps and mishaps among the Indians but also, in generous detail, of the ways of the Indians, their homes, costumes, manners, and particularly their civil and religious ceremonies.[3] But it is only an accident of the calendar and of one memorable romantic event that has made him loom so large in the story of American literature. He was not a colonist. He was a gentleman adventurer; his goings and comings to America were concluded sixteen years before his death in middle age; he wrote as an intelligent and amiable observer; and he was quite as willing in

---

[1] Smith, op. cit. p. 4. [2] Ibid. p. 13. [3] Ibid. p. 21.

the end to turn his back on the New World as for a while he was to turn his face toward it.

A man must sink into a region, identify himself with it, if he is to feel a local allegiance; the explorer must become a settler as John Hammond did. Twenty-one years, largely in Virginia and finally in Maryland, gave him the facts and put him in the mood to write the spirited defense which he published under a title which deserves quotation in full: "Leah and Rachel; or, The Two Fruitfull Sisters, Virginia and Mary-Land: Their Present Condition, Impartially stated and related with A Removall of such Imputations as are scandalously cast on those Countries, whereby many deceived Souls, choose rather to Beg, Steal, rot in Prison, and come to shamefull deaths, then to better their being by going thither, wherein is plenty of all things necessary for Humane subsistence."[1] Hammond was not a theorist about social conditions. He had a homely respect for the concrete, especially when it took the form of concrete human comfort. To him either Virginia or Maryland was a more comfortable place for the common man than London was. There was room for more people and need for more labor. He was happy while he was a colonist, and when he returned to the old country he was shocked both by the misery that he saw on every hand and by the unfairness of the current talk about conditions across the sea. In loyalty and good faith he must do what he might to offset the libelous misrepresentations and to show a way of escape to the luckless in England. To be sure, conditions had not always been ideal. Even the shepherds of the religious flock had been recruited from the ecclesiastics that Milton had already deplored in "Lycidas." For "many came, such as wore Black Coats, and could babble in a Pulpet, roare in a Tavern, exact from their Parishioners, and rather by their dissolutenesse destroy than feed their Flocks." But corrective measures had been taken, "and these Wolves in sheeps cloathing" had been "ques-

[1] John Hammond, "Leah and Rachel; or, The Two Fruitful Sisters," 1656. Reprinted in "Force Historical Tracts," Vol. III, No. XIV.

tioned, silenced, and some forced to depart the Country."[1] As to the hardships, Hammond was as free with promotional talk as John Smith, except that the resources were now much more largely the fruits of husbandry than of lavish nature unassisted, though "Grapes in infinite manner grow wild" as do nuts and small fruits "not known or grown in England." However, the vital feature of his pamphlet was not that the colonies were defensible, but that social hardship was so cruelly prevalent in England.

> Therefore I cannot but admire, and indeed much pitty the dull stupidity of people necessitated in *England*, who rather then they will remove themselves, live here a base, slavish, penurious life; as if there were a necessity to live and to live so, choosing rather then they will forsake *England* to stuff *New-Gate*, *Bridewell*, and other Jayles with their carkessies, nay cleave to tyburne it selfe; and so bring confusion to their souls horror and infamine to their kindred or posteritie, others itch out their wearisom lives in reliance of other mens charities, an uncertaine and unmanly expectation; some more abhorring such courses betake themselve to almost perpetuall and restlesse toyle and druggeries out of which (whilst their strength lasteth) they (observing hard diets, earlie and late houres) make hard shift to subsist from hand to mouth, untill age or sicknesse takes them off from labour and directs them the way to beggerie, and such indeed are to be pittied, relieved and provided for.[2]

There is a great deal more in this vein, the vein of the contented colonist. Why speculate on abstractions of church and state when one can be sure of a full dinner pail? Hammond leaves these questions for the doctors and pays his tribute to the land of plenty.

If Hammond is a genuine settler with a genuine enthusiasm for the sister colonies whose largesse he had enjoyed, George Alsop, gay back-trailer after only four years' residence, deserves and demands a hearing for his sober-titled piece of sprightliness, "A Character of the Province of Maryland."[3]

---

[1] Hammond, op. cit. p. 9.

[2] Ibid. pp. 17–18.

[3] George Alsop, "A Character of the Province of Maryland." Reprinted from the original edition of 1666 and edited by N. D. Mereness.

Alsop came across the water as an indentured servant twenty years old in 1658. He wrote home with zest about colonial conditions and alleged later that he had found "a commanding and undeniable enjoyment" in his four years of service. But as a Royalist he seems to have made his way back to England (then restored to monarchy) as soon as he could after he had earned his freedom. He must have made known his flourishing use of the pen by showing his "face upon the Exchange of conceited wits," for his little duodecimo on Maryland seems to have appeared under patronage. It was dedicated to Lord Baltimore; it was prefaced further with versified tributes to the author himself; it was addressed also to the merchant adventurers for Maryland; it included a rhymed address to the book itself; and it justified Alsop's observation that if it was wild and confused it partook of nothing less than the nature of its writer. It was also full of jocularity, mock heroics, and vulgarity, and rifted with smut. Mark Twain, whose "fancy stooped on rank suggestion," would have relished it; for it was earthy, with the broad humor of the undisciplined and with the sweeping rhythms of the man who writes from the elbow. Others had dilated on the abundance of Maryland's riches. Very well!

> He, who out of curiosity desires to see the Landskip of the Creation drawn to the life, or to read Natures universal Herbal without book, may with the Opticks of a discreet discerning, view *Mary-Land* drest in her green and fragrant Mantle of the Spring. Neither do I think there is any place under the Heavenly altitude, or that has footing or room upon the circular Globe of this world, that can parallel this fertile and pleasant piece of ground.[1]

Others had written of the prevailing peace and contentment. As for him:

> Here if the Lawyer had nothing else to maintain him but his bawling, he might button up his Chops, and burn his Buckrom Bag, or else hang it upon a pin untill its Antiquity had eaten it up with durt and dust: Then with a Spade, like his Grandsire *Adam*, turn

[1] Alsop, op. cit. pp. 32–33.

up the face of the Creation, purchasing his bread by the sweat of his brows, that before was got by the motionated Water-works of his jaws.[1]

Unregenerate soul that he was, England had been no home for him during the Protectorate; and writing from the security of Restoration England, he had his unique testimony to offer about the social and religious harmony that prevailed in the land of his sojourn. People were ruled with a strong hand and apparently with more success than in New England; rebellious theories were scotched whenever they peeped from under cover; none was ever allowed to erect itself, with the result that

. . . I really believe this Land or Government of *Mary-Land* may boast, that she enjoys as much quietness from the disturbances of Rebellious Opinions, as most States or Kingdoms do in the world: For here every man lives quietly, and follows his labour and imployment desiredly; and by the protection of the Laws, they are supported from those molestious troubles that ever attend upon the Commons of other States and Kingdoms.[2]

One fourth of the book is devoted (and in a more sober tone than most of it) to a demonstration of the peculiar blessedness that inheres in the state of servitude, with, of course, especial reference to the scriptural sanctions, Alsop displaying an altogether human alacrity to appeal to this authority in support of a social order of which he was now a beneficiary. As a historical document his little booklet is probably as unreliable as a book could be; but perhaps for that very reason the free play of mood, fancy, opinion, and rhetorical energy makes it one of the very few seventeenth-century colonial literary documents that can give the reader an hour of unalloyed pleasure. To reach this pleasurable point, however, it has been necessary to come far down the century. The years must be retraced to follow the slower-moving chronicle of the Northern colonial writers.

---

[1] Alsop, op. cit. p. 48.

[2] Ibid. pp. 45–46.

Northern Settlers

In contrast to the Virginians, the New Englanders were, on the whole, far more definitely concerned with finding a permanent place to live than with making fortunes. It is obvious that the England from which they came was an England of lively impulses, of widening imagination, and of imperial dreams, and that after the exciting achievements of the English explorers and discoverers the move across the Atlantic was inevitable; and it is natural, therefore, that the Puritans and the separatists should have been swept into it. It is also one of the most familiar matters of fact that the locating of the Plymouth plantation was a matter of accident and adverse winds. It is clear, too, that the settlers had come from the practical middle-class group of shopmen and traders and that they were perfectly capable of taking care of themselves in a practical world. The pat statement is well grounded that the New Englanders were interested in forests, furs, fish, and faith; and the kind of critical historian who is chiefly interested in the facts which are antithetic to accepted beliefs can go far in correcting a sometimes idealized and sometimes merely exaggerated picture of the Puritans and statement of their motives.

But no sober study of the seventeenth century can end by denying that the men who came to the Massachusetts Bay, the Plymouth, the Connecticut, or the New Haven colony were to a remarkable degree concerned with the problems related to their religious convictions. The colonies were headed by an extraordinary proportion of educated men. It has often been said that in the early decades of the century there was a larger population percentage of Cambridge University graduates in eastern Massachusetts than in any county of England. These men occupied positions of high strategic importance. They and their fellows, in contrast to the Southerners, were gathered into compact villages. The clergy were very frequently actual leaders of emigrant groups and frequently came over in answer to specific invitations from groups already in America who wished for their leadership, and they came with a compelling desire to contribute to a new and self-governing social order.

A reading of the various histories or history source books which they were given to compiling shows how insistent was the religious motive. Their statements on this theme have none of the perfunctory quality of similar utterances in the South. Said William Bradford:

> It was answered, that all great and honourable actions are accompanied with great difficulties, and must be both enterprised and overcome with answerable courages. It was granted ye dangers were great, but not desperate; the difficulties were many, but not invincible. . . . But their condition was not ordinarie; their ends were good & honourable; their calling lawfull & urgente; and therfore they might expect ye blessing of God in their proceding. Yea, though they should loose their lives in this action, yet might they have comforte in the same, and their endeavors would be honourable.[1]

Said John Winthrop, in scriptural language:

> . . . We must be knit together, in this work, as one man. We must entertain each other in brotherly affection. We must be willing to abridge ourselves of our superfluities, for the supply of others' necessities. We must uphold a familiar commerce together in all meekness, gentleness, patience and liberality.[2]

Edward Johnson, historian, reveals in the title of his voluminous work, "Wonder-Working Providence of Sions Saviour in New England," how definitely religious the venture of the Puritans seemed to him. God, he declared, "stood not as an idle spectator beholding his peoples Ruth and their Enemies rage; but as an Actor in all actions to bring

---

[1] Bradford, "History of Plymouth Plantation," p. 26; reprinted from the original manuscript, edited for the Massachusetts Historical Society by Charles Deane.

[2] John Winthrop's discourse, "A Modell of Christian Charity," written on board the *Arbella* in 1630, is reprinted in Stedman and Hutchinson's "Library of American Literature," Vol. I, pp. 304–307.

to naught the desires of the wicked. . . ."[1] The settlement of New England, he maintained, was a campaign of the church militant "for the Lord Christ intends to atchieve greater matters by this little handfull than the World is aware of . . ."[2] And Cotton Mather, writing nearly two generations later, opened his "Magnalia" with

> I shall yet give the Church of God a certain account of these *things*, which in America have been believing and adoring the glorious *Name* of Jesus; and of that country in America, where those *things* have been attended with circumstances most remarkable.[3]

Humanize the Puritan as you will, secularize him, commercialize him, materialize him, and he is still at bottom insistently mindful of himself as a soldier of the Lord.

Such an attitude inevitably leads to a literal belief in a personal Providence, pagan superstition having long ago graduated smoothly over into a primitive Christian credulousness. Every good fortune was an evidence of God's mercy, every mishap a proof of his displeasure, and the Providence who was aware of every sparrow's falling to the ground was a dispenser of minutiae and a director over the smallest details. Anthony Thacher, saved from shipwreck in Boston Harbor, could write devoutly "the Lord directed my toes into a crevice in the rock" without feeling that he attributed to the Most High an exceptional attention to his own body's welfare. It was inevitable that men with such a habit of thinking should evolve a tribal god whom they could evoke against any people or any person they chose to brand as an enemy. And the godly were surrounded by foes; for from the very start they were aware of insurgents and dissenters who were quite beyond their control, and they were quite unaware that in their attempt to achieve an unassailable formulation of faith and an unchanging social order

---

[1] Edward Johnson, "Wonder-Working Providence . . ." (edited by J. F. Jameson, 1910), p. 150.

[2] Ibid. p. 33.

[3] Cotton Mather, "Magnalia Christi Americana" (edited by Thomas Robbins, 1855), p. 41.

they might as well have undertaken to control the flow of the tides. The most interesting and the best-written pieces of seventeenth-century New England literature all give evidence of this irresistible current of change in human thought. It was one force over which Providence seemed to have no deterrent effect.

The Puritanism, to use the term in its looser sense, against which this rising tide of dissent developed was admirably embodied in William Bradford, the *Mayflower* Pilgrim who was more than thirty times governor of his colony, and the author of "A History of Plimouth Plantation." He was a brave, sober, devout leader with an abiding sense of the holy cause in which he was enlisted. His journal of the first year in America and his history are clearly and sometimes finely written, and give ample proof of his stalwart character, "fervent in spirit, serving the Lord," and not wholly overridden by the personal narrowness commonly ascribed to all Puritans. In his account, for example, of the reasons for the Pilgrims' removal from Leyden, he told of the hardships under which they had lived there, the encroachments of old age, the disturbing effects on the lives of the children of life in alien surroundings, and the great hope the elders entertained of advancing the church of Christ in some remote part of the world. He recounted many of the objections advanced against attempting settlement in America and concluded with the defense and exhortation already cited. Once arrived in the new land on the verge of winter, he sounded the note of rededication to a high emprise; but as a sober recorder of fact he did not gloss the aggravation of difficulties that arose from the Pilgrims' bent for interminable and fractious debate on every moot point. They were a group of individualists; all that they had been through and all that they faced wore them down near to or past the breaking point. To make matters worse, some of the survivors of the first winter were mean-spirited, and some of the new arrivals were too much for them to endure. There was Thomas Morton, for instance.

Morton would come down to us in Bradford's "History"

as just one of the thorns in the flesh of the Pilgrims if he had not left his own record behind him to offset the strictures of the governor chronicler. It is a half-pathetic fact that his "New English Canaan," published in Amsterdam in 1637, should stand out for vivacity of tone beyond anything else written in the same decade in America; for the best of it, the third book, is a savage satire on the Plymouth colonists. Morton, needless to say, was not a religious enthusiast. He was a restless, dishonest, irresponsible gentleman adventurer from London who gave his best energies to frustrating and annoying the Pilgrims on their own grounds. He started a fur-trading post at "Merry-Mount," just southeast of where Boston was to be; sold the Indians liquor and firearms; consorted with their women; and in wanton mockery set up a Maypole there and taught the Indians the English games and dances that were particularly offensive to their sober neighbors. But he did the Pilgrims more damage with his pen than with his naughtiness. He undermined their influence by treating them flippantly. He made fun of their costumes, derided their speech, ridiculed their religious formalities, held the valiant Miles Standish up to scorn by nicknaming him "Captain Shrimp," and dubbed Governor Endicott, "Captain Littleworth," and Governor Winthrop, "Joshua Temperwell." He went further and impugned their motives, their integrity in business, their sincerity in religion. Much of what he wrote was libelously unfair; he can never be accepted for his facts unless he is confirmed by other writers. The differences between his account of the arrest at Merry-Mount and that of William Bradford throw an illuminating light on the values of legal or historical testimony.[1] But beneath his clever abuse of the Puritans and their ways, there is a basis of truth, confirmed by the unprejudiced study of all the data. The brave, strong, self-denying serv-

[1] For comparative treatments of the Merry-Mount episode see Bradford's "History of Plymouth Plantation," Massachusetts Historical Society edition of 1856, pp. 236–243; and Thomas Morton's "New English Canaan," Prince Society Publications, Vol. XIV, Chap. XIV.

ants of the stern God they worshiped could stoop to sanctimony, cruel vengefulness, and low means to achieve the high ends by which they justified their tactics. At the very beginning of their life in America, Thomas Morton held these weaknesses up to view; and, so doing, he made his book an omen of the long, losing battle they were destined to fight. His effectiveness as a writer lies in the fact that however ill-behaved he may have been, he was disarmingly genial on the printed page. He was in truth a cheerful liar; but he lied like the writer of fiction who disregards the facts because he is telling a good story as well as he can and because the good story is based on real life if not on actual, verifiable event.

Churchman-Dictators

It is a simple and slight transition, hardly more than a shift in emphasis, from the early settler who stresses the conditions of settlement, making it an enterprise in the name of the Lord, to the early churchman-dictator who is trying to establish a state which is a secular adjunct to his church. It has already been stated that the religious enthusiasts who came to New England faced as their two chief undertakings the organization and control of the kind of church they believed in and the maintenance of a government in harmony with it, and it has been acknowledged that as rulers of an established order they had the normal embarrassment of coping with the liberal principles to which they had appealed when they were playing the role of rebels against another established order. History never repeats itself more clearly than it does in the succession of events that attend revolutions and postrevolutionary years. The pattern can be found as often as revolutions can be. A group who have risked everything for a change in the social order are certain to fight hard for what has been dearly bought. The consequence is that the day after freedom has been achieved the revolutionist sets about to lay down a new definition of freedom. In acquiring it he has found that it has become too expensive to squander. Joseph Hopkinson put the case in a nutshell when he wrote for the refrain of "Hail! Columbia,"

> Let Independence be our boast,
> Ever mindful what it cost.

The obvious analogy of the twentieth century is the attitude of mind and the political tactics that prevailed among the leaders of Soviet Russia. Like the Puritans who came to America, or like those who seized control of England in 1650, the soviet leaders were bent on setting up a new social order on the new pattern. The tactics which were the tactics of war for the achievement of a so-called revolution were only the first step in the long program. The next step was not merely to organize, but to foil any countermovement. Constructive measures were attended with complementary repressive measures. The struggle in their minds committed them to ruthlessness. The atmosphere of struggle created enthusiasm but engendered intolerance. They were bound to believe that the scheme of life they were fighting for was unsurpassable and, with fanatical zeal, to devote themselves to the regeneration of the world. It is a mistake even to say that the Puritan leaders and the soviet leaders were striving on different levels, that the one were religious and the others secular; for it is the agreement of all dispassionate observers that communism as conceived by the Russian revolutionists has for them substantially amounted to a religion. When it is remembered further that the New England leaders were intense believers in a revealed religion, and that the Puritan mind could look back over centuries of evolution in which Christian leaders had sought their authority in the Scriptures and had developed a capacity for finding what they wanted there, the attitude and the tactics of the Puritans need no further explanation.

Out of the multitude who could be cited in detail, two will serve as well as a dozen. The first is John Winthrop, who came over in 1630 as governor of the Massachusetts Company in the little fleet of vessels on which, according to one historian,[1] had embarked the most eminent group "of wealthy and cultivated persons that have ever emigrated in any one voyage from England to America." These were the prosperous English Puritans, men of means and social position, who came to America with the sole motive, if any group so came, of establishing a church-state to their liking. Winthrop was a product of Cambridge University, a Puritan Presbyterian who believed in the rule of the elders, which was far from a pure democracy. Like Governor Bradford of Plymouth Colony, he left behind him a year-by-year history of the events which took place in his jurisdiction, but, unlike Bradford, he was distinctly interested in a theory of his government and the theory of liberty. It is in a passage on this theme that in 1645 he made his most famous utterance. Some time earlier he had been charged with having exceeded his powers as deputy governor. In his speech before the General Court, by which he was acquitted of the offense, he made the distinction between natural and civil (or federal) liberty, and insisted that the belief in a man's right to do what he chooses without restriction is inconsistent with authority and intolerant of the least restraint.

> If you stand for your natural corrupt liberties, and will do what is good in your own eyes, you will not endure the least weight of authority, but will murmur, and oppose, and be always striving to shake off that yoke; but if you will be satisfied to enjoy such civil and lawful liberties, such as Christ allows you, then will you quietly and cheerfully submit unto that authority which is set over you, in all the administrations of it, for your good. Wherein, if we fail at any time, we hope we shall be willing by God's assistance to hearken to good advice from any of you, or in any other way of God; so shall your liberties be preserved in upholding the honor and power of authority amongst you.[2]

The element in the question which he did not discuss (possibly because he felt that he could assume an agreement among

---

[1] Moses Coit Tyler, "A History of American Literature, 1607–1765," Vol. I, p. 129.

[2] John Winthrop, "History of New England," Vol. II, p. 282.

his auditors) was the exact nature of the "civil and lawful liberties" sanctioned by the founder of the Christian faith; and as the nature of these was subject to interpretation and to such differences of opinion as were arising and were certain to arise, the utterance of the governor, though satisfactory to the general court, was in point of permanence a structure built on shifting sand.

John Winthrop's fellow soldier in the army of the Lord, Nathaniel Ward, was an equally zealous believer in a firm and centralized control of the church-state, and a far more intense advocate of the kind of firmness that resorts to harshness. Winthrop wrote an eloquent little treatise on "Christian Charity." Ward was suspicious of charity as the devil's approach to flabby complacency in the face of the devil's advocates. Like Winthrop he was a graduate of Cambridge University, a liberal, and a Puritan who in time fell under the disfavor of Archbishop Laud. A churchman, he was disciplined first in 1631, and again two years later, when he joined the Massachusetts Bay Company and remained with it for a dozen years. All his quaint, belligerent, gnarled and knotted jocosity and preciosity are packed into a little duodecimo of eighty pages and prove that godliness can be as animated and amusing as the gay worldliness of an Alsop or the jaunty perversity of a Morton. Ward propounded his conservative views under the title "The Simple Cobler of Aggawam in America. Willing To help mend his Native Country, lamentably tattered, both in the upper-Leather and sole, with all the honest stitches he can take. And as willing never to bee paid for his work, by Old English wonted pay. *It is his Trade to patch all the year long,* gratis. Therefore I pray Gentlemen keep your purses."

In a way the reputation of the book suffers from the presence of two passages that are so uniquely quotable that they have been emphasized out of all proportion. They are, in fact, irresistible. But in fairness they should be regarded as purple patches, and the whole fabric should first be held up to view. The book is written as from Aggawam (now Ipswich, Massachusetts), but it is written, nevertheless, as by an Englishman to Englishmen. It opens with the conservative's typical alarm at the menace of change. It continues with a section of mingled sprightliness and seriousness on the danger of conceding in the least measure to the apostles of liberalism. It proceeds then to a carefully considered formulation of policy, after an irrelevant interpolation on women's fashions, and inquires whether the crisis in England in the 1640's can be averted by "reformation," by "composition," by "cessation," or whether it must be pursued to "prosecution." "Reformation" he uses as a term for a resolute search for harmony within the church and for Christian virtues in the individual:

> When States are so reformed, that they conforme such as are profligate, into good civility: civill men, into religious morality: When Churches are so constituted, that Faith is ordained Pastor, Truth Teacher, Holinesse and Righteousnesse ruling-Elders: Wisdome and Charity Deacons: Knowledge, love, hope, zeale . . . admitted members, and all their opposites excluded: then there will bee peace of Country and Conscience.[1]

"Composition" is Ward's term for a spirit of concession from the king toward the people, coupled with the timely warning that "it is enough for God to be Infinite, too much for man to be Indefinite. He that will flye too high a quarry for Absolutenesse, shall stoope as much too low before hee remounts his proper pitch."[2] "Cessation," he declares, can be achieved only after "composition." If the will of a king "be not a foot and halfe lesser than the Will of his Councell, and three foot lesser tha[n] the Will of his Parliament it is too big. I thinke it were well for a King if he had no will at all, but were all reason."[3] Much as he yearns for peace finally, he has no hope for it; and he calls for "prosecution" with the closing appeal:

---

[1] Ward, "The Simple Cobler . . .," 1647, pp. 39–40.
[2] Ibid. p. 47. [3] Ibid. p. 62.

Goe on therefore Renowned Gentlemen, fall on resolvedly, till your hands cleave to your swords, your swords to your enemies hearts, your hearts to victory, your victories to triumph, your triumphs to the everlasting praise of him that hath given you Spirits to offer your selves willingly, and to jeopard your lives in high perills, for his Name and service sake.[1]

There are local applications to Ward's invectives against the doctrine of toleration and against the frivolity of women's fashions. The first twenty-three pages form a diatribe on the former topic. Religious toleration, he says, is an insidious device of Satan, who "loves to fish in royled waters." As a spokesman for New England, however, which has been much maligned, he ventures to proclaim "that all Familists, Antinomians, Anabaptists, and other Enthusiasts, shall have free Liberty to keep away from us, and such as will come to be gone as fast as they can, the sooner the better."[2] The advocate for freedom of opinion, "if he examines his heart by daylight, his conscience will tell him, he is either an Atheist, or an Heretique, or an Hypocrite, or at best a captive to some lust."[3] One agrees with him at a halfway point in his jeremiad when he asks, "But why dwell I so intolerable long about Tolerations?" And enough has doubtless been cited.

It is in the following section, devoted to the ladies, that his style and his humor caper and frisk in highest abandon. The woman with only enough squirrel's brains to help her "frisk from one ill-favor'd fashion to another," he looks on as "the very gizzard of a trifle, the product of a quarter of a cypher, the epitome of nothing. . . ."[4] He tries without success "to speak moderately" of women who "have so little wit, as to disfigure themselves with such exotick garbes, as not onely dismantles their native lovely lustre, but transclouts them into gant bar-geese, ill-shapen shotten shell-fish, Egyptian Hieroglyphicks, or at the best into French flurts of the pastery. . . ."[5] But he knows what he is doing. At the

[1] Ward, op. cit. p. 71. [2] Ibid. p. 3. [3] Ibid. p. 5. [4] Ibid. p. 25. [5] Ibid. p. 24.

end of the volume, after a bloodthirsty and lamentable page on the treatment of the Irish Papists, in a section entitled "Errata at non Corrigenda" he cites some faults in the foregoing which he elects not to mend but to commend.

> To speak to light heads with heavy words, were to break their necks. . . . Ye make such a noise there, with Drums and Trumpets, that if I should not speak loud, yee could not hear me. . . . If I affect termes, it is my feeblenesse. . . . I hold him prudent, that in these fastidious times, will helpe disedged appetites with convenient condiments. . . .[1]

Ward's sense of humor is so ready that one can easily suspect him of digressing on "futilous womens phansies" with covert reference to the "cladments" in which his sober thesis is arrayed. For if he had not dressed it in "the gyblets of perquisquilian toyes" it would have been lost in the troop of sober-garbed Puritan documents.

Active Dissenters

Two points may be recalled as one turns from churchman-dictators, leaders of the oft-mentioned ecclesiastical oligarchy, to the active dissenters who were the chief source of trouble to the men in power. The first is that the churchmen were in theory averse to the ways of the tyrant and the oppressor. In theory they resorted to them only in defense of revealed religion; but since religion involved both belief and behavior, and the state functioned as the right arm of the church, they felt that a system of control was demanded of them which reached far and wrought fiercely. Their fierceness is not hard to understand. It was derived from the concept of law and power in which they had been bred; it was justified in the anathematory psalms, and hence divinely sanctioned; it was written into the penal code of England and had been practiced on them in the Rule of Thorough as fiercely as they were ever to practice it; and it could always be condoned

[1] Ward, op. cit. pp. 74–77.

by allusion to the scriptural statement that "whom the Lord loveth he chasteneth." It should not be forgotten that Winthrop is justly distinguished for his definition of liberty as he conceived it, and that Ward, for all his brashness, counseled moderation in the use of power.

The other point is by way of reminder that the oligarchy were forced into a struggle with misconduct and dissent from the very outset. Hawthorne's picture of an early New England holiday in "The Scarlet Letter" introduces the smoking, drinking, swaggering sailors, on whom no restraint was attempted. The court records prove that depravity, whether natural or diabolical, was more than a thin abstraction. And in the realm of opinion, in addition to unsanctioned preachers, avowed heretics, illiterate babblers, and fanatical and ranting sectarians, whom the powers dared to deal with in the stocks, on the pillory, or at the whipping post and cart's tail, there was a far more insidious menace in the preachings and teachings by certain university men who had the same training as the conservative leaders and equal prestige with them. Thus Anne Hutchinson could be summarily disposed of, but men like Thomas Hooker and Roger Williams offered a more reverberating problem.

Hooker,[1] for example, was a Cambridge product; had been one of the disturbing "lecturers" who discussed questions of theology and church polity under the roof of the church but without its sanction until they were suppressed; had met with the disfavor of Archbishop Laud; and had come to Massachusetts Bay in 1633 after a sojourn in Holland. The date of his arrival may well have had something to do with the exact shade of his convictions. Before coming he had become a Congregationalist, but a nonseparatist. He arrived, fresh in his theories, after the first leaders had seen three years of experiment in statesmanship. They were, on

[1] A modern reinterpretation of Hooker is by Perry Miller, "Thomas Hooker and the Democracy of Early Connecticut," *New England Quarterly*, Vol. IV (1931), No. 4.

the whole, still committed to the Presbyterian rule of the elders and the elect, though the Congregational way was eventually to prevail. Hooker's inclination was naturally to apply his theory to the situation and to express his misgivings at its not being fully applied. Moreover, Hooker was dynamic and humanly impulsive. His hearers were swept away by his eloquence in the pulpit. He was used to sweeping methods and restive at opposition. It was probably no coincidence that within six months of his installation over his Newtown (now Cambridge) parishioners they complained that they were crowded by neighboring communities, and petitioned for the right to remove. Not being granted permission, they, together with other groups, committed a "breach of the covenant" which had bound them to the colony, and in 1636 went with their pastor to Connecticut. This was secession. It was separatism with a vengeance; and in Connecticut Hooker carried Congregationalism into politics, following to its conclusion his particular issue — that as the government was carried on in behalf of the people, the people were entitled to decide what laws the officers should enforce. "If you tether a beast at night," John Cotton had said of the magistrates, "he knows the length of his tether before morning." Hooker was even less inclined than Cotton to let the rulers run at large. He wrote nothing that cries out to be read as literature today; but on account of its disturbing influence, his thinking and his subsequent action stimulated the Winthrops and the Cottons and the Wards to their more readable productions. And more exciting than Thomas Hooker was the incorrigible protestant Roger Williams.

A man of later birth, whose life span of eighty years bridged the reigns of the Stuarts and the intervening Protectorate, he bore witness once more to the liberal influence of Cambridge University, from which he was graduated in 1627. Educated for the ministry, he refused to enter the service of the Anglican church and came to America in 1631, occupying a pulpit at Plymouth for the next two years, when he removed thence to Salem. Although he was only twenty-nine years of age, he was ready to stand on his own feet in behalf of a series of opinions which were far more subversive than any advanced by Hooker. The Massachusetts Bay Colony openly owed its land tenure to the powers of the crown. Nathaniel Ward was one of scores who occupied large acreages bestowed by the king. Williams took the honest and humane position that the land belonged to the Indians and could be legally acquired only by honest purchase. The colony recognized the English tradition combining church and state. Williams contended that an established church was doomed to corruption. The courts of the state invaded the realms of theology and religion. Williams asserted that the powers of the magistracy might not extend to the conscience of the subject, but must be limited to his body and his property. For one young man, in a series of outrageous thrusts, to stab at the validity of the royal charters, the integrity of the church, and the jurisdiction of the courts was more than any colony could be expected to endure, and the harsh fist of the community was shaken at him so fiercely that in midwinter of early 1636 he took flight to Rhode Island. Hooker had gone into the boundless West, settling on the shores of the Connecticut a hundred miles from Boston. Williams fled to the hill-circled headwaters of a deep bay forty miles to the southeast and only half that distance inland from Plymouth; but it was beyond the limits of either of the older colonies. The town he settled, with the tiny surrounding state, formed a pocket between Massachusetts to the north and east, Connecticut to the west, and the wide refuge to the south which for generations was open to the various kinds of liberals who could find no other haven in New England. It was too liberal a region for even the democrats of Connecticut — a fact that was made clear by the pointed exclusion of Rhode Island from the United Colonies of New England, the confederacy formed in 1643 by the Massachusetts Bay, Plymouth, Connecticut, and New Haven colonies.

Thus excluded, Rhode Island, the Ishmael of the settlements, felt the need of recognition from the crown, and Williams was its inevitable representative. The England to which he returned was the conflict-ridden country over which Nathaniel Ward was soon to express his concerns. Williams was never a man to keep his thoughts to himself, and once more he probed below the surface to reach the core of the troubles. He presented his findings in a document which he called "Queries of Highest Consideration," addressed to Parliament. They were Socratic questions with an introduction which was not so mild as the title. "Most Renowned Patriots, You sit at Helme in as great a Storm, as ere poor England's Commonwealth was lost in: Yet . . . all your Consultations, Conclusions, Executions, are not of the Quantity of the value of one poor drop of water. . . ."[1] He challenged the rulers of England to do something better than follow "the patterns of either French, Dutch, Scotch or New-English churches," and queried whether they could find any authority for a national church in the teachings of Jesus and whether it were not the true mark of a false church to persecute in the name of the faith.

Most celebrated of his publications is his controversy with John Cotton, in which he had the first and the last word. An English prisoner in Newgate assailing persecution for cause of conscience had been answered by John Cotton. Then followed Williams's "The Bloody Tenent of Persecution for cause of Conscience, discussed in a Conference between Truth and Peace" (1644); Cotton's reply, "The Bloody Tenent washed and made white in the Blood of the Lamb" (1647); and Williams's rejoinder, "The Bloody Tenent yet More Bloody: by Mr. Cottons endeavor to wash it white in the Blood of the Lambe" (1652). The whole process of argument by both the reverend gentlemen was to set their literal English minds to work at analyzing and expounding Biblical passages which were full of Oriental richness of

[1] Publications of the Narragansett Club, Vol. II, p. 254.

imagery. But Williams frequently rose above the homiletic level to a plane of simple eloquence. He was primarily interested in maintaining an orderly community in which freedom of conscience was assured. He succeeded in gaining for Rhode Island a charter which defeated the desire of the Massachusetts men to establish control over their neighbors to the south. Sometimes, to his own discomfort, he remained steadfast to his doctrine of toleration; and by acting in partial agreement with John Winthrop's definition of liberty subject to law, he kept order by insisting that religious liberty did not emancipate the citizen from civic responsibility.

The Massachusetts colonies were relatively successful in imposing their Mosaic law on the body of the settlers; but the policy of compulsion and the policy of exclusion cost them the loss of Hooker to Connecticut and Williams to Rhode Island, and demonstrated that the more liberal theories were workable theories. In so doing they taught the American people one of their first lessons in the philosophy of pragmatism.

Early Verse

Among the generalizations about the early settlers, and especially about the early New Englanders, the broad statement that they were indifferent to all forms of art must be taken with more than a grain of salt. In the South it is too easy to confute. In the North it is at least easy to qualify. Domestic architecture, from the first, progressed in the adaptation of use to beauty. Church architecture after the time of the great fire in London reflected the influence of Christopher Wren and Inigo Jones in the rebuilding process. The gay and brightly decorated home interiors, the simple dignity of line set out by dark woods against white paint in the meetinghouses, relieved the somberness of the conventional picture. The most that can be safely said is that in the North the Puritans were on guard against the carnal and the frivolous; that hence they disapproved of dancing, "play-acting," secular poetry, secular music. On the other hand, there is every kind of evidence that the early settlers in both regions had the universal inclination to indulge in the sort of rhyming that in its elementary forms is related to playing card tricks or solving crossword puzzles. Thus, naturally enough, along the stern and rock-bound coast "the earthly element, the passion, the carnal taint, the vanity, the weariness . . . exhaust[ed] itself in the sly dissipation of writing verses."[1]

They composed memorials of the most ingenious and intricate sorts. Cotton Mather wrote of John Wilson's

> Care to guide his *Flock*, and feed his *Lambs*,
> By, *Words*, *Works*, *Prayers*, *Psalms*, *Alms* and *Anagrams*:
> Those *Anagrams*, in which he made to start
> Out of meer *Nothings*, by *Creating Art*,
> Whole *Words* of Counsel; did to *Motes* unfold
> *Names*, till they Lessons gave richer than Gold.[2]

There is less verse sprinkled through the unregenerate Morton's "Canaan" than in the intolerant Ward's "Cobler." The old conservative never wrote more wisely than in his so-called song:

1.

> They seldome lose the field, but often win,
> Who end their wars, before their wars begin.

2.

> Their Cause is often worst, that first begin,
> And they may lose the field, the field that win.

3.

> In Civill wars 'twixt Subjects and their King,
> There is no conquest got by conquering.

4.

> War ill begun, the onely way to mend,
> Is to end the War before the war doe end.

---

1 Tyler, "A History of American Literature," Vol. I, pp. 267, 268.

2 "Handkerchiefs from Paul: Being Pious and Consolatory Verses of Puritan Massachusetts . . . " (edited by Kenneth B. Murdock), p. liv.

5.

They that will end ill wars, must have the skill,
To make an end by Rule, and not by Will.

6.

In ending wars 'tween Subjects and their Kings,
Great things are sav'd, by losing little things.[1]

The first volume in English printed in the Western Hemisphere (printing of Spanish books in Mexico had long preceded) was the "Bay Psalm Book," Cambridge, 1640.[2] This represented a conscientious attempt (for which there were distinguished precedents) to contribute to the service of worship a literal translation of the Psalms. The worst passages are all too frequently cited as evidence of the inability of the Puritans to compose or appreciate good verse, and this in spite of the oft-quoted and charmingly phrased apology in the preface by the editors, Thomas Welde, John Eliot, and Richard Mather:

If therefore the verses are not alwayes so smooth and elegant as some may desire or expect; let them consider that Gods Altar needs not our pollishings: Ex. 20. for wee have respected rather a plaine translation, then to smooth our verses with the sweetnes of any paraphrase, and soe have attended Conscience rather then Elegance, fidelity rather then poetry, in translating the hebrew words into english language, and Davids poetry into english meetre; that soe wee may sing in Sion the Lords songs of prayse according to his owne will; untill hee take us from hence and wipe away all our teares, & bid us enter into our masters joye to sing eternal Halleluiahs.

Some commentators, moreover, seem to derive satisfaction in quoting passages from Michael Wigglesworth's "Day of Doom" (1662) as added proof that the Puritans were incapable of writing felicitous verse. It is true that this grave and pretentious composition is no more mellifluous than the

[1] Ward, "The Simple Cobler," pp. 43–44.

[2] A facsimile reprint of the first edition of the "Bay Psalm Book" is published by the New England Society in New York (n.d.).

name of the author; but it should be remembered that it was only a mode of popularizing the Calvinistic theology, and that its extraordinary vogue proves how deep-seated is the response to rhyme and rhythm. The full title reads "The Day of Doom, or, a Description of the Great and Last Judgment with a short discourse about Eternity. Eccles. 12, 14. For God shall bring every work into judgment with every secret thing, whether it be good, or whether it be evil."[1] It is composed of two hundred and twenty-four eight-line stanzas with a somewhat jaunty rhythm and a leonine rhyme. After an invocation and an announcement of the day of doom, the dead come from their graves before the throne of God. There the "sheep," who have been elected for salvation, are placed on the right, and the wicked "goats" appear in groups to hear the judge's verdict. These include hypocrites; civil, honest men; those who died in youth before conversion; those who were misled by the example of the good; those who did not understand the teachings of the Scriptures; those who feared martyrdom more than the prospect of hell torment; those who despaired of salvation; and, finally, those who died as babes. All are sternly arraigned from the throne, and all are swept off to a common eternal doom except the infants, for whom a relenting deity reserves "the easiest room in hell."

Two facts should be considered in interpreting "The Day of Doom." The first is that Wigglesworth composed it as a teacher and not as a poet:

> Reader, I am a fool,
> And have adventured
> To play the fool this once for Christ,
> The more his fame to spread.
> If this my foolishness
> Help thee to be more wise,
> I have attained what I seek,
> And what I only prize.

---

[1] The most accessible edition of "The Day of Doom" is a reprint of the sixth edition (1715) by the American News Company, 1867.

The second point is that in versifying a sermon for Puritan worshipers he had his model in the "Bay Psalm Book," which had appeared some twenty years earlier and which was familiar to all his readers. The translators of Psalm CXXI wrote, for example,

> 1. I to the hills lift up mine eyes,
> from whence shall come mine aid
> 2. Mine help doth from Jehovah come,
> which heav'n and earth hath made.

Wigglesworth took up the strain with

> No heart so bold, but now grows cold,
> and almost dead with fear;
> No eye so dry but now can cry,
> and pour out many a tear.

Wigglesworth's resort to so light-footed a measure was not a wanton choice: he undertook to write in a meter with which everybody was familiar a rhythmic summary of what everybody believed; and he was unqualifiedly successful. A final verdict on the rhyming theologian is usually pronounced on the basis of this single production, or, if any further attention is conceded him, the worst of his remaining output is adduced in confirmation.

Yet, in the never quoted lines immediately following the longer poem (a fragment without a title, on the vanity of human wishes), he gave evidence of human kindliness and of poetic power. In these he displayed a mastery of fluent verse, a control of poetic imagery, and a gentle yearning for the welfare of his parishioners' souls which is the utterance of the pastor rather than of the theologian. For a moment God ceases to frown, Christ stands pleading without the gate, and the good pastor meditates on the neglected theme that the kingdom of heaven extends to the human heart:

> Fear your great Maker with a child-like awe,
> Believe his Grace, love and obey his Law.
> This is the total work of man, and this
> Will crown you here with Peace and there with Bliss.

The rigors of "The Day of Doom," however, quite overshadowed the gentler tones and hues of Wigglesworth's other verse. It was the most popular book of the century in the colonies. People memorized its easy, jingling measures as they might have memorized ballads or, at a later day, Mother Goose rhymes; and the grim tableaux became "the solace," as Lowell put it, "of every fireside, the flicker of the pine-knots by which it was conned perhaps adding a livelier relish to its premonitions of eternal combustion."[1] The vogue of "The Day of Doom" serves as a reminder that in the decade when the Royalists were returning to power in old England, the Puritans were dominant in New England. The reaction marked by Morton, Ward, and Williams was only beginning to be significant. But it was irresistible. Just short of a century later the most popular book was Benjamin Franklin's "Way to Wealth."

Anne Bradstreet was the first poet in the colonies to write both extensively and poetically. Her father's post as steward to the Puritan earl of Lincoln gave her, during her girlhood in England, the privileges of a library which she seems to have enjoyed to the fullest. Married at sixteen, she came to America with her husband and her father in the year of the founding of Massachusetts Bay Colony. In public affairs both men became eminent; in the family they were probably the lords and masters of their day. Yet the young wife, her rhymed epistles show, was a passionately devoted helpmeet. She played her part as mistress of the pioneer household in one place after another, and when less than forty was the mother of eight children. Yet somehow in the rare moments of her crowded days — and one can imagine how far apart these must have been — she put into verse "a compleat Discourse and Description of the Four Elements, Constitutions, Ages of Man, Seasons of the Year; Together with an exact Epitome of the four Monarchies, viz., the Assyrian, Persian, Grecian, Roman [this means five long poems, not two] also

[1] "The Harvard Book," Vol. II, p. 158, quoted in Tyler's "Colonial Period," Vol. II, p. 35.

a dialogue between Old England and New concerning the late troubles; with divers other pleasant and serious poems."[1] Halfway between the publication of the "Bay Psalm Book" and "The Day of Doom" they were taken to London by her brother-in-law and there published in 1650 as the work of "The Tenth Muse Lately Sprung up in America."

The list of poets who are said to have influenced Anne Bradstreet bears witness to the use she made of girlhood reading. The chief influence according to her own acknowledgment was the French Du Bartas,[2] whose "Divine Week" had been translated into English by Joshua Sylvester. But, much as she admired him, she never quite undertook the lofty flights in which he was not as impressive to others as to her; and though she was aware of the English "metaphysical" poets and the American workers of acrostics and anagrams, she kept clear of the sort of versifying whose chief titles to attention are complexity and ingenuity. The painstaking elaboration of the "quarternions" interests the modern reader only as survivors of medieval intellectual jugglery. Chaucer had played with the same material; Ben Jonson had reverted to it. Once again she set these quartets in array and let them argue for supremacy: childhood, youth, manhood, old age; earth, air, fire, water; blood, phlegm, choler, melancholy; spring, summer, autumn, winter.

Yet her real claim to interest lies in the "divers other poems" in which she was less literary and more personal. Her "Contemplations" is as poetic in thought as Bryant's "Thanatopsis," or Lanier's "The Marshes of Glynn," or Millay's "Renascence," with which it stands in suggestive contrast in the pageant of the ages; and it was far nearer to the spirit of Bryant than Bryant was to the spirit of the latter two. Like Bryant, she dwelt instinctively on the idea that nature endures but that man is mortal. It was never long absent from the Puritan mind; though when it came

[1] "The Works of Anne Bradstreet in Prose and Verse," edited by John Harvard Ellis. 1867.

[2] See "Life of Guillaume de Salluste Du Bartas," by Urban T. Holmes.

to the average Puritan, it was likely to find no fitter form than in the epitaph

> The path of death it must be trod
> By them that wish to walk with God.

Anne Bradstreet, on the same theme, concluded with noble dignity:

> O Time the fatal wrack of mortal things,
> That draws oblivions curtain over kings,
> Their sumptuous monuments, men know them not,
> Their names without a Record are forgot,
> Their parts, their ports, their pomp's all laid in th' dust
> Nor wit nor gold, nor buildings scape times rust;
> But he whose name is grav'd in the white stone (Rev. ii, 17)
> Shall last and shine when all of these are gone.[1]

She was even more interesting as an early champion of her sex. She did not go so far as to assert equality of woman with man: that was beyond even her imagination; but she did contend that women should be credited for whatever was worthy "small praise."

> Let Greeks be Greeks, and women what they are
> Men have precedency and still excell,
> It is but vain unjustly to wage warre;
> Men can do best, and women know it well
> Preheminence in all and each is yours;
> Yet grant some small acknowledgment of ours.[2]

Naturally she took satisfaction in the achievements of Queen Elizabeth, writing proudly "In Honour of that High and Mighty Princess."

> From all the Kings on earth she won the prize.
> Nor say I more then duly is her due,
> Millions will testifie that this is true.
> She hath wip'd off th' aspersion of her Sex,
> That women wisdome lack to play the Rex;
> *Spains* Monarch, sayes not so, nor yet his host:
> She taught them better manners, to their cost.

---

[1] "The Works of Anne Bradstreet," op. cit. p. 381. [2] Ibid. p. 102.

The *Salique* law, in force now had not been,
If *France* had ever hop'd for such a Queen.
But can you Doctors now this point dispute,
She's Argument enough to make you mute.
Since first the sun did run his nere run race,
And earth had once a year, a new old face,
Since time was time, and man unmanly man,
Come shew me such a *Phoenix* if you can.[1]

She recites the proudest triumphs of Elizabeth, claiming her superiority over Tomris, Dido, Cleopatra, Zenobia, and concluding,

Now say, have women worth? or have they none?
Or had they some, but with our Queen is't gone?
Nay Masculines, you have thus taxt us long,
But she, though dead, will vindicate our wrong.
Let such as say our Sex is void of Reason,
Know tis a slander now, but once was Treason.[2]

This is new wine in old bottles, innovation in idea long preceding innovation in form. It is a constant in literary history that the rebel fights with the arms of his adversary and utters his protests in the rhetoric of his rulers. Anne Bradstreet was almost completely bookish. She emulated Du Bartas with her quartet of quaternions; she owed her "Four Monarchies" to Sir Walter Raleigh's "History of the World." She echoed a dozen of the minor Elizabethans. She was deep in debt to Spenser. Yet, with all her susceptibility to her masculine models, she possessed a grace that was quite her own and that displayed itself even when she was borrowing most freely. She moved straitly at the accepted pace along the paths laid out for the women of her day, but she was courtly in nature and in carriage. Her defects were the defects of her age. Her gifts gave her the "preheminence" in colonial letters that she was not quite bold enough to claim.

---

[1] "The Works of Anne Bradstreet," op. cit. pp. 358, 359. [2] Ibid. p. 361.

Book List

GENERAL

ADDISON, DANIEL D. The Clergy in American Life and Letters. 1900.

ANDREWS, CHARLES MCLEAN. The Colonial Period. 1912.

BELMONT, PERRY. Political Equality; Religious Toleration from Roger Williams to Jefferson. 1927.

BROWN, ALEXANDER. The Genesis of the United States, 1605–1616. 2 vols. 1891.

BRUCE, PHILIP A. Social Life of Virginia in the Seventeenth Century. 1907.

COCKSHOTT, WINIFRED. The Pilgrim Fathers: Their Church and Colony. 1909.

DEXTER, ELIZABETH A. Colonial Women of Affairs. 1924.

DEXTER, HENRY M. The Congregationalism of the Last Three Hundred Years. 1880.

FISKE, JOHN. The Beginnings of New England (new ed.). 1930.

FISKE, JOHN. Old Virginia and Her Neighbors. 2 vols. 1897.

FORD, PAUL LEICESTER. The New England Primer; a History of Its Origin and Development. 1897.

HOLLIDAY, CARL. Woman's Life in Colonial Days. 1922.

JERNEGAN, MARCUS W. The American Colonies, 1492–1750. 1930.

ORIANS, G. HARRISON. "New England Witchcraft in Fiction," *American Literature*, Vol. II, pp. 54–71.

PARRINGTON, VERNON L. The Colonial Mind. 1927.

PARRINGTON, VERNON L. "The Puritan Divines, 1620–1720." Cambridge History of American Literature, Vol. I.

PHILLIPS, JAMES D. Salem in the Seventeenth Century. 1933.

RICHARDSON, CHARLES F. American Literature, 1606–1885, Vol. I. 1893–1894.

ROWE, HENRY K. The History of Religion in the United States. 1924.

SPRAGUE, WILLIAM B. Annals of the American Pulpit, Vols. I, VII. 1857–1869.

STANARD, MARY N. Colonial Virginia: Its People and Customs. 1917.

TYLER, MOSES C. A History of American Literature during the Colonial Period, 1607–1765. 1897.

UPHAM, CHARLES W. Lectures on Witchcraft, Comprising a History of the Delusion in Salem in 1692. 1831.

WALKER, WILLISTON. A History of the Congregational Churches in the United States. 1894.

WENDELL, BARRETT. A Literary History of America. 1901.

WERTENBAKER, THOMAS J. Virginia under the Stuarts, 1607–1688. 1914.

SOUTHERN SETTLERS

Individual Authors

GEORGE ALSOP. A Character of the Province of Maryland. 1666.

[*Available Editions*]

A Character of the Province of Maryland, ed. by Newton D. Mereness. 1902.
"A Character of the Province of Maryland," edited by Clayton C. Hall. Narratives of Early Maryland, Vol. XI. 1910.

[*Biography and Criticism*]

BATES, ERNEST S. "George Alsop." Dictionary of American Biography, Vol. I, pp. 227–228.

JOHN HAMMOND. Leah and Rachel; or, The Two Fruitfull Sisters . . . 1656.

[*Available Editions*]

"Leah and Rachel." Force Historical Tracts, Vol. III. 1844.
"Leah and Rachel." Narratives of Early Maryland, Vol. III. 1910.

[*Biography and Criticism*]

MCCRADY, EDWARD. History of South Carolina under the Royal Government, 1719–1776. 1899.
SIMMS, WILLIAM GILMORE. History of South Carolina (rev. ed.). 1927.
SMITH, WILLIAM ROY. South Carolina as a Royal Province, 1716–1776. 1903.
National Encyclopedia of American Biography, Vol. X, p. 45.

JOHN SMITH. A True Relation (London, 1608); A Map of Virginia, with a Description of the Country (Oxford, 1612); A Description of New England (London, 1616).

[*Available Editions*]

ARBER, EDWARD (Ed.). Travels and Works of Captain John Smith. New edition with an introduction by A. G. Bradley. 1910.
TYLER, LYON G. (Ed.). "Narratives of Early Virginia." Vol. V of Original Narratives of Early American History. 1907.
WINSOR, JUSTIN (Ed.). Narrative and Critical History of America, Vol. III. 1884–1889.
Force Historical Tracts, Vol. II, Nos. 1 and 2. 1844.
Massachusetts Historical Society Collections, third series, Vol. VI.

[*Biography and Criticism*]

ADAMS, HENRY. "Captain John Smith," *North American Review*, January, 1867.
BRADLEY, A. G. Captain John Smith. 1905.
CHATTERTON, E. KEBLE. Captain John Smith. 1927.
FLETCHER, JOHN GOULD. John Smith — also Pocahontas. 1928.
FULLER, THOMAS. The Worthies of England, Vol. I, p. 275. 1662.
GARNETT, DAVID. Pocahontas: or, The Nonparell of Virginia. 1933.
WARNER, CHARLES DUDLEY. Captain John Smith — a Study of His Life and Writings. 1881.
WOODS, K. P. The True Story of Captain John Smith. 1901.

[*Anthologies*]

ALDERMAN, HARRIS, and others. Library of Southern Literature.

CAIRNS, W. B. Early American Writers. 1925.

DUYCKINCK, E. A. and G. L. Cyclopedia of American Literature, Vol. I.

FOERSTER, NORMAN. American Poetry and Prose (rev. ed.). 1934.

SPILLER, ROBERT E. The Roots of National Culture. 1933.

TRENT, W. P. Southern Writers. Selections in Prose and Verse. 1905.

TRENT, W. P., and WELLS, BENJAMIN W. Colonial Prose and Poetry. 1903.

TYLER, LYON G. (Ed.). "Narratives of Early Virginia." Vol. V of Original Narratives of Early American History. 1907.

WINSHIP, GEORGE P. Narratives of Voyages along the New England Coast, 1524–1624. With introduction and notes. 1905.

NORTHERN SETTLERS

Individual Authors

WILLIAM BRADFORD. History of Plymouth Plantation. First published in Massachusetts Historical Society Collections, fourth series, Vol. III.

[*Available Editions*]

Bradford's History of Plymouth Plantation. Printed under the direction of the Secretary of the Commonwealth from the Original MS. 1901.

Bradford's History of Plymouth Plantation, edited, with map and facsimiles, by William T. Davis. 1908.

The Mayflower Pilgrims . . . Compiled by J. T. Wheelwright in the year of the tercentenary. 1920.

[*Biography and Criticism*]

BASSETT, JOHN S. "The Historians." Cambridge History of American Literature, Vol. I, Book I.

BRADFORD, E. P. "Conscious Art in Bradford's History of the Plymouth Plantation," *New England Quarterly*, Vol. I, pp. 133–157.

PLUMB, ALBERT H. William Bradford of Plymouth. 1920.

SHEPARD, JAMES. Governor William Bradford and His Son, Major William Bradford. 1900.

USHER, ROLAND G. The Pilgrims and Their History. 1918.

WALKER, WILLISTON. Ten New England Leaders. 1901.

WINSOR, JUSTIN. Governor Bradford's History of Plymouth Plantation and Its Transmission to Our Times. 1881.

EDWARD JOHNSON. The Wonder working Providence of Sion's Savior in New England. 1654.

[*Available Editions*]

"Johnson's Wonder working Providence, 1628–1651," edited, with map and facsimile, by J. Franklin Jameson. Original Narratives of American History, Vol. X. 1910.

Johnson's Wonder working Providence, 1628–1651. With historical introduction and index by William F. Poole. 1867.

[*Anthologies*]

CAIRNS, W. B. American Writers. 1925.
DUYCKINCK, E. A. and G. L. Cyclopedia of American Literature, Vol. I.
FOERSTER, NORMAN. American Poetry and Prose (rev. ed.). 1934.
HOLLIDAY, CARL. Three Centuries of Southern Poetry, 1607–1907. 1908.
SPILLER, ROBERT E. The Roots of National Culture. 1933.
STEDMAN and HUTCHINSON. Library of American Literature, Vol. I.

[*Biography and Criticism*]

TYLER, MOSES C. A History of American Literature, 1607–1765, Vol. I, pp. 137–146.
Dictionary of American Biography, Vol. X.

THOMAS MORTON. The New English Canaan. 1632.

[*Available Editions*]

"The New English Canaan." Force Tracts, Vol. II, No. 5. 1838.
"The New English Canaan." Prince Society Publications, Vol. XIV. Introduction by Charles Francis Adams. 1883.

[*Biography and Criticism*]

ADAMS, CHARLES FRANCIS. Three Episodes of Massachusetts History. 1892.
SHEHAN, BESTON H. The Book of Gallant Vagabonds. 1925.
Dictionary of American Biography, Vol. XII.

JOHN WINTHROP. John Winthrop's Journal — a History of New England, 1630–1649.

[*Available Edition*]

Winthrop's Journal, edited by James K. Hosmer. Narratives of Early American History, Vols. VII and VIII.

[*Biography and Criticism*]

JOHNSON, EDGAR A. J. "Economic Ideas of John Winthrop," *New England Quarterly*, Vol. III, pp. 235–250.
MCPHAIL, ANDREW. Essays in Puritanism. 1905.
TWICHELL, JOHN H. John Winthrop, First Governor of Massachusetts. 1892.
WINTHROP, ROBERT C. Life and Letters of John Winthrop. 2 vols. 1895.

CHURCHMAN–DICTATORS

Individual Authors

JOHN COTTON. God's Promise to His Plantations, 1630; The Way of the Churches of Christ in New England, 1645; The Controversy Concerning Liberty of Conscience, 1646; The Bloody Tenent, Washed . . . 1647.

[*Available Edition*]

God's Promise . . . Reprinted in Old South Leaflets No. 53. 1894.

[*Biography and Criticism*]

ADAMS, CHARLES F. "The Antinomian Controversy." Three Episodes of Massachusetts History. 1892.

CALDER, ISABEL M. "John Cotton and the New Haven Colony," *New England Quarterly*, Vol. I, pp. 82–94.

M'CLURE, A. W. The Life of John Cotton. 1846.

NORTON, JOHN. Memoir of John Cotton. Preface and notes by Enoch Pond. 1842.

PARKES, HENRY B. "Cotton and Williams Debate Toleration," *New England Quarterly*, Vol. IV, pp. 735–756.

WALKER, WILLISTON. Ten New England Leaders. 1901.

[*Bibliography*]

TUTTLE, JULIUS H. "Writings of the Reverend John Cotton," Bibliographical Essays, a Tribute to Wilberforce Eames. 1924.

NATHANIEL WARD. The Simple Cobler of Aggawam in America. 1647.

[*Available Editions*]

"The Simple Cobler." Force Historical Tracts, Vol. III, No. 8. 1844.

"The Simple Cobler of Aggawam." A Reprint with Facsimile of the Title-page, Preface . . . , and an Essay by Thomas F. Waters. Publications of the Ipswich Historical Society, Vol. XIV. 1905.

[*Biography and Criticism*]

DEAN, JOHN W. A Memoir of the Reverend Nathaniel Ward. 1868.

JOHN WINTHROP. (See page 63.)

ACTIVE DISSENTERS

Individual Authors

THOMAS HOOKER. A Survey of the Summe of Church Discipline. 1648.

[*Biography and Criticism*]

ARCHIBALD, WARREN S. Thomas Hooker. 1933.

LOGAN, WALTER S. Thomas Hooker; the First American Democrat. 1904.

MILLER, PERRY. "Thomas Hooker and the Early Democracy of Connecticut," *New England Quarterly*, Vol. IV, pp. 663–712.

WALKER, GEORGE L. Thomas Hooker: Preacher, Founder, Democrat. 1891.

ROGER WILLIAMS. The Bloody Tenent of Persecution, 1644; The Bloody Tenent Yet More Bloody, 1652; Christenings Make Not Christians, 1645.

[*Available Editions*]

Letters of Roger Williams, 1632–1682. Now First Collected. Edited by John Russell Bartlett. Publications of the Narragansett Club, first series, Vol. VI. 1874.

In Publications of the Narragansett Club. 1866–1874. The Bloody Tenents. . . . Christenings Make Not Christians, edited by H. M. Dexter. Rhode Island Historical Tracts, first series, No. 14. 1881.

[*Biography and Criticism*]

CARPENTER, EDMUND J. Roger Williams; a Study of the Life, Times and Character of a Political Pioneer. 1909.

EASTON, EMILY. Roger Williams, Prophet and Pioneer. 1930.

ERNST, JAMES E. The Political Thought of Roger Williams. 1929.

ERNST, JAMES E. Roger Williams; New England Firebrand. 1932.

FREUND, MICHAEL. "Roger Williams, Apostle of Complete Religious Liberty." Rhode Island Historical Society Collections, Vol. XXVI, pp. 101–133.

GUILD, REUBEN A. An Account of the Writings of Roger Williams. 1862.

HALL, MAY E. Roger Williams. 1917.

STEAD, GEORGE A. "Roger Williams and the Massachusetts-Bay," *New England Quarterly*, Vol. VII, pp. 235–257.

STRAUS, OSCAR S. Roger Williams; the Pioneer of Religious Liberty. 1894.

STRICKLAND, ARTHUR B. Roger Williams: Prophet and Pioneer of Soul Liberty. 1919.

[*Anthologies*]

CAIRNS, W. B. Early American Writers. 1925.

FOERSTER, NORMAN. American Poetry and Prose (rev. ed.). 1934.

SPILLER, ROBERT E. The Roots of National Culture. 1933.

STEDMAN and HUTCHINSON. Library of American Literature, Vol. I.

TRENT and WELLS. Colonial Prose and Poetry. 1903.

EARLY VERSE

General

EARLE, ALICE MORSE. The Sabbath in Puritan New England. 1896.

FISHER, WILLIAM ARMS. Ye Olde New England Psalm Tunes. 1930.

KOUWENHOVEN, JOHN A. "Some Unfamiliar Aspects of Singing in New England, 1620–1810," *New England Quarterly*, Vol. VI, pp. 567–588.

SCHOLES, PERCY A. The Puritans and Music in England and New England. 1934.

SCHOLES, PERCY A. "The Truth about the New England Puritans and Music," *Music Quarterly*, Vol. XIX, pp. 1–17.

STAPLES, SAMUEL E. The Ancient Psalmody and Hymnology. 1880.

TUCKER, SAMUEL M. "The Beginnings of Verse." Cambridge History of American Literature, Vol. I.

Individual Authors

THE BAY PSALM BOOK

[*Available Edition*]

EAMES, WILBERFORCE (Ed.). The Bay Psalm Book: Being a Facsimile Reprint of the First Edition. 1903.

ANNE BRADSTREET. The Tenth Muse lately sprung up in America; or Several Poems, compiled with great variety of Wit and Learning, Full of Delight . . . by a Gentlewoman in those parts. 1650.

[*Available Editions*]

The Works of Anne Bradstreet, in Prose and Verse, edited by John H. Ellis. 1867.

The Works of Mrs. Anne Bradstreet, together with her prose remains; with an introduction by Charles Eliot Norton. 1897.

[*Biography and Criticism*]

Caldwell, Luther. An Account of Anne Bradstreet. 1898.

Campbell, Helen. Anne Bradstreet and Her Time. 1891.

Cambridge History of American Literature, Vol II.

Dictionary of National Biography, Vol II.

Benjamin Tompson. New England's Crisis. 1676(?).

[*Available Editions*]

Hall, Howard J. (Ed.). Benjamin Tompson, His Poems. 1894

Hunnewell, J. F. New England's Crisis. With Prefatory Essay on the Early Poetry of the Provinces. The Club of Odd Volumes. 1894.

Murdock, Kenneth B. Handkerchiefs from Paul: Being Pious and Consolatory Verses of Puritan Massachusetts, including Unpublished Poems by Benjamin Tompson, John Wilson, and Anna Hayden; together with Other Poems by Samuel Torrey and Samuel Danforth and John Wilson. Reprinted from Rare Originals. 1927.

[*Biography and Criticism*]

Green, S. A. Benjamin Tompson, a Graduate of Harvard College. Massachusetts Historical Society Collections. 1895.

Michael Wigglesworth. The Day of Doom; or, a Description of the Great and Last Judgment, . . . (1662); Meat Out of the Eater; or, Meditations concerning the necessity, end and usefulness of Afflictions unto God's Children, . . . (1670); God's Controversy With New England (1662); Vanity of Vanities (appended to third edition of "The Day of Doom").

[*Available Edition*]

The Day of Doom, edited, with Cuts of Inscriptions from early New England Gravestones. 1929.

[*Biography and Criticism*]

Dean, John W. Memoir of the Reverend Michael Wigglesworth. 1871.

Green, Samuel A. Michael Wigglesworth, Earliest Poet among Harvard Graduates. Massachusetts Historical Society Collections. 1895.

Matthiessen, F. O. "Michael Wigglesworth, a Puritan Artist," *New England Quarterly*, Vol. I, pp. 491–504.

Murdock, Kenneth B. Introduction to Reprint of "The Day of Doom." 1929.

[*Anthologies*]

Aiken, Conrad. American Poetry, 1671–1928. 1929.

Boynton, Percy H. American Poetry. 1918.

Cairns, W. B. Early American Writers. 1925.

Duyckinck, E. A. and G. L. Cyclopedia of American Literature, Vol. I.

FOERSTER, NORMAN. American Poetry and Prose (rev. ed.). 1934.
KREYMBORG, ALFRED. Lyric America. 1930.
PRESCOTT, FREDERICK C., and SANDERS, G. D. An Introduction to American Poetry. 1932.
SPILLER, ROBERT E. The Roots of National Culture. 1933.
STEDMAN and HUTCHINSON. Library of American Literature, Vol. I.
TRENT and WELLS. Colonial Prose and Poetry. 1903.

[*Bibliography*]

OTIS, WILLIAM B. Bibliography appended to his American Verse, 1625–1807.
WEGELIN, OSCAR. Early American Poetry. 1903. Early American Poetry, 1800–1820. 1907. Revised and enlarged. 1930.

LITERARY TREATMENT OF THE PERIOD

Drama

BARKER, JAMES NELSON. The Indian Princess; or, La Belle Sauvage. 1808.
BARNES, CHARLOTTE M. The Forest Princess. 1848.
BROUGHAM, JOHN. Pocahontas, or The Gentle Savage. 1855.
CUSTIS, G. W. P. Pocahontas; or, The Settlers of Virginia. 1830.
LONGFELLOW, HENRY W. The New England Tragedies: John Endicott, Giles Corey of the Salem Farms. 1868.
OWEN, RICHARD D. Pocahontas. 1837.

Essays

ADDISON, ALBERT C. The Romantic Story of the "Mayflower" Pilgrims. 1921.
BLAXLAND, GEORGE C. "Mayflower" Essays. 1896.
LAWRENCE, HENRY W. The Not-Quite Puritans. 1928.
LOWELL, JAMES RUSSELL. "New England Two Centuries Ago." Works, Vol. II.
WASHBURN, ROBERT C. Prayer for Profit. 1930.

Fiction

CARLISLE, HELEN GRACE. We Begin. 1932.
COOKE, JOHN ESTEN. My Lady Pocahontas. 1885.
HAWTHORNE, NATHANIEL. "Endicott and the Red Cross."
HAWTHORNE, NATHANIEL. "The Gentle Boy."
HAWTHORNE, NATHANIEL. "The Gray Champion."
HAWTHORNE, NATHANIEL. The House of the Seven Gables.
HAWTHORNE, NATHANIEL. "Legends of the Province House."
HAWTHORNE, NATHANIEL. The Scarlet Letter.
HAWTHORNE, NATHANIEL. "Young Goodman Brown."
JOHNSTON, MARY. Audrey.

JOHNSTON, MARY. The Great Valley.
JOHNSTON, MARY. To Have and to Hold.
JOHNSTON, MARY. Prisoners of Hope.
MOTLEY, JOHN LOTHROP. Merry Mount, a Romance of the Massachusetts Colony. 1849.
SIMMS, WILLIAM GILMORE. The Cassique of Kiawah. 1857.
TAYLOR, I. IMLAY. Anne Scarlet, a Romance of Colonial Times. 1901.
WHITTIER, JOHN G. Leaves from Margaret Smith's Journal. 1849.

Poetry

FIRTH, CHARLES H. (Ed.). An American Garland: Ballads Relating to America, 1563–1759.
HOLMES, OLIVER W. "The Deacon's Masterpiece."
LONGFELLOW, HENRY W. The Courtship of Miles Standish.
STEVENSON, BURTON E. Poems of American History. 1908.
WALLINGTON, N. U. American History by American Poets, Vol. I. 1911.

CHAPTER III

The Eighteenth Century to the Revolution

The Turn of the Century

THE student of the colonial period who is not willing to dwell indefinitely on the seventeenth century may take a long jump at this point to certain characters whose lives bridged the centuries and bear witness to the changes which were taking place. Roger Williams, the latest-born of the men thus far cited, lived from 1604 (before the first colonial settlement in America) to 1684, from the beginning of the reign of James I almost to the end of Charles II's. In this period the little settlements scattered along the seacoast from Virginia to the north had slowly spread back from the tide-water regions toward the foothills. The population of the colonies was reaching toward a quarter of a million, more than a third of whom were settled in Virginia and Maryland. Trade, commerce, and agriculture were tending toward the first outcropping of a leisure class. Harvard College could already count its lifetime in generations; William and Mary was founded; Yale was to come in 1702.

In the South the relatively liberal rule of the landed gentry had, with the notable exception of Governor Berkeley's mistaken regime, encountered no fundamental challenge; but in New England the hold of the churchman-dictators was being slowly and reluctantly relaxed. In the old country, in spite of the restoration of kingship in 1660, the Puritan uprising had been markedly effective; for after the Protectorate the arbitrary power of king and council was increasingly restrained. There was a parallel movement in the democracy of the English colonies. American settlers with a highly developed sense of justice resented a bad royal governor like Andros, and were able to force his withdrawal; and they resented unreasonable domination by the clergy, and were independent enough to shake it off. In the years near 1700 Harvard College became for the first time something more than a training school for preachers; the right to vote in Boston was made to depend on moral character and property ownership instead of on membership in the church; and in the midst of the Salem witchcraft hysteria judges and grand jurymen caught their balance and refused any longer to act as cat's-paws of the fanatics. The passage to the eighteenth century was therefore more notably than usual a time of transition in common thinking, and the record of the change is clearly discernible in the literary writings of the old-line conservatives Cotton and Increase Mather; in the "Diary" of Samuel Sewall, who was able to see the light and to change slowly with his generation; and in the "Journal" of Sarah Kemble Knight, who represented the silent unorthodoxy of hundreds of other well-behaved and respectable people.

The "Diary" of Samuel Sewall, which carries a consecutive story from 1673 to 1729, is the richest single document for this period and hardly to be rivaled in the colonial centuries. It was written without bias (for Sewall had no thought of publication), and it was not printed until a hundred and fifty years later.[1] Sewall's "Diary" is in American literature a close parallel to that of John Evelyn in English letters. The more famous diary of Pepys, nearly simultaneous, covers only a decade; but Evelyn's life and his diary covered almost exactly the same years, and the writers occupied similar positions in society. Both were educated men (Sewall was a graduate of Harvard), and both held positions of trust and honor. Sewall at one time was librarian at Harvard, though probably not burdened by his duties. He was son-in-law of one of the richest men in the colony. He moved through successive posts in the law from justice of the peace to chief justice of Massachusetts. He sat in the witchcraft cases at Salem. He was a pillar of the church.

---

[1] Reprinted in full only in Massachusetts Historical Society Collections, fifth series, Vols. VI–VIII.

In this bulky source book of history, which his "Diary" has become, there are two leading elements: the writer, and the social order of which he was a part. As to Sewall himself, historians have taken two views. The most industrious historian of colonial literature, writing in the spirit of the eulogist, dubbed him "great by almost every measure of greatness."[1] The most substantial historian of the whole course of American letters denied him either greatness or originality and called him "a Puritan embodiment of Defoe's merchant ideal."[2] The truth is somewhere between. Tyler disarmed himself critically by writing in a mood of funeral laudation; Parrington supplied a negative answer to the question as to whether any man can be a hero to the critical reader of his diary. The facts seem to be that Sewall was a solid, industrious, thrifty conservative, and a beneficiary of the social system as it was.[3] He was a capitalist and concerned in the protection of property; he was an officeholder and, barring certain rubs and frictions of a personal nature, satisfied with the organization of the state. As a churchman he was a devout worshiper, and he was undisturbed by theory or speculation in any field. Even on the bench he was advanced to high eminence not because he was an expert in the law but because he was a man of good judgment. In only two respects did Sewall distinguish himself sufficiently to stand out against the background of his times. He did write a little pamphlet, "The Selling of Joseph," which was probably the first antislavery utterance printed in America, and he did at one time show unusual candor and courage. This was in 1697, five years after the Salem witchcraft trials, when, repenting of his part in them,[4] he chose to impose upon himself the humiliation usually reserved for disreputable offenders by standing before the congregation while the pastor read his "Petition of Penitence."

---

[1] Tyler, "American Literature, 1607–1765," Vol. II, p. 99.
[2] Parrington, "Main Currents," Vol. I, p. 91.
[3] N. H. Chamberlain, "Samuel Sewall and the World He Lived In."
[4] Ibid. Chap. X.

More important than the self-portrait of the man, however, is the picture of his times. It is the material, of course, and not the picture itself; for it lacks anything in the way of composition, as the facts of ordinary daily life do in the order of their occurrence. The sober but not unrelieved background of the times is a composite of various strands. Religion was its strongest fiber. Few weeks passed in which he made no record of sermon, fast, christening, wedding, funeral, or special celebration. These were among the chief social happenings of the calendar. Funerals, as well as more festive occasions, were accompanied with gifts of gloves and rings; refreshments were ample if not lavish; and the bill for strong drinks was likely to be a heavy item, for prohibition is of recent origin, and among the Puritans self-control made drunkenness as infrequent as drinking was common. Against frivolity too they set their minds; and Sewall's "Diary" registered his protests at "tricks" and dancing and May festivals, and even the celebration of Christmas and Easter, which were triply hated because they had their origins in pagan tradition and had come to the present through the Church of Rome and the Church of England. Yet the objections to these practices and festivals show that they were real disturbances in Sewall's Boston, as was the roistering of sailors and other strangers in town. Any fifty pages will do as well as any other for a sampling of the monumental work. It is best read selectively and with the aid of an index. Carefully perused, it reveals the growth of a human community humanly presented. Just how distinctively local this community was can be seen by comparing it in imagination with any English community of the time or any Southern plantation.

It is hard to free a discussion of the Mathers — Richard, Increase, Cotton, and Samuel — from the "rancors of dead partisanships" and the gossip of old wives' tales; for the middle two, who brought the family from celebrity to notoriety, were hot in controversy for a round half-century and have been belabored and belauded ever since. A recital of bare facts is therefore a particularly important preliminary to an attempt at interpretation.

There were four members of the "dynasty": Richard (1596–1669) was an Oxford graduate who came to Boston in 1635, escaping from England after encountering the heavy hand of Laud. He was independent enough to have been forced to this move, and "tonitruous" enough in the pulpit to be called promptly to a Dorchester parish, over which he presided until his death. Increase (1639–1723), after completing his Harvard course, was sent abroad in the closing years of the Protectorate, received a master's degree at Trinity, Dublin, served as chaplain in Cromwell's army, and after the Restoration returned to Boston. He was pastor of the North Church from 1664 till his death; president of Harvard (1685–1701); colonial agent to London in negotiations for a new charter (1688–1692); author of nearly two hundred books and pamphlets. Cotton (1663–1728) was a Harvard A.B. and A.M.; associate pastor with his father (1684–1723); successor till his death five years later; an F.R.S., and recipient of an honorary degree from the University of Aberdeen; a Bay Colony man without travel; author of over four hundred books and pamphlets. Samuel, born in 1704, carried on the family tradition without distinction. He was a Boston preacher until 1784.

The Mather name owes its emergence in colonial history to the joint careers of Increase and Cotton, and its controversial importance, to the qualities of their minds, which made them champions of a declining order and which unfortunately identified them with the tragic events of the Salem witchcraft episode.[1] They were extraordinarily erudite students and, in what passed for scientific inquiry, quite up to the progress of their day. Yet the characterization of the

---

[1] R. and L. Boas, "Cotton Mather," Chap. IV; G. L. Kittredge, "Notes on Witchcraft," American Antiquarian Society Proceedings, Vol. XVIII, pp. 148–212; K. B. Murdock, "Increase Mather," Chap. XVI; W. F. Poole, "Cotton Mather and Salem Witchcraft"; C. W. Upham, "Salem Witchcraft and Cotton Mather"; Barrett Wendell, "Cotton Mather, Puritan Priest," Chap. VI.

medieval churchman cited on the opening page of this volume is perfectly applicable to them. Even in eighteenth-century Massachusetts it can be said that the spirit of two leading divines "seemed to rely on everything except its sin-crushed self . . . trusted everything except its senses; . . . in the earthly Church beheld the heavenly, and in fleshly joys discerned the devil's lures." The variations are slight; the essential picture is the same; and the picture should be shown against a background of the times and of the immediate past.

For popular superstition still ran riot, and the belief in a personal providence and a personal devil added to the confusions of ignorance. Medicine, slowest to join the learned professions, displayed hardly a vestige of science. Physicians depended for honest effects on a few herb remedies and on powerful emetics and the letting of blood. The populace trusted in curatives like the royal touch for the "king's evil," or the anointing of implements instead of the cuts or bruises made by them. Sir Kenelm Digby, courtly subject of Charles II, reported that he overcame a persistent illness by having the fumes of camomile poured into his ear. The same sort of primitive speculation ruled the interpretations of natural and biological science. Witchcraft flourished in this soil. Between 1560 and 1600 in the little kingdom of Scotland, with a population hardly larger than Connecticut's today, there were eight thousand executions for witchcraft, an average of nearly four a week; and James I, who was Scotland's gift to England, was author of a royal work on demonology.

It is natural, then, that Increase Mather should have written on "The Fearful Sights and Signs in Heaven . . . Presages of Great Calamities at Hand" (1683); "A Discourse concerning Comets . . . and the Remarkable Events which have followed" (1683); or his more celebrated "Essay for the Recording of Illustrious Providences" (1684) or his "Cases of Conscience concerning evil Spirits" (1693). Natural too that his son Cotton should have compiled his "Wonders of the Invisible World" (1693) and included chapters on "Illustrious Wonderful Providences" in his monumental church history, with its monumental name "Magnalia Christi Americana: or, The Ecclesiastical History of New England, 1620–1698." The two shorter books and the section on things supernatural in the longer work loom into tragical significance on account of the focusing of primitive superstition distorted by religious credulity on the Salem witchcraft episode of 1691–1692.[1] This started in the household of the Reverend Samuel Parris, a contentious minister of Salem who had as servants an Indian and his half-breed wife. Through them ten girls, most of them from twelve to seventeen years of age, were "afflicted." Their behavior first marked them as no more than naughty nuisances. To escape punishment, they claimed to be bewitched. Challenged as to their persecutors, they specified certain old women, and then, emboldened by the success of their accusations, they progressed to people higher in the social scale. The sensation they produced moved rapidly to a case of fearful social hysteria in which the credulity of the judges before whom the accused were brought was as flagrant as that of the most illiterate. Early in the proceedings the court nevertheless requested an opinion from the clergy. This opinion was written by Cotton Mather, and on the whole was remarkably judicial. In its eight articles it advised caution at several points which, if observed by the court, would have prevented the extreme penalty in every case. Yet it concluded:

> 8. Nevertheless, we cannot but humbly recommend unto the government, the speedy and vigorous prosecutions of such as have rendered themselves obnoxious, according to the directions given in the laws of God and the wholesome statutes of the English nation for the detection of witchcrafts.[2]

Unfortunately this closing article more than offset the cautions that preceded it. Before the autumn of 1692 nineteen victims met the death penalty; one died of ill-treatment in prison; and Hecuba, the half-breed servant, was sold into

---

[1] For a brief account see John Fiske's "New France and New England," Chap. V.

[2] Ibid. p. 172.

slavery by her godly persecutors to meet the costs of her imprisonment. Only a fortunate interruption of the proceedings by the court calendar gave time for sober thought and the inevitable reaction. The place of the Mathers, then pre-eminent among the clergy of the colony, was thus a complicated one. Credulous with their generation, they were cited as believers in witchcraft and as instigators of the proceedings, in spite of the cautions which they counseled; and an unhappy story, that one of them was seen on horseback grimly witnessing an execution, provided just the dramatic touch to implicate them in the popular mind as complete subscribers to the tragic miscarriage of justice.

If the events of 1692 were not enough to condemn them, Increase Mather's "Illustrious Providences" of 1684 and Cotton Mather's "Wonders of the Invisible World" of 1693 stood as grim documentary evidence. The episode of a little more than six months' duration was followed by long-drawn controversy, of which a typical exchange was Robert Calef's "More Wonders of the Invisible World" with the rejoinders by Deodat Lawson in defense of the clergy.[1]

So the Mathers, father and son, were passed down into historical ignominy. It became the fashion to deride and decry them. Irving took his fling at them in "The Legend of Sleepy Hollow"; Whittier, in the "Double-Headed Snake of Newbury"; and Fitz-Greene Halleck reached the climax in an abusive passage on the author of the "Magnalia" when he described him as

> . . . a chronicler of tales more strange than true,
> New England's chaplain, and her history's father;
> A second Monmouth's GEOFFREY, a new
> HERODOTUS, their laurelled victor rather,
> For in one art he soars above them high:
> The Greek or Welshman does not always lie.[2]

---

[1] A good cross section of the controversy is presented in Stedman and Hutchinson's "Library of American Literature," Vol. II, pp. 75–189, containing passages from the Mathers, Sewall's "Confession," and excerpts from Calef and Lawson.

[2] Fitz-Greene Halleck, "Connecticut" (an unfinished poem), stanza XVIII.

These latter days have inclined to restore to the Mathers some of their lost prestige. Whatever measure of fame they enjoyed at the height of their careers was due to the measure in which they represented the political, ecclesiastical, and cultural character of their times. Whatever they lost gave evidence of the cruel capacity of the people to turn upon any popular favorite who meets their displeasure. Seen at this distance Increase and Cotton Mather were remarkable and remarkably fallible. They were industrious to an extraordinary degree. They did a prodigious amount of study which resulted in a prodigious amount of print and talk. They were learned in the learning of their day and as ostentatious in their erudition as one might expect from men who were more learned than wise. They suffered from extreme popularity and from a loss of balance that comes from continuously breathing an atmosphere of adulation. By this they became somewhat intoxicated, and at times they both talked and acted like children. They were at once the products and the victims of their generation — gifted enough to profit for a while by their opportunity, but so far lacking in largeness of nature that they had to suffer at the hands of the people, which had been calloused for long by unreserved applause.

Thus far the figures in the pageant have almost all been considered as predominantly religious characters, and all but one has been a member of the dominant sex. Sarah Kemble Knight, in her breezy journal,[1] is a reminder that by 1700 the American colonist who put pen to paper could be secular minded; and that a woman could live a vigorous, independent life and could hold her position discreetly in the community while she entertained a good many mental reservations that she was astute enough not to express to her own disadvantage. Mrs. Knight was widowed in 1703, at the age of thirty-seven. In the next year she undertook a business trip, apparently for the purpose of settling her estate. This involved her in a seven-day journey to New York, with a

[1] "Journal of Madame Knight," edited by W. H. Learned, 1865.

leisurely stop there and shorter stays in New Haven, where she was level-headed and persistent enough to carry through her negotiations. She recorded the chronicle of this round trip to New York in a journal which did not get into print until 1825. After reading this account one is not surprised to learn that for seven years she conducted a dame school in Boston, and that she had the courage then to remove to New London, Connecticut, where the records show that she was involved in land transactions on a rather generous scale, and where she doubtless had a hand in marrying her daughter into one of the leading families.

Whether it was a matter of choice or accident, it is no doubt a fact that her later years were more comfortable than they might have been if her journal had been published during her lifetime; for her tone was frequently frivolous and irreligious and would doubtless have been condemned as blasphemous by the churchmen of her day. One need only read the painful soul searchings in the diaries of the Mathers, or of Jonathan Edwards, or of John Woolman to realize how it would have rasped the sensibilities of the average worshiper. Crossing the river in a cranky canoe, she dared not lodge her "tongue a hair's breadth more on one side of my mouth than tother, nor so much as to think on Lott's wife; for a wry thought would have oversett our wherey."[1] Facing the prospect of another rough fording, she imagined herself doused "like a holy Sister Just come out of a Spiritual Bath in dripping Garments."[2] Informed that the innkeeper at Kingston was named Devil, she questioned whether she ought to "go to the Devil to be helpt out of affliction."[3] Disturbed at another inn by noisy tipplers in the next room, she composed some couplets the burden of which was the wish that they might drink themselves into stupor and silence.

But she was not merely a quipster: she revealed a genuine intercolonial consciousness. She was interested in the trading and the social customs in Connecticut and recorded them at

1 "Journal of Madame Knight," op. cit. p. 27. 2 Ibid. pp. 27–28. 3 Ibid. p. 37.

considerable length. New York was a foreign city to her, with the stamp of Dutch architecture and domestic life still evident and with a cosmopolitan tone quite unlike anything at home. Her little book is one of the few vivacious documents that survive from early eighteenth-century New England. It reveals the writer as a transition character; a witness to the persistent secularizing process that was going on; and, in her readiness to travel and to shift her colonial allegiance, an early exemplar of the widening country of which William Byrd and others to come are further representatives.

The Widening Country

William Byrd — A Tale of Two Colonies

The turn to William Byrd, Gentleman, of Virginia is a turn not only to a different brand of colonist but to a different social order; for the South was dominated in his lifetime (1674–1744), as it had been from the outset, by the gentry rather than by the clergy. The emphasis here was on the mansion house, the center of a great estate, rather than on the meeting house, the center of the village. Christenings, weddings, and funerals were conducted under the ancestral rooftree rather than before the altar; and even in the little towns the house of worship was so modest that it could be noted in one community that fifty pounds had been spent on the church and five hundred on the tavern. "A man," said one Virginian, "might be a Christian in any church, but a gentleman only in the Church of England."[1] Sabbath observance was expected, to be sure, and the support of church and parson was provided for in the taxes. Nonconformists had to pay twice if they were not, as sometimes happened, ostracized or banished; but the Southerner did not live "as ever in his great Taskmaster's eye," and his God had to share his attention with his lady and his honor.

Amusement and recreation found a very definite place in

---

[1] M. W. Goodwin, "The Colonial Cavalier," p. 219.

his program. Gambling was as prevalent as in the London of the eighteenth century; horse racing, "the sport of kings," was the favorite sport of the planter; for the commoners it was cockfighting and gouging, the most brutal form of personal combat. In William Byrd's latter years the theater found a home in Charleston, Williamsburg, and Annapolis, a hundred years before it met with equal hospitality in Philadelphia, New York, or New England. At William and Mary College there were ordinances which would have been unintelligible at Harvard, against the owning of race horses by students and against the keeping of fighting cocks. In a Virginia gazette of 1737 there was a village program for St. Andrew's Day that included a horse race, singlestick fighting, a fiddlers' competition, foot races, a beauty contest, and the singing of a "Quire of Ballads . . . by a number of songsters, all of them to have liquor sufficient to clear their wind-pipes."[1] The South was never in need, as Hawthorne wrote in 1850 that the whole nation was, "to learn again the forgotten art of gayety."

Nevertheless, there was a brutal grimness in legal statutes which the South shared with the North, because both shared it with the mother country. The stocks, the pillory, the whipping post were all employed, extreme penalties for minor offenses were common, and the death penalty was invoked for an extraordinary number of violations.[2] But the law was not especially arrayed against infractions of the ecclesiastical code, and the Southern gentleman was ready to blink at legislation directed at gambling, dueling, and the other peccadilloes of his kind.

William Byrd, author of "A History of the Dividing Line" and the briefer records called "A Journey to the Land of Eden" and "A Progress to the Mines," was a distinguished example of the leisure class in the South,[3] the apex, with his

---

[1] Goodwin, op. cit. pp. 151, 152. [2] Ibid. pp. 245 ff.

[3] The discussion of social origins in Virginia has been pursued at length by P. A. Bruce, "Social Life in Virginia in the Seventeenth Century," and T. J. Wertenbaker, "Patrician and Plebeian in Virginia" and "The Planters of Colonial Virginia." The former stresses aristocratic lineage, and the latter the rise of the merchant class.

lady, of the social order. Born to the purple, educated in England, elected to the House of Burgesses before his majority, he became a leading citizen and a pre-eminent landholder, the inevitable representative of the colony in disputes with its neighbor to the south. He was not in the remotest sense a frontiersman, though he lived on the very edge of the frontier, penetrated it deeply, and was an intimate observer of it. For he was completely equipped to resist it; his farthest west was only three hundred miles from the sea; and he was at heart an Easterner, a prosperous member of the creditor class, a respected representative of an established social order.

Throughout his writings his frequent references to religion reveal the worldly tolerance of the Anglican, in marked contrast with the inflexibility of the dissenter, solicitous for the orthodoxy of his recent invention or adoption. The only touch of complacency emerges in an allusion to paganism in a neat innuendo concerning the myrtle, laurel, and bay trees which, "sacred to Venus and Apollo, grow commonly in a very dirty soil."[1] He was more generous than many of his neighbors to the Quakers, commending them (as Franklin might have done) for their diligence and frugality; noting (as Roger Williams would have) that they acquired their land by purchase from the Indians, thus at a very low price purchasing "the credit of being more righteous than their neighbors"; and acknowledging with the wry face of the militarist that their pacifist principles put into practice had "saved them from many wars and massacres wherein the other colonies have been indiscreetly involved."[2] His tongue was clearly in his cheek in his discussion of the evangelizing of the Indians. He could give no good account of it, he said, and he could recommend nothing better than, and nothing so good as, the policy of intermarriage endorsed by "the most Christian king" of the French colonial possessions.

---

[1] Byrd, "Journey to the Land of Eden . . ." (edited by Mark Van Doren), p. 35.

[2] Ibid. p. 25.

I may safely venture to say, the Indian women would have made altogether as honest wives for the first planters, as the damsels they used to purchase from aboard the ships. It is strange, therefore, that any good Christian should have refused a wholesome, straight bedfellow, when he might have had so fair a portion with her, as the merit of saving her soul.[1]

At the conclusion of the "History of the Dividing Line," where some devout subscription was conventionally appropriate, Byrd paid his respects to the king of England rather than to the ruler of the Kingdom of Heaven.

Byrd's lack of self-righteousness as a religionist is more than offset by his pharisaism as a Virginian. He charged the delegates from Carolina with shiftless and irresponsible tactics which were more of an obstruction than an aid in establishing the boundary line between the colonies; and he rather enjoyed the thought that they were, if anything, too good for the social flotsam and jetsam they represented. It was a policy in the province, he wrote, to settle runaway slaves, debtors, and criminals along the border, for they made good buffers; a clergyman could fare no better there than spiders in Ireland; the poor whites were depleted in health by the unwholesome swamp airs, and loitered their lives away "like Solomon's sluggard." It was not surprising, therefore, he alleged, that the commissioners who joined the Virginians on the arduous job of running the line through the pestiferous jungle should have wearied of it and found flimsy pretexts for backing out. But the stalwarts on the northern side of the boundary served notice that they would complete the task by themselves; the Carolinians might take their survey findings or leave them; the Virginians would at least have something to go on for the future in boundary disputes. Things came to a head on a Sunday:

The gentlemen of Carolina assisted not at our public devotions, because they were taken up all the morning in making a formidable protest against our proceeding on the line without them. When the divine service was over, the surveyors set about making the plots of

---

[1] Byrd, op. cit. p. 102.

so much of the line as we had run this last campaign. Our pious friends of Carolina assisted in this work with some seeming scruple, pretending it was a violation of the sabbath, which we were the more surprised at, because it happened to be the first qualm of conscience they had ever been troubled with during the whole journey. They had made no bones of staying from prayers to hammer out an unnecessary protest, though divine service was no sooner over, but an unusual fit of godliness made them fancy that finishing the plots, which was now matter of necessity, was a profanation of the day. However, the expediency of losing no time, for us who thought it our duty to finish what we had undertaken, made such a labor pardonable.[1]

A man who writes with the vivacity of William Byrd invites a second glance. He is more likely to be enjoyable as a contributor to literature than he is to be valuable as a source of historical material. Byrd offers a nice illustration. While on his uncomfortable joint survey of the "dividing line" he kept a diary, circumstantial and no more than normally prejudiced. Ten years later he expanded it to twice its length. The two versions, printed parallel, show what literary embellishment did to humdrum fact.[2] To make his diary readable (it is the second version that survives), he supplied a lively introduction, eliminated most of the references to a troublesome Virginia commissioner and a quarrel among the Virginians, and amplified and supplemented his contemptuous observations on North Carolina and the Carolinians.[3] What Byrd saw in the colony to the south was its grosser frontier characteristics, alien to the disposition of the master of Westover; what he did not see, or saw fit not to acknowledge, was that North Carolina had its gentry, its learning, its wide estates, its regard for the social amenities. Unfortunately, what North Carolina did not have was a witness to its virtues who could write as well as its Virginia neighbor could.[4]

[1] Byrd, op. cit. pp. 124–125.

[2] "William Byrd's Dividing Line Histories," edited by W. K. Boyd.

[3] Ibid. For the quarrel, pp. 125–143, 179–187; for added anti-Carolina material, pp. 50, 52, 54, 56, 58, 64, 66, 68, 70, 72, 74, 76, 80, 92, 94, 96, 104, etc.

[4] Two North Carolina contemporaries of Byrd were John Lawson, "History of North Carolina," 1708 (reprinted, Charlotte, North Carolina, 1903); and John Brickell, "Natural History of North Carolina," 1731.

Mrs. Knight in her journeyings was aware of yokels and dullards all along the route; William Byrd, who forced his way farther back from tidewater, noted a still rougher and cruder element. Neither was much of a theorist; each was subject to provincial loyalty. If anyone had tried to involve the great landlord in a debate with the Madame he would probably have surrendered the field with a smiling thought of the echo rock at Wicco-quoi creek "that, like a fluent help-mate, will return her good man seven words for one, and after all be sure to have the last." For he was a courtly, suave male aristocrat, with a tinge of the social pharisaism that is the not unenviable endowment of the man who is utterly secure among his fellows and before his king.

Jonathan Edwards — Connecticut and New Jersey

Jonathan Edwards comes into the picture in the early half of the eighteenth century with a violence of contrast that throws him almost completely out of perspective. The comparison with Benjamin Franklin is inevitable, but it is also misleading. Franklin appears as type and spokesman for trade and commerce, for thrift and industry, for applied science, for morality rather than religion, for deism rather than Calvinism, for the school and library rather than the church, for the newspaper and almanac rather than the sermon or the tract; and Edwards dedicated his remarkable powers primarily to the defense of a medieval theology. But Franklin's way of life did not sweep Edwards's way of life out of its path. Calvinism was doomed, but it was doomed under a suspended sentence; it survives yet in wide reaches of America. It may have been swept out of the studies of certain liberal ecclesiastics and out of the market places and main streets of a few of the larger towns through which the tides of travel and traffic poured most freely. But in original or modified form it was deeply implanted in the minds of the lesser clergy; and it was transmitted from generation to generation in the homes of the majority, who always find it easier to accept the old than to analyze, amend, or reject it.

Edwards was thus the propounder of an accepted faith which was being amended or rejected by the most alert minds of his day but which was in general favor among the docile and the inert. Perhaps the most striking distinction between him and the church leaders who preceded him was that they were fundamentally more concerned with church polity, and he was more absorbed in religious theory and religious experience. The obvious distinction between him and the rising tide of materialism is that like his near successor, John Woolman, he was relatively indifferent to social and political life. A man who could declare that "the work of God in the conversion of one soul . . . is a more glorious work than the creating of the whole material universe" could hardly be otherwise. In the preface to his "Freedom of the Will" he wrote, while disclaiming that he was a disciple of Calvin, "I should not take it at all amiss to be called a *Calvinist* for distinction's sake." In his personal narrative he recorded that from "childhood up, my mind had been full of objections against the doctrine of God's sovereignty, in choosing whom he would to eternal life, and rejecting whom he pleased; leaving them eternally to perish, and be everlastingly tormented in hell. It used to appear like a horrible doctrine to me."[1] In some mysterious way, however, by inner assurance rather than by any conscious process of reasoning, he became satisfied as to this sovereignty. And now there followed a strangely irreconcilable discrepancy between the sense of a just God (and an angry one) and a benign and gentle one. The effort has been made to reconcile them, as if it were necessary or desirable to reduce any man to consistency in all his utterances. But it is time wasted, except as an engaging exercise in casuistry.[2] Why not let them stand either as lyric utterances, or as expressions of moods, or as evidences of changing points of view?

---

[1] "Personal Narrative" ("Works of President Edwards," New York, 1843, Vol. I, p. 15).

[2] F. I. Carpenter, "The Radicalism of Jonathan Edwards," *New England Quarterly*, Vol. IV, pp. 629–644.

. . . I have often, since that first conviction, had quite another kind of sense of God's sovereignty than I had then. I have often since had not only a conviction, but a delightful conviction. The doctrine has very often appeared exceeding pleasant, bright, and sweet. . . . The first instance that I remember of that inward, sweet delight in God and divine things that I have lived much in since, was on reading these words, I. Tim. i. 17, *Now unto the King eternal, immortal, invisible, the only wise God, be honor and glory for ever and ever, Amen.* As I read the words, there came into my soul, and was as it were diffused through it, a sense of the glory of the Divine Being. . . . Not long after . . . I walked abroad . . . in my father's pasture, for contemplation. And as I was walking there, and looking up on the sky and clouds, there came into my mind so sweet a sense of the glorious *majesty* and *grace* of God, that I know not how to express. I seemed to see them both in a sweet conjunction; majesty and meekness joined together; it was a sweet and gentle, and holy majesty; and also a majestic meekness; an awful sweetness; a high, and great, and holy gentleness.[1]

Edwards's adult life was now to be devoted to reconciling this idea of a sweetly beneficent God to the idea of the harsh God of the Calvinists. How he became subject to this vengeful deity, he acknowledged, he "never could give an account." The fact remains, however; and the young mystic, full of beatific adorations, gradually succumbed to the maturing theologian who strove to delve into the psychology of religious experience instead of accepting its ecstatic visions, and to buttress with metaphysical speculations the stern God for whom he felt the need of a justification. It was a dilemma for even a greater mind than his. His mind was orderly with an instinct toward observation and deduction, of which it had given precocious proofs. His emotions were rarefied and intense, lifting him from the laboratory to the mount of vision. Some way must be found to reconcile himself to himself. He could not forgo his gracious God; he could not surrender to the forces of reaction the hallowed doctrines of salvation by election and the necessary corollary of natural

[1] Edwards, op. cit. Vol. I, pp. 15, 16.

depravity. If man could not earn salvation by his own efforts and his own deserts, it must be that he had no freedom of will. Edwards proved this to his own satisfaction. If God in his goodness was condemning fallen man to ineffable and endless punishment, it must be that man was infinitely sinful. Edwards satisfied himself of this by the simple reasoning that it was infinitely sinful to offend against infinite goodness.

It remained for him to bring these lessons home to his auditors, for he doubtless in his day reached a larger public by the spoken word than by his printed treatises. In his sermons Edwards displayed extraordinary art. It was part of the pulpiteering method of his century and the preceding ones to indulge in vainglorious parades of erudition. Edwards stripped his discourses of pedantry and sermonic display. He knew his audiences and what they could understand. Starting from assumptions that their Calvinist creed committed them to, he moved on by simple, intelligible, unescapable steps through the "exegesis," or explanatory stage; and when he came to the "application" he drove home his point — that he was not talking vague abstractions but fearful truths — with terrifying pertinence to the men and women sitting before him. Had they ever thought of eternal torment? Let them think for a moment of a flame; of putting a finger into one, a hand, an arm, a whole body; of enduring the pain a moment, several minutes, an hour, a day, a week, a year, a century, an eternity. This prospect faced them.

You have offended him infinitely more than ever a stubborn rebel did his prince; and yet it is nothing but his hand that holds you from falling into the fire every moment; it is ascribed to nothing else, that you did not go to hell the last night; that you was suffered to awake again in this world, after you closed your eyes to sleep; and there is no other reason to be given, why you have not dropped into hell since you arose in the morning, but that God's hand has held you up; there is no other reason to be given why you have not gone to hell, since you have sat here in the house of God, provoking

> his pure eyes by your sinful wicked manner of attending his solemn worship; yea, there is nothing else that is to be given as a reason why you do not this very moment drop down into hell.[1]

Again and again his calmly, coldly delivered, but relentless iterations reduced his hearers to utter fright.

Holmes in the story of the "one-hoss shay" wrote lightly of such logical discourses and the theology beneath them. It was perhaps a direct achievement of Edwards that he made his sermons so awfully conclusive and invulnerable to logical attack that the only way to overthrow them was to undermine the assumptions on which they were constructed. This in itself was logical; there is no quicker way to demolish an argument than to deny its original premises. Edwards's proofs were so unassailable that, once held up to application as few but he could hold them, they were also intolerable; and being intolerable they were doomed. Once more the medieval mind reasserted itself in this Connecticut theologian and philosopher, still relying on everything but its sin-crushed self, still feeling life's terror and its pitifulness, still oppressed by the terror of the Judgment Day.

But colonial America was clearly a land of opportunity. It did not need the theology of a king-ridden, priest-ridden Europe. The forests were cleared; the Indians were in retreat. It was high time for a new gospel, the gospel of action. Before turning to this, however, it is necessary to pause for a moment, at least, with another of the expounders of unworldliness — John Woolman, the itinerant Quaker, long-remembered for his so-called journal, which is more nearly an autobiography. In general it seems to have been a book which, for the last century and a half, has been mentioned almost with bated breath. Charles Lamb was lyric in his references; Henry Crabb Robinson, likewise; Whittier was one of its editors and admirers. It has been included in model libraries and modern library series. It is, nevertheless, a book for a special type of reader whom Moses Coit Tyler

[1] Edwards, "Sinners in the Hands of an Angry God" ("Works," Vol. IV, p. 318).

fairly characterized when he wrote, "Certainly, the power of this book cannot be conveyed by detached passages, and in all cases must be without effect, save upon natures that are prepared for it." So prolonged has been this chorus of praise that dissent from it cannot quite fully be expressed by mere omission. A literary independent is under the same impulsion felt by the signers of the "Declaration" who admitted that "a decent respect to the opinions of mankind" required a decent explanation from the dissenters.

John Woolman, who lived from 1720 to 1772, was a Quaker who, with a deepening singleness of purpose, sought to attain simplicity of life, fought the institution and practice of slavery, traveled as an emissary among his fellow worshipers in the colonies, preached to the Indians, and died while on a self-imposed mission among his brethren in England. He seems to have been universally respected and loved. He seems to have lived a Saint Francis without Saint Francis's joyousness. As an individual he is to be regarded exclusively in terms of his religious fervor and devotion. His days were marked by the same insistent, exacting self-criticism to which the youthful Edwards subjected himself. Like Edwards, he was a mystic and inclined, in the manner of the mystic, to detach himself from a life of material interests and activities. Thus in his day he stood out like Edwards against the tendencies which were increasingly dominant: a devotee of the inner life at a time when action was becoming the distinctively American trait; a widely traveled man, yet oblivious to social influences or local impressions, for he was a totally unworldly figure. In all these respects he may legitimately be an object of admiration to "natures that are prepared for" him.

But it is hard to see, in spite of all the encomiums that have been showered upon it, why his journal should be admired as a piece of English pure and undefiled. It is not the utterance of a simple unlettered man telling of his own experiences or speaking his own heart in simple, direct utterance. The style, as a matter of fact, is not simple or plain.

It is full of the set phrases which obscure the expression of a sectarian worshiper as unhappily as legal locutions do the documents of a lawyer, or as the technical jargon of pedagogy and social science do the writings of the pedagogues and the sociologists. Woolman lacks directness as a rule, and concreteness in both figurative and literal passages as a practice. On shipboard, for example, he is seasick, uncomfortable, and homesick. He describes his condition as follows:

> My Appetite failing, the Trial hath been the heavier; and I have felt tender Breathings in my Soul after God, the Fountain of Comfort, whose inward Help hath supplied, at Times, the Want of outward Convenience: And strong Desires have attended me, that his Family, who are acquainted with the Movings of his holy Spirit, may be so redeemed from the Love of Money, and from that Spirit in which Men seek Honour one of another, that in all Business, by Sea or Land, we may constantly keep in View the coming of his Kingdom on Earth, as it is in Heaven; and, by faithfully following this safe Guide, shew forth Examples, tending to lead out of that under which the Creation groans![1]

Safe in England, he was moved to speak with eloquence in various meetings. He can find no better simile for it than this:

> . . . my Heart was like a Vessel that wanted Vent; and for several Weeks, at first, when my Mouth was opened in Meetings, it often felt like the raising of a Gate in a Water-course, where a Weight of Water lay upon it.[2]

This is the style which Lamb, Channing, Robinson, Whittier, and scores of others have applauded for its simple purity. Apparently their enthusiasm for the author was transmitted to his book. Good men are not necessarily good writers, and John Woolman was evidently better than his word.

Benjamin Franklin — Boston and Philadelphia

Although it is risky business to indulge in the kind of literary generalizations which allege that a man was the first of his kind or the "father" of a type of literature, it is safe

[1] Woolman, "Journal" (Everyman Edition), p. 143. [2] Ibid. p. 151.

to say of Benjamin Franklin that he was the first genuinely international figure to emerge in America, the first to achieve solid permanence in literary fame, and the first to offer a widely influential challenge to the religious life by the secular life. And in this latter connection it can be said further that he was the first eminent American writer who was an apostate from Puritanism. It is in the nature of the apostate that he is rebelling against a tradition to which he is a subscriber up to the moment of his apostasy.[1] He is, therefore, not an entirely different manner of man from his teachers, but the same manner of man with strongly marked differences. It is not surprising, therefore, but altogether natural, that Franklin's character had certain points of identity with the character of the Puritans. He shared their will-to-power, and, with a benignancy which was not theirs, he exercised his power when he had achieved it. He shared their belief in self-discipline, but with a balance which they did not enjoy. He thought of self-discipline as a means to an end and took no stock in asceticism as an end in itself, and in his thrift and his efficiency he was so like his Presbyterian parents that he could draw a lesson from them in the epitaph he compiled, and couple industry with faith in his injunction to

> Be encouraged to diligence in thy calling
> And distrust not Providence.

His life is divisible into the period covered by his "Autobiography," which is simultaneous with the life of Jonathan Edwards, and the period from then to the end of his career, which included his years of greatest "usefulness." Yet the whole earlier period may be estimated as a more or less conscious training toward the end of usefulness and a succession of experiences which in modern terms could be classified as phases in Franklin's "adult education."

Although he enjoyed the least of formal schooling — for he was set to work at the age of ten — he received a sound edu-

[1] Bertrand Russell, "On Catholic and Protestant Sceptics," *Dial,* Vol. LXXXVI, pp. 43–49.

cation, not merely in practical experience but in the learning which is drawn from the library and the laboratory. Two years in his father's shop gave him a glimpse of the rudiments of business; in his teens he was reading Bunyan, Burton, the Mathers, Locke, Shaftesbury, Defoe, Xenophon and Plutarch, Addison and Pope. Five years' apprenticeship in a printer's shop drilled him in accuracy and gave him the foundation for his self-conducted courses in arithmetic and composition. He schooled himself too in the elements of logic, and for a while applied them so assiduously in discussion that he made himself a nuisance to his friends. His residence in London while he was from eighteen to twenty years old widened his vista. He was always reading, — borrowing books until he enjoyed the service of a circulating library which he founded himself, — the only source of recreation he indulged in after his return to Philadelphia. His attempt to develop sound moral habits amounted to a profitable course in applied ethics. At the age of twenty-seven he began the study of languages and acquired in succession a reading knowledge of French, of Italian, and of Spanish. Finally, in the way of technical and deliberately acquired learning, came his investigations in the field of electricity.

Moreover, his capacity for learning and his alertness of mind led to the enrichment of his education through the fronting of definite problems, the visiting of various countries, and contact with the best minds of western Europe, England, and America. From a surprisingly early age he had come into acquaintance with well-known men. He knew Cotton Mather the theologian, Whitefield the evangelist, Rush the physician, West the artist, Webster the lexicographer, and Jay, Adams, Jefferson, Washington, and a host of other statesmen. In England, sometimes in conflict and sometimes in coöperation, he encountered men and minds of no less distinction; and in France his acquaintances included the most brilliant men and women of the time. All the while in the scientific world he was led into exchange of ideas with physicists in England, Holland, Germany, France,

Italy, and Spain. His mind, his studies, and his wider experiences developed him into a wise and accomplished citizen of the world.

Yet wide as his education was, it was the education of a thrifty and industrious man whose interests were focused on the acquiring of "useful attainments." He escaped being a poet, he stated, but prose writing was very useful to him. The sole allusions in the "Autobiography" to poetry were to certain pat couplets of Pope and to a passage in Thomson ridiculing the ambitions of would-be poets. There are almost no references to the theater, the drama, fiction, music, painting, sculpture, or architecture. There is no instinctive resort in his writings to the illuminative facts or principles of history, the broad reaches of philosophy; seldom to the larger implications of science. One need only compare Franklin's range of interests with those of Burke or Talleyrand or Jefferson, or with those of his fellow townsman, Francis Hopkinson, to realize how relatively limited it was in point of cultural variety.

But there was flexibility in these men which belonged to a somewhat later generation. Franklin belonged by natural affiliation to the more prosaic and practical period that preceded theirs. In the half-century before his birth England had passed through an exhausting experience which the colonies had partly shared. It had seen the political rise and fall of the Puritans, the return to power of the Stuarts, and the further rebellion against James II. The fine fervor of religious enthusiasm, culminating with the Commonwealth, had waned. By the end of the century religion had yielded the right of way to politics. Little newspapers had been established in surprising numbers, the coffeehouses had become centers for discussion of the ways of the world, and a common-sense age had settled down to a rather sordid and commonplace existence. The intelligent public, weary of dissension, read the "gazettes"; the frequenters of the coffeehouses beguiled the time in endless and aimless discussion; and Addison made it his ambition to bring his common-sense "philosophy" down from the clouds into the field of daily thinking. This was Franklin's way in Franklin's world.

While still a boy in Boston he wrote for *The New England Courant* the fourteen "Dogood Papers," which were the first published fruits of his discipleship to Addison. In Philadelphia, in his twenty-third year, he started the "Busy-Body Papers" and wrote six before he surrendered the continuing series to Joseph Breintnal. The two sets of little informal essays and sketches were an extraordinarily prompt reflection in the colonies of a way of writing which was to prevail in England throughout the century, but which had been initiated during the young American's boyhood. And it was fairly illustrative of Franklin's activities as a whole; for it represented an enterprise and an effective application of a literary device to a social need or a potential social demand. In all his life to middle age Franklin was living in the manner of the good journalist and the resourceful inventor; and both types thrive on quick appreciation of needs and demands and effective responses to them. There was nothing of the contemplative in Franklin except as he contemplated contrivances and organizations. Before he had reached the half-century mark he had freed himself from the need of daily earning; he had founded an academy, established a journal, organized a debating club, a philosophical society, and a circulating library, devised the lightning rod, invented a stove, improved the lighting of streets and the fighting of fires; he had held public office from justice of the peace to member of the common council in his city and representative in the colonial assembly; and he had progressed from these to the post of deputy postmaster general of America, in which latter service he, of course, greatly improved the whole system of handling the mails. One accepts it as a normal performance for Franklin that he founded the longest-lived periodical in American history and the most successful almanac of the period.[1]

---

[1] See also pages 96, 138, 149, 189.

The Popular Press

Almanacs, Newspapers, Magazines

During the period of the Widening Country, men and women who crossed freely from colony to colony or who changed their residence from one to another typify the spreading of intercolonial connections. There was need of such bonds. The first feelings were of rivalry if not of hostility. For generations the little settlements were sparsely populated and separated by days of laborious travel. The deep harborages and inlets along the Atlantic coast were such barriers that a long journey between could best be made by cutting back toward the foothills, where the fordings and ferryings were easiest; and travel by sea was slow and often perilous. So the printing press in its modest way served to anticipate the modern bridge in supplying connections while travel was limited to the adventurous few. Common news, common songs, and common anecdotes were harbingers of common opinions and common interests. The spread of these was slight and slow; and on account of the mode of settlement, and the schooling that developed a reading public, the first steps were taken in the North.

An "almanac calculated for New England, by Mr. Pierce" was the second piece of printing in the colonies when it was issued by Stephen Daye at Cambridge in 1639. For thirty-seven years it was unrivaled, until in 1676 one was issued in Boston. Philadelphia followed in 1686, New York in 1697, Rhode Island in 1728, and Virginia in 1731. In 1726 the Ameses, father and son, started on their fifty-year series; in 1733 Benjamin Franklin introduced "Poor Richard" to a public which annually welcomed him in spite of the fact that he now had many a competitor. There were thousands of households into which no other current printing found its way; but the almanac on the mantel or hanging on the wall was thumbed for its information on sun and moon and tides, for its advertisements, and for its astrology, its farm talk, its tall stories, its wit and wisdom, and its quoted and original verse.[1] Of all the series printed before the Revolution, those of the Ameses in Dedham, Massachusetts, and of Franklin in Philadelphia, are pre-eminent. The distinguishing features are, of course, the incidental material. "Poor Richard's" circulation, Franklin said, was about ten thousand, and

> observing that it was generally read, scarce any neighborhood in the province being without it, I consider'd it as a proper vehicle for conveying instruction among the common people, who bought scarcely any other books; I therefore filled all the little spaces that occur'd between the remarkable days in the calendar with proverbial sentences, chiefly such as inculcated industry and frugality, as the means of procuring wealth, and thereby securing virtue; it being more difficult for a man in want, to act always honestly, as, to use here one of those proverbs, *it is hard for an empty sack to stand upright.*[2]

The casting of many of these sayings into the harangue of Father Abraham, prefixed to the almanac of 1757, resulted in popularity for Poor Richard many times multiplied, for it was reprinted on all sides — in the colonies, in Great Britain, and in France. The Ames productions contained more verse, every month being preceded with a selection; and often there were essays on matters of improving knowledge, of which the 1758 "THOUGHT *upon the* past, present *and* future State of North America" is remarkable among colonial utterances for its eloquence, its prophetic substance, and its quiet Yankee humor. As its conclusion shows, it was on a loftier level than Franklin's platform of virtue assured by prosperity:

> So Arts and Sciences will change the Face of Nature in their Tour from Hence over the Appalachian Mountains to the Western Ocean. . . . O! Ye unborn Inhabitants of America! Should this Page escape

---

[1] For a discussion of early American almanacs see Isaiah Thomas's "History of Printing in America," Vol. I, pp. 46 ff., and G. L. Kittredge's "Old Farmer and His Almanack," Chaps. I and II.

[2] Franklin, "Autobiography" (edited by P. H. Boynton), p. 116

its destin'd Conflagration at the Year's End, and these Alphabetical Letters remain legible, — when your Eyes behold the Sun after he has rolled the Seasons round for two or three Centuries more, you will know that in Anno Domini 1758, we dream'd of your Times.[1]

The newspaper came far later than the almanac;[2] not until the firm hand of government was forced to relax enough to permit an approach to open expression of opinion and open publication of news. It was the faint approach to that freedom of the press that in the belief of some would result in social revolution, and in the opinion of others would mark the social millennium. Boston took the lead in 1704 with the *Boston News-Letter* and in 1719 with the *Boston Gazette.* Philadelphia followed in 1719 and 1721; New York, in 1725. From 1727 to 1763 journals were established in both South and North, and by the year of the Stamp Act (1765) forty-three had been issued: ten from the Southern colonies, thirteen from Pennsylvania and New York, and twenty from the New England region. Most of them were weeklies, and most of them confined themselves discreetly to news and advertisements, fearful of suppression if they ventured into editorial comment on political issues. Occasionally they risked an opinion under the guise of an open correspondence. But they were quick to reprint what was interesting and harmless or wholesome and improving; so that they were soon contributing to the inculcation of thrift, frugality, and morals, and reinforcing in the American character the ethical sobriety which is at the basis of so many of its judgments and which always adorns and often disguises so many of its practices.

Later than either almanacs or newspapers came the colonial magazines. The irreducible minimum of fact about the pioneers in this field can be culled from a recent exhaustive

---

[1] "The Essays, Humor and Poems of Nathaniel Ames (edited by Samuel Briggs, 1891) . . .," p. 286.

[2] For early newspapers see Frederic Hudson's "Journalism in the United States," pp. 44–49.

study of them.[1] There seem to have been no less than thirty-seven founded in this period. But so small was their circulation and so slender their revenue that they suffered a heavy rate of infant mortality. Sixteen survived less than a year; ten more, less than two years; seven others, less than three years; three died at less than four; and the leviathan and the Methuselah of them all lived to be only eight.

The majority revealed in their secondary descriptive titles that they intended to supplement the journals in their inclusion of foreign and domestic political news, their historical essays (frequently in extended serials), and their discussion of manufacture, trade, and commerce. A few included quite casually the words "amusement" and "entertainment." Several were exclusively religious, one of these in German. The single children's magazine lasted for only four issues. Most of them evidently relied on scissors and paste pot for much of their material, particularly the literary and poetical; for example, the *American Museum, or Repository of Ancient and Modern Fugitive Pieces &c. Prose and Poetical.* At the end of two years this subtitled itself, "Containing Essays on Agriculture — Commerce — Manufactures — Politics, Morals — and Manners. Sketches of National Characters — Natural and Civil History — and Biography. Law Information — Public Papers — Proceedings of Congress — Intelligence, Moral Tales — Ancient and Modern Poetry, &c. &c."; and the most prosperous and long-lived periodical of the whole era, the *Massachusetts Magazine,* professed on its title page to be "a Monthly Museum of Knowledge and Rational Entertainment. Containing, Poetry, Musick, Biography, History, Physick, Geography, Morality, Criticism, Philosophy, Mathematicks, Agriculture, Architecture, Chymistry, Novels, Tales, Romances, Translations, News, Marriages, Deaths, Meteorological Observations, &c. &c."

Two matters of literary interest emerge from an examina-

---

[1] The most complete study is by Lyon N. Richardson, "A History of Early American Magazines, 1741–1789." See particularly his bibliography, pp. 362–375. See also F. L. Mott's "History of American Magazines, 1741–1850."

tion of them. One is the evident influence of the popular English poets and essayists of the eighteenth century. The allusions are frequent to Addison, Blair, Dryden, Goldsmith, Gray, Johnson, Milton, Pope, Richardson (though not to Fielding, Smollett, or Sterne), Steele, and Swift; and there are various essays in criticism of poetry, drama, and fiction. The other main feature is that while they lasted, however slight these passing ventures were, they served as outlets to the conspicuous writers of their day — not merely those whose reputations depended on them, but those whose contributions lend them distinction even now: men like Joel Barlow, H. H. Brackenridge, Timothy Dwight, Benjamin Franklin, Francis Hopkinson, Philip Freneau, John Trumbull, and such commentators on the American language as Noah Webster and John Witherspoon.[1]

Of the three kinds of publications the magazines were the latest and the least important in public influence. The newspapers reached a greater number. The almanacs, earliest of the types, were far more widely distributed; and in so far as they attempted to deal with anything more than time and tide, they were much the most successful in communicating it to the great body of homely homesteaders.

Crèvecœur—Interpreter of the Frontier

Everything thus far recorded here from the pens of eighteenth-century colonial writers represents the point of view of the settled country of old churches, old homes, old families. Yet it was a new country of untold opportunities with a westward expanse of unexplored and unexploited territory. The Seven Years' War had increased the English possessions by about a quarter of a million square miles, an area that England was loath to garrison, trying to prevent settlement there by a futile edict of 1763. The old age of the Old World was utterly different from the youth of the new one, for it was rooted in control of the land, most of which

[1] M. M. Mathews, "The Beginnings of American English," 1931.

was in the hands of a few great proprietors. As control of government was largely in the same hands, the people could neither enjoy the fruits of their labor, pitilessly reduced by rents and taxes, nor make any effective peaceful protest in behalf of change. The American Revolution was to be the voice of the colonies in protest against the possible repetition of such conditions in America, and the French Revolution was to be the outcry of a downtrodden people calling for redress.

Michel Guillaume Jean de Crèvecœur was egregious among the colonists in knowing both sets of conditions at first hand. Born in France and partly educated in England, he came to English America by way of French Canada, settled and prospered on his own land, and for a while was so delighted with his life as citizen and farmer that he wrote his long series of "Letters from an American Farmer." Until 1925 all these were supposed to be included in the volume of 1782, the twelve which earned him his distinguished place in early American literature. The later installment, apparently written at the same time with the others but withheld then from publication, supplement and modify our understanding of the man. But from either set, as well as from both, the reader can see that Crèvecœur was an enthusiast; a sentimentalist, with a grasp of actualities in the New World, who wrote at one time emotionally and at another with the sober desire to tell the unvarnished facts.[1]

As an immigrant pioneer he was doubly a pioneer in his inclination to theorize on the frontier and to look westward beyond the visible horizon. When he did dilate on the nature of the American and the perils and distresses of the frontier, the result was what is now recognizable as a typical compound of frontier writing in its combination of sober fact and sentimental theory. As for the theory, Crèvecœur had a pleasant one which he expressed with genuine eloquence:

---

[1] Quotations from Crèvecœur are from the most accessible edition of the "Letters from an American Farmer," in Everyman's Library. The added volume, "Sketches of Eighteenth Century America; More Letters from an American Farmer," is edited by Henri L. Bourdin and others.

What then is the American, this new man? He is either an European, or the descendant of an European, hence that strange mixture of blood, which you will find in no other country. I could point out to you a family whose grandfather was an Englishman, whose wife was Dutch, whose son married a French woman, and whose present four sons have now four wives of different nations. *He* is an American, who, leaving behind him all his ancient prejudices and manners, receives new ones from the new mode of life he has embraced, the new government he obeys, and the new rank he holds. He becomes an American by being received in the broad lap of our great *Alma Mater*. Here individuals of all nations are melted into a new race of men, whose labours and posterity will one day cause great changes in the world. Americans are the western pilgrims, who are carrying along with them that great mass of arts, sciences, vigour and industry which began long since in the east; they will finish the great circle.[1]

He was thrilled that the New World was an asylum for the oppressed; that a chance to own land, to enjoy the whole product of their labor, and to share in the government made them free and glad and energetic and resourceful; furthermore, that while the country was in the making, no alien was an alien, because he could join a community of his own people, speak his own language, maintain his own customs, and prosper. He could become bigger and better too in the bigness of the land; and he could afford to be generous because there was enough for everyone. All the laws were reasonable because they were of his own making; the America of the future was to be of his making too. There was no problem of assimilation, for the whole country was fluid; he gave what he was and he took what he wanted. He sat in the lap of plenty, unconstrained. Nothing that might happen could disturb his comfort. He could write about melting all the races of the earth into a new nation and forget that life offers more comfortable experiences than being melted and fused.

But Crèvecœur was an actual immigrant who bought land and cleared it, and rubbed up against his neighbors, and

[1] Crèvecœur, "Letters from an American Farmer," pp. 43–44.

took time off to visit newer neighborhoods, some of them quite remote. When he wrote about what was actually taking place, he was unembarrassed by the discrepancy between fact and theory, describing without reserve the human sacrifice demanded of the pioneer. On the farthest frontier he noted men driven there by misfortune who were idle, drunken, contentious, wretched. They made no laws for themselves, and they were out of reach of the laws to the east. Their life was shameless and hideous. They were a forlorn hope, a vanguard ten or a dozen years ahead of the main army. They would perform the first heavy labor and then either gravitate up to prosperity or be pushed on by their successors into a new front line of semi-savagery. "Such is our progress, such is the march of the Europeans toward the interior parts of this continent. In all societies there are off-casts; this impure part serves as our precursors or pioneers." [1] Theory begins to run away until he recalls that his father was a pioneer. But it is an imaginary father, for his own never came to America; and he salvages the imaginary one by making him an honest and respectable exception.

As a farmer Crèvecœur again oscillated between sentimental pictures and hard fact. With his baby boy ingeniously rigged before him on the plow, he reckoned the increase of his fields, herds, flocks, hives, and acknowledged his inferiority "only to the Emperor of China, ploughing as an example to his kingdom." Then, looking beyond his own little acreage, he hinted at future industries. He was tilling the surface; there must be further treasures beneath. He and his neighbors were weaving the natural wool; some chemist must make and prepare colors. Commerce must follow on the heels of abundant production; "the avenues of trade are infinite." And in time the deep vast of the West, about which men had yet such feeble and timid fancies, must be explored and subjugated in its turn.

---

[1] Crèvecœur, op. cit. p. 47.

Here we have in some measure regained the ancient dignity of our species; our laws are simple and just, we are a race of cultivators, our cultivation is unrestrained, and therefore everything is prosperous and flourishing. For my part I had rather admire the ample barn of one of our opulent farmers, who himself felled the first tree in his plantation, and was the first founder of his settlement, than study the dimensions of the temple of Ceres.[1]

In the meanwhile, however, he was a dirt farmer, and in his "Thoughts on Various Rural Subjects," one of the "letters" omitted from the original series, he was a practical and circumstantial husbandman.

Crèvecœur displayed some powers of observation as to flora and fauna; but on this side he swung much farther in the direction of sentimentalism than he did in connection with field, forest, and frontier. He was never content to look on nature "as in the hour of thoughtless youth"; he never rose to the level on which he could feel its sublimity; but between these extremes he mounted a platform of eighteenth-century construction on which he could moralize and idealize ad libitum.

Who can listen unmoved to the sweet love tales of our robins, told from tree to tree? or to the shrill cat birds? . . . The astonishing art which all birds display in the construction of their nests, . . . always makes me ashamed of the slovenliness of our houses; their love to their dame, their incessant careful attention . . . remind me of my duty could I ever forget it. Their affection to their helpless little ones, is a lively precept; and in short, the whole economy of what we proudly call the brute creation, is admirable in every circumstance; and vain man, though adorned with the additional gift of reason, might learn from the perfection of instinct, how to regulate the follies, and how to temper the errors which this second gift often makes him commit. . . . I have often blushed within myself, and been greatly astonished, when I have compared the unerring path they all follow, all just, all proper, all wise, up to the necessary degree of perfection, with the coarse, the imperfect systems of men.[2]

This is the very ecstasy of the nature lover. And the wide divergence from the facts by a man who knew a good deal

---

[1] Crèvecœur, op. cit. p. 12.

[2] Ibid. pp. 33–34.

about natural phenomena simply shows the lengths to which a man can ride a closet formula in a moment of lyric enthusiasm. In saner moments he enumerated the damages done to farm and garden by marauding beasts, birds, and insects, as well as by climate, or recounted the murderous warfare of one part of animal nature on another with quite other implications than that the whole economy of brute creation "is admirable in every circumstance." He was, in short, such a man of moods that no single passage, on whatever theme, can safely be taken as an index of his convictions on the subject. And this, of course, is a chief reason that his pages are so readable, not excluding the half-dozen essays on the manners, customs, and employments of the Nantucket islanders or the people of "Charles-town," South Carolina. For even in his expositions he was always personal, always an interpreter.

The four loyalist sketches and the group of dramatic "Landscapes" in the volume of added "Letters" throw light on the closing unit in the original series. It is quite probable, if the entire set were ready in 1782, that they were more than a publisher cared to venture; for the author was unknown. It is also reasonable, as the modern editors suggest, to believe that in the midst of the war it seemed good business policy to omit the portions that involved the rights and wrongs of the war as well as the more technical essays on farming. One kind might bore the general reader and the other kind might estrange the partisan. The original set steered clear of both dangers; and the final essay, "Distresses of a Frontier Man," was adroitly ambiguous. It is on the distresses of the frontier man who finds himself forced either to take sides in the war or to run away. The author decided to push on farther west and risk a life among the Indians until peace had been restored. He was thoroughly frightened; he was afraid of picking the losing side and suffering the consequences; and he felt that no loyalty was so compelling as loyalty to the interests of his wife and children. Read by itself it is a convincingly dramatic presentation of a panic-stricken man's state of mind. But Crèvecœur's "Landscapes" plus four other sketches prove beyond question that his sympathies were all with the loyalists. They are added evidence of his skill as a writer, but they do not add to his stature as a man. When he was completely in doubt, there was more justification for flight. With clearly defined sympathies he clearly turned his back on anything but self-interest. His own retreat was, in fact, even more complete than the one he projected for the frontier man. He left his wife and younger children in the care of neighbors; made his way to France with his oldest son; and returned to the United States at the close of the war neither as loyalist nor as revolutionist, but as consul from France. In 1790 he returned permanently to the land of his birth and disappeared from the American picture.

Good writers need not be heroes, however. The estimate of Crèvecœur's courage or lack of courage has little to do with the estimate of his two volumes on life in colonial America. These are unsurpassed. And in his fine fervors and prophetic outreachings, his essay on "What is an American?" is an eloquent and challenging summary of what an American might be or what he may be in the days of the millennium.

The Theater before the Revolution

A professional theater is necessarily a late development in any society. Only the professional orchestra and the opera are as slow, and the reasons are obvious. They all depend on an elaborate plant and a complex organization. The play, the opera, or the symphony is expensive in money and in skilled group effort. Even of these three, moreover, the theater in America is the only venture which has had to support itself entirely from paid attendance. Thus colonial history offered no possibility for drama until several conditions could be met. There must be a number of fairly large communities; these must be fairly prosperous, and in them the play spirit in a double sense must prevail. It was not until just about 1750 that all these conditions were combined in any one district; for up to that time New England, with its larger towns, was hostile to the theater, as it continued to be, and up to that time the South was hospitable but too scattering in population.

Nevertheless, even in New England there are signs that the love of pageantry was trying to assert itself. It seems that in 1714 some rash souls had projected a dramatic entertainment and suggested presentation at the very stronghold of authority, the Council Chamber at Boston. This was too much, wrote Samuel Sewall to a friend. Even the Romans, fond as they were of dramatic performances, were not "so far set upon them as to turn their Senate-House into a Play-House. . . . Let not Christian Boston," he continued, "goe beyond Heathen Rome in the practice of shamefull Vanities."[1] Evidently his counsel prevailed; for a prologue to a Charleston, South Carolina, play[2] of twenty years later contains a pleasant innuendo in its concluding quatrain:

> No *real* Virtue blames the pleasing strife,
> To blend Amusement with the Shades of Life;
> Wise, innocent, serene, she smiles at Ease,
> Nor hanging Witches, nor adjuring Plays.[3]

The interchange of compliments between Massachusetts and South Carolina, Puritan and Cavalier America, was already well under way. Yet old truepenny ghost of the drama would not submit to banishment. An act of the Massachusetts General Court showed that he was busy underground. Else why should an act have been passed in 1750 "for preventing and avoiding the many great mischiefs which arise from publick stage plays, interludes and other theatrical entertainments, which not only occasion great and unnecessary expenses, and discourage industry and frugality, but likewise

---

[1] "Letter-Book of Samuel Sewall," Massachusetts Historical Society Collections, sixth series, Vol. II, p. 30.

[2] Eola Willis's "Charleston Stage in the XVIII Century" records the earliest theater activity in the South.

[3] Ibid. p. 14.

tend generally to increase immorality, impiety, and a contempt for religion"? The penalties called for a fine of twenty pounds on any owner of property who allowed it to be used for such purposes, and for a fine of five pounds on any actor or any spectator at a dramatic event where more than twenty people were gathered. It is quite evident that though the craving for pleasure bowed its head before this admonition, it did not do so meekly. And while Massachusetts was, to use its own diction, getting its dander up, the ungodly Rhode Island — Puritan influenced but not Puritan bound — had built a theater, sanctioned professional players, and contributed to dramatic humor by adopting a device for eating the cakes and having its virtue too. This was by means of the "moral dialogue" subterfuge. Thus, for example, there was advertised in Newport, Rhode Island, in 1762 a performance of "Othello" disguised as "Moral Dialogues in Five Parts, Depicting the evil effects of jealousy and other bad passions, and proving that happiness can only spring from the pursuit of virtue."[1] Yet it was an ill-omened venture even in liberal Rhode Island, and it was near the end of the century before another successful attempt was made to invade the land of Roger Williams.

Real professional beginnings were less impeded in the Cavalier South. It is a matter of record that in Williamsburg, Virginia, there was a building known as the theater which stood from 1716 to 1745. What went on in it is almost unknown; but the bare fact itself is significant, for it must have been intermittently used in the course of these twenty-nine years. From Charleston, South Carolina, the records are more complete; for there are data for 1732 and records of series of plays in 1735, 1736, and 1736–1737. Philadelphia comes into the picture toward the end of 1749 with the so-called Murray and Kean Company, which played in Philadelphia and New York in that winter, and which, from the historian's point of view, pursued a baffling and elusive career

[1] Quoted in full in Arthur Hornblow's "History of the Theatre in America," Vol. I, pp. 110–112.

for many years, having just vitality enough to survive and just too little to lift it out of obscurity or make it more than a theatrical will-o'-the-wisp. In 1751 a Robert Upton, setting out as advance agent for an English company, found the prospect so promising that during the winter he assembled a company and enjoyed his little day before disappearing permanently from the records. At last in 1752 the Hallam Company, an English organization with twelve adult performers, arrived in America with a repertory of twenty plays and eight afterpieces, the full-length plays including six by Farquhar and four by Shakespeare, the remaining ten by post-Restoration English playwrights.

Even by this date a consecutive history in the American theater was not reached; for the Hallam Company, which survived with many changes for the better part of a half-century, retired to the West Indies for two four-year breaks (1754–1758 and 1762–1766) before the Revolutionary War. A survey of the slender and incomplete records up to the closing of the theaters after action of the Colonial Congress in 1774 shows that out of something less than five hundred and fifty recorded productions there were three chief groups. Shakespeare was the unchallenged favorite, appearing either in the main plays or in the afterpieces of just about a third of the productions. Eleven English dramatists of the late Restoration and early eighteenth century were represented in nearly half the total, and the remaining fraction was made up of scattering plays and authors, of which it is necessary to record only that every English play had been already tried out on the London stage. No phase of colonial culture was so completely dominated by English tradition as the theater; but with a conventionalized stage and conventional ways of producing effects on it, with an English tradition of acting and the leading actors generously recruited from England, with an abundant dramatic literature available from England or from the Continent, and with an America that was play-starved, receptive, and docile, it is no wonder that at first and for a long time producers contented themselves with following well-trodden paths. In the whole long period up to the war the American playwright contributed only two plays for a total of three recorded performances. Yet two of the early efforts deserve mention because they represent long-persistent tendencies of American authors and producers. The first romantic drama and the first American play to be acted professionally was Thomas Godfrey's "The Prince of Parthia." It was presented in the "Southwark" Theater, Philadelphia, a playhouse no more imitative in its name than the play was in its nature. "The Prince" shows traces of "Hamlet," signs of "Macbeth," evidences of "The Maid's Tragedy," touches of the Restoration interest in the pseudo-Oriental. It is a precocious bit of imitative writing, in which the youthful Godfrey compares well with his contemporaries and with many of his successors. The type of poetic drama he attempted recurred persistently in the works of such dramatists as R. M. Bird, N. P. Willis, G. H. Boker, Julia Ward Howe, who, with many others of their like, fared far afield with no clear starting point or goal.

Robert Rogers's "Ponteach: or the Savages of America," published in London in 1766, was again a typical play. Its nonproduction may probably be laid to managerial timidity; for a sharp indictment of English colonial policies so soon after the French and Indian War could have had no more chance for presentation than a pacifist play in 1921. If it had been an indictment of the French, American audiences might have greeted it "with universal applause." Yet, though unpresented, as an Indian play it has had many successors; Pocahontas alone was the theme of five, and became celebrated enough to be subject of a popular burlesque. As a race play it broke the trail for both Indian and Negro dramas, and as a problem-purpose play it was the first contribution in this country to a never ending series.

A Continental Congress war measure of 1774 was quaintly indicative of the general standing of the theater and the drama, with its recommendation that the colonists "discountenance and discourage all horse-racing, and all kinds of gaming, cock-fighting, exhibitions of shows, plays, and other expensive diversions and entertainments." Until well toward the end of the war this recommendation was effective in checking theatrical enterprises on the part of the colonists. The beginnings up to this point were modest, indeed, but they serve as a straw in the wind; for beyond all other forms of art the theater is an evidence of organized cultural activity, demanding, as it does, not only public attention but active support in dollars and cents. When the war was over, it seemed at first as if little headway had been gained in all this preliminary campaign. The modest playhouses had to be rebuilt and conservative prejudice reconquered; but the records show that the progress was much faster and that the theater was at last to become indispensable in American life.[1]

Book List

GENERAL REFERENCES

ANDREWS, CHARLES MCLEAN. Colonial Folkways. 1920.

CHAMBERLAIN, NATHAN H. Samuel Sewall and the World He Lived In. 1897.

COBB, SANFORD H. The Rise of Religious Liberty in America. 1902.

DEXTER, HENRY M. The Congregationalism of the Last Three Hundred Years as Seen in Its Literature. With Bibliographical Appendix. 1880.

EARLE, ALICE MORSE. Child Life in Colonial Days. Last edition. 1927.

EARLE, ALICE MORSE. Colonial Dames and Good Wives. 1895.

EARLE, ALICE MORSE. Curious Punishments of Bygone Days. Last edition. 1922.

EARLE, ALICE MORSE. Customs and Fashions in Old New England. 1898.

EARLE, ALICE MORSE. Home Life in Colonial Days. 1898.

EARLE, ALICE MORSE. Stage-coach and Tavern Days. 1900.

FISKE, JOHN. New France and New England. 1904.

JONES, HOWARD MUMFORD. American Prose Style: 1700–1770. Bulletin No. 6 of the Huntington Library.

KITTREDGE, GEORGE L. Witchcraft in Old and New England. 1929.

MASSON, DAVID. Life of John Milton. 1859–1880. (Valuable for English background of Puritanism.)

MORAIS, HERBERT M. Deism in Eighteenth-Century America. 1934.

OSGOOD, HERBERT L. The American Colonies in the Eighteenth Century. 1924.

PARRINGTON, VERNON L. The Colonial Mind. 1927.

[1] See pages 185–188.

RICHARDSON, CHARLES F. American Literature, Vol. I. 1897.
TYLER, MOSES C. A History of American Literature, Vol. I, Chaps. XII, XIII. 1897.
UPHAM, CHARLES W. Salem Witchcraft. 2 vols. 1867.
WALKER, WILLISTON. Ten New England Leaders. 1901.
WENDELL, BARRETT. A Literary History of America. 1901.
WENDELL, BARRETT. "Were the Salem Witches Guiltless?" Stelligeri and Other Essays. 1893.
Services of the Mathers in New England Religious Development. American Society Church Historical Papers, first series, Vol. V.

THE TURN OF THE CENTURY

Individual Authors

INCREASE MATHER. An Essay for the Recording of Illustrious Providences. 1684.

[*Available Editions*]

History of King Philip's War, edited by Samuel G. Drake. 1862.
Letters of Increase Mather. Massachusetts Historical Society Collections, fourth series, Vol. VII. 1868.
Remarkable Providences . . ., edited by George Offor. Library of Old Authors. 1890.

[*Biography and Criticism*]

MURDOCK, KENNETH B. Increase Mather, the Foremost American Puritan. 1925.
VAN NESS, T. "Increase Mather," *Outlook*, Vol. LXXV, pp. 549–554.

[*Bibliography*]

HOLMES, THOMAS J. Increase Mather; a Bibliography of His Works. 1931.

COTTON MATHER. The Wonders of the Invisible World. 1693. Magnalia Christi Americana; or, The Ecclesiastical History of New England, 1620–1698. 1702.

[*Available Editions*]

Diary of Cotton Mather. 2 vols. Massachusetts Historical Society Collections, seventh series, Vols. VII, VIII. 1911–1912.
Magnalia Christi Americana. 2 vols. Library of Old Authors. 1853.
Selections from Cotton Mather, edited by Kenneth B. Murdock. American Authors Series. 1926.
Wonders of the Invisible World. Library of Old Authors. 1862.

[*Biography and Criticism*]

BOAS, RALPH and LOUISE. Cotton Mather: Keeper of the Puritan Conscience. 1928.
KITTREDGE, GEORGE L. "Cotton Mather's Scientific Communications to the Royal Society." Proceedings of the American Antiquarian Society, new series, Vol. XXVI, pp. 18–57. 1916.

MARVIN, ABIJAH P. The Life and Times of Cotton Mather. 1892

MURDOCK, KENNETH B. "Cotton Mather, Parson, Scholar, and Man of Letters." Commonwealth History of Massachusetts. Edited by A. B. Hart. 1928.

STEDMAN, EDMUND C. "Wendell's Cotton Mather." Genius and Other Essays. 1911.

TUTTLE, JULIUS H. "The Libraries of the Mathers." Proceedings of the American Antiquarian Society, new series, Vol. XX, pp. 269–356. 1910.

VAN NESS, T. "Cotton Mather," *Outlook*, Vol. LXXV, pp. 552–555.

WENDELL, BARRETT. "Cotton Mather, New England Puritan," *Quarterly*, Vol. CCVIII, pp. 32–48.

WENDELL, BARRETT. Cotton Mather: the Puritan Priest. 1926.

SAMUEL SEWALL. Diary. From 1674 to 1729.

[*Available Editions*]

Diary of Samuel Sewall. 3 vols. Massachusetts Historical Society Collections, fifth series, Vols. VI–VIII. 1878–1882.

Letter-Book of Samuel Sewall. 2 vols. Massachusetts Historical Society Collections, sixth series, Vols. I, II. 1886.

Samuel Sewall's Diary, edited by Mark Van Doren. An American Bookshelf. 1927.

[*Biography and Criticism*]

CHAMBERLAIN, N. & H. Samuel Sewall and the World He Lived In. 1897.

SARAH KEMBLE KNIGHT. Journal of Madam Knight. From the Original Manuscripts written in 1704. Edited by T. Dwight. 1825.

[*Available Editions*]

The Journal of Madam Knight, edited by George P. Winship. 1920.

The Private Journals Kept by Madam Knight, edited by W. R. Deane. 1858.

[*Biography and Criticism*]

BROOKS, GERALDINE. Dames and Daughters of Colonial Days. 1900.

CAULKINS, FRANCES M. History of New London. 1852.

GUNN, SIDNEY. "Sarah Kemble Knight." Dictionary of American Biography, Vol. X.

Bostonian Society Publications, Vol. IX. 1912.

[*General Anthologies*]

CAIRNS, WILLIAM B. Early American Writers. 1925.

DUYCKINCK, E. A. and G. L. Cyclopedia of American Literature, Vol. I.

FOERSTER, NORMAN. American Poetry and Prose (rev. ed.). 1934.

SPILLER, ROBERT E. The Roots of National Culture. 1933.

STEDMAN and HUTCHINSON. Library of American Literature, Vols. I–III.

TRENT and WELLS. Colonial Prose and Poetry. 1903.

THE WIDENING COUNTRY

Individual Authors

WILLIAM BYRD. The History of the Dividing Line, 1728–1729; A Journey to the Land of Eden, 1733.

[*Available Editions*]

BASSETT, JOHN S. The Writings of Colonel William Byrd of Westover in Virginia, Esqr. 1901.
BOYD, WILLIAM K. William Byrd's Histories of the Dividing Lines. 1929.
VAN DOREN, MARK (Ed.). A Journey to the Land of Eden. An American Bookshelf. 1928.
WYNNE, T. H. (Ed.). The History of the Dividing Line. 2 vols. 1866.

[*Biography and Criticism*]

BEATTY, RICHMOND C. William Byrd of Westover. 1932.
WERTENBAKER, THOMAS J. "William Byrd." Dictionary of American Biography, Vol. III. 1929.

JONATHAN EDWARDS. Sermons and Essays, variously edited (see below).

[*Available Edition*]

Most available of the collected editions of Edwards's works is that in four volumes (last edition, 1881). The valuable sections are Vol. I, pp. 1–27 (biographical), and Vol. IV, Sermons.

[*Biography and Criticism*]

ALLEN, ALEXANDER V. G. Jonathan Edwards. 1889.
FAUST, CLARENCE H. "Jonathan Edwards as a Scientist," *American Literature*, Vol. I, pp. 393–404.
GARDINER, H. NORMAN. Jonathan Edwards, a Retrospect. 1901.
HAROUTANIAN, JOSEPH G. "Jonathan Edwards; a Study in Godliness," *Journal of Religion*, Vol. XI, pp. 400–419.
HOLMES, OLIVER W. Pages from an Old Volume of Life. 1891.
JAMES, WILLIAM. The Varieties of Religious Experience. 1902.
JOHNSON, T. H. "Jonathan Edwards and the 'Young Folks' Bible,'" *New England Quarterly*, Vol. V, pp. 37–54.
McGIFFERT, ARTHUR C., JR. Jonathan Edwards. 1932.
MACPHAIL, ANDREW. Essays in Puritanism. 1905.
PARKES, HENRY B. Jonathan Edwards, the Fiery Puritan. 1930.
RILEY, I. WOODBRIDGE. American Philosophy: the Early Schools. 1907.
RILEY, I. WOODBRIDGE. American Thought. 1915.
WALKER, WILLISTON. Ten New England Leaders. 1901.

BENJAMIN FRANKLIN. Poor Richard Improved. 1757. Later issued as "Father Abraham's Speech"; over 150 editions and reprints are recorded. Autobiography. First issued in Paris. 1791.

[*Available Editions*]

Works of Franklin compiled and edited by John Bigelow. 10 vols. 1887–1888.

Franklin's Autobiography is variously edited for students. Some recent editions are:

The Autobiography of Benjamin Franklin. With introduction by Percy H. Boynton. American Authors Series. 1926.

The Autobiography of Benjamin Franklin, edited by Oral S. Coad. 1927.

The Autobiography of Benjamin Franklin, and Other Selections from His Writings, edited by Nathan G. Goodman. 1932.

Poor Richard's Almanac. Facsimiles. Edited by Phillips Russell. 1928.

The Wisdom of Benjamin Franklin. 3 vols.: (1) The Autobiography; (2) Political and Economic Essays; (3) Moral, Social, and Scientific Essays. Edited by John J. Murphy. 1927.

The Writings of Benjamin Franklin (10 vols.), edited by A. H. Smyth. 1905–1907.

[*Biography and Criticism*]

BRUCE, WILLIAM C. Benjamin Franklin Self-Revealed. 1917.
BUTLER, RUTH LAPHAM. Doctor Franklin, Postmaster General. 1928.
CLOYD, DAVID E. Benjamin Franklin and Education. 1902.
ELIOT, CHARLES W. Four American Leaders. 1906.
FAŸ, BERNARD. Franklin: the Apostle of Modern Times. 1929.
FAŸ, BERNARD. The Two Franklins: Fathers of American Democracy. 1933.
FORD, PAUL LEICESTER. The Many-Sided Franklin. 1899.
HALE, E. E. and E. E., JR. Franklin in France. 2 vols. 1887–1888.
MCMASTER, JOHN B. Benjamin Franklin as a Man of Letters. 1887.
MORE, PAUL ELMER. Benjamin Franklin. 1900.
MORSE, JOHN T., JR. Benjamin Franklin. American Statesmen Series. 1889.
RUSSELL, PHILLIPS. Benjamin Franklin, the First Civilized American. 1926.
SAINTE-BEUVE, C. A. Portraits of the Eighteenth Century. 1832–1848.
SHERMAN, STUART P. Americans. 1922.
SMYTH, J. HENRY, JR. The Amazing Benjamin Franklin. 1929.
STEELL, WILLIS. Benjamin Franklin of Paris, 1776–1785. 1928.
STIFLER, JAMES M. The Religion of Benjamin Franklin. 1925.

[*Anthologies*]

CAIRNS, WILLIAM B. Early American Writers. 1925.
DUYCKINCK, E. A. and G. L. Cyclopedia of American Literature, Vol. I.
FOERSTER, NORMAN. American Poetry and Prose (rev. ed.). 1934.
SPILLER, ROBERT E. The Roots of National Culture. 1933.
STEDMAN and HUTCHINSON. Library of American Literature, Vols. II–III.
VAN DOREN, CARL. Benjamin Franklin and Jonathan Edwards. Selections. Modern Student's Library. 1920.

JOHN WOOLMAN. Works. In two parts (1774). Some Considerations on the Keeping of Negroes (1754); Part II (1762). Considerations on Pure Wisdom, and Human Policy; on Laborers; on Schools; and on the Right Use of the Lord's Outward Gifts. 1768. Considerations on the True Harmony of Mankind; and How it is to be Maintained. 1770. Serious

Considerations on Various Subjects of Importance. 1773. A Word of Remembrance and a Caution to the Rich. 1793.

[*Available Editions*]

The Journal of John Woolman. Friends Book Association. 1892.
The Journal with Other Writings, edited by Vida Scudder. Everyman's Library. 1910.
The Journal, edited by John G. Whittier. 1871. Reprint, 1909.
Letters and Essays, edited by Amelia M. Gummere. 1923.

[*Biography and Criticism*]

DUNCAN, DAVID. "John Woolman." A paper read at the Friends' Institute, Manchester. 1871.
JONES, RUFUS. The Quakers in the American Colonies. 1911.
JONES, RUFUS. The Faith and Practice of the Quakers. 1928.
MORLEY, F. V. "John Woolman," *Saturday Review of Literature*, Vol. II, pp. 521–522.
SHARPLESS, ANN. John Woolman; a Pioneer in Labor Reform. 1920.
TREVELYAN, GEORGE M. Clio, a Muse, and Other Essays. 1913.
TYLER, MOSES COIT. Literary History of the American Revolution, Chap. XXXVIII. 1897.

MICHEL GUILLAUME JEAN DE CRÈVECŒUR. Letters from an American Farmer; Written for the Information of a friend in England. Edited by J. Hector St. John. 1782.

[*Available Editions*]

Letters from an American Farmer, edited by Ludwig Lewisohn, with prefatory note by W. P. Trent. 1925.
Letters from an American Farmer, edited by Ernest Rhys. Introduction by W. B. Blake. Everyman's Library, 1926.
Sketches of Eighteenth Century America, edited by H. L. Bourdin, and others. 1925.

[*Biography and Criticism*]

BOURDIN, HENRY L., and WILLIAMS, S. T. "Crèvecœur and the Susquehanna, 1774–1776," *Yale Review*, Vol. XIV, pp. 552–584.
BOYNTON, PERCY H. "A Colonial Farmer's Letters," *New Republic*, Vol. III, pp. 168–170.
MITCHELL, JULIA POST. St. Jean de Crèvecœur. 1916.
MOORE, JOHN B. "The Rehabilitation of Crèvecœur," *Sewanee Review*, Vol. XXXV, pp. 216–230.
TYLER, MOSES COIT. The Literary History of the American Revolution, Vol. II, Chap. XXVII. 1897.

[*Anthologies*]

CAIRNS, WILLIAM B. Early American Writers. 1925.
FOERSTER, NORMAN. American Poetry and Prose (rev. ed.). 1934.
SPILLER, ROBERT E. The Roots of National Culture. 1933.
STEDMAN and HUTCHINSON. Library of American Literature, Vol. III.
TRENT and WELLS. Colonial Prose and Poetry. 1903.

THE POPULAR PRESS: EIGHTEENTH CENTURY

[*Newspapers*]

BLEYER, W. G. Main Currents in the History of American Journalism. 1927.

DILL, W. A. The First Century of American Newspapers. 1925.

DUNIWAY, CLYDE A. The Development of Freedom of the Press in Massachusetts. 1906.

HUDSON, FREDERIC. Journalism in the United States from 1690 to 1872. 1873.

LEE, JAMES M. History of American Journalism (new ed.). 1923.

MARTIN, C. M. and B. E. "The New York Press and Its Makers in the Eighteenth Century." Historic New York, Vol. II. 1899.

PAYNE, GEORGE H. History of Journalism in the United States. 1920.

RUTHERFURD, L. John Peter Zenger. 1904.

SCHUYLER, LIVINGSTONE R. The Liberty of the Press in the American Colonies before the Revolutionary War. 1905.

SPAULDING, E. W. "*The Connecticut Courant*: a Representative Newspaper in the Eighteenth Century," *New England Quarterly*, Vol. III, pp. 443–463.

THOMAS, ISAIAH. History of Printing in America; with a Biography of Printers and an Account of Newspapers (2 vols., 2d ed.). 1874.

THWAITES, REUBEN G. "The Ohio Valley Press before the War of 1812–1815," Proceedings of the American Antiquarian Society, Vol. XIX, pp. 309–369. 1908–1909.

WROTH, LAWRENCE C. The Colonial Printer. 1931.

[*Almanacs*]

BRIGGS, SAMUEL. The Essays, Humor, and Poems of Nathaniel Ames, Father and Son, of Dedham, Massachusetts, from their Almanacs, 1726–1775. 1891.

BRIGHAM, CLARENCE S. An Account of American Almanacs and Their Value for Historical Study. 1925.

KITTREDGE, GEORGE L. The Old Farmer and His Almanack. 1904.

MORISON, SAMUEL E. "Squire Ames and Doctor Ames," *New England Quarterly*, Vol. I, pp. 5–31.

[*Magazines*]

MOTT, FRANK L. History of American Magazines, 1741–1850. 1930.

RICHARDSON, LYON N. A History of Early American Magazines, 1741–1789. 1931.

SMYTH, ALBERT H. The Philadelphia Magazines and Their Contributors, 1741–1850. 1892.

THE THEATER BEFORE THE REVOLUTION

[*History of the Drama and Stage*]

BROWN, BENJAMIN W. The Colonial Stage in New England. Bulletin No. 76 of the Newport Historical Society. 1930.

BROWN, T. ALLSTON. A History of the New York Stage. From the First Performance in 1732 to 1901. 3 vols. 1903.

CLAPP, WILLIAM W. A Record of the Boston Stage. 1853.

DUNLAP, WILLIAM. History of the American Theatre. 2 vols. 1832.

DYE, W. S. "Pennsylvania *versus* the Theatre," *Pennsylvania Magazine of History and Biography*, Vol. LX, pp. 333–372.

HORNBLOW, ARTHUR H. A History of the Theatre in America, Vol. I. 1919.

IRELAND, JOSEPH N. Records of the New York Stage from 1750 to 1860. 2 vols. 1866–1867.

ODELL, GEORGE C. D. Annals of the New York Stage, Vol. I. 1927.

PATTEE, FRED L. "The British Theater in Philadelphia in 1778," *American Literature*, Vol. VI, pp. 381–388.

POLLOCK, THOMAS C. The Philadelphia Theatre in the Eighteenth Century. 1933.

QUINN, ARTHUR H. A History of the American Drama from the Beginnings to the Civil War. 1923.

SEILHAMER, GEORGE O. History of the American Theatre. 3 vols. 1888–1891.

WILLIS, EOLA. The Charleston Stage in the Eighteenth Century. 1924.

[*Bibliography*]

HILL, FRANK P. American Plays Printed, 1714–1830. 1934. (A bibliographical record.)

WEGELIN, OSCAR. Early American Plays, 1714–1830. A Compilation of the Titles of Plays and Dramatic Poems Written by Authors Born in or Residing in North America Previous to 1830 (2d ed., revised). 1905.

[*Literary Treatment of the Early Theater*]

COOKE, JOHN ESTEN. The Virginia Comedians. 1854.

LOVELACE, MAUD HART. The Charming Sally. 1932.

CHAPTER IV

The Revolution, 1762-1807

Pre-war Songs and Ballads

A SPREAD of interest in the printed literature of the frontier and in the songs and ballads that passed from lip to ear reached almost faddish proportions in the United States in the 1920's. As far as surviving evidence goes, however, the colonial frontier seems to have depended for its familiar songs on Old World folk sources. Certainly many of the old English and Scottish ballads seem to have had centuries of oral transmission in this country, and many others of the most popular printed songs and ballads were imported and survived on paper. It is hard to believe that life was unaccompanied by native folk ballads and folk melodies; but so far as is known nothing of this sort survives from colonial times.

For the period that we are dealing with, therefore, the student must be content with printed songs and ballads, and these are almost exclusively concerned with national and political themes.[1] They were quite numerous, — increasingly so after the middle of the century and the outbreak of the French and Indian War, — and they serve as a running accompaniment to the main sequence of events. At the outset unqualified colonial loyalty prevailed in all of them. Braddock and Wolfe were heroes and martyrs. The subjects of Britain were fighting the wars of the Lord. With the

---

[1] For a record of eighteenth-century American song see Percy H. Boynton, "American Poetry"; William Chappell, "Old English Popular Music"; William McCarty, "Songs, Odes and Other Poems on National Subjects"; Frank Moore, "Songs and Ballads of the American Revolution"; and the anthologies entitled "Songs for the Whig Celebration" (1834), "The American Naval and Patriotic Songster" (1841), "The Eagle and Harp" (1812).

middle of the 1760's, however, signs of an unrest began to appear, and with the passage of the Stamp Act "freedom," "liberty," and "tyranny" loomed large. The most popular songs were all set to melodies then current in old England, sometimes occurring in sequences: the first, a parody of the English song, the next the parody of a parody, and so on. Soon the vocabulary of abuse was drawn on with "villains," "rascals," "banditti," "brats," "bunters," furnishing the ammunition for the loyalists; and "tyrants," "despots," "manacles," "scourges," and "dungeons" for the counterblasts of the rebellious. Still the extreme suggestion of either faction was political insurrection rather than military revolt. As the break came nearer, the attitude of the leading Tories was notably conciliatory.

With 1776 came the inevitable word "independence" and a farewell to all attempts toward sparing the king at the expense of Lord North. The colonials became truculent, though the loyalists continued to deprecate and deplore until the alliance with the French and the revulsion of feeling caused by their own hardships transformed their sorrow into anger. Now the loyalist Jonathan Odell blazed out his "Congratulations" of November, 1779, and "The American Times" of 1780, rivaling Freneau's "British Prison Ship" and "The Political Balance" in vitriolic bitterness. In the closing years of the war the colonial verse relapsed into complacency, and the loyalist either into sullen silence or into a pathetic effort to make the best of a bad matter.[1]

The ways in which the verses were put into circulation are various and interesting. As always with "occasional" poetry, the regular journals and periodicals were the most effective instruments of distribution: such publications as *The Virginia Gazette, The Pennsylvania Gazette, The Pennsylvania Packet,* and *The Pennsylvania Journal, The Boston Gazette, The Freeman's Journal,* or *New Hampshire Gazette,* and, for the Tories, *Towne's Evening Post* and *Rivington's Royal*

---

[1] See page 157.

Gazette. The difficulties, after 1776, of getting loyalist material printed and distributed made Rivington, who was safe behind the British lines, the chief agent. Many of these songs were originally delivered at social gatherings, winter dinners, and summer outings, or as prologues or epilogues to plays, or were circulated by means of handbill "broadsides." One was included in a cantata; one was put out as a pasquinade — simply written out and conspicuously posted; and one, the most famous of all, was almost a folk poem or ballad in origin. For "Yankee Doodle," although attributed originally to Edward Bangs, a Harvard sophomore, undoubtedly had the ballad experience of being modified and varied, as all ballads have been by this process. This experience was, of course, in some degree, common to all the songs and jingles which were widely repeated or sung. "Yankee Doodle" was simply the pre-eminent example. Others from among this immediate group are "The Boston Tea Party," "The Fall of John Burgoyne," and "The Dance," all of which are in conventional ballad meter, with a half-primitive ruggedness of form and content; and "Nathan Hale," more elaborate in form and more self-conscious in tone, a good eighteenth-century treatment of ballad material which, if not actually "trimmed in the gorgeous eloquence of Pindar," was at any rate quite appreciably dressed up.

In any discussion of the literary qualities of these verses of conflict and loyalty the frequently adopted device of writing new words for old melodies may be regarded as next of kin to the balladry of "Yankee Doodle." In the revolutionary days, as in every generation, there were a few popular favorites which it was impossible not to copy. The situation is well illustrated today by the general practice in connection with college and fraternity songs. A good new melody is invariably pirated before its third season, and old ones sometimes have as many as five or six sets of more or less inferior verse composed to them. The popular songs of the late eighteenth century furnished a fair stimulus to at least respectable song writing. Perhaps the most famous then and now were "Hearts of Oak," "Lords of the Main," and the toast "Here's to the Maiden of Bashful Fifteen," still familiar to the modern theatergoer, as sung by Charles Surface in "The School for Scandal." These and their like were all well turned and graceful, with dashes of rather magniloquent heroism and strains of tender sentiment. They were not vulgar in tone or content; still less were they vulgar in the neat rotundity of their form. It was fortunate for the literary quality of revolutionary song that the standard types of the day were not doggerel or modern concert-hall drivel.

The fortunes of a single song, David Garrick's "Hearts of Oak," are typical. This was first sung in public in a pantomime of 1759. Seven years later came the first American version, dedicated, as was natural for 1766, to both Loyalty and Liberty. By 1768 the issues were drawn, and a sequence of three versions appeared, the first lines of which reveal them:

> July, "Come, join hand in hand, brave Americans all,"
> September, "Come, shake your dull noddles, ye bumpkins, and bawl,"
> October, "Come, swallow your bumpers, ye Tories, and roar."

A further Tory rejoinder appeared in January, 1769, a retort courteous:

> "Come, cheer up, my lads, like a true British band."

Then silence in contributions to this measure and melody until Joseph Stansbury's song of 1774 or 1775:

> "When good Queen Elizabet governed the realm,"

followed by a sympathetic word from England counseling nonbelligerency:

> "Come, listen, my cocks, to a brother and friend,"

and an incendiary American response,

> "Come, rouse up, my lads, and join this great cause."

The final version during the war came from the Tory side:

> "Here's a bumper, brave boys, to the health of our King."

But the series was to be resumed. Francis Hopkinson's "The New Roof" (see page 139) inspired a song on the same metaphor:

> "Come, muster, my lads, your mechanical tools."

Susannah Rowson celebrated a naval victory over the French ship *Insurgente* in 1799:

> "When Freedom, fair Freedom, her banner displayed";

and three echoes and re-echoes resounded during the War of 1812.

"Lords of the Main" and "Here's to the Maiden" had similar paraphrases and parodies. Sometimes a good melody was used without attempt to parody the original words or sentiment. The tune "Derry Down," in the prevailing anapaestic measure, for which were written the "Satire on the Liberty Pole" of 1770 and the satirical "Epilogue" of 1778, could carry several other of the selections by the mere addition of the burden "Derry down, down, hey, derry down"; and the iambic "Maggie Lauder" could accompany not only "Cornwallis Burgoyned" but any other of the conventional ballad verse which was not otherwise engaged. Of the songs as a whole, from Wolfe's "How Stands the Glass Around" to those of Freneau and Hopkinson forty years later, it is fair to say that they were thoroughly English in form and sentiment. Manly strength, feminine grace, the cheering influence of the social glass, and a traditionally aristocratic point of view were implicit in them. By accident they were dedicated to a struggle for and against a democratic principle; but these song writers, by common consent with the rest of the radical vintners of their day, poured their new political wines into old literary bottles.

Perhaps the metaphor can be pursued a step further; for wine is not only pleasurable to the palate, but is a stimulant that braces courage, opens the heart, and sets the tongue to wagging. The sentiments in the songs were no more important than the sentiment stirred by singing them. A general familiarity along the seaboard with these insurgent rhymes, and the common zest that came with singing them, would never have been enough to bring about the Revolution; but, coupled with a half-dozen other and deeper incentives, the songs and ballads of the period no doubt contributed their share toward converting revolutionary spirit into revolutionary action.

Spark and Tinder in the Pre-war Years

While the people were reading the little gazettes and newspapers and the earliest of the magazines and singing their songs and talking matters over in the taverns and the churchyards and on the street corners, they were converting themselves into the tinder that oratory could inflame. The public mind was being prepared; public opinion was in the nebular stage; public events interpreted in public speech were to stir emotions that would eventuate in public action; and all this took time — years of time.

Yet the policies of George III and his ministers that were to be scathingly listed in the Declaration of Independence roused resentments promptly after his accession. Hardly a year had passed before the sparks began to fly in the Boston smithy. The Bay colony, haven of refuge to the insurgents against the rule of Charles I, had long been a breeding ground for rebels in the making. They had clung to the old faith; they were rigorous disciplinarians of others and of themselves; in the passage of the generations many of them, if not most, had forgotten how to play; and, believing vaguely that pleasure was self-indulgence and that self-indulgence was transgression, they had been driven to all sorts of indirections for the condoning of their carnalities and frivolities. But they had kept alive the spirit of the Roundheads — a natural spirit for controversy and the zest for a good fight in the name of a principle, and they were typically British in identifying high principle with personal interest.

It was a boy from Cape Cod, a Harvard graduate of 1743 and a master of arts three years later, a young classicist with a special predilection for prosody, who dramatized the situation in 1761 when the new king renewed to the customs officers the writs of search and seizure which had expired with the death of the second George. Here was a principle to fasten on, as James Otis was to demonstrate both in his protests and in the tragic wrecking of his career by the violent hands of His Majesty's officers. In arguing his case young Mr. Otis (he was in his thirties) spoke from the conviction which had already led him to resign as advocate general.

> I renounced that office, and I argue this cause, from the same principle; and I argue it with the greater pleasure, as it is in favor of British liberty . . . and as it is in opposition to a kind of power, the exercise of which, in former periods of English history, cost one king of England his head, and another his throne.[1]

He assailed the regranting of offensive powers to the customs officers, because the writ was illegal, universal, perpetual, and put tyrannical and unchallengeable authority in the hands of "menial servants" of the crown. Eight years later he was assailed in a Boston tavern by some of these menials and so brutally beaten that he suffered permanent mental derangement.

The momentous fact about James Otis is that he was both a legalistic defender of colonial rights and the most effective of speakers. John Adams could not say too much of this: Otis used "a style of oratory that I never heard equalled in this or any other country"; "Otis's oration against writs of assistance breathed into this nation the breath of life"; "Otis was a flame of fire."[2] He persisted as a lawyer in watching for invasions of Massachusetts liberties and in flaming in protest against them. The next occasion came in

---

[1] Quoted in Tyler's "Literary History of the American Revolution," Vol. I, pp. 33–34.

[2] John Adams, "Works," Vol. X, p. 362.

the next year when the royal governor, Bernard, quite efficiently took an extralegal step in fitting out an armed vessel to meet an emergency when the legislature was out of session. Nothing could be more natural or innocent; but in the act Otis saw a usurpation of the legislature's exclusive right to initiate public expenditures. At the next session Otis cried out so vehemently that the phrases in which he "disrespectfully brought into question . . . the sacred and well-beloved name" of His Majesty were stricken out of the records at the governor's request. But when the governor also insisted on his emergency prerogatives, Otis drafted for a legislative committee "A Vindication of the Conduct of the House of Representatives," and enunciated in the first half of it the principles of the preamble to the Declaration of Independence and the grounds for the bill of grievances that followed. For the first five of Otis's ten propositions ostensibly about human rights were these:

> (1) God made all men naturally equal. (2) The ideas of earthly superiority, pre-eminence and grandeur are educational; — at least acquired, not innate. (3) Kings were, — and plantation governors should be, — made for the good of the people, and not the people for them.

There is a rising tide of jocosity in the statements that follow. The fourth and fifth prepare the way for the second quintet:

> (4) No government has a right to make hobby-horses, asses and slaves of the subjects, nature having made sufficient of the two former . . . but none of the last, — which infallibly proves they are unnecessary. (5) Though most governments are "de facto" arbitrary, and consequently the curse and scandal of human nature, yet none are "de jure" arbitrary.[1]

These have served as rules of conduct and principles to allege at all times since Otis laid them down. As a legalist he could and did argue them inexorably. As an orator, a rhetorician, he could bolster them up not only with invective

[1] Tyler, op. cit. Vol. I, p. 42.

but with the gayest sallies of irony, as witness the remaining "propositions." These were to the effect that the British constitution, the king of Great Britain, and all his colonial governors were agents and instruments of complete political felicity, and that per contra one needed only to glance across the English Channel. Nominally Otis confined his recital and his protest to the king's servants and their ways, and made deep obeisance to his royal master. But this pamphlet was composed after his short and ugly treatment of the "sacred and well-beloved name" had been repudiated by the House. It is as well that Otis indited this document and that Samuel Adams at his request "quieu-whewed" it; for when he was expressing his deference for King George his tongue was so far in his cheek as to have almost obstructed vocal utterance.

The value in literary history of these two arguments of Otis is that they defined an issue which was fought out in the resort to arms between the colonists and the king after the Declaration of Independence, which was resumed in the conflict between the Republicans and the Federalists after the adoption of the Constitution and the Bill of Rights, and which is at the basis of every clash between capital and labor. While the military revolution was on, and during the civil revolution that preceded and followed, polite literature was pretty well ignored, and writers were conscripted to serve the interests of the contending factions. Otis, the classical scholar and the rhetorician, was one of the first to be drafted.

To pursue here the steps in the political debate that ensued on the rostrum and in a shower of pamphlets; to be lured from letters to politics, to discussion of Oxenbridge Thacher, the "Gentleman from Halifax," John Dickinson, the Pennsylvania "Farmer," Daniel Leonard, "Massachusettensis," John Adams, "Novanglus" and other anonymous or pseudonymous debaters, — would be once more to follow the drum of the recruiting officers to the camp and the battlefield. Literary history must limit itself to the writing that in form or substance represents something more than the excitement of the moment. And there were many in this loquacious period who wrote what is still readable as they turned from the Addisonian essay, social satire, ballads and lyrics, society verse, and early excursions in dramatic or epic composition to bend their talents and these forms to the exigencies of the time.

Provincial Echoes in the Pre-war Years

There is every evidence that if peace had prevailed in the reign of George III, there would have been a large output of conventional writing in the colonies. Long before the war Francis Hopkinson was taking his pen in hand to address the gentle reader with such pretty lyrics as his "Morning Hymn," his "Ode to Music," and his "Advice to Amanda." John Trumbull turned out nearly sixty contributions to his "Meddler" and two "Correspondent" series. Philip Freneau and H. H. Brackenridge jointly achieved their commencement colloquy on "The Rising Glory of America" in 1771; and Freneau wrote on "The Power of Fancy" and decided in jejune world-weariness to retire to a cottage — the ideal cottage in the ideal retirement that most youthful poets have yearned for as part of their poetic experience. If Trumbull's memory was correct when he annotated his collected poems in 1820, Timothy Dwight and Joel Barlow had already written,[1] — the one his "Conquest of Canaan" and the other his "Vision of Columbus," and they both had planned to have them published in London before Trumbull addressed his "Lines" to them in the autumn of 1775:

> Pleased with the vision of a deathless name,
> You seek perhaps a flowery road to fame;
> Where distant far from ocean's stormy roar,
> Wind the pure vales and smiles the tranquil shore,
> Where hills sublime in vernal sweetness rise,
> And opening prospects charm the wand'ring eyes,[2]

---

[1] The best illustrative volume for this group is "The Connecticut Wits" (edited by Vernon L. Parrington), in the American Authors Series.

[2] Trumbull, "Poetical Works" (1820), Vol. II, p. 105.

where, in short, these two young eighteenth-century British subjects were to see everything with their "wand'ring" eyes exactly as nature was seen in England, and where they were to record what they saw in the exact tropes that were to persist as the thinning currency of poetic diction until Wordsworth reassayed it. In these years Trumbull alone composed a substantial piece of verse which was not sweetened or fattened by the redundant adjectives that cluttered up most pentameters of the day, and which pranced in quadrupedal lines across the surface of a domestic theme — "higher education," as pursued in Connecticut, with especial and caustic reference to Yale College.

Yet this is a minor exception. The most that can be said of the development of the arts as the century approached its closing quarter is that the colonists were finding time and feeling the mood to cultivate them in the fashion of the best English models. It was the inevitable colonial attitude; it was the natural fashion for the ex-frontier, which, when it turns to the adornments of life, looks to the seat of fashion for its dress and its manners and for the dress of its thought even after its manners have begun to change. Colonial architecture, so called, revealed it; for the best colonial architecture was a modified Georgian. Colonial painting showed it; for it was founded on the English school, and attained its highest distinction in Benjamin West, who actually became president of the Royal Academy. Colonial music was an echo of the anglicized German Handel, and of Haydn and Mozart, who were so nicely expressive of the formalism of the English eighteenth century. Colonial hymnology was dignified by the same practice. And this complete cultural allegiance was to persist long after the years when the American Revolution was politically successful. In 1815 John Adams, in his renewed friendship with Thomas Jefferson, wrote that the war "was no part of the revolution; it was only an effect and consequence of it. The revolution was in the minds of the people, and this was effected from 1760 to 1775, in the course of fifteen years, before a drop of blood was shed at Lexington."[1] Yet in 1807 Barlow republished his long-cherished and much-expanded "Columbiad," which had first found its way into print twenty years before and which had been ready for publication a baker's dozen of years before that. It was still an echo; still a fulfillment of Trumbull's modest hope that the writers in the new world might

> bid their lays with lofty Milton vie;
> Or wake from nature's themes the moral song,
> And shine with Pope, with Thompson and with Young.
> This land her Swift and Addison shall view,
> The former honors equalled by the new;
> Here shall some Shakespeare charm the rising age,
> And hold in magic chains the listening stage;
> A second Watts shall string the heavenly lyre,
> And other muses other bards inspire.[2]

Thus in these pre-war years Francis Hopkinson of Philadelphia emerges as a "curious, ingenious" man with an interest in the arts that perplexed and tantalized the single-minded John Adams. "I wish I had leisure and tranquillity of mind to amuse myself with those elegant and ingenious arts of painting, sculpture, statuary, architecture, and music. But I have not."[3] Behind all his prose and verse there appears always a charming and complex personality. He had accomplishments enough to qualify him as a full-fledged dilettante, but abilities enough to make him an astute and learned judge. There was a good deal of Franklin in him — his erudition, his interest in science and literature, his humor, his complete and practical devotion to the things of the day. And there was a good deal in him, also, of Chesterfield, in his love of the refinements of life and in his mastery of the arts of getting on. His social graces brought him political favors from Lord North which his native strength enabled

---

[1] John Adams, "Works," Vol. X, p. 172.
[2] Trumbull, op. cit. Vol. II, pp. 159–160.
[3] John Adams, "Letters Addressed to His Wife," quoted in Tyler's "Literary History," Vol. I, p. 163.

him to sacrifice for the colonial cause. He had the qualities of heroism but none of its manners.

Two and a half of the three volumes of his collected works[1] are filled with prose essays which are worth reading both as literature and as cultural history. They include meditations, reveries, dreams, and innocuous light essays of the Addisonian type, personal satires, essays on music, discourses on education, grave and gay, popular commentaries on science and statecraft, and a program extending all the way from a "Speech of a post in the assembly room" to "Observations on the bill for amending the penal laws." As a poet Hopkinson stands in contrast to his contemporaries in his never attempting sustained flights. There are Miltonic imitations, songs, sentiments, hymns, a fable, and a piece of advice to a young lady. There are occasional poems, including birthday and wedding greetings, prologues and epilogues for plays, elegies and epitaphs. There is an "Epigram on the death of a favorite lap-dog" and "Verses written in a blank book which once belonged to Shenstone"—verses which betray Hopkinson's opinion that Shenstone wrote other books which were not blank.

These verses of the stock varieties possessed many of the excellences of their kinds. Hopkinson was never pompous, his sense of humor restrained him from the use of long and empty locutions, he was almost always facile and graceful, and he was always in control of his emotions:

My gen'rous heart disdains
The slave of love to be,
I scorn his servile chains,
And boast my liberty.
This whining
And pining
And wasting with care,
Are not to my taste, be she ever so fair.[2]

---

1 The work of Hopkinson is not available in reprint. The best study is George E. Hastings's "Life and Works of Francis Hopkinson."

2 Francis Hopkinson, "Works," Vol. III, p. 190.

It was an attitude of mind that was well adapted to the composition of light satire; and it accounts for Hopkinson's extraordinary effectiveness, to which we shall return when we come to the literary chronicles of the war.

The antebellum John Trumbull[1] was so like the antebellum Hopkinson that a group of short poems written between 1770 and 1774 might easily be attributed to the Philadelphian. Quite naturally he translated from Vergil; most of the English poets since the Restoration had taken side excursions into this field. As a young and orthodox New Englander he matched Hopkinson's hymns with Biblical paraphrases. He wrote two fables, like Gray, and offered his advice not to one lady but "to ladies of a certain age." With the echoes of Gray's "Elegy" in his ears, he too wrote his elegy on a friend, St. John, thereby indulging à la mode in the pleasurable melancholy of the "graveyard poets."

In "The Progress of Dulness," however, composed in the midst of these other performances and published in the year of the second series of "Correspondent" papers, he came down to facts as he had noted them in New Haven; and in the "keen spirit of critical observation" which he later attributed to himself, he began his work as a satirist. This production is on the interwoven careers of Tom Brainless and Dick Hairbrain and of Harriet Simper, who, after a varied experience as coquette, was first jilted by Dick and then doomed to an inglorious marriage with the dullard parson, Tom. There is a canto for each of the trio. Tom, an incompetent, was sent to college by his fond parents. Stupid and lazy, he survived to receive his degree at the end of

> Four years at college dozed away,
> In sleep and slothfulness and play,[2]

and was ultimately pushed into the pulpit as he had been shoved into the classroom.

---

[1] Trumbull's verse is not available in full except in his own edition in two volumes of 1820. References here are to this edition.

[2] Trumbull, op. cit. Vol. II, p. 23.

Of the academic leopard's spots Dick was a larger and darker one. Aware of the joys a "liberal education" was to afford him, he broke out on his arrival in rapturous salutation to the halls

> Where wealth and pride and riot wait,
> And each choice spirit finds its mate.[1]

Trumbull interrupted his tale for frequent strictures on the college. He agreed with Franklin, Hopkinson, and Freneau in deploring the domination of the classics, and took the aggressive against most of the other subjects in the curriculum, vaguely feeling that something was amiss but not asking himself what a college should contribute to the life of Connecticut. In Dick's case the only serious application it inspired was in the extracurricular activities:

> His talents proved of highest price
> At all the arts of cards and dice;
> His genius turned with greatest skill
> To whist, loo, cribbage and quadrille.[2]

With an indictment that rejected the studies as useless and the recreations as pernicious, Trumbull's criticism gave ample historical ground for New England's establishing of a day of prayer for colleges. There is a Grecian completeness in the punishment of Harriet.

This was genuine, home-made satire. Yet "The Progress of Dulness" reveals its imitativeness in its very title. There is a whole anthology of "progress" art and literature, from the rake's to the pilgrim's, hellward and heavenward;[3] there is another anthology of diatribes against dullards and dullness, from "MacFlecknoe" to "English Bards and Scotch Reviewers";[4] and there is a third vast collection of verse writ-

---

[1] Trumbull, op. cit. Vol. II, p. 36.

[2] Ibid. Vol. II, p. 50.

[3] R. H. Griffith, "The Progress Pieces of the Eighteenth Century," *Texas Review*, Vol. V (1919–1920), pp. 218–233.

[4] R. P. Bond, "-Iad: a Progeny of the Dunciad," *PMLA*, Vol. XLIV (1929), pp. 1099–1105.

ten in the contemptuous gallantry with which the eighteenth century addressed "the fair," and an array of portraits from Steele's "Biddy Tipkin" in "The Tender Husband" to Mrs. Lennox's "Arabella" in "The Female Quixote." Trumbull's "Progress" was thus local in its idiom and British-provincial in its type. In its day it was good satire; for the modern reader it is like all authentic satire, — an informative historical document; and it is distinctly readable. Its greatest value, however, is that it demonstrated to Trumbull's friends that his satirical gifts might be applied to more vital subjects. An experience as law student in John Adams's office at Boston brought him from the college yard to the city square and finally to the point where, quite reluctantly, he responded to the call of the literary recruiting officers to become the author of "M'Fingal," of which there is more to be said in due course.[1]

Freneau,[2] the young Princetonian, was traveling the same well-beaten path with Hopkinson of the college in Philadelphia and with Trumbull, the Yalensian, but with a difference. For Freneau was epic and romantic from the start. Hopkinson's college-commencement effusion is not recorded, though he seems to have had a place on the program; but there is record of an undergraduate oration from him on "Education in General." Trumbull, on receiving his master of arts degree, delivered "An Essay on the Use and Advantages of the Fine Arts," in which he defended devotion to the arts in a time of political unrest. Freneau, absent from graduating exercises, was the chief author of the poetic dialogue on "The Rising Glory of America," which was recited by H. H. Brackenridge. It is on the level to be expected from such a theme in the hands of a nineteen-year-old boy; but it foretells his reach of imagination and contains a quotable passage in the concluding poetic flight:

---

[1] See pages 143, 144, 160.

[2] The most nearly definitive edition of Freneau's poems is by Fred Lewis Pattee, for the Princeton Historical Association (3 vols.), 1902. The most accessible volume for students is "The Poems of Freneau" (edited by Harry Hayden Clark), in the American Authors Series. References here are to this edition.

— I see, I see
Freedom's established reign; cities, and men,
Numerous as sands upon the ocean's shore,
And empires rising where the sun descends! —
The *Ohio* soon shall glide by many a town
Of note; and where the *Mississippi* stream,
By forests shaded, now runs weeping on,
Nations shall grow, and states not less in fame
Than Greece and Rome of old! [1]

The country was not only to be widespreading and populous: Paradise was to flourish anew, "by no second Adam lost."

Freneau was an excessively serious youth writing in the post-adolescent solemnity with which his years were endowed. Already he felt some vague implications in the possibilities of the new paradise. He subscribed to the thesis of primitive nobility and explained away the homely and ignoble realities of primitive savagery. In "The American Village" and again in "Discovery" he maintained that the savage was never savage until he learned his lesson at the bloody hands of the conquering white man; and in the abysmal depression of discovery that the world was out of joint, he could make for solitude, saying over his shoulder,

Seek some new world in some new climate plac'd,
Some gay *Ta-ia* on the watery waste,
Though Nature clothes in all her bright array,
Some proud tormenter steals her charms away: . . .
Howe'er the groves, howe'er the gardens bloom,
A *monarch* and a *priest* is still their doom.[2]

In all these early effusions Freneau was a belligerent pacifist, dowered with the hate of hate; and an inevitable consequence of this temper was that when conflict came he became also a combatant pacifist. He was a moth before the flame of conflict. Yet though he could never resist the awful fascination of it, he also had a natural bent for a dreamy contemplation of long reaches of time, vast reaches of space

[1] "The Poems of Freneau" (edited by H. H. Clark), p. 13. [2] Ibid. p. 20.

and the poetic subject whose remoteness enveiled it in romantic glamour. He stood in fancy as a youth of seventeen before "The Pyramids of Egypt" and wrote upon them, concluding that God alone would endure

> when Genius, and *Time*,
> (Time not immortal, but a viewless point
> In the vast circle of eternity)
> Are swallowed up, and, like the pyramids,
> Leave not an atom for their monument! [1]

He composed his "Pictures of Columbus" (eighteen of them) and noted the ironic contrast between epic achievement and contemporary renown. He wrote on "The Power of Fancy," reduced all creation to "Fancies of the Power Divine," and attributed half his happiness to its emancipating magic. There was nothing but his vehemence in these early years to suggest that surrounding circumstance would ever be anything but a point of departure for him. When Fancy ceased to satisfy, there was the further refuge of books. "The American Village" opened with a low bow to Goldsmith; "The Deserted Farm House" was a frank echo of Gray. He was "unfit for cities and the noisy throng"; he would live with Milton, Shakespeare, Dryden, Spenser, Pope, Addison, and Goldsmith. So he fondly thought; but no such peaceful career awaited him, as we shall see before long.[2]

The War Draft of the Wits, 1773–1783

Even these adorners of life were conscious of the surrounding turmoil that was soon to engulf them. Events had been moving fast since James Otis stated the issues in 1761 and 1762. In 1764 had come the Sugar Act for the acknowledged purpose of raising revenues from the colonies. In 1765 the Stamp Act had followed, the first tax imposition that involved

---

[1] "The Poems of Freneau" (edited by H. H. Clark), p. 207.

[2] For further discussion of the writers named above see, for Brackenridge, pp. 174–176; for Dwight, pp. 163–168; for Freneau, pp. 141–143, 157, 168, 169; for Hopkinson, pp. 139–141, 152; for Trumbull, pp. 143, 144, 160.

all parts of all the colonies. The repeal in 1766 had been accompanied by an express repudiation of the colonial claim to an exclusive right to self-taxation. In 1767 modified revenues on a limited list of imports were pledged to the support of the local governments, but they were bracketed with a renewal of the hated writs of assistance and with provisions for quartering soldiers sent to enforce collection. A general policy of law evasion and of offensive violation ensued, culminating in 1770 with the Boston Massacre, in which the people were the aggressors. Then, for three years, all offensive imposts but the tax on tea were withdrawn, and the merchants breathed a sigh of relief, hoping that victory had been won. It might have been, if in 1773, in behalf of the East India Company, the last straw had not been added with the granting of a monopoly, even though in circumstances which actually reduced the cost to the consumer. But the colonists were legal-minded. They resented the implications of the act in the spectacular demonstration of the Boston Tea Party. The port was closed, other drastic punitive measures followed, the Revolution was in full procedure, and the resort to arms was inevitable.

In the meanwhile Boston and Philadelphia had been active in journalistic controversy. The country was divided in terms of commercial self-interest and sentimental loyalty. The advocates of peaceful settlement had come within hoping distance of a solution. Charges of tyranny had been met with countercharges of treason. "Valerius Poplicola," "Sincerus," "Monitor," and "The Centinel," champions of the oppressed, had been answered by "Censor," "Marcus Aurelius," "Freeman" (but not a protesting one), and even by "Eleutherina," who rose to defend His Majesty's servants.

While the newspaper letter writers were venting themselves, others, a little more deliberate, literary, ambitious, attempted the dramatic form. There was hardly anything dramatic about their works beyond their dialogue form and the emotional intensity that was responsible for them; and there is no record of performances at the time. But they filtered along through the whole war period; some of them were produced after the smoke of battle had settled, and some were published before the firing began. Mercy Warren was the most dramatic of the authors, and her works are the most vitriolic; for she was sister to James Otis, was committed to his cause, and was lamenting his complete breakdown consequent to the assault on him in 1769. The "History of the Rise, Progress and Termination of the American Revolution, Interspersed with Biographical, Political and Moral Reflections," which she published not till 1805, was written with the same animus. She was an Otis, married to a Warren, friend of the Adamses. They were honest people, devoted to a noble cause. Those who opposed them could not be honest and noble; at best they could be no more than "The Adulateurs," and to the best of her limited abilities she dramatized them toward the end of 1773. Naturally John Adams approved, and wrote to her husband: "Tell her that God Almighty (I use a bold style) has intrusted her with powers for the good of the world, which in the course of his providence he bestows on very few of the human race . . . it would be criminal to neglect them."[1] She had demonstrated the heavenly dispensation in a play which opened in "Upper Servia" with a conversation between four gentlemen with Roman names who were known to represent James Otis, the two Adamses, and John Hancock, and which closed with a speech of Otis to the effect that "murders, blood and carnage" were to be loosed on the country by "monsters" who would be crushed in the ruins of their making. Mrs. Warren had much the same thing to say in a more explicit dialogue entitled "The Group," of two years later;[2] and when she was not writing she was stimulating others to speech and action.

---

[1] Mercy Warren, letter of March 15, 1775, in "Works," Vol. IX, p. 356.

[2] The work of Mercy Otis Warren was published as "Poems, Dramatic and Miscellaneous," 1790; and "The History of the Rise, Progress and Termination of the American Revolution . . .," 1805. "The Group" is reprinted in Moses's "Representative Plays by American Dramatists," Vol. I.

Now in this exciting year, 1773, while Trumbull was completing his tale of Tom, Dick, and Harriet,[1] Franklin in London wrote two bits that were as blithe in spirit as anything of Trumbull's, and in their blitheness were far more effective than the invectives of Mercy Warren or "Mucius Scaevola" or "Usurper" or the other pseudonymous ranters. He was on his second long mission to England, from 1765 to 1775, and he had been conducting himself with the baffling urbanity that as a young man he determined to acquire. In the year of the Stamp Act he had written, on the credulity of Englishmen to hearsay stories of travelers, the gay open letter that included the fine passage on the cod and whale fishery in the inland lakes in which "the grand Leap of the Whale in that Chase [of the codfish] up the Fall of Niagara is esteemed, by all who have seen it, as one of the finest Spectacles in Nature. Really, Sir, the World is grown too incredulous."[2] The pamphlet on Franklin's "Examination . . . in the British House of Commons, relative to the Repeal of the American Stamp Act" had been generally received as the most informative document of the day because of its tact, good humor, and lucidity. It was time for more of the same in 1773, and more came in "Rules by which a Great Empire may be reduced to a Small One" and "An Edict by the King of Prussia," published in the *Gentleman's Magazine* in September and October of that year. The "rules" were a generalized statement of the tactics applied by England to the American colonies during recent years; the "edict" was a declaration directed at England as from the king of Prussia which closely paralleled the edicts launched at the colonists. Since England was hardly more unified as to the proper course in America than the Americans were as to the wise policy toward England, and since there were peace lovers on both sides of the ocean, the effectiveness of these two little boomerangs was very great. And their effectiveness as examples of dialectic is recorded in the number of utterances in this vein which

[1] See pages 131–133.
[2] Franklin, "To the Editor of a Newspaper," May 20 [1765].

soon and continuously appeared from the colonial writers who were capable of the lighter controversial touch.[1]

Hopkinson had found the tone a natural one. "Errata; or the Art of Printing incorrectly" needed only to be paralleled for equally devastating comments on the art of ruling incorrectly. Andrew Steuart, the printer, had felt the sting of this curious and ingenious little man; but the little man was big in heart and learned in law and government. In the autumn of 1774, shortly after the opening of the first Continental Congress, he published "A Pretty Story, written in the year of our Lord 1774, by Peter Grievous, Esq., A.B.C.D.E. Veluti in Speculo." It is prefaced by an introduction in which Hopkinson employed the figure of the house, to which he was to return in "The New Roof," his symbol for the Constitution contrived by a later congress. This time the house was his own book; but he abandoned the metaphor and left matters in the hands of the public. Let the reader, he observed, finish the preface to his own liking. And if he liked he might resort to the eighteenth-century convention of pretending that the manuscript had been written reluctantly at the urgency of friends, or dashed off without thought of publication, or found in an old desk, or dug out of a ruin, or discovered in a hermit's cave.

At all events the "Pretty Story" has to do with a nobleman, who is George III; and a shop, which is foreign trade; and a large family, his subjects and estates, including a wild tract far enough from home to stand for the American colonies. His wife is Parliament; his steward, the prime minister. One can gather the drift and the closeness of technique not only to Arbuthnot's "History of John Bull," to which this story is always compared, but also to the derisive indirection of those two sketches by Franklin that had echoed on both sides of the Atlantic within the year. In

[1] Reprints of representative work of Franklin are most accessible in "Selections from Benjamin Franklin and Jonathan Edwards" (edited by Carl Van Doren), in the Modern Student's Library. The "Autobiography" is edited by P. H. Boynton. American Authors Series, 1926.

terms of "The Old Farm and the New Farm," the unhappy complications summarized in "Rules by which a Great Empire may be reduced to a Small One" are detailed at greater length; and with the very latest development the chronicle comes to a close, without coming to a conclusion, with the abrupt statement that the rest is lacking. Hopkinson, the versatile, had found one of the ways in which he could contribute to the cause. While others of his services were more soberly performed, it is doubtful if any of them were more valuable in their effect on the war morale of the revolutionists.[1]

Some of the first readers of Hopkinson's skit were no doubt among the grave members of the Continental Congress who respected him for his professional prestige and wondered how he could do so many things and be so gay about them in those busy, somber times. They went on with their business, girding themselves for the coming fight, counseling preparedness and economy, revealing their interest in the arts by banning exhibitions of plays along with horse racing, gaming, cockfighting, "and other expensive diversions." Shortly after their adjournment a mild revenge was won by the author of a Tory quip in dramatic form, "A Dialogue between a Southern Delegate and his Spouse on His Return from the Grand Continental Congress. A Fragment Inscribed to the Married Ladies of America, By their most sincere and affectionate Friend and Servant, Mary V. V." The spouse is loquacious (in rhymed couplets), very much of a Tory, anything but docile, and not so much resolved to have hand or voice in politics as to keep her husband from raising a disturbance that would eventually reach to the drawing-room and the kitchen and the nursery. A Northern Tory followed promptly with another dialogue in the same temper, equally undramatic, equally disarming in his ac-

[1] Hopkinson's complete works have not been reprinted since the "Miscellaneous Essays and Occasional Writings of Francis Hopkinson," 1792. 3 vols. "The Old Farm and the New Farm" was edited by B. J. Lossing in 1857. Representative shorter poems appear in P. H. Boynton's "American Poetry," 1919.

knowledgment of the fact in the title: "The Americans Roused in a Cure for the Spleen, or Amusement for a Winter's Evening. Being the Substance of a Conversation on the Times over a Friendly Tankard and a Pipe" between a dozen participants (named in the title), reported verbatim by "Sir Roger de Coverly." It was not because these were two Tory skits that one was in rhymed couplets and the other in Addisonian conversation.[1] No one writing in America undertook to express himself in an American style. There was no such style short of the backwoods, and the backwoods were yet to become in the slightest degree articulate. The townsman was an Englishman, engaged in a civil struggle, utterly unconcerned with artistic innovations and utterly incapable of achieving any. As the months went on they rolled round to April of 1775 and to the nineteenth. For the rest of the year one voice rose above all the others in America.

Oddly enough this was not the voice of a New Englander but of the Philadelphian, Philip Freneau, a new Freneau dragged down to facts by the ruthlessness of surrounding facts, indignant and vociferous at having to abandon the cottage retreat his fancy had furnished. He came out in June in rude anapaests with "A Political Litany": deliver us, O Lord, from dependence on Britain, but also from a lot of definite, immediate abominations, like the royal council, and like the colonists inclined to take it seriously, and like marauding English ships, and English soldiers quartered on land, and English bishops who are grown butchers, and Lord North:

From a kingdom that bullies, and hectors, and swears,
We send up to heaven our wishes and prayers
That we, disunited, may freemen be still,
And Britain go on — to be damned if she will.[2]

---

[1] "A Dialogue between a Southern Delegate and his Spouse" exists in an old print of 1774. Anonymous. "The Americans Roused in a Cure for the Spleen" has been ascribed to Jonathan Sewall, 1775?

[2] "The Poems of Freneau" (edited by H. H. Clark), p. 21.

In July he published "American Liberty." He realized that revolutions must be policies converted into action, that a practical undertaking was ahead, that Congress was the body delegated to employ all its wisdom while the American army exerted all its strength. It was a sober appeal, following the first splenetic outburst, too sober for his temper, and offset soon by successive appeals to the groundlings in the form of assaults on General Thomas Gage, the first of that unheroic succession of British commanders on whom King George was unlucky enough to rely. "General Gage's Soliloquy" appeared in August, and the general turned out to be not half so confident as a victorious leader of invincible troops might be. In September he was described as holding "The Midnight Consultation," in which his greatest solicitude was over the lack of beef and mutton, though grazing herds were in sight, for the general could not get at them. On the theme of "The Conqueror of America Shut up in Boston" Freneau dwelt with savage pleasure. He was not a playful man; he never had been; but he had a kind of humor and a heavy keenness of delivery. He was a commentator on himself when he made Gaine the printer say:

> I printed some treason for Philip Freneau, —
> Some damnable poems reflecting on Gage,
> The king, and his council, and writ with such rage,
> So full of invective and loaded with spleen,
> So pointedly drawn and so hellishly keen,
> That at least in the judgment of half our wise men,
> Alecto herself made the nib to his pen.[1]

Call it spleen-loaded pen or clenched fist, Freneau was pressing the attack with the utmost zest and to the delight of the multitude when in mid-autumn of 1775 someone struck back. It appeared at once that Freneau had the thin skin that so often goes with the heavy hand. Bewildered, enraged, pitifully hurt, he came out with "McSwiggen" against his

---

[1] "The Poems of Freneau" (edited by F. L. Pattee), Vol. II, p. 201.

anonymous and unidentified assailant. It was a piece of poetical billingsgate that combined all the worst qualities of Pope at his worst with none of the good ones, and concluded with the resolve to go to balmier climes and more hospitable surroundings,

> Safe from the miscreants that my peace molest,
> Miscreants with dullness and with rage opprest.[1]

Fortunately his friend Captain Hanson of Vera Cruz had invited him to just such surroundings; and the so-called "poet of the Revolution" slipped away for a visit of two years and more, leaving the field until 1778 to the McSwiggens and the more robust defenders of liberty.

1776

One of these was the less truculent but on the whole less volatile author of "M'Fingal." During this year of 1775, when for a while Freneau was rushing into print with such gusto, the eyes of the country were focused upon Boston. Trumbull had served his short legal apprenticeship there the year before in the office of John Adams, returning to New Haven when his chief set out for the assembling of the Continental Congress in Philadelphia. The situation was his to describe as it could be only to a close observer; yet he showed no inclination to write about it until Silas Deane, Connecticut member of the first and second congresses, urged him to follow up his "Elegy on the Times," composed in his Boston sojourn, with a satire on General Gage. He did so, and it was published in the *Connecticut Courant.* Months later, and with every sign of diffidence, he sent to Deane his draft of the first installment of "M'Fingal," which was to appear in January, 1776.[2] He thought it harmless; Deane had suggested the idea; other friends had urged him

---

[1] "The Poems of Freneau" (edited by F. L. Pattee), Vol. I, p. 206.

[2] See, further, Alexander Cowie, "John Trumbull as a Revolutionist," in *American Literature,* Vol. III (1931), pp. 287–295. Trumbull's two major poems are reprinted in "The Connecticut Wits" (edited by V. L. Parrington), in the American Authors Series, 1926.

on. He felt that it was long, tedious, badly written; he was heartily tired of it. Would Deane, amend, cut, or suppress it? And would he be sure to let no one, "unless Mr. J. Adams," know of the authorship?

This most famous single satire of the Revolution is built around the dissensions in a typical New England town between Whigs and Tories, led by Honorius, the archrebel, and M'Fingal, the loyalist. The first two cantos, in its final form, were the fifteen hundred lines first published without division. These were on the daylong debate between the leaders, interrupted only by noon adjournment for luncheon. Honorius made the time-honored appeals to the Englishman's love of liberty, and M'Fingal retorted with addresses to his traditional respect for law and authority. Despite their length the speeches were vigorous, full of barbed personal and local allusions, and so turned that whether spoken with the fervor of Honorius or the abusive maladroitness of M'Fingal, they were equally effective in fanning rebellion in the breasts of those who were already rebellious. The debate was adjourned in general confusion sine die, and the poem was left thus unconcluded for six years.[1] To Trumbull's surprise it was greeted with loud applause. It was reprinted soon in London, where, with prejudices reversed, it could be read with almost equal satisfaction. It was subsequently (after its completion) to run into scores of editions. And its original appearance came in a month which welcomed the most sensational document, and the most momentous, to precede the Declaration of Independence. The time was ripe for a clarion call in reiteration of the principles declared by James Otis, echoed with varying degrees of partial effectiveness by all sorts and conditions of remonstrants ever since.

The call came with the publication of "Common Sense." Nobody seems to have loved Thomas Paine; but nobody loves skyrockets or meteors. Paine has been vilified for his early career, envied for his middle-life achievements in the

---

[1] See page 160.

colonies, and converted into a bogeyman for his utterances on religion and his adoption by the French. The literature of personal abuse has accumulated around him as it has around the two Mathers or Poe or Whitman. It is interesting perhaps because it is symptomatic of the critical bias of his assailants and his defenders; but it has no primary relationship to what Paine accomplished with "Common Sense" in 1776 or with "The American Crisis" in the seven years to follow. It is enough in passing to remember the advent in late 1774 of this rather shabby and certainly undistinguished clerk and artisan after an undistinguished and rather shabby thirty-seven years in England; to recall that within five months of his arrival the battle of Lexington had taken place; and to note that just after New Year of 1776 he persuaded one "R. Bell, in Third-Street," Philadelphia, to print and sell a pamphlet with the somewhat pedantic title page:

Common Sense: Addressed to the Inhabitants of America, On the following Interesting Subjects, viz.: I. Of the Origin and Design of Government in General; with Concise Remarks on the English Constitution. II. Of Monarchy and Hereditary Succession. III. Thoughts on the Present State of American Affairs. IV. Of the Present Ability of America; with some Miscellaneous Reflections. Written by an Englishman.

A prefatory word suggests that Paine did not realize any better than Trumbull how explosive American sentiment was at the moment. The time, he thought, might not *yet* be ripe for such sentiments as these. Opinions were divided. At any rate he would not, like Trumbull, encourage further division by personal compliments or personal censure. He would approach the problem as an intellectual. The pamphlet has the trappings of a legal brief. But the last sentence of the introduction betrays that Paine is a jury lawyer, for he is already enlisting the sympathetic attention of "every man to whom nature hath given the power of feeling." In this capacity for feeling he appeals almost at once and on almost every page to the titillation that greets the well-turned phrase which in itself is an appeal to a deeper feeling: "Society is produced by our wants and government by our wickedness," "Government, like dress, is the badge of lost innocence . . . ," "It is the pride of Kings which throws mankind into confusion," "*It is wholly to the constitution of the People, and not to the Constitution of the Government* that the Crown is not as oppressive in England as in Turkey." "Government by Kings . . . was the most preposterous invention the Devil set on foot for the promotion of idolatry." He counters the scripturalists' "Render unto Caesar the things which are Caesar's" with "*We have added unto our sins this evil, to ask a king.*" The discussion of monarchy and hereditary succession is approached from the point of view of the doctrine of natural rights. The thoughts on the present state of American affairs are thoughts on an intolerable situation irremediable in any way but one: "the period of debate is closed. . . . Everything that is right or reasonable pleads for separation. The blood of the slain, the weeping voice of nature cries, *'Tis time to part.*" He has declared his resolution to refrain from personal praise or censure; he reiterates that he wishes to avoid giving unnecessary offense, but in the full flood of his enthusiasm he does not refrain from the old partisan device of impugning the minds and the motives of the opposition: It is composed of "interested men, who are not to be trusted, weak men who *cannot* see, prejudiced men who *will not* see, and a certain set of moderate men who think better of the European world than it deserves." In the final section he argues America's potential strength, offers military and legislative advice in quite extended detail, and concludes with four reasons why "however strange it may appear to some, or however unwilling they may be to think so, matters not, but . . . nothing can settle our affairs so expeditiously as an open and determined DECLARATION FOR INDEPENDANCE" ("Common Sense," passim). Thus completely did the Englishman who wrote and signed this identify himself with the Revolution; and though he had had no part in the struggle, his challenge at this strategic moment proved to be the inciting word. The

Declaration was only six months away; and in these intervening months, while over one hundred and twenty thousand copies of "Common Sense" were being conned, other writers were swelling the chorus of protest.[1]

There are far too many to discuss or list; a few may serve as types. In February, John Leacock, a Philadelphian, came out with his ambitious chronicle play "The Fall of British Tyranny."[2] There was no chance of its being played; the Continental Congress had frowned on the extravagance of the theater two years before; only Tory plays could be played — behind the British lines. But Leacock's play could be read; and the casual purchaser, flicking through the little booklet, might see the epilogue first, and from that might start back at the beginning:

> Are ye not men? Pray, who made men, but God?
> Yet men make kings — to tremble at their nod!
> What nonsense this — let's wrong with right oppose,
> Since naught will do, but sound, impartial blows.
> Let's act in earnest, not with vain pretence;
> Adopt the language of sound COMMON SENSE,
> And with one voice proclaim INDEPENDENCE![3]

"The Fall of British Tyranny" could not be staged; but up in Boston, while the town was still in the dubious possession of the invaders, General Burgoyne, one of the British conquerors shut up there, had written a satirical sketch called "The Blockade," which had been produced by the soldiery. Since then the seventeenth of March had passed; it was St. Patrick's Day, but it became also Evacuation Day, marking for the second time in history an expulsion of the

---

[1] Quotations are from the most accessible reprint of Paine's writing, "Selections from the Works of Thomas Paine" (edited by Arthur W. Peach), in the American Authors Series, 1928.

[2] Leacock's play "The Fall of British Tyranny" is reprinted in Moses's "Representative Plays by American Dramatists," Vol. I. Burgoyne's play was not printed. "The Blockheads," published in 1776, has been doubtfully ascribed to Mrs. Warren.

[3] Moses, op. cit. p. 350.

unwelcome. "The Blockheads" appeared before the month was out, jeering at the comically futile invaders:

> By yankees frighted too! oh dire to say!
> Why yankees sure at red-coats faint away!
> Oh yes — they thought so too — for lack-a-day,
> Their gen'ral turn'd the *blockade* to a *play*;
> Poor vain poltroons — with justice we'll retort,
> And call them *blockheads* for their idle sport.[1]

"Now B——e," says one of the fleeing malcontents in this dramatized retort, "here is more matter for humor, you may now give us a *second edition* of your farce." The author borrowed some of the descriptive names for his dramatis personae from Mrs. Mercy Warren, but proved abundantly by his text what he also acknowledged in his prologue, that "such an attempt [he] never made till now." The title is the best feature of it, a bit of broad humor that won instant circulation. It was three months to a day from this seventeenth of March to the anniversary of Bunker Hill, with the anniversary of the battle of Lexington between — stirring days to remember.

The scene of military action was still in the Boston region, but the center of liveliest controversy was Philadelphia. Here, for example, beginning in April, Provost Smith of the College dissented long and loud from Paine's views in eight "Letters of Cato, to the People of Pennsylvania." Smith, like many of the educators of the day, was a clergyman; unlike many, an Anglican. In 1776 that was enough to make him suspect. He was defending the status quo, said the cynics, in the hope of becoming a bishop. This was too much for Francis Hopkinson. In May he wrote "A Prophecy," a Biblical parody — not a Bostonian device. A tree, which is British government, has been planted in a far land; but a north wind has shattered it, and blight has followed, and the people have been called to cut away the remains. "Then a certain wise man shall arise and call himself Cato"; and he

[1] "The Blockheads," last lines of the Prologue.

will "persuade" and "harangue," and when "every insinuating art" has failed he will "threaten." (And he will have his answerers, among them "The Forester," who is Thomas Paine himself, in four open letters over this signature.) However, in the end the tree will be rooted up, and a wall will fend off the north wind, "And Cato and his works shall be no more remembered amongst them. For Cato shall die and his works shall follow him."[1]

The Continental Congress was in session again and had appointed a committee, with the thirty-three-year-old Thomas Jefferson at its head, for the purpose of drawing up the last and greatest of the three famous documents in which his hand appears. It is the proclamation called for in "Common Sense." Jefferson had become a member of the Congress only a year before. He had made friends by wise and faithful work in committee and perhaps also by his silence on the floor, for he was no speechmaker. He was well known, however, for deftness with the pen. He had done well with it in the Virginia House of Burgesses; with John Dickinson since coming to Philadelphia in the declaration on taking up arms against England; with Franklin, Adams, and Lee in reply to Lord North's proposals for conciliation. He was versed in the principles involved and in the facts leading to the crisis. His committee was appointed in June. At the opening of July they were ready.

Too much has been said in ecstatic generalization about the Declaration, and too little in specific detail. A generation ago Moses Coit Tyler referred to "the American people . . . hearing its repetitions in ten thousand different places at least once every year." "Nothing," he wrote, "which has not supreme literary merit has ever triumphantly endured such an ordeal."[2] What was true, however, before the war with Spain is no longer true after the World War. The old-fashioned Fourth of July celebration is no more. Even in

---

[1] Francis Hopkinson, "Miscellaneous Essays and Occasional Writings," Vol. I, pp. 94–97.

[2] Tyler, "Literary History of the American Revolution," Vol. I, p. 520.

those days the reading was usually fragmentary and none too intelligible. Now the document is alluded to as a glorious expression, and left unread, more often than not as preliminary to further references to the Constitution, which also is a document to allude to rather than to read.

The Declaration opens with a sentence acknowledging that "a decent respect to the opinions of mankind" demands an explanation of the momentous step. There follows a paragraph stating the broad principles underlying the decision and asserting that these have been grossly violated. The third and longest portion — half the manifesto — is a recital of the specific grievances suffered at the hands of "the present King of Great Britain." The fourth part declares that the colonists have been long-suffering and deliberate in action. Finally comes the resolution itself, "that these united Colonies are, and of right ought to be, free and independent states; that they are absolved from all allegiance to the British crown, and that all political connection between them and the state of Great Britain is, and ought to be, totally dissolved."

Its distinction today rests, and must rest, mainly on the second paragraph, which is about as long as Lincoln's equally famous Gettysburg speech. The remainder is a legalistic paper expressed with a combination of eloquence and dignity. This preamble is a compendium of liberal political theories current in England and the colonies during the eighteenth century. It was so intended, for it was a colonial and not a personal statement; only so would it open with the observation that the signers "hold these truths to be self-evident." Such truths are obviously few in number: that men are created equal; that they are endowed with natural, and hence "unalienable" rights; that "life, liberty, and the pursuit of happiness" are among these, and for the purposes of the moment the only ones to be enumerated; that the consent of the governed is the basis of a government's just powers and of the right "to alter or to abolish" an unjust one. They are set forth in a hundred words, of which four, in one phrase, are in any way unusual: "the pursuit of happiness." The prevailing trio of rights had been life, liberty, and property. The phrase was and is, no doubt, a romantic intangible, hardly to be dealt with in terms of law or government. It does not occur again in official discourse, and, in the provisions of the Constitution, property was so completely restored that the chief provisions for the individual had to be supplied in the promptly formulated first ten amendments. The doctrine of "created" equality was slower to give way, and as a slogan was often and again appealed to with immense effect. In general Tyler is right in declaring that "it was the preamble of the Declaration of Independence which elected Lincoln, which sent forth the Emancipation Proclamation, which gave victory to Grant, which ratified the Thirteenth Amendment."[1]

On the publication of the Declaration on the Fourth of July, which became the most famous anniversary date in American history, the reception was first of all emotional and unrelated to its specific ideas or language. The fateful word was said at last; the challenge of the king was accepted. Every notable event or document in the controversy of the preceding fifteen years had contributed toward this end. For those who were deliberate enough to read and consider it, there were probably three grounds for enthusiasm: the familiar doctrines on human rights and democratic government, the exciting list of offenses charged against a tyrant, and the ascription of long-suffering patience and forbearance to the reluctantly militant colonists. Nothing could have been better calculated: noble principles invoked in behalf of the secessionists, definite and demonstrable wrong long endured by them, and an ultimatum forced on the majority by the deliberate and repeated use of force against them. It is well to recall that the Declaration did represent only a majority of the colonists, with more than a third of the wealth and respectability taking the conservative stand that

[1] Tyler, op. cit. Vol. I, p. 517.

the favored portion of any social order always assume — in this case the stand of the loyalists. And it is wholesome to recall also that this element was hounded and harried during the war and hated after, large numbers of them preferring refuge out of the country to ostracism if not active oppression within its borders.[1] But it was the uttered conviction of an honest majority, expressing their political convictions, their sense of wrongs endured, and their very human inclination to commend themselves at the expense of their opponents. It was fortunate that so gifted a penman as Thomas Jefferson was at hand to state their case in rhythmic, noble, memorable prose.

> the principle
> That all men are created free and equal . . .
> That's a hard mystery of Jefferson's.
> What did he mean? Of course the easy way
> Is to decide it simply isn't true.
> It may not be. I heard a fellow say so.
> But never mind, the Welshman got it planted
> Where it will trouble us a thousand years.
> Each age will have to reconsider it.[2]

In the months that followed there was a lull in literary activity, in contrast with the rapidity with which things were happening under arms. They were sober months of steady British aggression and American retreat, culminating with the crossing of the Delaware in early December. There were typical dramatized satires; a loyalist farce on "The Battle of Brooklyn" in August; and in October H. H. Brackenridge's "Battle of Bunker's Hill," a reminder of colonial military prowess of which there was all too much need that autumn. Francis Hopkinson, too, was audible once more: in early December with a conciliatory "Letter to Lord Howe," protesting against the pillaging and ravaging of the civilian

[1] No better literary treatment of this topic can be found than in the recent Crèvecœur material, "More Letters from an American Farmer," edited by Henri Bourdin, 1925.

[2] Robert Frost, "The Black Cottage," in "North of Boston," pp. 52, 53. Henry Holt and Co.

population, and a couple of months later with a more characteristic "Letter Written by a Foreigner on the Character of the English Nation," a genial anticipation of Washington Irving's bland caricatures of John Bull. Hopkinson had signed the Declaration, was as serious as anyone, but sought relief from the universal sobriety of the moment. Someone else was to speak in a tone to which people could more naturally respond.

Thomas Paine opened the year with "Common Sense"; he was to conclude it with the first of the long series called "The American Crisis." It was mid-December, Washington was in retreat, a grim winter was coming on. "These are the times that try men's souls. The summer soldier and the sunshine patriot will in this crisis shrink from the service of his country; but he that stands it *now*, deserves the love and thanks of man and woman." It is within a week of Christmas when this first of the series by "Common Sense" describes the American withdrawal of troops through New Jersey as a strategic retreat in the course of which new support was gained and almost nothing lost. It is a call to action just as the January appeal was a call for decision, and with it ends the literary chronicle of this "most immemorial year."

1777–1783

The year ends, but Paine is beginning again. "The American Crisis" is to run for sixteen numbers in all, extending over almost exactly seven years, with intervals sometimes of a few weeks, sometimes of eighteen months. Paine does not know what he has launched. He writes at the needed occasion and in the appropriate way. The New Year is hardly begun before the second installment appears on January 13. This is a letter to Lord Howe or, better, a letter at Lord Howe and to the American people. It is good propaganda. Paine commiserates with the noble lord, enumerates the insuperable difficulties he faces in attempting to occupy a vast territory with a handful of troops, turns on him with rage and scorn for his responsibility as a wanton marauder and pillager, and sympathizes again on the hopelessness of his undertaking, mocks, advises, and blasts once more. The first "Crisis" attempts to reconstruct American confidence in its own powers; the second, to dismiss the fear of the invader. The third returns, and at great length, to a discussion of the political principles at stake.

Now the long military struggle is launched; the political issue is defined not only in terms of ideas but also in terms of that sharp alignment of people that only a war can bring about. 1776 was like a gorge through which all the events and sentiments and convictions of the years before had been made to flow at forced speed. With 1777 the stream spreads, the speed declines, the observer can stop to take breath and look about more deliberately. And the progress of Paine's series of "Crisis" papers is characteristic of the whole subsequent course of events and of the accompanying printed commentary. These sixteen pamphlets extend from December, 1776, to December, 1783. They fall into three time groups: seven in the first two years; three, with an interval of a year and a half of silence on either side, between March and October, 1780; six in the last twenty-one months. The first group is divided between defiance of British power and enunciation of political doctrine. The middle trio is designed to discourage England and to reinflame the colonists with fresh military zeal. The last six press the offensive and lead up to the discussion of peace.

Throughout them and in his subsequent work Paine displayed in extraordinary degree the gifts of the journalist.[1] He shared in events and in the actual dangers as well as the hardships of the troops. He knew "his stuff" when he wrote of the army. He was a man of the people and constantly among them when he was away from the military front. He could share their emotional reactions and could measure his appeals to their intellects. In this is one of the marks of his

[1] H. H. Clark, "Thomas Paine's Theories of Rhetoric," in Transactions of Wisconsin Academy of S. L. and A., Vol. XXVIII, pp. 307–339; also, "Toward a Reinterpretation of Thomas Paine," in *American Literature*, Vol. V, p. 144.

distinction: that he did not write over the heads of the multitude and at the same time he did not write down to them. He realized that in critical times the people want to deal with ideas, and realized the terms in which they could be addressed. He was political theorist, ethical leader, sentimental exhorter. Emphatically a dissenter in religious creedal matters, he addressed his readers in terms of their orthodoxy, reserving his personal opinions for "The Age of Reason." Headed for a career in behalf of liberty that later horrified the stabler element in America, he concentrated during the fighting years on the concrete issues of the moment. And, in the fashion of a genuinely contemplative man, when the end came he not only accepted the dramatic fulfillment of his first challenge — "the times that try men's souls are over" — but went on in thought to the future, in which the real revolution was to be wrought out in slow, often baffled and frustrated, and finally constructive thinking, planning, acting.

> To see it in our power to make a world happy — to teach mankind the art of being so — to exhibit, on the theatre of the universe, a character hitherto unknown — and to have, as it were, a new creation intrusted to our hands, are honors that command reflection, and can neither be too highly estimated, nor too gratefully received.
>
> In this pause then of recollection — while the storm is ceasing, and the long-agitated mind vibrating to a rest, let us look back on the scenes we have passed and learn from experience what is yet to be done.[1]

The journalist is an index to his public. He is made by his readers; what they will not read he may as well not write. Paine's wide and continuous influence on the rebelling colonists therefore reveals quite as much about them as it does about him. It reveals that the colonists were of an intellectual caliber that was willing and interested to attend to an appeal to reason as well as an appeal to passion. Paine led them past the maze of mere political theory in the abstract to a political theory based on realities. Did the relationship with the king

[1] Thomas Paine, "The Crisis," in "Selections" (edited by A. W. Peach), pp. 218–219.

pay? Had he done his duty by his subjects or had he been an expensive luxury? Did kingship itself pay? Did the balance between king and Parliament work or did it only make the king more subtle without making him more just? What other solution was there than independence? Paine clearly made his choice between high principle based on pure concepts and the working principles that could honestly be invoked in behalf of a desirable program; and he made no pretense of not appealing to self-interest and expediency. Yet he did appeal to reason; he did write a substantial body of discussion that with all its emotional content demanded thoughtful attention. It has been said of the Constitutional Convention of 1787 that it represented a high level of intellect quite out of proportion to what could be assembled in a like convention today; for in fair comparison the present assembly would need to be equally distinguished in average membership and forty times as large. It might also be said that journalistic writing like that in either "Common Sense" or "The Crisis" could hardly achieve such influence today. Paine's reading public had been schooled in the uses of adversity. Nations strive for national security and the kind of prosperity that brings in its train what is called a high standard of living. The lack of either security or enviable prosperity in the colonies, and the continuous discussion of ways and means to achieve them, seem to have engendered an enviable activity of mind that peoples are unlikely to enjoy in less exacting times.

With the war well launched, the flood of controversial writing naturally subsides. In 1777 Paine and Hopkinson maintain a kind of balance — Paine with three of the "Crisis" papers in January, April, and September; and Hopkinson with his characteristic variations on the same themes in a "Political Catechism" in February, a counterproclamation to General Burgoyne in July, and a verse follow-up of Burgoyne's surrender, in November. In 1778, the year of Hopkinson's most hilariously applauded "Battle of the Kegs" and the closing trio of the first group of "Crisis" papers, Freneau returns from the West Indies and in his belated "America Independent; and Her Everlasting Deliverance from British Tyranny and Oppression," excitedly announces his rediscovery of what is going on. Mr. Robert Bell, the publisher, cannot be the only reader to think back two years to a bolder document issued while Freneau was nursing his wounded feelings. The deed being now accomplished, he declaims:

> 'Tis done! and Britain for her madness sighs —
> Take warning, tyrants, and henceforth be wise,
> If o'er mankind *man* gives you regal sway,
> Take not the rights of human kind away.[1]

His "Lines on the New American Frigate, Alliance" are more genuine and less declamatory, for Freneau is a salt-water man. He is to be more vociferous later. For the moment H. H. Brackenridge is getting into action that is to be increasingly impressive as the years go on. He writes "Six Political discourses Founded on the Scripture," taking a leaf out of Hopkinson's book, and in 1779 becomes editor of the *United States Magazine*; Mrs. Warren, if surmise is correct, resumes dramatic satire with "The Motley Assembly," and on the Tory side Jonathan Odell, bitter as Freneau, re-enters the fray with "Congratulations" and "The American Times," savage in resentment for his own hard usage at the hands of the revolutionists, and as abusive as Freneau till the end of the war. The Tories are paying for their convictions now, and are losing confidence in the outcome. The war drags on endlessly for them; they are safe only behind the British lines; and hope of victory, long deferred, is making their hearts sick and their voices shrill. By 1780, on the other hand, colonial supporters begin to take fresh courage. Paine sounds a new trumpet call in his three "Crisis" appeals after eighteen months of silence; Freneau sings a hymn of hate in "The British Prison Ship"; and the last phase of the struggle begins.

---

[1] "The Poems of Freneau" (edited by H. H. Clark), p. 24.

In the midst of all this vociferating one more temperate voice is raised, that of Colonel Robert Munford, author of "The Candidates" and "The Patriots." This latter is a remarkably cool and detached presentation of the fire-eating bigot of nationalism.[1] It is summarized in a speech by one Tackabout:

> Where is the man that has done more than I have? I have damn'd the ministry, abus'd the king, vilified the parliament, and curs'd the Scotch. I have raised the peoples' suspicions against all moderate men; advised them to spurn at all government: I have cried down tories, cried up whigs, extolled Washington as a god, and call'd Howe the very devil. I have exclaimed against all taxes, advised the people to pay no debts; I have promised them success in war, a free trade, and independent dominion. In short, I have inspired them with the true patriotic fire, the spirit of opposition; and yet you say it is expected that I should do something.[2]

Munford's candor, however, was probably reserved for the ears of his intimates at the time. "The Patriots" seems to have been written in 1777, when the extravagances of the hundred-percenters might well have received some check; but there is no record of publication until the later 1790's. Such honest satire released during the war years would have been welcomed only by the enemy, who were finding what comfort they could from the reiteration of confidence in British prowess and of contempt for both the fighting powers and the financing of the revolutionists. There was plenty to say about the latter, and Rivington's *New York Gazette* did not miss the opening. The depreciation of the "rag money" was going on apace, as everyone knew. The Continental Congress had no revenue-collecting powers even in payments of its own currency. Why should not the Tories advertise this paper money as a cheap substitute for wallpaper and commiserate with Charon, who was silly enough to accept some at face value for ferrying a group of congressmen over the Styx?

---

[1] A now rare volume is a collection of the Plays and Poems by Munford, printed by William Prentiss, Williamsburg, Virginia, 1798. It contains "The Candidates" and "The Patriots" and some miscellaneous poems.

[2] Robert Munford, "Plays and Poems," p. 76.

On another feature of the struggle the Tories were commenting in oscillations between alarm and contempt — the alliance of the French. England's historic foe found it expedient to champion the cause of liberty when it could do so to the embarrassment of John Bull. There were big possibilities at stake. The smart of heavy French losses at the conclusion of the Seven Years' War was still keen. Here was a chance for revenge and recoupings. To the Tories there was a whole catalogue of objections to such an alliance. The French, every Briton knew, were frivolous, unscrupulous, effeminate, yet brutal; godless, yet subjects of the Pope; frog-eating chatterers in an unintelligible gibberish. An alliance with them if followed by victory, which the objectors were willing to concede, would substitute an alien tyrant for a British ruler who was falsely alleged to be a tyrant. In the end he would Romanize his new allies, who would perforce be his subjects; prohibit the reading of the Bible in English; set up an inquisition; and conscript soldiers for duty in the French possessions and students for schooling in the Catholic faith.[1] But the alliance was actually concluded, and was all too sobering for the English, and particularly for the loyalists in the colonies. What if the revolt should succeed? What if their temporary refuge behind the British lines should be prelude to permanent exile, total loss of property? One can understand the sighs of relief at the first year's lack of achievement — relief so great that the Tories could pretend to the magnanimity of victors. One of them wrote an "Epilogue" to the transactions of the ill-fated Continental Congress: the farce was over; the strutting on the field of arms had been a comic bit of acting; George of Virginia and George of England would better be reconciled; independence was blown to the winds; ho, for a new friendship![2] Next year the tone was not quite so kindly. The curtain had stayed up

---

[1] Summarized from the *New York Gazette*, for March 17, 1779, quoted in Tyler's "Literary History of the American Revolution," Vol. II, pp. 75–77.

[2] For this anonymous "Epilogue" see Frank Moore's "Songs and Ballads of the American Revolution," pp. 220–223.

on the farce, wearisomely. D'Estaing's dilatory fleet had at last come into action and had most ingloriously failed. The Tory lyrist greeted the fiasco in the measure of Hopkinson's "Battle of the Kegs" and with the same contemptuous jocosity. There is a laugh in both jingles, but it is a jeering, sneering laugh; and it was coming to be the turn of the side which should laugh last. With the surrender of Cornwallis at Yorktown the military chapter of the Revolution was all over except for guerrilla skirmishing, renewed reprisals on the loyalists, and the long jockeying for terms of peace. A chorus of despair, with intermingled notes of resignation, rose from the defeated, and the victors gloated noisily over their victory.

Among them was John Trumbull, who had been none too eager to enter the fray and since January, 1776, had been a noncombatant in both deed and word. The first draft of "M'Fingal" had left the story unresolved at midday. The issues were defined; there was no telling what might happen by sunset. Trumbull, in that winter before the declaring of independence, was just where Hopkinson was when he wrote "Cetera desunt" as the concluding words of the "Pretty Story": the outcome was in the hands of time and fate. Now that time and fate had done their work, he resumed the tale. Honorius, champion of the cause of liberty, is no longer in the picture; his cause has been won by something more convincing than oral argument. It remains only to subject M'Fingal to ex post facto humiliation. He is roughed and tumbled, tarred and feathered, and left sticking to the liberty pole from which for a while he has been suspended. He makes his way to his own cellar, and there by night is haranguing his few followers when he is routed even from that dingy refuge, and slips away in the darkness to Boston, seat of the largest element of irreconcilables, most of them soon to become refugees. There is little that is inspiring in the literary obligato to the closing years of the war. Washington and the French fleet had kept it alive and brought it to a conclusion. No jingo could have sung in those days, "We've got the ships, we've got the men, we've got the money, too."

Yet by a miracle one great heart had bound to himself a little company of fighting followers and had fought down not so much the enemy as hardship, poverty, disloyalty, and despair, and with the ships and the money of a foe to his foe had come to a point where Thomas Paine could mistakenly say that the times that tried men's souls were over.

The Continuing Revolution

New trials were ahead and unforeseen complications. The little group of seaboard colonies, in whose peaceful moments a set of religious ideas and a system of personal ethics had long unconsciously prevailed, had been shocked into substituting for them a set of political ideas and a system of statehood. A revolution had been generated and a straggling series of battles had been dignified into a revolutionary war and crowned with success. Now the parson had been forced into the background and the commoner had been drawn forward; not the common worshiper either, but the common citizen, and this citizen had felt some power and heard hints of vague possibilities. To add to his confusions, he found himself cut off by harsh prejudice and deep resentments from the source of most of his inherited ideas, and found himself under obligation to a nation that he had been bred to suspect, detest, and fear. It was a time for the literate leaders to say what they might to restore order and re-establish standards. The religious, political, and literary chronicles of the next several years all record this phase of the continuing revolution. The religious influences and reactions and the political ones, although closely related, are distinguishable enough in kind to be considered separately in the interplay between France and America during the last quarter of the eighteenth century.[1]

The zealous religious bigotry of the seventeenth-century colonists had declined in the eighteenth, giving way to a spirit

[1] For a full and authoritative discussion of French influences in this period see Howard Mumford Jones's "America and French Culture," Chaps. X–XV.

of toleration which had risen in England, Germany, and France, as well as in America, and which was itself related to a spreading commerce that overstepped religious barriers; to the slow incursions of science, which would not brook the negations of medieval dogma; and to the onward march of democratic theory. All these, in Mr. Jones's terminology, were "cosmopolitan" responses. "By 1789 it was the hope of liberal European minds, whether they were domiciled in the New World or the Old, that the brotherhood of man might obliterate national and sectarian divisions."[1] American Protestantism, therefore, which had some of its roots in French culture but onto which had been grafted twin scions of distrust in French character and in French Catholicism, was first liberalized within its own confines, then, invaded by the principles of deism, became relaxed in respect for authority, secular or religious, and in its tendency toward indifference became less hostile toward Catholicism. The bars against French influence were temporarily let down; with the close of the war they were totally dropped for a while; but with the post-bellum demoralization the results were so startling, and the alarmed conservatives were so typically inclined to charge all ills to a single convenient and long-distrusted cause, that a chorus was raised against anything faintly tinged with French. This was promptly followed by earnest asseverations of native integrity and, before long, by a countermovement in American churchdom that narrowed all the old straitness and intensified all the old pharisaisms.

To picture the situation in all its complexities would result in drawing no picture at all. Let us admit that there was every shade of orthodoxy and heterodoxy in the uniting colonies at the end of the war. Let us admit that the South was already heading toward statesmanship as a leading vocation and settling into a literary reticence that long restrained it not from authorship but from publication. Let us remember that the printed records of authorship are therefore to

[1] H. M. Jones, "America and French Culture," pp. 385–386.

be sought largely from Philadelphia northward, and that Connecticut was for a time the most loquacious of the states. Let us remember that in New England Saxon moralism had forced the theology of Calvinism to share the sober center of the stage. We can dismiss whatever doubts may persist by a glance at the two sections in Dwight's "Greenfield Hill," in which the farmer and the parson successively exhort the villagers to adopt the precepts of Franklin and of Edwards. Let us recall that the elder generation were still resisting the baleful influence of the play and the novel and, in their editorial capacity, were upholding the ethical standard: "The American Museum . . . containing Essays on Politics, Morals — and Manners; The Massachusetts Magazine . . . Geography, Morality, Criticism; The Children's Magazine: Calculated for the Use of Families and Schools; The Christian's, Scholar's and Farmer's Magazine." And, finally, let us hold in mind, turbulent as the storm was for a quarter-century after the war, that when the Revolution was completed and the new democracy was in the saddle, religious orthodoxy was in the saddle again, and French so-called "atheism," French so-called "popery," and the debased morals that were supposed to accompany both had been complacently repudiated.

By 1788 the dangers seemed to be accumulating; and Timothy Dwight,[1] the stalwart, was sounding the battle cry of the old guard. He wrote on "The Triumph of Infidelity," and was perfectly true to type in his emotional and mental processes. A grandson of Jonathan Edwards, without Edwards's intellectual scrupulousness, he proceeded by the blanket method of reasoning. The true faith was to be found in the Connecticut valley. This, however, for purposes of argument could safely be ascribed to America as a whole, America being the thirteen states then existent. Any departure from this was infidelity. Infidelity was agnosticism, atheism, what you will; the baleful fact about whatever it

[1] Representative poems from Dwight appear in "The Connecticut Wits," edited by V. L. Parrington.

might be called was that, lacking the moral restraints of the true faith, — which was not a faith but a code, — the infidel was not only capable but guilty of every conceivable wickedness. And Dwight capped the climax by including a violent attack on the Pope in a jeremiad against infidelity.[1]

This was no more confused than the combinations of thought and feeling that prevailed in these confusing times. If the foundations had not dropped out from beneath the old certitudes, they were fearfully undermined. The radicalism of the younger generation, who had never known the rock of ages and were allured to shifting sands, was particularly distressing. At Princeton in 1782 there were only two professing Christians in the little student body. Columbia was a seat of deism. A bit later when Lyman Beecher entered Yale, the students, according to the liberal President Stiles, were "gay, jovial, tumultuous young Men"; according to young Beecher most of them were "infidels, and called each other Voltaire, Rousseau, D'Alembert etc." By this time Thomas Paine had left the country and had been enlisted in the French Revolution. This was a damaging fact in the eyes of Americans, who were harvesting the aftermath of a revolution themselves. Paine was now author of "The Rights of Man," a theory of government quite in harmony with that of the author of the Declaration of Independence. But Paine was also author of "The Age of Reason," a book which was not only subversive of any of the Protestant orthodoxies, but which was expressed in a sophomorically offensive style that appealed to a generation of sophomores. The boys were all reading him. Paine must therefore be repudiated with his doctrines. He was aiding and abetting "the cause of impiety and irreligion"; but he was composer of "Common Sense" and "The Crisis." The best way to compound the case was to account for it by laying the blame on France. He had become contaminated by foreign contacts; by "the infidel philosophy which led to the French Revolution of 1790, and

[1] The question of infidelity is further illustrated in a "Memoir of John Codman," quoted in Jones's "America and French Culture," p. 381.

which found its way across the Atlantic in the writings of Voltaire for the learned, and Paine for the illiterate." So much for the college students of the day; illiterates! But Paine must be discredited at any cost.

Just as New England identified the whole country with itself, it now identified all Europe with France.

> "See this glad world remote from every foe,"

chanted Timothy Dwight in "Greenfield Hill,"

> "From Europe's mischiefs, and from Europe's woe!"

It is the magnificent isolation thesis:

> Th' Atlantic's guardian tide repelling far,
> The jealous terror, and the vengeful war.[1]

In a more secure mood, then, the solicitous conservative reassured himself that though foreign contagion had threatened American health no fundamental harm had been done, could be done. Here is a part of the outline, or "argument," for the triumphantly concluding book of this poem:

> Happiness of U.S. contrasted to Eastern Despotism. Universal Prevalence of Freedom. Unfortified, and therefore safe, state of U.S. Influence of our state of Society on the Mind. Public Property employed for the Public Benefit. Penal Administrations improved by Benevolence. Policy enlarges its scope. Knowledge promoted. Improvements in Astronomica and other Instruments of Science. Improvements of the Americans, in Natural Philosophy — Poetry — Music — and Moral Science. State of the American Clergy. Manners refined. Artificial Manners condemned. American Women. Cultivation advanced. Other Nations visit this Country, and learn the nature, and causes, of our happiness. Conclusion.

New England was to be shocked and horrified again with the turn of the century and was to repudiate Jefferson by the same formula that it employed with Paine, and with reason; for a sober historian records that "it was his five years'

[1] Timothy Dwight, "Greenfield Hill," Part VII, lines 87–90.

residence in France, before the outbreak of the Revolution, that gave the freethinking Southerner an insight into the possibilities of materialism when carried to its logical outcome," and it appears that only "his fundamental deism" saved him from the atheism of Diderot.[1] It was not merely a political France but a terribly freethinking France which was seeking at the time of Washington's farewell address to involve the new republic in an entangling alliance.

For a while, however, to turn from the religious aspects of the situation to the political, hostility to France was not needed to fan the flames of controversy. Indeed, in the first years after the withdrawal of the British troops friendliness prevailed. Although there was some bickering with Paris over the terms of peace with London, it was between the negotiators rather than the nations. France concluded a commercial treaty with the United States long before England did, and won good will as a bonus. France's role as the villain of the melodrama was usurped in the years between Yorktown and the adoption of the Constitution by the obstructors of a genuine federation and by the malcontents who had sacrificed heavily in the war and wanted the pay that their Continental scrip mockingly represented.

A series of stern rebukes to these troublemakers was dealt by the authors of "The Anarchiad," which appeared in the *New Haven Gazette and the Connecticut Magazine* in 1786–1787. Four of the "Hartford Wits" are regularly said to have been the authors: David Humphreys, Lemuel Hopkins, John Trumbull, and Joel Barlow.[2] It came along in twelve numbers with a somewhat remarkable symmetry of structure for a succession that could hardly have been

---

[1] W. Riley, "American Thought," p. 80.

[2] No doubt the first two of these were the principal contributors; possibly Trumbull was also, although there is little of his playfulness in the lines; Barlow had a hand, perhaps, the Hesper in certain of the units being the same spirit of the Western world who presides in "The Vision of Columbus," already written; but the ponderous and abusive hand of Timothy Dwight seems also apparent, especially in Part X, itself a speech of Hesper. The identifiable Wits are represented in Parrington's selections, already referred to.

planned in full. The authors were intent on two matters: that the wavering alliance between the states should be converted into a national unity, without which civil war and foreign invasion were certain; and that commercial security should be assured by some sort of rational financial policy which must be based on sound money. Their method was the perennial one for the startled conservative: that of belaboring and vilifying their opponents.

"The Anarchiad" is literature only in the most generous interpretation of the word, but as it enlisted the energies of writers who were known for other excursions into verse the scheme deserves a brief survey. Massachusetts, seat of Shays's Rebellion, is a realm of chaos and mob rule (I); Connecticut is no less ridden by "chiefs, mobs, conventions" (II); Rhode Island is a "realm, of rogues, renown'd for fraud and guile" (III); but Hesper, spirit of the Western world, rebukes Anarch, and Columbia reassures her that new heroes "terrific in their rage, will crush" these factions (IV); so a song to the Genius of America is interpolated (V); after which Wronghead, General Erastus Wolcott, receives new precepts from the Anarch, including instructions to suppress popular education, hang the Wits, and drive Congress into the sea (VI); personal abuse prevails in the next installments, and is followed by a soliloquy from Anarch in which he admits the strength of "young Hamilton's unshaken soul" and relies on his own stupid but obstinate supporters (IX); Hesper warns against the twin dangers of the tyrant and the demagogue (X); and the concluding sections identify the anti-Federalists with the hosts of hell. The tactics of the series were brutal, but no one can deny that in the critical year before the adoption of the Constitution the doctrine of a need for national unity was sound. "The Anarchiad" is apparently confusing to some readers on account of its frequent use of the words "federal" and "federalism." All that the authors could have meant at this time was the need of a centralized government strong enough to hold together somehow. The Hartford Wits were later Federalists in the technical sense of the term; but that is another matter. Even Barlow could subscribe to their views on national unification in 1786; but in 1787 he left for a seventeen-year residence abroad, and the erstwhile friend of Timothy Dwight was henceforth to be classified with such radicals and insurgents as Philip Freneau and Thomas Paine.

A mention of these dangerous members of the opposition brings us back to France and the French influence. First, for Freneau. He helped chant the song of approaching victory as the war came to its close, and then, in his restless way, for six years after the conclusion of peace he was working off his redundant energies in the Atlantic coast trade. Now he was due for an interval of journalism, in the course of which between 1790 and 1798 he was connected with four papers, of which the *National Gazette* (August, 1791–October, 1793) was pre-eminent. Freneau's anti-Federalism was therefore concerned not in opposing the establishment of a secure government, but with the nature of that government now that it had been established. He had returned to the later stages of a controversy, just as he had returned to the later stages of the war. It is a fact to be remembered in face of the claims of his admirers that he was an unceasing champion of democracy and revolution; on the contrary, he was a notably intermittent fighter.[1]

In his work on the *National Gazette* he was doing a definite piece of political propagandizing under the official patronage of Thomas Jefferson. Hamilton had subsidized one John Fenno as editor of the *United States Gazette* to propound the Federalist policies. Jefferson undertook to offset this influence with a counter-journal and a counter-subsidy. One was for English alliance and the firmest of centralized control; the other, for French affiliation and the strongest offensive against everything savoring of aristocracy. Naturally Jefferson was enthusiastic about his poet-editor. "His paper," he declared, "has saved our constitution, which was gal-

[1] For a divergent and exceptionally eulogistic characterization of Freneau, see the discussion in V. L. Parrington's "Colonial Mind," pp. 368–381.

loping fast into monarchy, and has been checked by no other means so powerfully as by that paper." Naturally Washington was offended; agreed with Timothy Dwight, who called him "a mere incendiary, or rather . . . a despicable tool of bigger incendiaries"; and branded him as "that rascal Freneau." There is no doubt of his sympathies or his convictions.[1] As for the French Revolution, he celebrated in meter the successive anniversaries of Bastille Day; and as for French sentiments, so branded, he sang the praises of Thomas Paine, cried up Jefferson to the skies, aligned himself against a government dedicated to property and privilege, harped on the current theme of political justice, and, in regular eighteenth-century journalistic fashion, culled from the vocabulary of abuse whether dealing with opinions or with the men who held them. Fenno became "Shylock Ap-Shenkin"; William Cobbett, content with "Peter Porcupine," adopted the name himself. It is not surprising that Washington came in for some plain and ugly words; that was the way of controversy. But in moments of suspended controversy Freneau paid both Franklin and Washington the highest of personal tributes.[2] By the end of Jefferson's administration Freneau was through as an effective controversialist. He was discredited; there was no place for him in the scheme of things; but he was also burned out. Hither and yon throughout his career he had written simple lyrics and descriptive bits that last. Conflict had recruited a poet as a journalist. It was to do so later with Whittier; but though Freneau lived to greater age than Whittier, he did not have the recuperative powers of the Quaker to fulfill his poetic ambitions after the political struggle was over.

In the meanwhile what of Joel Barlow? While the "Anarchiad" group were scolding and blustering in 1786–1787,

[1] For these quotations and a discussion of Freneau the journalist, see H. H. Clark's introduction to "The Poems of Freneau," pp. xxxii-xxxiii. Freneau's recently discovered open letter disavowing any personal arrangement with Jefferson seems disingenuous and unconvincing.

[2] For verse illustrative of all these points see selections in "The Poems of Freneau" (edited by H. H. Clark), pp. 112–170 passim.

Barlow may have contributed to their ebullitions the idea of Hesper, who figures largely in his long-cherished "Vision of Columbus," published in the latter year. It is always, and naturally, classified with Dwight's "Conquest of Canaan" and "Greenfield Hill," which preceded and followed. The epic efforts concur in the assumptions that the elder countries had failed and that the new republic was the land of promise; but even at the outset Barlow was neither so truculent nor so complacent as Dwight, never so provincial. He regarded the United States as more of an experiment than an achievement, and was therefore far less afraid to pursue the trial-and-error method. Moreover, he was not purely philosophical in his attitude, and laid up a very comfortable fortune by speculating in the French funds while foreign representative of one of the earliest Western land companies of which little flattering can be said. While he was abroad the French Revolution came to a head, and in 1792 he came out with two startlingly revolutionary documents. The less important was in verse, "The Conspiracy of Kings":

> Of these no more. From orders, slaves and kings,
> To thee, O Man! my heart rebounding springs; . . .
> Freedom at last, with Reason in her train,
> Extends o'er earth her everlasting reign;
> See Gallia's sons, so late the tyrant's sport,
> Machines in war and sycophants at court,
> Start into men, expand their well-taught mind,
> Lords of themselves and leaders of mankind.[1]

However, one allows for poetic madness even in rather unpoetic verse. Prose utterance is a different matter; and Barlow published in prose an extended commentary on his thesis under the title "Advice to the Privileged Orders in the Several States of Europe, Resulting from the Necessity and Propriety of a General Revolution in the Principles of Government."

The "Advice" is in many ways comparable to Paine's "Common Sense" and "Rights of Man." All proceed from

---

[1] "The Connecticut Wits," (edited by V. L. Parrington), p. 348.

the theory of natural rights; of common wealth, or welfare; of social responsibility for the individual; of government as a social compact. Both Barlow and Paine regard Edmund Burke as the spokesman for the old order, though Paine's lighter treatment is the more damaging. They regard the ills of society as not only inherent in the monarchical system but as capable of being dismissed with it, and they indulge in easy presumptions about the common will as certain to choose and maintain the commonweal. Democracy, in fact, thinks Barlow, will transcend national lines; it will assure not only domestic harmony but also international peace; and he theorizes happily in this direction. But though he is no realist here, not having the extended experiment to observe, he is distinctly the realist in his fivefold indictment of the privileged orders in terms of The Feudal System, The Church, The Military, The Administration of Justice, and Revenue and Public Expenditure.

As the end of the century approached and passed, Barlow waxed in vigor while the other men of Connecticut waned. Trumbull, never eager for the fray, went on to a career of moderate distinction on the bench, and at the age of seventy collected and edited the verse he had completed a full generation before. Dwight enjoyed a long presidency of Yale and compiled a source book for future historiographers in his four volumes of "Travels in New England and New York." Humphreys, after a decade as minister to Portugal and to Spain, became a sheep breeder and prosperous mill owner and laureate of "The Industry of the United States of America." Hopkins made his contributions to the medical profession in the days before it had risen to the level of the other pursuits of the learned. They were substantial men, under an increasingly substantial regime, even while Jefferson was first a menace and then a reality; there was little reason for them to agitate themselves, but they were not the kind to keep complete silence. They could put the unanointed in their places with an occasional contemptuous word of derision. From 1791 to 1805 they maintained in the *American Mercury* a casual series which in 1807 they reissued in volume form from the appropriate house, the Porcupine Press.[1] They called it "The Echo," and began it with a rather precious design to make fun of rhetorical fustian. The first installment was merely this; but as the politicians supplied them with abundant examples they combined form and substance and jeered at John Hancock, Jefferson, the Jacobins, and whoever uttered anti-Federalist sentiments in extravagant terms. Each number accompanied the original expression with a verse parody; and they are mildly amusing, but they partake of the very carpings at style and nibblings at detail that the youthful Trumbull had deprecated in English critics of the youthful Dwight and Barlow in 1770. There was nothing muscular about "The Echo"; it was the comfortable after-dinner chucklings of a well-fed group of old cronies who were satisfied with their larders and their wine cellars and their housing — even with their idioms of speech — and were inclined to wax jocose about the vulgar, who were guilty of different ideas, manners, diction.

Not so Joel Barlow. He was intensely concerned with the interests and the rights and the hopes of the vulgar; and he was always an evangelist. Even his most popular and most quoted single composition is not so frivolous as it sounds. Barlow wrote "Hasty Pudding," says the hasty reader, because he was lonely in a distant land and pined for home cooking. But he dedicated it to Martha Washington. He likened it to "The Deserted Village," which is a piece of exhortation. He contended that he would not have taken the pains to put "so many rhymes together" if he had not "had hopes of doing some good." And the good he sought was "to rank *simplicity of diet* among the virtues," with the endorsement of the first lady of the land. There is the same urgent design in his epic of the New World in its final revised and extended form, "The Columbiad," in 1807. It was written before the

[1] Appropriate because the press derived its name from Peter Porcupine, who was William Cobbett, editor of the *Porcupine Gazette*, and persistent propounder of Federalist principles, an especial *bête noir* of Philip Freneau.

American Revolutionary War. It was published, with what changes we do not know, in 1787, before the French Revolution. In its final form it was presented to demonstrate the advance in civilization over the days of the Iliad and the Aeneid: the progress from nations of subjects to nations of citizens. Lest the lesson be missed, he stated it in the preface:

> The real object . . . is to inculcate the love of rational liberty, and to discountenance the deleterious passion for violence and war; to show that on the basis of republican principle all good morals, as well as good government and hopes of permanent peace, must be founded.

In contrast to the stand-pattism of the Federalists he spoke for liberalism:

> The theoretical question of the further advancement of human society . . . is held in dispute and still unsettled only because we have had too little experience of organized liberty in the government of nations to have well considered its effects.[1]

To believe in the achievability of what is socially desirable, he concluded, is the first step toward bringing it to pass.

This readiness to suspend judgment, to await the issues of time, to assume that progress and change are allied though not identical, and to lay much weight on the creative power of social faith, accounts for the relative vitality of Barlow as compared with his early associates. He was no less explicit than they in announcing the Saxon insistency of his moral purposefulness;[2] but he was less of a pharisee, more of a

---

[1] J. Barlow, "The Columbiad," preface, p. x.

[2] For example, in an open correspondence to Bishop Gregoire after publication of "The Columbiad" he wrote: "I judge not my poem as a work of genius. . . . But I *know* it as a moral work; I *can* judge and *dare* pronounce upon its tendency, its beneficial effect upon every candid mind." (Letter to Henry Gregoire, etc. (1809), p. 8.)

A detailed study of the revisions from "The Vision of Columbus" to "The Columbiad" offers proof of the complete change in Barlow's philosophy. The earlier was saturated with theology; the latter, with political theory. The earlier accepted the idea of war; the latter revolted from it and dwelt upon its horrors. The earlier was built on faith; the latter extolled reason. The docile subject gave way to the emancipated citizen.

believer in the multitude, in whom the Federalist-Calvinists could perceive only the menace of natural depravity let loose and given the reins of government; and he was far more of a realist in his actual knowledge of a humankind that was fallible yet worthy of trust, and subject to the guidance of aspiration as well as to the rule of fear. After his return to this country and his adoption of the national capital as his home town he was recognized as expert in European affairs and used as confidential adviser. For he was cosmopolitan in spirit and experience, unhandicapped by provincial complacency. He contributed to neither of the twin fallacies which persisted among his countrymen for more than a century after the Revolution: the magnificent-isolation theory, which exempted the Republic from responsibility in world welfare, and the manifest-destiny illusion, which, in distorted form, tended to exempt the average American from any sense of civic responsibility and made militancy the sole expression of patriotism.

The remaining critic of national life who demands attention from this period stands as a connecting link between the political theorists or satirists and the novelists. Hugh Henry Brackenridge was the classmate of Freneau who read "The Rising Glory of America" at the 1771 commencement in Princeton. He was the author of "Modern Chivalry," which appeared in 1792, 1793, and 1797, the years contemporary in part with the "Echo" series from the Connecticut Wits. Brackenridge was less partisan than either — not afraid of democracy and not afraid to hold up to view its extraordinary shortcomings in the early years of the experiment. His literary vehicle was the half-allegorical, half-expository combination of which Hopkinson gave a brief foretaste in his "Pretty Story" of 1774 and Jeremy Belknap offered a modest example in "The Foresters" in 1792. The long, rambling chronicle is carried on through the observations of one Captain Farrago, spokesman for the author, and the more definite experiences of his Irish servant and companion, Teague O'Regan. Taken in its entirety, the four original volumes amount to a long compendium of defects in the American political and social system, an admirable supplement and foil to Dwight's slightly later "Travels in New England and New York." The first three sections present a social background against which the upstart, the charlatan, and the demagogue have every chance of being thrown into favorable relief. Teague has no qualifications for preferment but unbounded self-assurance — forerunner of a roster of characters from Cooper's Aristabulus Bragg to Lewis's Elmer Gantry. Like them he has his ups and downs, in the course of which an indictment is drawn not so much against the exploiter as against the public, which is willing to be exploited. The low and scurrilous tone of the press, the ineffectiveness of the educator, the ignorance of the judiciary, the incompetence of the ministry, the general futility of the legislator, the "levelling phrenzy" of the mob, are successive objects of attack. The final part, more definitely suggestive of Swift and Defoe also more definitely represents the democracy of the frontier. Brackenridge had settled at Pittsburgh in 1781. In this concluding volume he pictured a new settlement and the problems arising in it, partly as local and partly as comparable to early colonial and national history. In the final preface he stated his "moral" for the benefit of those who might otherwise have missed it. He deplored, on the one hand, the surviving spirit of monarchy and, on the other, the dangers of the demagogue.

> The demagogue in a democracy, and the courtier in a monarchy, are identical. . . . I shall have accomplished something by this book, if it shall keep some honest man from lessening his respectability by pushing himself into public trusts for which he is not qualified; or when pushed into public station, if it shall contribute to keep him honest by teaching him the folly of ambition, and farther advancement. . . . This is in great part the moral of this book; if it should be at all necessary to give a hint of it.

Brackenridge wrote, he acknowledged, after the manners of Hume and Swift and Fielding. The surface likenesses to

Cervantes are too obvious to need exposition. "Modern Chivalry" is an elephantine production, a jumbled thesaurus of Americana. It could be used, with an index, as a cyclopedia. It is related to every phase of contemporary social history, and in the history of American literature it is related to formal satire, to native humor, and to the evolution of fiction.[1]

The long Revolutionary struggle did not end here; but it tapered off, changed emphasis. During its course it had usurped most of the attention and energy of the writers, as it had of all the intellectual class. It probably prevented some from entering the pursuit of polite letters. It certainly diverted many from it for a time or for all time. For a generation, too, the mind of America had been diverted from thoughts of salvation to problems of citizenship. But the fundamental habits of thought were unchanged; political revolutions are much more readily achieved than cultural ones. Although the name of God was omitted from the Constitution and the church was given no official standing in the state, a sweeping churchly reaction reasserted itself against both infidelity and Catholicism. It was a moral driving force limited, even within Protestantism, to the narrowness of the nonconformists. A touch of cosmopolitanism had frightened the country to take retreat in Anglo-colonial cultural traditions. The result was to determine the interpretations of art and literature and to direct cultural development in America for most of the next century.

---

[1] Brackenridge's book appeared as "Modern Chivalry: Containing the Adventures of Captain John Farrago, and Teague O'Regan, His Servant." Philadelphia . . . MDCCXCII. 2 vols. A third and a fourth volume appeared in 1793 and 1797. It was reprinted in 1804, 1805, 1807, 1808, 1815, and 1819. A recent reprint, edited by Ernest Brennecke, is in the Rogues' Bookshelf, 1926.

Book List

GENERAL REFERENCES

ADAMS, HERBERT B. Thomas Jefferson and the University of Virginia. 1888.
ADAMS, JAMES TRUSLOW. Revolutionary New England. 1923.
CHAMBERLAIN, JOSHUA L. Universities and Their Sons: the University of Pennsylvania. 1901.
FISKE, JOHN. The Critical Period of American History. 1888.
HAZELTON, JOHN H. The Declaration of Independence: Its History. 1906.
JACKSON, M. KATHERINE. Outline of the Literary History of Colonial Pennsylvania. 1906.
JONES, HOWARD M. America and French Culture. 1927.
MORAIS, HERBERT M. "Deism in Revolutionary America," *International Journal of Ethics*, Vol. XLII, pp. 434–453.
OBERHOLTZER, ELLIS PAXSON. Literary History of Philadelphia. 1906.
PARRINGTON, VERNON L. The Colonial Mind. 1927.
PATTERSON, SAMUEL WHITE. The Spirit of the American Revolution as Revealed in the Poetry of the Period. 1915.
TUCKER, SAMUEL M. "The Revolution." Cambridge History of American Literature, Vol. I, Book I.
TYLER, M. C. The Literary History of the American Revolution. 1897.
VAN TYNE, CHARLES H. The Loyalists in the American Revolution. 1902.
WENDELL, BARRETT. Literary History of America. 1900.
WERNER, DOROTHY LEEDS. The Idea of Union in American Verse (1776–1876). 1932.
For the spirit of the times read "Familiar Letters of John and Abigail Adams," edited by Charles Francis Adams. 1876.

[*General Bibliography*]

WEGELIN, OSCAR. Early American Poetry (revised and enlarged). 1930.
Cambridge History of American Literature, Vol. I, pp. 457–467.

PRE-WAR SONGS AND BALLADS

[*History and Comment*]

CHAPPELL, WILLIAM. Old English Popular Music, Vol. II. 1893.
DAVEY, HENRY. History of English Music, Chap. VIII, "The Period of Patriotic Songs." 1895.
HOOD, GEORGE. History of Music in New England. 1846.
HOWARD, JOHN TASKER. The Music of George Washington's Time. 1931.
HOWARD, JOHN TASKER. Our American Music, Chaps. I–III. 1931.

[*Early Collections*]

The Masque, a New Song Book. 1767.
Songs, Composed for Use and Edification. 1768.
The New Song Book. 1771.

American Harmony, or Royal Melody Complete. 1773.
The Humming Bird, or New American Songster. 1790.
The Columbian Songster. 1798.
The American Miscellany. 1798.

[*Anthologies*]

Boynton, Percy H. American Poetry. 1918.
Brooks, Henry M. Olden-Time Music. A Compilation from Newspapers and Books. 1888.
Eggleston, George Cary. American War Ballads and Lyrics. 1889.
McCarty, William. Songs, Odes and Other Poems on National Subjects. 1842.
Moore, Frank. Songs and Ballads of the American Revolution. 1857.
Otis, William B. American Verse, 1625–1807. 1909.
Paget, R. L. (pseud.). Poems of American Patriotism. 1898. Seventh impression. 1907.
Sargent, Winthrop. The Loyal Verses of Joseph Stansbury and Jonathan Odell. 1880.
Sargent, Winthrop. Loyalist Poetry of the Revolution. 1857.
Stedman and Hutchinson. Library of American Literature, Vol. III.
Stevenson, Burton E. Poems of American History. 1922.
Winslow, Ola. American Broadside Verse from Imprints of the 17th & 18th Centuries. 1930.

THE CONNECTICUT WITS

Individual Authors

Joel Barlow. The Vision of Columbus; a Poem in Nine Books. 1787. Advice to the Privileged Orders in the Several States of Europe. Resulting from the Necessity and Propriety of a General Revolution in the Principles of Governments. 1792. The Conspiracy of Kings: a Poem Addressed to the Inhabitants of Europe from Another Quarter of the Globe. 1792. The Hasty-Pudding; a Poem in Three Cantos. 1792. The Columbiad: a Poem. 1807.

[*Available Editions*]

The best single edition of these writers is V. L. Parrington's The Connecticut Wits. 1926.
The Hasty-Pudding. With Memoir by D. J. Brown. 1847.

[*Biography and Criticism*]

Miller, Victor C. Joel Barlow: Revolutionist in London, 1791–1792. 1932.
Todd, Charles B. Life and Letters of Joel Barlow. 1886.
Tyler, Moses Coit. Three Men of Letters. 1895.
Wilson, Beckles. "Barlow." America's Ambassadors to France, 1777–1927. 1928.
Zunder, Theodore A The Early Days of Joel Barlow . . . from 1754 to 1787. 1934.

TIMOTHY DWIGHT. The Conquest of Canaan: a Poem in Eleven Books. 1785. The Triumph of Infidelity: a Poem. 1788. Greenfield Hill: a Poem in Seven Parts. 1794. Travels in New England and New York; 1796–1815. 4 vols. 1821–1822. No recent editions.

[*Biography and Criticism*]

ADDISON, DANIEL D. The Clergy in American Life and Letters. 1900.
BEERS, HENRY A. The Connecticut Wits, and Other Essays. 1920.
CLERICUS (pseud.). An Inquiry into the Nature of Sin, as Exhibited in Dr. Dwight's Theology. 1829.
HOWE, M. A. DEWOLFE. "Timothy Dwight." Classic Shades. 1928.
SILLIMAN, BENJAMIN. A Sketch of the Life and Character of President Dwight. 1817.
TYLER, MOSES COIT. Three Men of Letters. 1895.

LEMUEL HOPKINS. The Anarchiad: a New England Poem. With Humphreys and others. 1786. The Democratiad, a Poem, in Retaliation . . . by a Gentleman of Connecticut. 1795.

[*Biography and Criticism*]

PARRINGTON, VERNON L. "Introduction." The Connecticut Wits. 1926.

DAVID HUMPHREYS. The Anarchiad. With Hopkins and others. 1786–1787. A Poem on the Happiness of America; Addressed to the Citizens of the United States. 1780. Miscellaneous Works of David Humphreys. 1804.

[*Biography and Criticism*]

HUMPHREYS, FRANCIS L. Life and Times of David Humphreys: Soldier-Statesman-Poet, "Belov'd of Washington." 2 vols. 1917.
MARBLE, ANNIE R. "David Humphreys: His Services to American Freedom and Industry," *New England Magazine,* February, 1904.
SWIFT, LINDSAY. "Our Literary Ambassadors," *Book Buyer,* June, 1910.

JOHN TRUMBULL. Poetical Works. With Memoir of the Author. 2 vols. 1820. The Progress of Dulness, Part I, 1772; Part II, 1773; Part III, 1773. M'Fingal: a Modern Epic Poem, Canto I, 1775. M'Fingal: a Modern Epic in Four Cantos. 1782.

[*Available Editions*]

M'Fingal; an Epic Poem. Introduction and notes by B. J. Lossing. 1881.
Poetical Works of John Trumbull. Reprinted from the original edition of 1820. Andiron Club. 1922.

[*Biography and Criticism*]

COWIE, ALEXANDER. John Trumbull, Connecticut Wit. 1935.
GREY, LENNOX. "John Adams and John Trumbull in the 'Boston Cycle,'" *New England Quarterly,* Vol. IV, pp. 509–514.
MARBLE, ANNIE R. "John Trumbull; Satirist and Scholar." Heralds of American Literature. 1907.
TRUMBULL, JAMES H. The Origin of M'Fingal. 1868.
TRUMBULL, JOHN. Autobiography, Reminiscences, and Letters from 1756 to 1841. 1841.

Works in Collaboration

The Anarchiad: A Poem on the Restoration of Chaos and Substantial Night. A series of twelve papers in the *New Haven Gazette and the Connecticut Magazine*, 1786–1787. By Joel Barlow, Lemuel Hopkins, David Humphreys, and John Trumbull. Collected and published by Luther G. Riggs, with introduction. 1861.

The Echo, with Other Poems. A political satirical poem in twenty numbers, by Richard Alsop and Theodore Dwight, with the aid of Lemuel Hopkins, Mason Cogswell and Elihu Smith. Appeared in the *American Mercury* from 1791 to 1805. Collected and published. 1807.

The Political Greenhouse for the Year 1798, by Alsop, Dwight, and Hopkins. 1799.

[*Comment on the Group*]

KING, WINNIFRED B. "The First American Satirists," *Connecticut Magazine*, Vol. X, p. 403.
OTIS, WILLIAM B. American Verse, 1625–1807. 1909.
PARRINGTON, VERNON L. "Introduction." The Connecticut Wits. 1926.
PARRINGTON, VERNON L. Main Currents in American Thought. 1927.
PATTERSON, SAMUEL W. The Spirit of the American Revolution as Revealed in the Poetry of the Period. 1915.
WILLIAMS, STANLEY T. "The Literature of Connecticut." A History of Connecticut, edited by N. G. Osborn. 1925.

[*Anthologies*]

BOYNTON, PERCY H. American Poetry. 1918.
CAIRNS, WM. B. Early American Writers. 1925.
EGGLESTON, GEORGE C. American War Ballads and Lyrics. 1889.
FOERSTER, NORMAN. American Poetry and Prose (rev. ed.). 1934.
PAGET, R. L. (pseud.). Poems of American Patriotism. 1898.
PARRINGTON, VERNON L. The Connecticut Wits. American Authors Series. 1926.
PRESCOTT, F. C., and NELSON, J. H. Prose and Poetry of the Revolution. 1925.
PRESCOTT, F. C., and SANDERS, G. L. An Introduction to American Poetry. 1932.
SPILLER, ROBERT E. The Roots of National Culture. 1933.
STEDMAN and HUTCHINSON. Library of American Literature, Vols. I, III.

BENJAMIN FRANKLIN. (See pages 113–114.)

FRANCIS HOPKINSON. A Pretty Story. 1774. A Prophecy. 1777. The New Roof. 1778. Miscellaneous Essays and Occasional Writings. 3 vols. Vol. III contains his Poems on Several Subjects. 1792.

[*Available Edition*]

The Old Farm and the New Farm, edited by B. J. Lossing. 1864. A reprint of A Pretty Story.

[*Biography and Criticism*]

DORR, BENJAMIN. Historical Account of Christ Church, Philadelphia. 1859.

HASTINGS, G. E. The Life and Works of Francis Hopkinson. 1926.

HILDEBURN, C. R. A Biographical Sketch of Francis Hopkinson. 1878.

MARBLE, ANNIE R. "Francis Hopkinson, Man of Affairs and Letters," *New England Magazine*, Vol. XXVII, pp. 289–302.

SANDERSON, JOHN. Biography of the Signers of the Declaration of Independence. 1823.

SONNECK, OSCAR G. Francis Hopkinson, the First American Poet-Composer. 1905.

TYLER, MOSES C. The Literary History of the American Revolution, Vol. I, Chaps. VIII, XII, XXII; Vol. II, Chap. XXX. 1897.

THOMAS PAINE. Common Sense. 1776. The Crisis, December, 1776; January, April, September, 1777; March, October, November, 1778; March, June, October, 1780; March, May 22 and 31, October, 1782; April, December, 1783.

[*Available Editions*]

Life and Works of Thomas Paine. Patriot's Edition. With a biography. 10 vols. 1925.

Selections from the Works of Thomas Paine, edited, with introduction, by Arthur W. Peach. American Authors Series. 1928.

Selections from the Writings of Thomas Paine, edited, with introduction, by Carl Van Doren. Modern Library. 1922.

The Writings of Thomas Paine, collected and edited by Moncure D. Conway. 4 vols. 1894–1896.

[*Biography and Criticism*]

BEST, MARY AGNES. Thomas Paine, Prophet and Martyr of Democracy. 1927.

BRADFORD, GAMALIEL. Damaged Souls. 1923.

CLARK, HARRY H. Thomas Paine's Relation to Voltaire and Rousseau. 1932. (Pamphlet.)

CLARK, HARRY H. "Toward a New Interpretation of Thomas Paine," *American Literature*, Vol. V, pp. 133–145.

CREEL, GEORGE. Tom Paine — Liberty Bell. 1932.

GOULD, FREDERICK J. Thomas Paine. Roadmaker Series. 1925.

MERRIAM, CHARLES E. "Political Theories of Thomas Paine," *Political Science Quarterly*, Vol. XIV, pp. 389–403.

ROPER, R. C. "Thomas Paine — the First to Urge the League of Nations," *Public*, Vol. XXII, pp. 488–489.

TYLER, MOSES C. The Literary History of the American Revolution. 1897.

PHILIP FRENEAU. The Poems of Philip Freneau. 1786. The Miscellaneous Works of Mr. Philip Freneau. 1788. Poems Written between the Years 1768 and 1794, by Philip Freneau, . . . 1795. Poems Written and Published during the Revolutionary War, and Other Pieces not heretofore in Print. By Philip Freneau. 2 vols. 1809. Poems Written between the Year 1797 and the Present Time. By Philip Freneau. 2 vols. 1815.

[*Available Editions*]

Poems of Freneau. American Authors Series. Edited by H. H. Clark. 1929.
The Philosopher of the Forest. Edited by H. H. Clark. 1929.
Poems of Philip Freneau. 3 vols. Edited by F. L. Pattee. 1902–1907.

[*Biography and Criticism*]

BRENNER, RICA. "Philip Freneau." Twelve American Poets before 1900. 1933.
CALVERTON, V. F. "Philip Freneau; An Apostle of Freedom," *Modern Monthly*, Vol. VII, pp. 533–546.
CLARK, HARRY H. "Literary Influences upon Philip Freneau," *Studies in Philology*, Vol. XXII, January, 1925.
CLARK, HARRY H. "What Made Freneau the Father of American Poetry?" *Studies in Philology*, Vol. XXVI, January, 1929.
DELANCEY, EDWARD F. "Philip Freneau, the Huguenot Patriot-Poet of the Revolution." Proceedings of the Huguenot Society of America, Vol. II, No. 2. 1891.
FORMAN, SAMUEL E. "The Political Activities of Philip Freneau," *Johns Hopkins University Studies in Historical and Political Science*, twentieth series, Nos. 9–10. 1910.
HEARTMAN, CHARLES (Ed.). Unpublished Freneauana. 1918.
MORE, PAUL ELMER. Shelburne Essays. Fifth series. 1908.
PATTEE, FRED L. "The Modernness of Philip Freneau." Sidelights on American Literature. 1922.
PATTERSON, SAMUEL W. The Spirit of the American Revolution as Revealed in the Poetry of the Period. 1915.
SMITH, FRANK. "Philip Freneau and *The Time-Piece and Literary Companion*," *American Literature*, Vol. IV, pp. 270–287.
TYLER, MOSES COIT. The Literary History of the American Revolution. 1897.

[*Bibliography*]

PALTSITS, VICTOR H. Bibliography of the Separate and Collected Works of Philip Freneau, together with an Account of His Newspapers. 1903.

HUGH HENRY BRACKENRIDGE. The Rising Glory of America. Written with Philip Freneau. 1771. The Battle of Bunker's Hill. 1776. Modern Chivalry: Containing the Adventures of Captain John Farrago, and Teague O'Regan, His Servant. 1792, 1793, 1797.

[*Available Editions*]

"The Battle of Bunker's Hill." Moses's Representative Plays by American Dramatists. 3 vols. 1918–1925.
Modern Chivalry, edited, with introduction, by Ernest Brennecke. Rogues' Bookshelf. 1926.

[*Biography and Criticism*]

EAKIN, MYRL I. "Hugh Henry Brackenridge, Lawyer," *Western Pennsylvania Historical Magazine*, July, 1927.
LOSHE, LILLIE D. The Early American Novel. 1907.
NEWLIN, CLAUDE M. The Life and Writings of Hugh Henry Brackenridge. 1932.

QUINN, ARTHUR H. A History of the American Drama from the Beginnings to the Civil War. 1923.

VAN DOREN, CARL. The American Novel. 1921.

VENABLE, W. H. Beginnings of Literary Culture in the Ohio Valley. 1891.

[*Bibliography*]

HEARTMAN, CHARLES F. A Bibliography of the Writings of Hugh Henry Brackenridge. 1917.

[*Anthologies*]

CAIRNS, WILLIAM B. Early American Writers. 1925.

FOERSTER, NORMAN. American Poetry and Prose (rev. ed.). 1934.

PRESCOTT and NELSON. Prose and Poetry of the Revolution. 1925.

SPILLER, ROBERT E. The Roots of National Culture. 1933.

STEDMAN and HUTCHINSON. Library of American Literature, Vol. III.

[*Commentaries on the War in Dramatic Form*]

The Adulateur. Mercy Warren. 1773.

A Dialogue between a Southern Delegate and his Spouse. "Mary V. V." 1774.

The Americans Roused in a Cure for the Spleen. Jonathan Sewall (?). 1775.

The Group. Mercy Warren. 1775.

The Fall of British Tyranny. John Leacock (?). 1776.

The Blockade. General Burgoyne. 1776.

The Blockheads. Anonymous. 1776.

The Patriots. Robert Munford. 1776.

The Battle of Bunker's Hill. H. H. Brackenridge. 1776.

The Death of General Montgomery. H. H. Brackenridge. 1777.

The Motley Assembly. Mercy Warren (?). 1779.

LITERARY TREATMENT OF THE TIMES

[*Drama*]

ANDERSON, MAXWELL. Valley Forge. 1935.

BROWN, WILLIAM. West Point Preserved. 1797.

BURK, JOHN DALY. Bunker Hill. 1797.

DUNLAP, WILLIAM. André. 1798.

FITCH, CLYDE. Major André. 1903.

FITCH, CLYDE. Nathan Hale. 1899.

LOW, SAMUEL. The Politician Outwitted. 1789.

MACKAY, CONSTANCE D. Benjamin Franklin, Journeyman. 1925.

MACKAYE, PERCY. Washington, the Man Who Made Us. 1925.

NICHOLS, J. HORATIO. The Essex Junto. 1802.

ROWSON, SUSANNA. Slaves in Algiers. 1794.

ROWSON, SUSANNA. The Volunteers. 1795.

TYLER, ROYALL. The Contrast. 1787.

[*Retrospective Fiction*]

ATHERTON, GERTRUDE. The Conqueror. 1901.

BIRD, ROBERT M. Nick of the Woods. 1837.

BOYD, JAMES. Drums. 1928.

CHURCHILL, WINSTON. The Crossing. 1904.

CHURCHILL, WINSTON. Richard Carvel. 1899.

COOPER, JAMES FENIMORE. Lionel Lincoln. 1825.
COOPER, JAMES FENIMORE. The Pilot. 1823.
COOPER, JAMES FENIMORE. Satanstoe. 1845.
COOPER, JAMES FENIMORE. The Spy. 1821.
FORD, PAUL LEICESTER. Janice Meredith. 1900.
HARTE, BRET. Thankful Blossom. 1877.
JEWETT, SARAH ORNE. The Tory Lover. 1901.
JOHNSTON, MARY. Audrey. A Story of Colonial Virginia. 1902.
JOHNSTON, MARY. Lewis Rand. 1908.
KENNEDY, JOHN PENDLETON. Horse-Shoe Robinson. 1835.
MITCHELL, S. WEIR. Hugh Wynne. 1897.
SIMMS, WM. GILMORE. The Partisan. 1835.
SIMMS, WM. GILMORE. The Scout. 1854.
STOWE, HARRIET BEECHER. Oldtown Folks. 1869.
THACKERAY, WILLIAM MAKEPEACE. The Virginians. 1858–1859.

[*Poetry*]

STEVENSON, B. E. (Ed.). Poems of American History. 1922.
WALLINGTON, N. U. (Ed.). American History by American Poets. 2 vols. 1911.

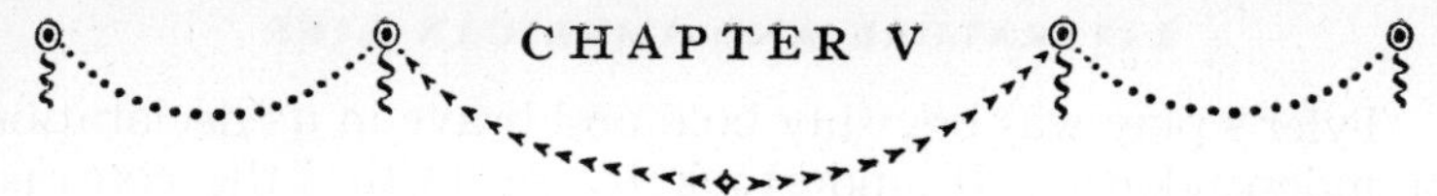

CHAPTER V

Provincial Independence

Post-Revolution Drama and Fiction

THE resort to dramatic sketches as political documents during the Revolutionary conflict has already been noted.[1] One or two outstanding plays after the fighting was over reveal the national self-consciousness that accompanied complete cultural allegiance to England. Royall Tyler's "Contrast," for example, was a success of 1787 and the first of many successes in the comedy of manners. Its purport was proudly indicated in the opening lines of the prologue:

> *Exult* each patriot heart! — this night is shown
> A piece, which we may fairly call our own;
> Where the proud titles of "My Lord! Your Grace!"
> To humble Mr. and plain Sir give place.
> Our Author pictures not from foreign climes
> The fashions, or the follies of the times;
> But has confined the subject of his work
> To the gay scenes — the circles of New York.

This complacency of pioneership would have been welcome to Freneau, whose 'Literary Importation" of only a year earlier had protested at the uneven balance of intellectual exchange:

> Can we never be thought to have learning or grace
> Unless it be brought from that horrible place
> Where tyranny reigns with her impudent face;
> And popes and pretenders,
> And sly faith-defenders
> Have ever been hostile to reason and wit,
> Enslaving a world that shall conquer them yet.[2]

---

[1] See pages 140–141, 147–148, 157–158.

[2] "The Poems of Freneau" (edited by H. H. Clark), p. 94.

Tyler's play was boyishly bold and brave in its declaration of independence. It undertook to set forth "the contrast between a gentleman who has read Chesterfield and received the polish of Europe and an unpolished, untraveled American." This is reinforced by parallels between an unscrupulous coquette and a feminine model of all the virtues, and between a popinjay servant and a crude countryman, the original stage Yankee. The play points its moral not because the good characters are admirable but because the bad ones are so vapid. Manly, the hero, is well disposed of by his frivolous sister's comment before she becomes sadder and wiser: "His conversation is like a rich, old-fashioned brocade, — it will stand alone; every sentence is a sentiment." And Maria, the blameless heroine, is revealed in her observation that "the only safe asylum a woman of delicacy can find is in the arms of a man of honor." Yet in the insistent and complacent contrasts between the unmitigated American and the Anglomaniac, Tyler's noble sentiments as to the homespun fabric of his play were offset by his English tailoring; for, with all its native complacency, the comedy was modeled after "The School for Scandal," and clearly indebted to O'Keeffe's "Poor Soldier" and Farquhar's "Provoked Husband." However, it cleared the way for American comedies of manners and for the succession of plays, descriptive rather than satirical, that carried New York in title as well as in content, and that themselves doubtless looked back to the repeated stage successes of Pierce Egan's "Life in London."

Dunlap's "André" (1798) is the other marked success of the time and the last early dramatic landmark. It was another hothouse plant exhibited as a wildflower:

> A Native Bard, a native scene displays,
> And claims your candour for his daring lays.

He took heed, as Rogers seems not to have done, of the risk in entering the straits of political controversy in which "Ponteach" was stranded before it reached the theater: [1]

---

[1] See page 109.

Oh, may no party-spirit blast his views,
Or turn to ill the meanings of the Muse;
She sings of wrongs long past, Men as they were,
To instruct, without reproach, the Men that are;
Then judge the Story by the genius shown,
And praise, or damn it, for its worth alone.

This was the time when party feeling ran high over the claims of "The Rival Suitors for America," as Freneau called them in his verses of 1795. "Hail Columbia," song of prudential patriotism ("Let independence be our boast, Ever mindful what it cost"), made an immediate hit when sung at an actor's benefit less than four weeks later than the production of "André." And Dunlap, after a slip of judgment in the opening performance, kept clear of politics and showed tact as well as daring by making the Briton heroic, though a spy, and by his fine treatment of the unnamed "General," who was evidently Washington. Dunlap's play, with its ready appreciation of theatrical effects, is the work of playmaker rather than poet, and the verse has little of the elevation of Godfrey's or Rogers's; but it is better than the declamatory stage efforts of Mercy Warren, Leacock, Low, and Brackenridge, and is the best early specimen of the historical romance.

True to his time, Dunlap was more illustrative of dramatic dependency than of emancipation. As a producer from 1795 to 1803 he was a salesman studying his market. When he could not find drawing plays, he undertook to write them; when he could not write drawing plays, he could translate and adapt; and he is chiefly memorable in this connection for tapping a new source — the German. He turned Schiller's "Don Carlos" into English, and it failed; but he made a striking success of Zschokke's "Abaellino! or, the Great Bandit" (later to be quite differently re-employed by Cooper in "The Bravo"), and he translated no less than thirteen plays by Kotzebue. For five years (1798–1803), almost entirely through Dunlap's activities, German adaptations were not only the largest element of recorded performances on the New York stage, but in one year they were in the actual majority. Then the vogue suddenly ceased, although "Pizarro" was a favorite for a full generation, and "The Stranger," variously Englished, like "Pizarro," survived even to rejuvenation as a moving picture. Nor did Dunlap limit his Continental indebtedness to Germany; for he drew also on France, anticipating John Howard Payne in this direction.[1] However, whether the foreign model was English, German, or French, the American public was still as slow to become theater-minded as Tyler's Jonathan in "The Contrast." The colonial attitude was hard to overcome. The average citizen was on guard against an institution long charged with being ungodly, carnal, and frivolous.

The same prejudice was naturally transferred to prose fiction in the colonies and the youthful states, and supplemented the "cultural lag" and the newness of the type to delay novel-writing in America. In fact, the first popular response in the reading public roused quick and eager reactions from the censors of morals.

> Nearly every grade of sophistication applied itself to the problem. The dullest critics contended that novels were lies; the pious, that they served no virtuous purpose; the strenuous, that they softened sturdy minds; the utilitarian, that they crowded out more useful books; the realistic, that they painted adventure too romantic and love too vehement; the patriotic, that, dealing with European manners, they tended to confuse and dissatisfy republican youth.[2]

The discussion was so general and so insistent that in "The Power of Sympathy," the first American novel, it was echoed in two long dialogues filled with cautions and admonitions to the young ladies, for whom that tale was composed.[3]

---

[1] Between 1821 and 1826 Payne adapted for production at Covent Garden and Drury Lane theaters in London ten plays from the French, seven of which were staged in New York with extraordinary promptness. Among them was "Clari; or the Maid of Milan," which contained "Home, Sweet Home"; and surpassing them all in vogue was "Brutus"—a mosaic from five previous versions, three English and two French.

[2] Carl Van Doren, "The American Novel," p. 3.

[3] See "The Power of Sympathy," original version of 1789, or facsimile reprint of 1894, Vol. I, pp. 32–40; Vol. II, pp. 1–15.

On all the earliest effusions the influence of English novelists was especially obvious; for the early development of a new type is no time for innovation, the type itself being nothing but a loose set of innovations. The chief models were supplied by the leading English pioneers in the field, and their three kinds of products were laboriously emulated: the sentimental, with emphasis on feeling, or "sensibility," and the attempt to dispense poetic justice à la Richardson; the Gothic romance, sentimentalism with the trappings of melodrama in the manner of Mrs. Radcliffe; and the humorous-realistic, with character and incident in balance and satire ever at call, of which Fielding was exemplar.[1] The first of these was the overwhelming favorite, and the third was seldom followed, though on rare occasions it stimulated some of the best results.

The ball of home-made fiction was set rolling in America in 1789. Its course is usually and conveniently pursued in terms of novels, doubtless because, few and slight as they were before 1800, they are more easy to examine than the shorter and less formal tales which can be found in the rare files of the magazines. This pursuit is not misleading, for periodical and book fiction followed parallel paths. Apparently the preoccupation of the public with problems of the state prevented American energies from flowing into this newest form of polite literature until the Constitution had been drafted and adopted. At any rate, fiction-writing did not develop until after these events. Mathew Carey's magazine the *American Museum*, which ran for the six full years 1787–1792, serves as a barograph of the shifting interests. Paine, Hopkinson, Franklin, Freneau, featured its early numbers. The Constitution was greeted with a salvo of applause and followed with contributions on American history. Then, in the middle of 1788, sighs replaced huzzas in the pages of *The Museum*. The political section started on its way toward the appendix. A sentimental approach to woman-

[1] These types are differentiated in W. L. Cross's "Development of the English Novel," Chaps. II, III.

hood and women readers was made by "The Visitant" and by the author of "Hints for Married Women," both heavily moralistic counselors. After a year and a half of hesitation on the springboard a bold leap was taken into the pool of fiction, a leap which came during the first celebrity of the first formal American novel, "The Power of Sympathy."

Carey, the astute, watching the taste of his subscribers, was changing his plan "in conformity with the sentiments of a number of friends" who wanted more of it "devoted to entertainment." For two full years he met the market demand, anticipating the kind of tale with which Mrs. Rowson was belatedly to supplement "The Power of Sympathy" with "Charlotte" in 1794, and Mrs. Foster with "The Coquette" in 1797. But before these came Carey saw signs of surfeit; and in 1792 he launched a countermove against "the common trash of novels under which the press has groaned . . . which have been so hurtful to young minds, particularly to the female sex."[1] He followed this in the next number with an article, "Interesting Comparisons between the Works of Richardson and Fielding," in which he established Richardson's moral superiority and suggested him as an antidote to "the trash daily pouring out for the circulating libraries." The deluge was evidently from England; there was as yet only a rivulet from American pens, and the first successors to "The Power of Sympathy" were largely didactic, like Hitchcock's "Memoirs of the Bloomsgrove Family"; allegorical, like Belknap's "Foresters"; or satirical, like the first installment of Brackenridge's "Modern Chivalry." Carey as a journalist was blazing the same smooth, conservative path that Brockden Brown was soon to follow[2] and that was still being trodden in 1850, when the *Mother's Magazine and Family Journal* for November chinked in between a moral anecdote and a religious poem:

Novel-Reading. — A writer in the American Messenger makes the following just and weighty objections to novel-reading: —

---

1 *The American Museum,* November and December, 1792. 2 Pages 198–203.

1. Novel-reading produces undue mental excitement. 2. Novel-reading enfeebles the mental powers. 3. The novel-reader is apt to imbibe erroneous and corrupt sentiments. 4. Novel-reading tends to unfit one for a happy and useful life. 5. The practice of novel-reading unfits one for the duties of religion.

A consequence of this prejudice was that those who wanted to indulge in fiction-writing and win the approval of the happy, the useful, and the religious, resorted to "true" stories, identifying factual and truthful, and insisted on drawing lessons from them. Those who were less solicitous made fun of the tendency. "Perhaps a novel writer," wrote Helen Maria Williams in the *Philadelphia Minerva* (May, 1798), "by the aid of a little additional misery, and by giving the circumstances which actually happened a heightened colour — by taking his pallet and dashing with the full glowing red what nature had only tinged with pale violet, might almost spin a volume from these materials." Another consequence was that the most widely popular and generally approved novels compounded a sort of literary felony by combining the factual, the moral, and the purple-patched.

The pioneer of them all in these respects was "The Power of Sympathy; or, the Triumph of Nature, Founded in Truth," the truth being in general a trueness to life, but notoriously the too truthful account of a scandal involving Perez Morton and his sister-in-law.[1] Thus the full title accounts in part for the vogue of Mrs. Rowson's outstanding success, "Charlotte, A Tale of Truth," the legend that the luckless heroine's tombstone stood in Trinity churchyard adding to its effect and starting it on its career of one hundred and four editions. And thus Mrs. Foster profited by example when she composed "The Coquette; or, the History of Eliza Wharton: A Novel; Founded on Fact," one of

[1] It is partly the incredibility of this scandal's being employed by the offended loyal wife, Sarah Wentworth Morton, and partly the evidence of textual examination that has convinced H. M. Ellis and, through him, the writer, that this novel was actually written by William Hill Brown. See "Philenia; the Life and Works of Sarah Wentworth Morton," by Milton Ellis and Emily Pendleton, for details.

the "facts" being the tradition that Eliza's mother was related to Charlotte.

The fullest bibliography of early American fiction[1] includes less than two hundred and fifty titles published before 1830, half or more of these coming in the last decade. Of the one hundred before 1820 some have disappeared, flimsily printed in small editions and read to pieces. From about sixty of the survivors some generalizations can be made that would probably hold for the rest. First, as to their contents in the broad.

Starting doubtfully and far away, there is an element of romances of other lands scattered all along the period: aboard ship, on a desert island, in the Mediterranean, stories alleged to have happened in Russia, Persia, China, the romantic feeling expressing itself in gropings for any place but home. In contrast to these, only two tales have to do with the richest of American material, the frontier; and in both of these the frontier is quite incidental. There is a third small group of overwhelmingly didactic narratives (for the moral or intellectual lesson is undercurrent in all) on education, on getting on in the world, on the control of a guiding Providence, — treatises costumed in narrative, but not disguised. There are a half-dozen historical tales: on the Pocahontas story; one just round the corner from it, on the hardly concluded War of 1812; and a trio of historical allegories. There are three lively social and political satires, including "Modern Chivalry," already discussed. And finally, predominantly, half the entire list is composed of sentimental domestic tales. In the period from 1789 to 1820 these start slowly in proportion to the others, reach their height in 1797–1799, and taper off between 1810 and 1820. In general they are on the stock romantic love-story pattern: two rewards of virtue, hero and heroine each for the other, a wide variety of obstacles human and natural, and wedding bells.

---

[1] Oscar Wegelin, "Early American Fiction, 1774–1830" (3d ed., corrected and enlarged), 1929.

There are definite patterns within the domestic tales. Most popular in the 1790's was the seduction story — theme of the much discussed subnarrative of Ophelia in "The Power of Sympathy," of "The Coquette," and, most popular of all, of "Charlotte." The seduction tale offers the reward-of-virtue formula in reverse. Virtue flags and the heroine loses caste or sanity or life, or all three; but poetic justice is vindicated in the utter ruination of the villain. This use of the awful example could be justified on moral grounds. The pattern of sentimental tragedy, like life, was more puzzling. One finds that "the invisible hand" is not working benignly or beneficently. It is the heavy hand of circumstance that weighs on the heroine, who deserves a reward withheld from her. Sometimes heaven is promised as a belated recognition of the continence which is the virtue mainly stressed. Yet in many of these tales there is a marked absence of the employment of Providence as paymaster to the righteous. In many, but not in all, the largest element is still made up of the completely sentimental romance. Mrs. Rowson compensates handsomely for "Charlotte" with "Rebecca" — after sacrificing "Sarah; or, the Exemplary Wife" on the wheel of fortune. Brockden Brown deals kindly with "Clara Howard." "A young lady of the State of New York" anonymously dispenses happiness to Henry Villars and all other deserving characters in "The Fortunate Discovery." The same can be said for "Cynthia" and "Amelia" and "Ferdinand and Elmira" and "Constantius and Pulchera" and many another. These happy-ending chronicles taper over to Cooper's first literary venture, written in the vogue which, after many uncertainties, assures a perfect union to Emily and Lord Pendennys.

If there is a single generalization to make about the content of these early American novels, it is that little but the bibliographical facts can be cited as evidence that they were novels written by or for Americans. This is reinforced by Royall Tyler's prefatory statement for "The Algerine Captive," a homespun story containing the romantic adventure suggested in the title, introducing Franklin and Paine in person, and following with satirical commentary the rovings of a character who must often have crossed the paths of Captain Farrago and Teague O'Regan. The American public, said Tyler, had been converted to fiction, but it was an exotic fiction:

> The worthy farmer no longer fatigued himself with Bunyan's Pilgrim up the "hill of difficulty" or through the "slough of despond"; but quaffed wine with Brydone in the hermitage of Vesuvius, sported with Bruce on the fairy land of Abyssinia.

This was travel literature which led over naturally to the work of the novelist.

> Dolly, the [dairy] maid, and Jonathan, the hired man, threw aside the ballad of the cruel stepmother, over which they had so often wept in concert, and now amused themselves into so agreeable a terrour, with the haunted houses and hobgoblins of Mrs. Ra[d]cliffe, that they were both afraid to sleep alone.

Tyler had offered "The Contrast" as an antidote to Anglomania; now, ten years later, he proffered "The Algerine Captive" as an antidote to the romantic moonings of the novelists, whether foreign or native.

The American product was even less indigenous in method than in matter, a point that can be illustrated again from the sentimental tales, as the other types are built in the same fashion. Plot development depends on complicating and prolonging the story and on resolving it. The complicating elements are composed of devices for postponing wedding bells until the last chapter or page. How simple they became then! First of all was parental objection, usually by the heroine's father; a deathbed promise to the mother was equally effective; social inequality was almost as good. But these were in the abstract. The separation of the lovers must ensue; and it did, by grace of the indirections of scandal (whispered or by letter) or through abduction, banishment, and all the vicissitudes of travel, shipwreck, and capture. Chance meetings and timely rescues of all sorts could bring them together; more abductions, captures, shipwrecks, rend them from each other's arms again. The mechanics of conclusion in the happy-ending tales was a matter of barriers withdrawn — parental blessings, deaths of intervening husbands or wives, restoration of identities to the apparently ineligible but really highborn, bequests to the poverty-stricken; and, in the tragedies, broken heart, madness, suicide, and the accessory ruin of the villain, never omitted. The style was elevated, but should be read with reference to the elevation of the period, which, in literature, was almost universal.

One tiny booklet of the day which, at first glance, seems the worst of the whole crop, looks, at second glance, like a burlesque with the critical values that accompany good burlesque or parody. The title page reads, "A beautiful little NOVEL / The / History / of / Constantius and Pulchera, / or / Constancy Rewarded / An American Novel /." The dedication is a paraphrase of the dedication to "The Power of Sympathy." The masterly non sequiturs of the preface, professedly by the publisher, Charles Peirce of Portsmouth, New Hampshire, could be accidental, but hardly so in conjunction with the title page and the dedication; and the hundred and two large-type duodecimo pages make up a compend of all the most extravagant incredibilities of the type. The lovers, engaged with her father's approval, are suddenly frustrated by the advent of a villainous Frenchman. Defying him, they are immediately separated: he, a captive of "British barbarity"; and she, to be shipped abroad with the interloper. She is victim of several shipwrecks and several captures at sea. Once the lovers encounter on shipboard, only to be rewrecked and torn apart. For some months she is disguised as an officer, afloat and ashore. She survives incredible hardships on a wintry coast where, on one night, five feet of snow fall. Eventually the lovers re-encounter in Paris and hold repeated interviews, during which he fails to penetrate her disguise. Their return to America and to her father's blessing is the only voyage in the tale unpunctuated by tempest and armed foe. If "Constantius and Pulchera" was not intended as parody, it serves the purpose none the less.

Since the stories have so slight a claim to attention as literature, the only other question is whether they throw any light on the mind of the time and the region; whether they supplement or gainsay what else we know. The answer is that they are moderately supplementary. In the field of politics and statecraft, except for the satires and allegories, which are least fictional in quality, they contribute little; for this new type of story-telling was not used as often as drama for propagandist ends. On the whole, however, if one read them with the idea in mind, one might gather that democracy was on trial and crudely operative.

A cultural consciousness was vaguely allied with conscious nationalism, and connected with these was an awareness that, while fiction was addressed to an American public, it was particularly addressed to the women. The feminization of American culture is dimly foreshadowed in some of these books. For the women readers there was held up to view the conventional eighteenth-century "female." The Amelia who was ruined by "The Faithless Briton" (there was another Amelia who fared more happily) was characterized by "delicacy of form, mildness of aspect, exquisite harmony of soul, and symmetry of person." This delicacy, prime requisite of femininity, was so sensitive that Mrs. Foster, in "The Coquette," noted that it was inconsistent with going to the circus, "especially when performers of equestrian feats are of our own sex." Enos Hitchcock, who wrote "Memoirs of the Bloomsgrove Family," took the easy way of the gallant with womankind by making the lady celestial and futile. She was not inferior; he repudiated the suggestion with scorn; but "in all societies there must be one who stands at the head of the list. . . . Whether nature has assigned the task to our sex or yours, I refer to the decision of your own judgment."

A creature so delicate and irresponsible as this, it followed, should be protected not only from harsh experience but also from discordant or agitative ideas. On this theme the novelists seemed to agree that the American young lady was in peril. Mrs. Rowson, in "Sarah; or, the Exemplary Wife," testified with grief to one whose mind "became a chaos of romantic sensibility, enthusiastic superstition, and sceptical boldness." Lucy Osmond, central figure in the tale that bears her name, just escapes ruination as the result of her reading. Out of calamity she emerges an ascetic; out of asceticism she passes to death overshadowed with remorse. As her friends reflect on her sad fate one of them says, "The pupils of Rousseau and all of those sentimentalists, who, without his genius have adopted his faults, are all of the [same] school; their maxims are baneful to society in general, but to women absolute destruction." Brockden Brown deplored the foreign contagion in "Clara Howard"; and the appended advertisements to "The Invisible Hand" recommended long lists of religious and moral works, including a "Vocal Poetry," which was "a suitable collection for a father to put in the hands of his daughter."

In the realm of religion there seems to have been a distinct split between novels still holding to the Puritan concept of a personal Providence and those which were uncomfortably wrestling with the concept of impersonal fate; but the compromise was often adopted of allowing chance and whim every liberty in the prolongation of the plot, after which the balance was retrieved either by the interposition of an overruling God or by the practical equivalent of invoking the principle of poetic justice. Sentimentalism and religious orthodoxy came to the same conclusion; the skeptic and the elect were at one. Mrs. Rowson quoted the formula in "The Trials of the Human Heart":

> If there's a power above us,
> (And that there is all nature cries aloud
> Through all her works) he must delight in virtue.
> The soul secured in her existence, smiles,
> At the drawn dagger and defies its point.

In which easy solution fiction adopted thus early in America the romantic avenue of escape from the world's ills that was to prevail right down to the twentieth century in all but exceptionally and unpopularly truthful novels.

Charles Brockden Brown

Charles Brockden Brown is pre-eminent among these early excursionists into the field of fiction in mass of output, in contemporary prestige, and in substantial relationship to the thought of the time. Indeed he belongs so completely to his period that the outline of his short career becomes more than the literary gossip of most biographical detail.

He was born in Philadelphia just before the Revolutionary War. "His parents," wrote Dunlap, "were virtuous, religious people, and as such held a respectable rank in society,"[1] the rank which is least likely to promote independent thought. Delicate, precocious, he was cultivated into an infant prodigy. At sixteen he was well schooled in the classics, had versified parts of Job, the Psalms, and Ossian, had sketched plans for three epics, and had permanently undermined his health. At eighteen he was studying law, indulging in debate and philosophical speculation, and publishing his first magazine article. Soon he abandoned the law. In one mood he gave thanks that he was free from the temptations of the flesh because of his feeble health; in another, for the same cause contemplated suicide. Finally, to escape the too urgent counsels of his advisers, he took flight to New York City. Here he fell in with congenial literary companions; joined the Friendly Club, where he was marked for "disputatiousness and dogmatism"; and in the stirring period of the 90's was stirred by French thought, stimulated directly by William Godwin of "Political Justice" celebrity, and began to dream dreams of a new heaven on the old earth.

His active authorship was varied and incessant from 1797 to his death in 1810, though the best of it was crowded into

---

[1] William Dunlap, "Life of Charles Brockden Brown," Vol. I, p. 11.

the first four years. And the adoption of liberal ideas and reaction from them, which took place more slowly with his countrymen, was also crowded into these middle years of Brown's life. He wrote at the outset with the confidence of youth to a youthfully uncritical reading public, "filled with the rapture with which he held communion with his own thoughts," committing them to paper in a copious journal, in circumstantial letters, and in the rivulet which flowed from his pen into the forgotten gulf of magazinedom. In 1799, while editing the *Monthly Magazine and American Review*, he was working on five novels; and in these novels he was under the evident influence of William Godwin and Mary Wollstonecraft, playing up the role of "reason" in a world which was corrupted by human institutions, lamenting the defeat of justice, and contending that the play of natural and altruistic instinct should be allowed to overcome the rule of privilege and the oppressions that inevitably accompany it. Before he was thirty his reputation was established and his important work was done. In 1801 he returned to Philadelphia with achieved success as a retort to the friends who had tried to dissuade him from professional writing.

Then in 1803 he undertook another editorial venture in the *Literary Magazine and American Register*. From the excited young radical of a half-dozen years earlier, he had become by some reaction a fulfiller of his pious ancestry. In an editorial statement of principles he made it clear that he would rather be respectable than exciting in his sentiments. He referred to recent bold attacks on "the foundations of religion and morality"; declared that he would uphold the old standards and proscribe everything that offended against them; and concluded, in the editorial third person, "His poetical pieces may be dull, but they at least shall be free from voluptuousness or sensuality: and his prose, whether seconded or not by genius and knowledge, shall scrupulously aim at the promotion of public and private virtue." Even under the weight of this unmitigated morality, the magazine survived four years. Brown had declined from creative writing to dispensing commonplace conservatism and useful knowledge — a decline that continued through a seven-volume "General Repository of History, Politics and Science" toward a prospectus of an uncompleted "System of General Geography; containing a Topographical, Statistical and Descriptive Survey of the Earth." It is evident enough that when he died in 1810 his distinctive work was well in the past. Unless some amazing reversal of form had taken place, long life would have been only a long, industrious, ultra-conventional anticlimax to the promise of his young manhood.

Even within the four-year period of his novel-publishing, his best bolts were shot early, and his peculiar powers were fully displayed in the first three of his sextet. Brown resorted to the temper and technique of the Gothic romance, the first extravagant contribution of fiction to the romantic movement of the day: the tale of wonder and horror, of alternating moonlight serenities and midnight storms, of haunted castles and secret chambers, of woods and vales and caves and precipices, of apparent supernaturalism explained away in conscientious postscripts, and the same immaculate heroine and diabolical villain who had played leading roles for Richardson. The type had been developed by Horace Walpole and Mrs. Anne Radcliffe and "Monk" Lewis; and it had been freshly employed by William Godwin, who combined all this machinery into a kind of literary "tank" for the conveyance of a didactic gun crew, his "Caleb Williams" being little more than his thesis on "Political Justice" in narrative camouflage. This was a formula to Brown's taste, with his strong ethical bias and his liking for the mysterious.

The first to be published was "Wieland," a gradually increasing succession of horrors inspired by a mysterious voice. By the oracular demands of the unseen speaker, Wieland's double tendency to superstition and melancholy is deepened into calm fanaticism. In the end, obedient to what he thinks the voice of God, he murders wife and children, and on confession is acquitted as insane. In the conventional afterword a repentant villain explains events as the result of his irresistible inclination to practice his gifts as a ventriloquist. This tale of innocence victimized is offset by "Ormond" of the next year, a tale of feminine virtue triumphant. The element of horror is furnished by the yellow-fever plague; the apparently supernatural, by the omniscience of the arch-malefactor, who is simply an ingenious resorter to false partitions and secret doors.

Brown's most ambitious novel, "Arthur Mervyn" (two volumes of 1799 and 1800), carries as subtitle "The Memoirs of 1793." These days, according to the preface, were suggestive to "the moral observer," to whom they furnished new displays of the influence of human passions and motives. He used "such incidents as appeared to him most instructive and remarkable," believing that it was "everyone's duty to profit by all opportunities of inculcating upon mankind the lessons of justice and humanity." He believed in tragic realism on account of the Aristotelian "pity" which it might inspire. However, the plague of 1793 is incidental to the story, which is a somewhat clumsy imposing of a Godwinian plot against an American background. The first volume, the atmosphere of which is plague-infested, recounts the involvements of Mervyn with a consummate villain, Welbeck, just as the sins of the latter return on him. The second pursues certain unfinished stories of the first and dwells on the innocence of the reputedly wicked hero and on his efforts to atone for the offenses of the real sinner. The structure is not as firm as this would imply; it is an endless ramification of plots within plots, and stops without any sufficient conclusion. The long tale is evidently indebted to Godwin, of whose "transcendent powers" in "Caleb Williams" Brown was an ardent admirer. Yet Godwin was in turn quite as evidently under obligations to Smollett's "Roderick Random." In the light of history Brown seems to have been impressed by Godwin's book because it was popular while he was writing, and Godwin's book was popular on account of its political timeliness. Of Brown's three remaining novels, only one is of any moment — "Edgar Huntly." This is a good detective story, fresher than any of his others. A somnambulist who murders while sleep-walking supplies the horror and creates the mystery; and certain pictures of frontier life and Allegheny Mountain scenery, with an Indian massacre and a panther fight, are effectively home-made.

Brown was like a good many other novelists in possessing certain native gifts which he exercised without any self-discipline. He is quoted as saying to one of his friends, "Sir, good pens, thick paper, and ink well diluted, would facilitate my composition more than the prospect of the broadest expanse of clouds, water or mountains rising above the clouds." This suggests the steady craftsmanship of Anthony Trollope with his thousand words per hour; but Brown fell short of Trollope in both structure and style. His novels are full of inconsequences and loose ends; he was unblushing in his reliance on the long arm of coincidence. His plots, untangled from mazes of circumstance, are often weakly motivated. As he never wrote with painstaking care, his best passages are those which give the impression of passionate rapidity. When the subject rapt him clean out of himself he could transmit his thrill to the reader. The plague horrors that he had survived in New York made him forget to be "literary"; and he could re-create in himself and on paper the tense excitement of an actor in moments of suspense. His gifts strengthened his climaxes and emphasized the flatness of the intervening stretches. He had the weakness of the playwright who can write nothing but "big scenes." He was a journalist with a ready pen, doing his best work in the mood and manner of the gifted reporter without the creative imagination or the scrupulousness in detail of the artist. Yet this is stating the case too simply. He wrote, to be sure, in a declining fiction type which within a few years was to become a literary oddity. Scott was to continue in what he called the "big, bow-wow" strain and was to make his romances rational and human; Jane Austen was to write of ordinary life in the hearty contempt for the extravagances of the Radcliffe school which she expressed throughout "Northanger Abbey."[1] Yet in his period Brown was recognized on both continents; Godwin owed a return influence to him; Shelley read him with absorbed attention; Scott borrowed names for two characters. Moreover, in his pages there are distinct foretastes, in material and temper, of Cooper and Poe and Hawthorne. But with the gifts which these facts imply, Brown lacked either the self-discipline as a craftsman or the depth of conviction as a thinker to succeed in inculcating "upon mankind the lessons of justice and morality" which he undertook to do as a novelist. He oscillated between being a Poe and being a Stowe, and his pendulum came to a dead stop in the middle.

1800–1820—An Interim

Sydney Smith's fleering question as to whether there were any readers of American books[2] and John Bristed's less caustic but equally damaging observations on the paucity of American literature were peculiarly pertinent when they were put out just before 1820. No new reputations were perceptibly on the way to establishment and no old ones were being enriched. Bristed cited the slimness of the crop as proof of democracy's leveling influence. He echoed a typical British reaction at a time when British criticism of the American scene was gratifying to British readers in proportion to its disparaging tone and conclusions, though an American like Cooper or like Dennie could for one reason or another subscribe to the same explanation. Yet it is much more likely that the lack of creative output is due to the prevailing uncertainties of the period, which themselves could not be projected against a clear-cut tradition. It was a flickering picture on an undulating screen. With the opening of the century there had

---

[1] Chaps. I, XX ff.

[2] R. E. Spiller, "The Verdict of Sydney Smith," in *American Literature*, Vol. I, pp. 3–13.

been a temporary wave toward the restoration of the orthodoxies and conservatisms, but it was part of a back eddy rather than of a tide. Jeffersonian democracy was on the way to being supplanted by democracy of the Jacksonian brand. While the Methodists and Baptists were scattering and developing sects within sects, Catholics were gaining rapidly in numbers, and Calvinist Congregationalism was losing deserters to Unitarianism. An era of home industries was giving way to a factory era — an era of transportation by sail and horse to a future of transportation by steam. And the West was opening up distractingly. Few could detach themselves from participation in events long enough to indulge in meditation. The concrete life of America was so absorbing that there was little temptation to convert it into fiction, little mood to interpret it in poetry, little inclination to pause for solid, sober analysis. Yet one important process was going on in these lean years. Here and there in the cities the gregarious instinct was drawing the literary into coteries, and starting activities that were to develop readers and then writers and then more magazines which were a little less miscellaneous, undistinguished, and ephemeral than their eighteenth-century forerunners.

A few summarized facts about the periodicals started between 1790 and 1820 are worth recording because they do not seem to have been reduced to lowest terms elsewhere, as well as because of the inferences to be drawn from them.[1] In the thirty years there were 157 magazines established, almost equally divided among the decades — 47, 53, 57. Between 80 and 90 per cent of these were published in New England and the central-Atlantic states in a proportion of one to two, which is a way of roughly stating that New York City and Philadelphia each held its own against Boston. There was a small and not increasing quota from the South, which means Baltimore, Richmond, and Charleston; and an important new element when, in the 1810–1820 period, six

[1] The figures here are derived from Frank Luther Mott's "History of American Magazines 1741–1850," pp. 787–809.

were issued from the West, which then meant Cincinnati, Ohio, and Lexington, Kentucky.

There was a consistent gain in what the actuary calls life expectancy. By 1790 the earliest experimental period was over.[1] Between then and 1800 all but six of the magazine ventures collapsed within the first year, and three of the remaining six were dropped before the end of the fifth year. One survived just past the quarter-century mark. In the next decade a dozen lasted from two to five years; ten, more than five years; and of the three that passed the quarter-century, one endured until 1931 and another is still current. In the 1820–1830 stretch only a minority faded away in the first year; seventeen passed the ten-year mark; and of the ten which existed more than twenty-five years, seven passed the century mark and six are still current.

From another point of view, that of dominant purpose and consequent circulation appeal, more significant conclusions can be drawn. Whatever else the magazines might contain between 1790 and 1820, they depended pre-eminently on information. Current history, local history, national history, "natural" history, usurped the bulk of their pages. Morals and sentiment were regarded as proper accessories. Literature and aesthetics won little attention, and what they did win was an attention to transatlantic models and traditions. As the years passed, the zest for the informational made a place for specialized and professional publications, — military, legal, and particularly medical, — a high proportion of these lasting for several decades. And as a class the so-called religious periodicals were the most successful of all, for they combined in themselves the informational, the moral, the professional. In their appeal to the ministry of the various denominations under whose auspices they were issued they doubtless gained invaluable assistance in building and maintaining their subscription lists. Judging from the periodicals of the early nineteenth century, the American public was

---

[1] See pages 97–99.

sober, fact-hungry, ecclesiastically minded, morally inclined, and in a mood for the adult education to which the lyceum movement, beginning in the middle 20's, was to minister most effectively.

The magazinists naturally contributed to the discussion of what was to some of them the quite exciting subject of American speech, diction, and idiom, brought to a focus by the appearance of Noah Webster's dictionary in 1806. The discussion was so peppery that Webster soon made the rueful admission that men could feel as intensely about traditional speech and spelling as about traditional religion. His particular offense in the eyes of the purists was that he regarded himself as a recorder of developing usages instead of as a defender of established ones. Some of these were Americanisms; some were even localisms. "Is this *my* fault? And if local terms exist, why not explain them? Must they be left unexplained because they are local? This very circumstance renders their insertion in a dictionary the more necessary."[1] Those who passionately refused to distinguish between recording a usage and endorsing it, began their assaults on the lexicographer long before his work appeared. William Duane, editor of *The Aurora* (June 22, 1803), called him a "walking monument of human folly, tergiversation, and literary quackery," and suggested that he appropriately christen his "projected volume of foul and unclean things" Noah's Ark. Joseph Dennie, in the *Port Folio* (August 28, 1802), ironically offered a list of barbarous words and phrases, urging others to do their "duty as good patriots, and as fond lovers of provincial idioms, and colloquial meanness, and, in short, of every thing, hostile to English sense, and English stile." Dennie, of course, was a rabid Federalist, but political conservatism did not always rule in the linguistic discussion. David Humphreys published a glossary of nearly three hundred colloquialisms which he

[1] "The Beginnings of American English: Essays and Comments" (edited by M. M. Mathews), p. 49.

used in his play "The Yankey in England"; and John Pickering, son of Timothy, Secretary of State, discriminated between keeping the well of English pure and undefiled and making record of the defilements that he fished up from its depths. In spite of Webster's philological openness of mind, however, he revealed as a morally responsible New Englander a mental reservation and a consequent practice which John Cotton might have approved and which Timothy Dwight must have endorsed. He would admit, and felt that he should admit, innovations, simplifications, localisms, vulgarisms, because they existed in current speech; but not words that offended the proprieties — at this point he became a guardian of the morals of his countrymen. Whether current or not, and regardless of authority, a certain class of words must be expurgated:

> It was most injudicious in Johnson to select Shakespeare, as one of his principal authorities. Play-writers in describing low scenes and vulgar characters, use low language, language unfit for decent company; and their ribaldry has corrupted our speech, as well as the public morals. I have made it a main point to reject words belonging to writings of this character, and shall proceed as far as propriety requires, in cleansing the Augean stable.[1]

The persisting prejudice against the theater is a reminder of the same sober public for which Webster expurgated the language, and which patronized the religious and didactic magazines, though there were certain counterbalancing facts in the field of the theater. A playgoing public was being slowly developed[2] all over the country: in the less hospitable districts to the north and east; in the south, where opposition had been slightest; and, finally, along the western waterway of the Ohio and lower Mississippi rivers. The domination of foreign producer, actor, and playwright was so

---

[1] "The Beginnings of American English" (edited by M. M. Mathews), p. 50.

[2] The most extended original source for this subject is N. M. Ludlow's "Dramatic Life as I Found It," 1880. The most compact statement of recent scholarship is in R. L. Rusk's "Literature of the Middle Western Frontier," Chap. VIII.

strong that native plays or plays on native themes can be cited only now and then. They represent neither a tendency of the time nor even the broad contribution of a single author. James Nelson Barker[1] is often mentioned as a playwright who felt the need of a native drama and tried to meet it; but Barker at best was a playmaker who welcomed any material for a new production. He drew on Cervantes, on Scott, on lesser French dramatists; and when he turned to American themes he never turned twice in the same direction, composing a masque, a Puritan play, an Indian play, a Western play, a political play, a social comedy. It is easily explicable; he was, like all other American dramatists, struggling to keep his head up against the stream of foreign competition.

The repertory of the Park Theater, New York, between 1810 and 1820 shows how strong the current was running. Some of it had been a constant since before the closing of the colonial theaters in 1774. In addition to the Shakespeare plays, there were "Alexander the Great," "The Belles' Stratagem," "Douglas," "The Beggar's Opera," "Venice Preserved." There were favorites of a later era: "The Gamester," "The Rivals," "The School for Scandal," "The Heir at Law." There was abundant dramatization of Scott and Byron; exotic melodrama: "The Æthiop; or, the Child of the Desert," "Timour, the Tartar"; musical plays; pantomime ballets; and now and then, at long intervals, an American production.

With the exception of Dunlap, who was only a temporary venturer, the main producers were English; so were the main actors until the advent of Edwin Forrest in the 20's; so was the heavy element in the supporting casts of the stock companies; and the fact that the whole theatrical enterprise was so largely alien in theme and personnel made it the easier for the old churchly prejudices to persist — the sort of prejudices that first arose when the early English play left

[1] A good study of Barker is Paul H. Musser's "James Nelson Barker, 1784–1858," with a reprint of his comedy "Tears and Smiles."

the churchyard for the public square, that were revived by Gosson in the sixteenth century and by Collier in the seventeenth, and that have found fertile soil in provincial America up to the very present.

But the opening up of theatrical territory in the Ohio and Mississippi valleys seems to have encountered little of this; and the movement that took place on the Middle Western frontier was the first of any moment to establish a definite connection between the dominant English tradition of the Atlantic coast and the dominant French tradition at the mouth of the valley.[1] The records show that there was sporadic amateur playing from 1799 on, so casual and infrequent, however, as to be negligible except as vague foreshadowing. Lexington, Kentucky, earliest cultural center in the Ohio basin, was visited each year from 1810 to 1814 by a company "from Montreal and Quebec," as was Louisville, beginning with 1811. But the first real invasion and occupation of the new territory came with a company recruited in Albany and brought out by one Usher, who had been active as local manager for the earlier venture. In 1815 Usher brought this company westward. It took them nearly three years of advancing and retreating to reach the final goal of New Orleans, after they had visited and revisited Pittsburgh, Cincinnati, Lexington, Louisville, Nashville, Memphis, and smaller towns. From 1818 on, Lexington waned in importance, but there was a consecutive theatrical history in the other towns. The theater had won its permanent foothold, and the interesting feature of the campaign is that it so resembled that of the Hallams and their rivals on the coast two generations earlier. Producers, plays, and players all came from farther east. The personnel was largely American but not native to the region. The plays were practically as British as in the days of the Hallams. "The Busy Body" and "Jane Shore" start the list; it progresses to later repertories of colonial times; Goldsmith and Sheridan enter the

[1] See Lucile Gafford's "History of the St. Charles Theater in New Orleans, 1835–1843," introductory chapter. The University of Chicago Libraries, 1932.

picture; then Tobin and O'Keeffe; then Scott and Byron dramatized. There was the old combination of main play and afterpiece; the same interpolated "acts" and features; the same succession of impromptu and primitive playhouses; the same conclusion of the seasons with actors' benefits; the same eventual development of local stock companies and itinerant star actors depending on the locals for supporting parts. But by the early 20's there was a recognizable West for the theater as well as for the magazine.

The nation that had been politically first federated, then federalized, then democratized, was culturally still as sprawling and uncoördinated as any nursling. There was no dominant metropolis, not even any fixed capital city. And when one was determined on, the compromise choice became simply the national office for the transaction of business, and the literary capital was still to be found. Anyone anywhere could publish a book, and no one anywhere could look to a national market. The steady importation of English books and periodicals flooded what market there was, just as the importation of English producers, actors, and plays overwhelmed the stage. To some Americans of Tory-Federalist leanings this was as it should be; to most it was a source of vaguely irritated unrest. And as far as English comment was concerned there were ample grounds for annoyance. John Trumbull's resentments of 1775[1] were justified anew by men

> Like Fearon, Ashe, and others we could mention;
> Who paid us friendly visits to abuse
> Our country, and find food for the reviews.[2]

Moreover, English complacency was as offensive as English criticism. Americans could not strike with effect, because they could not make their blows felt. They were to fret and fume for half a century, their discomfort finding its ultimate expression in Lowell's lines:

---

[1] Page 172.

[2] Halleck, "Fanny," stanza lviii.

She *is* some punkins, thet I wun't deny
(For ain't she some related to you 'n' I?)
But there's a few small intrists here below
Outside the counter o' John Bull an' Co,
An' though they can't conceit how't should be so,
I guess the Lord druv down Creation's spiles
'Thout no *gret* helpin' from the British Isles,
An' could contrive to keep things pooty stiff
Ef they withdrawed from business in a miff;
I ha'n't no patience with sech swellin fellers ez
Think God can't forge 'thout them to blow the bellerses.[1]

It is a human luxury to have a grievance; but most foreign strictures had the added sting of being measurably fair, of being untactful rather than unjust. In a day of dizzying possibilities in farm, factory, and frontier, it was inevitable that the enterprising should be drawn into undertakings that were usually eager and unconsidered and often slipshod and shady. Business ethics were no higher then than now and collusion of business with politics no rarer. In the cities, and notably in New York, possessors of mushroom fortunes multiplied rapidly, bringing up vapid daughters like Halleck's "Fanny," who, in all the modern languages, was

Exceedingly well-versed; and had devoted
To their attainment, far more time than has,
By the best teachers, lately been allotted;
For she had taken lessons, twice a week,
For a full month in each; and she could speak

French and Italian, equally as well
As Chinese, Portuguese or German; and
What is still more surprising, she could spell
Most of our longest English words off-hand;
Was quite familiar in Low Dutch and Spanish
And thought of studying modern Greek and Danish.[2]

Her father, a man of newly affected silence that spoke "unutterable things," was established in a mortgaged house

[1] Lowell, "Mason and Slidell," lines 159–169.
[2] Halleck, op. cit. stanzas cxxi, cxxii.

filled with servants and "whatever is necessary for a 'genteel liver'" and buttressed with an unpaid-for coach and six.

At the same time the countryside was developing a native but not altogether admirable rural stock. The noble husbandmen of romantic dream appeared to Halleck, as he saw them in "Wyoming,"

> . . . good, honest, quiet men enough,
> And hospitable too — for ready pay;
> With manners like their roads, a little rough,
> And hands whose grasp is warm and welcoming, though tough.[1]

And at their worst Whittier looked back a half-century to 1818 to recall

> Shrill, querulous women, sour and sullen men,
> Untidy, loveless, old before their time,
> With scarce a human interest save their own
> Monotonous round of small economies,
> Or the poor scandal of the neighborhood;
> . . . .
> Church-goers, fearful of the unseen Powers,
> But grumbling over pulpit-tax and pew-rent,
> Saving, as shrewd economists, their souls
> And winter pork with the least possible outlay
> Of salt and sanctity; in daily life
> Showing as little actual comprehension
> Of Christian charity and love and duty,
> As if the Sermon on the Mount had been
> Outdated like a last year's almanac.[2]

Politics and political theory had long played their part in the thinking of intelligent Americans. Such a disturbing awareness of social shortcomings, a perennial growth that thrived lustily in this season of heightened national consciousness, supplied them a fresh common factor. A desire to express themselves imaginatively and improvingly impelled some of them to write and print. The isolated aspirant

---

[1] Halleck, "Wyoming," stanza iv.
[2] Whittier, Prelude to "Among the Hills," lines 72–76, 84–92.

was lost in the wilderness unless he joined some caravan; and the largest convoys could be found in Boston, New York, and Philadelphia.

In Philadelphia, for example, a good start had been made during and after the Revolution. Mathew Carey, writer and publisher, had set the stage, and Joseph Dennie was now to occupy it with him.[1] Carey, an indefatigable projector and performer, had joined forces with the anti-Federalists; avoided political controversy as editor of his *American Museum*[2] and entered it lustily as individual opponent of "Peter Porcupine" Cobbett; played peacemaker with his "Olive Branch, or Faults on both Sides, Federal and Democratic" at the end of the War of 1812; founded a long-lived publishing house; and was miscellaneously active in connection with many phases of writing, printing, and bookselling until his death in 1839. Up to 1823 or 1824 he was the obvious and desirable publisher to turn to in the United States. His firm's list included Mrs. Rowson, Noah Webster, Freneau, Irving, Cooper, Percival, Neal, and, later, Poe and Simms. As the reading public increased he did what he could to cope with the invading tide of English works by negotiating for advance copies of "every new work of popularity and particularly those of Miss Porter, Lord Byron, Miss Edgeworth, W. Scott, Leigh Hunt, Author of Waverley, Moore, Miss Burney, Mrs. Taylor, Lady Morgan, Dugald Stuart, etc., etc."[3] All told, he was a much bigger man than Joseph Dennie, whose Philadelphia residence he antedated and postdated and for whose opinions he had no sympathy; but he paved the way for this author of the imaginative "Farrago" series and the ethical "Lay Preacher" series, who was typical of his time and thus served for a while as the literary recruiting officer in Philadelphia.

---

[1] Accounts of these early publishers are Earl Bradsher's "Mathew Carey, Editor, Author and Publisher" (Columbia Press, 1912), and Milton Ellis's "Joseph Dennie and His Circle," Bulletin of the University of Texas, 1915.

[2] See pages 189–190.

[3] Bradsher, op. cit. p. 79.

Dennie was a Tory dilettante with a zest for talk like that of the Autocrat who was a hark-back of two generations later. He played his way through Harvard, nursing his temperament, and developing a persecution defense which he cherished throughout his life. He could not labor; to sell he was ashamed. He coquetted with the professions, had an affair with the law, and a scant flirtation with politics. In England, he felt, his peculiar gifts would have been appreciated. From time to time he vaguely threatened to leave America, finding to his repeated annoyance that his "attempt to be useful, by exhibiting truths in a plain dress to the common people," did not pay him as much as he felt that he deserved. For a while he served as personal assistant to John Adams's Secretary of State, Timothy Pickering. Here, according to his chief, "his insatiable appetite for knowledge, useful as well as ornamental," made him less effective than many a dull man could have been; and here, according to a journalistic and political enemy, he functioned as "a kind of literary Jackall paid out of the public Treasury." It was the same treasury from which Freneau had been paid for sentiments of the opposite sort. These sentiments of Dennie's in their extremest form were expressed in one of his rare letters to his parents: all his best friends were Englishmen; the Fourth of July, 1776, was a foul day; "True Americans" were "Picarooning pedlers," simpleton believers in republican government; and to a friend, Roger Vose, he confided that Jefferson was a victim of "miserable delusions," that the average congressman was filthy and stupid (with marked exception of the Connecticut members, who despised and avoided their colleagues), that the government was tottering, and that a return to monarchy was probable.

For a man of this temper literature was bound to be an American expression only in locality. To be American was to be un-English, which was to be vulgar. He was concerned at the prevalence of cisatlantic idioms of speech almost as much as at corresponding idioms of conduct. No wonder Thomas Moore commended him for "diffusing through his cultivated little circle that love of good literature and sound politics which he feels so zealously himself"; for Moore hated "the rabble to which they are opposed." No wonder that Dennie characterized his "Lay Preacher" sequence as "a series of essays, modelled after the designs of Addison and the harmless and playful levity of Oliver Goldsmith." No wonder that Washington Irving portrayed him with harmless and playful levity and with affectionate respect as Launcelot Langstaff;[1] and no wonder that the respectable conservatives of the day endorsed him for his devotion to polite literature and commended him for his insistence on the moral lesson, the instructive discourse, the familiar illustration of Biblical truth, respectfully distinguished from "the doctrines and discipline of the church . . . the citadel of christianity."

Dennie, in fact, was less of an agent than an instrument; not a productive instrument, but an indicator. He persisted for years in composing his little Addisonian commentaries, not merely the "Lay Preacher," but the "Farrago"; not only these, but the "American Lounger," "An Author's Evenings," "Colon and Spondee." They ran, in all, into the hundreds. Neglected at first, they were the main feature of the *Port Folio.* And the *Port Folio* reached a larger public and survived far longer (from eleven years before his death until fifteen years after) than any preceding magazine in America. In the first number the editor indulged in a sort of orchestral tuning up with an announcement of some sixty types of material on which he was to draw. It is a random list preparatory to Dennie's always random writing, but three themes emerge most clearly. One is political conservatism. "It must be understood, that the editor totally prohibits every thing *Jacobinical.*" Freneau and Barlow might do their worst, but the *Port Folio* would set itself steadfastly to "detections of Jacobinical forgery, falsehood and misrepresentation." A second was the natural attitude of respect

[1] Irving's use of Launcelot Langstaff in the "Crayon Miscellany" and also in the eighth "Salmagundi" paper is confirmed in Pierre Irving's "Life of Irving," Vol. I, pp. 183–185, as based on Dennie.

for the English model. The magazine was to include "economical essays, on the model of Count Rumford"; obituary articles "after the model in *The Gentleman's Magazine*"; humorous ballads "in the style of 'John Gilpin'"; "tender ballads in the manner of Dr. Percy's"; "mock odes in the manner of 'The Rolliad'"; "essays in the manner of Addison, Johnson or Goldsmith"; "Hudibrastic poetry"; "songs adapted to the taste of the Anacreontic group." The third note was the ethical: there would be "concise moral lessons" and "moral allegories, tales and romances."

Thus in Philadelphia, Dennie and his circle bore witness to the passage of the youthful country out from a period of exciting liberalism in politics and morals back to an interim in which the literary clan took refuge in politeness and elegance, divorced itself from the mob except for an occasional outburst of irritation, ignored the world of getting and spending but prepared the ground for the flowering of its finest specimen, Irving, and helped to develop a reading public which would one day relish something sturdier. The same sort of development was taking place in other cities.

Doings of this sort can be cited for these years in only one city farther to the south. A certain reticent aversion to public self-exposure led many a Southern gentleman to entrust his writing only to manuscript or to private circulation in print. Statesmanship was more to the taste of the region than authorship.[1] And these attitudes had more to do with the relative silence of the south-Atlantic states than the physical and economic conditions which one Southern historian has adduced as rendering "the production of a southern literature practically impossible" before 1825. But Baltimore was coming on. A theater was well established.

---

[1] For treatment of the Southern group here discussed see O. G. Sonneck's "Report on the Star Spangled Banner," T. O. Mabbott and F. L. Pleadwell's "Life and Works of Edward Coote Pinkney," Henry T. Tuckerman's "Life of John Pendleton Kennedy," and Victor Weybright's "Spangled Banner, the Story of Francis Scott Key."

Francis Scott Key had composed his excited lyric to the measure of the London Anacreontic Society song. John Neal had moved down from New England, and Jared Sparks, as Johns Hopkins was to do later. John P. Kennedy, debater, literary clubman, lawyer, joined with his partner, Peter Cruse, to put out from 1819 to 1821 the "Red Book," following the Salmagundists in the very year when the Croakers emerged and when Paulding tried to revive the earlier series. Kennedy was on the way to the writing of "Swallow Barn" (1832) and "Horse-Shoe Robinson" (1835) and to distinguished service of the state. Furthermore, one young naval midshipman, lawyer, editor, and professor of rhetoric and belles-lettres without pay, Edward Coote Pinkney, was showing not only the imitativeness that belonged to his youth but also unusual gifts, particularly in his early fragment, "Rodolph." It appeared in his single slender volume of poems in 1825 shortly before (in the way of his times) he was recruited as editor of a semiweekly, *The Marylander*, in a vain effort to stem the rising tide of Jacksonism, in behalf of the program of the second President Adams. Up to this moment Pinkney had revealed quite as much promise as Bryant, and much more fire. His premature death leaves open the doubt as to whether journalism would have submerged him; but during his lifetime he seems to have had almost as little as Poe of literary companionship in this most northern of Southern cities. Baltimore was the outstanding town to provide such fellowship then in the South. It was much more stimulating in New England and New York.

The local picture in Boston contains the same elements as in Philadelphia. There had been the same lethargy of spirit at the close of the war, the same revival of political fervors at the time of the Constitutional Convention. There was the same predilection among the respectable for a strongly centralized government and the same fear of anything smacking of democracy, a fear heightened by the dramatic episode of the rebellion led by Daniel Shays that swept through central Massachusetts in 1787. Shays, however, had his sympathizers, and democracy had supporters enough to keep discussion alive. In New England the "Hartford Wits" were still holding the center of the stage as the turn of the century came; Barlow was safely out of reach and for the moment inaudible; and "The Echo"[1] reverberated from the Connecticut coast to the Maine woods and from the Hudson River to the sea. Speaking for the whole region, "Peter Parley" reminiscently described the situation:

> We who are now familiar with democracy, can hardly comprehend the odium attached to it in the age to which I refer, especially in the minds of the sober people in our neighborhood. They not only regarded it as hostile to good government, but as associated with infidelity in religion, radicalism in government, and licentiousness in society. It was considered a sort of monster, born of Tom Paine, the French Revolution, foreign renegadoes, and the great Father of Evil. Mr. Jefferson, the founder of the party, had been in France, and was supposed by his political opponents to have adopted the atheism and libertinism of the revolutionists. His personal character and dangerous political proclivities, as I have said, were not then well understood. The greatest fear of him, at this time, was as to his moral, religious, and social influence. It was supposed that his worshippers could not be better than their idol, and it must be confessed that the democracy of New England in its beginning raked up and absorbed the chaff of society. It is due to the truth of history to state that men of blemished reputations, tipplers, persons of irregular tempers, odd people, those who were constitutionally upsetters, destructives, come outers, flocked spontaneously, as if by a kind of instinct, to the banners of democracy, about the period of Jefferson's first election, and constituted, for a considerable period afterward, the staple of the party. In due time and when they had increased in numbers, they gradually acquired respectable leaders.[2]

Intellectual life in Boston from 1793, the year of the opening of the theaters, was largely divided between the activities of the political conservatives, for whom Fisher Ames was the

---

[1] See page 172.

[2] Samuel G. Goodrich, "Recollections of a Life Time," Vol. I, pp. 117–120.

admired spokesman, and a romantico-literary group, who were ready hosts to Joseph Dennie when he came to town, subscribers to his *Port Folio*, and beginners of certain undertakings that were to last beyond the lifetimes and probably beyond the dreams of their founders.

In this community the voice of Fisher Ames[1] — "the Bible and Fisher Ames" wrote one enthusiast of the day — is significant, not only because it expressed contemporary sentiment but also because it so clearly was the voice of old Massachusetts Bay Colony projected into the present. Ames seems to have inherited his convictions from the theocratic rulers of the seventeenth century and to have maintained them without perceptible modification. He was as certain as ever John Cotton had been, of knowing the right. He was certain that his idea of right should be imposed on the state, and equally certain that he was of the elect through whom that right should be administered for the public weal. He might have cried his "Hear! hear!" to Cotton's "If the people govern, who shall be governed?" though he had a further answer in his fear of popular tyranny: "As to liberty, we are to have none — democracy will kindle its own hell, and consume in it."[2] Certain that Federalism was the only safeguard to American liberties, by which he meant (and acknowledged that he meant) American property, — and by American property he meant American proprietors, — he deprecated change or threat of change. Like the Puritans, he was the conservator of an ultimate truth. A political school, therefore, that could feel its way through political experience to improving systems and conditions was itself a mere system of muddling which lacked substantial basis because it could not justify itself in immobility on the grounds of unchanging moral law. What Virginia might venture, Massachusetts could not tolerate — not the Massachusetts

---

[1] The definitive edition of Ames is "The Works of Fisher Ames," edited by his son, Seth Ames, 1854. 2 vols. An excellent brief discussion is in Parrington's "Romantic Revolution," pp. 279–288.

[2] Quoted in Parrington's "Romantic Revolution," p. 281.

of Fisher Ames. To all of which the stout volumes of his treatises and letters bear witness for the few students who care to labor through them.

But what Ames was doing for respectability and sound sentiment, another more picturesque representative of the same social circle was busily undoing. By the irony of chance Robert Treat Paine christened his son with the name Thomas when christening day came in 1773. Young Paine[1] grew up somewhat erratically in and out of the Federalist fold. On graduation from Harvard, in 1792, he was ripe for revolutionary contagions and poetized as a Francophile on "The Nature and Progress of Liberty." This was at the age of nineteen. At twenty-two, in candidacy for his master of arts, he repudiated his youthful indiscretion with "The Invention of Letters," in the course of which he ridiculed the shoemaker, the hairdresser, the blacksmith, and the tailor as would-be legislators, and converted "Envy, that fiend, who hates the great and good," into a Jacobin. In this same year (1795) he published in the *Federal Orrery* a "Jacobiniad" in which he fell foul of a social club which horrified most of polite Boston because of the alleged immorality of its members, but which offended him because they represented the "gentility which is produced by ingrafting dollars upon village habits and low employments." He himself was a polite and finished *bon viveur*. Harvard, satisfied with him, in 1797 made him Phi Beta Kappa poet; and in response he wrote on "The Ruling Passion" — for poetry and poetry-writing. In the meantime, tainted by the unhappy connotation of a name which was now Jacobinical and atheistical and democratically disreputable, he became Robert Treat Paine, Jr., as befitted a young gentleman within the pale of ancient gentilities.

But there was an unfortunate streak in young Paine of

---

[1] Brief accounts of Robert Treat Paine, Jr., are in Justin Winsor's "Memorial History of Boston," Vol. III, p. 625, and H. M. Ellis and E. Pendleton's "Philenia: the Life and Works of Sarah Wentworth Morton," pp. 47–51. "The Works in Verse and Prose," of the late Robert Treat Paine, Esq., with notes, were published by J. Belcher, Boston, 1812.

Harvard, whether christened Thomas or redubbed Robert Treat, Jr., a side that respectable Boston could not forgive nor the Paine family condone. He was capable of declaring, when the colonial ordinance of 1750 against theaters was repealed the year after he graduated from college, that "the Vandal spirit of Puritanism" was overthrown in Boston. He was too convivial, too much given to genteel gaming. He adopted the theater as his especial charge; became master of ceremonies at the Federal Street playhouse; and when he married an actor's daughter and devoted himself to dramatic criticism, neither his name nor his politics nor the name of the theater could atone for the fact that he had stepped outside the pale, never to be readmitted. He was disinherited; and when he died, a little later, his widow and children turned not to the Paine family but to an actor's benefit for aid in their distress.

Possibly "Philenia," whose actual name was Mrs. Sarah Wentworth Morton,[1] was one of the patronesses of this performance. Her husband, the Honorable Perez, had behaved much more scandalously than Paine ever did; but, not having contracted a misalliance or estranged his long-suffering wife, he eventually brazened his way into the speakership of the Massachusetts House and the Attorney General's office. By the time Paine had died Mrs. Morton's slender performance was over except for the pallid collection called "My Mind and its Thoughts." She too had made her excursion into the land of romance with "Ouabi, or the Virtues of Nature" and had registered her return in "Beacon Hill" and "The Virtues of Society." These were all in the 1790's. In the next decade, matured, respected, a younger contemporary of the still active Mercy Warren and Abigail Adams, she served a useful end as endorser and contributor to the *Monthly Anthology*, which the Anthology Club were to maintain from 1801 to 1811 and which was to be continued in the more substantial *North American Review* after 1815. The literary clan was

[1] The definitive word on Mrs. Morton is in H. M. Ellis and E. Pendleton's "Philenia," 1931.

finding an outlet for its energies — first in conversation, then in print, and finally in reading.

There were active minds about. Those just mentioned, and the younger Nathaniel Ames, a name inseparably associated with the family almanacs;[1] and Jedediah Morse, geographer and father of Samuel the painter and inventor; and Jeremy Belknap, historian; and, in a younger group, the anthologists William Emerson and Abiel Holmes, fathers of Ralph Waldo and Oliver Wendell; and a Quincy and a Kirkland and a Buckminster and a Tudor, established families secure in the established order, ready and eager to turn to art and literature in the fashion of people on their social level. So they met and dined and talked and sifted out material for their publication, which they made theirs after one Phineas Adams had carried it on through the first perilous period. They went further, in the establishment of a library, founding the still flourishing Athenaeum with an Emerson and a Kirkland among the five trustees.[2] This proved to be a benevolently assimilative organization. In 1807 it purchased the scientific apparatus of the "Society for Cultivating Philosophical Knowledge." Ten years later the American Academy of Arts and Sciences deposited their library with the Athenaeum. And later something called the Theological Library, and the books belonging to King's Chapel, the Boston Medical Society, and the Massachusetts Scientific Association all came to this haven. More important still was the development that installed in its quarters the first permanent gallery and art collection known to New England. The Athenaeum was supported by a membership which had joined in condemning the divagations of young Paine and condoning those of Perez Morton; and the Boston democracy resented its exclusiveness. When the shadow of Andrew Jackson was gathering over the country, the *Boston News Letter and City Record* was inquiring:

---

[1] See pages 95, 96.

[2] The authoritative record of the early Athenaeum is Josiah Quincy's "History of the Boston Athenaeum," 1851.

> What literary advantages have the mass of our citizens derived from the Athenaeum? Who gets a peep within its lofty walls without a ten-dollar bill? [the annual fee] And what genius owes its expansion to the liberal facilities of the Boston Athenaeum? . . . Things are becoming quite royal in our venerable old city.[1]

These were fair questions but idle ones. Boston citizenry in the mass was challenged to envy what it did not really want. Things were not then becoming royal in the city. Quite otherwise; in the Athenaeum a certain ancestral exclusiveness was perpetuating itself in the midst of a rising democracy. With the possible exception of R. W. Emerson's, no genius had owed expansion to the enjoyment of its privileges; and at the time of the questioning Emerson's was a full decade from first fruitage. Yet among the accumulating resources in its alcoves and gallery a friendly acquaintance with literature was being built into experience; and ultimately it became one of the resorts where Hawthorne and Holmes, Hillard and Whipple, Bancroft, Prescott, Parkman, Palfrey, were among the readers whose talents expanded there. Seeds of liberalism were being sown in this old but undepleted soil.

Developments in New York City were comparable, but distinguished by the fact that New York was already becoming the metropolis of the country. It had no such unbroken tradition as the other leading cities, and as the leading port it harbored more passing strangers and adopted more aliens. It was on the way toward the prophecy made by Fenimore Cooper in one of his more expansive moments: "Nature herself has intended the island of Manhattan for the site of one of the greatest commercial towns of the world." It was a steadily increasing aggregate of people with steadily multiplying activities; and its strength was to be derived from its new recruits. It had its Van Cortlandts and Van Winkles, its Brinkerhoffs and Stuyvesants, but they figured slightly in the activities of the day. The merchant prince

---

[1] February 25, 1826; page 116.

was a newcomer, John Jacob Astor. He patronized two authors: one the son of immigrant parents, Irving; the other, Halleck, a temporary sojourner from Connecticut. Cooper was to come down to the city from the frontier of middle New York; Bryant, from the Berkshires of Massachusetts; and from other points Coleman, the journalist, S. F. B. Morse, the artist-inventor, John Howard Payne, the actor-playwright, Edwin Forrest, the tragedian. A consequence was that New York had fewer inhibitions than the other cities, a less assertive personality to defend or vindicate. The theater had a solider footing here than elsewhere in the country; playhouses were destined to multiply more rapidly; playgoers and non-playgoers to let each other divert themselves without reproach. As the town passed Philadelphia in size and forged into a permanent lead, it began its long progress toward becoming the pre-eminent publishing center in America and, through its publications, an index not to local but to national tastes.

Small as the city was in comparison with modern population figures (it grew from 33,000 in 1790 to 200,000 in 1830), it had no such recognizable communal convictions as the more provincial centers. Getting and spending were its dominant interests. Business usurped the stage, earlier occupied by religion and politics, and busyness became a cardinal virtue. Literature tended, therefore, to be not identifiable with the life of the community but separable from it, a quite external adornment or an avenue of escape. There was for a while a deliberate adoption of a "return to normalcy" program. New York's literary expression re-echoed in America the days and ways of Addisonian London — genteel conviviality, light talk, light satire, light essays.

In the 1790's, to glance backward for a moment, Brockden Brown had found his equivalent for the London coffeehouse group in the Friendly Club,[1] a little circle in which perhaps

[1] See "Early Literary Clubs in New York City," by Eleanor B. Scott, in *American Literature*, Vol. V, pp. 1–16; and "Author about Town," in "James Fenimore Cooper" (H. W. Boynton), Book II, Chap. II.

the names of Elihu Hubbard Smith, Noah Webster, and William Dunlap are still recognizable. Eight of Brown's friends, with the generosity of people with ideas for others to carry out, urged him to found a magazine. During the decade New York had seen eleven magazines founded, and had seen them all cave in; but Brown nevertheless made his attempt in 1799, tried to be literary in content, failed to get support either from subscribers or from contributors, and compounded with fate by doing what the little magazine-buying public wanted and purveying instruction for the rest of his editorial career. Brown was not gay enough to succeed at anything else; but on toward the end of the next decade the two Irvings, Washington and William, with James K. Paulding, thrived sensationally with their year of "Salmagundi" papers. Because they so patently did not wish to "instruct the young, reform the old, correct the town and castigate the age," which they announced as their purpose, they did so well in the year the whim lasted that their publisher battened on their cleverness as the town snapped up their irregular succession of numbers. The papers were good. The prose was easy, the verse neat, the impertinence as well as the pertinence of their comments on the current manners and fashions altogether effective. They too were clubbed together, The Nine Worthies, The Lads of Kilkenny, or whatever. Possibly they were in no other wise so clever as in stopping before their vogue waned; possibly they would not have been able to "keep it up"; Gotham is always quick to doubt the depth of any fresh springs of humor. This one was reopened a year later with the burlesque "Knickerbocker History of New York," the anonymous Irving playing so blithely with the Dutch governors and their surrounding dignitaries as to show himself capable, in Sydney Smith's *mot*, of speaking disrespectfully of the equator. The generation of the patroons had nothing but ancestral dignity to fall back on; a new set of Federalist leaders — Hamilton, Jay, King, Morris — were themselves out of the running. A Gulian Verplanck, as "Abimelech Coody," could write as frivolously of his fellow Federalists as of the Democrats, and even, in the opinion of the court, indulge in two hundred dollars' worth of riotous defense of free speech at a Columbia College commencement.[1] There were intense feelings among the New Yorkers, though hardly of Bostonian or Philadelphian intensity, and among the penmen none who mixed so much acid with their ink as young Paine or Joseph Dennie did.

For a while it seemed as if James K. Paulding might be turning into a successor as leader of the literary conservatives. In 1812, just as Paine and Dennie had both died, he contributed the first of a series of five volumes, scattered over fifteen years, to the long and querulous interchange of discourtesies between the United States and England.[2] Paulding was a good deal of a dabbler, who tried his hand unimpressively at various kinds of writing: at long poetical narrative in "The Backwoodsman," at a sequel to the first "Salmagundi" series, a parody of Scott, several novels, and a variety of approaches to the Anglo-American wrangle. The first of these was imitative, after the manner of Hopkinson's "Pretty Story" and Belknap's "Foresters,"[3] Paulding's effort being entitled "The Diverting History of John Bull and Brother Jonathan." The next, "The United States and England" (1815), was a sober argument; the third, "Letters from the South," in description of one section of the country, recurrently alluded to the controversy; the fourth, "A Sketch of Old England," was one of the worst of its kind, a miscellaneous diatribe on a country which Paulding had not visited; the last, "John Bull in America, or the New Munchausen," returned to the bland tone of the first. The whole series is significant only because it belongs to a particularly vigorous outcropping of this endless international family

[1] Dixon R. Fox, "The Decline of Aristocracy in the Politics of New York," pp. 160–165.

[2] See "The English Traveler in America, 1785–1835," by Jane L. Mesick; "As Others See Us," by John Graham Brooks; "British Criticisms of American Writings, 1815–1833," by W. B. Cairns; and "The American in England, 1776–1826," by R. E. Spiller.

[3] See pages 139, 140.

quarrel. Occasional generations rise above it, but in the period of American national adolescence almost no one succeeded in doing so. Bryant had his little fling in "O Mother of a Mighty Race"; Cooper was long and deeply involved;[1] Irving did not escape the subject, though he escaped the universal rancor. Paulding was chiefly concerned with it for years, and so impressed the powers at Washington that his future was provided for in a succession of appointments which ended with the Secretaryship of the Navy. Little was lost to literature when politics enmeshed him, for neither he nor any of his townsmen was more than incidentally interested in literature.

So there were none who started lasting publications like the *Monthly Anthology* and the *Port Folio*. The only New York periodicals that survived these years were New York's offering to a national market for religious magazines, so called, but actually informational magazines under sectarian auspices which were valuable in building up mailing lists. "The Knickerbocker School" of writers ostensibly dates from the "History" of 1809, but actually did not come into existence until the 1830's, when Irving returned with European prestige and the magazine of this name was established. Probably the most permanently significant personality of the time for New York in literary ways was William Coleman, editor of the *Evening Post*. He was a last-ditch supporter of the old-guard conservative in politics, but he was a ready ally of youthful talent, recognized John Howard Payne for the prodigy he was, opened his pages to the "Croakers" on purely literary grounds, and started Bryant on his journalistic career. It was the most distinguished literary event of a rather drab decade, though it was no great feat, when Coleman opened his columns to Fitz-Greene Halleck and Joseph Rodman Drake.

Halleck (1790–1867) is a perfect illustration of what could happen in his lifetime to a man who never passed beyond the

---

[1] See pages 255–257.

Salmagundi stage.[1] When he came to town from a Connecticut village at the age of twenty-one, he fell in with the literary virtuosos and cemented a friendship with Drake on his companion's jejune exclamation that "it would be heaven to lounge upon the rainbow and read Tom Campbell." He wrote verses and had them published: poems with such observations as

> When the bright star of peace from our country was clouded,
> Hope fondly presaged it would soon reappear,[2]

and

> The heart hath sorrow of its own, and griefs it veils from all,
> And tears that hide them from the world, in solitude, will fall.[3]

Confidential secretary of an unsuccessful and discredited business man and then protégé of a captain of finance, he was uncomfortably aware of the prosaic drive of American life and disposed to lament the wane of romance, a sentiment to which he somewhat feebly reverted throughout his career up to his valedictory "Young America."

Though his friendship with Drake thrived in their common liking for romantic poetry, the joint work for which they are known is "The Croaker Papers," a series of thirty-five contemporary satires in verse which appeared in the *National Advocate* and the New York *Evening Post* between March and July, 1819. These were smart and timely, spiced by the mystery of their authorship, — for they were signed "Croaker" and "Croaker, Jr.," — and they became more and more interesting because of the uncertainty as to the date and victim of each new one. The more general in theme had the same underlying good sense that belonged to the "Salmagundi" of a decade earlier; and in their simple

---

[1] Halleck has had adequate treatment in two studies: James G. Wilson's "Life and Letters of Fitz-Greene Halleck," 1869; and Nelson F. Adkins's "Fitz-Greene Halleck, an Early Knickerbocker Wit and Poet," 1930. "The Poetical Writings of Fitz-Greene Halleck" were edited by Wilson in 1869.

[2] Quoted from Wilson's "Life," in Adkins's "Fitz-Greene Halleck," p. 37.

[3] Adkins, op. cit. p. 40. Later incorporated in "Young America."

and often brutal directness they must have offered then, as they do now, a relief from the fashionable echoes of secondary English poets. To those who could not read anything American without looking for an English analogy, there was ground for comparison with Dr. John Wolcot, the famous "Peter Pindar," or, better still, with James and Horatio Smith, authors of "Horace in London" and, later, of the gay "Rejected Addresses."

At the end of this same year Halleck's "Fanny" appeared anonymously. It was a versified tale of the rise and fall in New York society of Fanny and her newly rich and quickly impoverished father. The likeness to "The Croaker Papers" as well as to Byron's "Beppo" was immediately cited by the critics. It was written, as a letter from Halleck reveals, to while away a flight to the suburbs during a yellow-fever epidemic; it was "spun out" to a volume of fifty pages at the urgency of a bookseller who "stated to me that I was the only writer in America, Irving excepted, whose works he would risk publishing." This opinion was founded, of course, on the popularity of "The Croakers." "Fanny" was equally successful and stirred up numerous imitators, as ebullitions of this sort always do.

In 1820 Drake died at the age of twenty-five, leaving as his literary bequest the inspiration for Halleck's memorial verses

> Green be the turf above thee,
> Friend of my better days!

his share in "The Croaker Papers," "The Culprit Fay," and certain shorter and less pretentious poems which show far more promise than this overrated attempt. The "Fay," according to a letter by Halleck, was a three-day production of 1816, written to demonstrate that the Hudson River scenery could be turned to literary account. Drake deplored that it had been

> left to minstrels of a foreign strand
> To sing the beauteous scenes of nature's loveliest land,[1]

[1] Drake, "Poems" (1847), p. 42.

the song being Campbell's "Gertrude of Wyoming"; and he urged Halleck to

> let vivid fancy soar,
> Look with creative eye on Nature's face,
> Bid airy sprites in wild Niagara roar,
> And view in every field a fairy race.[1]

Yet no line in "The Culprit Fay" is any more explicitly true of the Hudson region than of the Rhine country or the Norwegian fiords. It reads like pure fantasy hurriedly and carelessly written by an inexperienced hand. Nevertheless, when it was published it was extravagantly praised, Halleck adding his voice to the chorus with, "It is certainly the best thing of the kind in the English language, and is more strikingly original than I had supposed it was possible for a modern poem to be."[2] It was reserved for Poe, writing for the *Southern Literary Messenger* in 1834, to set down the genuinely critical estimate of it that was later reprinted in "The Literati" and that fairly condemns Drake as a culprit poet.

Halleck's surprise at originality in any modern poet marked the vital difference between Drake and himself. But though Drake tried for new effects, his best efforts were but strainings at the leash of eighteenth-century convention. His idea was apparently to escape from the drawing-room into the open, but in the open to weave, as it were, Gobelin tapestries for drawing-room use. He saw no gleam of essential poetry in democracy or in the crowded town, though in his vague craving for something better than Georgian iterations he showed that the revival of individualism was at work in him.

As fate would have it, the more independent of the pair was taken off before his prime, and Halleck, the survivor, settled down into complacent Knickerbockerism. People liked "Fanny"; so he wrote a supplementary fifty stanzas for a new edition in 1821. People had applauded "The Croakers"; so he returned to the Croaker vein in casual

---

[1] Drake, op. cit. p. 45.

[2] Wilson, "The Life and Letters of Fitz-Greene Halleck," p. 183.

effusions of 1821 and thereafter. While abroad in 1822 he fell on the suggestion for "Alnwick Castle" and wrote this half-sentimental, half-sophisticated poem. In 1823 he had a moment of fine fury, of which "Marco Bozzaris" was the record, "my *chef d'oeuvre,* the keystone of the arch of my renown, if renown it be."[1] He wrote his sister of the number of reprints, translations, quotations, recitations, culminating with the Philadelphia theft of it from an Edinburgh thief and the controversy over its original authorship. But all the applause failed to rouse him to any real productivity. Publishers besieged him for new manuscript; but editions trickled along of "The Croakers" and "Fanny" and "Alnwick Castle," and "Fanny" again, and "The Croakers" once more. His fellow authors challenged him to fulfill his early promise; at public dinners he sat at the head table, where the toastmasters acknowledged his presence; he dined out endlessly; but he is remembered for his anecdotes and his quotations rather than for anything original. And when, in 1848, his employer-patron died, leaving him a tiny annuity, he packed up and went back to Guilford, Connecticut, and the seclusion from which he had emerged. In the sixteen years of security and intellectual indolence that preceded his retreat, when every hand was poised to applaud Halleck, Edgar Allan Poe was never far from the verge of penury and starvation. For thirty years Halleck was only the faint echo of a faint promise. The promise was made in 1819, the year of "The Croakers" and "Fanny." "Thanatopsis" had appeared in 1817 in Boston. "The Sketch Book" was published in book form in that year in London. Cooper's "Precaution" was to appear in 1820. But Bryant had not yet come down to the city; Irving was abroad and there to remain for another dozen years; Cooper, the only one of the three in the neighborhood, did not know what fate had in store for him. These three were to lend their reputations to New York City, but they derived little from it. It was to be

[1] Quoted in Wilson's "Life," pp. 293–294.

a residence place for them and a working place, but it was not a cultural rallying center for them.

It was, in fact, irresistibly a commercial center and typical of the country from that time to the present. The leadership of the church-statesman had long passed, and with it the thought of such a man as the admirable American. The leadership of the philanthropic philosopher-statesman was passing; and, by one of the nice ironies with which history enlivens its course, the machinery of government was taken out of the hands of the champions of property and privilege just when they had piled up such big fortunes that they now had the means to persuade and control the democratic machine. "We do possess," so wrote John Adams in 1808, "one material which actually constitutes an aristocracy that governs the nation. That material is wealth. Talents, birth, virtues, services, sacrifices, are of little consideration with us."[1] It was in these years that two American formulas were about to take shape: the formula for the President of the United States, who had progressed "from the log cabin to the White House," and the formula for the captain of finance, who had been born of "poor but honest" parents. The military hero could still be cited, as Andrew Jackson was; but the popular ideal was the builder of a great fortune. The ideal of democracy was to start with equal opportunity but to achieve a maximum of property, privilege, and power. And the most popular American author of coming years paid homage to the most picturesque of the self-made men, in the tribute of Washington Irving to John Jacob Astor.[2]

Astor began, according to Irving, "on the narrowest scale"; but he was endowed with an imposing array of characteristics which included not only industry, economy, integrity, and "an aspiring spirit that always looked upward" but also "a sagacity quick to grasp and convert every circumstance to its advantage," and no end of self-confidence. Going into the Western fur business, he found the field

---

[1] John Adams, "Works" (edited by C. F. Adams), Vol. VI, p. 530.

[2] Irving's "Astoria," 1836.

occupied by a powerful and well-intrenched company. To cope with this he needed strong backing; so he offered, "if aided and protected by government, to turn the whole of that trade into American channels." He got the promise of this aid and secured the charter for a company with a million dollars of capital. The capital was his and so was the organization; "for, though he had a board of directors, they were merely nominal. . . . He preferred . . . the imposing and formidable aspect of a corporation."

When Irving had told the details of this story, he saw in the fashion of his day the need for justifying, if not sanctifying, a man of Astor's type. The age had supplied a formula that was to serve for generations in the United States: such a fortune builder deserved the gratitude of his less predatory fellow countrymen because he and his like "by their great commercial enterprises have enriched nations, peopled wildernesses, and extended the bounds of empire." Mr. Astor had adopted the formula himself, and Irving recited it with abundance of italics: "*Our enterprise is grand and deserves success, and I hope in God it will meet it.* If my object was merely gain of money, I should say, think whether it is best to save what we can, and abandon the place; *but the very idea is like a dagger in my heart.*" The project had its ups and downs both under Providence and under the government at Washington; but in the end "the venerable projector . . . had the satisfaction of knowing, ere his eyes closed upon the world, that the flag of his country again waved over *Astoria.*"[1]

A portrait depends as much upon the painter as upon the subject. This was Irving's in the 1830's. Here is a set of snapshots by James Truslow Adams in the 1930's. The subject is the same, but the verdict of history gives him a different aspect:

Although we usually hear much more of the Massachusetts ships than others, the greatest fortunes were built by men like Astor of

[1] See, for quotations, "Astoria" (Knickerbocker Edition), Vol. I, pp. 24, 26, 27, 40; Vol. II, pp. 255, 358.

New York and Girard of Philadelphia, who in the first decade of the century became America's first millionaires. Money was coming to count for more in American life and to spell power. . . . Astor was czar in the Far Northwest fur trade, where his power was greater than that of the Federal government.

Astor, in New York, what with his fur trading, his city real estate, and deals of one sort and another, was setting the pace.

Astor had been a foreign immigrant, scarcely able to read and write, yet there he was, rich as Croesus, and dictating to the government.

When the first Astor died in 1848, the $20,000,000 fortune left by him was a milestone in American financial and social history.[1]

In his day he could commandeer what he wanted — a dummy board of directors, "the imposing and formidable aspect of a corporation," government endorsement; or, when he wanted to be written up, the pen of the most popular writer in the land. And by this writer he was canonized as a figure to revere in the religion of Mammon, whose capital city was New York.

Book List

PROVINCIAL INDEPENDENCE

General References

Adams, James T. The Epic of America. 1931.
Adams, James T. New England in the Republic. 1926.
Brooks, John Graham. As Others See Us. 1908.
Cairns, W. B. British Criticisms of American Writings, 1815–1833. 1922.
Gafford, Lucile. A History of the St. Charles Theater in New Orleans, 1835–1843. 1931.
Goodrich, Samuel G. Recollections of a Life Time. 1856.
Irving, Washington. Astoria. 1836.
Irving, Washington. The Crayon Miscellany. 1835.
Irving, Washington. Salmagundi Papers No. VIII.
Ludlow, Noah M. Dramatic Life as I Found It. 1880.
Mathews, Mitford M. The Beginnings of American English. 1931.

---

[1] James Truslow Adams, "The Epic of America," pp. 132, 178, 185, 224, 315. By permission of The Macmillan Company, publishers.

MESICK, JANE L. The English Traveler in America. 1922.
MOTT, FRANK L. A History of American Magazines, 1741–1850. 1930.
MOWAT, R. B. Americans in England, 1935.
SPILLER, ROBERT E. The American in England, 1776–1826. 1926.
SPILLER, ROBERT E. "The Verdict of Sydney Smith," *American Literature*, Vol. I, pp. 3–13.

POST-REVOLUTION DRAMA AND FICTION

Drama

[*Biography and Criticism*]

BERNARD, JOHN. Retrospections of the Stage (2 vols.), edited by Mrs. W. B. Bernard. Reprinted, with additions, as "Retrospections of America, 1797–1811," with introduction by Lawrence Hutton and Brander Matthews. 1887.
BIRD, ROBERT MONTGOMERY. Life and Dramatic Works, edited by Clement E. Foust. 1919.
BROWN, HERBERT R. "Sensibility in Eighteenth-Century American Drama," *American Literature*, Vol. IV, pp. 47–60.
COAD, ORAL S. William Dunlap; a Study of His Life and Works and of His Place in Contemporary Culture. 1917.
COLBY, ELBRIDGE. Early American Comedy. Bulletin of New York Public Library, July, 1919.
CRAWFORD, MARY C. The Romance of the American Theatre. 1913.
DUNLAP, WILLIAM. History of the American Theatre. 2 vols. 1832.
FORD, PAUL L. "Washington and the Theatre." Dunlap Society Publications, second series, Vol. VIII. 1889.
GAFFORD, LUCILE. "The Boston Stage and the War of 1812," *New England Quarterly*, Vol. VII, pp. 327–335.
HORNBLOW, ARTHUR. A History of the Theater in America, Vol. I, Chaps. VIII–XIII. 1919.
MABBOTT, THOMAS O. "Richard Penn Smith's Tragedy of *Caius Marius*," *American Literature*, Vol. II, pp. 141–156.
MCCULLOUGH, B. W. The Life and Writings of Richard Penn Smith, with a reprint of his play "The Deformed." 1917.
MOSES, MONTROSE J. The American Dramatist. 1911.
MOSES, MONTROSE J. "American Plays of Our Forefathers," *North American Review*, Vol. CCXV, pp. 790–804.
MUSSER, PAUL H. James Nelson Barker, 1784–1858, with reprint of his comedy "Tears and Smiles." 1929.
ODELL, G. C. D. Annals of the New York Stage, Vol. II. 1927.
QUINN, ARTHUR H. "Dramatic Works of Robert Montgomery Bird," *Nation*, August 3, 1916.
QUINN, ARTHUR H. "The Early Drama." Cambridge History of American Literature, Vol. I, pp. 215–232.
QUINN, ARTHUR H. A History of the American Drama from the Beginning to the Civil War. 1923.
WINTER, WILLIAM. The Wallet of Time, Containing Personal, Biographical, and Critical Reminiscences of the American Theatre. 2 vols. 1913.

[*Anthologies*]

MOSES, MONTROSE J. Representative Plays by American Dramatists. 3 vols. 1918–1925.

QUINN, ARTHUR H. Representative American Plays (3d ed.). 1925.

[*Bibliography*]

ADAMS, WILLIAM DAVENPORT. A Dictionary of the Drama. 1904.

HILL, FRANK P. American Plays Printed 1714–1830. 1934.

QUINN, ARTHUR H. "Early Drama." Cambridge History of American Literature, Vol. I, pp. 490–507.

WEGELIN, OSCAR. "Early American Plays, 1714–1830; being a compilation of the titles of plays by American authors published and performed in America previous to 1830." Publication of the Dunlap Society, old series, No. XXVI, pp. 11–113; new series, Vol. X.

Fiction

[*Biography and Criticism*]

BOLTON, CHARLES K. The Elizabeth Whitman Mystery at the Old Bell Tavern in Danvers, a Study of "Eliza Wharton." 1912.

CLARK, DAVID LEE. Charles Brockden Brown: a Critical Biography. 1923.

ELLIS, MILTON. "The Author of the First American Novel," *American Literature*, Vol. IV, pp. 359–368.

ELLIS, MILTON, and PENDLETON, EMILY. Philenia; the Life and Works of Sarah Wentworth Morton, 1759–1846. 1931.

ERSKINE, JOHN. Leading American Novelists. 1910.

FIELD, VENA B. "Constantia: a Study of the Life and Works of Judith Sargent Murray, 1751–1820." University of Maine Studies, No. XXXIII. 1931.

LOSHE, LILLIE D. The Early American Novel. 1907. New ed. 1930.

MCDOWELL, TREMAINE. "The First American Novel," *American Review*, Vol. II, pp. 73–81.

MCDOWELL, TREMAINE. "Last Words of a Sentimental Heroine," *American Literature*, Vol. IV, pp. 174–177.

PRESCOTT, F. C. "Wieland and Frankenstein," *American Literature*, Vol. II, pp. 172–173.

SHURTER, ROBERT L. "Mrs. Hannah Webster and the Early American Novel," *American Literature*, Vol. IV, pp. 306–308.

SINGER, GODFREY F. The Epistolary Novel, Its Origin, Development and Residuary Influence. 1933.

VAN DOREN, CARL. The American Novel. 1921.

VAN DOREN, CARL. "Minor Tales of Charles Brockden Brown, 1798–1800," *Nation*, January 14, 1915.

[*Bibliography*]

LOSHE, LILLIE D. The Early American Novel, pp. 106–124. 1907. New ed. 1930.

VAIL, R. W. G. "Susannah Haswell Rowson, the Author of Charlotte Temple: a Bibliographical Study." Proceedings of the American Antiquarian Society, Vol. XLII, pp. 47–160. 1933.

VAN DOREN, CARL. The American Novel, pp. 272–274. 1921.

WEGELIN, OSCAR. Early American Fiction, 1774–1830 (3d ed.). 1929.

[*Available Editions*]

BRACKENRIDGE, HUGH HENRY. Modern Chivalry. Rogues' Bookshelf. Edited by Ernest Brennecke. 1926,

BROWN, CHARLES BROCKDEN. Edgar Huntly, or Memoirs of a Sleepwalker, edited by David L. Clark. 1928.

BROWN, CHARLES BROCKDEN. Wieland, or The Transformation, edited, with introduction, by Fred L. Pattee. American Authors Series. 1926.

ROWSON, SUSANNA (HASWELL). Charlotte Temple: a Tale of Truth . . . reprinted from the rare first American edition. Introduction, bibliography, etc. by Francis W. Halsey. 1905.

1800–1820 — AN INTERIM

Philadelphia

BRADSHER, EARL L. Mathew Carey, Editor, Author and Publisher. 1912.

ELLIS, MILTON. Joseph Dennie and His Circle. 1915.

ROWE, KENNETH W. Mathew Carey, a Study in American Economic Development. 1933.

The American Museum, 1787–1792.

The Port Folio, 1801–1827.

Baltimore

GILMER, GERTRUDE. "Maryland Magazines: 1793–1861," *Maryland Historical Magazine*, Vol. XXIX, pp. 120–131.

MABBOTT, THOMAS O., and PLEADWELL, F. L. The Life and Works of Edward Coote Pinkney. 1926.

SONNECK, OSCAR G. A Report on the Star-Spangled Banner. 1909.

TUCKERMAN, HENRY T. The Life of John Pendleton Kennedy. 1871.

The Marylander, 1827–1828.

The Red Book, 1819–1821.

Boston

AMES, FISHER. Works, edited by Seth Ames. 2 vols. 1854.

ELLIS, H. M. Joseph Dennie and His Circle. 1915.

PAINE, ROBERT TREAT, Jr. Works in Verse and Prose. 1812.

PARRINGTON, VERNON L. The Romantic Revolution, pp. 279–288. 1927.

QUINCY, JOSIAH. The History of the Boston Athenaeum. 1851.

WINSOR, JUSTIN. Memorial History of Boston, Vol. III. 1880–1881.

The Federal Orrery, 1794–(?).

The Monthly Anthology, 1803–1811.

The North American Review, 1815– .

New York

BOYNTON, HENRY W. James Fenimore Cooper, "Author about Town," pp. 106–125. 1931.

COOPER, JAMES FENIMORE. Home as Found. 1838.

COOPER, JAMES FENIMORE. Notions of the Americans Picked Up by a Traveling Bachelor. 1828.

FOX, DIXON R. The Decline of Aristocracy in the Politics of New York, pp. 160–165. 1919.

NEVINS, ALLAN. The Evening Post. 1922.

SCOTT, ELEANOR B. "Early Literary Clubs in New York City," *American Literature*, Vol. V, pp. 3–16.

FITZ-GREENE HALLECK. Works appeared as follows: Fanny, 1819; Alnwick Castle, with Other Poems, 1827; Fanny and Other Poems, 1839; Young America, a Poem, 1865; Lines to the Recorder, 1866.

[*Available Editions*]

The Poetical Works of Fitz-Greene Halleck (last ed.). 1859.

Poetical Writings of Fitz-Greene Halleck, with Extracts from Those of Joseph Rodman Drake, edited by J. G. Wilson. 1869, 1885. (These editions include the "Croaker Papers.")

[*Biography and Criticism*]

The standard life is "The Life and Letters of Fitz-Greene Halleck," by J. G. Wilson. 1869.

ADKINS, NELSON F. Fitz-Greene Halleck, an Early Knickerbocker Wit and Poet. 1930.

BRYANT, WILLIAM CULLEN. Some Notices on the Life and Writings of Fitz-Greene Halleck. 1869.

DENNETT, J. R. "The Knickerbocker School," *Nation*, December 6, 1867.

DUYCKINCK, E. A. "Fitz-Greene Halleck," *Putnam's*, February, 1868.

LEONARD, W. E. "Bryant and the Minor Poets." Cambridge History of American Literature, Vol. I, Book II.

POE, EDGAR ALLAN. "Fitz-Greene Halleck." Works, Vol. VIII.

TUCKERMAN, HENRY T. "Reminiscences of Fitz-Greene Halleck," *Lippincott's*, February, 1886.

WILSON, JAMES Y. Bryant and His Friends. 1886.

JOSEPH RODMAN DRAKE. Poems by Croaker, Croaker and Co., and Croaker, Jr. First printed in the New York *Evening Post*. 1819. Reprinted as a pamphlet. 1819. The Culprit Fay and Other Poems. 1835. The American Flag. 1861.

[*Available Edition*]

The Culprit Fay, and Other Poems by Joseph Rodman Drake. Edited for the Grolier Club. 1923.

[*Biography and Criticism*]

CORNING, A. ELWOOD. "Joseph Rodman Drake," *Bookman*, Vol. XLI, pp. 574–576.

HOWE, M. A. DEWOLFE. American Bookmen. 1898.

PALTSITS, VICTOR H. Bibliography of the Writings of Joseph Rodman Drake. Bronx Society of Arts and Sciences, Vol. I, Part IV. 1919.

POE, EDGAR ALLAN. "Fancy and Imagination." Complete Works, Vol. VII. 1902.

WELLS, JAMES LEE. Joseph Rodman Drake. 1904.

WILSON, JAMES G. Bryant and His Friends. 1886.
WILSON, JAMES G. "Joseph Rodman Drake," *Harper's*, June, 1874.
Papers and Proceedings of the Drake Memorial Celebration. 1919.

[*Anthologies*]

BOYNTON, PERCY H. American Poetry. 1918.
DUYCKINCK, E. A. and G. L. Cyclopedia of American Literature, Vol. II.
FOERSTER, NORMAN. American Poetry and Prose (rev. ed.). 1934.
KREYMBORG, ALFRED. Lyric America. 1930.
PRESCOTT and SANDERS. An Introduction to American Poetry. 1932.
SPILLER, ROBERT E. The Roots of National Culture. 1933.
STEDMAN and HUTCHINSON. Library of American Literature, Vol. V.

CHAPTER VI

Early Metropolitans

Washington Irving

WASHINGTON IRVING, American-born son of immigrant parents, was by temperament a dispassionate observer of life; and life on the whole seemed picturesque and amusing to him. It was comfortably permanent in its ways, too much so to be in need of change or in danger of it at the hands of men whose deep and intense convictions made reformers or revolutionists of them. He was carefree, and secure in his reliance on a beneficent guiding hand in the affairs of man. As an American who was not a product of any American tradition, he was not committed to any American program. He was a Briton in a one-time Dutch town; but he could whimsically sympathize with the Stuyvesants and the Knickerbockers, who, when all was said and done, had lost so little. He was a commoner of Scotch-Presbyterian paternity; but he could feel more at home with the Anglicans and the gentry than with shopkeeping Presbyterians or Calvinists. He could dabble rather fruitlessly in speculative business and speculative investments and shrug his shoulders when fate failed to fill his lap with gold. He could absent himself from America for seventeen years at a stretch and perfunctorily lament his exile without ever taking a step toward home; and when he did come home he could refrain from accepting the political honors that were offered him, aware of his incapacity to meet the obligations that went with them. He could spend months at the national capital without understanding the fundamentals of politics or government; and he could tour the country quite thoroughly and conscientiously without grasping the implications of westward expansion. He could find the same diversion in English life that he could in American; and he could write voluminously about Spain without any attempt to disclose the essentials of Spanish character. So far was he from desire for, or possession of, the critical instinct that he might have written at the end of his life what he wrote at the end of his first complete work:[1]

> I have too high an opinion of the understanding of my fellow-citizens, to think of yielding them any instruction; and I covet too much their good-will, to forfeit it by giving them good advice. . . . I look up to the world with the most perfect good nature, and my only sorrow is, that it does not prove itself more worthy of the unbounded love I bear it.[2]

It was a fortunate chapter in Irving's youth that temporarily burdened him with ill-health and sent him to Europe for two years of travel instead of into college or business. He had the temper of the macaroni, or dandy, and an interest in customs and manners. He was well-bred, companionable, and socially eligible. Europe for him was a round of cities, centers of polite life, separated by stretches of travel that were pleasantly eventful. It offered him a series of picturesque and amusing experiences and a set of comparisons to apply to his modest home town. There was an atmosphere of romance about it, and material for the mild realism that could be felt by a butterfly, which, in flitting about garden and meadow, becomes something of a connoisseur in odors and colors and flavors. On his return to New York he was ready, quite incidentally, to undertake with his brother William and his friend Paulding a little venture in light satire, "The Salmagundi Papers." These had none of the caustic quality of Swift or Pope or Churchill or Byron.[3] They were more

---

[1] Quotations are from the edition of Irving's "Works" published by G. P. Putnam's Sons, 1848; and from the "Life and Letters of Washington Irving" (4 vols.; Putnam's, 1864), by Pierre Irving.

[2] Irving, "Knickerbocker History," concluding passage.

[3] N. F. Adkins discusses this point in some detail in his "Fitz-Greene Halleck," Chap. V, sect. 2.

in the vein for which George Colman the Younger, J. H. Frere, and W. S. Rose in England are, one may say, forgotten; less in the temper of "The Anarchiad," which preceded them in America; and more like "The Croaker Papers," which were to follow. They are Addisonian in tone, quite evidently influenced by Goldsmith's "Citizen of the World."

The youthful authors announced in their introductory number that they proposed "to instruct the young, reform the old, correct the town and castigate the age." In the twenty-two papers that came out as pamphlets irregularly between January, 1807, and January, 1808, they commented on whatever struck their attention in the ways of the polite world. They held up to genial ridicule social types, fashions, and styles, particularly of ladies' dress; they burlesqued the current dramatic criticism and books of travel by foreign visitors, the passion for fruitless discussion that was converting the democracy into a "logocracy," and the lack of judgment and order that marked the political elections. It was the kind of superficial commentary on the ways of the town that London had been enjoying for the better part of a century, ever since Addison and Steele had made it popular in *The Tatler* and *The Spectator*. In the recurrent letters from Mustapha Rub-a-Dub Keli Khan, the Tripolitan observer of American life, they played with a literary device that was old even before it was employed by Goldsmith in the letters of Lien Chi Altangi, the Chinese contributor to "The Citizen of the World." "The Salmagundi Papers" are interesting, however, as early representatives of a longish series of light satires on the life of New York continuing via the days of Edmund Clarence Stedman and William Allen Butler to the present of *The New Yorker*. They were quite the talk of the town, and were discontinued only because the authors were unable to get a fair share of the proceeds from their unexpected success.

The effect of this success did not hurry Irving into professional authorship; writing continued to be an avocation until much of his best and all of his most spontaneous work was done. But the momentum from this joint enterprise carried him on through the "History of New York by Diedrich Knickerbocker," a much more extended and elaborate satire, which was published in the following year. A chronicle of the city under the Dutch governors, it offered him openings that he did not overlook for resuming the gibes on politics and political procedure which had featured the letters of Mustapha in the "Salmagundi Papers." In particular he was skeptical of popular rule,[1] popular assembly, freedom of speech, and freedom of the press. He pitied the elected officials who are targets "for every whipster and vagabond in the land"; he loathed "the bawling of patriotism," scorned "the dignity of the sovereign people," and could say nothing more scathing about a predicament in which William the Testy found himself than that

> Nothing was wanting but half-a-dozen newspapers and patriotic editors, to have completed this public illumination, and to have thrown the whole province in an uproar![2]

After the extremely laborious, pseudo-pedantic humor of the opening chapters, the "History" is gay, spirited, and highly readable. The three governors are completely individualized and are approached in quite different tempers. Walter Van Twiller is a sheer caricature; William Kieft is humanized and presented with a certain degree of sympathy; Peter Stuyvesant is pathetic but sturdily admirable. The liberties Irving took with all the "first families" of Dutch descent made the book more audacious than it seems today and gave it a kind of *succès de scandale*.[3] Irving was a young man of promise, a writer to be reckoned with. But for the next ten years he published nothing.

---

[1] For characteristic observations on politics in America, see "Salmagundi Papers," Nos. VII, IX, and the "History of New York," passim.

[2] Irving, "History of New York," Vol. I, Part I, Chap. V.

[3] A typical expression of local resentment, delivered in an anniversary discourse before the New York Historical Society in 1818, but considered important enough to be reprinted in 1833, can be seen in G. C. Verplanck's "Discourses and Addresses," pp. 63, 64. The "Knickerbocker History," it declared, afforded one of "the gross instances of national injustice," was "a coarse caricature," and demanded some kind of atonement.

During this time, after a brief excursion into the law, he was engaged in business with his brothers and was perhaps the most level-headed in a very unbusinesslike combination. In 1815, in connection with one of their various ambitious and unsuccessful schemes, he went abroad unsuspecting that he would be away until 1832 and that he would return a celebrated author widely read on two continents. In 1818, when business prospects finally flickered out, he had to turn to writing not merely as a polite avocation but as a possible source of income. The new articles he then wrote, together with several that he had accumulated in his leisure, were soon ready, but found no English publisher willing to risk them. Even the powerful influence of Irving's cordial friend Scott could not prevail with John Murray, "prince of publishers." Irving had naturally wanted the prestige of Murray's imprint to offset the severity of the critics and the neglect of the public toward works of American authorship. As soon, however, as the sketches were printed in New York in a set of seven modest installments, the attention of English readers was attracted to them, and rumors began spreading that a "pirated" English edition was soon to appear. The success of an edition that Irving managed to get out through an inefficient publisher was so marked that Murray soon saw the light, and from then on was eager to get the English rights for everything that Irving wrote and to advance him five, ten, and, in one case, fifteen thousand dollars.[1]

On the appearance of "The Sketch Book" Irving became popular alike with the reading public and with the elect. Few tributes are more telling than the one contained in a letter written many years later by Dickens, in which he refers to the delight he took in Irving's pages when he was "a small and not over particularly well taken care of boy." Even the austere *Edinburgh Review* endorsed the American[2] as a writer

---

[1] For the changing nature of Irving's relations with John Murray see Pierre Irving's "Life," Vol. II, passim, and Vol. III, p. 273.

[2] For English comment on Irving see W. B. Cairns's "British Criticisms of American Writings" (1815–1833), Chap. IV and passim.

of "great purity and beauty of diction." From the most feared critic in the English-speaking world to the neglected boy whose father was in a debtor's prison, Irving met with enough applause quite to turn the head of a less balanced man.

"The Sketch Book" includes about thirty papers, of four or five kinds; it is a representative work of the day and, taken with his earlier publications, foreshadows every sort of writing Irving was to attempt except his perfunctory volumes on Western subjects. Fifteen of the units are definite observations on English life and customs as seen in country towns and estates. Of the remainder, six are literary essays on varying themes; four are personal traveling reminiscences; three are the famous stories "Rip Van Winkle," "Sleepy Hollow," and "The Spectre Bridegroom"; and five, defying classification, are "miscellaneous."

As a contemporary document the sixth paper, "British Writers on America," deserves something better than the neglect it has received. Like all his countrymen who were aware of it, Irving was disturbed by the prevailing ill-nature of English critics and travel writers. He deprecated a practice that threatened to estrange the two peoples and to lose for England a friend with whom she could not afford to be at loggerheads. He was not unique in making the point; but he was rare in the temperateness of his language, which was probably an evidence less of his self-control than of his easy-going amiability. He proceeded from warning the English to warning his countrymen:

> Nothing is so easy and inviting as the retort of abuse and sarcasm, but it is a paltry and unprofitable contest. . . . The members of a republic, above all other men, should be candid and dispassionate. . . . Let it be the pride of our writers, therefore, discarding all feelings of irritation, and disdaining to retaliate the illiberality of British authors, to speak of the English nation without prejudice and with determined candor.[1]

[1] Irving, "British Writers on America" (paragraphs 15, 16, 20), in "The Sketch Book."

"The Sketch Book" as a whole can best be understood as an American's comments on England at a time when "retort of abuse and sarcasm" was highly in fashion. In the opening paper Irving did not come far short of it:

> A great man of Europe, thought I, must . . . be as superior to a great man of America, as a peak of the Alps to the highlands of the Hudson; and in this idea I was confirmed by observing the comparative importance and swelling magnitude of many English travelers among us, who, I was assured, were very little people in their own country. I will visit this land of wonders, thought I, and see the gigantic race from which I am degenerated.[1]

Irving's summarized impressions are contained in the thirtieth paper on "John Bull," a sketch of official England in terms of a squire and his establishment, comparable to Francis Hopkinson's "Pretty Story" and all its kind.[2] But there is the basic difference between the two men that Hopkinson had intense political convictions and wrote to create a breach between colonies and mother country, in contrast with Irving, who was more of a dilettante than a doctrinaire and had no interest in politics beyond its picturesqueness and its humors. In all his English sketches, whether in this volume or in "Bracebridge Hall," "Jonathan Oldstyle," "Tales of a Traveler," or "The Crayon Miscellany," Irving was chiefly attracted by the evidences of age-old tradition. Even the English scenery was "associated with ideas of order, of quiet, of sober, well-established principles, of hoary usage and reverend custom."[3] He was aware that the English gentleman was a costly luxury; the usurpation of the land disquieted him momentarily; but he consoled himself that abuses of this sort were "but casual outbreaks in the general system." England was still Merry England, the land of hot cross buns and valentines, roast beef and plum pudding, Bartholomew Fairs and Lord Mayor's

---

[1] Irving, "The Author's Account of Himself" (paragraph 5), in "The Sketch Book."

[2] See pages 139, 140.

[3] Irving, "Rural Life in England" (paragraph 14), in "The Sketch Book."

Days, of kissing under the mistletoe, all fours, Pope Joan, and Tom-come-tickle-me. It is no wonder that the youthful Dickens reveled in these papers, for the same England appealed to both writers: a boisterous, jolly England of romantic tradition, with a good deal of vulgarity that they were ready to condone and a good many vices that they chose to overlook in favor of its chief virtues — a hearty laugh, a blunt honesty, and a full stomach.

Irving and Dickens concurred[1] also in their liking for John Bull's readiness to "be moved to a sudden tear" and in their own attempts to move him. The vogue of "sensibility" derided by Jane Austen was at its height in America while it was declining in England, but both men helped to prolong it. For this sentimentalism and its free play of emotion in eloquence, sobs, sighs, blushes, and swoonings, Irving found an outlet in "The Wife," "The Broken Heart," "The Widow and her Son," and "The Pride of the Village." "The Wife," which deals with "the fortitude with which women sustain the most overwhelming reverses of fortune," is interpreted by a tearful husband who weeps at the loss of his wealth, fears to shock his spouse with the revelation, and opens the flood gates on her display of sportsmanship when the facts are revealed. Another sketch is a direct challenge to "those who have outlived the susceptibility of early feeling." The pride of the village fails to survive it, for she is introduced "in all the beautiful confusion of girlish diffidence and delight"; passes into a love affair punctuated with agonies, faintings, and hysterics; goes into a decline on the departure of her lover; and on his return looks upon him "with a smile of unutterable tenderness" and dies. The influence of these sketches in Irving's most popular book outlived his own interest in this kind of writing. He recurred to it seldom, and when he told the story of "Annette Delarbre" in "Bracebridge Hall" supplied an antidote in the reference to "the tender-hearted Lady Lillycraft, who knew the story by heart,

[1] For the interchange of friendly letters between Irving and Dickens see the "Life," Vol. III, pp. 164–187.

had led the way in weeping, and indeed had often begun to shed tears before they had come to the right place."

Two other types of work remain in "The Sketch Book." The first is the literary essay. From these five essays it appears that Irving was well read in the English literature of an earlier period, and that he liked to dwell on passages which were characterized (as his own work came to be) by "purity and beauty of diction." Yet in themselves, and in the absence of any later substantial supplements, they emphasize the non-critical nature of his mind. Unlike Addison or De Quincey or Lamb or Hazlitt, to whom in certain respects he invites comparison, Irving contributed nothing of moment to either the general statement or the specific application of aesthetic principles. Instead, he was content with the "Desultory Thoughts on Criticism" in "Wolfert's Roost."

The other type is the most famous in "The Sketch Book," the three stories, of which "Rip Van Winkle" is best known. "Rip" offered a happy release for Irving's full powers as an artist.[1] He told a good story that will long be read for its own sake, using a Continental folk theme but completely localizing it and giving it enduring fame as an American tale. It is chiefly distinguished as a very early prototype of the modern short story, America's prime contribution to the types of literature. "Rip Van Winkle" is strikingly different from its vague and shapeless forerunners, usually condensed novels not limited in time or developed in detail. After the introduction it is confined to two short periods — the few hours just before and just after Rip slept on the mountain. And the whole story leads to a single point — the relentless way life moves on regardless of the laggard. The years bridging the Revolution were the most effective to mark the change; and Rip's experience in finding that loyalty to a discarded monarchy could be treason to a new republic was the definite application of a general truth. It is not at all necessary to

[1] See J. B. Thompson's "Genesis of the Rip Van Winkle Legend," *Harper's*, Vol. LXVII (1883), pp. 617–622. The various dramatizations of the story are sketched in A. H. Quinn's "History of the American Drama," pp. 325–332.

assume that Irving chose the folk legend to expound a theme, or even that he was conscious of the completeness with which he did it. The fact remains that the tale was remarkable in its day for its clear compactness, and that it meets the test of enduring fiction in telling a good story well and of building the story out of elements that convey some truth about life.

"The Legend of Sleepy Hollow" is comparable to "Rip Van Winkle" only in the use of native material. It is, of course, only a make-believe ghost story, neither important nor well told, as narrative; but as a sketch and in its development of local atmosphere it holds its own with the rest of the volume. Ichabod Crane and the respectable townsfolk are content, like Rip, to live in a village where "population, customs and manners remain fixed; while the great torrent of migration and improvement, which is making such incessant changes in other parts of this restless country, sweeps by them unobserved." Ichabod is an interesting figure too, because his combination of learning and superstition is credited to the influence of Cotton Mather, and he is held up to derision as a type abhorred by all New Yorkers — the Puritan descendant strayed from home. Cooper's David Gamut is one of the same crop. The value of the sketch lies in its picture of simple country life. The scene at the Van Tassel home is as vivid as those at Bracebridge Hall or in "Snow-Bound" or "The Cotter's Saturday Night." Except in "Rip Van Winkle," Irving did not surrender to his material in telling ghostly or supernatural stories. Like the Gothic romancers, he explained his mysteries away, as in two of the "Sketch Book" trio, the first group of "Tales of a Traveler," or the "Crayon" paper "Don Juan — a Spectral Research."

Irving's richest period as a creative writer was over by 1824, when he had followed "The Sketch Book" with "Bracebridge Hall," "Jonathan Oldstyle," and "Tales of a Traveler." He was committed to authorship for his livelihood and wrote with unflagging industry but with declining zest. He first resorted to Spanish history, taking his place between two Americans: Ticknor, historian of the literature, and Prescott, chronicler of the New World conquests. He wrought faithfully with original sources; but though "The Conquest of Granada," the most readable volume on Spain, is colorful and dramatic at times, only in the by-product of his studies, "The Alhambra," did Irving write with anything like his old ease and spontaneity. "Mahomet" is rather more of a set task than the Spanish undertakings. "Washington" is distinctly unsuccessful. He could write well on the romantic youth of his subject; but his distaste for politics and his consequent ignorance disqualified him for an intelligent treatment of the conflicts over the Constitution and during the first presidency and marked the work as that of a "somewhat tired old gentleman . . . struggling to fulfil his contract with his publisher."[1] With "Goldsmith" he was more effective because once more he was dealing with a literary subject and with a favorite from his youth. But all these latter were written after his return to America.

After his long absence Irving came back to New York in a glow of patriotic enthusiasm. He brought fame and fortune with him, and the prestige that Americans have always been quick to bestow on a reputation made by one of their countrymen on the other side of the Atlantic. At the dinner of welcome arranged on his return he spoke feelingly of his satisfaction in escaping from an atmosphere of gloom and doubt and danger to a homeland "where everyone speaks of the past with triumph, the present with delight, the future with growing and confident anticipation."[2] For most of a year he tried to reacquaint himself with the country, traversing New England, the south-Atlantic and Gulf states, and the Ohio valley, and touring the prairies to the southwest — a fairly inclusive survey for the 1830's. For a winter he listened to congressional debates and watched the machinery of government in Washington. He did not want to be a Rip Van Winkle, and played with the idea that he was a liberal; but he was the kind of liberal who thoroughly approved of the conservatives

[1] Parrington, "Romantic Revolution," p. 211.
[2] Quoted in "Life and Letters," Vol. II, p. 490.

and shrank from any program of rebellion against what he once called "vile systems of falsehood in every relation of human affairs, that have been woven over the human mind." He was quite completely under the spell of the "manifest destiny" illusion. He deprecated violence in controversy and harshness of opinion, and considered what seemed like social and economic abuses as "phenomena . . . devised by an all-seeing Providence for some beneficent purpose."[1]

Irving's three books on the West were thus altogether foreign to his talents. "A Tour of the Prairies" was published with an explanation and an apology: he was fulfilling an expectation of the public that a book would be the fruits of his travels, though he had no desire to write one and no story to tell. For "Astoria" there was a little more of an inward impulse and far more of an outward one. The subject of the fur traders had appealed to him before John Jacob Astor urged him to undertake it and supplied both documents and funds; and there was romance in the career of this immigrant boy turned merchant prince. But he wrought in anything but the mood of the artist when he accepted the subsidy of the millionaire and revised the draft of his nephew Pierre for the volume to which his name is attached. Possibly it was because he was so steeped in the atmosphere of the eighteenth century that he was willing to allow this magnate to play patron to him as he was already doing to Fitz-Greene Halleck. Again, "The Adventures of Captain Bonneville" was an aftermath of "Astoria" and the reworking of another man's manuscript. The three books fail to recognize in the frontier the form and substance of the great drama that was being enacted at the time. The account of the tour is on the tour rather than on the prairies; and an appended paragraph to "Captain Bonneville," which looks back to the "romance of savage life" and laments the disappearance of "the gay, free trapper and his steed, decked out in wild array, and tinkling with bells and trinketry,"[2] reveals in its very diction

[1] Letter to Kimble, in the "Life," Vol. III, pp. 119 ff.
[2] Pierre Irving, "Life and Letters," p. 421.

that the romance of Spain was being grafted onto the epic of the plains. It is only less convincing than the succeeding fantastic prophecy that the "irreclaimable wilderness" between the Rockies and the Sierra would one day "produce hybrid races like the mountain Tartars of the Caucasus," which would in time "become a scourge to the civilized frontiers on either side of the mountains." Steeds and cavalcades, Tartars and scourges, the whole concept was like the setting for a melodrama — "Metamora," let us say, played by Forrest in a New York theater and viewed from seats supplied with the compliments of Mr. Astor, whose tactics in the West were not so far from a Tartar's.

For Irving was like Forrest in one important respect: his prosperity depended on public approval, and the public in the second quarter of the nineteenth century wanted polite literature and traditional plays. Forrest's offer of substantial prizes for plays on native American themes brought one American winner and then a miscellany of exotic subjects, reaching its extreme, as in Irving's case, with "Mahomet." Irving had a hand with John Howard Payne in playwriting, collaborating in a tale from "The Arabian Nights" and in "Charles II" and "Richelieu."[1] In spite of the long succession of appeals for a native output, little had yet come in the way of actual performance; and the little that was genuinely indigenous was the literature of the unliterary. Among the gentry the tradition of the gentle reader was undisturbed. Mrs. Trollope was bearing witness to this American trait when she wrote:

> Every American newspaper is more or less of a magazine, wherein the merchant may scan, while he holds out his hand for an invoice, "Stanzas by Mrs. Hemans," or a garbled extract from Moore's "Life of Byron"; the lawyer may study his brief faithfully, and yet contrive to pick up the valuable dictum of some American critic that "Bulwer's novels are decidedly superior to Sir Walter Scott's."[2]

---

[1] Irving's own account of his collaborations with John Howard Payne is recorded in Pierre Irving's "Life and Letters," Vol. II, pp. 166–176.

[2] Quoted in Rusk's "Literature of the Middle Western Frontier," Vol. I, p. 131.

So it was that Irving was most popular when he was most obviously the American Addison. Instead of experiencing the normal development of a maturing artist in a mature community, he was at his best in his imitative youth and in the middle years when he occasionally recaptured the original flair in such bits as "Mountjoy," in "The Crayon Papers"; "The Devil and Tom Walker," in "Tales of a Traveler"; and the Hudson River sketches, in "Wolfert's Roost." He was at his best in "Rip Van Winkle" and as Rip Van Winkle. He lived until, to every alert observer, the Civil War seemed an "inevitable conflict." But he sat in his study with his back to the future, and in his last years focused his dimming eyes on George Washington and the days of the Revolution. The America of his declining years returned the disregard. It was preoccupied with livelier matters. "The death of Irving," wrote Thoreau in "The Last Days of John Brown," "having occurred while these things were transpiring, went almost unobserved."

His latter middle age was filled with honors. He had already received the gold medal from the Royal Society of Literature and the degree of Doctor of Laws from Oxford University. Now he was to have the refusal of a succession of public offices, including a place in the cabinet, and the leadership of a "school" of writers. Diedrich Knickerbocker had become a household name that was applied to the Knickerbocker group of Irving's followers and used in the christening of *The Knickerbocker Magazine* (1833–1865). As a connecting link between the century of his birth and the century of his achievement he carried over the spirit and the manners of Addison into the New World, and the courtly manners of the Federalists into the rough-and-ready era of the Jacksonian democracy. With him these were natural modes of thought and ways of expression; but with his imitators they were affected and superficial, — so clearly so that the Knickerbocker school declined and *The Knickerbocker Magazine* went out of existence shortly after his death.

JAMES FENIMORE COOPER

James Fenimore Cooper is generally known as the author of "The Spy," possibly of "The Pilot," and of the Leather-stocking Series. Of the latter "The Last of the Mohicans" is the pre-eminent favorite, and in these three novels Cooper's literary reputation enjoys a popular survival which is buttressed by their inclusion in many a student reading list.[1] They were written early in his career, within the first fifth of his writing period — a war story, a sea story, and a frontier story. He is vaguely known to have written other kinds, to have returned to all three of these, and to have extended "The Last of the Mohicans" into a series which pursues the chronicle of the woodsman, the Indian, and the retreating frontier. Probably these popular generalizations are adequate concerning Cooper as a literary artist; but they fall far short of the whole truth, for they do not put Cooper's best work into relation with his work as a whole, nor Cooper himself into relation with his times. Such a study of the man reveals him as a tumultuous American who matured very slowly; who was intensely concerned with the facts and theories of life in a new democracy; who fell into novel-writing by accident, did his best work during the first flush of authorship, and, in the remainder of his career, was a critic of the social order who wrote novels largely to propound his views. So considered, Cooper becomes increasingly interesting; his best tales lose nothing of their value, and the rest of his work gains greatly in significance. For Cooper was the first widely read American author who saw his country from the point of view of the West.

He was the product of rival forces: inherited gentility and acquired republican sympathies; and they kept him in con-

[1] Quotations here are from the "Complete Works of James Fenimore Cooper" (Mohawk Edition; 32 vols.), published by G. P. Putnam's Sons, 1896. This covers all the fiction. Cooper's critical volumes appear separately. References to "A Letter to His Countrymen" and "The American Democrat" are to the first editions; references to "Notions of the Americans," to the edition of 1840.

stant turmoil. He was brought up on what was then the frontier in the tradition of the landed aristocracy, more like a Southerner than like a Northern townsman. He was tutored in preparation for college by an Anglican clergyman in Albany. Sent to Yale instead of to King's College (now Columbia), the young Anglican squire was a stranger in a Puritan town. He did not belong there; and though he was generously inclined, he never freed himself from his antipathy for the New Englanders. Leaving college after a career of wild extravagance in the middle of the four-year course, he followed the custom of the English gentry in making a choice between the law, the church, and the service, entering the navy. Upon withdrawal from the sea he married the daughter of a Royalist family and returned to the life of the landed aristocracy.[1]

When the product of this confusing experience — which prevented his taking the new United States altogether for granted — left his rural estate, he came to a town which was more likely to re-arouse doubts and indecisions than to settle him in his convictions. He came down past Peekskill and Harlem toward Staten Island and Spuyten Duyvil to the Anglo-Dutch town of New York, which had seemed so strange to Mrs. Knight in 1704 and whose Knickerbocker history Irving had recorded in 1809. If he had gone to Charleston, South Carolina, or Boston, Massachusetts, he would have been either assimilated or estranged. Through agreement or opposition his ideas would have been clarified and reinforced. Nevertheless, during these years up to 1826 he was more at ease in the Zion of his mind and more effectively productive than ever thereafter. It was then that he wrote "The Spy," "The Pioneers," "The Pilot," and "The Last of the Mohicans."

The results of Cooper's following seven years in England and Europe were quite normal in kind, though they were

---

[1] The standard older biography of Cooper is T. R. Lounsbury's "James Fenimore Cooper," 1882; later indispensable studies are H. W. Boynton's "James Fenimore Cooper," 1931, and R. E. Spiller's "Fenimore Cooper, Critic of His Times," 1931.

heightened in degree by the character of his education and the intensity of his nature. Like any traveler on his first foreign tour, he saw his own country anew in the light of the comparisons and contrasts that every day offered. He became equally aware of the graces and dignities that belong to aristocracies and of the social oppressions on which they depend. In addition to three novels written in criticism of Venetian, Swiss, and German life, — "The Bravo," "The Headsman," and "The Heidenmauer," — which were indifferent, bad, and worse, he indulged in a two-volume anonymous work entitled "Notions of the Americans, Picked Up by a Traveling Bachelor." Cooper's earliest novel, "Precaution," a dull tale of English life, had shown promise; the succeeding works had fulfilled his promise as a teller of tales and had met with an enthusiastic response. His countrymen were proud of him; he could vie with the author of "Waverley," more than hold his own with the author of "Scottish Chiefs" in the romantic treatment of native material. But residence in Europe precipitated all the conflict that had been brewing within him and set him at war with himself, at war with the champions of the old order in Europe, at war with his fellow citizens in the New World. He could see too much of both sides to satisfy himself or anyone else. He was so concerned with what he saw that he was involved in a further conflict between his gifts as a novelist and his ardors as a political theorist; and more often than not the political theorist won.

> I had had abundant occasion to observe that the great political contest of the age was not, as is usually pretended, between the two antagonist principles of monarchy and democracy, but in reality between those who, under the shallow pretense of limiting power to the *élite* of society, were contending for exclusive advantages at the expense of the mass of their fellow-creatures. . . . With these views of what was enacting around me in Europe . . . I determined to attempt a series of tales, in which American opinion should be brought to bear on European facts.[1]

---

[1] Cooper, "A Letter to His Countrymen," pp. 11–12.

Since this "American opinion" loomed so large in his life and his works, it is worth summarizing. It appears in the length and breadth of his writings, but most explicitly in certain writings, either nonfiction or with the thinnest of fiction veneers, composed between 1828 and 1838 ("Notions of the Americans," 1828; "A Letter to His Countrymen," 1834; "The Monikins," 1835; "The American Democrat, or Hints on the Social and Civic Relations of the United States of America," 1838; "Homeward Bound" and "Home as Found," both also 1838), and in most of his prefaces during this period and thereafter.

As Cooper was always certain of his dislikes and never slow to express them, it is natural that he espoused democracy because of his rejection of aristocracy. A privileged aristocracy was certain, he maintained, like any other government, to rule in its own interest; but a widely extended suffrage would result in reducing deliberate inequity and dispensing general justice, for public will and public interest would be likely to coincide. He believed in equality of opportunity under a democratic regime, but, Tory-fashion, felt that the obligations of leadership rested more heavily on the class who were endowed with wisdom, manners, and possessions. Thus in the section "On the Private Duties of Station" in "The American Democrat," he explained:

> It is peculiarly graceful in the American, whom the accidents of life have raised above the mass of the nation, to show himself conscious of his duties in this respect, by asserting at all times the true principles of government, avoiding, equally, the cant of demagogueism with the impracticable theories of visionaries, and the narrow and selfish dogmas of those who would limit power by castes.[1]

He declared himself to be "as good a democrat as there is in America," yet he regarded the country with critical eyes. He was not a believer, he said, "in the scheme of raising men very far above their natural propensities" and he composed the book "more in a spirit of censure than of praise, for its aim is correction."[2]

[1] Cooper, "The American Democrat," p. 92. [2] Ibid. Introduction, p. 5.

Unhappily Cooper was not one of those who could keep his head in solitude and his hands in society, maintaining an equal balance of personal independence and democratic sympathy. He soon discovered, to his intense discomfort, that "the mass of the nation" were not grateful for his censures. The rank and file of a Jacksonian democracy resented his saying that they were compounds of "intelligence, kindness, natural politeness, coarseness, and vulgarity," as well as his complacent assertion that "no rights can be dearer to a man of cultivation, than exemption from unseasonable invasions on his time, by the coarse-minded and ignorant."[1]

Cooper's views on property, moreover, were offensive to many a man of property; for, again in Tory fashion, he was a believer in the distinction of landed wealth in contrast with wealth gained from commerce or even from banking and, emphatically, in contrast with wealth derived from manufacture or shopkeeping. Thus he was a disturbing critic of the town, which was dominated by the tradesman, the producer, and the financier, and he was loud in his abuse of the post-frontier countryside where lowborn vulgarians had the effrontery to invade his acreage, criticize his behavior, ban his books, and even burn him in effigy.

He had originally seemed to think that the blessings of democracy would be gratefully and humbly received by a proletariat who were eager to submit to the leadership of the elite, as he designated his own class. He was forced to the slow and painful discovery that the tyranny of the autocrat was not so hateful as the tyranny of public opinion and that the public press was its most fearful instrument. Never a man with a natural capacity for general ideas, his change of attitude toward the American newspaper was wholly determined by his personal experience with it. Up to the writing of the "Notions," when he had been kindly treated, he felt that the press was dignified and respectful of private feelings in deference to public opinion which "has imperiously pre-

---

[1] Cooper, op. cit. p. 98.

scribed that, amidst the utmost latitude of discussion, certain limits shall not be passed."[1] By 1834 he wrote a most laborious and resentful reply[2] to an article in the New York *Courier and Enquirer* which was altogether friendly, mainly laudatory, and deplored only that Cooper the novelist should be distracted by public controversy. In "The American Democrat" four years later, he had been goaded to the point of alleging that "as the press of this country now exists, it would seem to be expressly devised by the great agent of mischief, to depress and destroy all that is good, and to elevate all that is evil in the nation."[3]

For many years he was warped completely out of his natural orbit by the controversy for which his hot head peculiarly unfitted him. Lacking the distinguished dignity of the aristocrat, whom he was continually holding up to admiration, he fell into an unhappy and avoidable conflict with his neighbors of Cooperstown and proceeded from this to a series of libel suits, in which he elevated a succession of newspaper editors into the honorable guild of the sued, until he became one of the most vilified men in America.[4] It is a pathetic story, because Cooper was honestly eager to contribute to the democratic experiment on which his country was launched, and his criticisms were mainly well-founded. The experiment was noble; the immediate results were far from perfect; but he followed the tactics of the impatient, sharp-tongued faultfinder. His manners were as bad as his original judgments were good; and when he let his temper run away with him he lost not only his sense of proportion but his chances of exerting a beneficent influence. Lowell's

---

[1] Cooper, "Notions of the Americans," Vol. II, p. 106.

[2] The "reply" was "A Letter to His Countrymen" (1834), of which the first thirty-five pages are specific exposition of the motivation of "The Bravo."

[3] Cooper, "On the American Press," in "The American Democrat" (1838), p. 134. An excellent reprint of "The American Democrat" appeared in the Americana Deserta Series, with an introduction by H. L. Mencken, 1931.

[4] For different discussions of this see E. R. Outland's "The 'Effingham' Libels on Cooper," and H. W. Boynton's "James Fenimore Cooper," Part IV, "Demos at Home," and, in particular, pp. 266–280, 290–298.

comments on this chapter in the novelist's career are fairly to the point:

> There is one thing in Cooper I like, too, and that is
> That on manners he lectures his countrymen gratis;
> Not precisely so either, because, for a rarity,
> He is paid for his tickets in unpopularity.
> Now he may overcharge his American pictures,
> But you'll grant there's a great deal of truth in his strictures;
> And I honor the man who is willing to sink
> Half his present repute for the freedom to think,
> And, when he has thought, be his cause strong or weak,
> Will risk t'other half for the freedom to speak,
> Caring naught for what vengeance the mob has in store,
> Let that mob be the upper ten thousand or lower.[1]

Aside from Cooper's political disquisitions and his various controversial pamphlets, six narrative works are the literary by-products of his hopes and fears for democracy. They all show how seriously his art suffered when he tried to make it do the work of argument. The first three, written on European themes, have already been mentioned, and his purpose in writing them has been quoted. Only the first, "The Bravo," deserves a reading on its own account; but, like the others, it is heavily loaded with long and frequent digressions on aspects of government, aristocracy, bureaucracy, feudalism, the function of official pageantry, the use of public ritual, and government of the people contrasted with government by the people. All were designed to reinforce the democratic thesis by reference to the practice of limited governments.

"The Monikins" (1835) is a thinly veiled satire on England and the United States — the Leaphigh and Leaplow of the story. After a whole preliminary volume, in which Cooper seems to have enjoyed writing narration and description for their own sakes, comes the actual Monikin story, reminiscent of the travels of Gulliver among the Houyhnhnms. He looks

[1] Lowell, "A Fable for Critics," lines 1079–1090.

upon Leaplow with solicitude as a young and imitative nation, sound in theory, building from the bottom, but lamentable in its popular aversion "to anything like an insulated effort of the mind, which is offensive, anti-republican, aristocratic, and dangerous."[1] It is a labored and humorless satire, interesting as a document on the character of the times and the mind of the author.

"Homeward Bound" and "Home as Found" are compendiums of neither hopes nor fears, but only of resentments. Shoddy and pretentious architecture, manners of the same description, shifty business, superficial learning, and questionable politics share his scorn with silly Anglomania and the invasion of personal liberties by the public and the press. Steadfast Dodge, journalist, is pictured as all that his name implies; and Aristabulus Bragg is offered as a typical product of the new democracy.

> This man is an epitome of all that is good and all that is bad, in a very large class of his fellow-citizens. He is quick-witted, prompt in action, enterprising in all things in which he has nothing to lose, but wary and cautious in all things in which he has a real stake, and ready to turn not only his hand, but his heart and his principles, to anything that offers an advantage. With him, literally, "Nothing is too high to be aspired to, nothing too low to be done." He will run for governor or for town clerk, just as opportunities occur, is expert in all the practices of his profession, has had a quarter's dancing, with three years in the classics, and turned his attention toward medicine and divinity, before he finally settled down into the law. Such a compound of shrewdness, impudence, common-sense, pretension, humility, cleverness, vulgarity, kind-heartedness, duplicity, selfishness, law-honesty, moral fraud, and mother-wit, mixed up with a smattering of learning and much penetration in practical things, can hardly be described, as any one of his prominent qualities is certain to be met by another quite as obvious that is almost its converse. Mr. Bragg, in short, is purely a creature of circumstances.[2]

Cooper was so rancorous that he located the returning European travelers, the accusers of America, in Templeton

---

[1] Cooper, "The Monikins," p. 230. [2] Cooper, "Home as Found," p. 10.

Hall, his own country place. He involved them in his own quarrel with the villagers and loaded on himself all the priggishness that he ascribed to them. The public naturally took it as a personal utterance when he made one of them say:

> I should prefer the cold, dogged domination of English law, with its fruits, the heartlessness of a sophistication without parallel, to being trampled on by every arrant blackguard that may happen to traverse this valley in his wanderings after dollars.[1]

Preoccupation with the ways of the hour; disturbance over political and social conditions; resentment at foreign criticisms of America; harsher resentment at domestic criticisms of himself, all conspired to distract and confuse him.[2] As early as 1828, in spite of his early successes in dealing with native romantic story, he had made the odd observation that, in America,

> There are no annals for the historian; no follies (beyond the most vulgar and commonplace) for the satirist; no manners for the dramatist; no obscure fictions for the writer of romance; no gross and hardy offenses against decorum for the moralist; nor any of the rich artificial auxiliaries of poetry. The weakest hand can extract a spark from the flint, but it would baffle the strength of a giant to attempt kindling a flame with a pudding-stone![3]

No wonder that his best period was early at an end. The only wonder is that he did not fulfill his threat of six years later to stop writing, that with amazing energy he continued his prolific output, and that now and again he approached the level of the work of his serener days.

To return to these days, his first colorless story, "Precaution," made so little impression on public or publishers that when his second novel was ready in 1821 he had to issue it at his own expense; and he made this next venture, "The Spy," in part, at least, because of his friends' comment — charac-

---

[1] Cooper, "Home as Found," p. 226.

[2] R. E. Spiller's biography stresses Cooper as social critic. See also J. F. Ross, "The Social Criticism of Fenimore Cooper," The Univ. of California Press, 1933.

[3] Cooper, "Notions of the Americans," Vol. II, p. 108.

teristic of that self-conscious period — that he would have been more patriotic to write on an American theme. To let Cooper tell his own story:

> The writer, while he knew how much of what he had done was purely accidental, felt the reproach to be one that, in a measure, was just. As the only atonement in his power, he determined to inflict a second book, whose subject should admit of no cavil, not only on the world, but on himself. He chose patriotism for his theme; and to those who read the introduction and this book itself, it is scarcely necessary to add that he [selected his hero] as the best illustration of his subject.[1]

With this story of the adventures of Harvey Birch, an actual character in the Revolutionary War, Cooper won his public, a fact amply proved by the sale of thirty-five hundred copies of his third novel, "The Pioneers," on the day of publication. This story came nearer home to him, for he was born and bred in the region where he placed it. Working in this familiar material based on the country and the developing life which were part of his very self, Cooper wrote the first of the famous Leatherstocking Series. Even in this field, but without disturbing consequences, he wrote from a knowledge of the frontier rather than as a frontiersman. His father was a land-breaker incidentally to becoming a landlord. There had been a time when he could claim that forty thousand people held land, directly or indirectly, under him; and another when he could be impeached (though unjustly, as public vindication belatedly proved) for coercing the votes of his debtors, some hundreds of them, by threats of foreclosure. The son did not cling to his father's Federalism, but he did not swing over to a conception of the frontier as the melting pot of a new democracy. Instead of thinking of it as the promised land for the westward sweep of civilization, he regarded it as the region from which the Indian was being banished and where such a pioneer as Natty Bumppo, hunter but not settler, could find refuge from the oppressiveness of

---

[1] Cooper, "The Spy," Introduction, p. xxix.

a compact society. In "The Pioneers" the most dramatic scene represents this "nature's nobleman" reproaching Judge Templeton (drawn from the elder Cooper) for invading the rights of him who had ranged the woods before the law had laid its hand upon them. Later he deplored the fortune-hunting movement across the prairies and the stay-at-home land speculators like Irving. His frontiersman, therefore, was a highly romanticized figure, a solitary seeking escape from the ways of the world; quite as much of a poet and philosopher as a marksman and woodsman; endowed with all the virtues of the nomad pioneer and with none of his defects.

In terms of the Indian, Cooper's five tales can be said to form a link in the epic between the treatment of Longfellow and the conclusion supplied by Joaquin Miller. For Cooper took up the chronicle where "Hiawatha" dropped it:

> Then a darker, drearier vision
> Passed before me, vague and cloudlike;
> I beheld our nations scattered,
> All forgetful of my counsels,
> Weakened, warring with each other:
> Saw the remnants of our people,
> Sweeping westward, wild and woful,
> Like the cloud-rack of a tempest,
> Like the withered leaves of autumn.[1]

Cooper did not seem to appreciate how rich a vein he had struck in "The Pioneers"; for within the next two years he wrote "The Pilot," a sea story, and "Lionel Lincoln, or the Leaguers of Boston," supposed to be the first of a series of thirteen colonial stories which were never carried beyond this point. However, in 1826 he returned to the theme with "The Last of the Mohicans," and in 1827 he published "The Prairie," on the last days of the scout. It was not until 1840 and 1841, when the hottest of his controversies were over, that he completed the series with "The Deerslayer" and "The Pathfinder." The stories deal in succession with five

[1] Longfellow, "Hiawatha," Part XXI, last lines.

episodes in the life of the hero, occurring in 1740–1745, 1756, 1756, 1793, and 1804.

To "The Last of the Mohicans" the verdict of time has awarded first place among his works. It is the book that is devoted most completely to the vanishing race. Three passages set and hold the key to the story. The first is from the author's introduction:

> Of all the tribes named in these pages, there exist only a few half-civilized beings of the Oneidas, on the reservations of their people in New York. The rest have disappeared, either from the regions in which their fathers dwelt, or altogether from the earth.[1]

The second is a speech from Chingachgook to Hawkeye in the third chapter, where they are first introduced:

> Where are the blossoms of those summers! — fallen, one by one: so all of my family departed, each in his turn, to the land of spirits. I am on the hilltop, and must go down into the valley; and when Uncas follows in my footsteps, there will no longer be any of the blood of the sagamores, for my boy is the last of the Mohicans.[2]

The third is the closing speech of the story, by the sage Tamenund:

> It is enough. Go, children of the Lenape, the anger of the Manitou is not done. Why should Tamenund stay? The palefaces are masters of the earth, and the time of the red men has not yet come again. My day has been too long. In the morning I saw the sons of Unamis happy and strong; and yet, before the night has come, have I lived to see the last warrior of the wise race of the Mohicans.

In his treatment of the Indian, the scout, and primitive nature, as in his economics, Cooper was an heir to eighteenth-century tradition, explaining his ideas and modifying them in terms of American life. His most famous Indian character, Uncas, is so nearly the "noble red man" of French romanticism that Cooper has been unfairly reputed to have idealized

---

[1] Cooper, "The Last of the Mohicans," Introduction, p. vi. [2] Ibid. p. 29.

the whole race. It has been insisted that the woodcraft with which he endowed the Indians was beyond possibility, though later naturalists have recorded marvels quite as incredible as those in Cooper's pages. It has been reiterated that the dignity, self-control, tribal loyalty, and reverence for age were overdrawn, though many an authority has testified to the survival of these virtues. And it has been charged that they were never such a heroic and superior people as Cooper made them, though he did not make them half as admirable as he is said to have done. Tamenund is simply a mouthpiece. Uncas and Chingachgook are the only vital Indian characters whom he holds up to respect. All the others, beneath their formal ways in family, camp, and council, Cooper presents as treacherous and bloodthirsty at bottom, a savage people who betray their real natures in the massacre at the fort, the chief historical event in the novel. Any lingering inclination to idealize the primitive man is tempered by the realization of his primitive ferocity.

The scout throughout the series is as much of an idealization as Uncas, but lacks the offset of more realistic frontiersmen. He is an out-of-door creature, intolerant of town life, skeptical of any book but the book of nature; a lover of the woods and mountains and a worshiper of the God who made them. His activities are all on the wilderness side of the cutting edge of the frontier. In the influence of primitive nature on his character he embodies a philosophy which, coming from its earlier home in Greece, took up its abode in the eighteenth century among the English deists, and joined in the migration of ideas from the Old World to the New. The conception of the scout as a deistic philosopher is thus fused with Cooper's conception of the heroic pioneer. He shares the benevolence of the deist and the self-reliance of the frontiersman. The hero of the Leatherstocking Series is blood brother to Harvey Birch in "The Spy," Long Tom Coffin in "The Pilot," Captain Truck in "Homeward Bound" and "Home as Found," and some similar character in most of the other stories.

He has drawn you *one* character, though, that is new,
One wildflower he's plucked that is wet with the dew
Of this fresh Western world.[1]

Quite in contrast with this wild flower is a potted plant of whom Cooper is almost equally fond. This is the polished gentleman, fine flower of civilization, such as Montcalm, who embodies the culture and particularly the manners that the New World needed. Cooper admired the type to the point of infatuation, but presented it very imperfectly. Recurrent in the novels, he is always an idea rather than a personality, a veneer of manners over no substance of character. One can feel no affection for him and very little respect. He is as offensive to the reader in his social complacency as Cooper was later to be to the American public. Of the other types one of the most persistent is the eighteenth-century pedant, a constant on the stage of the period: David Gamut in "The Last of the Mohicans," Dr. Sitgreaves in "The Spy," Owen Bat in "The Prairie," and variously recurrent elsewhere.

Finally, among the leading types must be mentioned the "females," the generic word in a day when "lady" was reserved to indicate class distinction, and "woman" had not become the common noun. Faithfulness to the manners of their time would be reason enough for the utter unreality of pre-Victorian women in English and American fiction. A striking evidence of how universally they were regarded as not only dependents but inferiors can be found in the relevant passages in Bartlett's "Familiar Quotations." The majority of the quoted passages are culled from poets who lived before the rise of what used to be called "the woman's movement," and the tone of the passages is prevailingly supercilious and condescending. "Women are lovely at their best," the poets seemed to agree, "but after all they are only women. And at less than their best the least said about them the better." Cooper was by no means behind his

[1] Lowell, "A Fable for Critics," lines 1049–1051.

times in his attitude; indeed, he was, if anything, rather ahead of them. His feeling seems to have been expressed in the famous passage from "Marmion," of which the first couplet is usually all that is quoted:

> O woman! in our hours of ease
> Uncertain, coy, and hard to please, . . .
> When pain and anguish wring the brow,
> A ministering angel thou!

In the ordinary situations in Cooper's novels the "females" were beings to patronize and flatter, for flattery never goes unattended by her sardonic companion; but in times of stress they showed heroic powers of endurance.

The three introduced in the first chapter of "The Spy" were endowed, according to the text, with "softness and affability," "internal innocence and peace," and expressed themselves by blushes and timid glances. The two "lovely beings" of "The Last of the Mohicans" are even more fulsomely described. "The flush which still lingered above the pines in the western sky was not more bright nor delicate than the bloom" on Alice's cheeks; and Cora was the fortunate possesssor of "a countenance that was exquisitely regular and dignified, and surpassingly beautiful." In the passages that follow they are never referred to simply, but always with a bow and a smile — "the reluctant fair one," "the dark-eyed Cora"; and as they finally disappear through the woods on horseback, the reader is expected not to laugh at the final tableau of "the light and graceful forms of the females waving among the trees." Of course the readers to whom Cooper addressed this did not laugh. They realized that in speaking of women he was using the conventional language of the day, which was not intended to mean what it said; that he was introducing a pair of normal, lovely girls, and that the most he required of a normal girl was that she should be lovely — only this and nothing more. There was no evidence that Cora and Alice had minds, for they were not expected to have them; instead they had warm hearts, female beauty, and an oversupply of "sensibility." Lowell was not unfair in his comment, at least on the women of birth and breeding, in writing,

> And the women he draws from one model don't vary,
> All sappy as maples and flat as a prairie.[1]

But it must be admitted that Cooper followed the model of his generation, that it was only in the novelist's old age that Lowell made his observation, and that not till then were women beginning in any large numbers to think for themselves. Almost at the moment that Lowell was composing this couplet in "A Fable for Critics" Mrs. Sarah J. Hale, editress of *Godey's Lady's Book* and spokeswoman for the majority of her sex, was writing:

> For myself I would assert nothing incompatible with the dignity or delicacy of my sex. I would not claim for it superiority of intellect. I would only urge that with proper cultivation the intellectual attainments of women may equal those of men. . . . Let me not be misunderstood. I speak not of what woman should be; I merely say what she is capable of becoming.[2]

It was a capability that Cooper, with the average man of his time, was willing to leave undemonstrated and untested.

Cooper's criticisms of American character and American conditions are indispensable to the student of cultural history. His novels hold the attention, in spite of his slight respect for native material, for the very simple reason that they are based on actual life and real people. They had, moreover, and still have, the added advantage of being based on a life that was fascinatingly unfamiliar to the great majority of his readers, so that though realistic in detail they exerted from the outset the appeal of distant romance. Throughout the eighteenth century, and particularly through the last third, literature had been inclining to dwell on the joys of life in field and forest. Addison and his successors

---

[1] Lowell, op. cit. lines 1063–1064.

[2] Quoted in Minnigerode's "The Fabulous Forties," p. 77.

had handed on the spell of the old ballads of primitive adventure. Pope had dabbled with the "poor Indian," and Goldsmith had written his celebrated line about "Niagára['s] . . . thundering sound." Collins and Gray had harked back to the romantic past, Burns and Wordsworth had confined their poems to the peasantry among whom they lived, and Chateaubriand and Rousseau had developed a romantic philosophy of the "natural man." Irving's reply to English writers on America alluded to the current popularity of books on distant lands and peoples. When Cooper began publishing his stories of adventure in untrodden lands he found an attentive public not only in America but in England, and not only in England but all over Europe, where his novels were reprinted in thirty-four cities.

With the asset of this invaluable material Cooper combined his ability to tell an exciting story. His special gift was in the narration of exciting episodes — a storm, a battle, a pursuit, a capture, an escape, a hand-to-hand conflict. He was master of vivid detail and rapid action; he could maintain the sense of rapidity even while protracting the account. And this was about the limit of his gifts. He was not skillful in the handling of plots. If complicated, they are confusing and cumbersome; if simple, they are composed of strings of stirring adventures which seldom arrive at any striking conclusion, do not so much conclude as die, and as a rule "die hard." "The Last of the Mohicans" has its best material for a conclusion in the middle of the book, with the restoration of Alice and Cora to their father at Fort William Henry; but the story is only half long enough at this point, so the author separates them again by means of the massacre and carries the tale on more and more slowly to the deaths of Cora and Uncas. For "The Spy" the last chapter was actually written, set up, paged, and printed some weeks before the latter part had even been planned. Cooper's devices for starting and closing scenes were overworked, to the point of justifying Mark Twain's derision at the "Broken Twig Series," as he rechristened the Leatherstocking Tales;

and Bret Harte's burlesque in his "Condensed Novels"[1] shows how broadly Cooper laid his methods open to the scoffers. Furthermore, his work is as defective in stylistic detail as it is in general construction. It was written hurriedly and carelessly. Sentences often fail to hang together, words are ill-chosen, attempts at dialect are as bad as the average of his day, and pseudo-archaisms are unfounded in any historical usage. A recent study of his revisions of "The Spy" for republication arrives at the sanely negative finding that "as Dr. Johnson remarked concerning Boswell's account of a woman's preaching, . . . the wonder is not that the thing is done so well, but that it is done at all."[2]

Yet few who have come to scoff could have remained to rival Cooper. He has enlisted millions of readers in dozens of languages; he has fascinated them by the doings of woodsmen who were as mysteriously skillful as the town-bred Sherlock Holmes; he has thrilled by the genuine excitement of deadly struggles and hairbreadth escapes; and the sale of his books, a hundred years after he first addressed the public, would gladden the heart of many a modern novelist.

Cooper's career was rounded out with the neat finality of a well-made plot. He began his life as a young Tory on the frontier; he concluded it with a valedictory admonition to the American people, written from Cooperstown the year before his death. After his first problem novel, his six years of richest productivity, his preoccupation with the dilemmas of democracy and the controversies he was plunged into, he returned to the completion of his most famous series, and in 1842 suspended his campaign against the public. Happily the public seemed willing enough to let bygones be bygones and to welcome the dozen stories that appeared up to 1849. In prefaces, in characterizations, and in frequent digressions

[1] For burlesque and satire on Cooper see Bret Harte's "Stories and Condensed Novels," Vol. V of the "Complete Works"; and Mark Twain's "Fenimore Cooper's Literary Offenses," in "Literary Essays," Vol. XXII of the definitive edition.

[2] Tremaine McDowell, "James Fenimore Cooper as Self-Critic," *Modern Philology*, Vol. XXVII, p. 516.

he held to his old convictions; and in "The Chain-bearer" he condemned the leveling effects of frontier life, following this in "The Crater" with his contribution to the long succession of Utopias in which the world-weary have taken refuge from a hateful social order.

Then, finally, in 1850 he published "The Ways of the Hour" in order, he explained, "to draw the attention of the reader to some of the social evils that beset us; more particularly in connection with the administration of criminal justice" (preface, opening sentence), and without the vanity of supposing that the book could exert a very serious influence. In the person of Thomas Dunscombe he said his last say on his beloved but misguided country. In the twelve years since the writing of "Home as Found" he had seen little to encourage him. The vulgarian was still in the saddle, the press was still uncontrolled, the demagogue was still unbridled. And to make matters worse, the tendency of legislation was to undermine the seats of authority: the rights of property were under assault, even the rights of a husband to the property of his wife! Economic and domestic chaos threatened. It was the message of an irreconcilable Tory. The temper of the whole book is indicated as it draws to a close in the celebration of a wedding "in one of those little temples reared by our fathers in the days of the monarchy, when, in truth, greater republican simplicity really reigned among us, in a thousand things, than reigns today."[1]

If Cooper had lived as long as Bryant did, or even as long as Irving, his distresses would have multiplied. He was the conservative patriot. If his love of the United States led him into a sea of troubles, it was the same love that made him the writer of a compelling series of American stories. It is the native character of the man that is worth remembering, and the native qualities of his works that earned him a wide and lasting fame.

---

[1] Cooper, "The Ways of the Hour," p. 387.

William Cullen Bryant

Bryant, like Cooper, faced an America which challenged him with differences from the America of his heritage and his childhood. Cooper did not succeed in either overcoming conditions that offended him or adjusting himself to them. Bryant, not so passionately committed to the past, was happier in his adjustments, and, not at odds with the community, was more influential though less enduringly significant as a critic of his times. Again, because of his ability to detach himself from his social opinions, his art was seldom tinged with them and seldom sacrificed to them. He was fortunate in his flexibility, for he was subject to many changes in point of view. He was born and bred a rural New England Calvinist and Federalist, with the necessity of making a living and a desire from early boyhood to devote himself to poetry. He died a metropolitan Unitarian, a political democrat, and a prosperous journalist, who was still in his leisure pre-eminently the poet.[1]

He came down to New York City from the Massachusetts Berkshires in 1826, midway in Irving's first long sojourn abroad and at the beginning of Cooper's. By this year the other two had both laid down the main lines on their literary charts and had established their courses. There were no striking achievements ahead for either of them, though their careers were young. In a way, too, Bryant had written some of his most distinctive poems, and as an artist was seldom to surpass them. He was not only to outlive Irving and Cooper but he was to belong to the nineteenth century as neither of them did, and was to be a participant in the developments of his lifetime rather than a passive observer like Irving or an obdurate protestant like Cooper.

If he had not been fortunate in the critical but encouraging guidance of his father, his consistent, mild discontent with

---

[1] The standard reference for Bryant is the "Poetical Works of William Cullen Bryant," edited by Parke Godwin, and "A Biography of William Cullen Bryant," by Parke Godwin. 2 vols. each, 1883.

his provincial surroundings would doubtless have freed him from them much earlier. He pined for Boston, where Dr. Bryant went as a member of the state legislature; he was drawn toward New Haven, where he wanted to go as a Yale student under the presidency of Timothy Dwight after a disappointing year at Williams. He was utterly unsatisfied with a country law practice; he had entered it because he was unqualified for teaching or preaching and had been advised against doctoring by his doctor father; and he gave up with utter relief the practice of a shabby profession, as he called it, and as it doubtless was in a small town rifted by "innumerable quarrels and factions which were springing up every day among an extremely excitable and not very enlightened population." [1] This discontent with the back country and its insufficiencies was not merely negative. It had been heightened by early recognitions from the outer world: the publication in the *North American Review* of "Thanatopsis," "To a Waterfowl," and a critical survey of American poetry,[2] and the modest celebrity which brought him in 1821 an invitation to deliver the Phi Beta Kappa poem at Harvard. Yet though his natural inclinations were toward Boston, an accident of acquaintanceship gave him introductions to New York; and here, after a brief excursion among the straits and shallows of magazine editing, he found himself embarked on what proved to be a long, distinguished, and prosperous career as newspaper editor and proprietor.

When Bryant became editor-in-chief of the New York *Evening Post* in 1829 he was thirty-five years old and had composed about a third of the poetry he chose to preserve, and about half the poems on which his reputation rests. In substance this fraction of his writing is the normal expression of a young man in its reflection of boyhood influences and in its naïve and insistent egocentricity. Although his father

[1] Quoted in W. A. Bradley's "William Cullen Bryant," p. 91.

[2] Tremaine McDowell, "Bryant and the *North American Review*," in *American Literature*, Vol. I, pp. 14–26.

was liberal-minded, the young poet was a direct heir to colonial religious dogma: the sternness of God, the imminence of death, the threat of eternal damnation, the sense of life as a prelude to eternity. His mind and imagination were therefore wide open to the influence of Kirke White and the other "graveyard poets." He belonged to a people whose earliest childhood prayer ended with

> If I should die before I wake,
> I pray Thee, Lord, my soul to take.

"Thanatopsis," a glimpse of death, was composed under the eye of this God. In setting down "When thoughts of the last bitter hour come like a blight over thy spirit," he was not indulging in any far-fetched fancy; he was alluding to what the minister brought home in two sermons every Sunday and to the theme of the midweek prayer meeting. And when he wrote, at seventeen, of approaching the grave, "sustained and soothed by an unfaltering trust," he was writing of a trust which needed to be especially strong to face the day of doom and the counter-thought of the slave scourged to his dungeon. The concluding lines of "Thanatopsis" were appended to the original draft.[1] The early stirrings of dissent had become more assertive nine years later. In 1819 Bryant wrote the first four-fifths of his "Hymn to Death," a meditation based on Calvinistic theology. All men die, he said, even those one loves; but death is really God's instrument to punish the wicked. Oppressors, idolaters, atheists, perjurers, revelers, slanderers, the sons of violence and fraud, are struck down.

> Thus, from the first of time, hast thou been found
> On virtue's side; the wicked, but for thee,
> Had been too strong for the good; the great of earth
> Had crushed the weak for ever.[2]

With the poem at this stage, his father died in 1820 while at the height of his powers, as the result of exposure in meeting

---

[1] Carl Van Doren, "The Growth of Thanatopsis," *The Nation*, Vol. CI, p. 432.
[2] Bryant, "Hymn to Death," lines 115–118.

his duties as a country doctor. In view of this calamity the poet's verses seemed a bitter mockery to him:

> Shuddering I look
> On what is written, yet I blot not out
> The desultory numbers; let them stand,
> The record of an idle revery.[1]

Bryant's inclination to interpret everything personally in these days raised him at moments to lyric heights. The stanzas "To a Waterfowl" have a general application for the devout who are in trouble, though they were specifically pointed in his mind by his need for aid to guide his steps aright in the choice of a vocation. But the "pleasurable melancholy" that commended him to Poe often reduced other lyrics from a level of emotional beauty to a level of sentimental self-consciousness. He devoted five stanzas to "The Yellow Violet," but concluded with three more of self-analysis. "The Fringed Gentian" roused his hope that he might do as the autumn flower and look to heaven when the hour of death drew near. The upshot of "June" was that it would be a beautiful month for his funeral. This youthful bent for self-centering was natural not only to the young Puritan, vaguely dissatisfied with the existence of a country lawyer; it belonged to the sentimentalists of the age. It led him to applaud himself in Cummington days for his "sensibility"; and later in New York, not long after his removal there, to reprint,

> I cannot forget with what fervid devotion
> I worshipped the vision of verse and of fame;
> Each gaze at the glories of earth, sky, and ocean,
> To my kindled emotions was wind over flame.[2]

It revealed itself, moreover, in his generalized social optimism and his insistence on the doctrine of poetic justice. His Harvard effusion on "The Ages" was exactly what might

[1] Bryant, "Hymn to Death," in "Works," Vol. I, p. 52.
[2] Bryant, "I Cannot Forget," op. cit. p. 165.

have been expected from a Berkshire Mountain youth, unschooled, inexperienced, and happily romantic: History had accumulated an array of error from which Europe might in time escape. America had never been overwhelmed by it. A benignant population of white invaders, magnificently isolated, manifestly destined, could laugh at enemies and live in the lap of happiness. It was a conventional oration of the 1820's put into Spenserian stanzas; and just as Bryant echoed the orators in his confidence for America's future, he echoed Byron in his enthusiasm for Greek independence, not once, but many times.

"Thanatopsis" was, of course, the remarkable product of this up-country period in Bryant's career; and the remarkable feature of "Thanatopsis" is not its conventional Calvinism of ideology with its afterthought of mental reservation, expressed in what are now the opening and concluding lines. It was egregious in its day for its form; it is memorable now for the fact that here and there in its blank verse it contains unforgettable and unsurpassable lines. The normal experience for the youthful artist is to accept the prevalent style of the period even when his sentiments are ahead of the times. Bryant had had his period of conventional enthusiasm for Pope, and he was to go back to Spenser, very likely through Byron, whose contagion he did not quite escape during the epidemic in the 1820's; but in lifting himself while still a boy out of the rut of rhyme, and in composing fluent and effective blank verse, he showed an independent responsiveness to Wordsworth that was remarkable at an age which is not only usually imitative, but imitative of current fashions. Wordsworth, of course, was only restoring an older fashion; but to Bryant's American generation it was as unfamiliar as the free verse which just a hundred years later was puzzling a good many readers because, though often no freer than Bryant's, it was printed in units of meaning instead of units of measure. Naturally Dana and Phillips of the *North American Review* were surprised that anything of the sort should have been written on this side the Atlantic.

Bryant did not execute an about-face as soon as he went to New York. He followed Wordsworth further in his retrospective glances, as in "Lines on Revisiting the Country," "The Conjunction of Jupiter and Venus," and "I Cannot Forget." But he had come to town in Halleck's heyday, and he dropped into the vein of "The Croakers" and "Fanny," the Byronic vein, with a very nice lightness of tone and touch. In his poetical works "The Death of the Flowers" is printed between "To a Mosquito" and "A Meditation on Rhode Island Coal." An excerpt from each in turn will do better than any passage in commentary:

At length thy pinions fluttered in Broadway —
  Ah, there were fairy steps, and white necks kissed
By wanton airs, and eyes whose killing ray
  Shone through the snowy veils like stars through mist;
And fresh as morn, on many a cheek and chin,
Bloomed the bright blood through the transparent skin.[1]

The melancholy days are come, the saddest of the year,
Of wailing winds, and naked woods, and meadows brown and sere.[2]

I sat beside the glowing grate, fresh-heaped
With Newport coal, and as the flame grew bright
  — The many-colored flame — and played and leaped,
I thought of rainbows, and the northern light,
  Moore's Lalla Rookh, the Treasury Report,
  And other brilliant matters of the sort.[3]

The rural moralist could evidently play the role of the urban satirist; he could have out-Hallecked Halleck if he had chosen to; but at heart he was still the moralist.

The fundamental thing which happened to him and which changed him was that he became committed to an active vocation in which he was vitally interested, and that (though he made it a point to divorce his work as a journalist from his expression as a poet, going to rather extreme lengths) the

---

[1] Bryant, "To a Mosquito," op. cit. p. 154.
[2] Bryant, "The Death of the Flowers," op. cit. p. 157.
[3] Bryant, "A Meditation on Rhode Island Coal," op. cit. p. 160.

change in his point of view was bound to be recorded in some of his verse. He would not use his verse-making gifts, as Halleck did, either as a social accomplishment or as a means of livelihood; he would not divert them, as Freneau and Whittier did, to propagandist ends; he would not even write poems for occasions, as every official and unofficial laureate has done. But he had not been long in the city before he made the same discovery that Wordsworth had made, that his God lived in the town as well as in the country and was God of life as well as of death.

> Thy Spirit is around,
> Quickening the restless mass that sweeps along;
> And this eternal sound —
> Voices and footfalls of the numberless throng —
> Like the resounding sea,
> Or like the rainy tempest, speaks of Thee.[1]

Then in "The Battle Field" (1837) and "The Antiquity of Freedom" (1842) he shook off some of the civic irresponsibility that went with the manifest-destiny American formula and with the Calvinistic concept of a personal and all-powerful Providence. He was not oblivious to the desirability of salvation; but he was enlisted in the struggle for justice and the need for liberal acceptance of fresh solutions for both theological and social problems. When he wrote, in "The Battle Field," "Truth, crushed to earth, shall rise again," he meant, as the context shows, not the established truth of the ages but the unfamiliar truth which the new age is setting on its throne. And he became committed to the eternal vigilance which is the price of freedom.

For a while after Bryant's settling in New York this theme seemed to have replaced the theme of death, which had colored his adolescence and early maturity. It emerged in "Earth" (1834) when, not so certain of the manifest destiny, he hoped for a fairer page in history to be written in his new land; it appeared in "The Antiquity of Freedom" (1842)

[1] Bryant, "Hymn of the City," op. cit. p. 224.

when he called for a civic militance that, properly interpreted, might yet give point to "Onward, Christian Soldiers" as chanted by churchgoers recurrently thrilled by the rhythms of the melody, but so thrilled as to be dulled to the significance of the words. "The Planting of the Apple Tree" (1849) hinted at the end of fraud and force and oppression; the "Rain Dream" started from thoughts of the same sort. The theme lapsed until the Civil War, when it was naturally resumed, and after which it seems to have been permanently dropped. The new consciousness did not replace the old, but only supplemented it, giving evidence from time to time that Bryant the poet was not totally unaware of what Bryant the journalist was daily involved in — the stirring events and problems of contemporary history.

On the whole, though, as a poet, he was still living in the home of his imagination where he had been born and bred; and on the whole the poems of his maturity are on the level of his less distinguished earlier writing, not fulfilling the promise of "Thanatopsis." They are sweet, conventional, impeccable in form and in substance, unstimulative of either thought or emotion. They almost completely fail to meet the requirements laid down in the best of all his later utterances, his verses on "The Poet." They seem to the reader much more like "the pastime of a drowsy summer day" than the fruits of hot emotion glowingly committed to the page. The last exclamation to which he stirs his reader in this critical comment in verse is:

> What witchery hangs upon this poet's page!
> What art is his the written spells to find
> That sway from mood to mood the willing mind![1]

"The Poet" seems like a well-intentioned answer to Lowell's gay comments in "A Fable for Critics"[2]:

> Unqualified merits, I'll grant, if you choose, he has 'em,
> But he lacks the one merit of kindling enthusiasm,

[1] Bryant, "The Poet," in "Works," Vol. II, p. 137.

[2] Lowell's full comment on Bryant in "A Fable for Critics" (1848) runs to three pages, 37–40.

with the remarks on Bryant's "supreme ice-olation," which makes one feel that he is "stirred up with the very North Pole"; for the "Fable" preceded "The Poet" by some fifteen years.

An unqualified merit of Bryant's poetry is that in his so-called "nature poems" he wrote accurately and specifically about birds and trees and flowers and seasons that he knew. Thoreau could have corrected few of his allusions to flora and fauna. One reads of the bright coloration of the bobolink and of his sober-feathered mate, of the six white eggs flecked with purple, and feels that Bryant has really observed them and the whole cycle of bobolink life. The reaction is similar in many other descriptive verses; but Bryant's nature poems seldom catch the imagination and carry it away with the flight of the waterfowl. Usually the poems on such themes fall into one of two categories: either they are versified descriptions such as might be made from entries in Thoreau's journals, with some little appended observation on life, or they are observations on life for which the natural object is chosen as a visible analogy. To Peter Bell the primrose by the river's brim was just stupidly and literally that, and nothing more. To Bryant the something more was a prosy bit of moralization; and this application was more likely than not to deal with the shortness of human life. There is no magic significance in these poems; they are too pedantic. Yet at long intervals and in special circumstances Bryant could write in the spirit of the poet. He is out, for instance, on one of his family visits to Princeton, Illinois. He is a long way from home and from the office of the *Evening Post*. Looking out over the prairie he suddenly realizes the anguished loneliness of the pioneer's wife, who has followed her man without choice and is losing him even while she seems to have him:

> These prairies glow with flowers,
>   These groves are tall and fair,
> The sweet lay of the mocking-bird
>   Rings in the morning air;

And yet I pine to see
  My native hill once more,
And hear the sparrow's friendly chirp
  Beside its cottage door.

And he, for whom I left
  My native hill and brook,
Alas, I sometimes think I trace
  A coldness in his look!
If I have lost his love,
  I know my heart will break;
And haply, they I left for him
  Will sorrow for my sake.[1]

The Bryant of "Thanatopsis" used often to be called the American Wordsworth; the Bryant who wrote this simple, unexpounded plaint of loneliness resembles the Wordsworth of the Lucy poems. But the world and the afterworld were too much with him to permit him often to write in this unpretentious, unpedantic, and genuinely emotional vein.

A full survey and appraisal of Bryant's contributions to the *Evening Post* is still to be made, but the main outlines have been drawn.[2] The paper to which he came as a young Federalist had been established and conducted with the help of Alexander Hamilton. Coleman, the editor who enlisted Bryant on the little staff, was committed to Hamiltonian doctrines. *The Post* and its new editor changed to support the doctrines of insurgent democracy; and Bryant's own leading recruits — William Leggett, Parke Godwin, and even John Bigelow — were more aggressively liberal than he. He believed in party government, and supported Jackson, but not in party subservience; and he championed the civil service reform that Jacksonian tactics made imperative. He created a legal precedent in his successful defense of the right of labor to group bargaining; he took an early stand

[1] Bryant, "Works," Vol. II, p. 67.

[2] The most complete treatment as yet is in "The Evening Post — a Century of Journalism," by Allan Nevins, in which Bryant appears as the major figure.

against slavery; he insisted on the right of free speech, and, of course, supported the free-soil element and opposed the Fugitive Slave Law. He turned with most ardent liberals against the Daniel Webster whom he regarded as an ambitious opportunist, and four years before the seventh-of-March speech he bolted the Democratic party in disgust. He was among the first of influential Easterners to rally to Abraham Lincoln and among the minority who were independent and bold enough to applaud the heroism of John Brown.

In his later years Bryant was regarded with something approaching reverence in New York. Throughout his career there he had insisted on writing in terms of principles and in keeping out of personal controversy. A certain social remoteness and a marked picturesqueness of appearance helped to make him a sort of living legend. Everyone could see him on the streets and on the platform; no one knew him. He was an old-fashioned orator of rotund periods, and was so often called on to deliver memorial addresses that he was affectionately known as "the old man eloquent."

Theater and Drama in the 1830's

In a survey on this scale it is out of the question to follow the whole story of the American drama or of the American stage. All that may be done is to continue, as in preceding chapters, to make occasional soundings in the wide stream of the national literature in the 1830's, in the 1850's, at the turn of the century, and in the more recent past. What comes up tells something of the constant and the variant factors in public taste as shown by what was written for the stage or acted upon it.

In the 1830's there were many recurrent phases and features from the earlier days. Generally speaking, for example, the censorious moralism of the straitly religious was still active toward plays and players. The contentions of Gosson and his successors were still lively. From time to time defenders tried to buttress the drama by saying how good and useful it was. Thus when a benefit performance for the elderly William Dunlap was proposed in 1833, the announcement in the *Knickerbocker Magazine* suggested the event and italicized it "as a testimony of respect for the character of Wm. Dunlap, Esq., and our esteem for the evidence which his dramatic works have furnished *for the moral influence of the stage*."[1] Thus in the next year the *North American Review* asserted, "the true object of the Drama is public instruction. Our sentiments ought to be more noble, our minds more pure and elevated, on leaving than on entering the theatre."[2] And thus even as late as November, 1840, and as far south as Richmond, Virginia, the *Southern Literary Messenger* published a fervent attack on the theater, calling it, in "An Evening Walk in the City," "a whited sepulchre, a gate to hell, within which a human being was bartering his soul for a brief shout of applause, oblivious to both virtue and religion."[3] Yet such expressions as these were becoming less frequent and were on the decline throughout the country, though most rapidly so in New York, the chief producing center. Yet even here, on the return of the favorite actress Mrs. Hilson in 1835, the New York *Evening Post* could ascribe the heartiness of the welcome to the fact that as a widow she came "with a name as bright as when she first appeared before us, 'a maid in the pride of her purity.'"[4]

A new critical note, moreover, was becoming audible — a note that reveals the increasing maturity of the American theater public. This was the perennial refrain of all ages, a lament over the decline of contemporary taste. Perhaps in greater measure than usual there was ground for this. While temporal distance lends enchantment to any view at any time, it is true that in the half-century of the long-lived Hallam Company the original rather select repertory of Shakespeare and the Restoration dramatists persisted for many decades and, on the whole, was supplemented or

---

[1] Vol. I, p. 323. [2] Vol. XXXIV, p. 335. [3] Vol. VI, p. 721.
[4] Odell, "Annals of the New York Stage," Vol. IV, p. 51.

gradually replaced by comparatively excellent plays, Farquhar giving place to Goldsmith, Congreve to Sheridan, Shakespeare holding his own. But as the theater became less of a rarity in the colonies and the states, the public was less inclined to buy seats regardless of the attraction; and the demand for the sensational, the spectacular, and the merely laugh-provoking became increasingly insistent. There were evidences of this tendency in the 1790's. They were generously multiplied by the 1830's; and the caviar to the general was wormwood for the critically minded. Let the trio of periodicals just cited bear witness again: *The Knickerbocker* announced of the 1835 season that "the most prominent attractions have been of the canine description. When Shakespeare said the dog would have his day, he little thought that that sagacious quadruped would usurp the province of the legitimate actor and bark his hour upon the stage."[1] The next year it protested in more rhetorical style that "inexplicable dumb show and noise have usurped the place once advantageously held by the brightest emanations of human genius."[2] *The Southern Literary Messenger*, in November, 1837, deplored dramatizations of the "Pickwick Papers," saying that they were prepared for "a generation which tolerates Jim Crow upon the stage, which would prefer Colman's broad grins to Goldsmith's racy humor, and substitutes the melo-drama, and the opera, and the spectacle, and broad farce, for the best tragedies of Shakespeare, and the finest productions of the comic muse."[3] And the *North American* rendered the harshest verdict with, "The English and American stage is now too degraded to be taken into the account in any estimate of literary merit."[4]

The competition for audiences brought about this lowering of standards. It was inevitable in connection with an art that had to be maintained as a business and that depended on public patronage. The more level-headed critics acknowledged that producers and managers must either sell what the

[1] Vol. VI, p. 559.
[2] Vol. VII, p. 10.
[3] Vol. VII, p. 678.
[4] Vol. LII, p. 496.

public would buy or withdraw from the market; and the managers proved that they had no prejudices against supplying the best the market could afford, by their extravagant competition for the most popular star actors and actresses, many of whom confined their repertories almost exclusively to tried and justly popular plays. In fact, this competition for the best as well as for the most sensational and least admirable was quite disastrous in the 1830's, particularly in Philadelphia;[1] for it resulted in excessive payments to the stars, ruinously low salaries to the supporting stock companies, and a tenuous margin between meager profits and actual deficits for the managers. Yet as long as the stars could be secured, the dramatic seasons had their high lights in plays as well as in players.

As the playgoing publics in Boston, New York, and Philadelphia were not large enough to absorb any attraction for a whole season, and as travel between them was now fairly rapid and easy, their programs for any season were largely overlapping and may be treated as one. The English and Continental performers were still in the ascendant, as the comments of the critics and the box-office returns testify; and the native-born element, while increasing in vogue, were, not unnaturally, more inclined to introduce not only fresh blood but also fresh features to the local stage.

Of these visiting players, Thomas Abthorpe Cooper, known to the American stage since the 1790's, could still draw an audience for his Shakespearean interpretations, though evidently past his prime. Charles and Frances Kemble were favorites in solid repertories — the father so obviously the English gentleman, the daughter strangely gifted in view of her half-contempt for the art and her complete dislike for her professional associates. The star of J. B. Booth was in the ascendant, eccentric as he was in his uncalculated effects, his unevenness within the limits of a single performance, his overwhelming powers when he chose to release them on an

[1] See William B. Wood's "Personal Recollections of the Stage" in various complaints about this abuse and its consequences.

audience. The first of the Wallacks passed and repassed the Atlantic until he finally settled in America as actor-manager. Ellen Tree too came in these years, and Tyrone Power, first of the name and first of the distinguished performers in Irish roles.[1] There were several of less repute who were skilled enough to hold their hours for successive seasons. And it may be said of these leading players that the distinction of their repertories was in close relation to their own distinction as artists. The public came to see them in famous and familiar roles; except for Power they were free from dependence on novelties. In what they played and the way they played they furnished a standard of comparison for the contemporary stage.

This standard of comparison throws into relief the most conspicuous of the American actors and playwrights and their contributions to a native stage and drama. The two leading developments stress the interaction of the groups and the futility of trying to make literary history by deliberate forethought. The first was Edwin Forrest's unsuccessful attempt to foster an American drama on native, aboriginal themes. From 1829 to 1837 he conferred prizes on plays written for his robustious acting. The "hero or principal character" was to be "an aboriginal of this country." In the first winning role Forrest strutted and roared as Metamora, an Indian chief; but in the next eight he appeared as an Inca prince, as a primitive Briton and a British highwayman, as a gladiator, a noble Roman, and a noble Greek, as a Central American, and as Mahomet. He had discovered that for an actor who wanted to out-Herod Herod and tear passions to tatters the American Indian was not the best character. He kept "Metamora" in his repertory for many years, but he was better suited for a Spartacus. So plays were built for him on Spartacan lines; they were by American authors for an American actor, and they were utterly exotic.

---

[1] Most of these players have their biographers. The most useful general references for them are Arthur Hornblow's "History of the American Theater" and A. H. Quinn's "History of the American Drama from the Beginning to the Civil War."

On the other hand, while this attempt to pulmotor some vitality into the American drama was failing, signs of spontaneous life were cropping out. A Yankee character strolled on the stage, appearing at first as a native variant of the Irish comic-relief servant who was a constant on the British stage. Since his first appearance the Yankee had figured now and then as Jonathan in "The Contrast,"[1] though he did not make much of a hit until Woodworth introduced him as Jonathan Ploughboy in "The Forest Rose" of 1825.[2] This character, like the long succession that followed, was drawn from life and appealed to native audiences. Though the Yankee first strayed into the action quite incidentally, he soon captured the center of the stage and was written into the center of the plot. He was a wandering figure roving through time and space, eventually to reach even King Arthur's court. There were plays on "Yankee Land" and "Yankee Hill at Home"; but he was more in his element as "The Yankee Traveller" or the "Yankee Pedlar," or in distant settings — at Niagara, in England, in Tripoli, in China, in 1776, in Time. He actually made careers for players like "Yankee" Hill and Dan Marble. He launched James H. Hackett and the last Joseph Jefferson on the way to fame. Sol Smith was to carry on the tradition until it was resumed by James A. Herne and Denman Thompson. Moreover, he strengthened the weak knees of native drama by winning the encouragement of foreign approval. England looked on and smiled as Hackett, Hill, Marble, and Silsbee triumphed in London with Yankee roles. The reason was simple: the Yankee was a spontaneous native growth in American literature. He flourished like the goldenrod.

Even in these years of the Yankee's rise to fame and favor the more ambitious American dramatists still seemed of a mind with Fenimore Cooper as to the lack of native material.[3]

---

[1] See pages 185–186.

[2] Quinn, "American Comedy Types, 1825–1860," Chap. XI.

[3] Quinn, "Boker and the Later Romantic Tragedy," Chap. XII; also E. S. Bradley's life of Boker.

It was a dictum that George H. Boker was to insist on as late as 1850 when he wrote his friend Stoddard, "Read Chaucer for strength, read Spenser for ease and sweetness, read Milton for sublimity and thought, read Shakespeare for all these things, and for something else which is his alone. Get out of your age as far as you can."[1] Believing this, the literary dramatists hunted miscellaneously for inspiration in the remoteness of time and space.

The titles of their plays tell enough of the story to satisfy any but the hardiest: Richard Penn Smith's "Caius Marius"; R. M. Bird's "Caridorf," "Pelopidas," "Broker of Bogota"; D. P. Browne's "Sertorius"; J. A. Stone's "Tancred, or the Siege of Antioch"; R. T. Conrad's "Jack Cade"; James Lawson's "Giordano"; Mrs. Ellet's "Teresa Contarini"; N. P. Willis's "Tortesa the Usurer." Why prolong the list? It could be pursued for three decades before the Civil War, up to Mrs. Howe's "Leonora, or the World's Own" and Boker's various efforts, of which none succeeded in its day, and only one, "Francesca da Rimini," was ever revived. A phase of this exoticism is apparent also in the widening flood of dramatized novels, and of plays based on poetic narrative, on short tales, and even on ballads. A single year in New York offered from Scott "Rob Roy," "Guy Mannering," "The Heart of Midlothian," "The Pirate," "Rokeby," "Woodstock," "The Bride of Lammermoor." Cooper was rewritten for the boards within a few months of publication and more often than appears at first glance; as, with "The Red Mask, or the Council of Three" from "The Bravo," and "The Wigwam" from "The Pioneers." Dickens, starting with various episodes from "Pickwick Papers," was to run through a long and varied career. And the middle thirties saw also "The Last Days of Pompeii," "The Yemassee," "The Spectre Bridegroom," and even "Tam o' Shanter."

These features thrived better than the poetic drama by students of Spenser, Milton, and Shakespeare, partly because

---

[1] E. S. Bradley, "G. H. Boker, Poet and Patriot," p. 79.

of their spectacular qualities and partly because, drawn from tried stories, they had genuine narrative interest. "Mazeppa," of course, owed its tremendous success to these facts, coupled with the introduction of the famous equestrian scene and, when played in its greatest days by Adah Isaacs Menken, to the beauty and notoriety of the actress, who made her final exit strapped to the back of the flying steed. But the "Mazeppa" of the 1830's prospered without these extra drawing qualities.

Two other aspects of the stage at this time are worth mentioning, both of them as indexes to the public taste of the day. One was the readiness of producers to turn themes of contemporary interest to account. In an industrial age there were a lot of vocational plays — homely productions, like "Luke the Laborer," "Teddy the Tiler," "The North-End Pilot," "The Factory Girl." Many of these were advertised as based on facts — the true-story device. History had been temporarily exhausted with the conclusion of the semi-centennials, 1825–1833; but politics supplied a skit, "Removing the Deposits," on the recent debatable exploit of President Jackson; and popular science and religion, skits on "Bumpology; the Victim of Science" and "Miller's Rights or Mormon Profits." This burlesque-satire[1] is a connecting link to the other straw in the wind of public taste — the growing vogue of burlesques which were based on the audiences' acquaintance with well-known plays or novels, the evidence of a modest degree of literary sophistication. Some were general in nature, like the popular "Deep, Deep Sea" with its variety of legendary characters from Neptune and Minerva, Perseus and Andromeda, to a Lieutenant of Minnows and a Sea Serpent. Some were personal and specific, like "The Bugs," which was Fanny Kemble's unhappy term for newspapermen, and which had for leading lady Fanny Journalism. But most of them were of the parody type:

[1] See Constance Rourke's "American Humor," pp. 119–131, also Walter Blair's "Burlesques in Nineteenth Century American Humor," in *American Literature,* Vol. II (November, 1930), pp. 236–247.

"The Death of 'Life in London'" (Pierce Egan), "Nigger Assurance" ("London Assurance"), "Buy it, Dear" ("La Bayadère"), and the more easily recognizable "Lady of Irons" and "Virginius, the Rum 'Un." Even this type of production gave the critics their bad moments, because the comic effects were so obvious and because the popular performers, like Reeve, fell into the bad habit of "gagging" their lines in all their parts. A writer in *The Knickerbocker* in August, 1836, speculated on whether the appetite for broad effects had been developed through the highly spiced diet of the opera, and tried to turn the burlesque to scorn by offering a scenario on the theme of Jack and Jill.

The ballet heightened the zest for thrill and color too. This was the decade in which Augusta came, and Celeste and Elssler and Taglioni and Vestris, each attracting audiences beyond the hopes of most actors, each soon followed by her child imitator, "La petite etc." Beyond and below these dramatic box-office attractions, and often interlarded through dramatic programs, were all sorts of vaudeville acts, monologues, songs, dances, legerdemain, trained-animal performances. Barnum was looming over the horizon; "Ethiopian Drama," commonly known as minstrelsy, was ascending the sky, no bigger than a man's black face. With these and ever developing fresh competitors the legitimate theater and drama had from now on to hold its own in the leading Eastern cities.

By the 1830's, however, the tale of the American theater could not be told in terms of seaboard centers only. The West, or what then was the West, had already been invaded; [1] the Ohio-Mississippi Valley had developed a long "road" for the itinerant actor; and at the extreme points of a fan-shaped Western theatrical territory were three towns which can serve as representative of this frontier in terms of plays and playhouses: New Orleans, St. Louis, and Chicago. Activities had begun in this order on the extreme Western front. New

---

[1] See pages 209–210.

Orleans, oldest of the three and French in allegiance as well as in culture and speech until the purchase of Louisiana Territory, had reluctantly succumbed to "Yankee" invasion in the years that followed, though it was not until this fourth decade of the century that the drama in English fairly rivaled the long-established drama in French. A round eighteen years of intermittent existence had passed over the English stage in New Orleans between the day of Ludlow's arrival with his company and the opening of Caldwell's St. Charles Theater there in 1835.[1]

Caldwell, the enterprising, was in continuous correspondence with people of the London stage, and resorted there for annual additions to his local repertory and the actors to present it. A summary of his seasons at the St. Charles is therefore fairly representative of what was running in London, and of the newer features, particularly of what had been tried out at the unlicensed theaters of the metropolis, in which novelties and experiments were more frequent than on the boards at Covent Garden and Drury Lane.

Except in the program elements which showed Caldwell's enterprising up-to-dateness, his methods and his lists of plays are an extraordinary example of history in repetition, his company retreading the paths of the Hallams and their fellow actors so closely that generalizations about what one company did in the 1750's on the seacoast and the other in the 1830's on the Gulf coast are confusable if not literally interchangeable. He operated with the conventional stock company drilled to support leading actors and actresses in a well-established list of standard plays. These included the main Shakespeare tragedies, "Much Ado" and "As You Like It" for the women's parts, and the Falstaff plays. A "New Way to Pay Old Debts" was still running strong, as were "Jane Shore," "The Busy-Body," and "The Wonder" from the original Hallam repertory. When one has listed also "Rule a Wife and Have a Wife," "Venice Preserved,"

[1] See Lucile Gafford's "History of the St. Charles Theater in New Orleans, 1835–1843." The University of Chicago Libraries.

"Douglas," and "George Barnwell," the mid-eighteenth century is apparently identified. Add the Goldsmith and Sheridan plays, Colman's "Heir at Law," and Tobin's "Honeymoon," retaining the others, and the turn of the century seems to be approaching. Yet as a matter of record all these, and all the leading favorites applauded in London and New York practically up to the moment, were in Caldwell's New Orleans programs.

Much the same may be said for the leading performers. Forrest came back here to the most important scene of his earlier training before the footlights; to New Orleans came Hackett and "Yankee" Hill and Dan Marble and Tyrone Power; so did Celeste and Elssler and Ellen Tree and old Mr. Cooper and the elder Booth. Remote as it was, the New Orleans of the 30's had its flowers from every bouquet that came to New York, if it did not now and then cull them first, and many of the weeds too; for the child actors and acrobats and vaudevillists of every description won their way in this old city which, though so emphatically Western in terms of geography, was in terms of culture anything but a frontier community. How far it was from this one can see by comparison with the St. Louis and the Chicago of the same years.

Like New Orleans, St. Louis had risen under the French flag. It was nearly forty years old at the time of the Purchase, and more than fifty when the first play in English was put on by a group of amateurs. Well north of the junction of the Ohio and Mississippi, the town of five thousand was on a spur from the Pittsburgh–New Orleans waterway; and it was not until 1818 that a professional company came to town by steamboat and not until 1820 that Ludlow came north with a troupe of his own. Up to 1835 the fortunes of the play waxed and waned, performances progressing from an abandoned smithy and a stable loft to a log house and an abandoned saltworks. From 1835 on, there were a hundred nights or more in the annual season, and in 1837 Ludlow finally raised the funds for an adequate theater. By the end of the decade St. Louis had achieved a history[1] which recapitulates what the Eastern cities had seen in the theatrical beginnings and what New Orleans had more recently survived. But it had been more crowded, and the first solid repertory had not established it so firmly or survived so long. In number the performances of Shakespeare were surpassed by those of J. B. Buckstone; the sensational play gained an earlier hold on the river audiences and the passing emigrants; and only the hardiest of the wandering stars were tempted to take their chances in this more nearly frontier town. St. Louis was an echo of New Orleans in these years, but a far fainter echo of New Orleans than New Orleans was of New York or even of London. As for Chicago, this city was still far from the main lines of travel. The panic year, 1837, saw its first theater, for the panic was slow in reaching these Western communities. But there were a dozen places in the north-Ohio valley that fared better than this lake port. Chicago is mentionable in theatrical history in the 1830's only because of the notable fact that there is so little to report of this coming metropolis. Its theatrical chronicles were soon to accumulate abundantly.

Book List

EARLY METROPOLITANS

WASHINGTON IRVING. Works. First complete edition. 21 vols. 1861. Chief titles appeared as follows: Salmagundi; or the Whim-Whams and Opinions of Launcelot Langstaff, Esq., and Others, 1807–1808; A History of New York from the Beginning of the World to the End of the Dutch Dynasty. . . , by Diedrich Knickerbocker (2 vols.), 1809; The Sketch Book of Geoffrey Crayon, Gent., 1819; Bracebridge Hall; or The Humorists . . ., 1822; Tales of a Traveller, 1824; A History of the Life and Voyages of Christopher Columbus (3 vols.), 1828; A Chronicle of the Conquest of Granada (2 vols.), 1829; The Alhambra: a Series of Tales and Sketches of the Moors and Spaniards (2 vols.), 1832; The Crayon Miscellany (3 vols.), 1835; Astoria; or Incidents of an Enterprise beyond the Rocky Mountains (2 vols.), 1836; The Life of George Washington (5 vols.), 1855–1859; Uncollected Miscellanies, 1866.

---

[1] W. G. B. Carson, "The Theater on the Frontier: Early Years of the St. Louis Stage," 1932.

[*Available Editions*]

PENNY, CLARA L. Washington Irving's Diary in Spain. 1926.
WILLIAMS, STANLEY T. Journal of Washington Irving, 1823–1824. 1931.
WILLIAMS, STANLEY T. (Ed.). Letters from Sunnyside and Spain. 1928.
WILLIAMS, STANLEY T. Washington Irving and the Storrows. Letters from England, 1821–1828. 1933.
The Alhambra, The Sketch Book, Bracebridge Hall, and Tales of a Traveller are variously edited for class use.
A History of New York, by Diedrich Knickerbocker, edited by Stanley T. Williams and Tremaine McDowell. 1927.
Irving's Works. Knickerbocker Edition. 27 vols. 1864–1874.
Poems of Washington Irving, brought together from various sources by William R. Langfeld. 1931.
Tales by Washington Irving. Selected and edited by Carl Van Doren. 1919.
A Tour in Scotland, 1817, and other manuscript notes by Washington Irving, edited, with critical introduction, by Stanley T. Williams. 1927.
Voyages and Discoveries of the Companions of Christopher Columbus, by Washington Irving. With foreword by Van Wyck Brooks. 1929.
Works of Washington Irving. Author's Revised Edition. 28 vols. 1872.

[*Biography and Criticism*]

BOYNTON, HENRY W. Washington Irving. 1901.
BRYANT, WILLIAM CULLEN. A Discourse on the Life, Character, and Genius of Washington Irving. 1860.
BURTON, RICHARD. "Washington Irving's Services to American History." Literary Likings. 1902.
CANBY, HENRY SEIDEL. Classic Americans. 1931.
CURTIS, GEORGE WILLIAM. "Irving's Knickerbocker," *The Critic*, Vol. III, 1883.
CURTIS, GEORGE WILLIAM. "Washington Irving." Literary and Social Essays. 1894.
HAWEIS, HUGH R. American Humorists. 1883.
HAZLITT, WILLIAM. "Elia and Geoffrey Crayon." The Spirit of the Age. 1825.
HELLMAN, GEORGE S. Washington Irving, Esqr., Ambassador at Large from the New World to the Old. 1925.
HOLMES, OLIVER W. "Irving's Power of Idealization," *The Critic*, Vol. III, 1883.
HOWELLS, WILLIAM DEAN. My Literary Passions. 1895.
LOWELL, JAMES RUSSELL. A Fable for Critics. 1848.
MACY, JOHN. The Spirit of American Literature, Chap. II. 1912.
PAYNE, WILLIAM M. Leading American Essayists. 1910.
THOMPSON, J. B. "The Genesis of the Rip Van Winkle Legend," *Harper's*, Vol. LXVII, pp. 617–622.
WARNER, CHARLES DUDLEY. Washington Irving. A. M. L. Series. 1881.
WARNER, CHARLES DUDLEY. "Washington Irving," *Atlantic Monthly*, Vol. XLV, pp. 396–408.
WILLIAMS, STANLEY T. Washington Irving. 2 vols. 1935.
The authorized life is Life and Letters of Washington Irving, by Pierre Irving. 4 vols. 1862–1864.

[*Bibliography*]

LANGFELD, W. R., and BLACKBURN, P. C. Washington Irving; A Bibliography. 1933.

LONG, SHIRLEY V. Cambridge History of American Literature, Vol. I, pp. 510–517.

JAMES FENIMORE COOPER. The chief works appeared originally as follows: Precaution, 1820; The Spy, 1821; The Pioneers, 1823; The Pilot, 1823; Lionel Lincoln, 1825; The Last of the Mohicans, 1826; The Prairie, 1827; The Red Rover, 1828; Notions of the Americans, 1828; The Wept of Wish-ton-wish, 1829; The Water-Witch, 1831; The Bravo, 1831; The Heidenmauer, 1832; The Headsman, 1833; The Monikins, 1835; Homeward Bound, 1838; Home as Found, 1838; The Pathfinder, 1840; Mercedes of Castile, 1840; The Deerslayer, 1841; The Two Admirals, 1842; Wing and Wing, 1842; Wyandotte, 1843; Ned Myers, 1843; Afloat and Ashore, 1844; Satanstoe, 1845; The Chainbearer, 1845; The Redskins, 1846; The Crater, 1847; Jack Tier, 1848; The Oak Openings, 1848; The Sea Lions, 1849; The Ways of the Hour, 1850.

[*Available Editions*]

The American Democrat. Introduction by H. L. Mencken. 1931.

Complete Works. Leatherstocking Edition. 33 vols. 1854.

Gleanings in Europe (England), edited by R. E. Spiller. 1930.

Gleanings in Europe (France), edited by R. E. Spiller. 1928.

Works. Mohawk Edition. 33 vols. 1895–1901.

The more popular tales are variously edited for school use; among them are the following printings:

The Deerslayer, edited by Gregory L. Paine. American Authors Series. 1927.

The Pathfinder. Everyman Edition. 1917. Edited by Tremaine McDowell, Modern Students' Library. 1931.

The Spy, edited by Percy H. Boynton. Modern Readers Series. 1930.

[*Biography and Criticism*]

BARBA, PRESTON A. Cooper in Germany. German American Annals. 1914.

BARNUM, H. L. The Spy Unmasked; or Memoirs of Enoch Crosby, Alias Harvey Birch, the Hero of Mr. Cooper's Tale of the Neutral Ground. 1886.

BOYNTON, HENRY W. James Fenimore Cooper. 1931.

BROWNELL, WILLIAM C. "Cooper." American Prose Masters. 1909.

BRYANT, WILLIAM CULLEN. "A Discourse on the Life and Genius of James Fenimore Cooper" (1852). Memorials of James Fenimore Cooper. 1852.

CANBY, HENRY S. "James Fenimore Cooper." Classic Americans. 1931.

CLEMENS, S. L. "Fenimore Cooper's Literary Offenses," *North American Review*, July, 1895. Also in "How to Tell a Story and Other Essays." 1897.

COOPER, JAMES FENIMORE. The Correspondence of James Fenimore Cooper, edited by his grandson. 2 vols. 1922.

ERSKINE, JOHN. Leading American Novelists. 1910.

GRIGGS, E. L. "James Fenimore Cooper on Coleridge," *American Literature*, Vol. IV, pp. 389–391.

HILLARD, G. S. "Fenimore Cooper," *Atlantic Monthly*, January, 1862.
HOWE, M. A. DEWOLFE. "James Fenimore Cooper." American Bookmen. 1898.
HOWELLS, WILLIAM DEAN. Heroines of Fiction. 1901.
LOUNSBURY, THOMAS R. James Fenimore Cooper. A. M. L. Series. 1890.
MCDOWELL, TREMAINE. "The Identity of Harvey Birch," *American Literature*, Vol. II, pp. 111–120.
MCDOWELL, TREMAINE. "Scott on Cooper and Brockden Brown," *Modern Language Notes*, Vol. XLV, pp. 18–20.
MACY, JOHN. The Spirit of American Literature. 1912.
MATTHEWS, BRANDER. "Fenimore Cooper." Gateways to Literature, 1912.
OUTLAND, ETHEL R. "The 'Effingham' Libels on Cooper." University of Wisconsin Studies in Language and Literature, No. 28. 1929.
PAINE, GREGORY L. "Cooper and the *North American Review*," *Studies in Philology*, Vol. XXVIII, pp. 799–809.
PATTEE, FRED L. "Cooper, the Critic," *Saturday Review of Literature*, Vol. V, pp. 1107–1108.
POE, EDGAR A. Cooper's "Wyandotte." Literary Criticisms, Vol. II, pp. 3–18.
ROSS, JOHN F. The Social Criticism of Fenimore Cooper. 1933.
SIMMS, WILLIAM G. "The Writings of J. Fenimore Cooper." Views and Reviews, first series. 1845.
SPILLER, ROBERT E. Fenimore Cooper: Critic of His Times. 1931.
STEDMAN, EDMUND C. "Poe, Cooper, and the Hall of Fame," *North American Review*, August, 1907.
TUCKERMAN, HENRY. "James Fenimore Cooper," *North American Review*, Vol. LXXXIX, pp. 289–316.
VAN DOREN, CARL. The American Novel. 1921.
VINCENT, LEON H. American Literary Masters. 1906.
WILSON, JAMES G. "Cooper Memorials and Memories," *Independent*, Vol. LIII, pp. 251–255.

[*Bibliography*]

LOUNSBURY, THOMAS R. "Bibliography." James Fenimore Cooper, pp. 290–299.
SPILLER, R. E., and BLACKBURN, P. C. James Fenimore Cooper: a Descriptive Bibliography. 1934.
Cambridge History of American Literature, Vol. I, pp. 532–534.

WILLIAM CULLEN BRYANT. Chief works appeared as follows: The Embargo; or, Sketches of the Times, 1808; Poems, 1821; Poems, 1832; Poems (5th ed.), 1839; The Fountain and Other Poems, 1842; Thirty Poems, 1864; The Little People of the Snow, 1873; A Happy New Year, 1877; Unpublished Poems of Bryant and Thoreau, 1907.

[*Available Editions*]

CASTLEMAN, J. H. (Ed.). Thanatopsis, Sella, and Other Poems of William Cullen Bryant. 1906.
Best single volumes are the Household Edition, 1909, and the Roslyn, 1910.

Poems of William Cullen Bryant, edited, with introduction and notes, by Nelson A. Crawford. 1924.

The Poetical Works of William Cullen Bryant. Roslyn Edition, with chronologies of Bryant's life and poems, and a bibliography by Henry C. Sturges . . . and R. H. Stoddard. 1910.

The Works of William Cullen Bryant, edited by Parke Godwin. 6 vols. Vols. I and II, Life; Vols. III and IV, Poetical Works; Vols. V and VI, Prose Writings. 1884–1889.

[*Biography and Criticism*]

BIGELOW, JOHN. William Cullen Bryant. A. M. L. Series. 1890.

BRADLEY, W. A. William Cullen Bryant. E. M. L. Series. 1905.

CURTIS, GEORGE WILLIAM. The Life, Character, and Writings of William Cullen Bryant. 1879.

GLICKSBERG, CHARLES I. "Bryant and the *United States Review*," *New England Quarterly*, Vol. VII, pp. 687–701.

KREYMBORG, ALFRED. Our Singing Strength. 1929.

LEONARD, WILLIAM E. "William Cullen Bryant." Cambridge History of American Literature, Vol. I, Bk. II.

McDOWELL, T. "Bryant and the *North American Review*," *American Literature*, Vol. I, pp. 14–26.

McDOWELL, T. "Cullen Bryant Prepares for College," *South Atlantic Quarterly*, Vol. XXX, pp. 125–133.

McDOWELL, T. "Cullen Bryant at Williams College," *New England Quarterly*, Vol. I, pp. 443–466.

McDOWELL, T. "The Juvenile Verse of William Cullen Bryant," *Studies in Philology*, Vol. XXVI, pp. 96–116.

McDOWELL, T. "William Cullen Bryant and Yale," *New England Quarterly*, Vol. III, pp. 706–716.

NEVINS, ALLAN. The Evening Post. 1922.

PATTEE, FRED LEWIS. Side Lights on American Literature. 1922.

POE, EDGAR A. "William Cullen Bryant." Complete Works, Vol. VIII. 1902.

SHICK, J. S. "William Cullen Bryant and Théophile Gautier," *Modern Language Journal*, Vol. XVII, pp. 260–267.

SMITH, FRANK. "Schoolcraft, Bryant, and Poetic Fame," *American Literature*, Vol. V, pp. 170–172.

STEDMAN, EDMUND C. Genius and Other Essays. 1911.

STEDMAN, EDMUND C. Poets of America. 1885.

TAYLOR, BAYARD. Critical Essays and Literary Notes. 1880.

VAN DOREN, CARL. "The Growth of 'Thanatopsis,'" *Nation*, Vol. CI, p. 432.

WILSON, JAMES G. Bryant and His Friends. 1886.

The standard life is by Parke Godwin, Vols. I and II of the Life and Works in 6 vols. 1883–1884.

[*Bibliography*]

STURGES, HENRY C. Prefixed to the Roslyn Edition of Bryant and also published separately. 1910.

Cambridge History of American Literature, Vol. I, pp. 517–521.

THEATER AND DRAMA

CARSON, WILLIAM G. B. The Theatre on the Frontier. 1932.
CLAPP, WILLIAM W. A Record of the Boston Stage. 1853.
COAD, ORAL SUMNER, and MIMS, EDWIN, JR. "The American Stage." The Pageant of America, Vol. XIV. 1929.
COWELL, JOE. Thirty Years Passed among the Actors and Actresses of England and America. 1844.
CRAWFORD, MARY C. The Romance of the American Theatre. 1913.
EATON, WALTER PRICHARD. The Actor's Heritage. 1924.
HORNBLOW, ARTHUR. A History of the Theatre in America from its Beginnings to the Present Time. 2 vols. 1919.
KEMBLE, FRANCES ANNE. Journal. 2 vols. 1835.
LUDLOW, NOAH M. Dramatic Life as I Found It. 1880.
MAYORGA, MARGARET G. A Short History of the American Drama. 1932.
MOSES, MONTROSE J. The Fabulous Forrest. 1929.
ODELL, GEORGE C. D. Annals of the New York Stage, Vols. III, IV. 1928.
POLLOCK, THOMAS CHARLES. The Philadelphia Theatre in the Eighteenth Century. 1933.
REES, JAMES. Life of Edwin Forrest, with Reminiscences and Personal Recollections. 1874.
SONNECK, OSCAR G. Early Opera in America. 1915.
WINTER, WILLIAM. The Wallet of Time, Containing Personal, Biographical and Critical Reminiscences of the American Theatre. 2 vols. 1913.
WOOD, WILLIAM B. Personal Recollections of the Stage. 1855.

9

THEATER AND DRAMA

CARSON, WILLIAM G. B. The Theatre on the Frontier. 1932.
CLAPP, WILLIAM W. A Record of the Boston Stage. 1853.
COAD, ORAL SUMNER, and MIMS, EDWIN, JR. "The American Stage," The Pageant of America, Vol. XIV. 1929.
COWELL, JOE. Thirty Years Passed among the Players in England and America. 1844.
CRAWFORD, MARY C. The Romance of the American Theatre. 1913.
EATON, WALTER PRICHARD. The Actor's Heritage. 1924.
HORNBLOW, ARTHUR. A History of the Theatre in America from Its Beginnings to the Present Time. 2 vols. 1919.
KEMBLE, FRANCES ANNE. Journal. 2 vols. 1835.
LUDLOW, NOAH M. Dramatic Life as I Found It. 1880.
MAYORGA, MARGARET G. A Short History of the American Drama. 1932.
MOSES, MONTROSE J. The Fabulous Forrest. 1929.
ODELL, GEORGE C. D. Annals of the New York Stage. Vols. III, IV. 1928.
POLLOCK, THOMAS CLARK. The Philadelphia Theatre in the Eighteenth Century. 1933.
REES, JAMES. Life of Edwin Forrest with Reminiscences and Personal Recollections. 1874.
SONNECK, OSCAR G. Early Opera in America. 1915.
WINTER, WILLIAM. The Wallet of Time, Containing Personal, Biographical and Critical Reminiscences of the American Theatre. 2 vols. 1913.
WOOD, WILLIAM B. Personal Recollections of the Stage. 1855.

PART II

The Middle Years

CHAPTER VII

New England — Left Wing

THE TRANSCENDENTALISTS

IN THE summer of 1837 Ralph Waldo Emerson, a young New Englander sixteen years out of college, enjoyed the distinction of delivering the annual Phi Beta Kappa address at Harvard College. He was a solid and hitherto respectable young man who had recently withdrawn from the pulpit to enjoy the privileges and perform some of the duties of a heretic. He had published a pleasant and somewhat poetical volume on "Nature" the year before, and now he was to speak before his own college on "The American Scholar." The first part of his discourse was not sensational; but when he went on to the duties of the scholar the heretic began to speak — nowhere more emphatically than when he said of his subject that he should never quit his belief that a popgun was a popgun, though the ancient and honorable of the earth affirmed it to be the crack of doom. Possibly the time when he spoke was no more of a transition period than any period is. Things were moving no faster than they are a hundred years later; but there was an urgency of problems and an urgent need of people acute and alert enough to study and meet them.

The country had just completed a half-century of democratic experiment. The making of a constitution had proved to be more of a task than the writing of a declaration of independence. Almost immediately human rights had been forced to compound their demands with the rights of property. In the running conflict that followed and climaxed in Jacksonian democracy the tyranny of a distant and unintelligent monarchy had been supplanted by the tyrannies of a near and unintelligent public opinion. The rule of a people was demonstrably as fallible as the rule of a monarch. In these same years bewildering industrial and economic changes had taken place. The rise of the factory, the problems of labor, the developments on the opening of what seemed like an illimitable West, had encouraged to a high degree what Lowell was to describe as "eye-dollar-try." There was enough in this field to occupy the best minds of America for the next generation; but this was only the beginning.

In the province of religion and the church, events were no less disturbing. Unlimited sectarianism in the United States had given rise to unlimited varieties of bigoted orthodoxy, and with the 1830's the conflict between freedom and authority was in some respects far more acute than it had been in the early days of less generally challenged churchly domination. Again, and involving state and market and church, came all the aggravations attendant on slavery and the desire to overthrow it. The economic worthlessness of the slave in the North, his plantation value in the South, the dependence of the Southern planter on the Northern banker, brought to the fore questions of natural right, of state sovereignty, of economic stability, of Christian charity. And in addition to these major problems two others which came to later settlement, one in temporary and one in permanent fashion, were looming over the horizon: the problem of controlling the use of alcoholics and the problem of equal suffrage. In the circumstances there was wide room for discrimination between popguns and cracks of doom.

As for the cracks of doom, the ancient and honorable were vehemently insistent on their orthodoxies. In the realm of government the United States of America must remain forever united. No loyal and right-minded man could dissent; yet there were distressing renegades: Emerson saying that the state was a good cow and must be fed with its fodder of taxes, but warning the cow that if she obstructed him as he crossed the meadow he would cut her throat; Thoreau going to jail rather than pay tribute to a government that was for extending slavery into Texas; Massachusetts soberly considering the possibility of nullification before South Carolina faced the question; South Carolina questioning whether to continue an alliance with so nefarious a state as Massachusetts.

The defenders of property were as vigilant as always. The manufacturer was calling for protection and getting it; the slaveholder was extending his territory and demanding that the non-slaveholder chase, capture, and return his fugitive property. The banker was fearful lest anything disturb the market; and as antislavery agitation was a disturbance, State Street, which was the Wall Street of that day, upheld the planter, and "cotton thread held the union together."

The defenders of the religious orthodoxies, especially in New England, were as violent in preaching the gospel of love as only startled conservatives could be. Believing in Christian forbearance, they smote the liberals on the one cheek to encourage them in turning the other. Congregationalists anathematized the Unitarians, who were the latest group of Protestant separatists; and the Unitarians, soon possessed of their own brand of orthodoxy, excommunicated the Transcendentalists and boycotted their most popular preacher. Of course the inevitable followed, — suppression is the one infallible stimulant of revolt, — and there sprang up a forced crop of heresies and heterodoxies, many of them wild enough. "Everybody had a Mission (with a capital M) to attend to everybody-else's business. . . . Communities were established where everything was to be common but common-sense. . . . Conventions were held for every hitherto inconceivable purpose."[1] Between the fireworks and the lightning it was a wise man who could keep his head and maintain his sense of direction.

But intellectual unrest was not disturbing the entire country. Only the more settled parts of a country can be unsettled by things of the mind. The regions invaded in the enterprise of Western expansion were too preoccupied with

[1] Lowell, Essay on "Thoreau," in "Literary Essays," Vol. I, p. 362.

urgent, immediate, practical problems to have much time for theorizing. Over the Alleghenies the United States was absorbed in the business of pioneering and settlement. New York was suffering from the growing pains of becoming a metropolis. The thinking of the country was being done along the eastern seaboard to the south and to the north. And in New England a group of thinkers became coherent and articulate enough to be thought of as a "school" and to be labeled with a name — the Transcendentalists.

In the years of the growing fame of Irving, Cooper, and Bryant there was growing in the neighborhood of Boston a generation of New Englanders with a different training from that of the New Yorkers. Many of them came from a long line of churchly ancestry, as Bryant did, but, unlike Bryant, almost all felt an early dislike and distrust for the sternness of the old creeds. Yet they had the Puritan character of mind that was "derived from the daily contemplation of superior beings and eternal interests," and the Puritan inclination toward rebelliousness. As a rule they had been to college, most of them to Harvard, and the glimpse of philosophy allowed them in senior year sharpened their taste for abstract thinking. Their reading was no longer chiefly in Pope, Addison, and Goldsmith; it was in the greater English writers who were not yet so well known — Coleridge, Carlyle, and Wordsworth — and in the French and German philosophers, in whom these Englishmen were versed.

Centering about Concord, Massachusetts, but by no means limited to it, was a so-called Transcendental movement for which Emerson was the prime spokesman.[1] Though the proper noun is used by common consent to refer to this impulse in eastern Massachusetts, the ideas for which their proponents stood were only an expression of world thought, one of the many outcroppings of the independence of spirit that had been developing for generations. The refusal of the

---

[1] The major studies of Transcendentalism in America are O. B. Frothingham's "Transcendentalism in New England," 1876, and H. C. Goddard's "Studies in New England Transcendentalism" (Columbia University Studies in English), 1908.

nineteenth-century mind to submit to a philosophy that limited man's faith to a knowledge derived through the senses had already brought about in Germany, France, and England a reaction which insisted on the right of man to believe much that he could not prove. The successive stages of revolt in the Christian world, of Protestantism from Catholicism, of the nonconformist sects from the Protestant Church of England, of Unitarianism from the nonconforming Congregationalists, had all led from deference to established authority to an insistence on self-reliance. The political history of Europe and England had been moving for centuries toward the replacement of the subject by the citizen. Out of these tendencies in western Europe — which provincially regarded itself as the whole civilized world — and out of the special applications of these movements in the New England church and state, developed the school of thinkers dubbed Transcendentalists, who espoused a system of thought based on the assumption of certain fundamental truths not derived from experience, not susceptible of proof, which transcend human life, and are perceived directly and intuitively by the human mind.

This stood in complete contrast with the faith of the Pilgrims and the Puritans, and yet in strong resemblance. Like the Calvinists, the Transcendentalists proceeded from a set of assumptions rather than from a set of observed facts, but, unlike the Calvinists, the Transcendentalists drew these assumptions from an inner revelation instead of from a set of dogmas distorted out of the Scriptures. They believed in a benign God, and they found his clearest expression in the spirit of man and in the natural surroundings where God had placed him. They believed that in each man was a spark of divinity. They were assailed because they did not acknowledge an utter difference between Jesus Christ and the average man, though their offense lay not in degrading Christ to the level of man but in exalting man potentially to the level of Christ. They believed that man was perfectible, and dwelt on the duty of each individual to develop the best that was in him on earth, thinking more of this life than of the life hereafter. They were inspired by the love of God rather than by the fear of him, and thus "for a dogmatic dread they substituted an illimitable hope."[1]

The significance of the Transcendental movement in New England, however, depends quite as much on the people it enlisted as it does on the ideas they propounded. For they were a lively set of individuals. Though they were accused by the theologians of being champions of "the latest form of infidelity," as if their sole interest were in ecclesiastical matters, and though they were somewhat derisively regarded by the laity as dreamers with their heads in the clouds, as if their philosophizing were an end in itself, they were actually searching critics of the life of the day. They were impatient of a community that fell so far short of its possibilities. Emerson, the mild and saintly, had, as his neighbors knew, a gift for cutting down to the core of an issue and speaking straight out, using the short and ugly words for parties and partisans, measures and men. Such talk offset his reputation for being a recluse and his own statement that meddling with public questions was a dissipated philanthropy which made him leave his work. Thoreau, the village eccentric, was also the notorious author of an essay on the duty of "Civil Disobedience," backing his conclusions with chapter and verse from current history.

Emerson and Thoreau, of course; but Bronson Alcott too, and Theodore Parker no less. Both individualists and philosophers of a sort, they represented the polar extremes of the group, if group it may be called. Alcott[2] was Transcendentalism sublimated, pursuing his theories to absurd conclusions; a householder and father but nothing of a "provider"; a vegetarian possessed with what Carlyle called his "damned potato-gospel," though it was not even this, for Alcott abjured all but "aspiring" vegetables. A pedagogical theorist,

---

[1] Barrett Wendell, "Literary History of America," p. 286.

[2] The standard life of Alcott is F. B. Sanborn and William T. Harris's "A. Bronson Alcott; His Life and Philosophy," 2 vols., 1893.

more indebted than is usually known to the Englishman Richard Lovell Edgeworth, but pushing his theory of innate wisdom to excessive lengths and offering evidence for it in his "Record of a School" and his incredible "Conversations on the Gospels." A dealer in more or less Coleridgian aphorisms, some of which have been rescued in "Table Talk" and "Concord Days," but most of which were tossed off in conversations that Emerson said were like writings of a slate pencil with a sponge on the blunt end which was forever erasing all but the last few words. Yet he showed at the attempted rescue of the fugitive slave Anthony Burns that he had a physical recklessness or courage that made him oblivious to danger; and he was subject to a love of ideas that made him an inspiration to his great Concord neighbor and, in his far old age, the chief motivating figure behind the Concord School of Philosophy.

Parker[1] was anything but this contemplative manner of man — a dynamo who burned himself out in early middle age. He was a prodigious person, driven by an insatiable desire for activity. Unable to afford the expenses of going to Harvard, he did at home the work of the Harvard undergraduate, and qualified for a degree. Entering the Unitarian pulpit, he went on incessantly with his studies, versed himself deeply in the theologies and philosophies, and roved amazingly far and wide as a linguist. He had something of Macaulay's capacities for reading and mastery of what he had read. Inevitably he amassed one of the largest private libraries of his day in Boston. Too liberal for the Unitarians, he was ostracized by them, carried on a voluminous controversy with them, established a people's church (misleadingly designated the Twenty-eighth Congregational Church of Boston), preached to far larger audiences than any other pulpiteer of the town, ministered personally to his followers, and was eminent in civic activities and an indomitable foe of slavery, especially when slavery invoked the right to invade Massachusetts in pursuit of fugitives.

[1] The standard study of Parker is O. B. Frothingham's "Theodore Parker: a Biography," 1874.

But Parker as a Transcendentalist was something of a paradox. In theory he was at one with Emerson in his respect for the power of truths which transcended experience and which neither could be proved nor needed proof; but as a scholar he was voracious in his appetite for facts, and as a controversialist, incessant in his appeal to them. In this respect there is a likeness between him and Thoreau. The author of "Walden" loved the natural scene, wanted to be content with contemplation of it, resented the inquisitiveness of the natural scientist, ultimately surrendered to his own passion for facts.[1] The author of "Theism, Atheism and Popular Theology" asserted the truths of intuition, but immersed himself in "The World of Matter and the World of Man." This was his dilemma.

> He remained to the end as transcendental as Whitman, and as experimental as Spencer, as intuitive as Jefferson, and as sensational as Franklin. He maintained the complete and unique validity of facts of consciousness and then proved them by facts of demonstration. He elaborated the absolute and submitted first principles to laboratory tests.[2]

In consequence of his extraordinary activity as scholar and citizen, at the age of fifty he died of exhaustion, worn out.

At the heart of the movement, as it became articulate in the pages of *The Dial*, was Margaret Fuller,[3] first editor. She lived a turbulent life from girlhood, overstimulated by an ambitious and autocratic father; through young womanhood, when she was taking over the family burdens which his death had thrust upon her; past the exigent days in New York, when she was writing for Horace Greeley's *Tribune*; and through her European pilgrimage, her marriage to a titled Italian puppet, and her tragic death by shipwreck. She was a bluestocking with a restless, urgent, eager mind.

---

[1] See pages 346–347.

[2] H. S. Commager, "The Dilemma of Theodore Parker," *New England Quarterly*, Vol. VI, pp. 257–277.

[3] For a treatment of Margaret Fuller see T. W. Higginson's "Margaret Fuller," in American Men of Letters Series, 1884.

Among the Transcendentalists she was the burden bearer, certain to take on the editorship of *The Dial* until she tottered under it and was relieved by Emerson. Almost at once she took her place with the early agitators for equal suffrage. She lectured, she conducted "conversations," and, between seasons of almost incessant talk, she wrote. The men half dreaded her. Hawthorne named a refractory heifer after her at Brook Farm. In her habit of establishing friendships rather magnificently she was a sort of spring flood who frequently submerged her helpless acquaintances, forcing Emerson, when she reproached him for being craglike and unassailable, to reply with all humility but possibly secret gratitude that God had made him so. When people contemn the Transcendentalists as being ineffectives and cloistered solitaries, they ignore Parker and Margaret Fuller.

And they ignore Elizabeth Peabody,[1] the most dynamic of the Peabody sisters, the other two marrying Nathaniel Hawthorne and Horace Mann. Like Miss Fuller, she was learned in advance of her time, a born teacher with an enthusiasm for history and another for the classics. At the bookstore which she and her father conducted in Boston, German and French philosophical publications could be found when no one else in the country supplied them. When Bronson Alcott founded the Temple School she volunteered her services, and it was she who compiled the two books on it for which Alcott receives chief credit. When *The Dial* threatened to founder in mid-career she undertook to be publisher for a while. James Freeman Clarke's comment on her was that she was always meeting some want that first had to be created; Emerson's, that she kept "a whole stud of Phoenixes on hand." Among these, at one time, was the kindergarten, to which she gave an impelling momentum in this country. At the end of her life she was championing the lost cause of the American Indians.

---

[1] Fair treatment of Elizabeth Peabody is to be found in G. W. Cooke's "Introduction to The Dial," Vol. I, pp. 140–157, 193–194. Adequate treatment is yet to be made.

There was another busy and effective woman in the circle, or on the edge of it — Lydia Maria Child,[1] known in her own right, but also, in the neighborhood, known as the brilliant sister of Convers Francis. The Transcendentalists were variously interrelated, often in blood as well as in spirit. Mrs. Child fell under the Transcendental spell of John S. Dwight, who must have his own word here. She regarded Parker as the greatest American of all time. She wrote for *The Dial.* She won a national reputation with her pen, and she wielded it untiringly in the antislavery cause, while editing journals for young and old and writing the kind of compendious books of information which were still in vogue and of which "Peter Parley" was the most prolific compiler.[2]

These people all had their publics; but the element in the ranks of the movement which enjoyed the most constant audience was the element of Unitarian ministers who were less belligerent than Parker and were disapproved without suffering expulsion. John S. Dwight[3] stepped out of the pulpit by his own choice, as Emerson had done; and he became eventually the editor of his own journal of music and a leading influence in the formation of musical taste in Boston. Others remained[4] in the pulpit: John Weiss; Cyrus A. Bartol; James Freeman Clarke, reformer and voluminous author; Frederic H. Hedge, one of the most eloquent of the group but learned withal, an original member of the Transcendental Club (sometimes called Hedge's Club, because Hedge's arrival in Boston from his Bangor parish was the signal for a meeting). But the way out was easy to take, as George Ripley took it when, in 1840, he became propounder and founder of the Brook Farm community. Ripley was one of the group, as were Charles A. Dana, Margaret

---

[1] Lydia Maria Child's personality and activities are sketched in Cooke's "Introduction to The Dial," Vol. II, pp. 166–169. Reprinted for the Rowfant Club, 2 vols., 1902.

[2] See pages 200, 218.

[3] G. W. Cooke has treated Dwight in his "Introduction to the Dial," passim, and in "John Sullivan Dwight, Brook-Farmer, Editor and Critic of Music," 1898.

[4] The minor Transcendentalists are also sketched in Cooke.

Fuller, and George William Curtis, who made a kind of retroactive contribution to the movement by later activity in journalism. Greeley had been watching the Brook Farmers; and when they scattered, Horace played the role of Maecenas and provided several of them with welcome and lasting jobs.

The number of this group who made their way west for longer or shorter sojourns in the Ohio valley testifies to their energy and adventurousness in other than philosophical sallies. There had long been a connection between Boston and the rising towns of this Middle West. Cincinnati, in particular, had become a kind of outpost of Boston liberalism, and Boston liberalism was inseparable from Transcendentalism in its personnel. Bartol; Clarke; two of the Channings, preacher and poet; Christopher P. Cranch, ex-preacher, who ended up as a painter, all came there. Moncure D. Conway, a sort of Crabb Robinson in his capacity for making literary friendships, there founded and conducted for a year a second *Dial*. It is not necessary to press the frontier motif in their connection. There was a little of the nomad in a good many of them, and in Cincinnati or Louisville they could find enough of their kind to be in the West and feel at home. The point is that they were energetic people, not the dreamy set of armchair philosophers that tradition has made them.

Fortunately for the contemporary influence of the group the Transcendentalists did not lay themselves open to attack from a host of critics who would have made the most of any offensive vagaries of conduct. Emerson was a saint; Thoreau, an ascetic; Alcott, a blameless philosopher; Parker, a social knight-errant without fear and without reproach; Margaret Fuller, a high-minded woman of letters. And the scores of their associates were just as devoted to a high religious ideal as any equal number of the early settlers at Plymouth or Massachusetts Bay.

Two definite undertakings chiefly focused the group activity of the Transcendentalists. One was *The Dial*,[1] a

[1] The most complete analysis of *The Dial* is Cooke's "Introduction" to the reprint, cited in the note on page 312. The reprint is fairly accessible.

quarterly that ran for sixteen numbers from July, 1840, to April, 1844. The so-called Transcendental Club, an informal group of kindred spirits, came toward the end of the 1830's to the need of an "organ" of their own, and undertook the publication of this journal of a hundred and twenty-eight pages. Its paid circulation was very small, never reaching two hundred and fifty; and when, in the hands of its third set of publishers, it had finally to be discontinued, Emerson personally met the last small deficit. It contained chiefly essays, but included in every issue a rather rare body of verse. The essays reflected and expounded German literature and thought and, to a lesser degree, Oriental thought, and discussed general problems in art, literature, and philosophy. The section devoted to criticism of current books, music, and painting is interesting for its quick reception of works which later years have in most instances proved and accepted. Possibly the nearest analogy of today to the old *Dial* is the *Hibbert Journal*, though this is unique in having achieved international circulation and self-support. *The Dial* stands as the literary notebook of the Transcendental movement in the United States from 1840 to 1844.

The other undertaking associated with the Transcendentalists was less formally their own venture. This was the Brook Farm Institute of Agriculture and Education in West Roxbury, nine miles out from Boston.[1] It was the venture of a small group of stockholders, of whom the Reverend George Ripley was the leader, and Nathaniel Hawthorne the man of widest later fame. It was an attempt at the start to combine "plain living and high thinking" on the theory that the group could do all their own work and maintain their intellectual life as well. During the first three years, from 1841 to 1844, it was carried on as a quiet community of idealists slightly withdrawn from the hubbub of the world. Farming was supplemented by other simple industries, a school was successfully conducted, and the people who lived there

[1] The record of the Brook Farm experiment is given in Lindsay Swift's "Brook Farm; Its Members, Scholars and Visitors," 1900.

were viewed and visited by many who looked on with sympathetic interest not untinged with amusement. The number in residence never exceeded a hundred and fifty. Of the five leading Transcendentalists, Margaret Fuller was the only one to be even casually identified with it. Parker was occupied with his multitudinous duties as student, preacher, and reformer; Thoreau attempted his own solution at Walden Pond, and Alcott, at his short-lived and ill-fated Fruitlands; and Emerson stayed in Concord with the comment[1]: "I do not wish to remove from my present prison to a prison a little larger. . . . I have not yet conquered my own house. It irks and repents me. Shall I raise the siege of this hencoop, and march baffled away to a pretended siege of Babylon?"[2]

In the latter half of its history Brook Farm was drawn into the communistic program elaborated by the French philosopher Charles Fourier and introduced to America by his enthusiastic disciple Albert Brisbane. But when the Farm became a "phalanx," as the Fourierite units were called, its whole nature changed, as it became part of a social project for transforming the world. An ambitious central building was erected in 1846, and by an irony of fate the uninsured "phalanstery" was burned down on the very day when its completion was being celebrated. This last financial blow broke the back of the enterprise, and it was abandoned in 1847. Yet it is significant of Brook Farm that, however complete a practical failure it may have been, it served as a gathering spot for a group of idealists who never ceased to recall their life there as a happy and fruitful experience.

So "Babylon" fell but Concord remained—"a little town," Emerson wrote in his "Journal," "and yet has its honors. We get our handful of every ton that comes to the city;"[3] and well it might, for it was less than twenty miles from Boston. In his address at the two-hundredth anniversary he dwelt on his pride in its history and character, tracing

---

[1] See note on page 319 for bibliographical note on Emerson citations.
[2] Emerson, "Journals," Vol. V, pp. 473–474.
[3] Ibid. Vol. VI, p. 383.

the earliest settlement, the partitioning of the land, the events leading up to the Revolution, and, in the presence of some of the aged survivors, the firing by the embattled farmers of "the shot heard round the world." The Concord institution that most appealed to him was the town meeting, where the whole body of voters met to transact the public business.

> It is the consequence of this institution that not a school-house, a public pew, a bridge, a pound, a mill-dam, hath been set up, or pulled down, or altered, or bought, or sold, without the whole population of this town having a voice in the affair. A general contentment is the result. And the people truly feel that they are lords of the soil. In every winding road, in every stone fence, in the smokes of the poor-house chimney, in the clock on the church, they read their own power, and consider, at leisure, the wisdom and error of their own judgments.[1]

Emerson noted that the English government had recently given to certain American libraries copies of a splendid edition of the "Domesday Book" and other ancient public records of England. A suitable return, he said, would be the printed records of Concord, not merely because Concord was Concord, but because Concord was America. "Tell them, the Union has twenty-four States, and Massachusetts is one. Tell them, Massachusetts has three hundred towns, and Concord is one; that in Concord are five hundred ratable polls, [that is, taxable voters] and every one has an equal vote."[2] In closing his address the orator of the day gave his reason for choosing when thirty-one years old to return for the rest of his life to "the fields of his fathers": "I believe this town to have been the dwelling place, in all times since its planting, of pious and excellent persons. . . . The benediction of their prayers and of their principles lingers around us."[3]

In his "Journal" he carried the general endorsement down to particulars, appraising the townsmen in terms of their independence:

> Here we have Mr. S., who is man enough to turn away the butcher who cheats in weight. . . . There is the hero who will not subscribe

[1] Emerson, "Historical Discourse at Concord," in "Works," Vol. XI, p. 49.
[2] Ibid. p. 50.
[3] Ibid. p. 86.

to the flag-staff or the engine, though all say it is mean. There is the man who gives his dollar, but refuses to give his name, though all other contributors are set down. There is Mr. H., who never loses his spirits, though always in the minority. . . . Here is Mr. C., who says "honor bright" and keeps it so. Here is Mr. S., who warmly assents to whatever proposition you please to make, and Mr. M., who roundly tells you he will have nothing to do with the thing.[1]

In this old town he found Hunts and Willards, Meriams and Hosmers, who had been part of its history from the beginning. The Thoreaus were among the newcomers. The Hoars were here; an ancestor had been an early president of Harvard. Samuel Hoar was to serve in the Massachusetts legislature; of Samuel's children, George Frisbie was to be senator from Massachusetts for many a term, and Ebenezer Rockwood to be one of the Bay State's most honored judges. And here were to come as residents the Hawthornes (first to the Old Manse and later to Wayside), and the Alcotts, and Ellery Channing, and Frank Sanborn. Here, too, as Emerson's fame spread, came "many men upon long pilgrimages to speak with him face to face."[2] Some were distinguished travelers who felt about Emerson as they did about Niagara, that he was one of the goals of an American tour. But too many, for Hawthorne, were men of whom he could write:

Uncertain, troubled, earnest wanderers through the midnight of the moral world who beheld his intellectual fire as a beacon, burning on a hill-top, and, climbing the difficult ascent, looked forth into the surrounding obscurity more hopefully than hitherto. . . . Never was a poor little country village infested with such a variety of queer, strangely-dressed, oddly-behaved mortals, most of whom took upon themselves to be important agents of the world's destiny, yet were simply bores of a very intense water. Such, I imagine, is the invariable character of persons who crowd so closely about an original thinker as to draw in his unuttered breath and thus become imbued with a false originality.[3]

---

[1] Emerson, "Journals," Vol. IV, p. 352.
[2] Hawthorne, "The Old Manse," in "Works," Vol. II, p. 41.
[3] Ibid. pp. 42–43.

These were the same sort that Emerson noted elbowing their way into Alcott's presence and eagerly assenting to what they thought that he had said. Yet there were others more competent to understand; and the final fruition of the Transcendental movement, the Concord School of Philosophy, included in its summer sessions from 1879 to 1888 not only Alcott and Sanborn but such thinkers as Thomas Davidson, whose influence was to be felt by many a better-known philosopher, and William T. Harris, who was later to be the first head of the United States Bureau of Education.

Concord has its sightseers by the thousand every year. They go to the bridge and the burying ground and to the houses where its famous citizens dwelt. Yet all but one in a thousand miss the most remarkable exhibit — the alcove in the Concord Public Library where stand books by local authors, the like of which cannot be shown in any other town in America.

Ralph Waldo Emerson

Emerson's first thirty-one years, from his birth in 1803 until he began residence in Concord in 1834, must have seemed like years of little positive promise to those who were most eagerly watching for signs of achievement. He had not been distinguished as a student or teacher; and when the resignation of the senior pastor put him at the head of an old and distinguished Boston church, it took him but three years to raise an issue with his congregation that resulted in his offer of resignation and their acceptance of it. A year of travel followed, in which the most momentous event was his meeting with the then unknown Thomas Carlyle, and a year of preaching and lecturing. He brought no brilliant promise with him when he took lodging under his grandmother's roof in the Old Manse.

These thirty-one years exhibit the life in Boston and Cambridge of a young American with a solid Puritan inheritance. His dominant traits were his rectitude and his independence. Like the boys of earliest colonial parentage, he was trained at home in the uses of adversity, given a careful schooling, and sent to college to be prepared for the ministry. His withdrawal from the pulpit did not forfeit him the love of the people he had been serving; his parishioners were more generous than their own grandfathers would have been or than some of Emerson's fellow ministers were at the time. Travel along the Atlantic seaboard and in Europe enriched his knowledge of the world, but only deepened his love of the home region; and here in his early maturity he settled down with his books and his friends to think about life and to tell what he thought.

It was therefore no accident that in three successive years — 1836, 1837, and 1838 — Emerson made three statements in summary of his ideas on men and things.[1] He was convinced that life had become too much a matter of unconsidered routine and that people should stop long enough to consider what it was all about. He offered no "system." He pleaded only that men begin to think again; so that if they followed in the footsteps of their fathers they should do so with their eyes open, or if they decided to strike off into new paths they should not be blind men led by the blind.

In this trilogy on self-reliance the approach in "Nature" was in terms of beauty and emotion; in "The American Scholar," in terms of truth and the intellect; in the "Divinity School Address," in terms of the moral nature and the will. Each opened with a poetical exordium, proceeded through a more systematic development than he was to pursue in his later writings, and ended with a spirited and prophetic peroration. They were utterances of the Emerson who had recently composed so logical an argument as his sermon in resignation of the Boston pulpit, rather than of the Emerson who was soon to abjure all argument.

---

[1] References are to the "Complete Works of Ralph Waldo Emerson," Centenary Edition (12 vols.), 1893; and to the "Journals of Ralph Waldo Emerson," edited, with notes and index, by E. W. Emerson and W. E. Forbes (10 vols.). The standard biography is the "Memoir of Ralph Waldo Emerson," by J. E. Cabot (2 vols.), 1887.

In the first, after considering nature as beauty, as the origin of all commodities, as the source of language, and as an agent for discipline, he anticipated a persistent debate of the twentieth century in his contention that the man who will understand nature must combine the exactness of observation which belongs to science with the reverence of feeling which is the basis of religion.

> When a faithful thinker, resolute to detach every object from personal relations and see it in the light of thought, shall, at the same time, kindle science with the fire of the holiest affections, then will God go forth anew into the creation. . . . So shall we come to look at the world with new eyes. . . . The kingdom of man over nature, which cometh not with observation, — a dominion such as now is beyond his dream of God, — he shall enter without more wonder than the blind man feels who is gradually restored to perfect sight.[1]

In the second, passing from the influences that surround the scholar — nature, the past, and life — and stressing the last of these as of prime importance, he demanded that the scholar know no loyalty that could challenge his loyalty to the truth:

> We will walk on our own feet; we will work with our own hands; we will speak our own minds. The study of letters shall be no longer a name for pity, for doubt, and for sensual indulgence. The dread of man and the love of man shall be a wall of defence and a wreath of joy around all. A nation of men will for the first time exist, because each believes himself inspired by the Divine Soul which also inspires all men.[2]

Rounding out his "philosophy" by a final application before the students of the Harvard Divinity School, Emerson spoke for a religion that was fresh, vivid, and personal, and went on to discuss the defects of "historical Christianity." These were that dogmatic Christianity differed from the simple teachings of Jesus, and that any fixed dogma was dangerous. "Men have come to speak of the revelation as of somewhat long ago given and done, as if God were dead."

---

[1] Emerson, "Works," Vol. I, pp. 74–77. [2] Ibid. p. 115.

The corrective again was in self-reliance. "Yourself a new-born bard of the Holy Ghost, cast behind you all conformity, and acquaint men at first hand with Deity."

> What hinders that now, everywhere, in pulpits, in lecture-rooms, in houses, in fields, wherever the invitation of men or your own occasions lead you, you speak the very truth, as your life and conscience teach it, and cheer the waiting, fainting hearts of men with new hope and new revelation? [1]

With this conclusion of his first message Emerson took his place as a pronounced liberal and reaped his reward in the denunciations of the conservative clergy.[2] To one of them, his friend the Reverend Henry Ware,[3] he wrote the seldom-quoted letter announcing his refusal, steadfastly maintained, to be drawn into polemical controversy. He would go on as before, seeing what he could, telling what he saw, and making the position of his opponents the more uncomfortable by his bland refusal to debate with them.

His one most definite reply was the essay on "Self-reliance," in his First Series, in which he repeated his contentions but without argument. Men should not pray, not be consistent, not travel, not imitate, not conform to society, but be Godlike, independent, searching their own hearts, and behaving in accord with the truth they found there. He was, of course, harping on the iron string that he alludes to in the essay on "Fate," saying what in another mood he was likely to gainsay, and in a third to reconcile with his original statement. So in his essay on "Society and Solitude," of thirty years later, he balanced his views of independence, acknowledging the claims of society on the individual and the dependence of the individual on the group. The concluding paragraph sums up his compensating views on the two ways of life and illustrates his mode of establishing a balance be-

---

[1] Emerson, "Works," Vol. I, pp. 150–151.

[2] Henry S. Commager, "Tempest in a Boston Teapot," *New England Quarterly*, Vol. VI, pp. 651–675.

[3] See "Uncollected Writings, Essays, Addresses, Poems, Reviews and Letters," by Ralph Waldo Emerson, pp. 197–199.

tween statements that little minds could magnify into hobgoblins of inconsistency:

> Solitude is impracticable, and society fatal. We must keep our head in the one and our hands in the other. The conditions are met, if we keep our independence, yet do not lose our sympathy. . . . But let us not be the victims of words. Society and solitude are deceptive names. It is not the circumstance of seeing more or fewer people, but the readiness of sympathy, that imports; and a sound mind will derive its principles from insight, with ever a purer ascent to the sufficient and absolute right, and will accept society as the natural element in which they are to be applied.[1]

Through the most fruitful of Emerson's years he lived quietly in Concord, writing in his journals in the mornings, walking and talking with his friends who lived there and with the increasing number of the more and less distinguished who visited him. But the three winter months he surrendered to lecturing, culling from his journals the series that he prepared for New York and Boston audiences and that he sometimes delivered as far west as Wisconsin and Missouri. These series, the first two with no other title, and others, such as "Representative Men," "The Conduct of Life," "Letters and Social Aims," "The Natural History of Intellect," expounded the principles his mind derived from insight. Reluctantly, but in answer to frequent demands, he stepped aside from his self-appointed task to apply these principles to society in a succession of special addresses in connection with events of the day. A reading of these shows that he was at home no less on the rostrum than in the study or on the lecture platform. His auditors heard him call the operation of the Fugitive Slave Law a damnable outrage, and their governor a trifler, and the Statehouse a playhouse, and the General Court a dishonored body. They heard him say that the vocation of statesman in America was become a presumption against a man; that all the statesmen were befriending liberty with their voices and crushing it with their votes.

---

[1] Emerson, "Works," Vol. VII, pp. 15–16.

They cried "Hear! hear!" to his charges that representative government was misrepresentative, the Union a conspiracy against the Northern states, and democracy and freedom fine names for an ugly thing that he called bilge water. They even heard him excoriate Daniel Webster, idol of New England.

Obviously Emerson can be understood only in relation to his period, — its theology, its philosophy, its political theory, — and not by identifying him with it, but by contrasting him. He was, indeed, a distinctly native product, for he was highly susceptible to influence and tradition, but he was also highly defiant of both. As he wrote always in the mood of the moment regardless of consistency, the ingenious can cull and piece together isolated passages to make him out conservative, liberal, or radical, orthodox or infidel, whig or tory, moralist or amoralist, belligerent or pacifist, patriot or traitor. But he can actually be known only as one knows him in all his moods, for his times were turbulent and his heritage was complicated.

This complexity appears in his inheritance of Puritanism[1] and his repugnance to it. In all his unconscious or partially conscious ways he was a chip from an old block. He had a deep-seated horror of the grosser vices. He observed the Sabbath and made his children observe it, even though he would not have them christened. He was sedate, temperate, methodical, conventional; he was practical in the management of his affairs; he was habitually law-abiding. He inherited these traits as naturally as he inherited the melodious baritone with which he greeted his neighbors on the streets.

But at the point where he began to consider the Puritans in their theology, the only Puritan trait left him was his bent for apostasy. He had none of their spiritual abasement, because his world was a different one from the world of Knox and Calvin. He had not the desire to mortify the flesh, because the American scholar had no impulse so to set himself

[1] See Stuart Sherman's essay "What is a Puritan?" in "The Genius of America," 1924.

off from a luxury-loving community. He had not the will to power, because there was no need of civil rebellion to restore the rights of the commoner. He had no belief in a vengeful God, because in the Western world a general distribution of civil rights and domestic comforts called for no such explanation of human affairs. The progress of science in the unfolding of natural laws disposed once for all of a personal Providence, with the primitive ideas of prayer and the primitive accounting for plague and famine, earthquake and lightning stroke. And the conviction that life was a matter of progressive change, and that truth was to be sought not in religious dogma but in intuition supplemented by knowledge, made him hate the intolerance of his ancestors and committed him to heterodoxy. He was, he declared in one of his extravagant moments,[1] to unsettle all things, recognizing no fact as either sacred or profane, simply experimenting, an endless seeker with no past at his back. Authority, whether of the church or of the Bible, was an idle word to him.

In reality, however, his whole literary output was written against the background of the past. In his theological rejections he used the past of medieval Christendom as a point of departure, because time and place demanded for contemporary American Christendom something quite different, retaining the essentials and sloughing off the accretions. It was on the issue of accepting or rejecting what seemed to him an alien and antiquated rite that he left the pulpit. And in the "Divinity School Address" he was for rejecting most of what nineteen centuries had interposed between a modern sect and an ancient prophet, in order to restore the prophecies in their primal clarity.

His rejections, however, were only incidental. He set aside the idea of revelation as something fixed and permanent in order to make way for a revelation based on intuitive truth. He was as insistent as any Puritan on morality, but his morality was not a set of imposed Hebraic regulations but the

---

[1] For his exact words see "Circles," in "Works," Vol. III, p. 297.

righteousness in conduct which is the natural expression of the religious sentiment. "Morals is the direction of the will on universal ends. He is immoral who is acting to any private end. He is moral — we say it with Marcus Aurelius and with Kant, — whose aim or motive may become a universal rule, binding on all intelligent beings."[1] When the champions of orthodoxy quoted the Psalmist that in the fear of the Lord was the beginning of wisdom, he could quote the Messiah to the effect that the truth would set men free. In his substitution of freedom for fear lay the difference between Emerson and his remote pastoral predecessor, Increase Mather. And the followers of Mather, with his wrathful God, were divided between those who feared Emerson would be lost and those who hoped he would be damned. The Congregational Church was bound to supply him with a point of departure. It was an insistently aggressive factor in his life. A meeting house dominated the town; the dominie was the town meeting's frequent moderator. He looked back on generations of clerical ancestry. Respectability was still popularly identified with pulpit tax and church attendance. He was an unfrocked minister and a stay-at-home. The circumstances of his life put him in the opposition.

But there was more than circumstance at work. His own intellectual optimism was utterly alien to a creed of pessimistic fatalism. A church which represented successive departures from old authorities had committed him to individualism. The system had done what systems are continually doing: it had developed in one of its offspring the spirit of opposition and provided him with something to oppose. It taught him to walk and "showed him the door." He left the meeting house for surroundings where he could see more clearly and speak more freely.

Outside the door Emerson found that in every direction but one the philosophers had committed themselves to

---

[1] Emerson, "Character," in "Works," Vol. X, p. 92.

dogmatisms as forbidding as those of John Calvin.[1] The experimental scientist had been progressively curbed by the metaphysicians until the existence of the mind was the one unchallenged fact left him. There followed the usual result when metaphysics runs counter to daily life; but the rejection this time was made by philosophy itself. Emerson followed the Kantian lead to the acceptance of fundamental truths intuitively perceived. It was the only road to emancipation for the speculative philosopher.

Now, being committed to the truth as revealed to the individual, he was in the comfortable position of being committed to himself.

> Bland angel as he was, he very much wanted his own way. One is tempted to say that he invented or elected his philosophy in order to get it. At all events it exactly suited him. He had no sentimental needs. It satisfies none. He had, to an inordinate degree — as how should he not have? — the pride of intellect. It magnifies mind. He was assailed by no temptations, knew no "law of the members." It contemplates none. He was impatient of constraint. It exalts freedom. He suffered from the pressure of traditional superstition. It lauds the leading of individual light. He felt acutely, with an extraordinary and concentrated intensity, the value, the importance, the dignity of his own soul. It invents the "over soul" — surely an exercise in terminology! — to authenticate it.[2]

This, which is a fair statement of Mr. Brownell's, savors of injustice only in its implication that Emerson was unique in his procedure. A similar approach to any other man's philosophy will demonstrate that to a large degree it is his vision of truth as seen through the lens of his own temperament.

For there was more than this in Emersonian philosophy. The Kantian transcendentalism, which in its acceptance of intuition emancipated the speculative thinker, also restored the material universe to the experimental scientist. Emerson was very much aware of what was going on among the astronomers, geologists, botanists, physicists, chemists. He was an

---

[1] See the discussion in Josiah Royce's "Spirit of Modern Philosophy," 1922.
[2] W. C. Brownell, "American Prose Masters," p. 152.

eager reader of their findings, and in them all he found happy confirmation of his inborn belief in the prevalence of universal law and the prevalence of progressive change. In his day it was his special and lonely role to demonstrate that a man could live in security in the "no man's land" between two camps; to go about his business in invulnerable serenity as the missiles whizzed by him. He accepted the universe before Margaret Fuller or John Burroughs did,[1] in his recognition of the laws of being, or fate. Everything reminded him of this, and he acknowledged every reminder. But he harped with equal insistence on the other string of "liberty, the significance of the individual, the grandeur of duty, the power of character." He was certain that both ideas were fundamental. As a mystic he was content to believe in them without attempting to reconcile them. But in the camps of the belligerents neither faction could forgive him for what he was willing to concede the other. To the theologians he was an infidel and an atheist; to the scientists, a transcendental dreamer, an impractical idealist.

To himself he was the quiet possessor of unassailable truth. Nature as revealed in its behavior by the men of the telescope and the microscope was a realm of majestic order, the irrefutable symbol of the majesty "whose dwelling is the light of setting suns, and the round ocean and the living air."[2] But he himself was a part of this natural universe, and the majestic power behind it had its residence also "in the mind of man." So he was assured that nature was the evidence of God, and that God was the creator of nature. He could go far with both Jonathan Edwards and Herbert Spencer. He went, in fact, along the path that Edwards might have followed all the way if the youthful scientist had not surrendered to the maturing theologian. And he attracted far more than he estranged, by his thinking.

---

[1] Compare Carlyle's sneer at Margaret Fuller's phrase ("Gad! She'd better!") quoted in John Burroughs's "Accepting the Universe," 1920.

[2] For Wordsworth on the "Oversoul," see "Lines Composed a Few Miles Above Tintern Abbey."

The inspiring quality of his thought is beyond all peradventure. His mind had the gift not only for sustaining itself on a high plane but also for lifting others, at least momentarily, to its own level. He was speaking to a community which was committed beyond any parallel in history to the maintenance of moral order and a subscription to the doctrines of self-control and self-government. However disturbing his philosophical anarchy and his theological revolt might be, in his own character he was a reassuring fulfillment of his convictions; and taken in their entirety his convictions might serve as stepping-stones to the millennium.

But, taken in part (as in the case of every great spiritual leader), they have been subjected to disconcerting distortions. In the immaculateness of his nature and the moralistic rigor of his essential self he could contend for intuitional perception of truth without being led into beliefs that had their source in the justification of the "natural man," with whom he had no acquaintance. Yet in the codes of later apostles of self-expression his gospel has led to Dionysian conclusions. He who needed no discipline resented the thought of discipline, not realizing that to proceed from himself to mankind was the most fallible of generalizations from a single particular. And he knew better, though he never brought his knowledge to bear when his favorite theme of the divinity in man was in question.

It is not quite so clear that he did know better in his carefree acceptance of the rightness of all intuitive concepts. He was as confident — he reiterated it endlessly — in the finality of individual judgments as was the Calvinist whose soul-searchings led him to the assurance of salvation. In the philosophical idiom of his day he gave all weight to "reason," or intuition, and none to "understanding,"[1] or the constructive approach to truth and the critical appraisal of it. There was no need in his belief for Aristotelian or Arminian or Baconian tests of what seemed to be true. As he followed

[1] Coleridge's "Aids to Reflection" is largely devoted to a distinction between these two concepts.

his thoughts wherever they chanced to lead him, writing "Whim" on the lintel of his door, challenging all and proving nothing, he chanced now and again to write as if he were expounding a system instead of uttering a series of lyric exclamations. And when he did so he strayed into the sort of philosophical ingenuities that he deplored in Swedenborg, and often became as unconvincing as Fourier, whom he accused of including "every fact save one — namely Life." Moreover, though he referred to himself as an experimenter and a seeker, he was neither of these, but a seer and an asserter; and as he declared that he wished to say what he felt and thought on any day, with the proviso that on the morrow he might contradict it all, it is only by studying him in extenso that one can be sure what was an expression of a mood and what was an abiding conviction.

Thus, as one looks for any sustained position on the living America about him, one might turn with impatience on reading that "Everything is beautiful seen from the point of intellect, or as truth. But all is sour if seen as experience. Details are melancholy; the plan is seemly and noble."[1] There are plenty to say that herein lies the reason for Emerson's blinking the facts of life. It would be a fair explanation if elsewhere he had not said that "no picture of life can have any veracity that does not admit the odious facts."[2]

He asserted them vehemently when he was sufficiently goaded, as we have seen; but his belief in the capacities of the average man led to an expectation of an ultimate democracy in spite of what he saw around him. Yet the deference paid the machinery of government sometimes disgusted him, as when he gave an ironic second to "I baptize thee in the name of the Governor, and of the Senate, and of the House of Representatives."[3] He did not set out to define the nature of government (not being given to definitions);

---

[1] Emerson, "Love," in "Works," Vol. II, p. 171.
[2] Emerson, "Fate," in "Works," Vol. VI, p. 19.
[3] Emerson, "Journals," Vol. VII, p. 204.

but in one passage, writing to a definite point, he came close to compressing his theory: "Let us stifle our prejudices against common sense and humanity, and agree that every man shall have what he honestly earns, and, if he is a sane and innocent man, have an equal vote in the state, and a fair chance in society."[1]

He respected the average man more in the unit than in the mass. Charles Eliot Norton marveled at what a universal talker Emerson was aboard their returning ship in 1873.[2] Thirty years earlier a journal entry accounted for his miscellaneous tastes:

> When, in our discontent with the pedantry of scholars, we prefer farmers, and when, suspecting their conservatism, we hearken after the hard words of drovers and Irishmen . . . this is alkali to our acid, or shade to our too much sunshine; but abide with these, and you will presently find that they are the same men you left.[3]

He did more than like the commoners: he insisted on their sound judgment and ripe intelligence and protested against talking down to them. Books they did not like should have been written differently. "The people — no thanks to them — are always nearly right, have a low sort of right, that of common sense and instinct; and the man of talents and transcendent ingenuity is wrong."[4]

Yet in the mass the populace depressed him. It hurt him that bad manners should prevail. When he looked at Washington's portrait in his dining-room he felt that this man had absorbed all the serenity in America and left none for his restless, flighty countrymen. And their manners were no worse than their standards. Perhaps no more could be expected of a nation dedicated to trade, whose conversation was all of hay and grain and pigs and corn and apples. It was not surprising that they could be so easily misled. Twice in 1854 came the word for word entry in the journal, "Alas for

[1] Emerson, "Journals," Vol. IX, p. 464.
[2] "Letters of Charles Eliot Norton," Vol. I, p. 503.
[3] Emerson, "Journals," Vol. VI, p. 142.
[4] Ibid. p. 293.

the majority, that old inevitable dupe and victim. What a dreary Iliad of woes it goes wailing and mad withal. Some dog of a Cleon or Robespierre or Douglas is always riding it to ruin."[1] His distress in the midst of a chaos due equally to the dull and the bad was increased by the epidemic of reform that was sweeping the land under the lead of "Madmen, madwomen, men with beards, Dunkers, Muggletonians, Come-outers, Groaners, Agrarians, Seventh-Day-Baptists, Quakers, Abolitionists, Calvinists, Unitarians and Philosophers."[2] He was so intent on the education of the individual that he felt that sympathy with a good cause need not involve partnership in it. Nor was it easy to see good in many of the more aggressive reform movements. He could only set in opposition his certainty that men in the aggregate could not be disposed of at the will of even the most benevolent despots. As for the "small, sour, and fierce schemes"[3] of the day, each with its set of little proprietors, Emerson's head was so high in solitude that only the distant hum of them reached his ears. "The criticism and attack on institutions," he said, "has made one thing plain, that society gains nothing whilst a man, not himself renovated, attempts to renovate things around him: he has become tediously good in some particular but negligent or narrow in the rest; and hypocrisy and vanity are often the disgusting result."[4]

It is natural that with his many generations of ministerial ancestry and his own initial experience Emerson's prose should have been composed as for oral delivery. Most of it found its way first to the public from the platform. What he meant to his auditors has been best said by Lowell in his brief essay on "Emerson the Lecturer":

---

[1] Emerson, "Journals," Vol. VIII, pp. 429 and 449.

[2] For discussion of the miscellaneous inclination to reform, see comments by contemporaries in such works as Emerson's "New England Reformers," in "Works," Vol. III; Lowell's essay on Thoreau, opening passage; and T. W. Higginson's "Period of the Newness," in "Cheerful Yesterdays," 1898.

[3] Emerson, "Notes on . . . New England," in "Works," Vol. X, p. 353.

[4] Emerson, "New England Reformers," in "Works," Vol. III, p. 261.

We used to walk in from the country [Cambridge, four miles out from Boston] to the Masonic Temple (I think it was) through the crisp winter night, and listen to that thrilling voice of his, so charged with subtle meaning and subtle music, as shipwrecked men on a raft to the hail of a ship that came with unhoped-for food and rescue. . . . To some of us that long-past experience remains as the most marvellous and fruitful we have ever had. . . . Did they say he was disconnected? So were the stars, that seemed larger to our eyes, still keen with that excitement, as we walked homeward with prouder stride over the creaking snow. And were *they* not knit together by a higher logic than our mere sense could master? [1]

If listeners were hard put to follow the drift of Emerson's discourses (and they often were), it was because most of these actually did drift. His method of composition was to set down his ideas as they came to him, capturing some as they passed. These were knit together, like the moon and the tides and the best time for digging clams; but when he assembled various paragraphs into lectures he took no pains, except in his earliest utterances, to make his connections clear. In his later years he assembled passages from earlier journals, relying on them to hang together, though his confidence was sometimes misplaced; and auditors of his latter years recall how as he passed from one page to the next a look of doubt and slight amusement would confess without apology to an utter lack of coherence.

His style, within these passages, however, was extremely simple and clear. Lowell is again worth quoting: "A diction at once so rich and so homely as his I know not where to match in these days of writing by the page; it is like homespun cloth-of-gold. The many cannot miss his meaning, and only the few can find it." [2] Which is a way of saying that anyone can understand him sentence by sentence, but only the wise can apprehend him as a whole; and this applies in greater degree to his poetry, as it does to all poetry.

About his poetry there has been wide disagreement, swinging all the way from the strictures of Matthew Arnold to the

---

[1] Lowell, "Works," Vol. I, pp. 354–356. [2] Ibid. p. 351.

unqualified praise of George E. Woodberry.[1] A good deal of the argument has been beside the mark in condemning Emerson on technical grounds instead of appraising him for his intrinsic values. In "Merlin"[2] Emerson stated his poetic thesis and threw out his mild challenge:

> Thy trivial harp will never please
> Or fill my craving ear;
> Its chords should ring as blows the breeze,
> Free, peremptory, clear.
> No jingling serenader's art,
> Nor tinkle of piano strings,
> Can make the wild blood start
> In its mystic springs.
> The kingly bard
> Must smite the chords rudely and hard,
> As with hammer or with mace.

As he did not lay prime emphasis on poetic grace, there is a resultant likeness between much of his verse and some of his most elevated prose. His prose frequently contains poetic flashes; his verse not seldom is spirited prose in both form and substance. Frequently, and with very few changes, he transcribed into verse the original entries in his journals. They are the poems of a philosopher whose first concern is with all-embracing truth. The utter compactness and starkness of his verse made it rugged and hard to grasp. "Brahma," a monologue of the Deity, rephrased from certain passages from the Vishnu Purana, quite bewildered many of its first readers. The poems are like Bacon's essays in their meatiness and unadornment. If they had been more strikingly different from ordinary measures, they would probably have been both blamed and praised more widely. Few of his poems have passed into wide currency, but many of the lines are quoted by speakers who have little idea of their source:

---

[1] For this comment see G. E. Woodberry's "Ralph Waldo Emerson," Chap. V, and Matthew Arnold's "Discourses in America" (third section).

[2] Opening lines.

Yet not for all his faith can see
Would I that cowlèd churchman be.[1]

Earth proudly wears the Parthenon,
As the best gem upon her zone.[2]

. . . if eyes were made for seeing,
Then Beauty is its own excuse for being.[3]

O tenderly the haughty day,
Fills his blue urn with fire.[4]

Time has wrought whimsically with Emerson's reputation. As an independent thinker he received in due course his first accolade when he was accused of "the latest form of infidelity." Because his conduct and his character made him immune to anything more than verbal abuse, and no tyranny of public opinion happened to make a scapegoat of him, he lost prestige for a while as his heterodoxies seeped into general acceptance. Of late, when America, with the rest of the world, began to take stock of itself, he was set down as a dealer in commonplaces and was reproached for not having been jailed or crucified. He was arraigned with the rest of his generation as a Puritan, a Victorian, a relic of the past. He had said, "Cast behind you all conformity"; he had said that he wanted to man his post on the battle front which every day encroaches on smug conservatism and "puts it out of countenance, out of reason, out of temper." He had said a dozen other things of the same sort, and for a half-century had been the horror of the respectable classes, whose "invincible depravity" he branded as the chief obstacle to progress; but the ultra-moderns lumped him with his generation. This was natural in an image-breaking age. The iconoclast must work with a kind of fury; afterwards comes the further business of picking up the pieces. This began well within the century

[1] Emerson, "The Problem," lines 5–6.
[2] Ibid. lines 33–34.
[3] Emerson, "The Rhodora," lines 11–12.
[4] Emerson, "Ode Sung in the Town Hall," lines 1–2.

mark of Emerson's first public utterance; and the first discovery seemed to be that he had not been smashed, was not badly battered, was not even tipped off his pedestal, was only for a moment covered in the general debris.

Those who subscribe to the significance of Emerson's doctrines today have as a rule, perhaps, a less carefree optimism than he often avowed and very much less acquiescence in the present order of things. They admit that it was his province to seek the truth and accept the obligation of applying it. For Time, his "little gray man," who could perform the miracle of continual change in life, has performed no miracle greater than persuading men to share the burden of creation, in doing which they are adopting Emerson's principles and Bryant's tactics, less capable than Emerson of independent thought but less fearful than he of dissipating their energies by plunging their hands in society.

Henry David Thoreau

On the title page for his "Walden" Thoreau quoted from the chapter on "Where I Lived and What I Lived For" a passage which is strangely omitted from the title page in most student editions; for it serves as a self-description and as a warning to his readers: "I do not propose to write an ode to dejection, but to brag as lustily as chanticleer in the morning, standing on his roost, if only to wake my neighbors up." Whitman, whose "Leaves of Grass" was to be published within a year, was talking in the same vein when he said, "I sound my barbaric yawp over the roofs of the world." In the middle of the 1850's the two men, in their own middle thirties, were equally dissatisfied — conscious rebels, a little theatrical, eager to attract attention, and willing to do and say what would make people look and listen.

At Harvard, from which Thoreau received his diploma in 1837, he had been out of patience with the narrow limits of the course of study and with the eagerness of his classmates for scholastic standing rather than for education. When he was in danger of faculty discipline, the president, supported by a letter from his townsman Emerson, backed him for his character in spite of his performance. When he came back to Concord he enjoyed shocking his neighbors by his brusque manners, abrupt ways, strange opinions startlingly expressed, and what they considered his shiftless unwillingness to work for money as long as he had any in his pocket. Yet he played at being more of an eccentric than he actually was, crowing from his roost whenever people were likely to notice him. For three years he taught school in Concord with his brother John, giving it up only with the failure of John's health; and, in spite of Emerson's implication to the contrary,[1] as long as he was able he kept a hand in the family business, first of pencil-making and later of preparing fine plumbago for electrotyping. He persisted in his pose, however, and ten years after graduation wrote the secretary of his college class:

> I don't know whether mine is a profession, or a trade, or what not. . . . I am a Schoolmaster, a private Tutor, a Surveyor, a Gardener, a Farmer, a Painter (I mean a House Painter), a Carpenter, a Mason, a Day-laborer, a Pencil-maker, a Glass-paper-maker, a Writer, and sometimes a Poetaster.[2]

Able to turn an honest penny whenever he needed one, and needing but few, he worked at intervals and offended many of his industrious townsfolk by spending long days talking and walking, studying the ways of plants and animals, and occasionally leaving the village for trips to Canada, to the Maine woods, to Cape Cod, to Connecticut, and, once or twice on business, to New York City.

After coming home from college he became a devoted friend and disciple of Emerson, living with the Emersons from 1841 to 1843 and again just after the Walden experience, when Emerson took his second trip abroad. At the outset the older man delighted in Thoreau's free and erect mind, which was capable of making an "else solitary afternoon

---

[1] Emerson, "Works," Vol. X, p. 425.
[2] "Memorials of the Class of 1837," by Henry Williams, 1887.

sunny with his simplicity and clear perception."[1] But the chanticleer traits of his companion gradually wore on Emerson. He had little sympathy with Thoreau's attempt at sensational martyrdom when he chose to protest at the United States' policy toward Mexico by inviting arrest with his refusal to pay his poll tax. And after this episode Emerson's journal contains various disappointed entries:

> Thoreau sometimes appears only as a *gendarme*, good to knock down a cockney with, but without that power to cheer and establish which makes the value of a friend.[2]

> Henry is military. . . . One would say that, as Webster could never speak without an antagonist, so Henry does not feel himself except in opposition. He wants a fallacy to expose, a blunder to pillory, requires a little sense of victory.[3]

> If I knew only Thoreau, I should think coöperation of good men impossible. Must we always talk for victory and never once for truth, for comfort, and joy? . . . Always some weary captious paradox to fight you with, and the time and temper wasted.[4]

On the other hand, a journal entry by Thoreau in 1853 is significant as to the widening rift between the two:

> Talked, or tried to talk, with R. W. E. Lost my time — nay, almost my identity. He, assuming a false opposition where there was no difference of opinion, talked to the wind — told me what I knew — and I lost my time trying to imagine myself somebody else to oppose him.[5]

In Thoreau's later years he was bewildered and hurt by the gradual wane of a friendship that had meant much to him, not realizing that it was largely due to his own somewhat aggressive smartness. But as the reader has powers of self-

---

[1] Emerson, "Journals," Vol. IV, p. 397. The citations from Thoreau are to "Thoreau's Writings," Walden Edition, 1906.

[2] Emerson, "Journals," Vol. VII, p. 303.

[3] Ibid. Vol. VIII, p. 375.

[4] Ibid. Vol. IX, pp. 15, 16.

[5] Thoreau, "Journals," Vol. V, p. 188. See J. B. Moore's "Thoreau Rejects Emerson," in *American Literature*, Vol. IV, pp. 241–256.

protection beyond those of the listener, for he can always close a book, the same quality that was oppressive in speech has proved attractive in print and has won him far more friends than it has estranged. Yet it is a quality not to forget either in interpreting single passages or in estimating broader values.

It should be remembered, too, that Thoreau actually prepared for publication only two of the twenty-odd volumes which bear his name, and that in "Walden" (especially the first third of it) he crows most shrilly because here he is first propounding his personal convictions at length. His other book, "A Week on the Concord and Merrimac Rivers," published five years earlier, was much more of a transcribed meditation than a public harangue. It is a meandering record of what he saw and what the sights suggested, and it failed equally to challenge attention and to achieve sales. A comparison of his later works, culled after his death from his notebooks, with "Walden" and with the few articles and discourses addressed directly to the public, makes it quite clear that in his natural mood he was given to a quiet enjoyment of out-of-door life; but that, like most children and like many shy adults, the presence of other people — even the thought of them — roused a certain perversity in him, stirring him to strut and crow.

His life from 1845 to 1847, when he was from twenty-eight to thirty years old, gave him the experience and most of the material for his most famous volume, though it was not to be published until seven years later. Externally an account of the two years and two months of his residence at the lakeside, it is really, like his sojourn there, a commentary and criticism on social life and life in the open. In the chapter on "Where I Lived and What I Lived For" he wrote:

> I went to the woods because I wished to live deliberately, to front only the essential facts of life, and see if I could not learn what it had to teach, and not, when I came to die, discover that I had not lived.... I wanted to live deep and suck out all the marrow of life, to live so sturdily and Spartan-like as to put to rout all that was not life, to cut

a broad swath and shave close, to drive life into a corner, and reduce it to its lowest terms, and, if it proved to be mean, why then to get the whole and genuine meanness of it, and publish its meanness to the world; or if it were sublime, to know it by experience, and be able to give a true account of it in my next excursion.[1]

The actual report includes the weeks of preparation when, with an ax borrowed from Bronson Alcott and on land owned by Emerson, he felled his timber, dismantled a railroad workman's shanty for boards and nails, later built a brick chimney, and secured a tight, dry, homely shelter for a very low cash cost. He learned, too, that it would cost very little in labor, for a single man to obtain the food he needed. "It is not necessary that a man should earn his living by the sweat of his brow, unless he sweats easier than I do."[2] There is no question that as one individualist in the midst of an established society he lived cheaply, easily, happily, independently; and no question that he could not have done so if the bricks and glass and nails in his shack and the tools he borrowed to build it with had not been the product of mine, factory, and kiln brought to him on the railroads and handled by the shopkeeper he scorned. He was the first to admit this as he returned to the family rooftree, satisfied with his experiment, and not recommending it to any follower.

But he was urgent and explicit in his indictment of a society that was dedicated to the pursuit and the protection of wealth. And in the parts of the book devoted to social theory (Chaps. I, II, V, VIII, and XVIII) he chanticleered vociferously: "The laboring man has not leisure for a true integrity." "The civilized man's pursuits are not worthier than the savage's." "The college student obtains an ignoble and unprofitable leisure, defrauding himself." "Thank God I can sit and I can stand without the aid of a furniture warehouse." "Men say a stitch in time saves nine, so they take a thousand stitches today to save nine tomorrow." "Society is commonly too cheap." "Wherever a man goes, men pur-

[1] Thoreau, "Walden," pp. 100–101. [2] Ibid. p. 78.

sue and paw him with their dirty institutions, and, if they can, constrain him to belong to their desperate, odd-fellow society."

He who had never known either social chaos or social overlordship offers again a striking comparison with Crèvecœur, refugee from oppressed France.[1] To the hearty immigrant of the eighteenth century the right to own land and to enjoy the fruits of his labor unburdened by oppressive taxes seemed almost millennial in contrast with Old World conditions; but to the New Englander private ownership of property seemed a burden in contrast with his own right to traverse field and forest without assuming the obligation of maintaining an establishment or "improving" an acreage. In Crèvecœur's France, where, for centuries, the people had lived on sufferance, tenure of the land seemed an inestimable privilege. Thoreau's United States stretched out so illimitably that he apparently supposed that land would always be "dirt cheap." Though one prized property and the other contemned it, they were alike in their failure to foresee the economic changes that the nineteenth century was to produce.

With a perversity that was a little deeper than Emerson thought and that was, after all, a not unusual trait, Thoreau was least tolerant of what was near. His country in the broad was too vague to stir his skepticisms or rouse his resentments as men and events in Concord could. And Concord never seemed so fair a community to him as when he was absent on Staten Island or in Canada. At home his notebooks show that he was irked at the surrounding pressure of his fellows — so much so that he must set down his resentments, not in defiance to his townsmen but as an outlet for his private feelings. Politics, he felt, was a vital function of society, but it should operate silently and unseen, like the functions of the body in health. Why should a thinker submit to be "rasped by the great gizzard of creation?"[2] The industrious man, applauded by the community because of his

---

[1] See pages 99–105.

[2] Thoreau, "Journals," Vol. III, p. 103.

mere doing, is more often than not only subserving the vanity of a richer neighbor. He himself was continually being called on to survey land. He could not see that the results were valuable, whether the survey was about private property or was an annual "walking of the lines" in company with the selectmen of Concord and adjoining townships. The selectmen seemed anything but select in what they thought and said.

As one reads the pages of the journals, written for no eye but his own, one is conscious of a sense of isolation in Thoreau that was far from self-satisfied. He did not take himself for granted; he was forever expounding himself to himself, reassuring himself, whistling to keep his self-reliance up. No man who is wholeheartedly independent would ever protest so much about independence. There is a hint of frustration in the pages of Thoreau's journals. He was like a willful child who yearns for parental support and resists parental restraint, harassed by a lack of internal harmony. In Thoreau this dissonance does not seem to have arisen from experience in the family. In the long list of his repugnances this one does not occur. On the other hand, his distrust and distaste for womankind were too insistent not to have had some definite ground. Young women attracted his eye, distracted his mind, failed to satisfy him with any genuine companionship, offended him with the arrogance of their conventional helplessness. Why rise when a woman with Olympian effrontery presumes to "elicit the miracle of seat where none is?"[1]

In the midst of small-town closeness of contact and meddlesomeness of interest he could only pretend to Olympian effrontery himself, keeping up the brave pretense until he confided to his journal. A town boy spoke to him impudently as he was passing the tavern; two men watched him with avid curiosity as he stood motionlessly contemplating a budding willow. Someone asked him why he did thus and so. All his conduct was a challenge to such behaviors, but he could

---

[1] Thoreau, op. cit. Vol. I, p. 192.

neither ignore nor comfortably endure the acceptances of his challenge. So he longed for the open road that should lead away from contact, away even from the reminder of land-ownership and possible trespass, to where the earth was not desirable to the lustful possessor and there was no need of fences. He dreamed of vagabondage, and took it out in dreaming. Liberty was alluring, but exile was too high a price for it. He would make a pilgrimage in his mind into the world of the imagination. His imaginary road led to a Sudbury and a Marlborough in the skies. But there was also an unfrequented road to a real Sudbury, only six miles away. So he played with the idea of Nootka and Lapland, Patagonia and Tierra del Fuego; and when far wanderers came back to town with tales of their tours, he rejoined with, "I have traveled a good deal in Concord."[1] In this it is hard to believe that Concord, for which he felt such combined affection and resentment, was quite so aggressively concerned with his ways as he persuaded himself; that he was not a victim quite as much of his self-consciousness as of their criticism.

His essay on "Walking" is characteristic. The first long fifth (for it is generous in its length) is spent in half-petulant, half-churlish half-recrimination at people who are not so devoted to daily walks as he is. He has, apparently, to fight his way out of this mood, as he might have to fight his way out of town during working hours in sight of toiling neighbors, conscious of what they may be thinking. Only when this mileage is passed and this mood is shaken off can he come with any real zest to his subject; and the subject of the essay, the pleasure of walking, is the reward of escaping from the town. Once out of it, however, he can stop talking negatively, in terms of resentments and escapes. He finds his direction is almost always toward the southwest, — not because of any attraction in the compass, but because for long reaches that direction promises him open country. And he finds, furthermore, that the trail toward the setting sun is a

[1] Thoreau, "Walden," p. 4.

mysteriously primitive one because it follows the commonest course of human migration. He is walking toward the frontier and away from Europe. "We go eastward to realize history and study the works of art and literature, retracing the steps of the race; we go westward as into the future, with a spirit of enterprise and adventure."[1]

This adventure toward a new and braver civilization is something he can pursue in Concord. And this is not all repudiations; for in the trenchancy of his criticisms of men and events and in the abundance of his utterances he stands shoulder to shoulder with the bravest men of his day. To think of Thoreau as author of "Walden" — even the most vociferous passages in "Walden" — and to forget or ignore him as the author of "Civil Disobedience" and "Life without Principle," is to miss the essential seriousness of the critic who may have crowed in the "Economy" of "Walden," but whose manner, deliberately adopted, proves that on occasion Jeremiah can play the role of Chanticleer.

In a period of miscellaneous reform projects, which Lowell has amusingly described in his otherwise unprofitable essay on Thoreau,[2] the Concord experimenter with life was immune to all formal promoters of idealism. In 1842 Emerson wrote with mild derision in *The Dial* on "Fourierism and the Socialists." With all the completeness of the scheme, he felt that the Frenchman "had skipped no fact but one, namely, Life." In 1843 Thoreau wrote in similar vein on the German Etzler's plan to redeem society by the simple expedient of perfecting the machine and its uses. In his article entitled "Paradise (to be) Regained," he refused to "be imposed on by this vast application of forces."[3] The scheme substitutes power for friendliness and machinery for faith. Yet "every machine, or partial application, seems a slight outrage against universal laws."[4] "What says Veeshnoo Sarma? 'He whose

[1] Thoreau, "Excursions and Poems," p. 218.
[2] Lowell, "Works," Vol. I, pp. 361–363.
[3] Thoreau, "Cape Cod and Miscellanies," p. 297.
[4] Ibid. p. 302.

mind is at ease is possessed of all riches. Is it not the same to one whose foot is enclosed in a shoe, as if the whole surface of the earth were covered with leather?'"[1] To the projects of Western reformers he opposed the wisdom of the East.

He richly repaid his debt to the Orient by his essay on "Civil Disobedience" (1849); for when a Hindu student of law read this in London a half-century later he was so impressed with it that subsequently, as Mahatma Gandhi, he adopted the phrase for a political policy that in its passive resistance has proved more irresistible than any machinery from Occidental arsenals.[2] Events around Thoreau had roused all the rebelliousness of the Puritan in him. The operations of the Fugitive Slave Law had touched him and his friends. His refusal to pay a poll tax that by implication involved him in approval of the Mexican War led him into his overnight imprisonment and his reluctant departure from jail.[3] The wage slavery in the near-by cotton mills of Lowell stirred him deeply. The experience of his townsman Senator Samuel Hoar, in being ushered out of South Carolina, where he had gone to protest at the detention of black citizens of Massachusetts, was a fresh and vivid grievance. All this and more led him to resent and suspect the machinery of government no less than the machines of industry. He was not an anarchist by conviction. He demanded, he said, not "at once no government, but *at once* a better government."[4] That better government, however, must reckon with men not as parts of a machine, without exercise of judgment or the moral sense, but as free agents with consciences. The truest men, therefore, will be committed from time to time to serve the government by resisting it; and this resistance may force them not simply into the expression of criticism, which is the privilege of the opposition party, but actually into individual secession.

---

[1] Thoreau, "Cape Cod and Miscellanies," p. 303.

[2] See "Gandhi of India: His Own Story" (edited by C. F. Andrews), pp. 193–196.

[3] Thoreau gives his own account at length in "Civil Disobedience," in "Cape Cod and Miscellanies."

[4] Thoreau, "Cape Cod and Miscellanies," p. 357.

"How does it become a man to behave toward this American government today? I answer, that he cannot without disgrace be associated with it."[1]

The great difference between Thoreau's radical doctrine and the leading radicalisms of these latter days was that it was not an economic radicalism and did not advocate the substitution of new governmental machinery for the machinery that he decried. He did not advocate a redistribution of either goods or power. He was consistent to his opening declaration: "That government is best which governs least."[2] He was insistent in his contention that the individual must be free to participate or refrain from participation. Theoretically it is a dangerous doctrine, for if it does not lead to the destruction of government it could lead to its disintegration; but actually it is the least dangerous of radicalisms for the reason that it demands moral independence and offers no material rewards. To demand of the citizen that he shall not reform society but that he shall reform himself is anything but an inflammatory doctrine. It is the doctrine that is reaffirmed in the essay "Life without Principle" published in *The Atlantic* the year after Thoreau's death.

Rebelling against the social order represented in the town of Concord, with its selectmen and its assessors and its constable and court and jail, Thoreau could escape, as none of his neighbors could, into a totally different world in the out-of-doors of Concord township. It was the escape from society to nature. Four hours a day, at least, he must be afoot, now and again with a congenial companion, but better by himself. He had keen senses and enjoyed himself through all of them, though, perhaps with a touch of asceticism, he has least to say of taste as it satisfies the palate and most as it merely adds to the data of the observer. The fullness of his records in the journal suggests that he had an appetite for facts like that of a statistician for figures.

---

[1] Thoreau, op. cit. p. 360. [2] Ibid. p. 356.

It has become a convention to enumerate proofs that as an observer he was faulty, a careless amateur. It is true that he committed mistakes with reference to flora and fauna, and that he lived most of his life without caring systematically to compass the main facts of botany. Yet when he chose to assemble his observations and draw deductions, he proved what many of the repeaters of this charge do not realize, that he had solid powers as an interpreter of scientific data. His address of 1860 on "The Succession of Forest Trees"[1] is unacknowledged by the generality of ecologists. They cite as the fundamental document on this subject a work published in 1895 at Copenhagen — Warming's "Ecological Plant Geography." Yet a full generation earlier Thoreau had studied the relations of trees to their surroundings — the water, the soil, and the physiography — and had anticipated the findings of the Danish scientist as to the sequence of stages from cottonwood to pine, black oak, red oak, and beech and maple. If Thoreau did not do more or better in the field of exact science, it should not be charged to inability; it should be ascribed to choice. But there was something fateful about his choice to be the poet of nature rather than the student of it; something parallel to his choosing to walk daily away from the haunts of men, and the nightly necessity for a return. He cites Ellery Channing, his most frequent walking companion, for his comment on taking notes in field and wood:

> In our walks C. takes out his note-book sometimes and tries to write as I do, but all in vain. He soon puts it up again, or contents himself with scrawling some sketch of the landscape. Observing me still scribbling, he will say that he confines himself to the ideal, purely ideal remarks; he leaves the facts to me. Sometimes, too, he will say a little petulantly, "*I* am universal; I have nothing to do with the particular and definite."[2]

This was in 1851, when Thoreau had but eleven years to live. He soon came to Channing's conclusion himself, as

[1] Thoreau, "Excursions and Poems," in "Writings," Vol. V, pp. 184–204.
[2] Thoreau, "Journals," Vol. III, pp. 98–99.

he reveals in entry after entry. Yet so strong had the habit of systematic observation become that he could not cope with it. Struggling against it, he writes that he must let his senses wander; they must saunter, as the good walker should. . . . The more he looks, the less he will observe. . . . He will look only with the side of his eye, or nature will become a Medusa and turn him into a scientific man of stone. . . . He murders in the name of science, and cannot forgive himself. . . . All the advantage is with the poet, the philosopher, the naturalist. . . . He has surveyed the land around Walden Pond so minutely that it has become to him only so many men's wood lots. He is afraid that the dry knowledge will affect his imagination. . . . He must forget his technical information and approach each natural object as something strange, that he may rediscover it. . . . The old naturalists had this ever youthful gift. "The greatest and saddest defect is not credulity, but our habitual forgetfulness that our science is ignorance."[1]

Yet in spite of this persistent iteration his notebooks of the latter years are filled to repletion with dry, exact records of things seen, heard, tasted, measured, counted. They have supplied the data for four books on the seasons in Massachusetts. And together they are less memorable than the single passage on the fall of the majestic pine tree that fills with drama the next to the last day of 1851. Yet though he was filled with emotion as he saw it crash to earth, he went at once to measure it, and the next day to remeasure. It was five feet longer than he had guessed. It was ninety-four years old. "The tears were streaming from the sapwood — about twenty circles — of each, pure amber or pearly tears."[2] So he mingled sentiment and statistics; not even then could poetry quite dismiss science.

There was the same conflict in Thoreau between the man of

---

[1] These paraphrases are based on passages in "The Heart of Thoreau's Journals" (edited by Odell Shepard), pp. 149, 150, 165, 166, 205, 212, 241, 293, 295, 322, 328.

[2] Thoreau, "Journals," Vol. III, p. 169.

nature and the man of culture in his attitudes toward primitive life. "I wish to speak a word for Nature," he prefaces the essay on "Walking," "for absolute freedom and wildness, as contrasted with freedom and culture merely civil, — to regard man as an inhabitant, or a part and parcel of Nature, rather than a member of society. I wish to make an extreme statement, if so I may make an emphatic one, for there are enough champions of civilization."[1] It is Chanticleer again; and he returns to the figure as he has applied it to himself: the monarch of the barnyard lives in the present, crows "the gospel according to this moment."[2] Was he aware of the appropriateness of selecting a domestic fowl for his symbol? Toward the end of this glorification of "absolute freedom and wildness" he declares, or confesses, "For my part, I feel that with regard to Nature I live a sort of border life, on the confines of a world into which I make occasional and transient forays only."[3]

Again there is the divided feeling toward the primitive man, the Indian, as he knows him. At times he rhapsodizes over the "noble red man" with all the fervor and unreality of the French romanticists. The Indian of the past lived closer to nature than we; his earthly life was as remote as heaven from ours. "I broke forth into an extravagant eulogy on those savage times."[4] "The charm of the Indian is to me that he stands free and unconstrained in Nature, is her inhabitant and not her guest, and wears her easily and gracefully."[5] Yet his three journeys into the Maine woods disillusionize him as to both the wilderness and the wild man. The Indian whom he found had nothing of the romantic picturesqueness of song and story; no feathered headdress or embroidered skins. He was shabby and dirty. Certain gifts of woodcraft he still possessed, but he made "a coarse and imperfect use . . . of nature. No wonder that their race is so soon exterminated. I already, and for weeks after, felt my

---

[1] Thoreau, "Excursions and Poems," p. 205. [2] Ibid. p. 246. [3] Ibid. p. 242.
[4] Thoreau, "Journals," Vol. I, p. 7. [5] Ibid. p. 253.

nature the coarser for this part of my woodland experience."[1] As always he returned with relief to Concord. "I long ago lost a hound, a bay horse, and a turtle-dove, and am still on their trail."[2] They are not to be found in the wilderness. Homes and shaded streets, tilled fields, gardens, and bookshelves for all but a few hours of the twenty-four.

And particularly bookshelves. Working in the garden at Walden with no time for books, he sustained himself by the prospect of future reading. By sheer insistence he importuned Harvard College to lend him books when he was no longer an enrolled student. As a reader his desire for freedom led him down the vistas of the past just as it led him away from the shadow of modern industrialism. He was enthralled, in the literary vogue of his day, with the Oriental Scriptures, making a mild affectation of putting the Hebrew Scriptures in their place beside the others. He wanted them all bound into one "Book of Books which let missionaries carry to the ends of the earth." He had been grounded in the classics at college and had survived the grim discipline with an honest liking for the literatures it released him into. The modern foreign languages were the dead languages for him; but he was well versed in the English classics from Chaucer and the old balladry to Shakespeare and the Elizabethans.

He studied books as assiduously as he studied nature, making a virtue of reading his Greek and Latin masters in the originals and speaking contemptuously of light reading and frivolous readers. "To read well, that is, to read true books in a true spirit, is a noble exercise, and one that will task the reader more than any exercise which the customs of the day esteem."[3] With his characteristic rejection of the near at hand he went on to possess himself of the "oldest and best," instinctively identifying the two. This identification led him to a rejection of fiction, with a fleering allusion to "The Skip of the Tip-Toe-Hop, a Romance of the Middle Ages, by the

---

[1] Thoreau, "Maine Woods," p. 133. [2] Thoreau, "Walden," p. 18. [3] Ibid. p. 112.

celebrated author of Tittle-Tottle-Tan,"[1] and to an almost complete ignorance of the books published in the United States during that richest of periods that included his "Week" and his "Walden." The pages of these two volumes are rich in allusion, but almost exclusively to the elder poets and prophets. Thoreau was apparently content with Emerson's estimate of Poe as "the jingle man," and of "In Memoriam" as no better than the condolences of prosperous Unitarians in the first weeks of bereavement. There is not a word of Hawthorne or Melville; none of "Uncle Tom's Cabin." There was none, when it appeared, of "Hiawatha."

But the one acknowledgment to books of the day is happily the only one whose omission would have been unforgivable in Thoreau. He paid a memorable tribute to Whitman and "Leaves of Grass," and did so in spite of the affront that was offered to his almost maidenly modesty:

> That Walt Whitman, of whom I wrote to you [he wrote to Harrison Blake in 1856], is the most interesting fact to me at present. I have just read his second edition (which he gave me), and it has done me more good than any reading for a long time. . . . He has spoken more truth than any American or modern that I know. I have found his poem exhilarating, encouraging. . . . On the whole, it sounds to me very brave and American, after whatever deductions. I do not believe that all the sermons, so called, that have been preached in this land put together are equal to it for preaching. . . . Though rude, and sometimes ineffectual, it is a great primitive poem — an alarum or trumpet-note ringing through the American camp. . . . Since I have seen him, I find that I am not disturbed by any brag or egoism in his book. He may turn out the least of a braggart of all, having a better right to be confident. He is a great fellow.[2]

The loneness of this exception increases its importance to this solitary, and in the estimate of him. Otherwise he paid as little respect to contemporary literature as he did to the contemporary press or to the news, at which he was continually twitting. But for books, old or new, he came out

[1] Thoreau, op. cit. p. 117. [2] Thoreau, "Familiar Letters," pp. 295–296.

from his solitude into the town. No resort to the wilderness for them. "Shall the world be confined to one Paris or one Oxford forever? Cannot students be boarded here and get a liberal education under the skies of Concord?" "To act collectively is according to the spirit of our institutions. . . . If it is necessary, omit one bridge over the river, go round a little there, and throw one arch at least over the darker gulf of ignorance which surrounds us."[1] In "Walden," as soon as the author has settled himself into his surroundings, he devotes the third chapter to "Reading."

The happiest result of all his erudition in books is that it did not make him bookish. The "Week" is overabundant in allusion and quotation, but this is the work of a very young man in very conscious possession of his learning. "Walden" and all the posthumous volumes culled from his journal show that what he had at first read, marked, and learned, he has now inwardly digested. And his mature style is as simple and unliterary as the speech of the plain man he was. Thoreau is, of course, important in the growth of the American spirit as one of the spokesmen for his age; but he spoke for it to posterity, achieving little of a hearing and too often only amused half-contempt of the sort Holmes indulged in in his lines on "Contentment." He would not be audible to posterity if he had not been a writer of fine, firm, beautiful prose, better than Emerson, better than any of the others labeled Transcendentalists, hard to surpass in his generation.

When he wrote best he was not being literary. He was either talking earnestly on paper about what he thought were the essential values, which he could do with extraordinary cogency and picturesqueness, or he was simply presenting pictures of the nature that rejoiced him. Take, for example, this bit from "The Pond in Winter," in which the last twelve words are as beautiful as the scene they describe:

Standing on the snow-covered plain, as if in a pasture amid the hills, I cut my way first through a foot of snow, and then a foot of

[1] Thoreau, "Walden," pp. 121, 122.

ice, and open a window under my feet, where, kneeling to drink, I look down into the quiet parlor of the fishes, pervaded by a softened light as through a window of ground glass, with its bright sanded floor the same as in summer; there a perennial, waveless serenity reigns as in the amber, twilight sky.[1]

Or, again, this prose poem quoted in Channing's book:

One more confiding heifer, the fairest of the herd, did by degrees approach as if to take some morsel from our hands, while our hearts leaped to our mouths with expectation and delight. She by degrees drew near with her fair limbs (progressive), making pretence of browsing; nearer and nearer, till there was wafted to us the bovine fragrance, — cream of all the dairies that ever were or will be: and then she raised her gentle muzzle toward us, and snuffed an honest recognition within hand's reach. I saw it was possible for his herd to inspire with love the herdsman. She was as delicately featured as a hind. Her hide was mingled white and fawn color, and on her muzzle's tip there was a white spot not bigger than a daisy; and on her side turned toward me, the map of Asia plain to see.[2]

The following passages fulfill the main tenets of the twentieth-century imagists:

I am no more lonely than the loon in the pond that laughs so loud, or than Walden Pond itself. What company has that lonely lake, I pray? . . . I am no more lonely than a single mullein or dandelion in a pasture, or a bean-leaf, or sorrel, or a horse-fly, or a humble-bee. I am no more lonely than the Mill Brook, or a weather-cock, or the north star, or the south wind, or an April shower, or a January thaw, or the first spider in a new house.[3]

The wind has gently murmured through the blinds, or puffed with feathery softness against the windows, and occasionally sighed like a summer zephyr, lifting the leaves along, the livelong night. The meadow-mouse has slept in his snug gallery in the sod, the owl has sat in a hollow tree in the depth of the swamp; the rabbit, the squirrel, and the fox have all been housed. The watch-dog has lain quiet on the hearth, and the cattle have stood silent in their stalls. . . .

---

1 Thoreau, op. cit. p. 313.

2 Channing, "Thoreau: the Poet-Naturalist," p. 65.

3 Thoreau, "Walden," p. 152.

But while the earth has slumbered, all the air has been alive with feathery flakes descending, as if some northern Ceres reigned, showering her silvery grain over all the fields.[1]

No yard! but unfenced nature reaching up to your very sills. A young forest growing up under your windows, and wild sumachs and blackberry vines breaking through into your cellar; sturdy pitch pines rubbing and creaking against the shingles for want of room, their roots reaching quite under the house. Instead of a scuttle or a blind blown off in the gale, — a pine tree snapped off or torn up by the roots behind your house for fuel. Instead of no path to the front-yard gate in the Great Snow — no gate — no front yard, — and no path to the civilized world.[2]

In the autumn of 1859 John Brown's raid at Harpers Ferry, his capture, conviction, and execution, roused Thoreau to his last vivid enthusiasm and gave him the occasion for three reassertions of his doctrine of freedom. The challenge to him was the greater because Brown had so few advocates, every shade of philistinism and timid conservatism hastening to condemn or repudiate him. Thoreau did not speak as an apologist; he took the offensive. Brown had not been "fed on the pap" furnished at Harvard. He had gone to "the university of the West where he pursued the study of Liberty," and "commenced the public practice of Humanity in Kansas."[3] The public and the press demeaned themselves in their comments on his exploit, incapable of recognizing that he was a superior man who valued life less than ideal things and would not obey unjust human laws that he was bidden to resist. Thoreau's vehemence rose as his plea for John Brown progressed. He gibed and jeered at his hearers and defied them, identified himself with every word and act of his hero. His voice rose to a snarl:

This event advertises me that there is such a fact as death, — the possibility of a man's dying. It seems as if no man had ever died in America before; for in order to die you must first have lived. . . .

---

[1] Thoreau, "Excursions," p. 163.
[2] Thoreau, "Walden," p. 142.
[3] Thoreau, "Cape Cod and Miscellanies," p. 411.

The best of them fairly ran down like a clock. Franklin, — Washington, — they were let off without dying; they were merely missing one day. I hear a good many pretend that they are going to die; or that they have died, for aught I know. Nonsense! I'll defy them to do it. They haven't got life enough in them. They'll deliquesce like fungi, and keep a hundred eulogists mopping the spot where they left off. . . . Do you think you are going to die, sir? No! there's no hope of you. You haven't got your lesson yet. You've got to stay after school.[1]

This is not Emerson's "bachelor of nature," nor Ellery Channing's "Poet-naturalist," nor Parrington's "Greek turned transcendental economist," nor the chanticleer of the "Walden" title page. It is a master of invective, passionately assailing the foes of human liberty. Down from the Walden woods he strides into the village, hands clenched as usual, his long hair tossing, not stopping at Emerson's or Alcott's or young Frank Sanborn's, who all agree with him but are not so aflame, mounts the platform in the vestry, and cries "For once we are lifted into the region of truth and manhood." That was Thoreau's abiding place.

John Greenleaf Whittier

Whittier, one of the seven New England men of letters who are accepted as the major nineteenth-century spokesmen for this district, did not belong to the group. He was not only different from all the rest; he was pretty well isolated from them. There is no mention of him in the indexes to Emerson's "Journals," Thoreau's "Journals," the first three volumes of Holmes's "Breakfast Table" series, almost none in the standard life of Longfellow. Between the Cambridge group and the so-called Concord group there were literary and personal contacts. Thoreau's gig was hitched to the star of Emerson. Emerson, Hawthorne, Longfellow, and Lowell were men of family, college bred, and, however responsive they may have been to the beauties of the countryside, urban in viewpoint.

[1] Thoreau, op. cit. pp. 434–435.

Of the six contemporaries and near neighbors who followed their careers in New England, only Lowell was apparently aware of Whittier or sympathetic to him until after the Civil War.

Whittier was a precocious country boy schooled in hard labor, bred in a tradition of the oppressed Quakers and a tradition of humanitarian Quaker liberalism. He knew this tradition not merely from hearsay but from careful study. What it was, described without resentment, he offered in his "Leaves from Margaret Smith's Journal." It holds up to view the relative sweetness and light of the more tolerant people of Maine; the dogmatic Hebraism of the Puritans in Massachusetts north of Boston; the hardships suffered by the Quakers, invited partly by their own passive resistance and partly by the goings on of the Ranters who helped to keep them in disrepute; and the savagery of the religious persecutors who quite lived up to the precedents supplied by their English forebears in the tactics of heresy-baiting. And it accounts in Whittier himself for his belief in democracy, freedom of person, speech, and conscience, as well as for his conviction that "prayer and action" should be one and that moral action was fruitless unless it was coupled with political.

His birth and breeding helped to fit him for his career as a popular spokesman for the people. His language was theirs and his images the ones they were used to. He knew the popular superstitions and the local legends: about the feuds with the Indians, the campaigns against the witches, the struggles to make the Calvinists' idea of the will of God prevail. He had studied court records and acts of legislation, and he could use them not as formidable documents but familiarly, as one employs allusion to the village events of day before yesterday. He had the sentimentalism, too, of the popular type: a belief not only in a beneficent Providence but in a "poetic justice" that could be evoked for everyone, a belief in the goodness of goodness, and an approval for the satisfaction in doing good that is on the brink of self-righteousness. He was given to the utterance of "sentiments," too—moral sentiments, too often appended to his tales in verse, noble sentiments, and touching sentiments, as in the tale (strangely quoted in full by one of his biographers) of the incurable drunkard who is commended to the reader for saving his dead mother's chair from a burning house. But all these tendencies and aptitudes were invaluable to a man whose career for thirty years was to involve him in incessant appeals to the mind and heart of the widest public.[1]

He showed an early inclination for writing verse, and had the thrill of seeing his words in print before he was nineteen.[2] He was actually laureate on the occasion of opening the new Haverhill Academy at the time that he was being admitted with its first class. Before he was twenty-one he had contributed about two hundred bits of verse, not only to local newspapers and a regional magazine but even to an annual published in Philadelphia. And he had enjoyed the distinction of having his verses — written in the fashion of the day under various pseudonyms — both reprinted and plagiarized. This youthful output was normally immature in quality. It reflected Milton, Scott, Byron, Mrs. Hemans, N. P. Willis, J. G. Percival, as he had encountered them in the poets' corners of country newspapers. It drew on many of these and on the Bible for romantic themes. It revealed the first flutterings of love and passion. It foreshadowed later work in using the lore and legend of the countryside and in treating the problems of the hour. The hortatory and moralistic verses were clear harbingers of the near future.

A succession of editorships promptly followed for the young countryman: on the *American Manufacturer*, in Boston; on the Haverhill *Gazette*; and for a year and a half, ending with January, 1832, on the *New England Review* of Hartford, Connecticut. These three years — 1829, 1830, and 1831 —

---

[1] Citations are to the Cambridge Edition of Whittier's "Works" in seven volumes. The authorized biography is "John Greenleaf Whittier," by S. T. Pickard, 2 vols., 1894.

[2] For the material in this and the next paragraph see Frances M. Pray's "Study of Whittier's Apprenticeship as a Poet": Introduction, pp. 1–110; a group of Selections, pp. 113–260.

marked his final period of preparation. He was just short of twenty-five, but he was wise in the ways of the journalist as both contributor and editor. As editor he could select material and make up an issue, and he could express opinions on the problems of the moment — express them so confidently, in fact, that one W. G. Snelling, in his "Truth, a New Year's Gift for Scribblers," wrote perhaps enviously at this time:

> The wax still sticking to his fingers' ends
> The upstart Wh—tt—r, for example, lends
> The world important aid to understand
> What's said and sung and printed in the land. . . .
> And, with God-only-knows-how-gotten light
> Informs the nation what is wrong or right.

For the *New England Review*, in addition to the political leaders, he wrote largely as a conscious New Englander who was in love with the picturesque past of the region. The chief product was his first published volume, "Legends of New England," 1831. It is a collection of eighteen pieces — "The Midnight Attack," "The Weird Gathering," "The Murdered Lady," "The Spectre Ship," and so on. The book was equally divided between prose and verse, the work of a legend lover and a rhymester. In later years Whittier destroyed every copy he could find. Not until he included two poems in the edition of 1888 did he see fit to reprint anything from it.

Throughout his life Whittier enjoyed making jingles for their own sakes. As a youngster he inventoried the family library in couplets. Fifty years later he lapsed into something less than poetry in more than one of his letters; as, for example, to Lucy Larcom:

> Pray give the "Atlantic"
> A brief unpedantic
> Review of Miss Phelps' book. . . .
> Say to Fields, if he ask of it,
> I can't take the task of it.[1]

---

[1] Quoted in Pickard's "Life," Vol. II, p. 563.

With pages more of the same. It is a slight detail but not a negligible one that in Whittier there was no necessary tie between his inclination to turn out verses and his gift for composing poetry. It accounts for a clear distinction between the two kinds of undertaking in the extremes of his work. It accounts for the shifts within the types that sometimes lift his verse to the level of poetry and sometimes drag his poetry down to the level of doggerel. Combined with the facts of his developing career, it quite disposes of the idea that for thirty years he patiently sacrificed his art to his convictions and chose to write popular verse when he naturally would have been writing elevated poetry. As a matter of fact he grew steadily from the lower order of writing up to the higher and was ready for his best creative work when the end of the Civil War released him for it.

By 1833, then, when he was swept into the antislavery campaign and into a long-continued but unofficial connection with state and national politics, he was an active and industrious young man with a creditable background as editor and with a facility in turning phrases in both prose and verse. He had written a large amount of fugitive rhyme that he was wise enough not to want to recapture. He had published a book of regional legends that he wished might go to oblivion. He had edited, too, with an introductory sketch, the "remains" of a now forgotten Connecticut poet.[1] And he had anonymously published the long verse tale "Moll Pitcher," writing it to beguile "such leisure as is afforded by indisposition" with a subsequent indisposition ever to republish it.

He was eager, he wrote to friends more than once, for celebrity; posthumous fame was not a satisfactory goal. When in 1832 the possibility of election to Congress was raised, and he was a few months short of the eligible age, he wrote, "Of poetry I have nearly taken my leave,"[2] and, again, "I have done with poetry and literature."[3] As there was a deadlock

---

[1] "The Literary Remains of John G. C. Brainard, with a Sketch of His Life," 1832.

[2] Pickard, "Life," Vol. I, p. 113. [3] Ibid. p. 117.

on the congressional election in his district, he hoped that it could be prolonged over the creeping weeks till he was old enough to enter the race. The truth of the matter, he wrote a friend, was that the thing would be peculiarly beneficial to him. It would be worth more to him then, young as he was, than almost any office after he had reached the meridian of life. Politics was his field.

But events did not work out as he hoped at the moment; and in 1833, with open eyes, he wrote his antislavery pamphlet "Justice and Expediency," printing it at his own expense.[1] It was a long, documented indictment of slavery, so substantial that it was at once copied in the monthly organ of the American Antislavery Society and circulated in a large extra edition. In the mind of the respectable North, Whittier had gained not celebrity but notoriety. Political preferment was now out of the question, and for twenty years he was to pay the price of championing an unpopular cause. Describing himself in "The Tent on the Beach"[2] (1867) when the turmoil was over, he wrote:

> And one there was, a dreamer born,
> Who, with a mission to fulfil,
> Had left the Muses' haunts to turn
> The crank of an opinion-mill.

Until the end of the Civil War he was now committed to the use of his political gifts in exerting effective pressure on men in public office. He was incessant in his reminders to the lawmakers that their constituencies were on the watch. He may not have believed in the resort to physical violence, but in the appeal to a coercive public opinion he was a past master. As a trained journalist he knew that the crank could best be turned in connection with exciting events and, as poet, for special occasions. In "Justice and Expediency" he had wrought an argument through an appeal to both intellect and emotion. In his antislavery verse he appealed almost

---

[1] Reprinted in the "Works," Vol. VII.

[2] "Works," Vol. IV, p. 230.

wholly to feeling; and he had no compunctions about descending to a plane a good deal lower than the angels'. Nor was he the gentle poet that some of his friends insist on. Of the North he used such ungentle words as "traitor," "recreant," "craven"; of the proslavery clergy, "paid hypocrites," "fat locusts," "parish popes"; of slavery, slave-hunting, slave-shipping, all the conventional language of tyrant and tyranny familiar to literature; of the South, all the abusive words that could fall within the vocabulary of decency. Until 1850, when the weight of Northern opinion began to swing in his direction, he was stirred to vehemence less by the opposition he faced than by the indifference and timidity he encountered. For twenty years, he wrote long after, he was abjured by booksellers and magazine editors.

It was an act of courage for Ticknor, the publisher, to issue in 1843 so otherwise inoffensive a volume as Whittier's "Lays of My Home," for it included the inflammatory "Massachusetts to Virginia." The genuinely controversial poems had to find harborage in avowedly antislavery publications — the Boston *Courier*, the Haverhill *Gazette*, the *New England Magazine*, the *Anti-Slavery Reporter*, the *Liberator*, the *Emancipator*; and in book form they appeared from presses committed to the campaign.

The "Poems" of 1838, published by Joseph Healy in Philadelphia, are typical of the period. The first half are on the great issue: "The Song of the Free," "Hunters of Men," "The Slave Ships," "Stanzas for the Times," and the like. Many were written as retorts: Lines, "written on reading 'Right and Wrong in Boston,'" "on reading the famous 'Pastoral Letter' of the Massachusetts General Association," "on reading the spirited and manly remarks of Governor Ritner of Pennsylvania," "on the adoption of Pinckney's resolutions in the House of Representatives"; and they were written for various antislavery occasions. They were not all excited and declamatory; several were hymns, gentle, reverent, devotional.

This little volume included also selections from his fugitive verse, printed as he wrote them, he explains, in self-defense. And they give point to a further description of himself in "The Tent on the Beach"[1]:

> For while he wrought with strenuous will
> The work his hands had found to do,
> He heard the fitful music still
> Of winds that out of dream-land blew.

But there is little distinction in them. He included only half of them in his edition of 1888, and only two or three of these are at all memorable. More memorable was the "Leaves from Margaret Smith's Journal" (1849), already alluded to. And more remarkable was the bulk of his prose and verse written during his eleven years as contributing editor of the *National Era* (1849–1860), generously interspersed through its pages but quite unrelated to the antislavery cause, of which it was, next to the *Liberator*, the leading organ. This included, in prose, "Old Portraits and Modern Sketches" (1850) and "Literary Recreations and Miscellanies" (1854), and five volumes of verse wholly or partly devoted to the life and legend of New England. In bulk alone it is an extraordinary achievement for a semi-invalid so deeply involved in politics and propaganda.

In his controversial rhymes, as a good journalist and rhetorician, he made his issues plain and simple with an avoidance of embarrassing qualifications. He appealed more and more to the Northerners as a people unanimously opposed to human bondage and not as a half-hearted and divided group. In a generation when the sense of statehood was much stronger than now he assumed a high level of altruism in the Bay State while rousing resentment against Virginia and South Carolina, as in "Expostulation" and "Massachusetts to Virginia." With the memories of the Revolution refreshed by a series of recent semi-centennials, he let his verse resound with scorn for repudiation of Revolutionary principles of freedom. In the opening lines of "The Crisis" he was skill-

[1] "Works," Vol. IV, p. 230.

fully suggestive in his paraphrase of the missionary hymn "From Greenland's Icy Mountains," and in the "Letter from a Missionary of the Methodist Episcopal Church, South, in Kansas, to a Distinguished Politician" he turned to contempt the resort to the Bible in defense of slavery:

> "Go it, old hoss!" they cried, and cursed the niggers —
> Fulfilling thus the word of prophecy,
> "Cursèd be Canaan."[1]

At times the heat of passion did its inevitable work. His disappointment at Webster's famous "Seventh of March" compromise speech in 1850 led him to the extreme of reproach which was felt by Northern liberals — an extreme from which he shared the common reaction of later years and for which he made the atonement of "The Lost Occasion," moved by "the consciousness of a common inheritance of frailty and weakness." The lowest level of his war verse was touched in his famous "Barbara Frietchie." The middle third of the ballad, which has to do with Stonewall Jackson, is partly libelous and partly ridiculous. He is represented as coming through the town like a stock melodrama villain, blushing with remorse at the challenge of the old woman, and capping the climax with a burst of cheap and unsoldierly rhetoric. No doubt it expressed at the moment what the passions of war could lead even a gentle Quaker to declare; no doubt also it was good war journalism; but it stands as evidence of the depths to which poetry can be degraded in war times.

"The Waiting" (1862) is in the loftier vein of one who does not reinforce himself by abuse of his foes. It is a lament of unfulfilled endeavor in an ideal cause. A really great lyric, it is both personal and general in its application. It expresses the despondency of the enfeebled and aging poet that he could not join "the shining ones with plumes of snow" in the good fight; in its reference to "the harder task of standing still" it alludes not only to his resignation at the moment but also to the patient policy that in former years had estranged the

[1] "Works," Vol. III, p. 178.

extremest abolitionists from him. It has been an immediate consolation to thousands who have been confronted by urgent duties that they could not perform; and in a broader way it has expressed the faith of "Ulysses" and "Abt Vogler," of "In Memoriam" and "Saul" and "Asolando," that "good but wished with God is done."

Though, like Philip Freneau, sometimes called "the poet of the Revolution,"[1] this poet of abolition won popularity through his controversial verse, his most permanent work has little to do with either noble or ignoble strife. He had written "Hampton Beach" (1843) and "Cassandra Southwick" (1846) during the heat of the conflict. By 1857 such poems as "The Last Walk in Autumn," "The Garrison of Cape Ann," and "Skipper Ireson's Ride" prove the persistence of the "fitful music" amidst all the din of outward circumstance. Yet the music was seldom unqualifiedly secular. He was not inclined to tell stories without some clear moral implication, and too often he expounded the implication, sermonwise, at the end. Thus he related with dignity and fine effect the legend of the Indian specters of Cape Ann, who were finally driven away by the prayers of the devout garrison after repeated volleys from their muskets had failed. In eighty lines the tale is told; an added stanza calls attention to the fact that there is a lesson in the ancient fiction; and two more, in a sort of subpostscript, indulge in a final burst of poetical exegesis. "Skipper Ireson," the best of his ballads, is no less pointed, but it was written with more art, for the "moral" is developed within the account instead of being tacked on after it. In 1867, again, in "The Tent on the Beach," Whittier refers to "Abraham Davenport" as having "a hint of the old preaching mood" in it, the "sort of sidelong moral squint" that some of his friends object to; but it is a squint that was never permanently overcome, as he betrayed in such of his latest poems as "Saint Gregory's Guest" and "How the Robins Came."

---

[1] See pages 133–135, 141–143, 157, 168–169

From "Memories" (1841), past "In School Days" (1870), to "The Reunion" (1885), Whittier took his readers along or across the borderlands of autobiography. Pre-eminent among his recollections of persons and places is "Snow-Bound." The snowfall, which Emerson celebrated as a thing in itself, Whittier adopted for the background of a winter idyl. The "Flemish pictures of old days" that he drew of his boyhood home are annotated in great detail by the poet; but their virtue lies not so much in their being true to a given set of facts as in their trueness to the rural life of Whittier's New England — just as the pictures in "The Cotter's Saturday Night" are true to the Scotland of Burns, and the pictures in "The Deserted Village" to the landlord-ridden Ireland of Goldsmith. And the contrast that can be drawn between the peasant life of Great Britain and the nearest thing to it that could be found in America furnishes Whittier's testimony to the practical virtues of democracy in his day. In this simple idyl, written with "intimate knowledge and delight," he combined truth and beauty as in no other of his poems.

For summarized criticism of Whittier as an artist his own "Proem" to the collected poems of 1849 and the contemporary comment in Lowell's "Fable for Critics" are suggestive. It is true that the older man had not yet reached his finest period, but this is a matter of balance of characteristics and involves no new trait. Whittier acknowledges the lack in his lines of "mystic beauty, dreamy grace" and of psychological analysis converted into poetry; Lowell confirms the judgment with

> Let his mind once get head in its favorite direction
> And the torrent of verse bursts the dams of reflection,
> While, borne with the rush of his metre along,
> The poet may chance to go right or go wrong,
> Content with the whirl and delirium of song.[1]

Whittier lays his best gifts on the shrine of freedom with an avowal of his love for mankind and his hearty and vehement

[1] Lowell, "A Fable for Critics," lines 901–905.

hatred of all forms of oppression, and Lowell properly qualifies the value of these gifts with the statement that the Quaker's fervor has sometimes dulled him to the distinction between "simple excitement and pure inspiration." Whittier deprecates the harshness and rigor of the rhythms that beat "Labor's hurried time, or Duty's rugged march"; but Lowell declares that at his best the reformer-poet has written unsurpassable lyrics. And both pronounce strictures on his rhymes, which have been conventionally repeated by most of the later critics who have commented on them at all.

Many of Whittier's apparently false rhymes, however (as the author of the "Biglow Papers" should have recognized), are perfect if uttered in accordance with local speech in Essex County. Lowell passes for a scrupulous writer of dialect in the line "This heth my faithful shepherd ben," but Whittier is smiled at for allowing the same final verb to rhyme with "Of all sad words of tongue or pen." Yet the sole difference is that one recognized the pronunciation in his spelling and the other assumed it. If Whittier had employed Lowell's method of transcription in "Barbara Frietchie," for example, he would have written,

> Quick, as it fell, from the broken sta'af
> Dame Barbara snatched the silken sca'af,

and he would have concluded with

> Peace and odda and beauty drawr
> Reound thy symbol of light and lawr;
>
> And evva the stahs above look deown
> On thy stahs below in Frederick teown!

For the *ou* sounds belong to Essex County, and all the others to Boston and even to hallowed Cambridge. False rhymes Whittier wrote in abundance, but by no means all the apparently defective ones should be condemned at first glance.

Until the publication of "Snow-Bound" (1866) Whittier's verse, though widely circulated, had brought him the most meager money returns. Now he was solidly established with the *Atlantic Monthly*, the leading literary magazine in the country, and with Ticknor and Fields, the leading literary publishers; and Whittier thrived in income as well as in the hearts of the reading public. For his verse had now, as always, the leading characteristics of fireside favorites, the only sort of poetry that is always certain of the sales to which no publisher or editor is indifferent. Their form is simple; common words and short sentences are cast in conventional rhythms with frequent rhyme; and they are therefore easy to memorize. In content they are easy to understand, not given to subtleties of analysis or philosophical abstractions. More often than not they are either narratives, like the war ballads and the New England chronicles, or strung on narrative threads, like "Snow-Bound." Almost always they contain vivid pictures; mention of "Skipper Ireson" or "Telling the Bees" or "Maud Muller" or "The Huskers" recalls tableaux first and then the ideas connected with them. And, finally, they contain the applied moral which the immature or unliterary American mind dearly loves, the very feature that proves irksome to the seasoned reader serving as an added attraction to the less experienced. On the other hand, in a little group of hymns Whittier proved how finely moral sentiment can be expressed in poetry.

It is easy to cite popular favorites that do not illustrate all, or even most, of these traits, but beyond doubt the great majority of universally popular poems contain most if not all of them. If poems with these features are also related to average experience or average emotional responses, people cherish them as they do the melodies to which some of them are fortunately set, or as they do those bits from Beethoven, Mendelssohn, Chopin, or Schubert which belong to every concertgoer's repertory. It is because Whittier — militant journalist until the close of the Civil War — wrote so much in this gentler vein that in his latter years the people acclaimed him beyond any of his contemporaries. He belonged to them.

Book List

GENERAL

ALCOTT, LOUISA MAY. Life, Letters, and Journals, edited by Mrs. E. D. Cheney. 1906.

ALCOTT, LOUISA MAY. Silver Pitchers, and Other Stories. 1905.

CARY, EDWARD. George William Curtis. A. M. L. Series. 1894.

CHRISTY, ARTHUR. The Orient in American Transcendentalism. 1932.

CODMAN, JOHN T. Brook Farm: Historic and Personal Memoirs. 1894.

COOKE, GEORGE WILLIS. John Sullivan Dwight, Brook-Farmer, Editor, and Critic of Music. 1898.

COOKE, GEORGE WILLIS (Ed.). The Poets of Transcendentalism; an Anthology. With introductory essay and biographical notes. 1903.

COOKE, GEORGE WILLIS. Unitarianism in America; a History of its Origin and Development. 1902.

FROTHINGHAM, OCTAVIUS BROOKS. George Ripley. A. M. L. Series. 1882.

FROTHINGHAM, OCTAVIUS BROOKS. Transcendentalism in New England, a History. 1876.

GODDARD, HAROLD CLARKE. Studies in New England Transcendentalism. 1908.

GOHDES, CLARENCE L. The Periodicals of American Transcendentalism. 1931.

HAWTHORNE, NATHANIEL. The Blithedale Romance. 1852.

HAWTHORNE, NATHANIEL. Passages from the American Note-Books of Nathaniel Hawthorne. 2 vols. 1868.

HIGGINSON, THOMAS WENTWORTH. Cheerful Yesterdays. 1898.

HIGGINSON, THOMAS WENTWORTH. Part of a Man's Life. 1905.

MARSHALL, HERBERT E. "The Story of the Dial," *New Mexico Quarterly*, Vol. I, pp. 147–165.

REED, AMY L. (Ed.). Letters from Brook Farm, 1844–1847, by Marianne Dwight. 1928.

SEARS, JOHN V. D. My Friends at Brook Farm. 1912.

SWIFT, LINDSAY. Brook Farm. Its Members, Scholars, and Visitors. 1900.

THE TRANSCENDENTALISTS

Individual Authors

AMOS BRONSON ALCOTT. Conversations with Children on the Gospels (2 vols.), 1836–1837; Tablets, 1868; Concord Days, 1872; Table-Talk, 1877.

[*Biography and Criticism*]

GOHDES, CLARENCE. "Alcott's 'Conversation' on the Transcendental Club and the *Dial*," *American Literature*, Vol. III, pp. 14–27.

PEABODY, ELIZABETH PALMER. Record of Mr. Alcott's School. 1874.

SANBORN, FRANK B. Bronson Alcott at Alcott House, England, and Fruitlands, New England (1842–1844). 1908.

SANBORN, FRANK B., and HARRIS, WILLIAM T. A. Bronson Alcott: His Life and Philosophy. 2 vols. 1893.

WARREN, AUSTIN. "Orphic Sage: Bronson Alcott," *American Literature*, Vol. III, pp. 3–13.

WILLIAM ELLERY CHANNING. The Works of William Ellery Channing, D. D. First Complete American Edition, with an introduction. 5 vols. 1841.

[*Biography and Criticism*]

CHANNING, WILLIAM H. Memoir of William Ellery Channing, with extracts from His Correspondence and Manuscripts. 3 vols. 1848, 1854.

PEABODY, ELIZABETH PALMER. Reminiscences of William Ellery Channing. 1880.

PEABODY, FRANCIS G. "The Humanism of William Ellery Channing," *Christian Register*, Vol. CIX, pp. 407–409.

SPILLER, ROBERT E. "A Case for William Ellery Channing," *New England Quarterly*, Vol. III, pp. 55–81.

SARAH MARGARET FULLER (OSSOLI). Conversations with Goethe in the Last Years of His Life, Translated from the German of Eckermann, 1839; Gunderode (a translation from the German of the correspondence between Canoness Gunderode and Bettine Brentano), 1842; Summer on the Lakes in 1843, 1844; Woman in the Nineteenth Century, 1845; Papers on Literature and Art (2 vols.), 1846; At Home and Abroad, or Things and Thoughts in America and Europe (edited by her brother, Arthur B. Fuller), 1856; Life Without and Life Within; or Reviews, Narratives, Essays, and Poems (edited by Arthur B. Fuller), 1860.

[*Biography and Criticism*]

ANTHONY, KATHERINE. Margaret Fuller: a Psychological Biography. 1920.

BELL, MARGARET. Margaret Fuller: a Biography. 1930.

BRAUN, FREDERICK AUGUSTUS. Margaret Fuller and Goethe. 1910.

EMERSON, RALPH WALDO, CHANNING, W. H., and CLARKE, J. F. Memoirs of Margaret Fuller Ossoli. 2 vols. 1852.

HIGGINSON, THOMAS WENTWORTH. Margaret Fuller Ossoli. A. M. L. Series. 1884.

MCMASTER, HELEN N. Margaret Fuller as a Literary Critic. 1928.

THEODORE PARKER. The Collected Works of Theodore Parker . . . containing his theological, polemical, and critical writings, sermons, speeches, and addresses, and literary miscellanies, edited by Frances Power Cobbe. 14 vols. 1863–1871, 1876.

[*Biography and Criticism*]

CHADWICK, JOHN WHITE. Theodore Parker, Preacher and Reformer. 1900.

COMMAGER, HENRY S. "The Dilemma of Theodore Parker," *New England Quarterly*, Vol. VI, pp. 257–276.

COMMAGER, HENRY S. "Tempest in a Boston Teapot," *New England Quarterly*, Vol. VI, pp. 651–675.

FROTHINGHAM, OCTAVIUS BROOKS. Theodore Parker; a Biography. 1874.

WEISS, JOHN. Life and Correspondence of Theodore Parker. 2 vols. 1864.

[*Magazines*]

The Dial: an Historical and Biographical Introduction, by George Willis Cooke. 1902.

The Dial: a Magazine for Literature, Philosophy, and Religion, Vols. I–IV. 1840–1844.

The Harbinger, Devoted to Social and Political Progress. 8 vols. 1845–1849.

[*Anthologies*]

Boynton, Percy H. American Poetry. 1918.

Cooke, George Willis. The Poets of Transcendentalism. 1903.

Foerster, Norman. American Poetry and Prose (rev. ed.). 1934.

Kreymborg, Alfred. Lyric America. 1930.

McDowell, Tremaine. The Romantic Triumph. 1933.

Prescott and Sanders. An Introduction to American Poetry. 1932.

Stedman and Hutchinson. A Library of American Literature, Vols. V, VI, VII.

Ralph Waldo Emerson. Chief volumes appeared as follows: Nature, 1836; An Oration Delivered before the Phi Beta Kappa Society, at Cambridge, 1837; Essays, 1841; Poems, 1847; Nature, Addresses and Lectures, 1849; Representative Men: Seven Lectures, 1850; English Traits, 1856; The Conduct of Life, 1860; May Day and Other Pieces, 1867; Society and Solitude, 1870; Letters and Social Aims, 1876.

[*Available Editions*]

The Complete Works of Ralph Waldo Emerson. Centenary Edition (the standard edition). Edited by Edward Waldo Emerson, with index. 12 vols. 1903–1921.

A Concordance to the Poems of Ralph Waldo Emerson. Arranged by George Shelton Hubbell. 1932.

Emerson: Representative Selections, edited, with introduction, by Frederic I. Carpenter. 1934.

Essays and Poems of Emerson, edited, with introduction, by Stuart P. Sherman. 1921.

The Heart of Emerson's Journals, edited by Bliss Perry. 1926.

The Journals of Ralph Waldo Emerson, edited by E. W. Emerson and Waldo Emerson Forbes. 10 vols. 1909–1914.

Light of Emerson: a Complete Digest with Key-word Concordance etc., edited by H. H. Emmons. 1930.

Uncollected Lectures by Ralph Waldo Emerson, edited by Clarence Gohdes. 1932.

The Uncollected Writings. Essays, Addresses, Poems, Reviews and Letters by Ralph Waldo Emerson. Edited by Charles C. Bigelow. 1912.

[*Biography and Criticism*]

Beach, J. W. Emerson and Evolution. 1934.

Boynton, Percy H. "Emerson in His Period," *International Journal of Ethics*, Vol. XXXIX, pp. 177–189.

Brooks, Van Wyck. Emerson and Others. 1927.

Brooks, Van Wyck. The Life of Emerson. 1932.

Brownell, William Crary. American Prose Masters. 1909.

Cabot, James Eliot. A Memoir of Ralph Waldo Emerson. 2 vols. 1887.

CANBY, HENRY SEIDEL. Classic Americans. 1931.
CARPENTER, FREDERIC I. Emerson and Asia. 1930.
CARPENTER, FREDERIC I. "Points of Comparison between Emerson and William James," *New England Quarterly*, Vol. II, pp. 458–474.
CHAZIN, M. "Quinet, an Early Discoverer of Emerson," *PMLA*, Vol. XLVIII, pp. 147–163.
CLARK, HARRY H. "Emerson and Science," *Philological Quarterly*, Vol. X, pp. 225–260.
FIRKINS, OSCAR W. "Has Emerson a Future?" Selected Essays. 1933.
FIRKINS, OSCAR W. Ralph Waldo Emerson. 1915.
FOERSTER, NORMAN. American Criticism. 1928.
FOERSTER, NORMAN. Nature in American Literature. 1923.
GARROD, H. W. "Emerson," *New England Quarterly*, Vol. III, pp. 3–24.
GRAY, HENRY D. Emerson: a Statement of New England Transcendentalism as Expressed in the Philosophy of Its Chief Exponent. 1917.
HOLMES, OLIVER WENDELL. Ralph Waldo Emerson. A. M. L. Series. 1884.
HOTSON, CLARENCE P. Emerson and Swedenborg. 1929.
JAMES, HENRY, JR. Partial Portraits. 1888.
KREYMBORG, ALFRED. Our Singing Strength. 1929.
LOWELL, JAMES RUSSELL. "Emerson, the Lecturer." My Study Windows. 1871.
MCQUISTON, RAYMER. The Relation of Ralph Waldo Emerson to Public Affairs. 1923.
MARCHAND, ERNEST. "Emerson and the Frontier," *American Literature*, Vol. III, pp. 149–174.
MICHAUD, REGIS. Emerson: the Enraptured Yankee. Translated by George Boas. 1930.
MORE, PAUL ELMER. "Emerson." Cambridge History of American Literature, Vol. I.
MUMFORD, LEWIS. The Golden Day. 1926.
PERRY, BLISS. Emerson Today. Vanuxem Lectures. 1931.
PERRY, BLISS. The Praise of Folly and Other Papers. 1923.
RUSSELL, PHILLIPS. Emerson: the Wisest American. 1929.
SANBORN, FRANK B. The Genius and Character of Emerson. 1885.
SANTAYANA, GEORGE. Interpretations of Poetry and Religion. 1900.
SCUDDER, TOWNSEND, III. "Emerson's British Lecture Tour, 1847–1848," *American Literature*, Vol. VII, pp. 15–36, 166–180.
SHERMAN, STUART P. Americans. 1922.
SUTCLIFFE, E. G. Emerson's Theories of Literary Expression. 1923.
THOMPSON, F. T. "Emerson's Theories and Practice of Poetry," *PMLA*, Vol. XLIII, pp. 1170–1184.
WAHR, FREDERICK B. Emerson and Goethe. 1915.
WOODBERRY, GEORGE EDWARD. Ralph Waldo Emerson. E. M. L. Series. 1907.

[*Bibliography*]

COOKE, GEORGE WILLIS. A Bibliography of Ralph Waldo Emerson. 1908.
Cambridge History of American Literature, Vol. I, pp. 551–556.

HENRY DAVID THOREAU. The chief works appeared as follows during Thoreau's lifetime: A Week on the Concord and Merrimack Rivers, 1849; Walden; or, Life in the Woods, 1854. Posthumous volumes: Excursions,

1863; The Maine Woods, 1864; Cape Cod, 1865; Letters to Various Persons, 1865; A Yankee in Canada, with Anti-Slavery and Reform Papers, 1866. Early Spring in Massachusetts, 1881; Summer, 1884; Winter, 1888; Essays and Other Writings, 1891; Autumn, 1892; Miscellanies, 1893; Familiar Letters, 1894; Poems, 1895.

[*Available Editions*]

On the Duty of Civil Disobedience, edited and printed by Carl P. Rollins. 1928.

The Heart of Thoreau's Journals, edited by Odell Shepard. 1927.

Little Essays from the Works of Henry David Thoreau, selected by Charles R. Murphy. 1931.

Manuscript Edition. 20 vols. 1906.

Thoreau: Philosopher of Freedom; Writings on Liberty by Henry David Thoreau, selected, with an introduction, by James MacKaye. 1930.

The Walden Edition. 20 vols. 1906. (Of these volumes the last fourteen are the complete "Journal," which includes what stands in Vols. V–VIII of the Riverside Edition as "Early Spring in Massachusetts," "Summer," "Autumn," "Winter."

"Walden" and the "Week" have been variously edited for school use.

The Writings of Henry David Thoreau. Riverside Edition. 11 vols. 1932.

[*Biography and Criticism*]

The standard life is by Frank B. Sanborn. A. M. L. Series, enlarged edition. 1919.

ADAMS, RAYMOND W. "Thoreau's Literary Apprenticeship," *Studies in Philology*, Vol. XXIX, pp. 617–629.

ATKINSON, J. BROOKS. Henry Thoreau: the Cosmic Yankee. 1927.

BAZALGETTE, LÉON. Henry D. Thoreau, Bachelor of Nature. Translated by Van Wyck Brooks. 1925.

BENTON, JOEL. "The Poetry of Thoreau," *Lippincott's*, May, 1886.

BURROUGHS, JOHN. Indoor Studies. 1889.

CANBY, HENRY S. "Thoreau, the Great Eccentric," *Saturday Review of Literature*, Vol. IV, pp. 337–339.

CANBY, HENRY S. "Thoreau, and the Machine Age," *Yale Review*, Vol. XX, pp. 517–531.

CHANNING, WILLIAM E. Thoreau, the Poet-Naturalist (new ed.). 1902.

COURNOS, JOHN. "A Comparison of Gauguin with Thoreau." A Modern Plutarch. 1928.

DE ARMOND, FRED. "Thoreau and Schopenhauer," *New England Quarterly*, Vol. V, pp. 55–64.

EMERSON, RALPH WALDO. Lectures and Biographical Sketches. Centenary Edition, Vol. X.

FOERSTER, NORMAN. "The Humanism of Thoreau," *Nation*, Vol. CV, pp. 9–12.

HAYDON, WALTER T. "Thoreau, Philosopher, Poet, Naturalist," *Bookman* [London], June, 1917.

HINCKLEY, EDWARD B. "Thoreau and Beston: Two Observers of Cape Cod," *New England Quarterly*, Vol. IV, pp. 216–229.

HUBBELL, GEORGE S. "Walden Revisited," *Sewanee Review*, Vol. XXXVII, pp. 283–294.

JONES, SAMUEL A. (Ed.). Pertaining to Thoreau. 1901.

LOWELL, JAMES RUSSELL. My Study Windows. 1871.
MACMECHAN, ARCHIBALD. "Thoreau." Cambridge History of American Literature, Vol. II, Book II.
MACY, JOHN. The Spirit of American Literature. 1913.
MARBLE, ANNIE R. Thoreau: His Home, Friends, and Books. 1902.
MOORE, JOHN B. "Thoreau Rejects Emerson," *American Literature*, Vol. IV, pp. 241–256.
MORE, PAUL ELMER. Shelburne Essays. First series. 1906.
MUMFORD, LEWIS. The Golden Day. 1926.
PATTEE, FRED L. American Literature since 1870. 1915.
SALT, HENRY S. "Gandhi and Thoreau," *The Nation and Athenaeum*, Vol. XLVI, p. 728.
SALT, HENRY S. Henry David Thoreau. 1896.
SANBORN, FRANK B. Life of Thoreau. A. M. L. Series. 1882.
SANBORN, FRANK B. The Personality of Thoreau. 1901.
STEVENSON, ROBERT LOUIS. Familiar Studies of Men and Books. 1882.
VAN DOREN, MARK. Henry David Thoreau: a Critical Study. 1916.
WOOD, JAMES P. "English and American Criticism of Thoreau," *New England Quarterly*, Vol. VI, pp. 733–746.

[*Bibliography*]

ADAMS, RAYMOND W. A Thoreau Checklist. 1930.
ALLEN, FRANCIS H. A Bibliography of Henry David Thoreau. 1908.
Cambridge History of American Literature, Vol. II, pp. 411–415.
Catalogue of a Collection of Books by, or pertaining to, Henry David Thoreau. 1927.

JOHN GREENLEAF WHITTIER. The chief works appeared as follows: Legends of New England, 1831; Justice and Expediency, 1833; Poems Written during the Progress of the Abolition Question in the United States, between the Years 1830 and 1838, 1837; Poems, 1838; Lays of My Home, 1843; Voices of Freedom, 1846; Songs of Labor and Other Poems, 1850; The Panorama, and Other Poems, 1856; Home Ballads, and Poems, 1860; In War Time, and Other Poems, 1864; Snow-Bound: a Winter Idyl, 1866; The Tent on the Beach and Other Poems, 1867; Among the Hills, 1868; At Sundown, 1892.

[*Available Editions*]

The Complete Poetical Works of John Greenleaf Whittier. Cambridge Edition. 1895, 1914.
Works of Whittier. 9 vols. 1892. (Includes the contents of the Riverside Edition plus the Life, by S. T. Pickard.)
The Works of Whittier. Riverside Edition. 7 vols. Vols. I–IV, Poetical Works; Vols. V–VIII, Prose. 1888–1889.

[*Biography and Criticism*]

The standard life is by Samuel T. Pickard. 2 vols. 1894.
BEST, MARY AGNES. Rebel Saints. 1925.
BURTON, RICHARD. John Greenleaf Whittier. 1901.
CANBY, HENRY S. American Estimates. 1929.
CANBY, HENRY S. Classic Americans. 1931.
CARPENTER, GEORGE RICE. John Greenleaf Whittier. A. M. L. Series. 1903.

CHRISTY, ARTHUR. "The Orientalism of Whittier," *American Literature*, Vol. II, pp. 47–57.

CLAFLIN, MRS. MARY B. Personal Recollections of John Greenleaf Whittier. 1893.

CURRIER, T. F. "Whittier and the *New England Weekly Review*," *New England Quarterly*, Vol. VI, pp. 589–597.

EASTBURN, IOLA KAY. Whittier's Relation to German Life and Thought. 1915.

FIELDS, MRS. ANNIE. Authors and Friends. 1896.

FLOWER, BENJAMIN O. Whittier, Prophet, Seer and Man. 1896.

HAWKINS, CHAUNCY J. The Mind of Whittier. 1904.

HIGGINSON, THOMAS WENTWORTH. Cheerful Yesterdays. 1898.

HIGGINSON, THOMAS WENTWORTH. Contemporaries. 1899.

HIGGINSON, THOMAS WENTWORTH. John Greenleaf Whittier. E. M. L. Series. 1902.

KENNEDY, WILLIAM SLOANE. John Greenleaf Whittier, His Life, Genius and Writings. 1882.

KREYMBORG, ALFRED. Our Singing Strength. 1929.

LAWTON, WILLIAM C. The New England Poets. 1898.

LINTON, WILLIAM JAMES. Life of John Greenleaf Whittier. 1903.

MACY, JOHN. The Spirit of American Literature. 1913.

MORDELL, ALBERT. Quaker Militant, John Greenleaf Whittier. 1933.

PICKARD, SAMUEL T. Whittier Land. 1904.

PRAY, FRANCES MARY. A Study of Whittier's Apprenticeship as a Poet, 1825–1835. 1930.

SCOTT, WINFIELD T. "Poetry in American: a New Consideration of Whittier's Verse," *New England Quarterly*, Vol. VII, pp. 258–275.

STEDMAN, EDMUND C. Poets of America. 1885.

STEVENS, JAMES S. Whittier's Use of the Bible. 1930.

TAYLOR, BAYARD. Critical Essays and Literary Notes. 1880.

UNDERWOOD, FRANCIS H. John Greenleaf Whittier: a Biography. 1884.

WENDELL, BARRETT. Stelligeri and Other Essays. 1893.

WHITMAN, WALT. Specimen Days. 1881.

WILLIAMS, CECIL B. The Historicity of Margaret Smith's Journal. 1933. (University of Chicago thesis.)

[*Bibliography*]

RISTINE, FRANK H. "Whittier Bibliography." Cambridge History of American Literature, Vol. II, pp. 436–451.

"A Bibliography of the Original Editions of the Works of John Greenleaf Whittier," *The Book Buyer*, Vol. XII, pp. 216–221. 1895.

[*Anthologies for the Transcendental Group and Whittier*]

BOYNTON, PERCY H. American Poetry. 1918.

COOKE, GEORGE WILLIS. The Poets of Transcendentalism. 1903.

FOERSTER, NORMAN. American Poetry and Prose (rev. ed.). 1934.

KREYMBORG, ALFRED. Lyric America. 1930.

McDOWELL, TREMAINE. The Romantic Triumph. 1933.

PRESCOTT and SANDERS. An Introduction to American Poetry. 1932.

STEDMAN and HUTCHINSON. Library of American Literature, Vols. V–VI.

CHAPTER VIII

The South Asserts Itself

THE TRADITIONS OF THE SOUTH

DURING the middle third of the nineteenth century, the latter years of Irving and Cooper and the maturing period of the New England group, the South became the most insistent and inescapable factor in the American equation. It was the factor most clearly derived from the latter 1700's and modified there from medieval sources. In the opening chapter of this survey the colonial debt to the Middle Ages was traced at some length. The determining influence in the Middle Ages, it appeared, was a religious belief which had degenerated into an excessively restrictive theological dogma. "The special bias of the Church Fathers toward historical and natural facts *closed their eyes to many phenomena, and focussed them on special interpretations of the rest. Knowledge of mankind or of nature could not be sought in a mood of open inquiry, for the conclusions of inquiry were predetermined.*"[1] In the years leading to the crisis of the Civil War an economic situation in the South had developed an economic dogma with a parallel result.

Up to 1861 the Southern people in the United States were living a notably simple life colored by medieval survivals.[2] The emigrant Cavaliers of the Commonwealth period were not, it is true, the sole ancestors of the pre-war aristocracy. These were largely descended from an energetic merchant class who had turned planter and who for a hundred and fifty years were enterprising profit seekers, speculators, exploiters of the public domain. But in the Revolutionary War

---

[1] See page 6.

[2] T. J. Wertenbaker, "Patrician and Plebeian in Virginia"; W. P. Trent, "Life of William Gilmore Simms," pp. 31–43; N. S. Shaler, "The Peculiarities of the South," *North American Review*, October, 1890.

generation the merchant spirit had once more given way to the spirit of the Cavalier. It was an evolution in which Colonel William Byrd[1] had had an early place and of which George Washington, planter, landholder, aristocrat, was the culminating figure. The dominant Southerners were from then on committed to the social order in which the landed estate was the prime element and overlordship the prime necessity. In manners, customs, education, religion, the Southern planter was thus a child of the English squire, a grandchild of the English baron.

Within this social order, of which he and a few score of his kind stood at the apex, he acknowledged no superior, no superlord above himself, the overlord. Within his circle he was subscriber to a limited Grecian democracy; but within his domestic establishment, almost too extensive to be so called, he was master of his family, of his related and adopted dependents, of his retainers and their dependents, of free hospitality to his casual guests. He lived on the land, and at least nominally drew his living from it. To his serfs, in return for their labor, he supplied roofs, a certain small share in the fruits of their toil, and no small measure of protection. An overseer of overseers, he spent his energy largely and his money lavishly at the dining table and the card table, at the hunt and the race track, in the ballroom, and possibly on the stump and in the legislature. The law did not recognize the claims of primogeniture; but the Southern planter did, assuming that younger sons should enter the army or navy or one of the professions, with the possibility of earning or marrying an acreage and an establishment. There was little in the social program of this gentleman that had not been anticipated by William Byrd, gentleman. Some of the material conditions were altered; the ideal of life on his own domain was unchanged.

But his political ideas were changed. The first necessity for a strong central government was passed. The Southern

---

[1] See pages 79–84.

aristocrat of the seaboard states began to feel the necessity for protecting himself both from the industrial North and from the democratically agrarian frontier. While the respectable, propertied North stood long for the federalism of Washington and Adams, the aristocratic South was swept reluctantly but surely over to the Jeffersonian doctrines of State rights. An early tie with the North was thus broken; and the adoption of politics as a gentleman's profession sent a disproportionate number of gifted Southerners to Congress, where they did not gain in respect for the North, whose legislative representatives were not so representative of its best mind and manhood. For the first half of the century the contingent from the old South stood for republican simplicity, economy in administration, decentralized power. As sectional consciousness grew stronger, while the Northern banker became the creditor of the plantation which the Northern antislavery element was assailing, a newer South took the aggressive, and took it in behalf of a propertied, privileged class with whom it would normally have been in jealous conflict. The solidarity of the South was effected in terms of its fondest conservatisms — the conservatisms of the squirearchy and, before them, of the baronage.

Thus intrenched in property, privilege, and custom, the Southern gentleman was the expositor also of an ornate social code which shared ancestry with the economic order. For its romantic chivalry turned back to a remote and idealized Arthurian age, while its own gallant self reverted to a nearer, world-weary and worldly-wise mid-eighteenth century. The remote past, — James Branch Cabell, Southern genealogist and romancer, explains at length, — in the idealized life to be found there, was the genuine age of chivalry, "a world-wide code, in consonance with which all estimable people lived and died. Its root was the assumption (uncontested then) that a gentleman will always serve his God, his honor, and his lady without any reservation."

It was a code under which gentlemen and ladies regarded themselves as children of an indulgent Father who was certain to deal out justice tempered with mercy; a code which later centuries outgrew, but which served society for long. It is the code which is implicit in most Southern romances and which prevails in Cabell's "Domnei," a concept of sublimated love to which, in certain hours of disaffection with the modern "tragi-comic mêlée," the romantically disposed modern mind reverts with almost religious devotion. Such a reversion is possible, however, only to those who can make it at a single, bold stride over the centuries. This done, such a book as "Domnei" becomes readable and credible, a fine fruit of Southern romantic faith. To fall short of this could result in "A Connecticut Yankee at King Arthur's Court," a natural product of a reactionary romantic skepticism.

Thus, when the Southerner lacked seven-century boots, which could carry him all the way to medieval chivalry, he recognized himself as a wayfarer from the eighteenth century, which was the ancestral home of Southern gallantry. What such a derivation means is suggested if we remember that "The Rape of the Lock" was an early utterance of the eighteenth century and "Sense and Sensibility" a posthumous message from it. Whatever the contributory origins of Southern speech and manners may have been, they have not even yet ceased to resemble those we associate with the days of Pope and Sterne and Jane Austen, all of whom regarded them with amused tolerance even while they practiced them. Both speech and manners in the old South were marked by a somewhat elevated formality of phrasing, an inclination to speak as from the rostrum, an opulent show of deference to beauty in women, a vocal insistence upon honor and chivalry, the stagey insincerity which follows hard on the heels of conventionalized speech. He who talks the language of gallantry today can do it only with the smile of one who is dancing a minuet, or with the covert contempt of one who is talking to intellectual inferiors. The South of "before the war" preserved to a remarkable degree an attitude of chivalrous deference to the ladies of the privileged class, while applying its phrases of gallantry to Southern womanhood in general.

Life is usually lived in a world of immediate circumstance and experience which is more or less affected by a set of inherited, traditionalized, and imperceptibly changing assumptions. The individual normally refuses to admit the discrepancies between fact and tradition, between reality and romance, though he may either oscillate between them or uneasily attempt to reconcile them, trying to adjust idioms of thought and speech which belong to another age to idioms of action which belong to the immediate present. Thus in New England at this middle third of the century, the problem, for those who saw it, was to uphold the tenets of nonconformist religious orthodoxy and to thrive on a system of wage slavery after the manner of a briskly developing industrial and commercial community. In the South the problem for the member of the dominant class was to play the knight and be the planter, dependent on a system of bond slavery though not without allusion to the Sermon on the Mount. Both New Englander and Southerner thus faced what our English cousins call a rather large order. Once again Mr. Cabell interprets the situation in "The Cream of the Jest," a book which is not only a most readable story but also a gloss on Southern history. Herein the central character lives in a modern world with a yearning for the romance which he finds nowhere about him. By means of a charm he makes off nightly to a world of dreams and romantic adventure. Then returning to daily life, with the mocking sophistication of an eighteenth-century-derived Virginian, he yet carries back with him enough of the chivalric code to be true to his love, disavowing constancy even while he practices it; to his Christian God, according to his own interpretation of him; and, between the two, to his own honor. Mr. Cabell makes this gallant much more convincing to himself than he is to the dispassionate observer.

But the doctrines of knightliness and courtliness could be more easily carried over into this nineteenth-century retrospective world — and with less debate — than the feudal doctrine of overlord and serf. For at this point the eighteenth century had actually interpolated counter-doctrines in the theories that men had natural rights and that all men were created equal; and the embarrassment was the worse because of the early enunciation of these theories from the South and because of the general condemnation of slavery there until a turn in agriculture and invention seemed to make it a necessity. The shift of Southern sentiment and the evolution of Southern argument are well known:[1] first, general disapproval of slavery and opposition to a continuation of the slave trade; then somewhat reluctant admission that slavery was an unfortunate necessity dictated by the demands of the general good; then an insistence that slavery was a divinely ordained institution, sanctioned in Holy Writ, beneficent to the slave, indispensable as a cornerstone of democracy. The whole procedure by the modern overlord and his delegated defenders — legislative, collegiate, and churchly — was a masterpiece of rationalizing, of seeking out principles to buttress an existing condition.

> He felt, but he did not think. At best he thought backwards, and, with his feelings for a guide, began to use his by no means inconsiderable powers of mind in the erection of a system of political and social philosophy which, as an exhibition of what wrong-headed honesty can accomplish in the way of self-stultification, has never had an equal in the world's history.[2]

Thus the heritage of the pre-Civil War South from feudal medievalism by way of the eighteenth century was inevitably expressed in reactionary thinking. The easygoing Cavalier of Virginia was forced by the aggressions of alien critics to join the fiery Southerner of the Carolinas in defense of a social system which seemed to be based on economic necessity. He could not admit the ruthless facts that proved it to be economically unsound. Even less could he admit that a system which was harsh on the slave and bad for the plantation

---

[1] T. V. Smith, in "The American Philosophy of Equality," traces the subject clearly and briefly in Chapter II. See also S. N. Elliott's "Cotton is King."

[2] W. P. Trent, "Life of Simms," p. 41.

was also demoralizing for the master. His eyes were closed to what he would not believe, and he would not tolerate open inquiry into social conditions, "for the conclusions of inquiry were predetermined." So had they been for the medieval products of patristic theology and learning. So had they been for the churchly dictators in seventeenth-century Massachusetts. A community dominated by men whose eyes and minds were closed to social and economic facts and inferences was no more likely to be a center for creative artistry than these others had been in the past. What were the effects on literary activity of this general situation? The answer must be made in two quite different sets of terms: (1) the Northern onslaught and the Southern reply; (2) the formal literature of the South.

The Northern Onslaught and the Southern Reply

The third decade in the nineteenth century was marked by rifts in the "era of good feeling" in the United States; and the next ten years saw the end of it. The change is a loose parallel of the developments leading up to the Revolution of two generations earlier, the South playing the role of the colonists and the North that of the controlling government. In both cases the conflict arose from rival economic interests and from a feeling on the part of the seceding group that they were being exploited and oppressed. In both cases there was a prolonged period of discontent, a shorter one of doubt, and an ultimate resort to arms; and in both cases a succession of events gave rise to controversy which drew the literary into the field of politics and statecraft.

The record of this widening cleavage starts with an industrial free-soil North committed to a policy of strong Federal control, and with an agricultural slave-state South devoted to a doctrine of State rights.[1] At the outset, however, in

[1] "Is it not the chief disgrace in the world, not to be an unit; . . . but to be reckoned in the gross, in the hundred, or the thousand, of the party, the section, to which we belong; and our opinion predicted geographically, as the north, or the south?" — Emerson, "The American Scholar" (1837), last paragraph

both sections the newer radical elements which eventually brought the conflict to a climax were balanced by the conservative and aristocratic defenders of the older traditions, who were relatively in agreement and intent on maintaining harmony, restoring it, finding peaceful solutions, avoiding open combat, if necessary evading issues, and at all costs preserving the Union. The history of the cleavage thus becomes the record of progressing from controversy within the sections to controversy between them; from friendly solicitude to hostile recrimination; from attempts to convince and coöperate to attempts to convict and discredit. And the record is punctuated by a series of happenings in American life which served as sparks to set off the ever accumulating tinder of regional prides, irritabilities, and resentments. From the election of John Quincy Adams, in 1824, every Presidential campaign fanned the embers. From the date of the Missouri Compromise, in 1820, every admission of a new state to the Union disturbed the balance of power, until it was completely overthrown. Henry Clay's unhappy "American plan" set going a tariff war which is not yet over, though it lasted no longer than 1832 before one Southern state propounded its doctrine of nullification. And a succession of proslavery and antislavery enactments and court decisions continued to puff at the flames started in these other ways. It is a chronicle worth following in terms of a few of the events and a few of the more notable utterances; for it involved casually most of the major Northern writers and it accounts for the heightening of Southern characteristics which in more harmonious circumstances might have waned or disappeared.

When Andrew Jackson was first elected, in 1828, men and women apparently could entertain opinions on slavery with little of sectional consciousness. In 1827, for example, the young widow Sarah J. Hale wrote a frank potboiler called "Northwood, or Life North and South, showing the true character of both." It was a tale in which the ways of New Hampshire were exhibited and explained to a visiting Englishman, and the ways of Charleston, South Carolina, were expounded in letters from visiting New Englanders. The comparisons were in favor of the North, but only mildly so. One of the weakest characters in the novel was a spoiled Northern woman; one of the most admirable, a Southern planter. In the end their son, who inherited the plantation, decided to Christianize his slaves with the help of his Northern wife and then to free them and colonize them in Liberia. It was the solution of the day. Nothing could have been more innocuous than this tale. It was so obviously inoffensive that in 1852 Mrs. Hale republished it in order, she hoped, to offset the exciting effects of "Uncle Tom's Cabin." Similarly, Fenimore Cooper's "Notions of the Americans"[1] of 1828 would give the impression, if it were a lone document, that the country was united in resenting foreign strictures on slavery in America. Europe, he wrote, had worse conditions to condone than America. Europe was originally to blame for the situation in America. Of course the illiterate black should not have the vote. General emancipation was remotely desirable, but level heads and wise measures were more desirable still. All this not from a Virginian or a Carolinian, but from a New Yorker eager to defend his country against critics from abroad. But this happy harmony was not to continue. Ten years after these two books were written, when Mrs. Hale became editor of *Godey's Lady's Book*, and Cooper author of "Homeward Bound" and "Home as Found," the rift between the sections was rapidly widening.

For most of the time from the first rift until the outbreak of the war the North had the double advantage of being the aggressor and of enjoying a well-developed literary tradition, with a large body of writers and all the machinery for publication. The conservatives of both sections wished to avoid open disagreement, but at the outset even the fire-eating Southerners wanted nothing better than to be let alone. No one ever rises to defend the status quo as long as it lacks assailants.

---

[1] Vol. II, pp. 340–367, 456–458.

In those opening years in the early 30's, the most extreme of the antislavery agitators sounded the note of pity for the slave, and at the same time stressed the imperative need for preserving the Union. These were sentiments that the conservatives of the North also could subscribe to, and most of the South as well, provided they were not uttered as from New England. There was little evidence of deep sectional feeling in 1830, when, on a tariff issue, Webster and Hayne indulged in their courtly asperities in the Senate chamber. Seven years later the *Southern Literary Messenger*,[1] in an article on Webster, could endorse his eloquent peroration: "one and inseparable, now and forever." And in these same years Northern extremists could be repelled as severely at home as in the South. No "right-minded" banker or manufacturer, clergyman or teacher, could take any stock, intellectual or emotional, in Garrison's *Liberator* when he came out with his explosive and capitalized I WILL BE HEARD in 1831. And though young Mr. Whittier's "Justice and Expediency" of two years later was widely distributed by the enthusiast Lewis Tappan, it was discounted and decried by the respectables on account of the enthusiasm displayed in its forensic style. In its general procedure it was an orderly document borrowing many of its arguments from the English debate that had just ended with emancipation in the British West Indies. It listed and deliberately dismissed the four methods that had then been offered for getting rid of slavery in the United States: reduction of the slaves to serfdom, fixed to the soil but not salable; gradual abolition; a boycott on slave-state products; colonization. And it proceeded to the conclusions that immediate abolition would be "a safe, just, and peaceful remedy" and that the South would be better off with free labor. Temperatures were rising, but matters had not yet come to a fever heat; if they had, the Richmond *Jeffersonian and Times* could not have quoted a passage from Whittier, nor have declared that "the morbid

---

[1] Vol. III, p. 760.

spirit of false and fanatical philanthropy" which it revealed was at work not only in the Northern states "but to some extent in the South." On the other hand, the stigma of fanaticism was promptly applied to the young reformer in his own state. A biographer long after said that he shrieked "like a temperance lecturer or a cheap politician."[1] Whittier's extended reply to his Richmond critics in the *Haverhill Gazette*[2] could satisfy only those who were predisposed in favor of discussion.

The author of "Justice and Expediency" was young, ambitious, and promising, but unknown. He could hurt his prospects, but he had little prestige to lose. The author of the first full volume in antislavery annals was in a very different position. In this year Lydia Maria Child entered the fray. She was a sister of Convers Francis, one of the Transcendentalists, who were notoriously sympathetic with "fanatical philanthropy." Her husband was no better in the eyes of the conservatives. In 1841 man and wife became joint editors of the *National Anti-Slavery Standard.* The title page of her book of 1833 is enough to reveal its inflammatory tone: "An Appeal in Favor of That Class of Americans Called Africans, by Mrs. Child, Author of The Mother's Book, The Girl's Own Book, The Frugal Housewife, etc.

> We have offended, Oh! My countrymen!
> We have offended very grievously,
> And been most tyrannous. From east to west
> A groan of accusation pierces Heaven!
> The wretched plead against us; multitudes
> Countless and vehement, and sons of God,
> Our Brethren."
>
> COLERIDGE

And it was dedicated to the Reverend S. J. May, another minor Transcendentalist, "as a mark of gratitude for his earnest and disinterested efforts in an unpopular but most righteous cause." It was offensive in every way: an acknowl-

[1] W. S. Kennedy, "J. G. Whittier," pp. 101 ff.
[2] Whittier, "Prose Works," Vol. III, pp. 58–86.

edged spokeswoman for the home circle deserting her proper sphere and quoting in the name of righteousness as bad a passage as Coleridge ever wrote. *The North American* deplored her abandoning her accepted role "and urging on a cause so dangerous to the Union, domestic peace, and civil liberty, as the immediate emancipation of the slaves at the South." Polite Bostonia was prompt in further punishment of her indiscretion. Her children's magazine, the *Juvenile Miscellany*, lost subscriptions till it died a lingering death. The Boston Athenaeum withdrew her free membership. She was thrust outside the pale of respectable society.

Yet in the next year (1834), while the conservatives of New England were harshly handling the assailants of slavery, the genial Virginian W. A. Caruthers could include in his novel "A Kentuckian in New York" a whole series of observations which might have been called fanatically philanthropical by the supersensitive in either North or South.[1] He conceded many virtues to the Northerners, recommended intersectional travel as an antidote to prejudice, acknowledged the superior prosperity of the North. He contended that slavery in the Carolinas was less benevolent than in Virginia, and admitted that "poor, exhausted, eastern Virginia" was in her economic dotage, "her impassable roads protect[ing] her alike from the pity and contempt of foreign travellers." With all his candor, however, he did not forget that he belonged to the South and that a harshly critical eye was fixed upon her:

> You know I am no *abolitionist*, in the incendiary meaning of the term; yet I cannot deny from you and myself that [the slaves] are an incubus upon our prosperity. This we would boldly deny, if a Yankee uttered it in our hearing; but to ourselves, we must e'en confess it. If I am, therefore, an abolitionist, it is not for conscience-sake, but from policy and patriotism.[2]

---

[1] Just how inoffensive to the Northern reader this novel was is indicated by the brief but cordial review in the *Knickerbocker Magazine* of August, 1834, Vol. IV, pp. 155, 156. For the following summary of Caruthers's attitude see "A Kentuckian in New York," Vol. I, pp. 72, 77, 115, 165, 181; Vol. II, p. 194.

[2] For a closely comparable passage of the same period see a speech by Meriwether in J. P. Kennedy's "Swallow Barn" of 1832 (1851 edition), pp. 455–460.

A nice example of what even mild sectional feeling can effect; for the American who inclined fondly to embrace any moral principle in support of his own views or actions here repudiated a principle, because the hussy had already been embraced by another man, and turned honestly but brazenly to self-interest. It is not the fact that is surprising, but the allegation.

It is not surprising, for events were moving steadily toward a first clear definition of issues. Slave importation had now been abolished in the country for twenty-five years. The Missouri Compromise of 1820 had drawn a bold line between North and South a decade before Webster and Hayne had had their set-to in 1830. In 1831 the Anti-Slavery Society had been established and *The Liberator* had been founded. In 1832 South Carolina had declared for nullification. In 1833 had come the abolition of slavery on British soil; but in 1835 free-Negro suffrage had been withdrawn in South Carolina. Finally, in 1836, Andrew Jackson's policies had been handed over to his chosen successor, Martin Van Buren; in the same year Texas had asserted independence, and the prospect of annexation had inevitably raised the companion question of the further extension of slave territory. Quite naturally, then, in this year the verbal controversy was redoubled.

By 1836 the burden of the Northern attack in the periodical field was being carried by the explicitly antislavery magazines and almanacs, of which eventually there were more than a dozen. These do not come within the province of this chapter. The standard publications were conservative and handsoffish, no doubt partly from conviction and partly with an eye to circulation. Yet the subject of slavery was so urgent that though it could be avoided, it could not be ignored. The way out was to print conciliatory and optimistic articles in the hope that they would please some and offend none. Thus *The Casket, or Flowers of Literature, Wit and Sentiment,* a mixed metaphor published in Philadelphia, reprinted in 1835 two articles from the *Saturday Evening Post* on the character and customs of the African Negro on his native soil. *The American Quarterly Review*, also Philadelphian, was continuing its policy of deploring sectional feeling, condemning talk of nullification, commending colonization, maintaining the tone that was said to turn away wrath. *The North American* was almost equally cautious, but, issued from Boston, could not resist printing the innuendoes of a lecture on "Slavery in Rome," which concluded, "Slavery had destroyed the democracy, had destroyed the aristocracy, had destroyed the empire; and now at last it left the traces of its ruinous power deeply furrowed on the face of nature itself" (October, 1834). And the *Southern Literary Messenger*[1] could publish at this period an enthusiastic tribute to the Liberian experiment in colonization and endorse Webster as an anti-nullificationist, but, issued from Richmond, could be goaded by Harriet Martineau's comments on slavery into declaring:

> "We have our slaves and mean to keep them" was never uttered by any southern gentleman by way of argument on the subject of slavery, but simply in answer to a party seeking to exercise a power ... upon a subject upon which the jurisdiction of the government is expressly denied by the southron.

This utterance in the *Messenger* touched on a theme that was expanded into a whole book by Beverley Tucker when he published in this year (1836) "The Partisan Leader." It was a direful prophecy of what was destined to happen under President Van Buren, just elected, in the continuance of encroachments by Federal authorities on Southern State rights. The South was putting its back to the wall; and it was bound to do so, for the literary assault was steadily gaining intensity. Witness Richard Hildreth's "The Slave, or Memoirs of Archy Moore," another publication of 1836, in which all the worst

---

[1] *The Casket*, August, September, 1835. *American Quarterly Review*, June, December, 1832; March, June, December, 1833. *North American Review*, January, July, 1833; October, 1834 ("Slavery in Rome," a lecture possibly by Theodore Parker, who was planning a book, never completed, on this theme); July, 1835; July, 1836; then silent on slavery for ten years. *Southern Literary Messenger*, February, 1836; November, December, 1837.

abuses of slavery were heaped on the innocent head of the quadroon of the title role. According to the advertisement of the second edition no bookseller could be found in New York who dared to publish it. In Boston it was printed and marketed without name of either publisher or dealer. The first edition was disposed of within a few months, and a second was regularly issued four years later. There was a ready market for such a work now. It was good propaganda; for the episodes were picturesque and lively, and a reader who was in the least inclined to sympathize could soon be lost in the trials of the pseudo autobiographer; and it opened and closed with an old-line forensic exordium and peroration. The first sentence gives a fair idea of the fine fury in which the book was composed: "Ye who would know what evils man can inflict upon his fellow without reluctance, hesitation or regret; ye who would learn the limit of human endurance, and with what bitter anguish and indignant hate, the heart may swell and yet not burst — peruse these Memoirs!"[1]

A piece of fiction shortly after, from R. M. Bird, may have afforded a little relief to the harassed Southerners. This was his much neglected social satire "Sheppard Lee." It was a gay and shallow piece of work in which the novelist by an ingenious device of transmigration, or transcarnation, of spirit presented passing views of the lives of seven typical men of the time, including a futile philanthropist who was kidnaped and carried South as an abolitionist, and a slave who was first happy but later an insurgent. These episodes, which occupy part of the second volume,[2] were written sympathetically to the South. The philanthropist was a good deal of a nincompoop; the slave turned against his indulgent master in an absurdly motivated uprising caused by an anti-slavery pamphlet which revealed to the blacks how badly off they were and promptly drove them to ruthless arson and murder. Bird's play "The Gladiator," of 1831, was a fervent plea for the bondsman; but the slave episodes in "Sheppard

[1] For a literary model note the opening address in Johnson's "Rasselas."

[2] R. M. Bird, "Sheppard Lee" (1838), Vol. II, pp. 135–211.

Lee" must have gone far to offset the effects of the drama. However, 1836 supplied one more bellows blast to the smoldering fire with the first volume of its kind, "Songs of the Free."

Few phases of the controversy are more interesting in a social or sociological way than the resort to group singing as a mode of stirring antislavery enthusiasm. It began early and continued straight on to war time; and it was an inevitable social expression that became audible for the same reason that patriotism and the spirit of worship express themselves in song. Every "cause" has its lyric accompaniment. So the technique of the Fourth of July celebration or of the religious revival was simply transferred to the antislavery gathering (some of whose attendants were teaching their children A B C's from abolition primers), as it was soon to be transferred also to the temperance meeting, and later to the equal-suffrage rally. Moreover, as such developments will, antislavery song started on a relatively high level, and degenerated as it became more popular, moving from the plane of the Sunday-morning church service to the plane of the camp meeting.

The difference is clear enough if we contrast "Songs of the Free" of 1836 with "The Anti-Slavery Harp" of 1854 and "Songs of Freedom" of 1855.[1] The first of these was edited by M. W. Chapman, with the subtitle "and Hymns of Christian Freedom." "Those who are laboring for the freedom of the American slave," says the foreword, "have felt their need of . . . the encouragement, consolation and strength afforded by poetry and music; . . . and they cannot allow the opponents of their principles the selection of the moral and intellectual powers with which it shall be carried on, — no, though this free use of their own souls should occasion men to call them agitators and fanatics." The editor was skillful in the kinds of material he included. For the churchly-minded there were well-known hymns from Reginald Heber, John Wesley,

[1] See pages 401, 402.

Felicia Hemans, Francis Keble, Harriet Martineau, and plentiful psalmody from Watts; for the more literary, poems of Bryant, Bulwer, Tom Moore, and the then popular Mrs. Barbauld and Lydia Sigourney; for the militant, songs by Garrison and Whittier and a paraphrase of "Scots wha hae wi' Wallace bled"; for the secular, paraphrases of John Howard Payne's "Home, Sweet Home." Favorite hymns, like "Greenland's Icy Mountains," "My Faith Looks Up to Thee," and "America," were used as models, bringing to the "cause" all the sentimental associations gathered into their melodies. The martial words and music of "Doddridge,"

> Awake, my soul! stretch every nerve,
> And press with vigor on:
> A heavenly race demands thy zeal,
> And an immortal crown,

were included under the heading "Emancipation," and "Blest be the tie that binds" under "Association." One can imagine the fervor at an antislavery rally when in "Montgomery," with its stirring tune, the singers came to

> He comes to break oppression,
> To set the captive free;
> To take away transgression,
> And rule in equity.

It was the practice of the abolitionists to hold a regular "Monthly Concert of Prayer for Emancipation," and for these events "Songs of the Free" includes no less than nine special hymns. These can hardly have been excited rallies; they were rather quiet resumptions of the siege which the singers were laying about the throne of their God, and the tone of the hymns for the monthly concert attests to this. But for other occasions they sang faster and louder; and by way of stimulating excitement the editor supplied a running accompaniment of footnotes and footnoted excerpts from relevant poetry, from classic-prose utterances, and from contemporary platform eloquence. "Songs of the Free" is a dignified publication calculated to inspire feeling, but fervor rather than violence of feeling, the sort of anthology that could enlist to the abolition cause quiet people who believed in philanthropy but shrank from fanaticism. They were more nearly in the mood of Jonathan Edwards than of Whitefield, of W. E. Channing than of H. W. Beecher. Twenty years of agitation were to change all this, as the antislavery songs of the middle 50's will show.

It was just before the end of 1836 that W. E. Channing, the elder, took his belated stand on slavery. Till then he had been content to disapprove slavery but to fear the effects of controversy. Finally he was goaded to action by an indignant reformer who admitted that he and his fellows were amateurs. "We Abolitionists are just what we are — babes, sucklings, obscure men, silly women, publicans, sinners. . . . It is unbecoming in abler men, who stood by, and would do nothing, to complain of us because we manage this matter no better."[1] There followed promptly in 1836 his little volume on "Slavery," an open letter on the abolitionists; in 1837 an open letter to Henry Clay on the annexation of Texas; and in the remaining five years before his death, in 1842, five more documents of the same sort.[2] He was at the end of a distinguished career, and he commanded wide respect and attention. He wrote as a gentleman and a scholar trying to avoid personalities and sectional prejudices and to restrict himself to the discussion of an economic system. To the student of today his discussions present with extraordinary fullness and clarity the problem as it appeared in New England. But it is evident, while he continued to be urbane in manner, that even in this short seven years of debate it was harder and harder for him to be dispassionate. If this change can be traced in such a man as Channing, it is natural to find it among the editors and contributors to the magazines.

In 1838 Cooper returned to the subject in "The American

[1] W. H. Channing, "Life of W. E. Channing," p. 529.

[2] Ibid. Part III, Chap. IV; and "Channing's Works" (Centenary Edition), pp. 679–924.

Democrat,"[1] with a set of conventional observations rather casually included in this general survey of American social conditions. In spite of the increasing agitation he was not really apprehensive. As a Tory he respected the rights of property; as a patriot he felt that special issues should be subordinated to national harmony; as a nationalist he held that the European kettle was quite as black as the American pot. He was so hard pressed in his own conflicts that the menace of the Northern press and the Northern proletariat seemed more important than the condition of the Southern body politic. Not so, however, with William Gilmore Simms, Cooper's Southern counterpart. Simms entered the fray in 1838 with a peppery review of Harriet Martineau's "Society in America" — a review published as a thin octavo "Slavery in America" and included fourteen years later in "The Pro-Slavery Argument, as Maintained by the Most Distinguished Writers of the Southern States." Simms is the only one of the four contributors to whom any distinction is still conceded, and none of it is due to this effusion. Yet it is a fine specimen for any museum of controversial pieces. Fully one third of the ostensible review was devoted to personal animadversions at the visiting Englishwoman, which forfeited any claim for Simms as a courtly Southerner. He twitted her on her deafness, he impugned her honesty, he crudely vilified her. Cooper defended the South against foreign critics; but Simms lumped Northern observers with foreigners as foes of the "Southron" (as literary Southerners of the period designated themselves in fervent moments). For a while he came down to specific discussion of some of Miss Martineau's allegations, not doing very well in his replies, often resorting to the formula it isn't true; supposing it were; but even if it is. . . . He reached his highest level of candor in his regretful admission that miscegenation was an inevitable fruit of slavery. But though resentful, his reply clearly belonged to an early stage in the debate, in his assumption that some day

[1] Three brief sections on slavery, pp. 173–178.

slavery would be abrogated. It was still regarded as an unfortunate necessity; not yet a divinely ordained institution.

With the late 30's a definite milestone was passed; and now for several years developments moved along on an established level. Still, and for many years to come, the offensive was taken by the North. In 1839 Mrs. Child returned to the assault with her "Evils of Slavery and Cure of Slavery," an iterative work which served only to remobilize her friends around her and her opponents against her. 1840 was productive of nothing new, but was marked by the issue of at least four antislavery anthologies, one of them edited by Whittier. The next year witnessed the issue of Longfellow's perfunctory little volume "Poems on Slavery," the sole significance of which was that the poet conscientiously recorded his stand on the issue, though he did it in as dull, conventional, and ineffective a book as he ever composed. But in the year of its issue there occurred an event which was to re-echo long and wide. This was the first famous episode of the arrest in Boston of a fugitive slave, George Latimer, seized without warrant on the demand of the Virginian who claimed to be his owner. Massachusetts was aflame. Sixty-five thousand signers from the Bay State petitioned Congress for legislation which would prevent the repetition of such an affront. In the height of the agitation county conventions were held throughout the state, and in Essex, Whittier's "Massachusetts to Virginia" was read to a wildly enthusiastic crowd. The closing stanzas included everything that the abolitionists could desire and that the slaveowner could resent: the established diction of the apostle of freedom — *manacles* and *gyves* and *fetters* and *pirates* and *bondsmen*; the assumption of virtue in the North and wickedness in the South; and the implication that God was with the righteous and that the righteous all lived on the Arctic side of Mason and Dixon's line. Almost simultaneously with Whittier's verses the same theme was treated with many of the same terms in a rude jingle set to the tune of "The Troubadour." And shortly after there appeared in Boston "The Virginia Philosopher, or Few Lucky

Slave-Catchers, by Mr. Latimer's Brother." As the years drew on, antislavery sentiment was roused more and more by definite events and the things said and sung about them. It was no longer necessary to appeal to broad principles. Logicians might reason about abstractions, but the great mass of men were given the images which they always want to be setting up or knocking down. The political South retorted to accusations by supplying new grounds for accusation; and still the literary South was relatively silent — for reasons which one of their writers was finally to present.[1]

With the approach of the middle 40's James Russell Lowell entered the lists, quite the most popular new entrant and the only one on either side to rival Whittier in wideness of appeal. For three months in 1843 he was editor of a moderate antislavery journal in Philadelphia. He was for a while contributing editor to another. But in the antislavery campaign it was Lowell's distinctive performance to act as a kind of brilliant cavalry reserve to the main army. The closing stanza of "The Present Crisis" of 1845 was in all likelihood the most quoted passage in the orations of the next decades. The new duties which the new occasion of Texan annexation had challenged were paralleled almost from year to year as the war drew nearer. And it was this same gift for writing sage couplets or quatrains which were applicable to one situation after another that marked the renewing successes of his series of "Biglow Papers," the first of which began appearing in 1846.[2] Hosea Biglow was a Yankee Doodle in appearance and speech, but he was as canny as Jack Downing and all the homely political critics who were to succeed that Yankee oracle.[3] As to slavery, he had by this time been persuaded of its viciousness so clearly that he did not argue about it, but went on directly to discussing how to overcome it and its

---

[1] See pages 404, 405.

[2] "The Biglow Papers," first series, appeared originally in the *Boston Courier*, June 17, 1846; August 18, November 2, December 28, 1847; and May 3, 1848; and in the *Anti-Slavery Standard*, May 4, June 1, July 6, September 28, 1848.

[3] See page 609.

advocates. This marked a distinct step in the argument. Lowell assumed, as all the later combatants were to do, that the sections were aligned against each. He was both anti-slavery and anti-Southern:

> May be it's all right ez preachin',
>   By *my* narves it kind o' grates,
> Wen I see the overreachin'
>   O' them nigger-drivin' states.

Yet he acknowledged that, even as late as 1846, candor could not allow him to ascribe all altruism to the North:

> Massachusetts, God forgive her,
>   She's akneelin' with the rest;

and he adjured the Bay State to sound a clarion call for tyrant haters and, if need be, to welcome disunion rather than subscribe to slavery.

Lowell's much quoted introduction to the second series of "Biglow Papers," in which he looked back to the origin of the first, is so notable as a statement of propagandist tactics that it is worth including here again:

> Thinking the Mexican War, as I think it still, a national crime committed in behoof of Slavery, our common sin, and wishing to put the feeling of those who thought as I did in a way that would tell, I imagined to myself such an upcountry man as I had often seen at antislavery gatherings, capable of district-school English, but always instinctively falling back into the natural stronghold of his homely dialect when heated to the point of self-forgetfulness. . . . I needed on occasion to rise above the level of mere *patois*, and for this purpose conceived the Rev. Mr. Wilbur, who should express the more cautious element of the New England character and its pedantry, as Mr. Biglow should serve for its homely common-sense vivified and heated by conscience. . . . Finding soon after that I needed some one as a mouthpiece of the mere drollery . . . I invented Mr. Sawin as the clown of my little puppet show. . . .
>
> The success of my experiment soon began not only to astonish me, but to make me feel the responsibility of knowing that I held in my hand a weapon instead of the mere fencing-stick I had sup-

posed. Very far from being a popular author under my own name, so far, indeed, as to be almost unread, I found the verses of my pseudonym copied everywhere; I saw them pinned up in workshops; I heard them quoted and their authorship debated; I once even, when rumor had caught up my name in one of its eddies, had the satisfaction of overhearing it demonstrated, in the pauses of a concert, that *I* was utterly incompetent to have written anything of the kind. . . . If I put on the cap and bells and made myself one of the court-fools of King Demos, it was less to make his majesty laugh than to win a passage to his royal ears for certain serious things which I had deeply at heart. . . . I endeavored, by generalizing my satire, to give it what value I could beyond the passing moment and the immediate application.[1]

The fame of the "Biglow Papers" and the oblivion into which Lowell's antislavery prose contributions have fallen are proofs of the effectiveness of his tactics. None but the student knows even now that for the seven years from 1843 to 1850 Lowell published more than fifty articles in the *Pennsylvania Freeman* and the *National Anti-Slavery Standard*; and everyone who knows anything about American history or literature is acquainted with Hosea Biglow and his collaborators. Yet Lowell was no more than a reserve fighter and a short-enlistment man. By 1850 he had withdrawn; reform could not take up the whole of him, he explained; and his place was left open for newer recruits.

There were plenty. Longfellow continued to confide antislavery sentiments to his diary, but Whittier was indefatigable in print. Melville, in his Mardian Odyssey of 1849, finally came to the "extreme south of Vivenza"[2] (his name for the United States) and admitted himself baffled. Humanity was crying out against slavery; the North could not be blamed for assailing it, nor the South for inheriting it. "It can not be, that misery is perpetually entailed; though, in a land proscribing primogeniture, the firstborn and last of

[1] Lowell, "Works" (Standard Library Edition), Vol. VIII, pp. 155–157.

[2] In Melville's "Mardi" there are cursory passages on slavery in Chapters LXIII, CXLVIII, CLVIII, CLIX, but the longest and most important passage is in Chapter CLXII, "They Visit the Extreme South of Vivenza."

Hamo's tribe must still succeed to all their sire's wrongs. Yes; Time — all-healing Time — Time, great philanthropist! — Time must befriend these thralls!"[1] But Theodore Parker had no such misgivings.[2] It is surprising that he should have been so late in taking up his pen; he had been active in deed for some years. However, abolition had not been his primary interest. In 1847 he became occasionally vocal, and from 1848 he was continually writing and speaking and with increasing vehemence. He said nothing new; but he brought his increasing prestige to the struggle, returning to the attack with each new provocation until he died from overwork in 1860.

One of these provocations was, of course, Webster's famous "Seventh of March" speech in 1850. History seems to have revised contemporary judgment on this utterance.[3] In its day it was generally regarded in the North as an unworthy piece of compromising, with the motive of paving Webster's way toward the Presidency at the election of 1852. Passions were so easily inflamed by this time that Whittier, of all men, led the abuse with his "Ichabod":

> All else is gone; from those great eyes
> The soul has fled:
> When faith is lost, when honor dies,
> The man is dead!

Emerson was no more generous: Liberty, he exclaimed, in Webster's mouth sounded like "love in the mouth of a courtesan," and Union, as he pronounced it, became "a ghastly nothing."[4] Holmes, writing more in sorrow than in anger, exclaimed,

> Illustrious Dupe! Have those majestic eyes
> Lost their proud fire for such a vulgar prize?[5]

---

[1] Melville, "Mardi," Vol. II, p. 252.

[2] For Theodore Parker's antislavery writings see the Centenary Edition, Vol. XI, "The Slave Power"; Vol. XII, "The Rights of Man"; Vol. XIV, "Saint-Bernard and Other Papers," Nos. 11–14.

[3] Claude M. Fuess, "Life of Webster" (1930), Vol. II.

[4] Emerson, "Journals," Vol. VIII, pp. 182, 186.

[5] Holmes, "The Statesman's Secret."

These were but straws on the gale of protest. At the Baltimore convention two years later Webster did not receive a single vote; his former disciples joined his enemies and, to Emerson's satisfaction, "drove Mr. Webster out of the world."

Between the delivery of this historic speech and its prompt political consequences there was enacted the Fugitive Slave Law, and there was published the most exciting document in the whole course of the struggle, "Uncle Tom's Cabin." Like part of the first series of "The Biglow Papers," it was released through an antislavery periodical, *The National Era* in this case, but it owed most of its success to its literary qualities and its publication as a book. It ran for eleven months, ending with April, 1852, and was issued in book form by a somewhat skeptical publisher as the last serial installment was coming off the press. The tale of its extraordinary circulation is a familiar one: a second edition within ten days, at least ten in America within the year; one hundred and fifty thousand copies sold in the first year in America, five hundred thousand within five years; and a larger circulation in Great Britain than at home. Such a distribution was inevitably accompanied by a chorus of praise and blame and a lengthening succession of criticisms and counter-criticisms. Simms jumped to the fore in the South with a review, in which he returned to the tactics he had used against Miss Martineau. He wrote with a vengeance. Mrs. Stowe had "shockingly traduced the slaveholding society of the United States," and he was simply acting on the defensive as he exposed "the miserable misrepresentations of her story." She was avaricious as well as mendacious and had forfeited the respect due to a lady. Wide as the chasm was growing between the sections, it was still quite clear that opinion was divided in both North and South. A Mr. Adams who significantly moved away from Charleston took up the cudgel for Mrs. Stowe in a review of her reviewers, with liberal reference to Simms.[1] Rumor, he wrote, had it that the book was "awful." "That

[1] "Uncle Tom at Home, a Review of the Reviewers and Repudiators of Uncle Tom's Cabin," by F. A. Adams, late of Charleston, 1853.

the whole 'nigger kingdom' of the South had been killed, smothered, torn to pieces by bloodhounds, ground up for bone manure; children dragged from mothers' breasts, and whole plantations turned into slaughter-houses, we fully expected; and yet *nobody had read it.*" Reading the story, the reviewer was forced to admit its essential truth. Shortly after Mrs. Stowe had followed up the novel with the apparently unanswerable documentations of "A Key to Uncle Tom's Cabin," "A Lady in New York" replied with "The Patent Key to Uncle Tom's Cabin." Mrs. Stowe's readers were "raving maniacs"; the book was a "firebrand"; the authoress was afflicted with a "craving pocket." She was also, of course (in the minds of many), an inspired prophetess; and, by and large, Northern objectors and Southern endorsers were rule-proving exceptions.

The whole output inspired by "Uncle Tom" is a fit subject for a monograph. Dramatizations began to appear within a few months[1] — two of them, by G. L. Aiken and H. J. Conway, running to hundreds of performances in a period when long runs were exceptional even for successful plays. At least eight versions were produced on the American stage, six of these before the beginning of the Civil War. It was produced, of course, in England, and had its successes in translation into German, French, Dutch, Flemish, Danish and Swedish, Spanish, Portuguese, Italian, Bulgarian, Polish, and Russian. A sentence in the preface to a catalogue of horrors — "The Down-Trodden, or Black Blood and White" — which was published in 1853 mentions "Aunt Phillis's Cabin," "Uncle Tom as He Is," "Uncle Tom in England," and "a thousand other evaporations." Whittier wrote to Garrison, "Thanks for the Fugitive Slave Law! Better would it be for slavery if that law had never been enacted: for it gave occasion for 'Uncle Tom's Cabin.'" And Garrison wrote in turn to Mrs. Stowe: "I estimate the value of anti-slavery writing by the abuse it brings. Now all the defenders of slavery have let

---

[1] Allston Brown, "History of the New York Stage," Vol. I, pp. 312–319.

me alone and are abusing you." The estranging effects of "Uncle Tom" can hardly be overstated. The crevasse was widened to a chasm.

Across this chasm certain plaintive sounds could be heard among all the noises of strife. These were the Negro songs by Stephen Foster,[1] of which the most famous, "My Old Kentucky Home," appeared in the same year with Mrs. Stowe's novel. Between 1848 and 1850 Foster, a man in the early twenties, had written thirteen songs on the lives and feelings of the Negro. Up to this time he had enjoyed no close contact with the slave. "Away Down Souf," "Oh! Susannah," "Old Uncle Ned," were idyllic songs of the happy black. However, in 1850 he went on his honeymoon trip through the Southern states and along the river; and from then on the darky was no longer a comic or an amusing character in his lyrics, for Foster had seen the pathos and the tragedy of bondage. Probably "My Old Kentucky Home" was composed without any thought of pointing a moral. It was a lyric that the Southerners could accept for its sympathetic understanding and that the Northerners could seize on for its somber implications. The opening stanza, in which the sun is shining bright, is in the tone of the earlier plantation lyrics. But the third stanza contained the sequence awaiting the slave who was to be sold down the river and to end his life in the cane fields:

> The head must bow and the back will have to bend,
> Wherever the darky may go;
> A few more days and the trouble all will end
> In the fields where the sugar canes grow.
> A few more days to tote the weary load —
> No matter! 'twill never be light —
> A few more days till we totter on the road
> Then my old Kentucky home, good night.

The song, no doubt, lacked the brisk militancy and the obvious moralism that the abolitionists wanted for their

[1] J. T. Howard, "Stephen Foster," 1933.

rallies, and it seems not to have been included in their collections of the next few years. Furthermore, it is often the fate of words for popular melodies to be sung without any sense of their meaning. But it can hardly have been true in the decade before the Civil War that the slave sympathizers missed the purport of this song of exile, or of "Way Down upon de Swanee River," or of "Old Black Joe."

In the meanwhile those who hankered for the camp-meeting style of song had an ample supply at hand — a very different supply from that of twenty years before. It was becoming standardized. In "The Anti-Slavery Harp" (Boston, 1854) and "Songs of Freedom" (Portland, Maine, 1855), twelve-and-one-half-cent pamphlets, there were twenty-nine songs in common. There was in these collections little of the dignified hymnology that prevailed in "Songs of the Free" of 1836, and not a single survivor from them. There are examples of the same sentimentalism, and a resort to a few of the old melodies; but for the most part the songs were for romping, roaring enthusiasts confident of success for their long crusade. All of them were set to familiar indicated tunes. "America" and "My Faith Looks Up to Thee" furnished the pattern more than once; so did the "Marseillaise" and "Sweet Afton" and "Scots wha hae wi' Wallace bled" and "Oft in the Chilly Night." Sometimes the doggerel made the songs ridiculous, as when "Auld Lang Syne" was the melody for

> I am an Abolitionist!
>   I glory in the name;
> Though now by Slavery's minions hissed
>   And covered o'er with shame.

Quite as often the jaunty tunes were perfect misfits, as when

> Lo! the Northern Star is beaming
>   With a new and glorious light,
> And its cheering radiance streaming
>   Through the clouds of misty night!

was set to "Oh! Susannah." Yet it is easy to imagine the zest with which a righteous band of philanthropists could shout the refrain

> O! Star of Freedom
> 'Tis the star for me,
> 'Twill lead me off to Canada,
> There I will be free.

There was an evident sense of exultation in these songs of the 50's, many of them having to do with the fugitive helped on his way along the Underground Railroad; many more, with blatant prophecy of the "Good Time Coming." That is doubtless one reason why the mood of "Rosin the Bow" and "Dan Tucker" and "Dandy Jim" and "Dearest Maie" and "Crambambule" seemed the natural one for the lyrists. It was the mood of the later crowds who found complete satisfaction in the songs by Ira D. Sankey — moral democracy rampant.

The decade of the 50's produced little new in the exchange of opinions or of recriminations. Each side felt abused at the aggressions of the other. Each cloaked itself in self-righteousness and felt that no evil was too foul to ascribe to the other. Argument gave way to threat, and threat to violence. It was the norm for public controversy at the stage which this had reached; and it was easier than usual to explain, because the aggressions of the South were still political and the affronts from the North were largely literary. Each was defenseless before the other; each, irresistible in its own field. Events climaxed in 1856, the year when the free-soil struggle came to a head; when Sumner was assaulted in the Senate chamber for his speech on "The Crime against Kansas"; when John Brown directed the executions at Pottawatomie; when the Dred Scott case went to the Supreme Court. At every point the South seemed to be gaining ground politically; with every gain the North became more vociferous; and in every instance the questions at issue shifted from the plantations of the South to the territories of the West and from the immediate problem of emancipation to the problem of national control and national survival.

Whittier had long ago lost his sense of perspective and was far on the way to the vilifications of "Barbara Frietchie." Now Emerson was to follow suit. Twice in 1856 he mounted the platform in spite of his reluctance to dissipate himself in political activity, and twice he went to extremes.[1] He belabored the assailants of Sumner as madcaps, vagabonds, bullies. "The whole state of South Carolina does not now offer one or any number of persons who are to be weighed for a moment in the scale with such a person as the meanest of them all has now struck down." As to the struggle for free soil in the West, "There is this peculiarity about the case of Kansas, that all the right is on one side." Yet, "in the free States, we give a snivelling support to slavery." He was glad that people were becoming less afraid of disunion and anarchy. In its heroic days Massachusetts was in fact an anarchy. He ended in a hysteria of protest:

> Send home every one who is abroad, lest they should find no country to return to. . . . When it is lost, it will be time enough then for any who are luckless enough to remain alive to gather up their clothes and depart to some land where freedom exists.

At this juncture Walt Whitman came to the verge of public abusiveness, with an ominous document, "The Eighteenth Presidency," but for one reason or another did not publish it.[2] He was disgusted with the political futility of the last two Presidents, and as the new election approached set about to wake the American workingman to the gravity of the situation. He was outraged by the occupants of the White House: "Never were publicly displayed more deformed, mediocre, snivelling, unreliable, falsehearted men." He had nothing but contempt for the Northern politician, and he was des-

---

[1] The two speeches by Emerson in 1856 were "The Assault on Mr. Sumner" (May 26) and "Speech at the Kansas Relief Meeting" (September 10). See "Works," Vol. XI, "Miscellanies," pp. 245, 253.

[2] C. J. Furness, "Walt Whitman's Workshop," pp. 87–113.

perate over the effrontery of Southern leaders and their tactics:

> . . . no end of blusterers, braggarts, windy, melodramatic, continually screaming in falsetto, a nuisance to These States, their own just as much as any; altogether the most impudent persons that have yet appeared in the history of lands, once with the most incredible successes, having pistol'd, bludgeoned, yelled and threatened America, the past twenty years into one long train of cowardly concessions, and still not through, but rather at the commencement.

There were six million workingmen in the country, but the country was being ruled in the interest of "three hundred and fifty thousand masters of slaves." "The people of the territories are denied the power to form State governments unless they consent to fasten upon them the slave-hopple, the iron wristlet and the neck-spike." The tirade ran on for pages; but it was never put into circulation. It is reasonably certain that Whitman could not have found editors or underwriters to distribute it. It seems unlikely that he lacked courage. It is probable that having vented his wrath on paper he was relieved, and on second thought acted on the conclusion he recorded next year,[1] to keep out of the political arena and to confine himself to fighting for principles.

If developments had not gone so far the South would, no doubt, by now have enlisted its penmen in a counter-attack. In October and November of 1856 the *Southern Literary Messenger* acknowledged a situation which many had vaguely felt but none defined so clearly. Southern writers as a class had failed to meet their sectional obligations. Slavery was a blessed institution; but a bombardment of slander, fanaticism, and malignity was being launched against it from an unholy citadel of falsehood.[2] The workshops of the North were resounding with the labors of those who were forging

[1] "Notes and Fragments Left by Walt Whitman" (edited by R. M. Bucke), p. 57.

[2] See the *Southern Literary Messenger*, October, 1856, "The Duty of Southern Authors," Vol. XXIII, pp. 241 ff.; and November, 1856, "An Inquiry into the Present State of Southern Literature," Vol. XXIII, pp. 387 ff. See, also, for similar articles of somewhat earlier date, *De Bow's Review*, 1852, "Southern School Books," Vol. XIII, pp. 258 ff.; and 1855, "Home Education at the South," Vol. XVIII, pp. 655 ff.

calumnies and hammering mendacities into semblances of truth. Poetry, drama, fiction, and essay should be marshaled in a counter-offensive; and, above all, "a great and comprehensive history of African slavery at the South" should be compiled in the interests of truth — a truth which apparently should keep the slaves in slavery. Thus much on the duties of Southern authors. The second article, "The Present State of Southern Literature," accounted for the lamentable remissness of the region. All her culture was purveyed to her from the hostile North. Textbooks were written there for the South. Her promising youths were sent to Northern colleges. Northern periodicals flooded the slave states. And the South for generations had poured her best energies into politics with the result that she was depending on a literature "devoted in a great measure to a crusade against an institution, the destruction of which, as she verily believes, would impoverish her purse, cripple her powers and corrupt her morals." The obvious fact, thus tardily acknowledged, was easier to acknowledge than to remedy. There were, of a truth, relatively few Southern authors to array against the North. The most vigorous of these, Simms, was not in high repute in his own district; the most gifted group, the poets, were apparently oblivious to what was going on; and one of the most popular, Kennedy, was a stanch Unionist. The sudden mustering of a battalion of effective writers was as impossible to realize as W. J. Bryan's later bland assurance of "a million men in arms by sunset" on a twelve-hour notice to a country of pacifists. As events proved, it was too late for the South even to begin such a mobilization. The eve of the Irresistible Conflict was at hand.

Though the titles pile up after the middle of the decade, there is little of significance to record. Mediocre novels, largely inspired by "Uncle Tom," accumulated from the hands of partisans on either side. Mrs. Stowe returned to the campaign in 1857 with "Dred, a Tale of the Great Dismal Swamp," a novel in which she dwelt on the evils of slavery to the slaveholder, introducing the increasingly insistent theme of mixed blood. New anthologies of antislavery verse

— Lays of Liberty, and Harps of Freedom, and Garlands of Freedom, and Poems for Reformers — were dismal effusions of wasted ink. The only memorable outcries of the literary, as the babel grew among the politicians and the militarists, came once more from Concord. Concord had been a station on the Underground Railroad, and had become a main supply-post for the belligerents in Kansas, largely through the efforts of young Frank Sanborn and young Thomas Wentworth Higginson. Finally, in 1859, John Brown, Connecticut Calvinist, rose before a startled country as a reincarnation of the colonial anarchists, for whom Emerson could not say too much. Then when the attack on Harpers Ferry was followed by Brown's speedy arrest and execution, Emerson and Thoreau[1] were only the most eloquent of the eulogists who waxed fervent in his praise. There was an outburst of verse from the younger and lesser lights — men and women like E. C. Stedman and C. S. Hall, Edna Dean Proctor and Louise Imogen Guiney; and Whittier, of course, cried out again.

From that time on, it was all over but the shooting. The last desperate steps were reluctantly taken, but there was no withdrawal from them. The extremists had brought the conflict on, but it could not be fought until the level heads had been won over. It was Northern agitator against Southern planter. Said Lincoln to Mrs. Stowe, when novelist was presented to war President, "So you are the little woman who brought on this great war." Maybe she did. If she was symbolic of the North, the South could offer no less picturesque a figure: white-haired Edward Ruffin,[2] scientific farmer, slaveholding planter, who sought for and was granted the honor of pulling the lanyard that released the first gunshot against Fort Sumter.

The Civil War Occasional Verse

The verse accompaniment to the Civil War naturally included little that is memorable. It deserves comment here only because it reinforces what the verse of the Revolutionary

[1] See pages 353–354.

[2] Avery O. Craven, "Edward Ruffin," 1932.

War demonstrated: that war lyrics have vitality while the events that evoked them are still exciting; that if they are designed to be sung they are after recognizable models. It does, however, appear from the run of Civil War verses that the models are different. The courtly quality of Revolutionary lyrics is gone; the nineteenth-century products are much more tinctured with sentimentalism and with the kind of godliness that appeals to a tribal god. The classification in the anthologies of Frank Moore's "Lyrics of Loyalty," "Personal and Political" and "Songs of the Soldiers" is available in any generalizings about either Northern or Southern war verse.

The lyrics of loyalty reveal a sober and usually elevated mood in the combatant poets. They progress in the North from the early calls to arms, like Tilton's "Great Bell Roland" and Edna Dean Proctor's "Who's Ready?" to Thomas B. Read's "Closing Scene" and William Winter's "After All"; and in the South, from St. George Tucker's "Southern Cross" to Father Ryan's "Sword of Robert E. Lee." They include, moreover, certain poems of sentiment, like George H. Boker's "Battle Hymn" or "Dirge for a Soldier," Ethel Lynn Beers's "Picket Guard," and the anonymous "Claribel's Prayer," which, though composed for war times, are, except for a few phrases, applicable to any time and any conflict.

The personal and political ballads are, on the other hand, most definitely localized. The "Farewell to Brother Jonathan" is incomplete till one has read Holmes's "Brother Jonathan's Lament for Sister Caroline." John R. Thompson's "On to Richmond" and "Farewell to Pope" refer to events just as definite as those behind Read's "Sheridan's Ride" or Whittier's "Barbara Frietchie." These recall aspects or phases of the war, events of sometimes national and sometimes individual significance, glimpses of great men, acts of heroism by the common soldiery. Their tone is less lofty than in the lyrics of loyalty, and they are bitter or jaunty, mournful or sublime, as befits the various subjects.

The songs for the soldiers are the most spontaneous fruits

of the war and, as a group, are far better known than other more literary products. "John Brown's Body," "Dixie," "Marching through Georgia," and "When Johnny Comes Marching Home" are known to millions now, as they were in war times, because spirited words were combined with inspiring tunes. They became folk poetry and experienced the changes, both through oral transmission and through deliberate composition of variants, to which the most popular songs are often subject. A nobler song, such as Julia Ward Howe's "Battle Hymn of the Republic," with which the populace was less inclined to be familiar, came out at the end of the war unscathed from the ordeal by song.

The authorship of the war verses was very widespread. If wars do not often stimulate great literature, they do, beyond doubt, awaken the sleeping doggerels that more peaceful times leave undisturbed. As parody offers a helping hand to the unoriginal by setting both a meter and a sequence of thought, many of the fireside favorites appeared in this masque of poesy in every degree of artistic, amusing, and grotesque disguise. Among the originals thus used were "America," "Dixie," "Excelsior," "The Night before Christmas," "The Star-Spangled Banner," "The Campbells are Coming," "John Anderson, My Jo," Gray's "Elegy," Hood's "Song of the Shirt," and even the "Hearts of Oak," which had done valiant service in the War of the Revolution. In this secondary zone of martial verse, however, there is almost nothing worth preserving which was not composed by authors who had at least sectional reputations. The freshest note from those who would otherwise be generally forgotten was struck by two Southerners: John R. Thompson, author of "On to Richmond" and "Farewell to Pope," and Albert B. Pike, author of the best of many versions of "Dixie." Thompson's work is excellent jovial satire. He has an easy mastery of verse, control of the double and multiple rhymes which are always effective in lighter moods, a pungent humor, and an abounding and infectious jollity. When at his best in this vein he challenges comparison with Lowell.

On the whole, all this verse, whether written by the most or the least eminent, proves again that the dust and smoke of battle are suffocating to the Muse. The poets who can soar on Pegasus are awkward on Bucephalus; and the lesser ones, who belong with the infantry, are unimpressive spectacles on any sort of steed.

The Formal Literature of the South

When it came to literary self-expression in this period of prolonged political agitation the Southern aristocrat had little to say, wished to say that only to his compeers, and was complete and perfect in his loyalty to English Augustan tradition with little poems, essays, and romantic excursions into realms that never were on land or sea. There was an analogy for this sort of thing in the North in the contents of the annuals; but one can forget these of the North. In the South the Old School felt no interest in the man who used his pen forthrightly during this middle third of the century. Writing did not offer a career for the planters or for their sons; others were outside the pale; and if they wrote with any originality they were put down as eccentrics. Even these eccentrics, moreover, were under the general American spell of imitativeness, only less imitative than the echoers of "Mr. Pope" and "Mr. Addison" and "Mr. Steele." The emergent figures were from among these social ineligibles: Poe and Simms and, after them, Hayne and Lanier and Timrod. A John P. Kennedy in a commercial city might thrive and enjoy political favor and amass a fortune and become a favorite among the elect; but if he did so he played with writing incidentally and deserves credit mainly for doing so well in the circumstances.

If in many respects the South could be fairly differentiated from the North in this period, there is, however, one dominant characteristic which they still shared in common — the Saxon insistence on a moralistic interpretation and justification of life. This most American trait was ever assertive. Poe referred to it as he defied it; Chivers apparently disregarded it, but expressed himself unfailingly (as Poe did) in terms of angels and devils and heavens and hells and rewards and punishments. The rank and file of Southern prose writers were unflagging in their running comments on the moral implications of every tale, every incident, every speech and action. This was not only an American trait; it was a trait of contemporary England; and with it was the complementary one that, while life was being interpreted as a matter of controls and disciplines and abnegations, life went on uncontrolled and undisciplined and left it to the author to supplement the clergyman in his professions of belief in the immediate exercise of divine and poetic justice.

The most distinguished writing that came from the South in this generation was, naturally, the little output that was least aggressively regional, sectional, provincial. The region was not interested in this, nor was any other region. The poets who wrote a little body of lyric and descriptive verse were either suffered to go on in obscurity, as Chivers did; or forced to resort to some other form of composition, as did Pinkney, obscure editor; and the editors Poe and Simms, who also took refuge in narrative and turned their hands to critical or controversial writing. Yet before 1840 it is hard to find in the North any equal number of poems to rival in genuine imaginative reach, emotional fervor, and felicity of form what Pinkney and Poe had written, what Simms, indefatigable versifier, indited at rare intervals, or what the turgid half-hysterical Chivers occasionally rose to in the course of his dizzy and ecstatic flights. Let us look closer at some of these Southern poets, see the leading characteristics of their poetry, and ask whether these characteristics belong to the poets because the poets belong to the region and the period. First for the trio of early lyricists: Pinkney, Poe, and Chivers.

Here is young Edward Coote Pinkney, who published a little volume in 1825, from whom in the next century two or three lyrics were quoted, but who was never again presented to the public until his "Life and Works" appeared after a lapse of a hundred and one years.[1] He was the son of a cosmopolitan Southerner, a diplomatist, and he was born in London, where he mainly lived until his father, minister extraordinary to the Court of St. James's, returned to America on the breaking of diplomatic relations in 1811. The boy's formal schooling was ended on his entering the navy as midshipman at the age of fourteen. It is a pattern picture: family, prestige, not too much education, entrance into the service. He had less than a dozen adult years in the service of his country, in the service of the Muse, in love, but most insistently and melodramatically in the service of his honor — protesting at naval discipline, protesting at reflections on his father, protesting at affronts to himself, brandishing revolvers, issuing defiances, posting cowards, doing everything but fight. In the meanwhile, somehow he found time to read extensively and to use the fruits of his reading in that showy erudition which had been the vogue with some and the subject of satire for others in the late eighteenth century. He was under the evident influence of Byron and Scott and Wordsworth. "The Indian's Bride" is Franco-romantic, and in one copy was preceded by a motto from Tom Moore; his "Prologue, Delivered at the Greek Benefit in Baltimore, 1823," was one of scores of politico-literary documents of the time. It was not so Byronic as "Italy" or as "Rodolph," despite the fact that Pinkney, young American, with altogether un-Byronic compunction, deprecated the fact that when Rodolph sighed "First *for*, next *with*, another's bride," "their loves were vices." He echoed the Lucy poems of Wordsworth, and preceded certain "Lines to Georgiana" with a long passage from "She was a phantom of delight." And his sole popular bits were songs of the serenader and a toast of the courtier. Yet what he gave in this slender volume was a promise, a definite one, of lyric gift, emotional intensity, and the innate sense of human

[1] "The Life and Works of Edward Coote Pinkney," edited by T. O. Mabbott and F. L. Pleadwell.

experience and its significance that a longer life might have fulfilled. The chief response in his day, however, was from the youthful Edgar Allan Poe, who imitated him early and applauded him later.

And what of Poe, the poet, against this Southern background? As poet he is to be almost completely differentiated from his other self, the writer of tales and journalistic criticism; and it is as poet that he appears to be the remote derivative of Southern life rather than the fugitive frequenter of Northern editors' offices. He was born outside the social pale and bred where he could look over and feel his ultimate exclusion the more bitterly. He was offered the privileges of the choicest Southern college, and was chiefly schooled there in gaming and drinking. Thrown off by his patron, he defied the code of the region and enlisted as a common soldier. Taken back by Mr. Allan, he adopted the code in securing admission to West Point. Two years after Pinkney's volume, came Poe's first, and two more at two-year intervals. He had already reached his stature as a poet and with no more recognition than his ill-fated predecessor. By 1833 he turned to prose and magazinedom, just as Pinkney had done; and the only later verse he wrote was either reminiscent of the work in the early neglected volumes or was meretricious stuff written "to run," like "The Raven" and "The Bells," or the utterance of combined poet and journalist, as in "Ulalume." He was, in short, the author of "Alone":

> All I lov'd — *I* lov'd alone.
> *Then* — in my childhood — in the dawn
> Of a most stormy life — was drawn
> From ev'ry depth of good and ill
> The mystery which binds me still;

and the author of "Romance," that "familiar bird" which

> Taught me my alphabet to say —
> To lisp my very earliest word
> While in the wild wood I did lie,
> A child — with a most knowing eye.

There was no wild wood except in his knowing eye; but in this fancied retreat he wrote not only "Tamerlane," after the manner of Byron, but a dozen romantic excursions, with Coleridge leading the way to Xanadu and adjacent realms. Poe's aloneness is comparable to the sense of isolation felt or imagined by any youthful poet, but it was intensified by the harsh facts of his own experience. Romance did lead him for long in wild woods and by shadowy lakes in retreat from that world which later he was not able to escape. Possibly, as recent critics have suggested,[1] his alphabet was taught him not by the painted paroquet but by wayfarers and in Negro cabins, where, as a boy, he may have caught his "flair for the bizarre, the concept that birds and animals were speaking characters, and that fear of graves and corpses and the paraphernalia of the charnel, so peculiarly a characteristic of the Negro, which haunted him through the rest of his life." It is not needful to look for the ghoul haunts at this folk source; the literature of horror was flourishing in Poe's day; yet a natural inclination may well have been intensified there, just as Poe's desire to escape from circumstance may well have been heightened by the habit of a community whose gaze was fixed upon the past. Whatever the case, Poe, the poet, was most essentially himself in fairyland, in dreamland, in the valley of unrest, in a haunted palace, in a city in the sea, in a dream within a dream, and in an occasional love poem in which his love emancipated him from his surroundings. These poems were the output of his early years, for the most part, before the pressure of daily need became irresistible and before his need for recognition in dollars and cents impelled him to write the potboilers which won him applause — potboilers for which he finally evolved a theory that was based partly on the motivation of the poet and partly on the motivation of the salesman.

If there was anything in the theory for Poe, — and it was

[1] Hervey Allen, "Israfel: the Life and Times of Edgar Allan Poe," Vol. I, p. 160; and Louis Untermeyer's "American Poetry from the Beginning to Whitman," p. 425.

ostensibly derived from a retrospect of "The Raven," which he had written "to run," — it naturally follows that he was a poet in the limited sense of one who is highly and consciously skilled in the achievement of poetic effects but, according to his own definition, wholly uninspired toward the presentation of poetic truth. If the creative gift is "to see life steadily and see it whole," Poe was as far from possessing it as mortal could be — as far, let us say, and as near as William Blake was. To say this, of course, is to estimate not Poe's performance but his sense of values. A letter to Lowell of 1844 once more presents the negative background against which his theory and practice are thrown into relief:

> I really perceive that vanity about which most men prate, — the vanity of the human or temporal life. . . . I have no faith in human perfectibility. I think that human exertion will have no appreciable effect on humanity. . . . I have no belief in spirituality. . . . You speak of "an estimate of my life," — and, from what I have already said, you will see that I have none to give. I have been too deeply conscious of the mutability and evanescence of temporal things to give any continuous effort to anything — to be consistent in anything. My life has been *whim* — impulse — passion — a longing for solitude — a scorn of all things present, in an earnest desire for the future.[1]

Accepting him therefore as a whim-directed devotee of literary technique, one may observe his performance in "Ulalume," a little later than "The Raven." It satisfies the formula of "The Philosophy of Composition," and is richer in meaning and in self-revelation. In length, tone, subject, and treatment it is according to rule. In ninety-four lines of increasing tension the ballad of the bereaved lover is sung. The effect toward which it moves is the shocked moment of discovery that grief for the lost love is not yet "pleasurable," but on this anniversary night is still a source of poignant bitterness. It is built around a series of unheeded warnings —

[1] G. E. Woodberry, "Life of Poe," Vol. II, pp. 91–93.

as "The Cask of Amontillado" is — which fall with accumulated weight when the lover's cry explains all the mistrusts and agonies and scruples of the unpacified Psyche. The effect is intensified by the use of the whole ominous first stanza in a complex of refrains. The employment of sound-sense words is more subtle and more effective than in "The Bells" or "The Raven"; and the event occurs in the usual circumscribed space — the cypress-lined alley that is blocked by the door of a tomb.

Beneath this surface is a piece of life history interpreted in its broad human application. The "I" of the ballad is the half of a divided personality that, for want of a better term, may be called the masculine element — self-confident, blundering, slow to perceive, brave in its blindness to any cause for fear. Psyche, the soul, is the complementary, feminine element — intuitive, timid, eager for the reassurance that loquacious male stupidity can afford her. They are the Macbeth and Lady Macbeth of the early half of the play; and the story in "Ulalume" is the story of "Macbeth" up to the time of the murder. Yet, and here is the defect in Poe, true as the analysis may be, in Poe's hands it becomes nothing more than that. It is like a stage setting by Gordon Craig — very somber, very suggestive, very "artistic," but so completely an artifice that it could never be mistaken for anything but an analogy to life. It is, in a word, the product of one whose "life has been *whim* — impulse — passion — a longing for solitude — a scorn of all things present." For with all Poe's multifarious activity in editing magazines and writing for them, he was still an isolated figure, a figure who had had innumerable contacts with life and had established no connections with it.

His briefer lyrics are written to a simpler formula, modified from that for the narratives. The resemblance is to be found mainly in the scrupulous nicety of measure, in the adjustment of diction to content, and in the heightened dream tone. The earlier of the two poems entitled "To Helen" is quite matchless in its beauty of sound and suggestion, but utterly vulnerable before the kind of hostile analysis to which he subjected the verse of any luckless contemporary who stirred his critical disapproval. One has no objective conception of "those Nicaean barks" nor why the beauty which attracts a wanderer homeward is like the ship that bears him back. The two fine lines in the second stanza reverberate sonorously, but they suggest no likeness to feminine loveliness; and the last mellifluous couplet is quite beyond comprehension. Read in the dream mood, however, which is unreasoning and unexacting, "To Helen" is as captivating as the sound of a distant melody.

In these far reaches Poe, the magazine editor, the cryptographer, the writer of detective stories, the meticulously intellectual, took refuge from himself and surrounding realities. In the mood of the parodist[1] he could make sardonic sport of such excursions, but in the mood of the poet he could make them serve as a complete avoidance of actuality. At times, when he was concerned only with the expression of his own emotional life, oblivious to the world and to his need for food and raiment, he could and he did succeed in the "rhythmical creation of beauty" more repeatedly and sustainedly than the Pinkney who stimulated his early attempts, and with a degree less of utterly exuberant extravagance than the Chivers who was his nearest poetic kin.

Chivers was born in the same year with Poe and issued the first of his many volumes of verse in 1832. He did not need the pressure of poverty to achieve his maladjustment with the world, living in what are known as comfortable circumstances. Poe and he were like-minded and were drawn to each other, though the relationship, which was never close, was complicated by Poe's willingness to share some of Chivers's money, and Chivers's readiness to accept Poe's critical endorsements. Their literary obligations to each other have been variously discussed by the few who con-

---

[1] See pages 421–422.

tinued to be aware of the less known of the pair.[1] To the casual observer the resemblance between Poe's "Annabel Lee" and Chivers's "Rosalie Lee,"

To my Lamb-like Rosalie Lee
To my Dove-like Rosalie Lee
To my beautiful, dutiful Rosalie Lee,

is startling enough, though hardly more so than the likeness of Poe's "Raven" to Chivers's "Isadore," with its recurrent "forevermore." Chivers at his wildest exceeds any of Poe's worst, in infelicity of figure, in gaudiness of diction, in wearisome tintinnabulation. They both revert to Israfel and Politian, both play the recondite, both adorn their verse with sounding and resounding coinages. But this is not all to be said of Chivers. He could write such a poem as "Apollo." For a moment the histrionic, attitudinizing effect-monger could forget himself in his theme and write with splendor. One can understand how Poe would be drawn to a man — one is forced to forgive much to a man — who could reach a level like this and hold it through an entire poem:

Like some deep, impetuous river from the fountains everlasting,
  Down the serpentine soft valley of the vistas of all Time,
Over cataracts of adamant uplifted into mountains,
  Soared his soul to God in thunder on the wings of thought sublime.
With the rising golden glory of the sun in ministrations,
  Making oceans metropolitan of splendor for the dawn —
Piling pyramid on pyramid of music for the nations —
  Sings the Angel who sits shining everlasting in the sun,
  For the stars which are the echoes of the shining of the sun.[2]

It was wild, undisciplined poetry of escape. In the decades before the Civil War the only verse from the South that was not quite banal was from a few men whose temperament re-

[1] J. A. Harrison (Ed.), "Poe and Chivers," in "Works of Edgar Allan Poe," Vol. XVII; A. G. Newcomer, "The Poe-Chivers Controversy Re-examined," *Sewanee Review*, January, 1904; S. Foster Damon, "Thomas Holley Chivers, Friend of Poe," Chaps. VII–X.

[2] "American Poetry to Whitman" (edited by L. Untermeyer), p. 390.

leased itself in such effusions. One must turn to the prose writers for anything more nearly related to the life of the times.

And the life of the times must be reached by the devious avenue of the journalistic work of Edgar Allan Poe. The whole approach to Poe — who he was, what he wrote, and how he wrote it — has been more insistently mist-ridden, obstructed, sidetracked, and confused than that to any other American author.[1] There are shelves of controversial material on the subject of his erratic, tragic life. His first biographer, ex-preacher and editor, set the match to the fuse by using him as a text for a moral discourse. As defenders appeared, facts were subordinated to prejudices, and a variety of conflicting legends sprang up. Poe ceased to be a man and became a bone of contention. After a generation of moralizing a generation of amoralists have tried to separate the wheat from the chaff, but have created new confusions by dealing with Poe not as immoral but as pathological, and by attempting to apply the methods of the psychologist and the psychiatrist without acknowledging either the limitations of the methods or the insufficiency of their data.

This latter group, moreover, having tasted of the fruit of the tree of knowledge of the normal and the abnormal, progressed from a study of Poe's life to an interpretation of his works and an accounting for them. They followed the tendency to stress the importance of biological determinism in the boom enthusiasm that always follows the opening of new regions with promising resources. They plunged like speculative investors on the elusive and incalculable in the hope of extraordinary returns. But they neglected the principle of choosing the simplest reasons for explaining a given situation, in their failure to take into account an increasing body of evidence that Poe was actuated for most of

[1] For the precipitation of the trouble see the chapter on "The Poe-Griswold Controversy," in Killis Campbell's "Mind of Poe," 1933. Originally published in *PMLA*, Vol. XXXIV, pp. 436 ff., September, 1919.

his productive career by one dominant motive, a definite ambition to which all his literary activities were subordinated. This was to become the owner and editor of a literary review of national circulation. It is shown in his repeated and effective work as critic on a succession of periodicals in Richmond, Philadelphia, and New York; it is recorded in his passionate desire to win the wide reputation that the editor of such a magazine should bring to it; it is revealed in his deliberate selection of ways and kinds of writing and in his comments on their success or failure; and it is capped by the hope that ended only with his life, when he seemed to have found a financial patron for the long-delayed project.

It would be a mistake to adduce these facts, which various scholars have brought to the fore but none has assembled,[1] as a total explanation for Poe's literary life and art. But they do account for very much, and they reduce the importance of other factors which may well be reduced without being ignored. They account for many of his stories; they lead to simple interpretations of many that have been complexly construed. And they fail in any way to take luster from the little residuum of prose and verse on which his reputation will stand or fall and which was tossed off as the casual by-product of a life of endeavor to succeed in a direction of far less importance. Poe did not devote himself to pure literature; but though in letters he was no less distracted than he was in his personal affairs, he unquestionably contributed to the literature on which he was accustomed to regard himself as pre-eminently a commentator.

No other major writer in America has had so large a place in the history of periodicals. His connection with four is the most distinguished fact that can be adduced for them. His poems, tales, sketches, and criticism appeared in at least forty-seven, and he served in the editorial offices of five. In the year and a half he was with the *Southern Literary*

[1] See J. B. Moore's introduction to "Selections from Poe's Literary Criticism"; J. S. Wilson's introduction to "Tales of Edgar Allan Poe"; Napier Wilt's "Poe's Attitude toward His Tales," in *Modern Philology*, Vol. XXV, pp. 101 ff.

Messenger the circulation increased from seven hundred to five thousand. In the year he worked with *Graham's Magazine* the gain was from eight to forty thousand. Five years later his critical articles were desirable enough to be used as a six months' series in *Godey's*, the most popular monthly in the country.

When he was first thrown on his own resources, after his early unwelcomed ventures in verse, estranged from Mr. Allan, married, and in penury, Poe undertook to study the literary market, the only one for which he had any wares. The result of his observations was a set of sixteen narratives, including "The MS Found in a Bottle," the prize winner in a *Baltimore Saturday Visiter* contest. John P. Kennedy, one of the judges, recommended publication of the whole collection to Carey, Lea and Carey; and, when they were refused, the submitting of some to the *Southern Literary Messenger*. In reply to the editor's criticisms of "Berenice," Poe wrote a letter of the utmost significance[1]:

> A word or two in relation to Berenice. Your opinion of it is quite just. The subject is by far too horrible. . . . The history of all magazines shows plainly that those which obtained celebrity were indebted for it to *articles similar in nature to Berenice*. . . . [Poe's italics.] You ask me in what does that nature consist . . . in the ludicrous heightened into the grotesque; the fearful colored into the horrible; the witty exaggerated into the burlesque; and the singular heightened into the strange and mystical. . . . You may well say that all of this is in bad taste. I have my doubts about it. . . . But whether the articles of which I speak are in bad taste is of little purpose. To be appreciated you must be *read* and these things are sought after with avidity. . . . The effect — if any — will be estimated better by the circulation of the magazine than by any comments on its contents.

In the letter he mentioned four examples which quite confirmed his statement: "The Man in the Bell," by William Mangin; "The Confessions of an English Opium Eater,"

[1] From a letter of Poe to T. W. White, April 30, 1835, published by Napier Wilt, *Modern Philology*, Vol. XXV, pp. 102–104.

by De Quincey; and "Monos and Daimonos" and "A MS Found in a Madhouse," "by no less a man than Bulwer." An examination by the scholar who discovered this letter shows that Poe could have multiplied this list manifold by allusions to current numbers of the *Dublin University Magazine, Fraser's, Blackwood's*, the *London*, the *New Monthly, Knickerbocker*, and *Godey's*.

A probable reason why the publishers refused to put out these tales of Poe in book form is that they were neither sober imitations nor broad burlesques, but somewhat elusively represented his contempt for the popular type. They contained many allusions to the fiction fashions of the day, many covert references to himself, many gibes at the critics. The whole formula, summed up three years before the letter to editor White, in "How to Write a Blackwood Article"[1] and illustrated therewith in "A Predicament," is also perfectly met in "Loss of Breath," one of the earlier Folio Tales to be published. This is "sensational"; based on alleged experience; "elevated, diffusive, interjectional" in tone; interlarded with recondite allusions, quotations, and similes; a complete example of the literary lollipop. And Poe wrote it with his tongue in his cheek. He used a subtitle in this case to indicate its burlesque quality — "A Tale neither in nor out of 'Blackwood.'" In others of the series none is needed to bring home the suggestions of Bulwer, D'Israeli, Irving, Hawthorne. He employed other subtitles as well: "A Parable," "In Imitation of the German," and so on.

But at times, as is inevitable with a creative writer who condescends to parody and burlesque, Poe surrendered so far to the possibilities of his theme that it teeters between sheer magnificence and sheer extravagance, between nonsense and reason. This is the case in "The Assignation," with the extraordinary aquatics of the diving rescuer, "muffled in a cloak," and the necessity for an almost equally swift descent downstairs of the Marquesa; with Poe's

[1] K. L. Daughrity, "Poe and *Blackwood's*," in *American Literature*, Vol. II, pp. 289–292.

description of the hero, so obviously himself, preceded by, "There are some subjects upon which I take pleasure in being minute"; with the suicide's gratuitous performance in swallowing "in rapid succession several goblets" of the poisoned wine. These are not slipshod blunders; no more is the suavely formal discussion with Metzengerstein carried on by the three attendants just described as frantically struggling with his fiendish charger. They are outbreaks of the imp of the perverse who was never far from Poe's elbow; the author trying to achieve the hyper-conventional, the imp whispering ironic perversities and forcing him to set them down. So if one read "Shadow" without the warning originally given by Poe when he entitled it "Siope — a Fable, in the Manner of the Psychological Autobiographists," he might be led to take it more seriously than Poe did. For with a properly solemn invocation of the sub-muses of symbolism and expressionism the lovely rhythms could lure one into ignoring the extravagances that are hardly exceeded in the famous trap-passage in the "Double-Barrelled Detective Story" by that other hoax perpetrator, Mark Twain.[1] And this same perversity rises above itself to the level of an artistic thesis in "Never Bet the Devil Your Head, a Tale with a Moral," another of the "Folio Club" series, with its ironic introduction and its explicit references to *The Dial* and the *North American Review*. This moral tale is again sympathetic with Mark Twain's improving observations on good little boys and bad little boys and his blithe defiance of poetic justice.

It is clear enough, then, that at the outset as a magazine contributor Poe was writing with more respect for his market than for his art. His dealings with editors and publishers naturally furnished him with ideas and aroused a wish to work as a free agent rather than as an employee; and his brief failure with the *Broadway Journal* stimulated this, for he failed as manager rather than as editor. The plan of

---

[1] See pages 637, 639, 641.

having his own publication is recurrent in his correspondence. In 1844 he wrote to Charles Anthon:

> Holding steadily in view my ultimate purpose, — to found a Magazine of my own, or in which at least I might have a proprietary right, — it has been my constant endeavor in the meantime, not so much to establish a reputation great in itself as one of that particular character which should best further my special objects, and draw attention to my exertions as Editor of a Magazine. . . .
>
> My sole immediate object is the furtherance of my ultimate one. I believe that if I could get my tales fairly before the public, and thus have an opportunity of eliciting foreign as well as native opinion respecting them, I should by their means be in a far more advantageous position than at present in regard to the establishment of a Magazine.[1]

In founding this magazine he felt that he would be keeping step with his generation; and he stated his theory in one of the "Marginalia":

> The increase, within a few years, of the magazine literature . . . is but a sign of the times — an indication of an era in which men are forced upon the curt, the condensed, the well-digested, in place of the voluminous — in a word, upon journalism in place of dissertation. We need now the light artillery rather than the "Peace-makers" of the intellect. . . . Hence the journalism of the age; hence, in especial, magazines. Too many we cannot have, as a general proposition.[2]

To Horton Patterson, prospective patron of *The Stylus*, he wrote, in 1849:

> We must aim high — address the intellect — the higher classes — of the country (with reference also to a certain amount of foreign circulation). . . . I need not add that such a Mag. would exercise a literary and other influence never yet exerted in America.[3]

Hope for monetary success as well as influence was expressed in this letter as well as in the reminiscent passage, of an earlier date:

---

[1] J. A. Harrison, "Life and Letters of Poe," Vol. II, pp. 178–180.
[2] Stedman and Woodberry, "Works of Poe," Vol. VII, pp. 264–265.
[3] Allen, "Israfel," Vol. II, pp. 809, 810.

In short I could see no real reason why a Magazine, if worthy of the name, could not be made to circulate among 20,000 subscribers, embracing the best intellect and education of the land. This was a thought which stimulated my fancy and my ambition. The influence of such a journal would be vast indeed, and I dreamed of honestly employing that influence in the sacred cause of the beautiful, the just and the true.[1]

With the ambition to control a literary magazine well defined, and the desire to establish a compelling reputation clear in mind, it was natural for him to study the public taste and to write on the level of it, in order to draw attention to his name. The author of the most complete recent biography of Poe discounts a statement from the would-be editor to F. W. Thomas. In the light of the foregoing, however, it is right to take quite seriously this comment of Poe on his most successful poem and his most successful story:

I send you an early number of the "B. Journal," containing my "Raven." It was copied by Briggs, my associate, before I joined the paper. "The Raven" has had a great "run" . . . but I wrote it for the express purpose of running — just as I did the "Gold Bug," you know. The bird beat the bug, though, all hollow.[2]

Between Poe's earlier stories, which were so clearly written with the literary fiction market in mind, and the less than twenty that represent his best prose narrative, there lies a dreary stretch of forced and mediocre work. Its shortcomings need not be stressed. It was potboiler writing, but though Poe was pathetically industrious he had slight gifts for turning out narrative on demand. Before coming to the cream of his creative prose it is pertinent to turn to the other phase of his journalistic reputation-building — his current criticism. And this, in fairness, should be considered with a clear distinction between the statements of his literary theories and most of the tom-tom beating by means of which he was drumming up his audience.

---

[1] Harrison, op. cit. Vol. II, p. 177.
[2] Ibid. Vol. II, p. 205.

Poe's critical writings were addressed to an American audience which could pillory Cooper for his aggressive patriotism, which could ignore Thoreau and Whitman and Melville, and which would have left Emerson in privation if he had needed to live by his pen. It was slowly being swept into civil controversy and civil war, but it shrank from general ideas and the discussion of them. Poe's partial journalistic success as critic was unimpeded by general ideas. He had little or nothing to say about the state, the church, the family, or the market; he made only a single fumbling attempt to think in philosophical terms; he was the assailant of individual literary reputations, a swashbuckler, cutting and thrusting, and strutting about a stage on which he played the villain to his complete satisfaction. And his public enjoyed him in the role, enjoyed the flaying and blood-letting, and excluded themselves from any generalizations about the stupidity of the larger public.

His abusive and scurrilous personalities made good "copy" for his editors. He wrote of Headley's "Sacred Mountains,"[1] "The book is written in the kind of phraseology in which John Philpot Curran when drunk, would have made a speech at a public dinner." He called Cornelius Mathews a "turkey gobbler," declared that Lewis Gaylord Clark was "as smooth as oil, or a sermon from Dr. Hawks," and described Christopher P. Cranch as "one of the least intolerable of the school of Boston transcendentalists." He used Hawthorne as a cue for falling foul of public intelligence: "The author of 'Twice-Told Tales' is scarcely recognized by the press or the public, and when noticed at all, it is merely to be damned by faint praise." It was this circulation-drawing aspect of Poe that his nearest twentieth-century parallel, H. L. Mencken, once took exception to in saying that "he was enormously ignorant of good books, and, moreover, he could never quite throw off a congenital vulgarity of taste, so painfully visible in the struttings of his style." The quite

[1] Headley's "Sacred Mountains" was a pedantic and unctuous work on the mountains referred to in Biblical narrative.

logical result was that when as an utter amateur he made his pretentious ill-directed excursion into the field of intellectual speculation he betrayed his lack of knowledge and discipline, and won no reading for the "Eureka," of which he had wanted to have fifty thousand printed. Yet for popular journalistic consumption Poe's defects as critic served as his virtues. A certain savagery in all but the exceptional reader is sated by bad manners, irritability, truculence, sectional prejudice vented in the name of some ostensible principle. Even his egocentricity, which led him to declare a good deal of nonsense at the expense of individuals or of New England or of the whole American public, and which was far short of G. B. Shaw's in later years, seemed to allure more than it estranged.

To turn from the surface to the substance, Poe's criticism was, first of all, fresh in its dissent from both American humility and American bumptiousness in literature. He had his own idea of what was good and applied it (with such exceptions of bias as have been noted) to the new books that passed before his eye. He was anything but the perfunctory and amiable book reviewer; he was anything but the critic or the student of the best in literature. His literary thesis he presented at some length and with characteristic finality in his two almost valedictory essays, "The Philosophy of Composition" and "The Poetic Principle." Limiting the realm of pure literature to the realm of taste, and limiting its possibilities to the expression in brief form of a brief emotional experience; limiting the emotional experience to moments in which beauty and melancholy are combined; limiting the setting of his narratives to circumscribed spaces, and the expression of them to conventional and established forms; he limited his own problem by the arbitrary exclusion of whatever did not interest him. In the exercise of his criticism in specific cases he went still further by limiting his attention almost exclusively to the examination of details; and this in spite of his insistence on the importance of the total effect and the determination of the dominant mood and tone.

Thus in his satisfying disposition of Drake's overrated "Culprit Fay" he assembled in a final indictment all the fallacious and inconsistent metaphors in that hasty hodge-podge. And in the works of Elizabeth Barrett, of whom he was one of the earliest champions, he discussed diction, syntax, prosody, and single lines of distinction in the minutest detail. Seldom in these critiques did he rise to the exposition of principles, and more seldom still to the discussion of any principles of life. Always it was the cameo, the gold filigree, the miniature under the microscope. And his predilection for a "pleasurable melancholy" led him to delight chiefly in the mortuary beauties of his fellow poets.

Aside from commendation of this sort and on this scale, Poe's application of critical theory was like the theory itself — largely negative. It was his business, he said, to hold up the model of supreme excellence, but as a rational critic he must look less at merit than at demerit. The statement is half confusion, half paradox, akin to his attempt to subordinate the ethical or intellectual content to the aesthetic, yet preserve its independence. Akin, too, to his statement in the *Penn Magazine* prospectus, in which his positive thesis is offset and overbalanced by the vehemence with which he declares he will resist what is irresistible for him — the venting of his antipathies:

> . . . a criticism self-sustained; guiding itself only by the purest rules of Art; analyzing and urging those rules as it applies therein; holding itself aloof from all personal bias; acknowledging no fear save that of outraging the right; yielding no point either to the vanity of the author, or to the assumptions of critical prejudice, or to the involute and anonymous cant of the Quarterlies, or to the arrogance of those organized *cliques* which, hanging like nightmares upon American literature, manufacture, at the nod of our principal booksellers, a pseudo-public opinion by wholesale.[1]

The purest rules of art for him were rules for technical proficiency. He made less of a demand on the inherent pos-

[1] Allen, op. cit. Vol. II, p. 468.

session of beauty in the artist than he did on intelligence enough to achieve a technique and ethical integrity enough to maintain it. If one looks in Poe's thesis or his creative writing for any beauty other than the enjoyment of pleasurable melancholy, he will find it in an opulence of sensuous enjoyment, in excitement rather than in elevation, in dizziness rather than in loftiness, with no place for high devotion or high aspiration.

Poe's best tales, considered in the broad, were conceived in the spirit of his poetry or in the spirit of his criticism. The highest genius, he declared, could be best displayed in the composition of a rhymed narrative; and in "mere prose" the "tale proper" offered the finest field. "Ligeia," "Berenice," "Morella," are examples of the poet's work in prose, the first of these, like "The Assignation" and "The House of Usher," including one of his lyrics. They are cast in the misty mid-region between life and death, with none of the pleasures of the one except as foils to the reduplicated horrors of the other. In construction they are comparable to "The Raven" and "Ulalume," as also in general effect. Like the poems too, these tales inspire no human interest, unless this be derived from the consciousness that the spokesman in the first person is drawn in the image of Poe — a claim on the attention to which the stories as works of art have no title. Again, poems and tales are of the same family in their subordination of event to mood and in the employment of every accessory that contributes to a sense of shivery horror.

Perhaps, to indulge in a classification after the manner of Poe, a connecting group might be mentioned between the extreme types. This is the sort of tale that substitutes the horrors of crime and its consequences for the horrors of death, centering on the malignance of hatred and of fear. It deals with crime as distinct from sin and, if it involves conscience, introduces the conscience that doth make cowards of us all, a torturer rather than a guide. Neatest of these, "The Cask of Amontillado" is a complete fulfillment of its author's narrative formula. It is cut on the pattern of "The Raven";

"The Philosophy of Composition" can be applied to it by the substitution of the specific and relevant allusions. And it is equally inhuman. Montresor, the avenger, is an incarnate devil; Fortunato, the victim, a piece of walking vanity. In tone the slow murder is conceived "during the supreme madness of the carnival season," is pursued in grim mockery, and is concluded with ironic laughter and the jingling of the foolscap bells. Finally, to free the tale from any least relation to life, the assassination does "trammel up the consequence, and catch with his surcease, success."

The tales that display the mind of critic rather than poet, the best of which come in his later career, are in different fashions riddle solutions, pre-eminently "The Murders in the Rue Morgue," "The Mystery of Marie Roget," "The Gold Bug," and "The Purloined Letter," early examples of the detective story. In their elaboration Poe combined his gifts as story-teller with the powers that appeared equally in deciphering codes, discrediting Maelzel's chess player, dealing with the complications of "Three Sundays in a Week," or foreseeing from the opening chapter the outcome of "Barnaby Rudge." Still, as in the earlier types, they are composed of the things that life is made of, and still they are uninformed with the breath of life. The detective story has been cited as a concession to the moral sense of the reading public, following the paths of the older romance of roguery but pursuing the wrongdoer to prison or gallows instead of sharing his defiance of the social order. But in this concession Poe had no hand. For him detection was an end in itself; he was like the sportsman who is stirred by the zest of the hunt and shoots to kill, but at the day's end hands over the bag to a gamekeeper.

In a comparable way the creating of effects was an end in his more poetic writings. He wanted to win an audience, and he wanted to wield an influence over that audience; but there was nothing positive that he wanted to say to it or do with it. It may be said that though he was an alien in a materially minded generation, his desire for success was as avid and as objectless as that of any money-grubber of his despising. Desperate and defiant, he struggled desperately to capitalize his mood. But "there is nothing very sinister in Poe, except the desire to produce sinister effects";[1] and there is nothing deeply tragic about him because he does not represent a fall from any high estate. In his day he deserved more for his independence and his artistry than his generation conceded him. Since his day he has been awarded honors quite beyond his deserts.

Europe has exclaimed over him because he wrote exceptional and extravagant tales and verses and because these seemed unique from an American. France, with its proclivity for stressing form, gave him applause from a secondary critic, Gautier, and translations from a *fin de siècle* admirer, Baudelaire. America has re-echoed and magnified this attention. Thrill hunters turn to him perennially, and pathology hunters periodically. By an accident of emphasis one of the first expounders of the short story, or Short Story, or Short-story, made him the Aristotle of this genre and was quoted by scores of successors who quoted the same passage or two with the same unbalance of discrimination. But in point of the magnitude of the man or the magnitude of his achievement, Poe subsides to his proper level on a moment's comparison with such of his neglected contemporaries as Whitman or Melville. His technical proficiency endures the test, but his substance dwindles to gauds and baubles. And as one looks at the three together these others stride on into the future, leaving the author of "The Raven" and the would-be editor of *The Stylus* shrilly gesticulating in a baffled argument with the imp of the perverse.

Quantitatively speaking, William Gilmore Simms was the most imposing Southern poet of all. Between 1825 and 1860 his bibliography shows eighteen titles of poetry,[2] most of them books, with a two-volume collected edition in 1853. In

---

[1] W. C. Brownell, "American Prose Masters," p. 257.
[2] W. P. Trent, "Life of Simms" (A. M. L. Series), pp. 331–342.

recording which all has been recorded of Simms's poetry, except that one bit from it has survived, "The Lost Pleiad" (not to be confused with poems of the same title by Chivers and H. M. Stephens), which like the seventh of the Pleiades hangs almost invisible above the southern horizon. For Simms had nothing but his fervor to sustain him in his verse. He was historian, chronicler, raconteur, rhetorician — anything but poet; and a loose kind of prose was the natural medium for his turbulent vitality. There was no time or fitting mood for poetic art in a thirty-five-year authorship which also produced two plays, thirty-one volumes of prose fiction, nine volumes of history and biography, and ten separately published miscellanea, and which included editorial connection from time to time with a newspaper and five periodicals.

Simms, particularly the Simms of the 1850's, has often been compared to Dr. Samuel Johnson. There was a resemblance in lowliness of origin, in burliness of body, in brusqueness of manner and pugnacity of disposition, in dogmatism, and in local eminence among the bookmen. There is a similarity too in a thinness of skin for which these assertive traits were none too effective protection; but Simms failed to carry off the role so well as his London prototype. Instead of accepting his lack of social prestige in traditional terms and building his own prestige on his own terms, he strove to "better himself," surrendered to the ambitions of the overlord, was never so happy as when he was dividing his energies between playing author and playing host on the estate which he first shared and then fell heir to from his second father-in-law, and was never more rancorously belligerent than when he was living on the hottest of diets in correspondence with the matchless fire-eater, Beverley Tucker. He was a complete spokesman for the aristocratic South, by which he was never unreservedly accepted.

Even in the years of his greatest prosperity his own district was not supporting him as an author. Only one of the five periodicals he undertook lasted more than two years, and that was dead in six. He had to brave a mob away from the office of the Charleston *City Gazette*. Charleston could publish his poetry and ignore it, but all his successful fiction was issued in New York and Philadelphia. Here, or near these cities, he read all his proofs, not daring to depend on the unreliable mails; here he made his stimulating literary acquaintances; here friends arranged lecture engagements for him until he estranged all hearers by his sectional effrontery and arrogance. And from here he returned to the Charleston whose gentry accepted all his overflowing energies in the cause of the South but never completely accepted the man himself.

Consider the beginnings of his career as a prose writer. He had published five volumes of poems in Charleston, and the last of these—"Atalantis"—had attracted attention enough, in the words of his biographer, to tempt him "away from South Carolina to the more literary North." He settled in New Haven and, casting about for material, decided to rework a partly factual serial of his, on the "Confessions of a Murderer." The result was "Martin Faber," one of the stories built on "the fearful colored into the horrible" which, according to Poe,[1] was a popular type of the day. Simms started as Cooper did, with an accepted form. And now, as Cooper did, he moved over to the field which was native to him, the memories of his own region. In a little over four years (1834–1838) he completed and published five tales of the Old South: "Guy Rivers, a Tale of Georgia," "Richard Hurdis, a Tale of Alabama," "The Partisan, a Tale of the Revolution," its sequel, "Mellichampe," and "The Yemassee, a Romance of South Carolina," which reverted farthest, to the seventeenth century. Cooper eventually wrote a long succession of sea tales, using the experiences of his young manhood on the ocean. Simms before long made use of his observations on the westering border line, which he had crossed and recrossed when as a boy he visited his nomad father in the Southwest. Cooper wrote a history of the navy;

[1] See page 420.

Simms compiled several biographies. Cooper spent enormous energy in social criticism and controversy; so did Simms. But the parallel could be pursued too far, and forced too far. Cooper's nation was the United States of America; Simms's became the Confederate States of America; and their positions were reversed in the fact that Cooper, starting as landlord and inheriting the point of view of overlord, — in which respect he more nearly resembled the average Southern gentleman than the average in the North, — had to compound his convictions in favor of democracy with his prejudices as an aristocrat; whereas Simms, one of the common herd, longed to become egregious socially as well as intellectually, and in the end went down to defeat with the other landlords.

Probably it was their difference of parentage that accounts for the striking contrast between their most successful tales of the frontier; for, after all, Cooper's "anti-rent" novels were afterthoughts. Cooper, as has been indicated,[1] although he lived for a time in the settled ex-frontier, wrote of the Western border always from the point of view of the West; and his pre-eminent character was at one with the Indians in resenting and receding before the invading forces of civilization. Simms, in "Richard Hurdis," "Border Beagles," "Beauchamp," and "Charlemont," regarded the borderlands from the viewpoint of the settler, and while he acknowledged the abominations of early white settlement, he was solicitous not over what the Indian suffered at the hands of his conqueror but over the delays progress had to endure at the hands of the land pirates. In the opening chapter of "Charlemont," the last-written of the border tales, Simms revealed a sense of the frontier process which was far more explicit, if not more acute, than anything displayed by Cooper. He had seen the facts through his own eyes and with his father as a guide — a very different guide from Judge Cooper.

[1] See pages 263, 264.

But Simms's stories were as confused, hectic, turbulent, and indeterminate as his career. While his whole theory of life was shifting, events were undermining the life built upon that theory. Unsupported by the section which he vainly championed; estranged from the North, which fed him until he alienated it; impoverished with all his neighbors, he suffered a series of frustrations. And his failure to achieve at any one point as he aspired to is pointed by the paradox of his lone literary achievement. His major romances, as such, may be regarded as documents in political and social history and as evidences of certain tendencies in literary history. Yet, writing with the materials that he knew, he made his real contribution not to the romance of the Old South, not to the portrayal of Southern heroes or courtiers. Thackeray could bone up on local topography and give the flavor of courtly life in the South.[1] Simms's contribution came from the other end of the social scale — the horde of blackguards, sharpers, outlaws, and border buccaneers who ravaged and slew in the name of war when wars were in progress, and who plied the same tactics beyond the reach of the civil authority while the frontier was edging toward the west. Honest men clashed with them; and in Simms's hands both sets of characters became men whose speeches and actions smacked of the soil. They were subordinate figures in romance or they were major figures only on account of their villainy; but they were more genuine and far nearer to history than the gilt and tinsel gentry of Simms's pages. Even conceding this, however,— the romancer's concession to realistic portraiture,— there is no clear reason why any reader should turn to Simms today except the student of history, the student of literature, or the enthusiast over local traditions in the regions traversed in his pages.

The decade of the 1830's was the most prolific in Southern romances, with Simms far in the lead of all competitors;

[1] E. M. Gwathmey, "John Pendleton Kennedy," Chap. IV, "Kennedy and Thackeray."

but in this decade two works by others appeared which seem now to be significant in themselves and symptomatic of an attitude and a change — John P. Kennedy's "Swallow Barn" of 1832 and A. B. Longstreet's "Georgia Scenes" of 1835. This was just after the return from his long sojourn abroad of Irving, the most polite and the most popular of American authors, who was continuing the tradition of Addison and Goldsmith. Where in the country should he be more cordially read than in the region of eighteenth-century traditions? And by whom in the South more than by potential men of letters? Kennedy was a young gentleman who had had his baptism of fire in the War of 1812; had dallied with the law; in the very year of the "Sketch Book" had started a two-year venture with a sort of Southern "Salmagundi," the Baltimore *Red Book*; and who now, in 1832, followed the pictures of Sir Roger de Coverley's household and of Bracebridge Hall with a comparable "rivulet of story wandering through a broad meadow of episode. Or, I might truly say, . . . a book of episodes with an occasional digression into the plot."[1] Longstreet was prepared for Yale at a Southern academy, studied law in Connecticut, at thirty-two was a judge of the supreme court in his native state of Georgia, and a dozen years later (in 1835) issued serially his own sketch book, "Georgia Scenes." Both men departed from the Southern main-traveled road of sentimental romance about the South. Neither in doing so wrote under his own signature, and each found in the North the publisher who would venture to put his lucubrations into book form. Both, furthermore, wrote quite definitely to preserve pictures of a life that was passing; and each in his own way was chary of violating the prejudices of the gentle reader in the subjects or the details of his realism.

Kennedy, choosing "Mark Littleton" for pen name, sent his proxy into the Virginia he himself had often visited, and

[1] See the concluding paragraph in Kennedy's "Word from the Author to the Reader," in "Swallow Barn" (1851 or 1861 edition), p. 11.

made a record of a society that he felt was losing certain happy provincial qualities before what he called "the progress." A Baltimorean, he was not identified with the land; he belonged to a city that was commercial in its dominant interests, and he had married the daughter of a rich manufacturer. He was a sympathetic observer of a social order of which he had been a friendly neighbor, not a member, and he registered, especially in the two preliminary sections, a polite regret at its decline. He described in Meriwether and Hazard a pair of country gentlemen of modest circumstances, but he deferred to them as to men of superior clay and acknowledged their ancestral traditions in such chapter headings as "Traces of the Feudal System," "Knight Errantry," "A Joust at Utterance," and "The Last Minstrel." He made Bel Tracy, the leading lady of the successive tableaux, a romantic and finicky creature,[1] "like the king's daughter in the ballad," and he made her lover sue her in a protracted series of courtly indirections, which were "in the very best strain of a cavalier devoted to his lady-love; and had more true chivalry in them than all the formal courtesies in the world."[2] The difference between "Swallow Barn" and the other tales of Virginia in its day was that it was less ornate and unreal than they. It is a picture of the gentry, for the gentry, by one of the gentry, and is realistic only as it divests them of some of their trappings and presents them as simple, fallible, moderately uncultured country squires.

Longstreet, too, wrote as a recorder of historical material. "Georgia Scenes" is less unified than Kennedy's scenes of Virginia. Seven of the nineteen sketches are native pictures

---

[1] See Kennedy's "Swallow Barn," Chaps. IX, XII, XXXI, XXXVIII, etc., in which the author treats his heroine with the typical attitude of the indulgent and semi-contemptuous gallant. Kennedy's "Quodlibet" (1840), with its subtitle and signature, "Containing some annals thereof. Edited by Solomon Second Thoughts, Schoolmaster, Phila.," is again after the manner of Irving. The resemblance, of course, is to the "Knickerbocker History" and the political satire of the "Salmagundi Papers," though "Quodlibet," a satire on Jacksonian democracy, has more of the political acumen of Brackenridge's "Modern Chivalry" than anything of the like by Irving.

[2] Kennedy, "Swallow Barn" (1851 or 1861 edition), p. 394.

of the Georgia villager or countryman, dancing, fighting, horse-swapping; at the shooting match, the gander-pulling, or the barbecue. The rest are of the more conventional eighteenth-century essay type. There is an eccentric humorist, a remote relative of the Will Wimble, Launcelot Langstaff genus, or a sort of caricature of Kennedy's Ned Hazard. There are some sketches of the gentry, dancing, drilling, debating, racing, hunting — sketches drawn in complete want of sympathy with frivolity, indulgence, and the pomp of power. The sketches of the ladies, particularly those who have been "finished" at Northern schools, are done in the same temper. The conventional comments on "Georgia Scenes" misleadingly imply that the whole collection has the rough simplicity of subject that is to be found only in the few sketches of the commoner. Longstreet displayed marked timidity in these departures from the paths of elegant literature. He wrote for the newspapers under three pen names; he proclaimed in his preface to the collected sketches that he was preserving data for the historian of social manners, declaring that the ephemeral newspaper pieces were reissued only on the urgency of friends, and apologizing for the colloquial language and the occasional masked profanity. All this was explicable on pure literary grounds.

But Longstreet was eventually more than the literary purist: he was the complete religious moralist. He resigned from the bench to enter the church, now preaching and now serving as clerical college president. And in the latter role he was no tolerant eighteenth-century parson but an unctuous nonconformist who never failed to point his morals as he adorned his tales. The fighters' fearful practice of gouging each other's eyes out, he presented only in a pantomime rehearsal of a would-be bully. He ended the spirited account of a real fight, which included all tactics but gouging, with the observation that such doings were a disgrace to civilization and were being done away with, "thanks to the Christian religion, schools, colleges and benevolent associations."

Candor constrained him to condemn drunkenness, and he did so repeatedly. And for the frivolities and excesses of the upper class he had a stern but tempered word on frequent occasion. Careful culling of the pages of forgotten journals has recently furnished a second volume by Longstreet which is quite properly entitled "Stories with a Moral." There is a disquisition in narrative form on the abominations of the press and the gossip-mongering Yankee editor that would have warmed the cockles of Cooper's heart; another on the viciousness of oral gossip; another that ends "No danger of the child that can't sleep till he prays for his father and mother"; two by college-president Longstreet on the fatal ravages of dissipation on William Mitten, student; and so on and so on. It is quite apparent that "Georgia Scenes" was something of a happy accident; that its present repute rests on a casual fraction of the whole.

Georgia was fertile ground for folk pictures, since it had no antecedent social distinction to compare with Virginia's. Longstreet, in the younger community, looked down from the secure heights of an embattled clergyman and educator, smiled at the vulgar sinners below, but elected to reform them rather than to depict them. Kennedy, in the older one, looking down from the equal security of social eminence, never forgot that he was a gentleman; allowed Ned Branch to indulge in a lively fisticuffing without mussing his hair or disturbing his cravat while vindicating the honor of a futile old landholder; and bade good-by to the present as he reverted in two subsequent romances to the past of the Revolutionaries and Cavaliers. Yet, casual as they were, these early snapshots of the South are worth recording, if only for their rarity at the time.

Sectional loyalties, however, do not thrive best on a basis of sectional realism; they find better rooting in prejudice against opposing sections and in unleashed idealizing of local tradition. The Southern inclination to look to the past was restimulated by the embarrassment of looking too acutely at the present. Such was the case with W. A. Caruthers, for example, by inclination a frank, freehearted Virginian. On the publication of his all too candid "Kentuckian in New York"[1] something happened to Caruthers; and it is hard to believe that the occurrences did not include tart remarks from his neighbors.[2] At any rate, within a few months he offered an antidote in "The Cavaliers of Virginia, or The Recluse of Jamestown," a tale of Bacon's rebellion comfortably located a century and a half in the past. It was in these years (1833–1835) that Simms was pouring out his romantic memories of the colonies; and in 1836 Kennedy was to depart from the shabby-genteel of "Swallow Barn" — the hall door too heavy for its hinges, the horse-nibbled plum trees on the driveway, the barn decrepit, the barnyards knee-deep in litter — and to revert to the Revolutionary days of "Horse-Shoe Robinson." Caruthers and Simms were to follow with more in the 40's, and Simms with redoubled zeal in the early 50's. And then from 1854 on was to come John Esten Cooke of "Virginia Comedians" fame. Cooke piled on the adulation of the fine old South so heavily that even as late as 1858 George W. Bagby essayed, in the Richmond *Whig*, his "Unkind but Complete Destruction of John Esten Cooke, Novelist." Bagby was proud of his ancestry, he protested; but he was bored by seeing them praised at the expense of himself and his own times. "Therefore I desire that Effingham Cooke shall sell out his old stock, close business in the Behind, and set up in the New." Moreover, he continued, "Mr. Cooke's eyes are not only set in the back of his head, but they are also afflicted with a pair of rose-colored goggles of enormous magnifying powers."[3] How, he asked, could a South so degenerate that he and Cooke were representative of it have descended from such a super-ancestry as Cooke described in his novels?

---

[1] See page 385.

[2] It is not stretching a point to presume that Caruthers's first novel must have provoked some resentments in Virginia, and that these hastened the publication of the second, even though he had been planning to write this even before "The Kentuckian" was published.

[3] J. O. Beaty, "John Esten Cooke," pp. 69–70.

Cooke went on his way, issuing three tales in 1854 and two more before the end of the decade, all of the sort that evoked Bagby's strictures. By 1854 Melville and Hawthorne had both achieved; and still Cooke pursued his hard-beaten path of conventionalized and sterilized romance. Moreover, literary convention was soon overtaken, as with Longstreet, by religious fervor. While completing "The Virginia Comedians" Cooke suddenly joined the church, professing the Episcopal faith with all the fervor of a Southern Methodist. He wrote of his first novel, "Leather Stocking and Silk" (a tale compounded of Cooperian matter and Irvingesque style), "If the book be found entertaining and (above all else) the spirit of it pure, the writer will be more than satisfied."[1] He had already written a short story called "Peony," which was a forerunner of Harte's "M'liss" with an extra measure of saccharin. And now in 1855—at the end of a five-year period which had seen not only the best of Hawthorne and Melville but also "Uncle Tom's Cabin" and "Walden" and "Hiawatha" and "Leaves of Grass"—Cooke produced "Ellie," a long elaboration of the regenerative powers of childhood, and the worst of combinations of moralism and sentimentalism. What might have been an honest and innovating picture of Richmond life became a series of homilies on the ways of the hour. Cooke continued on his sentimental route, dashing off his tales in an average of six weeks of effusiveness. Moreover, he established and held his market with the consumers of the sentimentally uplifting, Northern publishers and editors snapping up his work. But before the war he was already a respectable competitor with the authors of Beadle's Dime Novels and the other sensationalists, a sobering witness of the wide chasm that so often yawns between popular success and permanent achievement.

One literary event of antebellum days remains to be recorded here. In 1857 there had gathered around Simms and his friend John Russell, bookseller, a group who became for

---

[1] Beaty, op. cit. p. 36.

Charleston, South Carolina, what the frequenters of the Old Corner Book Store were to Boston,[1] and rather more than what the "Bohemians" of Pfaff's restaurant were to New York. Russell's became a daytime rendezvous for the best people — possibly for business, certainly for talk — and an evening literary clubroom; and *Russell's Magazine* was the natural expression of the group, just as the *Atlantic Monthly* (also founded in 1857) was for the Bostonians, and the *Saturday Press* (1856–1860) for the New Yorkers. For the three years before it was choked out by the oncoming war, *Russell's* compared well in purpose and substance with the more fortunate Northern monthly. Simms fostered the Charleston project; two younger Charlestonians, Henry Timrod and Paul Hamilton Hayne, were stimulated by what was going on.[2]

Book List

GENERAL

CABELL, JAMES BRANCH. Chivalry. 1921.

CABELL, JAMES BRANCH. Gallantry; an Eighteenth Century Dizain. 1907.

CHANDLER, JULIAN A. C., and others (Eds.). The South in the Building of the Nation. 13 vols. 1909–1913. Vol. VII, Literary and Intellectual Life of the South; Vol. VIII, History of Southern Fiction; Vol. X, History of the Social Life of the South.

COUCH, W. T. (Ed.). Culture in the South. 1934.

DAVIDSON, DONALD. "The Artist as Southerner," *Saturday Review of Literature,* Vol. II, pp. 781–782.

DODD, WILLIAM E. "The Social Philosophy of the Old South," *American Journal of Sociology,* Vol. XXIII, pp. 735–746.

HART, ALBERT BUSHNELL. Slavery and Abolition. 1906.

HART, ALBERT BUSHNELL. The Southern South. 1910.

HOWARD, JOHN TASKER. Stephen Foster, America's Troubadour. 1934.

LANDRUM, GRACE W. "Notes on the Reading of the Old South," *American Literature,* Vol. III, pp. 60–71.

MACY, JESSE. The Anti-Slavery Crusade; a Chronicle of the Gathering Storm. 1919.

[1] See "Library of Southern Literature," Vol. V, pp. 2278–2284, a portion of the excerpts from Paul Hamilton Hayne's articles in the *Southern Bivouac* for September, October, November, 1885.

[2] See pages 574–577.

PAGE, THOMAS NELSON. The Old Dominion, Her Making and Manners. 1908.

PAGE, THOMAS NELSON. The Old South. 1900.

PAGE, THOMAS NELSON. Social Life in Old Virginia before the War. 1898.

RUTHERFORD, MILDRED L. The South in History and Literature. 1907.

SHALER, N. S. "The Peculiarities of the South," *North American Review*, Vol. CLI, pp. 477–488.

SMITH, THOMAS VERNOR. The American Philosophy of Equality, Chap. II. 1927.

STEARNS, BERTHA M. "Southern Magazines for Ladies, 1819–1860," *South Atlantic Quarterly*, Vol. XXXI, pp. 70–87.

TRENT, WILLIAM P. "Dominant Forces in Southern Life," *Atlantic*, Vol. LXXIX, pp. 42–53.

WERTENBAKER, T. J. Patrician and Plebeian in Virginia. 1910.

NORTHERN ONSLAUGHT AND SOUTHERN REPLY

Individual Works

NOTE. It seems to be of more value to present the following list in order of time rather than of authors and alphabet.

HALE, SARAH J. Northwood, or Life North and South, Showing the True Character of Both. 1827. 1852.

COOPER, JAMES FENIMORE. Notions of the Americans, Picked Up by a Travelling Bachelor. 1828.

SHANKS, C. L. "The Biblical Anti-Slavery Argument of the Decade 1830–1840," *Journal of Negro History*, Vol. XVI, pp. 132–157.

WHITTIER, JOHN G. Justice and Expediency. 1833.

CARUTHERS, WILLIAM A. A Kentuckian in New York. 1834.

TUCKER, BEVERLEY. The Partisan Leader. 1836.

HILDRETH, RICHARD. The Slave, or Memoirs of Archy Moore. 1836.

BIRD, ROBERT MONTGOMERY. Sheppard Lee. 1836.

Anti-Slavery Song Books: Songs of the Free, 1836; Freedom's Lyre, 1840; Envoy from Free Hearts to the Free, 1840; Hymns and Songs for Friends of Freedom, 1842; Anti-Slavery Hymns, 1844; The Liberty Minstrel, 1845; Lays of Liberty, 1854; The Anti-Slavery Harp, 1854; Songs of Freedom, 1855.

CHANNING, WILLIAM ELLERY. Anti-Slavery Papers. 1836–1842.

CHILD, MRS. LYDIA MARIA. The Evils of Slavery and Cure of Slavery. 1836.

MARTINEAU, HARRIET. Society in America. 1837.

COOPER, JAMES FENIMORE. Homeward Bound, 1838; Home as Found, 1838; The American Democrat, 1838.

WHITTIER, JOHN G. "Massachusetts to Virginia." 1840.

LONGFELLOW, HENRY W. Poems on Slavery. 1842.

Anonymous. The Virginia Philosopher, or Few Lucky Slave-Catchers, by Mr. Latimer's Brother. 1843.

EMERSON, RALPH WALDO. Miscellanies. Works, Vol. XI: "Emancipation in the British West Indies, " Address at Concord, August 1, 1844; "The Fugitive Slave Law," Address at Concord, May 3, 1851; "The Assault on Kansas," Cambridge, September 10, 1856; "Speech on Affairs in Kansas," Cambridge, September 10, 1856; "Speeches on John Brown," Boston, November 18, 1859, and Salem, January 6, 1860.

LOWELL, JAMES RUSSELL. "The Present Crisis." 1845.

WHITMAN, WALT. The Uncollected Poetry and Prose. Vol. I (edited by Emory Holloway, 1921): "Slavers and the Slave Trade," 1846; "New States: Shall They be Slave or Free?" 1847; "American Workingmen versus Slavery," 1857.

LOWELL, JAMES RUSSELL. The Biglow Papers. First series, June, 1846–September, 1848.

MELVILLE, HERMAN. Mardi. 1849.

PARKER, THEODORE. Anti-Slavery Papers. Centenary Edition, Vols. XI, XII, XIV. 1847–1860.

STOWE, MRS. HARRIET BEECHER. Uncle Tom's Cabin. 1852.

SIMMS, WILLIAM GILMORE, and others. The Pro-Slavery Argument. 1852.

STOWE, MRS. HARRIET BEECHER. A Key to Uncle Tom's Cabin. 1853.

ADAMS, FRANCIS C. Uncle Tom at Home, a Review of the Reviewers and Repudiators, etc. 1853.

A Lady in New York. The Patent Key to Uncle Tom's Cabin. 1853.

HALE, SARAH J. Liberia; or Mr. Peyton's Experiments. 1853.

SUMNER, CHARLES. "The Crime against Kansas." 1856.

WHITMAN, WALT. "The Eighteenth Presidency." 1856. (Written but not published at the time. See "Walt Whitman's Workshop," edited by C. J. Furness, pp. 87–113.)

Anonymous. "The Duty of Southern Authors" and "An Inquiry into the Present State of Southern Literature," *Southern Literary Messenger*, Vol. XXXIII (October and November, 1856), pp. 241, 387.

STOWE, MRS. H. B. Dred, a Tale of the Great Dismal Swamp. 1856.

HELPER, HINTON R. The Impending Crisis of the South: How to Meet It. 1857.

STOWE, MRS. H. B. The Minister's Wooing. 1859.

CIVIL WAR VERSE

General

ELLINGER, ESTHER P. The Southern War Poetry of the Civil War. 1918.

HOLLIDAY, CARL. A History of Southern Literature. 1906.

HOLLIDAY, CARL. Three Centuries of Southern Poetry. 1908.

MATTHEWS, BRANDER. "The Songs of the Civil War." Pen and Ink. 1894.

MOSES, MONTROSE J. The Literature of the South. 1910.

PREBLE, GEORGE H. "National and Patriotic Songs." History of the Flag of the United States. 1880.

SINE, EDWARD W. The Civil War Poetry of the North, 1861–1865. University of Buffalo Studies. 1932–1933.

Older Collections

ALDERMAN, E. A., and others. "Fugitive and Anonymous Poems." Library of Southern Literature, Vol. XIV, pp. 6081–6129.
BRAINERD, C. S. Old War Songs, North and South. 1887.
BROCK, SALLIE A. The Southern Amaranth. 1869.
BROWNE, FRANCIS F. Bugle-Echoes: a Collection of the Poetry of the Civil War. 1886.
EGGLESTON, GEORGE CARY. American War Ballads and Lyrics. 1889.
FAGAN, WILLIAM L. Southern War Songs. 1890.
HUBNER, CHARLES W. War Poets of the South and Confederate Camp-Fire Songs. 1896.
MASON, EMILY V. Southern Poems of the War. 1867.
MOORE, FRANK. Songs and Ballads of the Southern People, 1861–1865. 1886.
SIMMS, WILLIAM GILMORE. War Poetry of the South. 1866.
TRENT, WILLIAM P. Southern Writers. Selections in Prose and Verse. 1905.
WHARTON, HENRY M. War Songs and Poems of the Southern Confederacy. 1904.
WHITE, RICHARD GRANT. Poetry of the Civil War. 1866.

More Recent Anthologies

BOYNTON, PERCY H. American Poetry. 1918.
FOERSTER, NORMAN. American Poetry and Prose (rev. ed.). 1934.
PAGET, R. L. (pseud.). Poems of American Patriotism. 1925.
PRESCOTT and SANDERS. An Introduction to American Poetry. 1932.
STEVENS, RUTH D. and DAVID H. American Patriotic Prose and Verse. 1917.
STEVENSON, BURTON E. Poems of American History (rev. ed.). 1922.
WANN, LOUIS. The Rise of Realism. 1933.
WYNN, WILLIAM T. Southern Literature; Selections and Biographies. 1932.

THE FORMAL LITERATURE OF THE SOUTH

General

ALDERMAN, E. A., and others (Eds.). The Library of Southern Literature. 17 vols. 1909–1923.
BASKERVILL, WILLIAM M., and others. Southern Writers. 1896–1911.
BRADSHAW, SIDNEY E. On Southern Poetry Prior to 1860. University of Virginia Studies in Literature, No. I. 1900.
ECKENRODE, H. J. "Sir Walter Scott and the South," *North American Review*, Vol. CCVI, pp. 598–603.
FULTON, MAURICE G. Southern Life in Southern Literature. 1917.
HARRISON, M. C. Social Types in Southern Prose Fiction. 1931.
HOLLIDAY, CARL. A History of Southern Literature. 1906.
LANDRUM, GRACE W. "Sir Walter Scott and His Literary Rivals in the Old South," *American Literature*, Vol. II, pp. 256–276.

MINOR, BENJAMIN B. The Southern Literary Messenger. 1905.
MOSES, MONTROSE J. The Literature of the South. 1910.
RUTHERFORD, MILDRED L. The South in History and Literature. 1907.
SMITH, C. ALPHONSO. Southern Literary Studies. 1927.
WYNN, WILLIAM T. (Ed.). Southern Literature. Selections and Biographies. 1932.

Writers

WILLIAM ALEXANDER CARUTHERS. The Kentuckian in New York, or The Adventures of Three Southerns (2 vols.), 1834; The Cavaliers of Virginia, or The Recluse of Jamestown (2 vols.), 1834–1835; The Knights of the Horse-Shoe; a Traditionary Tale of the Cocked Hat Gentry, 1845.

[*Available Edition*]

Knights of the Horse-Shoe. 1927.

[*Biography and Criticism*]

ALLEN, E. P. "Notes on William Alexander Caruthers," *William and Mary Quarterly*, Vol. IX, pp. 294–297.
JOHNSON, JAMES G. Southern Fiction Prior to 1860. 1909.
PARRINGTON, VERNON L. "William Alexander Caruthers, a Virginia Liberal." The Romantic Revolution in America, pp. 41–46. 1927.

THOMAS HOLLEY CHIVERS. Chief works: The Lost Pleiad; and Other Poems, 1845; Eonchs of Ruby. A Gift of Love, 1851; Memoralia; or Phials of Amber Full of the Tears of Love, 1853; Virginalia; or, Songs of My Summer Nights, 1853; Conrad and Eudora; or, The Death of Alonzo. A Tragedy in five Acts. Founded on the Murder of Sharpe by Beauchampe, in Kentucky. 1834.

[*Available Edition*]

"Thomas Holley Chivers; a Selection," edited by Lewis Chase. The Oglethorpe Book of Georgia Verse. 1929.

[*Biography and Criticism*]

BELL, LANDON C. Poe and Chivers. 1931.
BENTON, JOEL. In the Poe Circle. 1899.
DAMON, S. FOSTER. Thomas Holley Chivers, Friend of Poe. 1930.
HUNEKER, JAMES G. "A Precursor of Poe." The Pathos of Distance. 1913.
NEWCOMER, ALPHONSO G. "The Poe-Chivers Controversy Re-examined," *Sewanee Review*, Vol. XII, No. 1.
RICHARDSON, WARFIELD C. "Who Was Chivers?" *Boston Transcript*, April 24, 1897.
TOWNSEND, JOHN W. "Thomas Holley Chivers." Library of Southern Literature, Vol. II, pp. 845–849.

JOHN ESTEN COOKE. Chief novels: The Virginia Comedians (2 vols.), 1854; Surrey of Eagle's Nest, 1866; Hilt to Hilt, 1869; Mohum, 1869; Stories of the Old Dominion, 1879.

[*Available Editions*]

Hilt to Hilt. 1896.
Surrey of Eagle's Nest. Popular Edition. 1894.
The Virginia Comedians. 1883.

[*Biography and Bibliography*]

BEATY, JOHN OWEN. John Esten Cooke, Virginian. 1922.
WEGELIN, OSCAR. A Bibliography of the Separate Writings of John Esten Cooke. 1925.

JOHN PENDLETON KENNEDY. Chief titles: Swallow Barn: or, A Sojourn in the Old Dominion, 1832; Horse-Shoe Robinson: a Tale of the Tory Ascendency, 1835; Rob of the Bowl, a Legend of St. Inigoes, 1838; Quodlibet, 1840; At Home and Abroad: Essays, with a Journal in Europe, 1867–1868, 1872.

[*Available Editions*]

Horse-Shoe Robinson (rev. ed.), 1883. Condensed for Schools. Standard Library Series, Vol. X. 1897.
Swallow Barn, edited, with introduction, by Jay B. Hubbell. American Authors Series. 1929.

[*Biography and Criticism*]

GWATHMEY, EDWARD M. John Pendleton Kennedy. 1931.
MOORE, JOHN R. "Kennedy's Horse-Shoe Robinson: Fact or Fiction?" *American Literature,* Vol, IV, pp. 160–167.
TUCKERMAN, HENRY T. Life of John Pendleton Kennedy. 1871.
UHLER, JOHN E. "Kennedy's Novels and His Posthumous Works," *American Literature,* Vol. III, pp. 471–479.
WINTHROP, ROBERT C. (Ed.). Tributes to the Memory of John Pendleton Kennedy. 1870.

AUGUSTUS BALDWIN LONGSTREET. Georgia Scenes, 1835; Stories with a Moral (n. d.).

[*Available Editions*]

Georgia Scenes (new ed.). 1897.
Stories with a Moral, edited by Fitz R. Longstreet. 1912.

[*Biography and Criticism*]

PARRINGTON, VERNON L. "Augustus Longstreet." The Romantic Revolution in America. 1927.
WADE, JOHN D. Augustus Longstreet, a Study of the Development of Culture in the South. 1924.

EDWARD COOTE PINKNEY. Rodolph and Other Poems, 1823; Poems, 1825; Poems (2d ed.), 1838; Miscellaneous Poems, 1844.

[*Available Edition*]

"Poems and Literary Prose." Mabbott Life of Pinkney. 1926.

[*Biography and Criticism*]

HUBNER, CHARLES W. Representative Southern Poets. 1906.

MABBOTT, THOMAS O., and PLEADWELL, F. L. The Life and Works of Edward Coote Pinkney. A Memoir and Complete Text of His Poems and Literary Prose. 1926.

MELTON, W. F. "Edward Coote Pinkney," *South Atlantic Quarterly*, Vol. XI, pp. 328–336.

ROSS, C. H. "Edward Coate Pinkney," *Sewanee Review*, Vol. IV, pp. 287–298.

WILLIAM GILMORE SIMMS. Chief titles: Guy Rivers: a Tale of Georgia (2 vols.), 1834; Charlemont; or, The Pride of the Village, 1856; Richard Hurdis; or, The Avenger of Blood (2 vols.), 1838; Beauchampe; or, The Kentucky Tragedy (2 vols.), 1842; Border Beagles: A Tale of Mississippi (2 vols.), 1840; The Yemassee: A Romance of South Carolina (2 vols.), 1835; The Cassique of Kiawah. A Colonial Romance, 1859.

[*Available Editions*]

Works of Simms. Uniform Edition. Illustrated by Darley. 20 vols. 1853–1866.

The Yemassee, edited for school use. Standard Library Series. 1898.

The Yemassee. Johnson's English Classics. 1911.

[*Biography and Criticism*]

ERSKINE, JOHN. Leading American Novelists, pp. 131–274. 1910.

TRENT, W. P. William Gilmore Simms. A. M. L. Series. 1891.

VAN DOREN, CARL. The American Novel, pp. 60–66. 1921.

WHALEY, G. W. "A Note on Simms's Novels," *American Literature*, Vol. II, pp. 173–174.

[*Bibliographies*]

SALLEY, A. S. A Bibliography of William Gilmore Simms. 1897.

TRENT, W. P. William Gilmore Simms. 1891.

Cambridge History of American Literature, Vol. I, pp. 540–544.

[*Anthologies for the Southern Group*]

ALDERMAN and others. Library of Southern Literature, Vols. II, VII, IX, XI.

BECKER, MAY LAMBERTON. Golden Tales of the Old South. 1930.

FOERSTER, NORMAN. American Prose and Poetry (rev. ed.). 1934.

FULTON, MAURICE G. Southern Life in Southern Literature. 1917.

McDOWELL, TREMAINE. The Romantic Triumph. 1933.

MIMS, EDWIN, and PAYNE, B. R. Southern Prose and Poetry. 1910.

WYNN, WILLIAM T. Southern Literature. 1932.

EDGAR ALLAN POE. The chief works appeared as follows: Tamerlane and Other Poems, 1827; Al Aaraaf, Tamerlane and Minor Poems, 1829; The Narrative of Arthur Gordon Pym of Nantucket, 1838; Tales of the Grotesque and Arabesque, 1840; The Prose Romances of Edgar A. Poe, 1843; The Raven and Other Poems, 1845; Tales, 1845; Eureka: a Prose Poem, 1848; The Literati, 1850.

[*Available Editions*]

The Works of Edgar Allan Poe. Virginia Edition. Edited by James A. Harrison. 17 vols. 1902.

The Works of Edgar Allan Poe, edited by E. C. Stedman and G. E. Woodberry. 10 vols. 1894–1895.

Best single-volume editions are:

The Book of Poe; Tales, Criticism, and Poems, edited, with introduction, by Addison Hibbard. 1929.

The Poems of Edgar Allan Poe, edited by Killis Campbell. 1917.

Poems of Edgar Allan Poe, edited by J. H. Whitty. 1917.

Poems of Edgar Allan Poe, edited, with introduction, by Howard Mumford Jones. 1929.

Selected Poems of Edgar Allan Poe, edited, with introduction, by Thomas O. Mabbott. 1928.

Selections from Poe's Literary Criticism, edited by J. B. Moore. 1926.

Tales of Edgar Allan Poe, edited by J. S. Wilson. 1927.

[*Biography and Criticism*]

The standard life of Poe is by George E. Woodberry. 1884.

ALLEN, HERVEY. Israfel: the Life and Times of Edgar Allan Poe. 2 vols. 1926.

BAUDELAIRE, CHARLES. Edgar Poe, sa vie et ses œuvres. 1856.

BOYNTON, PERCY H. "Poe and Journalism," *English Journal*, Vol. XXI, pp. 345–352.

BROWNELL, WILLIAM CRARY. American Prose Masters. 1909.

CAMPBELL, KILLIS. "Edgar Allan Poe." Cambridge History of American Literature, Vol. II, Book II.

CAMPBELL, KILLIS. The Mind of Poe, and Other Studies. 1933.

DAUGHRITY, K. L. "Poe and *Blackwood's*," *American Literature*, Vol. II, pp. 289–292.

FORREST, WILLIAM M. Biblical Allusions in Poe. 1928.

FRANCE, ANATOLE. La vie littéraire, Vol. IV. 1925.

GATES, LEWIS E. Studies and Appreciations. 1900.

GRISWOLD, RUFUS W. Memoir of Poe (with Poe's Works). 1850–1856.

HARRISON, JAMES A. Life and Letters of Poe. 1903.

HUNGERFORD, E. "Poe and Phrenology," *American Literature*, Vol. II, pp. 209–231.

HUTTON, R. H. Contemporary Thought and Thinkers. 1900.

INGRAM, J. H. Life, Letters, and Opinions of Poe. 1880.

KENT, CHARLES W. Poe the Poet. Vol. VII of Virginia Edition of Poe's Works. 1902.

KRUTCH, JOSEPH WOOD. Edgar Allan Poe, a Study in Genius. 1926.

LANG, ANDREW. Letters to Dead Authors. 1886.

LAUVRIÈRE, E. Edgar Poe: sa vie et son œuvre. 1904.

MACY, JOHN. Edgar Allan Poe. Beacon Biographies. 1907.

MINOR, BENJAMIN B. The Southern Literary Messenger, 1834–1864. 1905.

MORE, PAUL ELMER. Shelburne Essays. First series. 1906.

MOSES, MONTROSE J. Literature of the South. 1910.

PATTEE, FRED LEWIS. Side-lights on American Literature. 1922.

POPE-HENNESSY, UNA. Edgar Allan Poe, . . . a Critical Biography. 1934.

STOVALL, FLOYD. "Poe as a Poet of Ideas." University of Texas Studies in English No. 11. 1931.

WENDELL, BARRETT. Stelligeri and Other Essays. 1893.

WILT, NAPIER. "Poe's Attitude toward His Tales: a New Document," *Modern Philology*, Vol. XXV, pp. 101–105.

WOODBERRY, GEORGE EDWARD. America in Literature. 1908.

Poe articles in *American Literature*, March, 1934: Louise Pound, "On Poe's 'The City in the Sea'"; Ernest Marchand, "Poe as Social Critic"; Joseph S. Schick, "The Origin of 'The Cask of Amontillado.'" "Notes and Queries," by Lewis Chase, Joy Bayless, Emma K. Norman, William S. Hoole.

Studies in English No. 10. University of Texas Bulletin No. 3026. July, 1930. Several Poe articles.

[*Bibliography*]

CAMPBELL, KILLIS. "Poe Bibliography." Cambridge History of American Literature, Vol. II, pp. 452–468.

HEARTMAN, CHARLES F. A Census of First Editions and Source Materials of Edgar Allan Poe in American Collections. 1932.

ROBERTSON, JOHN W. Bibliography of the Works of Edgar Allan Poe. 2 vols. 1934.

STEDMAN, E. C., and WOODBERRY, G. E. Works of Poe, Vol. X.

CHAPTER IX

Metropolitan Convention and Revolt

Theater, Drama, and Press in the 1850's

THE decade before the Civil War was a time of unfulfillments. There was a promise in the 1830's, an expectation in the 1840's. At the passing of the mid-century mark the prospect was brilliant. The seven years (1849–1855) that included "Mardi" and "Moby Dick," "The Scarlet Letter" and "The House of the Seven Gables," "Uncle Tom's Cabin," "Walden," "Hiawatha," and "Leaves of Grass" are hard to rival in the annals of America. But the early 1850's were merely harvest time for the preceding decades. Only "Uncle Tom" was generated by the times; only "Hiawatha" was also popular. For the rest neither the works nor the authors were influential on the American people. Melville slipped out of the picture, in which he had been only a faint background figure, Hawthorne left the country for the last seven years of the decade, Lowell withdrew from the arena to the study, Whitman decided to keep out of the fray. And the foreshadowings of the war were quite as inimical to the arts as the actual years of fighting. It was a time for statistics of progress and prosperity. The population increased by a third during the decade; United States patents, by 300 per cent; railroad mileage, equally fast. The Western Union Telegraph Company linked the Atlantic coast with the Pacific; Field's ocean cable linked New York with London. Magazine subscriptions were multiplied fourfold. The theater gained a permanent footing on the Gold Coast.

Perhaps that is the most memorable fact to recite about the theater in the 50's: like everything else in the country, it expanded. It did not improve; nor did it in any distinguished way add to its stature by the increase in native plays, though they multiplied almost as fast as the magazine circulation was doing. Yet stage and drama deserve passing attention once more; for they represented, as the periodicals also did, the active popular taste of the day. So considered, of course, two questions should be asked about them with reference to any period: What do they reveal on the average? What do they reveal in terms of the best?

With reference to the theatrical map two facts are important: since the 1830's Chicago had become a center of more significance than St. Louis and shared the same general features with Boston and New York stagedom; and San Francisco was big enough in population and lavish enough in rewards to attract the Eastern players who had any dash of adventure in them, and was getting ready to offer a practical education to one of the pre-eminent coming producers, David Belasco. In the 1830's if one looked westward from a New York stage, he looked to the Ohio and Mississippi rivers and, eventually, to New Orleans. In the 1850's he looked to the foot of the Great Lakes, across the plains, and eventually to Salt Lake City and the Pacific coast.

The already cited[1] public avidity for shows instead of plays in the main producing centers was waxing with the years; and of course it was being capitalized as nothing in the amusement world had ever been capitalized before by the prince of advertisers and exploiters, P. T. Barnum. His achievement in "selling" Jenny Lind to the American public in 1850 was without parallel; and the excellence of the musical commodity which he offered then gave him a prestige which enhanced the values of everything else he had to offer — from the various freaks in his exhibition halls, culminating with directions "to the Egress," to the various songs, acts, and plays with which he enriched the programs of his so-called museums. But Barnum was meeting a rival attraction in the

---

[1] Pages 284–286.

vogue of the minstrel show and the growth of what was described as Ethiopian drama. Neither the men who gave the shows, nor the dialogue, nor the music were Ethiopian or even honest American Negro; fidelity to these details and the extensive use of Negro actors in light or serious drama had to wait until the present century, but the patter and the pattern of the minstrel show won their audience and held their form for a round half-century. In the meanwhile the "animal shows" continued to draw their audiences, child actors were still attempting their interpretations of adult roles, and women were still affecting men's parts.

In organization the theaters continued to be run by means of resident stock companies, opening and closing seasons with their own productions, but largely supporting the itinerant stars; and these stars continued to supply the stage with a measure of standard drama, as the standard plays supplied them with parts through which they could display their virtuosity. This practice maintained Shakespeare as a constant in the seasons' repertories, while many of the other older favorites were going into decline. Of the eighteenth-century plays only Goldsmith's and Sheridan's held their own through the decade; and, in spite of all advertising, none of the nine Forrest prize plays[1] succeeded in the struggle for survival. Native drama was not yet a staple product in America. Of a hundred and twelve plays presented in Chicago in one season at the middle of the century, ninety-one were English, five were French and German, and sixteen were American. Moreover, of the American plays seven were Yankee dramas, the most popular being "Sam Patch in France," and three of the remaining nine were in foreign settings.

As the decade ran on, one fresh application of an old type of comedy appeared. This was the "Life in London" potpourri done over into the American idiom. Pierce Egan had paved the way for the type, and the various Jonathan plays prepared the entrance for the character when Baker's

[1] See page 287.

"Glance at New York" proved to be the first big success at a city play centering round a grown-up street urchin, Mose the Fireman. Before long Mose became a recurrent figure, like the Yankee of former days; and, like the Yankee, he wandered — to Philadelphia, to California, to China. He recurred in "Mose, Three Years After," and he revived his English predecessors in "Life in New York, or Tom and Jerry on a Visit." He was a sign of the times, too, in replacing the rural comic favorite with a comic urban character. Chicago welcomed him in the original plays, but soon had a "Chicago Fireman" of her own, just as she soon had "Chloroform, or Chicago One Hundred Years Hence" from a similar Manhattan prototype; there was a "Boston Fireman," too, as well as, for this port, a "Boston Caulker."

Plays of the sort would seem to indicate that the American stage was freeing itself at last (in this modest way at least) from the long domination of British playwrights, actors, and producers; but the two most energetic and original figures in the picture at this time point to the contrary, for they were a pair of roving Irishmen — Dion Boucicault and John Brougham. They were both born in the Emerald Isle; both first trained on the foreign stage; both, in decreasing scale, playwright-actor-producers; both professional sources of supply for the current stage, much as William Dunlap had been[1] and as Augustin Daly and Clyde Fitch and Augustus Thomas were to be.[2] Like these others, they were barometers for the taste of the times because their powers and their originalities were largely confined to supplying what theatergoers wanted, and their energies largely expended as adapters and dramatizers rather than as creative authors. There were no creative artists writing for the American stage in those days; but neither were there any in England. None can be named to correspond with the leading poets or novelists.

In these dull days, then, Boucicault and Brougham came to New York, both arriving in the early 1840's, leaving a

---

[1] Pages 186–188.

[2] Page 825.

country which seemed not to offer them careers, and bringing to the New World nothing fresh beyond fresh personalities, enthusiasm and energy, and a gift, which belongs peculiarly to the journalist, of finding out how the winds of fashion were shifting and how to trim their sails thereto. One further talent was of great importance: both of them "knew their theater," and could give the genuinely dramatic touch which made plays playable as well as merely recitable. Naturally enough they became dominant dramatic modistes for New York and, through New York, for the country.

For example, dramatized narrative was established in public favor before either Boucicault or Brougham came to America. Byron and Scott were popular on the stage in the 30's;[1] Irving, Cooper, Dumas, Charlotte Brontë, Bulwer Lytton, were among the early contributors of plots; Dickens was pirated onto the stage from the day when "Pickwick Papers" was first launched on the series of twenty-seven recorded versions in the American theater. Of them all he was the most fruitful source for the playwright, from one to eight versions of each of his novels and six of his shorter tales appearing on the boards in this country. This being the case, Boucicault took his toll with "Dot" and "Smike" in 1859 (from "The Cricket on the Hearth" and "Nicholas Nickleby"); Brougham, with "Dombey" in 1848 and 1850, "David Copperfield" in 1851, and "Bleak House" in 1853. With the climax of Dickens's popularity in the United States, after the readings in the early winter of 1867, Brougham returned to the vein in "The Old Curiosity Shop" and "Our Mutual Friend." British craftsmen were supplying the American public with an Englishman's stories. Again, Boucicault and Brougham both saw the turn in preferences that was to bring the French drama in America back to the position it had enjoyed through the efforts of Dunlap and Payne.[2] Boucicault adapted from this source even more than Payne did, and in his enthusiasm translated a French drama-

[1] Page 289.

[2] Page 188.

tization of Dickens without recognizing its origin. Impartial as to their material, they drew it also from the land of their adoption: Boucicault with the popular city plays, with "The Octoroon" (a slavery play), and later with "Bell Lamar," a Civil War play in which he anticipated the best effects in "Shenandoah," "Secret Service," and "Alabama"; Brougham with his own city plays, with "Franklin," with his slave play "Dred." It was characteristic that Mrs. Stowe led the way for both the imported playwrights in treatment of the slavery problem, that neither attempted an arrangement of "Uncle Tom," and that both followed at a respectful distance of several years when the ground was well trodden. As Irishmen they did bring something to the American stage. Brougham was most distinguished as an actor of Irish gentlemen. Boucicault, beginning with "Colleen Bawn" in 1860, contributed a whole succession of Irish plays to the stage on both sides of the Atlantic. And there were plenty of playgoers of Irish descent along the American seacoast to acknowledge them as part of the American heritage.

However, their richest contribution was in the writing and playing of the burlesques, which they raised to new levels by their joint talents. These were Brougham's compositions, though he was simply carrying on a practice already established. No popular story was free from the risk of literary caricature. "Mazeppa" and "Uncle Tom's Cabin" were inevitably parodied. So were "Esmeralda," "The Bohemian Girl," and "Camille." Shakespeare, of course, was a target, with a "Hamlet" and a "Macbeth" and a "Much Ado about the Merchant of Venice." This last was Brougham's, as were "Don Kayser de Bassoon" and "Lucy Did Sham Amour." He did a "Metamora" and a "Hiawatha" too, but he was particularly proud of his "Columbus" and particularly successful in his "Po-ca-hon-tas," which he played with Boucicault. Memory still echoes the uproarious delight of the winter audience who saw these two comedians carry through a production of the early Virginia story on an occasion when the leading lady had seen fit to elope, and the seasoned veterans, meditating aloud on her failure to pick up cues, carried the performance to a triumphant conclusion. These burlesques, according to report, were almost perfect of their kind and pointed the way down the years toward Weber and Field and the tabloid parodies in the more recent "reviews."

It remained, however, for Boucicault to take one step in theatrical management that was perhaps of more widespread and lasting influence than anything he or Brougham ever wrote. Like many another impractical man, he was much concerned with money returns, though incapable of fully collecting them or of saving what he did collect. In 1860, eager to increase his earnings as an author and unprotected by adequate copyright provisions for dramatists, he undertook to send out from New York a traveling company with one of his plays. The plan worked, and its consequences were to be beyond anything Boucicault intended or could have foreseen. First of all, as traveling companies became the norm, the old resident stock companies, which supported traveling stars, were gradually superseded. This in turn meant that the main school of the thespian, in which he played with leading actors in a great number of standard productions, was discontinued; and that the average player needed in the future to know little if anything about the acting drama or the best of stage tradition. It affected the playwright too, as well as the player; for, with the period of long runs now established, a production could hold the stage in New York for most or all of a season, other companies could tour the country with it, and the motive for presenting new plays either in the theatrical center or on the road was weakened. There is little in the mid-century period to make the modern student think that many masterpieces were lost as a result of this, but it did doubtless reduce the dramatic output in terms of staged plays. In a word, an immigrant producing playwright, eager to fill his own perennially empty purse just at a time when the railroad mileage had been multiplied manyfold, had an idea which, by putting complete productions on the theatrical circuit, resulted in reorganizing the theater business, the actor's education, and the dramatic output of the country. A full generation later these developments were to evolve into the formation of a theatrical syndicate which turned the theatrical field into a vast booking agency under which playwriters, players, and producers were puppets manipulated from behind the box office.[1]

Of the periodicals of the 1850's the generalizations are substantially the same as of the theater. Broadly speaking, the taste of the American magazine reader was not asserting itself in a demand for anything native in quality. The most marked measure of the decade is quantitative: in 1850 there were about one hundred monthly periodicals; in 1860, just short of three hundred. Of all these less than one tenth survived until 1870, and only a quarter of that fraction until 1933. In fact, the mortality of the longest-lived was particularly heavy after the World War; they so evidently partook of another age, and died either of senescence or of ill-advised experiments in rejuvenation.

The magazines as a group were the output of a generation of publishers who considered that their subscribers wanted particularly the informative and the edifying. The eclectic, scissors-and-pastepot periodicals flourished on the reprinting of foreign matter which the looseness of copyright regulations still permitted without payment. *Littell's Living Age* was thriving; and *Harper's Magazine*, founded as the decade opened, belonged in this class until it learned that the encouragement of native contributors would pay better. Among the edifying publications were, of course, the magazines of particular causes, notably of temperance and of antislavery, the latter at the height of their activity in these years and certain of discontinuation when the cause was won in the 60's. In contrast to these controversial monthlies, the rank and file of periodicals with original material, evidently seeking

---

[1] Robert Grau, "The Business Man in the Amusement World," 1910.

for large and steady subscription lists, were frankly committed only to the negative policy of printing nothing that would estrange readers who had fixed convictions about the problems of the day. They were inevitably flabby and opinionless. The most popular of them all, *Godey's Lady's Book,* compounded with fate, however, by the ingenious method of creating its own causes and espousing activity or reform on matters hitherto undiscussed, like the completion of Bunker Hill Monument, the improvement of home architecture (which it helped to debase), higher education for women, labor-saving for the housewife.

With the exceptions of *Godey's,* which boasted in 1850 that it was sent to every state and territory in the country, and of the *Spirit of the Times* (of which more later), the periodicals of the decade were either frankly or implicitly sectional in circulation and in tone. *The North American Review* seemed since its founding, in 1815, to have contracted its idea of the continent to Boston and its environs, amply justifying Holmes's quip about "the Hub of the Universe." *The Southern Quarterly* was forced by the pressure of Northern literary aggression and the provincial militancy of its editor, Simms,[1] to concentration on the policies and the "peculiar institution" of the South. In the literary field *The Knickerbocker* acknowledged its local allegiance in its title. *Graham's* drew for its material on many of the same contributors; supplemented it generously from its Philadelphia townsmen; built up a Northern circulation on which it thrived for most of the 40's and 50's; and forfeited what *Harper's* had not won from it when the editor, failing to recognize that by 1852 the North was anti-Southern and antislavery in sentiment, vigorously condemned "Uncle Tom's Cabin" as a graceless, untimely, unfair, inflammatory assault upon the South. In all the circumstances the *Southern Literary Messenger* was remarkable for its effort to proceed on a level emotional keel, though it was evidently enough a coastwise vessel sailing

---

[1] See pages 430–434.

from Richmond, Virginia. Even in the realm of agriculture there was no national journal. Three periodicals of those days are still extant. *The Prairie Farmer*, established in 1841, was circulated to a Western constituency from Chicago; the *Rural New Yorker*, 1849, reached the North and New England from Rochester; the *Southern Field and Fireside*, 1859, weathering the invasion soon to come, was published from Augusta, Georgia.

Three notable monthlies were founded in the decade—*Harper's* (1850); *The Atlantic* and *Russell's* (1857). The latter two represented Boston and Charleston, Massachusetts and South Carolina, with about equal distinction for the three years before *Russell's* was forced to discontinue — each the product of a highly localized group, each distinctly the work of a highly literary group, each committed to the tradition of polite letters addressed to a polite urban public. The early history of *Harper's Magazine*, when it was satisfied with borrowings from abroad, is significant in this connection; for it shows that in spite of the efforts of Graham and other magazinists the periodicals were almost as completely under English influence as were the theaters. This being so, the monthly which fostered American contributors was likely to foster the Brother Jonathans who were least different from the literary John Bulls.

Harper's was started in 1850, according to one of the members of the house of Harper, "as a tender to our business." The firm "saw an enormous reading public in a country of cheap literature and an immense store of material at their disposal in England, more various and more attractive than the home supply; and they resolved to bring the two together." With an unsung genius for a circulation manager they gained fifty thousand subscribers within six months and one hundred and fifty thousand within three years. They pirated serials from England or bought advance rights from English publishers who joined the Americans in defrauding English authors of all returns from American publication. The foreign contributions had the double advantage of costing little or nothing and of coming from authors of glamorous reputation. Occasional American contributors were engaged to write didactic articles that served as vehicles for the wood engravings with which each number was "embellished." Thus in the 50's *Harper's* figured partly as a menace and partly as a model for the magazine publishers who tried to promote native authorship. Only the adventurer or the outlaw would think of attempting to regale the American reader with essays or tales that genuinely smacked of the soil rather than of the dust from the bookshelf.

William T. Porter was such a literary adventurer, and his *Spirit of the Times*, which ran under three different titles and editorships from 1831 to 1861, supplied in the magazine field a perfect parallel to the Yankee, Jim Crow, and frontier plays and sketches in the theater of the same generation. The parallel is reinforced by the facts that Porter's patrons were the patrons of Yankee Hill and Dan Rice, and that formal criticism usually deplored or ignored both expressions of native Americanism. Porter and his weekly had to wait for polite recognition even longer than Mark Twain — until the very recent revival of interest in the frontier and the frontier development of native types.

Starting as a systematic borrower of British products, the *Spirit of the Times* announced in one subtitle that it was "A Gazette of the Literary, Fashionable and Sporting World," and in another that it was "A Chronicle of the Turf, Agriculture, Field Sports, Literature and the Stage." But before 1850 it evolved into something quite different — "the nucleus of a new order of literary talent . . . who furnished most valuable and interesting reminiscences of the pioneers of the far West . . . and in the course of a few years . . . the correspondents of *The Spirit of the Times* comprised a large majority of those who have subsequently distinguished themselves in this novel and original walk of literature."[1] In 1851 Porter was able to boast that among his

[1] W. T. Porter, "The Big Bear of Arkansas" (preface).

contributors, who included lawyers, doctors, journalists, soldiers, boatmen, and explorers, were eighteen members of Congress. As these contributors came from, or had lived on, the frontier, and as the weekly was published in New York, *The Spirit* was clearly national in its appeal. It was the appeal of the familiar to those who shared in the life it described; but also of the romantic to such a bookish enthusiast as the eulogist of Porter who wrote that the vein he had tapped "sparkled from the cheerful leisure of the easy scholar — poured in from the emulous officer in the barracks, or at sea — emanated spontaneously from the jocund poet — and flowed from every mead, or lake, or mountain — in the land where the rifle or the rod was known."[1] In the best collection of such sketches, "Tall Tales of the Southwest," almost a third were published or reprinted in Porter's weekly; and the doubtful reader may rest assured that they had none of the traits of easy scholarship or of the spontaneous jocundities of the poets, and that in them meads were called fields, rifles were called guns, and rods were called fishing poles. They were spontaneous and jocund, but they were the emanations of Southern and Western yarn-spinners. In this fact lay the distinction which, for the time being, made them unworthy in the minds of those who still were of the opinion that America afforded no material for literature — the gentry, like George H. Boker, who were saying, "Get out of your age as far as you can."

Herman Melville

If you seek [wrote Herman Melville[2]] to ascend Rock Rodondo, take the following prescription. Go three voyages round the world as a main-royal man of the tallest frigate that floats; then serve a year or two apprenticeship to the guides who conduct strangers up the Peak of Teneriffe; and as many more respectively to a rope-dancer, an Indian juggler, and a chamois. This done, come and be

[1] "Tall Tales of the Southwest" (edited by F. J. Meine), p. xxviii.

[2] References are to the Standard Edition of Melville's "Works" (16 vols.), Constable, 1922–1924.

rewarded by the view from our tower. How we got there, we alone know. If we sought to tell others, what the wiser were they? Suffice it, that here at the summit you and I stand. Does any balloonist, does the outlooking man in the moon, take a broader view of space? Much thus, one fancies, looks the universe from Milton's celestial battlements.[1]

It was Melville's comment to those who care to reach his vantage point and share his view. He was looking back on a hard, short, varied struggle among men, and he was on the verge of giving it up. Circumstance, even from boyhood, had always hemmed him in and frustrated him. In youth he had restively shipped on a merchantman. The attempt on his return to settle into village life had been fruitless. Soon he had set off again on a whaleship, this time for years on a broken voyage to the South Seas; and always thereafter the spell of the ocean had been upon him. It had given him story after story to tell, and it had given him time and place to make up his mind about life. Though he never returned to the sea, he never escaped from it. The life of the landsman was a life of restraint. The tyranny aboard ship surpassed any tyranny on land, and yet the seafarer was free; for the sea was a symbol to him of the innumerable dreams and shadows and far excursions of the soul that are the lives of men. Like a surrounding mystery it encircled his world and was itself the deep and fathomless soul that includes nature and mankind. To a symbolist and mystic it offered "glimpses . . . of that mortally intolerable truth; that all deep, earnest thinking is but the intrepid effort of the soul to keep the open independence of her sea; while the wildest winds of heaven and earth conspire to cast her on the treacherous, slavish shore."[2] It was in the brief years of his major tales of the sea that he did his lasting work. Starting with direct narrative and moving steadily toward allegory, he combined the two in one matchless book. Drawn back to "the treacherous, slavish shore," his narrative lost direction

---

[1] Melville, "Piazza Tales," p. 199.
[2] Melville, "Moby Dick," Vol. I, p. 133.

and his thinking, clearness. For the most part after the writing of "Moby Dick" he was fumbling along a fogbound coast.

"Typee" and "Omoo," a continuous chronicle, were the first literary result of Melville's experiences on the high seas and foreign soil. The escape from a luckless whaler and a tyrannical captain to the uplands of the island Nukuheva, the exposures and hardships of the first flight, the encounter with the cannibal natives, the idyllic life for months as captive-guest, and the sudden, thrilling escape occupy the earlier and better volume. The second tale records vicissitudes with a semi-mutinous crew on a run-down ship, a much mitigated penal captivity ashore, a vagrant and picturesque companionship with whites and Tahitians, and a further embarkation.

These tales of a traveler, "Typee" in particular, are an extraordinary achievement for a youth in the middle twenties. Without apparent effort he put character and action on the printed page, life and color so simply and vividly presented that they have never been surpassed for these islands. They offer a picture of a life to allure any victim of a driving northern civilization: soft climes and balmy airs, a relaxed and indolent people, a whole male population who loafed and invited their souls, and women who had little to do but exercise their graces. If ever natural conditions could permit such a life, it would be in this part of the world; here the island folk, neither savage nor noble, peacefully idled away their lives.

Coming from the realm of thrift and industry, Melville nevertheless wished them nothing better than their happy sloth; and because something much worse had been wished upon them by an invading race, he used his narrative as a vehicle for explosive information and opinion. It was not enough to describe the delights of South Sea life: he must inveigh against the civilization he had come from. Tongue in cheek, he compared the Typees with the unco guid of Anglo-Saxondom.

In truth, I regard the Typees as a back-slidden generation. They are sunk in religious sloth, and require a spiritual revival. A long prosperity of bread-fruit and cocoa-nuts has rendered them remiss in the performance of their higher obligations. The wood-rot malady is spreading among the idols — the fruit upon their altars is becoming offensive — the temples themselves need rethatching — the tattooed clergy are altogether too light-hearted and lazy — and their flocks are going astray.[1]

It is a mild parody of "Lycidas."

There was slight hope for the natives before the invading sailors, merchants, consuls, and missionaries. All contributed zealously to the downfall of the decadent paganism. They usurped and "improved" the best of land; for the natives never cultivated anything deliberately — neither coconuts, nor breadfruit, nor the vices of the civilized. On the heels of evangelization followed disease and depopulation that warfare could hardly rival.

Behold the glorious result! — The abominations of Paganism have given way to the pure rites of Christian worship — the ignorant savage has been supplanted by the refined European! Look at Honolulu, the metropolis of the Sandwich Islands! — A community of disinterested merchants, and devoted, self-exiled heralds of the Cross, located on the very spot that twenty years ago was defiled by the presence of idolatry. What a subject for an eloquent Bible-meeting orator! . . . Not until I visited Honolulu was I aware of the fact that the small remnant of the natives had been civilized into draught horses, and evangelized into beasts of burden.[2]

Recurrent observations of this sort led later critics into discussion of the romanticism of the humanist as over against the romanticism of the naturalist; at the moment they led representatives of church, state, and commerce to recrimination of Melville that resulted in numerous excisions by the timid publisher in the second edition of "Typee."[3] But the young author had documents behind his charges; and it would have been quite out of character if he had not,

---

[1] Melville, "Typee," p. 241. [2] Ibid. p. 264.
[3] Lewis Mumford, "Herman Melville," pp. 75–78.

for he was to become a confirmed, and sometimes it seems, incorrigible expositor and documentarian. He was a born factmonger. He knew nothing of the economy and unity that are always listed in the rhetorics as cardinal virtues of narrative.

> Sadly discursive as I have already been, I must still further entreat the reader's patience, as I am about to string together, without any attempt at order, a few odds and ends of things not hitherto mentioned, but which are either curious in themselves, or peculiar to the Typees.[1]

"Typee" and "Omoo" are stories; they are books of information; and they are books of opinion — the opinion, perhaps not broadly generalized, that life along the Hudson River has little to offer life in the mid-Pacific.

"Not long ago," Melville wrote in January, 1849, "having published two narratives of voyages in the Pacific, which, in many quarters, were received with incredulity, the thought occurred to me of indeed writing a romance of Polynesian adventure, and publishing it as such; to see whether the fiction might not, possibly, be received for a verity."[2] The result was "Mardi," the work in which the author, retaining all his feeling for the sea and the poetry thereof, passed over into the realm of allegory, from which he was not to return. At generous length the opening narrative parallels the opening events in the early third of "Typee": a seaman on a whaler endures the monotony of an unending voyage until at last he deserts. He survives the perils of the open ocean and comes to land. All this for a hundred and fifty pages is circumstantial and credible.

But the land to which he comes is a sort of cyclopedia of the known world, and his experiences are in the use of this vast reference book. As he enters the coastal waters he encounters a boat in which a priest and his attendant worshipers are taking to sacrifice a beautiful maiden, Yillah. He slays the priest and frees the maiden, who is Unattainable Beauty, and is soon lost, never to be recaptured. The re-

---

[1] Melville, "Typee," p. 304. [2] Melville, "Mardi" (preface).

mainder of the story is the quest, in which he is pursued by the avengers of the priest, and continually lured by the messengers of Carnal Love, Hautia.

The quest itself is a strange and fascinating Odyssey, made by five pilgrims: the narrator, a king, a poet, a teller of old chronicles and quaint tales, and a garrulous philosopher. They course through the world in search of Yillah on a voyage that seems at first unplanned, but that in fact is as systematic as a book of reference. In the early stages it is to a series of islands that represent types of living — the islands of the revelers, of the dreamers, of rogues, of gourmands, of the rich, of the warlike; the island of litigation; the island of civil strife. Then the world ceases to be typified and is localized. The voyagers, still seeking Happiness, go to Porpheera — Europe with all its recognizable kingdoms; to Dominora — England, with its adjacent Kaleedoni and Verdanna; and, farther away, to Vivenza, or America. Yillah is in none of these; could not survive in any. Finally the voyagers come to Serenia, a consistently Christian land; but in their worldly wisdom they reject it as a manifestly impracticable community, and Taji, the narrator, undeterrable in his quest, fares on alone, though not until he has discovered that the carnal love of Hautia is no compensation for the lost Yillah.

Now and again Melville offers reminders of what lies beneath the fantastic tale:

"And pray, what may you be driving at, philosopher?" interrupted Media.

"I am intent upon the essence of things; the mystery that lieth beyond; the elements of the tear which much laughter provoketh; that which is beneath the seeming; the precious pearl within the shaggy oyster. I probe the circle's center; I seek to evolve the inscrutable."[1]

"Meditate as much as you will, Babbalanja," [says the king at another time] "but say little aloud, unless in a merry and mythical

[1] Melville, "Mardi," Vol. II, p. 36.

way. Lay down the great maxims of things, but let inferences take care of themselves. Never be special; never, a partisan. In safety, afar off, you may batter down a fortress; but at your peril you essay to carry a single turret by escalade."[1]

Or once more:

"Now, then, Babbalanja," said Media, "what have you come to in all this rhapsody? You everlastingly travel in a circle."

"And so does the sun in heaven, my lord; like me, it goes round, and gives light as it goes."[2]

From "Mardi" to "White Jacket" was a natural step for Melville, and it was taken very quickly. After the experiences of "Typee" and "Omoo," which were factual though unbelieved, he made his return to the United States on a frigate. The voyage furnished the basis for "White Jacket." Like the first two stories, it is based on fact; like the third, it is filled with allegory; and like the coming "Moby Dick," it is cyclopedic in its information. It is the chronicle of a voyage with no superimposed plot. The frigate *Neversink* becomes what Mardi was, a microcosm of the world. The white jacket becomes the motley individuality which one may never discard, a thing of rags and patches, a disguise, a protection, a fateful burden. The book is compounded of meditation, myth, and maxim; but at one point it disregards the admonition of King Media, and attempts with signal success "to carry a single turret by escalade." Melville's indictment of the practice of flogging seamen resulted in congressional action that ended this abuse in the American navy.

There are fine characters and characterizations in the book. Jack Chase, captain of the top, is a splendid figure. There are thrilling episodes told with masterly skill. Yet through them all, sometimes subordinated but never forgotten, is pursued "the one proper object," to picture "the world in a man-of-war." This world is freighted with passengers who, though fate-ridden, are yet possessed of free will. After his life in the forecastle Melville could not be other than sobered

---

[1] Melville, "Mardi," Vol. II, p. 56. [2] Ibid. p. 161.

and sophisticated. Yet he came out from the years of duress with a simple, homely, still orthodox creed: fate rules impartially, but fate itself is controlled by mankind. "I have a voice that helps to shape eternity; and my volitions stir the orbits of the furthest suns. . . . Ourselves are Fate."[1] He turns frank exhorter in the anticlimactic passage with which the chronicle ends:

> Oh, shipmates and world-mates, all round! we the people suffer many abuses. Our gun-deck is full of complaints. In vain from Lieutenants do we appeal to the Captain; in vain — while on board our world-frigate — to the indefinite Navy Commissioners, so far out of sight aloft. Yet the worst of our evils we blindly inflict upon ourselves; our officers cannot remove them, even if they would. From the last ills no being can save another; therein each man must be his own saviour. For the rest, whatever befall us, let us never train our murderous guns inboard; let us not mutiny with bloody pikes in our hands. Our Lord High Admiral will yet interpose; and though long ages should elapse, and leave our wrongs unredressed, yet, shipmates and world-mates! Let us never forget, that
>
> Whoever afflict us, whatever surround,
> Life is a voyage that's homeward bound.[2]

"Typee" was written, "Omoo," and "Redburn," the tale of his earliest voyage of all; beyond the chronicles of fact the romantic allegory "Mardi," great achievement, was written; "White Jacket" was written, and allegory was united with fact as well as with romance. But as yet Melville had not resorted to the richest of all his materials — whalers, whales, and whaling. In the order of things it was for him to turn to this next. "But we that write and print," he recorded in a letter of the time, "have all our books predestinated — and for me, I shall write such things as the Great Publisher of mankind ordained ages before he published the World!"[3] In such mood he undertook "Moby Dick."

> . . . If by any possibility, there be any as yet undiscovered prime thing in me; if I shall ever deserve any real repute in that small but

[1] Melville, "White Jacket," p. 404. [2] Ibid. p. 504.
[3] Melville, letter to Duyckinck, London, December 14, 1849.

high hushed world which I might not be unreasonably ambitious of; if hereafter I shall do anything that, upon the whole, a man might rather have done than to have left undone; if, at my death, my executors, or more properly my creditors, find any precious MSS. in my desk, then here I prospectively ascribe all the honour and the glory to whaling; for a whale-ship was my Yale College and my Harvard.[1]

So he declares in the midst, characteristically, of his greatest work. Beyond a doubt it was in this Odyssean college that he learned the way to proceed with his story: "There are some enterprises in which a careful disorderliness is the true method."[2]

There are few adventures among masterpieces equal to sailing the high seas with Captain Ahab. Like most other colossal stories, "Moby Dick" has its offering to submit to every degree of literary acumen. On the surface it is the story of Captain Ahab, long ago maimed in an encounter with the terror of the South Seas, of his consuming hatred for the monster, and of the voyage for revenge that ends in fatal conflict with the foe. Two thirds of the chapters have been culled to present this chase in the form of a so-called "boys' book." Yet even so presented the story contains more than meets the eye.

Beneath this tale of whaling adventure, greatest of its kind, is the story of Eve or of Prometheus, the perennial story of man's struggle for spiritual victory in a world of harassing circumstance and in a world where fate opposes the individual in the form of his own thwarting self. "All visible objects, man," says Ahab, desperately, "are but as pasteboard masks. But in each event — in the living act, the undoubted deed — there, some unknown but still reasoning thing puts forth the mouldings of its features from behind the unreasoning mask. If man will strike, strike through the mask! How can the prisoner reach outside, except by thrusting through the wall?"[3] So Ahab maneuvers for the stroke, combats the world about him, seeks the unattainable revenge, even as the

[1] Melville, "Moby Dick," Vol. I, p. 139. [2] Ibid. Vol. II, p. 101. [3] Ibid. Vol. I, p. 204.

voyagers in "Mardi" seek the unattainable happiness, and meets the fate of Eve and Prometheus and Beelzebub.

It is sometimes said that "Moby Dick" is not an allegory. It is not merely a discoverable allegory, but in Melville's procedure it was as definitely and avowedly an allegory as "The Divine Comedy" or "Paradise Lost" or, for that matter, as "Pilgrim's Progress" or "Gulliver's Travels" or "The Ancient Mariner."[1] And it is as didactic in the pursuit of its sustained and applied metaphors as it is in its carefully documented chapters on the lore of the whale and all the analogies derived from it. The ocean is the boundless truth; the land is the threatening reef of human error. The whiteness of the great whale figures forth the ghostly mystery of infinitude. Human life is the product of the loom of time, wherein the warp is necessity, the shuttle-driven thread is free will, and the staff that pounds the woof thread to its place is chance. The whale, again, is symbol of all property and all privilege. Melville takes no chances at having these elements misunderstood or overlooked. He expounds them at length and recurs to them often. If it be a sin to write prose allegory, never man sinned as Melville. If it were a sin, it would be a sin of splendor and not of bathos; but as a matter of fact the only literary sinfulness in writing allegory consists in writing bad allegory, particularly if in so doing an otherwise good piece of narrative is spoiled — as narrative is often spoiled in purpose novels and problem novels, which are akin to allegory.

"Moby Dick," however, is superbly successful as a story, regardless of the secondary purpose. In spite of a thousand digressions the whole tale moves with grim ruthlessness to its tragic outcome. Captain Ahab is more than an incarnate spirit of revenge. He is a terribly human being. He has none of the actuality of the fiction types in whom one may recognize contemptible or detestable acquaintances; but he is undeniably real, with the reality of a Richard or an Oedipus. He pervades the ship with his unseen presence before he

[1] See, for example, W. S. Gleim, "A Theory of Moby Dick," *New England Quarterly*, Vol. II, pp. 402–419.

emerges on deck. He quells dissent with the irresistible power of a head wind at Cape Horn. He bends to his will those whom he cannot enlist in his cause. As the end comes near he is eager to joust with death. He carries the reader with him as he carries his crew; and he leaves a vast silence behind him.

In 1852, three years before the publication of "Leaves of Grass," Melville, an exact contemporary of Whitman, published "Pierre, or the Ambiguities." He had come back from the sea to "the treacherous, slavish shore." It was an attempt to combine the struggle of the human spirit against its own weaknesses with the struggle against the surrounding social order, a task for which Melville was unfitted. Though "Pierre" has a carefully devised plot (perhaps because of this) and moves toward its tragic end with relentless inevitability, it is not an effective story, for it does not present a single thoroughly human major character; and it is not effective allegory, for it is not sufficiently detached from life nor clearly enough superimposed upon it. It deals with the conflict between the claims of the conventional social order and the duties and claims of the individual. A rich young aristocrat is adored by his mother and by a lovely girl of his own class to whom he is engaged. Suddenly he learns of an illegitimate sister, beautiful and poverty-stricken. Without explaining fact or motive, in an evasive effort to protect his mother's pride he wounds it to death by befriending the sister as her nominal husband. The mother dies after disinheriting him; and he lives out his last miserable days, before suicide, with the sister, for whom he now feels an overwhelming passion, and with the abandoned love, who has now abandoned all to join the outcasts in platonic devotion.

It is too much and too little to ask anyone to read. The characters are waxwork figures. They put Madame Tussaud's chamber of horrors to the blush. They are less convincing than hers because they are made to move and talk, ornately rhetorical talk, with the strides and gestures of clumsy automatons. If the theme were overwhelmingly big, it might somehow overshadow the characters; but it is not. Pierre is a blundering and melodramatic ninny. His mother's alleged colossal pride is only a futile vanity. Pierre's first love is too stupid to see through his transparency. His sister, though a duskily alluring beauty who often serves as the author's spokesman, is no more than the occasion for the blunders and futilities of the others. Yillah, Unattainable Beauty? Yes, but not the disheveled Isabel. Captain Ahab, incarnate hatred? Yes, he is a splendid madman; but Pierre is a quixotic lunatic. And yet the book contains so much in the way of autobiographic clues and of critical comment on the America of the 1850's that one cannot understand Melville nor climb Rock Rodondo without using these elements in the tale as steps in the ascent.[1]

Melville at thirty-three was through with effective authorship. "Israel Potter" was to come, but it added nothing to his fame. "Piazza Tales" was to come, a kind of potpourri with one or two striking units and a good deal of featureless writing. "The Confidence Man," laborious pseudo-narrative treatise. But "Pierre" was Melville's last real and audible word published during his lifetime; and even "Pierre" was an epilogue. He was headed for a life of speculation in obscurity; and "Pierre," though in a measure autobiographical, had in it more of the future than of the past. He called it "The Ambiguities"; he wrote it in scorn of the conventional novels which were spinning intricate veils of mystery, only to unravel and spool them at the end, and in avowed scorn of the compensation school of philosophy, which held that clouds are provided solely for the making of rainbows. He was a skeptic as to the ways of the Philistine world, more or less of an agnostic as to the operations of Providence, and in one state of mind as much of a mystic in his ultimate optimism as the "compensationist" Emerson himself. While in this state of mind he declared that "human life doth truly come from that, which all men are agreed to call by the name of *God*; and that it partakes of the unravellable unscrutable-

[1] See most specifically Chapters XVII, XVIII, XIX. And R. S. Forsythe's introduction to "Pierre" in the Americana Deserta Series, pp. xxi–xxviii.

ness of God."[1] "We lie in nature very close to God."[2] "From each successive world the demon Principle is more and more dislodged; he is the accursed clog from chaos. . . . Want and woe, . . . with their sire, the demon Principle, must back to chaos, whence they came."[3]

But in the state of mind which finally prevailed he wrote that for the enthusiastic youth there must come a time when faith falls into conflict with fact, "and unless he prove recreant, or unless he prove gullible, or unless he can find the talismanic secret, to reconcile this world with his own soul, then there is no peace for him, no slightest truce for him in this life."[4] The talismanic secret, he went on to say, has never yet been found. Melville was neither recreant nor gullible. There followed the long period of retirement and obscurity which has been melodramatized by sentimental interpreters into prolonged, soul-cankering despair.

Honestly regarded, it appears to have been less tragic than this, though at the outset he seems to have been prepared for worse than came to him. While composing "Moby Dick" he wrote to Hawthorne that during the last seven years he had been constantly and consciously unfolding within himself. "But I feel that I am now come to the inmost leaf of the bulb, and that shortly the flower must fall to the mould." In the midst of "Pierre" he allowed Isabel to recite for him what it may not be improper to reprint in verse form:

I have suffered wretchedness,
But not because of the absence of happiness,
And without praying for happiness.
I pray for peace — for motionlessness — for the feeling of myself,
As of some plant, absorbing life without seeking it,
And existing without individual sensation.
I feel that there can be no perfect peace in individualness.
Therefore I hope one day to feel myself drunk up
Into the pervading spirit animating all things . . .

I feel I am an exile here.[5]

---

[1] Melville, "Pierre," p. 199.
[2] Ibid. p. 151.
[3] Ibid. p. 44.
[4] Ibid. p. 290.
[5] Ibid. p. 167.

This mood of quiet despair is balanced in the same book by the mood of contempt revealed in his chapter on the American critics, editors, and publishers at whose hands he was suffering. Despair was to be the undercurrent in "Benito Cereno," "Bartleby," and "The Encantadas" in "The Piazza Tales," the most skillful in this volume; but contempt was to dominate "The Confidence Man," and may even account for the dull drabness in the execution of this cynical satire. In Melville's own external life the despair of the Ishmael and the exile was to give way to the contempt of the recluse, and this, in time, to a quiet acceptance of things that was nearer to happiness than to the mere resignation of defeat. He had written great prose, and it had not sold. Whatever reputation he enjoyed was based on his authorship of "Typee" and "Omoo" and the fact that he had been to the places he described. But he refused to live on "Peedee and Hullabaloo" and, of his own volition, to "go down to posterity as the man who had lived among cannibals."[1] Writing what he wished to could not earn him a living. It had not earned one for Poe; it was not doing so for Whitman; Hawthorne had apparently laid down his pen and was battening on a consul's fat fees. Rather than try to be a Nathaniel Parker Willis or a Fitz-James O'Brien he would give up the struggle. This he did, living for some years on a kind of manna from heaven — some of it delivered via his mother's family, the Gansevoorts, and his wife's, the Shaws. And when, later, there came an appointment to the New York custom house, and at last a legacy, he was as detached in his non-resentment and as serene in his security as Bronson Alcott in those same protected years. If this sound more invidious than it is intended to, one can say that he had accepted the universe, as Margaret Fuller had done before him and as John Burroughs was later to do. And his universe was not a mere philosophical concept: it included the circumstances of daily life, which he seems to have accepted like many another domesticated male.

---

[1] Melville, letter to Hawthorne, quoted in Mumford's "Life," p. 155.

In 1856–1857 he made a leisurely trip to the Holy Land and beyond to Constantinople and Cairo; in 1866, now custom house inspector and sure of bread and butter, he put to use the material then collected in his long, philosophical poem "Clarel." In 1876, through the subsidy of an uncle, this was published. He was struggling herein with what preoccupied the best minds of his day — the unsettlement of the old faith and the unsatisfactoriness of the invading sciences:

> Yea, long as children feel affright
> In darkness, men shall fear a God; . . .
> Is't ignorance? This ignorant state
> Science doth but elucidate —
> Deepen, enlarge. . . .[1]

And again,

> Much as a lightship keeper pines
> Mid shoals immense, where dreary shines
> His lamp, we toss beneath the ray
> Of Science's beacon. This to trim
> Is now man's barren office.[2]

He was more nearly reconciled to near circumstance than to the remoter problems, but he was not in either respect the pessimist that he has carelessly been called. He was a doubter, and in doubt there is always potential the element of hope. Final emancipation came for him with the inheritance that freed him from the burdens of the "provider." Again he took his pen to write as he chose. He reverted to the sea at once; and in "Billy Budd," which he left behind him in manuscript, he wrote a tale which was full of the sweep and vigor of his early work, a final resurgence of his energies not without parallel in the annals of genius. The dramatic feature of Melville's long period of obscurity was that America allowed him so completely to disappear. But only ingenious sentimentalizing can convert this period into a personal tragedy.

---

[1] Melville, "Clarel," Vol. I, p. 126.

[2] Ibid. p. 255.

Healed of my hurt, I laud the inhuman sea —
Yea, bless the Angels Four that there convene;
For healed I am even by their pitiless breath
Distilled in wholesome dew named rosemarine.[1]

As for what should have been his public, it was so sheeplike that because for a generation there was no shepherd to lead them back to Herman Melville, the next generation, and the next, passed him by. Bookish elders, gentle readers of the Old School, recalled him with vague disapproval as the grandson of Holmes's "Last Leaf," a renegade from the courtly traditions of the old three-cornered hat, and the breeches, and all that. He had gone to sea, not like a patriot or a merchant voyager, or a convalescent gentleman such as young Dana, but as a South Sea vagabond. And he had written things that were not for gentle readers, with none of the gentility that belonged to Taylor and Stedman and Stoddard, or even to young Dana, who wrote of the faraway world as of something to be contemplated in retrospect or in the distance from a club window. Conscientious historians made perfunctory mention of the author of "Peedee and Hullabaloo," absolving themselves with paragraphs or half-pages from which one might gather that the author was a good deal lower than the angels; lower than the antebellum trio, Cooper, Poe, and Hawthorne; lower than William Gilmore Simms; lower than young Dana; perhaps on a level with James Hall and Timothy Flint, to be reported as among those present in literary surveys. When in 1891 people heard that Herman Melville had just died, they listened as to the distant echoes of an old melody, mused a moment, and forgot again.

But at last the inevitable happened: the demonstration that what is permanently good may not be permanently forgotten. With the hundredth anniversary of his birth the reading public had been awakened to feel the wind of the spirit when it blew in the direction of Melville and Captain

[1] Melville, last lines of "John Marr and Other Sailors," in "Poems," p. 244.

Ahab. Tradition had been so upset in the years just past that a challenger of tradition and an inquirer into the ways of God found hearers. He had many rediscoverers. One who read "Moby Dick" for the first time in 1920 can be quoted for them all:

> I hereby declare, being of sane intellect, that since letters began there never was such a book, and that the mind of man is not constructed so as to produce another; that I put its author with Rabelais, Swift, Shakespeare and other minor and disputable worthies; and that I advise any adventurer of the soul to go at once to the . . . prolonged retreat necessary for its deglutition.[1]

So the pilgrimage was started toward Rock Rodondo, and every year brings more votaries.

Walt Whitman

Whitman was thirty-six years old when he wrote

> Bearded, sun-burnt, gray-neck'd, forbidding, I have arrived,
> To be wrestled with as I pass for the solid prizes of the universe.[2]

The facts about these thirty-six years have been by no means veiled in obscurity. Everyone knows that certain periods in Whitman's upgrowth have not been fully brought to light, are sometimes only vaguely and tantalizingly hinted; but the inquirer has been fairly well informed about his unimpressive parentage and his simple family life, the briefness of his formal schooling, the variety of his early excursions in self-support, his rather lazy acceptance of life and his talents as a loafer, his liking for the crowd and his homely friendships, and the succession of his newspaper jobs, North and South. It is familiarly known that for part of his young manhood he was conventional in dress, in point of view, and in literary style; that his "Franklin Evans, or The Inebriate" was a hastily written piece of fiction or fabrication

---

[1] London *Nation*, January 22, 1921.

[2] Whitman, "Starting from Paumanok," sect. 16.

that was as bad as the worst of its type; and that his early prose and verse gave no promise of his later fruition.[1]

The sunburned wrestler could not have been more strikingly in contrast with the dapper journalist of only a few years earlier. Some of the verse reads like burlesque; might be so regarded if Whitman's lack of this kind of humor were not so clear. More of it is sugary sentimentalism. He leaned to "graveyard" poems, recurring frequently to the theme of his own demise. He flouted ambition; he doted on children; as late as 1846 he fearfully paraphrased "The Star-Spangled Banner" for a local celebration. In 1848, when his exact contemporary, Lowell, had shown evidences of maturity in "A Fable for Critics" and "The Biglow Papers," Whitman was as unpromising in verse as any Poets' Corner contributor to a village weekly.

In these same years (the 1840's) his prose was no more distinguished. "The Sun-Down Papers" (1838–1841) are Addisonian in scheme and overflowing in the sentimentalism that the Addisonians reveled in. Observations on death and the vanity of human wishes alternated with diatribes against smoking and coffee-drinking, attacks on capital punishment, defenses of slavery, and rhapsodies on human and natural innocence. In these effusions people wend their ways, focus their gentle orbs on pale emblems of decay, and say "whilome," "certes," and "ycleped."

However, there is a difference between early traits, which are positive features, and faint, early symptoms which become significant when seen in the light of later performance. Two changes began to take shape while Whitman was yet in the early twenties: an ambition to become a public speaker affected his style, steering him away from elegance toward force and clearness; and the desire to say some-

[1] References and quotations, unless otherwise indicated, are from the Inclusive Edition of "Leaves of Grass," by Emory Holloway, 1925; "Whitman's Complete Prose," published by Mitchell Kennerley, 1924; the "Uncollected Poetry and Prose of Walt Whitman," edited by Holloway, 1921; Holloway's "Whitman: an Interpretation in Narrative . . .," with portraits and facsimiles of Whitman's letters etc., 1926.

thing that men would listen to led him from pleasant nothings in the direction of bardic and prophetic utterance.

As to his style, the report of an outdoor political speech by the youthful journalist in 1841 is nearer his mature style and broader in sentiment than most of his writing in the 1840's:

> My fellow citizens: let this be an afterthought. I beseech you to entertain a noble and more elevated idea of our aim and struggles as a party than to suppose that we are striving [to raise] this or that man to power. We are battling for great principles — for mighty and glorious truths. I would scorn to exert even my humble efforts for the best democratic candidate that ever was nominated, in himself alone. It is our creed — our doctrine, not a man or set of men, that we seek to build up.[1]

The recently discovered notes for prospective lectures[2] — on lecturing and oratory, on religion, on democracy, and on literature — are further evidence of his never-to-be-satisfied ambitions as a speaker, and explanatory of the rhetorical qualities of his later verse. As the years advanced toward 1850 there were definite promises in such poems as "Wounded in the House of Friends" and "Resurgemus."

In his speech before the Brooklyn Art Union in 1851 he quoted from the latter, and so offered a striking parallel of what he that day chose to put forth as verse and what he offered as prose. There is little to distinguish these passages:

> Not a grave of those slaughtered ones,
> But is growing its seed of freedom,
> In its turn to bear seed,
> Which the winds shall carry afar and resow,
> And the rain nourish.
> Not a disembodied spirit
> Can the weapons of tyrants let loose,
> But it shall stalk invisibly over the earth,
> Whispering, counselling, cautioning.[3]

---

[1] Holloway, "Uncollected Poetry and Prose," Vol. I, p. 51.

[2] The final evidence of Whitman's careful workmanship is revealed in "Walt Whitman's Workshop," edited by Clifton J. Furness.

[3] Holloway, op. cit. Vol. I, pp. 29–30.

> It is the school of all grand actions and grand virtues, of heroism, of the death of captives and martyrs — of all the mighty deeds written in the pages of history — deeds of daring, and then enthusiasm, and devotion, and fortitude. Read well the death of Socrates, and of a greater than Socrates. Read how slaves have battled against their oppressors — how the bullets of tyrants have, since the first king ruled, never been able to put down the unquenchable thirst of man for his rights.[1]

Both might be printed in rhythmic units or in block prose, and both belong to the rostrum.

Parallel with the change in form is the growth in substance and in the capacity for general ideas which must belong to poet or critic. At twenty-one Whitman was exclaiming, "Light has flowed in upon me. I am not quite so green as I was. The mists and clouds have cleared away, and I can now behold things as they really are."[2] The particular profundity he had just arrived at was that "it is a very dangerous thing to be rich."[3] In the next few years he became aware of several other obvious dangers, and carped and caviled irritably at them. But his *Brooklyn Eagle* editorial articles soon began to reveal an international altruism, and among the notebook memoranda of 1847 is an eloquent passage on a "vast and tremendous" scheme that "involves no less than constructing a nation of nations."[4] This expansiveness of spirit was encouraged with his journey down the Ohio and Mississippi in 1848. He partook of the amplitude of the reaches through which he traveled on the trip out and on the return; and he came to a sense of America as a whole.

He was getting ready to give an affirmative answer to his own questions:

> Have you studied out the land, its idioms and men? . . .
> Do you see who have left all feudal processes and poems behind them,
> and assumed the poems and processes of Democracy? . . .
> Have you vivified yourself from the maternity of these States?
> Have you too the old ever-fresh forbearance and impartiality?[5]

---

[1] Holloway, op. cit. Vol. I, p. 246. [2] Ibid. p. 38. [3] Ibid. p. 37.
[4] Ibid. Vol. II, p. 76. [5] Whitman, "Leaves of Grass," pp. 293–294.

These questions, elaborated from the first "Leaves of Grass" preface, were published in 1856, the year in which he wrote a remarkable document, "The Eighteenth Presidency." It was a virulent and abusive attack on the political code and the political leaders of the year.[1] There is no positive proof as to whether Whitman failed to get this published, or decided to withdraw it; but the presumptions are strong that he vented his wrath in the writing of it and that "forbearance and impartiality" rendered a verdict against its circulation. From now on he was to be "neither for nor against institutions."[2]

There is no poet in connection with whom the distinction should be more clearly kept between the examination of his theory and method of writing and the enjoyment of his completed work. It is easy for the critic to emphasize technique at the expense of content, and it is not impossible for the poet to do the same thing. But Whitman's importance in the field of technique is relatively as great as his importance in the province of poetic thought; though the way he wrote must be of less significance than what he had to express, it is almost uniquely deserving of study.

Whitman was never unaverse to expounding his theories of poetry and the poet. In an introduction written for an English edition but not published until nearly forty years after his death, the poet set down as a prediction what had already happened in his own country: "At first sight, the form of these verses, not only without rhyme, but wholly regardless of the customary verbal melody & regularity so much labored after by modern poets, will strike the reader with incredulous amazement."[3] In the preface to "Leaves of Grass" in the first edition (1855) he had stated his theory of evolving a new form for a new nation:

> The poetic quality is not marshalled in rhyme or uniformity or abstract addresses to things nor in melancholy complaints or good precepts, but is the life of these and much else and is in the soul. . . .

---

[1] Furness, "Walt Whitman's Workshop," pp. 88–113.
[2] Whitman, op. cit. p. 107.
[3] Furness, op. cit. p. 150.

The rhyme and uniformity of perfect poems show the free growth of metrical laws and bud from them as unerringly and loosely as lilacs or roses on a bush, and take shapes as compact as the shapes of chestnuts and oranges and melons and pears, and shed the perfume impalpable to form. . . .

The art of art, the glory of expression and the sunshine of the light of letters is simplicity. Nothing is better than simplicity. . . . To carry on the heave of impulse and pierce intellectual depths and give all subjects their articulations are powers neither common nor very uncommon. But to speak in literature with the perfect rectitude and insouciance of the movements of animals and the unimpeachableness of the sentiment of trees in the woods and grass by the roadside is the flawless triumph of art. . . .

The old red blood and stainless gentility of great poets will be proved by their unconstraint. A heroic person walks at his ease through and out of that custom or precedent or authority that suits him not. Of the traits of the brotherhood of writers savans musicians inventors and artists nothing is finer than silent defiance advancing from new free forms. . . .

The great poets are also to be known by the absence in them of tricks and by the justification of perfect personal candor. . . .

The poems distilled from other poems will probably pass away. . . .

The soul of the largest and wealthiest and proudest nation may well go half-way to meet that of its poets. The signs are effectual. There is no fear of mistake. If the one is true the other is true. The proof of a poet is that his country absorbs him as affectionately as he has absorbed it.[1]

The absorbing was anything but rapid. Derision interfered at first — the sort of derision that greets any innovation in art. Timidity followed. Whitman's bust was at last installed in the "Hall of Fame" in the spring of 1931.

Obviously, then, the form of "Leaves of Grass" was not, as loosely charged, the result either of laziness or of inability to use the established measures. Throughout his work are recurrent passages in regular, and often rhymed, meter. "O Captain! My Captain!" (1865), "Ethiopia Saluting the Colors" (1871), and the song of "The Singer in the Prison"

[1] Whitman, op. cit. pp. 493–507, passim.

(1864) are deliberate resorts to the old ways. More likely to escape attention are unlabeled bits scattered through poems that are in prevailingly free verse: the opening of the "Song of the Broad-Axe"; the first four lines of section 14 in "Walt Whitman," or "Song of Myself."

He theorized his versification in some detail, referring to his lines as apparently "lawless at first perusal, although on closer examination a certain regularity appears, like the recurrence of lesser and larger waves on the sea-shore, rolling in without intermission, and fitfully rising and falling."[1] His feeling, — and this is the right word for a question of artistic form, — his feeling was that the idea should govern from moment to moment the form into which it is cast, since a fixed pattern must inevitably impose a constraint. As in any poet with a theory and a generous output, the test of the one by the other shows uneven results. In many a descriptive passage there is a succession of nice adjustments of word and rhythm to subject. The flight of birds, the play of waves, the swaying of branches, the thousandfold variations of motion, are easy to reproduce and easy to recognize in verse — easier than the rhythms appropriate to abstract ideas. Such a passage as the following displays Whitman at the height of his powers. It is reproduced exactly except that it is broken into lines that correspond with the rhythmic units.

I too many and many a time cross'd the river of old, [7]
        Watched the Twelfth-month sea-gulls, [3]
        saw them high in the air [3]
        floating with motionless wings, [3]
        oscillating their bodies, [3]
        Saw how the glistening yellow [3]
        lit up parts of their bodies [3]
        and left the rest in strong shadow, [3]
        Saw the slow-wheeling circles [3]
      and the gradual edging toward the south, [4]
    Saw the reflection of the summer sky in the water, [5]
    Had my eyes dazzled by the shimmering track of beams, [5]

[1] Quoted in B. Perry's "Walt Whitman," p. 207.

Look'd at the fine centrifugal spokes of light round the shape of
  my head in the sunlit water, [9]
Look'd at the haze on the hills southward and south-westward [6]
Look'd on the vapor as it flew in fleeces tinged with violet, [6]
Look'd toward the lower bay to notice the vessels arriving, etc.[1] [6]

But Whitman went far beyond these objective rhythms to the innate suggestions of things and ideas. At the same time — not to be preoccupied in a search for variety which might end in chaos — he adopted a succession of pattern rhythms, taking simple, free measures and modifying them in the reiterative form often used by Emerson and common to "Hiawatha." There was some acumen in Mrs. Whitman's comment that "if 'Hiawatha' was poetry, perhaps Walt's was"; for Longfellow's assumption of "frequent repetitions" was a reversion to the parallelism prevalent in folk poetry, which is the warp of Whitman's patterns.

In execution he was, of course, more or less effective. He wrote scores of passages full of splendor, of majesty, of rugged strength, of tender loveliness. In general the lines that deal with definite aspects of natural and physical beauty are most effective — lines of which "Out of the Cradle Endlessly Rocking" offers the purest type; but many of the poems and sections in which concrete imagery is summoned to the explication of a general concept are often finely impressive, as in his stanzas on the poet, or on himself, the "divine average":

My foothold is tenon'd and mortis'd in granite,
I laugh at what you call dissolution,
And I know the amplitude of time.[2]

Whitman was quite as conscious in choice of words as in his selection of measures. Poetry, he agreed with Wordsworth, was choked with outworn phrases; the speech of the people should be the source of poetic diction. From this he would evolve a "perfectly clear, plate-glassy style." But no new style, whatever its merits, ever seems transparent to

[1] Whitman, "Leaves of Grass," p. 135. [2] Ibid. p. 41.

people who are used to looking through something else. To the hostile critic Whitman offered an abundance of lines for unfriendly quotation, as every prolific poet has done. Furthermore, he offered for attack all the long series of "catalogue," or "inventory," passages, in which he abandoned the artistic principle of selective suggestion and overwhelmed the reader with cascades of casual detail apparently poured out in a careless effervescence of improvisation. For these Whitman has paid the penalty of being branded a slovenly, hasty writer.

Yet the most remarkable contribution[1] of recent Whitman scholarship is the revelation of his painstaking and almost painful processes of composition, the overthrow of the legend that he wrote with the ease and extravagance of a free-flowing pen. Long lost manuscripts and notebooks belatedly brought to light reveal an almost unparalleled evolution in writing, from chaotic thought to orderly expression — a procedure laborious and protracted in its random jottings, iterative recurrences, tentative phrasings, listings of undetermined variant words, trial drafts, and repeated emendations. No poet ever brooded more solicitously over his materials or more carefully economized his resources. His whole body of prose and verse will give confirmation to the attentive student. A careful reading of the preface to the first edition of "Leaves of Grass" and the poem "By Blue Ontario's Shore" will serve as illustration to both the incredulous and the inquirers who would like to look but not to look too long.

The derision with which readers treated Whitman's manner of writing was a slight matter compared with their resentment at his unprecedented frankness in matters of sex; for their knowledge of precedent was confined to their own age and land. The Victorian habit of shrouding the subject in unwholesome silence had converted a central element in human experience into a subject of morbid curiosity and furtive indulgence. This bred vicious ignorance, distorted half-knowledge, and, among other by-products, hysterical

---

[1] See the Furness study in detail for the methods of Whitman's craftsmanship.

protestations at any open violation of the code in action or in speech. People seemed to feel that they were vindicating their own probity by the shrillness of their invective. So Whitman was made scapegoat, just as Byron had been; and the merits of the controversies are obscured by the fact that however much at fault the poets may have been, their accusers were no less in the wrong. Out of the babel of discussion one clearest note emerged in the form of a letter from an Englishwoman to W. M. Rossetti, who had lent her "Leaves of Grass":

> I rejoice to have read these poems; and if I or any true woman feel that, certainly *men* may hold their peace about them. You will understand that I still think that instinct of silence I spoke of a right and beautiful thing; that it is only lovers and poets (perhaps only lovers and *this* poet) who may say what they will — the lover to his own, the poet to all, because all are in a sense his own. Shame is like a very flexible veil that takes faithfully the shape of what it covers — lovely when it hides a lovely thing, ugly when it hides an ugly one.[1]

This judgment exerted no effect in its day, and is significant now largely because of its rarity then. What the objectors failed to appreciate then was that only a few score lines were responsible for all the turmoil, and that only a morbid supersensitiveness could cause them to color a reader's whole concept of Whitman.[2]

The remaining complaint in the general indictment of the poet was lodged against his "colossal egoism," a subject more for interpretation than defense. If all his "I's" should be

---

[1] Anne Gilchrist, quoted in Perry's "Walt Whitman," pp. 189–190.

[2] Mrs. Gilchrist's repeated allusions to silence and shame (by which she seems to mean modesty) are the habitual locutions of her period. Even in her guarded defense of Whitman she was violating both. Ludwig Lewisohn has gone a step farther in alluding, with a good deal of a flourish, to Whitman's homosexuality. As a Freudian, Mr. Lewisohn characteristically attributes too much to the influence of this. It was explicit in "Calamus"; but only to the psychoanalyst was it implicit in Whitman's work as a whole. And it is absurd to say that on account of it he "has never been accepted by the folk"; for until very lately few Americans have even been aware of the practice. Even the notoriety of Oscar Wilde did not really bring it to light. See Ludwig Lewisohn's "Expression in America," pp. 198–201.

read literally they would offer no more than an unusual degree of frankness in the artist. Every creative artist is of necessity an egoist. He is bound to believe in the special significance of what he has to express and in the rightness of his expression. The whole anthology on poets and poetry is an array of supreme egoisms, even though most of them are written in the third person. Whitman cast aside the regular locution without apology. But his "I's" do not always mean the same thing. Sometimes they are explicitly personal, as in,

> I, now, thirty-seven years old in perfect health begin,
> Hoping to cease not till death.[1]

Sometimes they stand just as explicitly for the average man. This he made clear enough again and again and explained in the preface to the edition of 1876:

> I meant "Leaves of Grass" as published, to be the Poem of Identity, (of *Yours*, whoever you are, now reading these lines). . . . To sing the Song of that divine law of Identity, and of Yourself, consistently with the Divine Law of the Universal, is a main intention of those "Leaves."[2]

Finally, the "I" is often a symbol of the religious mysticism at the basis of his faith. Without an understanding of this factor in Whitman he cannot be known.

> Place yourself [said William James in his lecture on Bergson] at the centre of a man's philosophic vision and you understand at once all the difficult things it makes him write or say. But keep outside, use your post-mortem method, try to build the philosophy up out of the single phrases, taking first one and then another, and seeking to make them fit, and of course you fail. You crawl over the thing like a myopic ant over a building, tumbling into every microscopic crack or fissure, finding nothing but inconsistencies, and never suspecting that a centre exists.

It is James again who gives the exact cue to Whitman's mysticism, this time in a chapter on "Varieties of Religious Experience." It is the experience of the mystic, he explains,

[1] Whitman, "Leaves of Grass," p. 24.

[2] Ibid. pp. 517–518.

to arrive in inspired moments at a height from which all truth seems to be divinely clarified. This revelation is not a flash-light perception of some single aspect of life, but a sense of the entire scheme of creation and a conviction that the understanding of it has been miraculously revealed. It is clear, like the view from a mountain top, but, like such a view, it is elusive of adequate expression in words. It is "an intuition," and now the vague generalization is Whitman's, "of the absolute balance, in time and space, of all this multifarious, mad chaos of fraud, frivolity, hoggishness — this revel of fools, and incredible make-believe and general unsettledness, we call *the world*; a soul-sight of that divine clue and unseen thread which holds the whole congeries of things, all history and time, and all events, however trivial, however momentous, like a leashed dog in the hand of the hunter."[1] It was the fashion of speech of the Hebrew prophets, when thus inspired, to preface their declarations with "Thus saith the Lord"; Whitman, with his simpler "I say" or "I tell you," regarded himself as no less a mouthpiece for the Most High. The vision made him certain of an underlying unity in all life and of the coming supremacy of the law of love; it made him equally certain of the mistakenness of human conditions and unqualifiedly direct in his verdicts.

This sense of the wholeness of life — a transcendental doctrine — made all the parts deeply significant to him who felt their relationship. The same mystic consciousness prevails in these passages and all the others like them:

I celebrate myself, and sing myself,
And what I assume you shall assume,
For every atom belonging to me as good belongs to you.[2]

. . . .

The wild gander leads his flock through the cool night,
Ya-honk! he says, and sounds it down to me like an invitation,

---

[1] Whitman, "Complete Prose" (1914), p. 167.
[2] Whitman, "Leaves of Grass," p. 24.

The pert may suppose it meaningless, but I listening close,
Find its purpose and place up there toward the wintry sky.[1]

. . . .

I believe a leaf of grass is no less than the journey-work of the stars,
And the pismire is equally perfect, and a grain of sand, and the egg of the wren,
And the tree-toad is a chef-d'œuvre for the highest,
And the running blackberry would adorn the parlors of heaven,
And the narrowest hinge in my hand puts to scorn all machinery,
And the cow crunching with depressed head surpasses any statue,
And a mouse is miracle enough to stagger sextillions of infidels.[2]

This sense of oneness explains, too, the otherwise bewildering excesses of the "inventory" passages, which, for all their apparent unrelatedness, are always brought up with a unifying, inclusive turn. In the universe, then, — and Whitman thought of the word in its literal sense of a single, great design, — man was the supreme fact to whom all its objects "continually converge." As man was God-created, Whitman was no respecter of persons but a lover of the common folk, in whom the destiny of humankind resided more than in presidents or kings; and since he considered the race in the light of ages upon ages, the generating of life seemed to him of holiest import.

For the carrying out of such a design the only fit vehicle, he felt, was the purest sort of democracy; all other working bases of human association were only temporary obstacles to the course of things; and as Whitman felt that the nearest approach to the right social order was being made in his own country, he was an American by conviction as well as by accident of place. The essential difference between his type of loyalty and the loyalty that normally has its roots in this something less than coincidence, is, of course, that Whitman's allegiance was primarily to an idea that was potential in the United States but extremely far from realization.

His government, or any government, he felt, was a neces-

---

[1] Whitman, "Leaves of Grass," p. 34.

[2] Ibid. p. 50.

sary convenience, and so-called rulers were servants of the public from whom their powers were derived. The greatest driving power in the state was public opinion, and his respect for this was great, though not as a daily agency for political ends. He respected it less as a dynamo than as dynamite and, even at that, less as a useful explosive than as a source of terror. The great city was

> Where the populace rise at once against the never-ending audacity of elected persons,[1]

and he declared that he would

> make a song for the ears of the President, full of weapons with menacing points.[2]

Public opinion was a certain and final fiat to be pronounced against "the frivolous judge," "the corrupt Congressman, Governor, Mayor," and "the mumbling and screaming priest" on the popular day of judgment. Until that day abuses might persist without any reforming check from the poet, who would observe in silence "all the meanness and agony without end."

This estimate of public opinion as a kind of millennial voice ignored any assumption of immediate responsibility toward the state. If Whitman was at all interested in the rights or duties of the voter,— as he seemed to be when he wrote the unpublished outburst on "The Eighteenth Presidency,"— he kept his sentiments to himself. The one civic duty he emphasized was the most obvious and primitive, that of the soldier. Yet even at this point his militarism was highly sublimated. He never talked "preparedness"; he never talked national honor; he had no thought of conquest for territory, much less for the extension of trade. The army in his mind was a shining host with plumes of snow whose warfare was to be a holy crusade.

This fine abstraction fitted well the loose federation of states that composed Whitman's America. He liked to

[1] Whitman, "Leaves of Grass," p. 160.

[2] Ibid. p. 15.

dwell on the provincial differences in race, climate, occupation, with the still surviving differences of character.

> I will make a song for these States that no one State may under any circumstances be subjected to another State,
> And I will make a song that there shall be comity by day and by night between all the States, and between any two of them.[1]

The America Walt Whitman loved was clearly a community rather than a government. His new democracy was a composite of personalities, in each of whom he was interested on his own account, and even more because, taken together, they were the stuff from which nations were made. Thus he held to the conventional view of children and immigrants as potential Americans and to the less conventional one that all are necessary to the whole, and none are irredeemable.

In his approval of activity Whitman resembled Carlyle more than Emerson. He did not rise to Ruskin's belief in spiritual growth through excellence of craftsmanship, but he held for muscular and spiritual exertion as admirable in themselves. In a primitive way he therefore distrusted the sedentary intellectual man — though he believed in the poet and the "philosoph," and he applauded the open-air laborer because the man of brawn was developing himself in doing the work of the divine average in wresting the world's food from the soil or in digging and delving to make the earth a better place to live on. The farther labor was removed from the soil, the less he cared for it; hunter, fisher, miner, mariner, farmer, then the mechanic, then the clerk, then the priest and the professor. Yet his fear of the nicer refinements was not the mere distrust or envy of the churl. It was born of the fear of decadence, of "elegance, civilization, delicatesse." The vandal did not attract him by his vandalism but by his restless, vandalic strength. He would rather trust the future to an Attila than to a Nero.

This brings us nearer the heart of his social philosophy.

---

[1] Whitman, "Leaves of Grass," p. 15.

The state was a spiritual entity containing the hope of the future. America was his promised land, the cradle of universal liberty. As he looked on its occupants he stood as in the presence of a young Olympian.

America, curious toward foreign characters, stands by its own at all hazards,
Stands removed, spacious, composite, sound, initiates the true use of precedents,
Does not repel them or the past or what they have produced under their forms,
Takes the lesson with calmness.[1]

Like most of his countrymen in the nineteenth century, he believed in the manifest destiny of his country, and he relied on it in the way of the pacific philosopher. The future of America was safe because the race was safe, and the future of the race was safe because God willed it so. On this theme he sang with epic fervor, relying on the

Unseen moral essence of all the vast materials of America, (age upon age, working in death the same as in Life),
You that, sometimes known, oftener unknown, really shape and mould the New World.[2]

In his cloud-topped optimism he offered his poems as an offset to Jay Gould's railroads, extolled labor while Jay Gould employed it, loafed and invited his soul while Jay Gould made money. Jay Gould's vast projects extended only to the Pacific; Whitman's dream reached "beyond the sunset and the baths of all the western stars." They are the antithetic types of their generation: the complete captain of finance who in the name of progress crushes competitors to the glory of God, and the abstract philanthropist who in the name of brotherhood damns competition by the same formula. If Jay Gould was a harbinger of Andrew Carnegie and John D. Rockefeller, without their expiatory benevolence, Whitman was a forerunner of several million less

[1] Whitman, "Leaves of Grass," p. 288. [2] Ibid, p. 177.

prosperous Americans whose vociferative loyalty is still largely based on passive hopefulness.

In his American point of view he was characteristically committed to the companion of the manifest destiny fallacy — that of magnificent isolation. He was by nature and experience utterly devoid of any sense of internationalism. He was, to be sure, aware of his limitations, and he made continual and, in a way, pathetic attempts to overcome them; but he succeeded in hardly more than enumerating geographical names. There was no one in his social vista between Peter Doyle on a street-car platform and the "presence . . . whose dwelling is the light of setting suns." What he knew of America he knew down to the ground, but of the rest he was grossly ignorant, and of Europe he had no clear conception. His view of the world was like a landscape without any middle distance. Here was America, in which the problems of the future were to be solved while Europe stood yonder in admiring expectancy. In the fullness of time all the other nations would follow after this people, who had shown nothing but contempt for the Old World and a desire to be kept uncontaminated by it. So his idea of the state is baffling at some points and obviously insufficient at others. It is fragmentary and inarticulate, and in these respects representatively American. In its optimism also it is American, as in its individualistic theory of life. Program makers crop up on every side; his work was not theirs. Were he living he would be singing indomitably:

> Have the elder races halted?
> Do they droop and end their lesson, wearied, over there beyond the seas?
> We take up the task eternal, and the burden and the lesson,
> Pioneers! O pioneers! [1]

Moreover, his assumption would still be strongly advanced that the teacher of the lesson for the New World must be the poet, or bard. And his lesson must be based on

[1] Whitman, "Leaves of Grass," p. 194.

the values and the rewards of love. His expression was primitively physical. He was a shoulder-rubber. He reveled in the crowd. His enormous service in war nursing was the perfect fulfillment of his desire to identify friendliness with contact.

> When he appeared, in passing along, there was a smile of affection and welcome on every face, however wan, and his presence seemed to light up the place as it might be lit by the presence of the Son of Love. From cot to cot they called him, often in tremulous tones or whispers; they embraced him, they touched his hand, they gazed at him.[1]

It was no vague altruism he was writing about, but a definite hand-clasping brotherhood:

I hear it was charged against me that I sought to destroy institutions,
But really I am neither for nor against institutions,
(What indeed have I in common with them? or what with the destruction of them?)
Only I will establish in the Mannahatta and in every city of these States inland and seaboard,
And in the fields and woods, and above every keel little or large that dents the water,
Without edifices or rules or trustees or any argument,
The institution of the dear love of comrades.[2]

To the bard who was to establish this institution he attributed knowledge of science and history (more than he himself commanded) and, beyond that, wisdom:

He bestows on every object or quality its fit proportion, neither more nor less. . . .
He is no arguer, he is judgment, (Nature accepts him absolutely,)
He judges not as the judge judges, but as the sun falling round a helpless thing,
As he sees the farthest he has the most faith.[3]

He is no writer of polite rhymes; he is the propounder of

the idea of perfect and free individuals,
For that, the bard walks in advance, leader of leaders,
The attitude of him cheers up slaves and horrifies foreign despots.[4]

---

[1] Holloway, "Whitman," p. 206.
[2] Whitman, "Leaves of Grass," p. 107.
[3] Ibid. pp. 291–292.
[4] Ibid. p. 292.

In self-reliance he lived up to his own creed. Sustained by the mystic's sense of revealed truth and a conviction that it was his duty to show men a new heaven and a new earth, he went confidently on his way. Emerson wrote of self-reliance in general, "Adhere to your act, and congratulate yourself if you have done something strange and extravagant, and broken the monotony of a decorous age." Yet he remonstrated with Whitman, and in the attempt to modify his extravagance used arguments that were unanswerable. Nevertheless, said the younger poet, "I felt down in my soul the clear and unmistakable conviction to disobey all, and pursue my own way;"[1] in doing which he bettered Emerson's instructions by ignoring his advice. Hostile or brutal criticism left him unruffled, reinforcing him in his conclusions and cheering him with the assurance that they were receiving serious attention.

His daily preoccupation with "superior beings and eternal interests" gave him some of the elevations and some of the complacent certainties of the Puritan fathers. It leads far to think of Whitman as a Puritan stripped of his dogma. It accounts for his daily absorption in things of religion, his democratic zeal, his disregard for the adornments of life, even for his subordination of romantic love to a zest for perpetuation of the race. He dwelt on the broad and permanent factors in human life, regarding the finite and personal only as he saw them in the midst of time and space. And this leads to the man in his relation to science, with which Puritan dogma was at odds. Whitman was not in the usual sense a "nature poet." Although any counter of allusions can muster a formidable list of references to birds, plants, flowers, stars, and sea, the only relation of natural fact to the essential Whitman was intellectual rather than sensuous. He had nothing to say in detached observations on the primrose, or the mountain tops, or the sunset. But through the aid of science nature was, next to his own in-

---

[1] Whitman, "Complete Prose" (1914), p. 184.

tuitions, his source of deepest truth. The dependence of biological science on the material universe did not shake his faith in immortality. He simply took what knowledge science could contribute and understood it in the light of his transcendental faith. Among modern poets he was one of the earliest to chant the paean of creative evolution:

Rise after rise bow the phantoms behind me,
Afar down I see the huge first Nothing, I know I was even there,
I waited unseen and always, and slept through the lethargic mist,
And took my time, and took no hurt from the fetid carbon.
. . . .
Before I was born out of my mother generations guided me,
My embryo has never been torpid, nothing could overlay it.

For it the nebula cohered to an orb,
The long slow strata piled to rest it on,
Vast vegetables gave it sustenance,
Monstrous sauroids transported it in their mouths and deposited it with care.

All forces have been steadily employ'd to complete and delight me,
Now on this spot I stand with my robust soul.[1]

The slow and steady growth of Whitman's influence is impressive. John Burroughs tells of the staff of a leading newspaper in New York waiting to be paid off one Saturday afternoon in 1855 and greeting the passages read to them from "Leaves of Grass" with "peals upon peals of ironical laughter." Young men, like Thoreau and Burroughs, were moved to admiration in their obscurity, but their opinion counted for nothing with the multitude. Emerson was the single man of standing to recognize that he was at "the beginning of a great career." On publication of the enlarged edition of 1856, labeled with Emerson's endorsement, ultra-respectable people of the Jaffrey Pyncheon type were eager to hound Whitman and his publishers out of society. During the decade of the Civil War he neither gained nor lost fame.

[1] Whitman, "Leaves of Grass," pp. 68–69.

It became clear that he was not to be popular, but that the poets were to take him seriously. A Whitman vogue began to develop among the consciously literary, just as a Browning vogue did in the same years. As 1870 passed, essays and reviews in England and Germany enhanced Whitman's reputation in the United States.

By the middle of the 80's he had become a monumental fact that no critic of American poetry could overlook, even though the sight of him filled the spectator with alarm. Richardson, in 1886, was evidently perturbed and paid him the high compliment of denying that he would mold the future song of America. Stedman, the year before, had been hard pressed by the consciousness of Whitman's growing reputation and betrayed the grounds for his uneasiness — that Whitman was not a poet of gentility. In spite of which he wrote, "He is, in a sense, the poet of the over-refined and doctrinaires . . . and appeals most to those who long for a reaction, a new beginning."[1] To this charge Barrett Wendell returned in 1900, but without either the generosity or the urbanity of Stedman, seeming to feel that Whitman had forfeited all claim to good manners from the well-mannered, and abusing him roundly. He was the last to show just this critical bias toward the poet.

Within the next few years Whitman was, as it were, elected to the Academy by his inclusion in the English and the American Men of Letters Series, with G. R. Carpenter's incisive analysis and Bliss Perry's respectful treatment; and foreign attention, in criticism and reprint, multiplied greatly. Finally, the latest word has been said not by the critics but by the poets. In 1905 Huneker had written, "If we have no great school of literature in America we can at least point to Poe as the progenitor of a half-dozen continental literatures." But by 1919 Untermeyer's "New Era in American Poetry" could almost be described as a series on Whitman in relation to his literary progeny. Granting the difference

[1] Stedman, "Poets of America," p. 394.

in bias between the commentators, the striking fact is that Huneker's dictum was true when he pronounced it and that Untermeyer's was equally sound fourteen years later; for it was Poe who had a peculiar vogue with the "decadents," and it is Whitman who has been the animating force in contemporary poetry.

Bohemians and Knickerbockers

If one were to pick out of the past the emergent names from mid-nineteenth century New York, the poll would make Greeley and Bryant, two newspaper editors, the outstanding figures in the intellectual stratum; Nathaniel Parker Willis and Fitz-Greene Halleck the most popular; Henry Clapp and Charles T. Congdon the cleverest. But in the New York of the period no one who knew anything about it would accept the selection. For this is a nonpartisan ticket, and New York was irreconcilably partisan at the mention of such names as these.

By 1850 the Knickerbocker group were past their prime, conservators of a dying tradition. Irving was still alive, and Halleck, and so were James Kirke Paulding and Charles Fenno Hoffman and Gulian C. Verplanck and the Clark twins, Willis and Lewis. *The Knickerbocker Magazine* survived — was to survive until 1866, though its obituary was prematurely pronounced as early as 1859. By 1867 a contemporary could say of the magazine and its contributors that the magazine had not done anything either very fine or highly valuable for American culture, though the concession could be made that "if we are not sorry that it exists no longer, we may very well be glad that it once existed."[1] This was an offensive verdict in a town where the Knickerbockers were not all under the sod, where many of them represented the dignities of the Old School, and where the Century Club provided their enviably exclusive gathering point.

---

[1] J. R. Dennett, "Knickerbocker Literature," *The Nation*, December 5, 1867.

But it was a welcome sentiment for the former frequenters of Pfaff's Restaurant, where the Bohemians foregathered with their Prince, Henry Clapp. The men who gathered there were variously loyal to New York as an emancipated metropolis among American cities, and they were variously conscious of Boston. The most violent said that the thought of it made them as ugly as sin. Fitz Hugh Ludlow of "The Hasheesh Eater," the American version of De Quincey's "Confessions," Fitz-James O'Brien of "The Diamond Lens," Launt Thompson, sculptor, George Arnold, poet, concurred; and the anti-Bostonian bitterness prevailed in the editorial office of their short-lived periodical, *The Saturday Press*.

The Bohemians and their journal attracted a third group who did not quite belong to them and finally left them — a group who represented New York in letters rather more completely than the Bohemians and became in a way successors to the Knickerbockers. This included William Winter, Nathaniel Parker Willis, Richard Henry Stoddard, émigrés from Bostonia; Aldrich, who left New England only to return in mid-career to the "Hub"; Edmund Clarence Stedman; and, intermittently, Bayard Taylor. Aldrich was on the staff of the *Press* for a time; Stedman, Stoddard, and Winter contributed to it; so did William Dean Howells. But they were not at home in this company; they were too conscious of Boston in their own way. Howells spoke for more than himself in recording, "I remember that as I sat at that table, under the pavement, in Pfaff's beer cellar, and listened to the wit that did not seem very funny, I thought of the dinner with Lowell, the breakfast with Fields, the supper at the Autocrat's, and felt that I had fallen very far."[1] To which reminiscence Winter, who did not belong but resented the implication, replied fiercely, "No literary circle comparable with the Bohemian group of that period, in ardor of genius, variety of character, and singularity of achievement, has since existed in New York, nor has any group of writers any-

[1] Howells, "Literary Friends and Acquaintances," p. 76. See also pages 69–79.

where existent in our country been so ignorantly and grossly misrepresented and maligned."[1] Aldrich was of like mind with Howells, readily accepted Osgood's invitation to the editorship of *Every Saturday* in Boston, and wrote years after to Bayard Taylor: "I miss my few dear friends in New York, but that is all. There is a finer intellectual atmosphere here than in our city. . . . The people of Boston are full-blooded *readers*, appreciative, trained"; and later to Stedman: "I did not find more than two or three such in New York, and I lived there fifteen years. It was an excellent school for me — to get out of."[2] Boston was his native heath in spite of his quip: "Though I am not genuine Boston, I am Boston-plated." Stedman too caught the infection: "I was very anxious to bring out my first book in New York in Boston style, having a reverence for Boston, which I continue to have."[3]

One thing was true of all these variants of the genus New York: that in their conception of literature New York had hardly any place. Irving had not granted it any in his mature years, and his Knickerbocker successors did not. The Bohemians fared equally far afield. They failed even in criticism when Whitman offered them their chance. They offered him a kind of support more in perversity than in love, making him the occasion for forcible-feeble defiance of the orthodox. For the others "The Ballad of Babie Bell," "Ximena, or The Battle of the Sierra Morena, and Other Poems," "Poems of the Orient," "Poems Lyric and Idyllic," "The Book of the East," "The Blameless Prince," "The King's Bell," "Königsmark, and Other Poems," were their characteristic output; in which they wrote in harmony with the playwrights who were producing their Leonoras and Francescas and Tortesas and Brokers of Bogota.[4]

---

[1] Winter, "Old Friends," p. 138.

[2] Ferris Greenslet, "Life of Aldrich," pp. 81, 101.

[3] Stedman and Gould, "The Life and Letters of Edmund Clarence Stedman," Vol. I, p. 211. For varying sentiments about Bohemia, note the references above in their contexts, as well as Ferris Greenslet's "Life of Aldrich," pp. 37–47.

[4] See page 289.

Of the permanently enlisted recruits to literary New York, Richard Henry Stoddard was probably the most devoted to a fanciful Muse. The criticisms of Holmes and Lowell served as correctives to the artificialities of Aldrich and Stedman, and the latter served as a kind of metropolitan laureate. But Stoddard, in spite of his contacts with journalism and politics, regarded poetry as altogether detached from life, ignoring or avoiding the facts of daily existence. Though now and again his poems show signs of becoming mildly erotic, they have no passion in them. Rather they exhibit the chaste delights of the virtuoso, who takes up one object after another from the glass-covered cabinets in the museum which his fancy has furnished, looks it over fondly, admires its form and color, and sets it back with even pulse until he shall choose to gaze on it again. These lyrics are sometimes nature descriptions and sometimes nature fantasies. Often they are about the idea of love — rather than about love itself — and about wine — but not about conviviality. In the abstract there is a negative tone, as in

> Man loses but the life he lives
> And only lives the life he loses,[1]

or in

> There is no life on land or sea
> Save in the quiet moon and me;
> Nor ours is true, but only seems
> Within some dead old World of Dreams.[2]

And this dream world was an abandoned unreality and not a hope for something better.

Taken at its best, Stoddard's verse is conventional and reminiscent. It suggests many measures from many periods. In only a few poems, which purport to be themselves imitations from the East, he wrote what seems fresh and new. His real gift was in the composition of little poetic cameos, bits of from four to a dozen lines, the dainty ornaments of literature.

---

[1] Stoddard, "Poems" (Complete Edition), p. 394. [2] Ibid. p. 49.

In a tributary essay on "My Friend Bayard Taylor"[1] Stoddard wrote:

> My favorite poet was Keats, and his was Shelley, and we pretended to believe that the souls of these poets had returned to earth in our bodies. My worship of my master was restricted to a silent imitation of his diction; my comrade's worship of his master took the form of an "Ode to Shelley," which I thought, and still think, the noblest poem that his immortal genius has inspired. It is followed in the volume before me . . . by an airy lyric on Sicilian Wine, which was written out of his head, as the children say, for he had no Sicilian wine, nor, indeed, wine of any other vintage.[2]

Taylor's most genuine work was written out of his travels; for he was one of the foremost to make known the fascinations of the Old World to the American public, not only in books but in hundreds of lyceum lectures; but much of his voluminous output of over forty volumes was written out of his head, and a great proportion of it out of his immense and tireless industry. He was an indefatigable worker, driven by the desire of establishing a manorial estate in Pennsylvania; continually on the go, getting up new lectures abroad, delivering them all over the country, buzzing around New York, dying abroad of overwork in what should have been the prime of life. He knocked out more than a dozen volumes of verse, nearly a dozen books of travel, guidebooks too, four novels in which he mildly visited on his countryside his mild resentments at their provincial ways. From 1850 to 1870 he cherished the project of translating Goethe's "Faust" and made the achievement of it his most distinguished work. If he had done half as much, he might have done twice as well. Probably his insatiable desire for activity would have whirled him out of any environment, but it is idle to theorize. The fact seems clear that Goethe supplied him with a task so definite and so superbly exacting that it elicited all that was best in his artistry. Left to himself he was like a beltless driving wheel, demolished by its own centrifugal force.

[1] Stoddard, "Recollections Personal and Literary," pp. 50–67.
[2] Ibid. p. 56.

Aldrich's literary career began and ended with the writing of poetry, but what he did in the interims of poetical silence contributed to the character of his work. As a reader and editor he was schooled in the exercise of a taste so exacting in detail that *The Atlantic* under his direction was described by a foreign critic as "the best-edited magazine in the English language."[1] Thus trained, he gave no quarter to what he had produced with zest if it did not ring true to his critical ear. "The vanilla-flavored adjectives and the patchouli-scented participles" criticized by his kindly senior, Dr. Holmes, were pared away. So in the little engravings that are the best expressions of his talent there is a schooled simplicity. And herein lie the shortcomings of Aldrich's poetry — that it is merely the poetry of accomplishment. As a youth in New York, writing while Halleck's popularity was at its height, he was not independent enough to be more original than his most admired townsman. The verses in "The Bells: a Collection of Chimes" are most of them clearly imitative; and from the day of "Babie Bell" on, whatever of originality was Aldrich's belonged to the library and the drawing-room and the literary club.

It is natural, then, that his longer narrative poems have least of his own stamp in them. They are literary grass of the field and establish no more claim on the primary attention of a modern reader than do the bulk of prose short stories written in the same years by Aldrich and his fellows. It is natural too that in his more ambitious odes — such as "Spring in New England" and the "Shaw Memorial Ode," which open and close the second volume of his poems — he did not appear to the best advantage. War odes are adequate only if written with epic vision, but the best that Aldrich did was to indulge in heartfelt tributes to the nobility of his fallen friends. Read Moody's "Ode in Time of Hesitation" beside Aldrich's slender lyric based on the same man and the same memorial, and the difference is self-evident.

---

[1] Ferris Greenslet, op. cit. p. 147.

In writing on personal and local and occasional themes Aldrich dealt with more congenial material, addressing the choicest of the limited public in which he was really interested. The kind of folk he cared for "drank deep of life, *new books* and hearts of men," like Henry Howard Brownell. As a youth he wrote delightedly of a certain month when he could see "her" every day and browse in a library of ten thousand volumes. He was a literary poet for literary people. As such he was most successful in poems which ranged in length from the sonnet to the quatrain. In the tiny bits, like "Destiny," "Heredity," "Identity," "Memory," "I'll Not Confer with Sorrow," "Pillared Arch and Sculptured Tower," he achieved a fulfillment of the wish recorded in his "Lyrics and Epics":

I would be the lyric
Ever on the lip,
Rather than the epic
Memory lets slip.

No more charming tribute was ever paid Aldrich than this of Whittier's narrated by a friend who had been visiting for a week with the poet in his old age:

Every evening he asked me to repeat to him certain short poems, often "Destiny," and once even "that audacious 'Identity,'" as he called it; but at the end he invariably said, "Now thee knows without my saying so that I want 'Memory,'" and with his wonderful far-off gaze he always repeated after me: "Two petals from that wild-rose tree."[1]

In his address[2] at a meeting held in memory of Edmund Clarence Stedman in January, 1909, Hamilton Mabie struck the keynote in two complementary statements: "Mr. Stedman belongs with those who have not only enriched literature with works of quality and substance, but who have represented it in its public relationships," and, "Stedman was by

[1] Ferris Greenslet, "Life of Aldrich," p. 258.
[2] Stedman and Gould, op. cit. Vol. II, pp. 495–499.

instinct and temperament a man of the town." He elected to live in Manhattan just as deliberately as Aldrich elected to live in Boston; and in this distinction lies something much broader than the mere difference between the two men.

Stedman took the consequences of settling in the commercial capital of the United States. While the members of the Saturday Club were lending distinction to Boston, the members of the Ornithorhyncus Club and the Bohemians were receiving the impress of New York. Thus it came about that Aldrich contributed to Boston what he brought there, but that Stedman was "made in New York." Both were war correspondents, but Aldrich admitted the war into his poetry only rarely, and then without much success. On the other hand, the first eighth of Stedman's collected poems are entitled "In War Time," and, with the poems of Manhattan, of New England, and of special occasions, amount to nearly one half the volume. Moreover, of the poems by Stedman which are generally known and quoted, quite the larger portion are included in utterances which are representative of literature "in its public relationships."

A timely admonition from Lowell, as valuable as the one from Holmes to Aldrich, helped to keep Stedman out of the byways in which he was inclined to stray. In 1866 he was proud of his "Alectryon," a blank-verse poem on a classic theme which had appeared in one of his books three years before.

> He at once said that it was my "best piece of work," but "no addition to poetic literature," since we already have enough masterpieces of that kind — from Landor's "Hamadryad" and Tennyson's "Œnone" down to the latest effort by Swinburne or Mr. Fields. So I have never written since upon an antique theme. Upon reflection, I thought Lowell right. A new land calls for new song.[1]

Stedman wrote, however, in full consciousness of all the wealth of Continental literature and the splendors of Old World tradition. Perhaps there was no single work into which he put more ambition than into his uncompleted

[1] Stedman and Gould, op. cit. Vol. I, p. 372.

metrical version from the Greek of the Sicilian Idyllists. His "Victorian Poets" and the anthology which followed were undertaken by way of making a workmanlike approach to the poetry of his own countrymen. As a reader he had the scholar's attitude toward literature; as a poet he felt a respect approaching reverence for the established traditions of his art. And yet he wrote no single essay which better demonstrated his sanity and his suavity of mind and manner than his discussion of Walt Whitman. Although he felt an innate distaste for much of Whitman's writing and for the way most of it was done, he succeeded in applying a fair mode of criticism. Counter to the cheap fashion of his day, of beginning with ridicule and ending with truculence, Stedman did himself the honor of coming out with " . . . there is something of the Greek in Whitman, and his lovers call him Homeric, but to me he shall be our old American Hesiod, teaching us works and days." The measure of Stedman's poetry should therefore be made in the light of two characteristics: his instinctive love of the town, as this determined his choice of subject matter, and his feeling for the elder poets, as this affected his sense of artistic form.

His less important work was the succession of verses which were written in the spirit and, in some cases, at the speed of the journalist. "The Diamond Wedding," for example, was done in an evening and was the talk of the town thirty-six hours later. But, more than that, it was actually good light satire — as good a piece of its kind as had appeared in New York since Halleck's "Fanny." So, too, "Israel Freyer's Bid for Gold" was published three days after the idea had first occurred to him. These, like the "Ballad of Lager Bier" and "The Prince's Ball" and even "How Old Brown Took Harper's Ferry," represented the high spirit of youth rollicking on paper in the fashion of the "Salmagundi" and "Croaker" satires. "Bohemia" and "Pan in Wall Street," though composed in this same general period, are more sober, deliberate, and genuinely poetical. In both Stedman dealt with the romantic potentials of city life.

During the last dozen years of his life poetry could not be his natural form of expression, for the world was too much with him. A great deal of the time when he was not getting or losing on 'Change he devoted to service on all sorts of boards and councils of good works, speaking and versifying for special occasions, editing miscellaneously (even a "Pocket Guide to Europe"), and giving advice and encouragement to younger poets. He was admirably representing literature in its public relationships and paying the price which is always exacted of an ambassador of any sort in the complete sacrifice of independent leisure. There is something pathetic in his oft-repeated protests in these latter years at being called a "banker-poet" or "broker-poet"; for he had failed to become rich as he had hoped, and he had enjoyed on the whole less security than many of his acquaintances who had attached themselves to literature in some professional way. This, however, had been a mistake not so much of judgment as of temperament. Unless his voluminous biography utterly misrepresents him he had no true capacity for leisure. He was an intellectual flagellant; and his poetry, although he was in theory devoted to it, was in reality a proof of the love of art which continually tantalized and distracted him but never won his complete allegiance.

Richard Watson Gilder was almost exclusively a lyric poet. His units are very brief, — there are more than five hundred in the one-volume "Complete" Edition, — very few extending to the one hundred lines ordained by Poe. Even among lyrics, moreover, he set distinct boundaries to his field. Among his metropolitan fellows he was notable in not writing imitative and reminiscent poetry. They must have been in his mind when he wrote:

Some from books resound their rhymes —
  Set them ringing with a faint,
  Sorrowful, and sweet, and quaint
Memory of the olden times,
Like the sound of evening chimes.[1]

[1] Gilder, "Poems" (Household Edition), p. 19.

His love lyrics remind one of Stoddard's. It is a chaste and disembodied passion that he celebrated in frequent groups of song. The lady is a delight to the eye — modest, timid, and yet all-generous; the lover — eager, gentle, adoring, and inspired to nobility.

> I love her doubting and anguish;
> I love the love she withholds;
> I love my love that loveth her
> And anew her being molds.[1]

A poet of so rarefied a sentiment hangs on the brink of sentimentalism, but Gilder seldom fell over.

His regard for nature was urban or suburban. The reader is conducted from the "Dawn," with which his first volume opened, past "Thistle-Down" and "The Violet," to the poems of Tyringham, his summer home; and then to "Home Acres" and "The Old Place," which had no rival; and ends "In Helena's Garden" between "The Marble Pool" and "The Sundial," to drink tea with eleven pretty girls at a table made from a granite millstone. The sun shines brightly; the flowers are in bloom, their odor mingling with that of the souchong; the conversation is facile; everybody is amiable and complacent. From such a catalogue one might expect sappy and emasculated nature poems, but once again Gilder's sanity rescues him. Even in Helena's garden he is rather a worker at ease than a sybarite. Poetry was not solely the record or the evidence of beauty for him. Although his only markedly personal allegiance in poetry was an allegiance to Keats, it was a fealty to Keats taken off before his prime. Gilder lamented the wrong that fate had done the youthful genius and did not content himself with reiterating that "a thing of beauty is a joy forever."

For Gilder seldom, even in his most ecstatic moods, set art above life. Though his work does not show the marked changes which have developed in many evolving careers,

---

[1] Gilder, op. cit. p. 226.

there is a clear emergence of philosophic and then social and civic interest in his progressive volumes. His sense for the need of a brave integrity comes to the surface in such poems as "Reform," "The Prisoner's Thought," "The Heroic Age," "The Demagogue," "The Tool," "The New Politician," "The Whisperers," and "In Times of Peace." To such themes as these and to his poems of heroism and of the reunited country, Gilder brought the same delicacy of touch as to his poems of love and art and nature, and he brought into view in them the latent vigor which saved the others from being merely pink and mellifluous.

In poetry written on the scale of Gilder's there is need of fine workmanship. There is no chance for Turneresque effects:

> The foreground golden dirt,
> The sunshine painted with a squirt.[1]

His craftsmanship becomes interesting in the history of versification. For Gilder was facile with the more complex forms of traditional verse and an early experimenter in the freer forms. Some rhythmic prose appears in his earliest volume, but the sonnet prevails at the beginning of his authorship; and at the end it almost utterly disappears in favor of the freest sort of blank verse — irregular and unrhymed iambic measures, suggestive of but distinct from Whitman's, and of frank prose-poetry, not even "shredded prose" (in the language of Mr. Howells) but printed in solid paragraphs.

The philosophy of Gilder was the philosophy of his most enlightened contemporaries. There is in it much of Emerson, whom he called the "shining soul" of the New World, and there is much of Whitman, though it is not clear whether their likeness does not lie in their common accord with Emerson rather than in a direct influence from "the good gray poet" to Gilder. The immanence of God in nature and in the heart of man ("The Voice of the Pine"); the unity of all natural law ("Destiny"); the conflict between religion

[1] O. W. Holmes, "Contentment."

and theology ("Credo"); and a faith in the essentials of democratic life — these are the elements of belief shared by Emerson and Whitman and Gilder. Gilder is not their most impressive or prophetic expositor. He is a lesser voice in the choir. The point of distinction for him is that he combined the work of a literary editor with the life of a good citizen and still kept the current of his song serene and clear.

Book List

THEATER, DRAMA, AND PRESS IN THE 1850'S

Theater and Drama

BRADLEY, EDWARD S. George Henry Boker, Poet and Patriot. 1927.
CLAPP, HENRY A. Reminiscences of a Dramatic Critic. 1902.
DURANG, CHARLES. The Philadelphia Stage. Third series. 1830–1855.
JEFFERSON, JOSEPH. Autobiography. 1897.
LUDLOW, NOAH M. Dramatic Life as I Found It. 1880.
MCVICKER, JAMES H. The Theatre; Its Early Days in Chicago. 1884.
MOWATT, MRS. ANNA C. Autobiography of an Actress. 1854.
MURDOCK, JAMES E. The Stage; or Recollections of Actors and Acting. 1880.
ODELL, GEORGE C. D. Annals of the New York Stage, Vols. VI–VII. 1931.
PYPER, GEORGE D. The Romance of an Old Playhouse. (Salt Lake City.) 1928.
QUINN, ARTHUR H. A History of the American Drama from the Beginning to the Civil War, Vol. II. 1923.
RYAN, KATE. Old Boston Museum Days. 1915.
TOMPKINS, EUGENE, and KILBY, QUINCY. The History of the Boston Theatre, 1854–1901. 1908.
VANDENHOFF, GEORGE. Leaves from an Actor's Note-book. 1860.
WALLACK, LESTER. Memories of Fifty Years. 1889.
WARE, RALPH. American Adaptations of French Plays on the New York and Philadelphia Stages from 1834 to the Civil War. 1930.
WINTER, WILLIAM. Other Days. 1908.

Collections of Plays

MOSES, MONTROSE J. Representative Plays by American Dramatists, Vols. II and III. 1918–1925.
QUINN, ARTHUR H. Representative American Plays. 1917. 1925.

Press

BLEYER, WILLARD G. Main Currents in the History of American Journalism. 1927.

DAVIS, ELMER. History of the *New York Times*, 1851–1921. 1921.

DILL, WILLIAM A. The Growth of Newspapers in the United States. 1928.

FLEMING, HERBERT E. Magazines of a Market-Metropolis; a History of Literary Periodicals and Literary Interests of Chicago. 1906.

GARWOOD, IRVING. American Periodicals from 1850 to 1860. 1931.

LEE, JAMES M. History of American Journalism. 1917.

NEVINS, ALLAN. *The Evening Post* — a Century of Journalism. 1922.

O'BRIEN, FRANK M. The Story of *The Sun*, 1833–1928. 1928.

TASSIN, ALGERNON. The Magazine in America. 1916.

YOUNG, JOHN P. Journalism in California. 1915.

MELVILLE

HERMAN MELVILLE. Chief works in book form in Melville's lifetime were these: Typee: a Peep at Polynesian Life, 1846; Omoo: a Narrative of Adventures in the South Seas, 1847; Mardi: and a Voyage Thither (2 vols.), 1849; Redburn: His First Voyage, 1849; White-Jacket: or, The World in a Man-of-War, 1850; Moby-Dick, or, The Whale, 1851; Pierre: or, The Ambiguities, 1852; Piazza Tales, 1856; The Confidence Man, 1857; Battle-Pieces and Aspects of the War, 1866.

[*Available Editions*]

The Apple-Tree Table and Other Sketches, edited, with introductory note, by Henry Chapin. 1922.

Family Correspondence of Herman Melville, edited by Victor H. Paltsits. Bulletin of the New York Public Library. 1929.

John Marr and Other Poems, edited, with introduction, by Henry Chapin. 1922.

Selected Poems, edited by Mark Van Doren. 1929.

The Shorter Novels of Herman Melville, edited by Raymond M. Weaver. 1928.

Some Personal Letters of Herman Melville, edited, with introduction, by Meade Minnegerode. 1922.

The Works of Herman Melville. Standard Edition (Constable). 16 vols. 1922–1924.

Among various reprints of the novels these are notable:

Moby Dick. Introduction by Raymond Weaver. 1925.

Moby Dick. Illustrated by Mead Schaeffer. 1922.

Moby Dick. Illustrated by Rockwell Kent. 1930.

Pierre, edited by Robert S. Forsythe. Americana Deserta Series. 1930.

Pierre. Preface by H. M. Tomlinson; introduction by John B. Moore. 1929.

Typee. Illustrated by Guido Boer. Aventine Classics. 1931.

Typee. Introduction and glossary by Sterling Leonard. 1920.

[*Biography and Criticism*]

BOYNTON, PERCY H. More Contemporary Americans. 1927.

BROOKS, VAN WYCK. Emerson and Others. 1927.

CANBY, HENRY S. "Conrad and Melville." Definitions. 1922.

CANBY, HENRY S. "Hawthorne and Melville." Classic Americans. 1931.

CURL, VEGA. Pasteboard Masks: Fact as Spiritual Symbol in the Novels of Hawthorne and Melville. 1931.

DAMON, S. FOSTER. "Why Ishmael Went to Sea," *American Literature*, Vol. II, pp. 281–283.

FREEMAN, JOHN. Herman Melville. E. M. L. Series. 1926.

GLEIM, W. S. "A Theory of Moby Dick," *New England Quarterly*, Vol. II, pp. 402–419.

HOMANS, G. C. "The Dark Angel; the Tragedy of Herman Melville," *New England Quarterly*, Vol. V, pp. 699–730.

MCCUTCHEON, R. P. "The Technique of Melville's 'Israel Potter,'" *South Atlantic Quarterly*, Vol. XXVII, pp. 161–174.

MATHER, FRANK J. "Herman Melville," *The Review*, Vol. I, pp. 276–278, 298–301.

MORDELL, ALBERT. "Melville and 'White Jacket,'" *Saturday Review of Literature*, Vol. VII, p. 946.

MORISON, SAMUEL E. "Melville's 'Agatha' Letter to Hawthorne," *New England Quarterly*, Vol. II, pp. 296–307.

MORRIS, LLOYD. "Melville: Promethean," *Open Court*, Vol. XLV, pp. 513–526, 621–635.

MUMFORD, LEWIS. Herman Melville. 1929.

PATTEE, FRED L. "Herman Melville," *American Mercury*, Vol. X, pp. 33–43.

RIEGEL, O. W. "The Anatomy of Melville's Fame," *American Literature*, Vol. III, pp. 195–204.

THOMAS, RUSSELL. "Melville's Use of Some Sources in 'The Encantadas,'" *American Literature*, Vol. III, pp. 432–456.

VAN DOREN, CARL. "Melville before the Mast," *Century*, Vol. CVIII, pp. 272–277.

VAN VECHTEN, CARL. "The Later Works of Herman Melville," *Double Dealer*, Vol. III, pp. 9–20.

WAINGER, B. M. "Herman Melville: a Study in Disillusion," *Union College Bulletin*, Vol. XXV, pp. 35–62.

WATSON, E. L. G. "Melville's 'Pierre,'" *New England Quarterly*, Vol. III, pp. 195–234.

WATSON, E. L. G. "Melville's Testament of Acceptance," *New England Quarterly*, Vol. VI, pp. 319–327.

WEAVER, RAYMOND M. Herman Melville: Mariner and Mystic. 1921.

[*Bibliography*]

"Bibliography." Minnegerode Edition of Letters, pp. 93–195.

A Bibliography of First Editions of the Prose Works of Herman Melville, compiled by Michael Sadlier. 1923.

Melville Bibliography, compiled by Robert Forsythe and John H. Birss.

WHITMAN

WALT WHITMAN. Chief titles: Leaves of Grass, 1855; ten successive enlarged editions appeared during Whitman's lifetime: 1856, 1860–1861, 1867, 1871, 1876, 1881 (Boston), 1881 (Philadelphia), 1888, 1889, 1891; Drum-Taps, 1865; Democratic Vistas, 1871; Specimen Days and Collect, 1882–1883; November Boughs, 1888; Good-bye, My Fancy, 1891.

[*Available Editions*]

Complete Prose Works of Whitman. Authorized by the executors. 1914.
The Complete Writings of Walt Whitman. 10 vols. Edited under the supervision of R. M. Bucke, T. B. Harned, and H. L. Traubel. 1902–1903.
Franklin Evans; or, The Inebriate, edited, with introduction and notes, by Emory Holloway. 1929.
The Gathering of the Forces. Editorials, Essays, etc. 2 vols. Edited by Cleveland Rodgers and John Black. 1920.
I Sit and Look Out. Editorials from the *Brooklyn Daily Times*, by Whitman. Selected and edited by Emory Holloway and Vernolian Schwarz. 1932.
In Re Walt Whitman, edited by Whitman's literary executors: H. L. Traubel, R. M. Bucke, and T. B. Harned. 1893.
Leaves of Grass. Inclusive Edition. Edited by Emory Holloway. 1931.
Letters of Anne Gilchrist and Walt Whitman, edited, with introduction, by Thomas B. Harned. 1918.
Specimen Days in America. World's Classics. 1932.
Uncollected Poetry and Prose of Walt Whitman. 2 vols. Edited by Emory Holloway. 1921.
Walt Whitman and the Civil War. A Collection of Original Articles and Manuscripts. Edited by Charles I. Glicksberg. 1933.
Walt Whitman's Diary in Canada. With Extracts from other of his Diaries and Literary Note-books. Edited by William S. Kennedy. 1904.
Walt Whitman's Workshop. A Collection of Unpublished Manuscripts. Edited, with introduction, by Clifton J. Furness. 1928.

[*Biography and Criticism*]

BAILEY, JOHN CANN. Walt Whitman. E. M. L. Series. 1926.
BARRUS, CLARA. Whitman and Burroughs, Comrades. 1931.
BAZALGETTE, LÉON. Walt Whitman; the Man and His Work. Translated by Ellen FitzGerald. 1920.
BINNS, HENRY BRYAN. A Life of Walt Whitman. 1905.
BLODGETT, HAROLD W. Walt Whitman in England. 1934.
BRADFORD, GAMALIEL. "Portraits of American Authors. II. Walt Whitman," *Bookman*, Vol. XLII, pp. 533–548.
BRADLEY, E. S. "Walt Whitman on Timber Creek," *American Literature*, Vol. V, pp. 235–246.
BROOKS, VAN WYCK. America's Coming of Age. 1915.
BUCKE, RICHARD MAURICE. Walt Whitman. 1883.
BURROUGHS, JOHN. Whitman; a Study (2d ed.). 1902.
CANBY, HENRY SEIDEL. Classic Americans. 1931.

CARPENTER, GEORGE RICE. Walt Whitman. E. M. L. Series. 1909.

DE SELINCOURT, BASIL. Walt Whitman; a Critical Study. 1914.

FOERSTER, NORMAN. American Criticism. 1928.

FOERSTER, NORMAN. Nature in American Literature. 1923.

FURNESS, CLIFTON J. "Walt Whitman's Estimate of Shakespeare," *Harvard Studies and Notes in Philology and Literature,* Vol. XIV, pp. 1–33.

FURNESS, CLIFTON J. "Walt Whitman's Politics," *American Mercury,* Vol. XVI, pp. 459–466.

GOHDES, CLARENCE L. "Whitman and Emerson," *Sewanee Review,* Vol. XXXVII, pp. 79–93.

HOLLOWAY, EMORY. "Whitman as Critic of America," *Studies in Philology,* Vol. XX, pp. 345–369.

HOLLOWAY, EMORY. Whitman: an Interpretation in Narrative. 1926.

HOWARD, LEON. "Walt Whitman and the American Language," *American Speech,* Vol. V, pp. 441–451.

HUNGERFORD, EDWARD. "Walt Whitman and His Chart of Bumps," *American Literature,* Vol. II, pp. 350–384.

KELLER, ELIZABETH L. Walt Whitman in Mickle Street. 1921.

KENNEDY, WILLIAM SLOANE. Reminiscences of Walt Whitman. 1896.

LOWELL, AMY. "Walt Whitman and the New Poetry," *Yale Review* (new series), Vol. XVI, pp. 502–519.

MABBOTT, THOMAS O., and SILVER, R. G. "Mr. Whitman Reconsiders," *Colophon,* Vol. IX, February, 1932.

MACY, JOHN. The Spirit of American Literature. 1913.

MOORE, JOHN BROOKS. "The Master of Whitman," *Studies in Philology,* Vol. XXII, pp. 77–89.

MORE, PAUL ELMER. "Walt Whitman." Shelburne Essays. Fourth series. 1906.

MORRIS, HARRISON S. Walt Whitman: a Brief Biography with Reminiscences. 1929.

MUMFORD, LEWIS. The Golden Day. 1926.

O'HIGGINS, HARVEY. Alias Walt Whitman. 1929.

PARRINGTON, VERNON L. Main Currents in American Thought, Vol. III. 1930.

PATTEE, FRED LEWIS. American Literature since 1870. 1915.

PERRY, BLISS. Walt Whitman: His Life and Work. A. M. L. Series. 1906.

POUND, LOUISE. "Walt Whitman and Italian Music," *American Mercury,* Vol. VI, pp. 58–63.

ROGERS, CAMERON. The Magnificent Idler. 1926.

SANTAYANA, GEORGE. "The Poetry of Barbarism." Interpretations of Poetry and Religion. 1900.

SAUNDERS, HENRY S. An Introduction to Walt Whitman. 1933.

SHERMAN, STUART. Americans. 1922.

STEDMAN, EDMUND C. Poets of America. 1885.

STOVALL, FLOYD. "Main Drifts in Whitman's Poetry," *American Literature,* Vol. IV, pp. 3–21.

TRAUBEL, HORACE. With Walt Whitman in Camden. 3 vols. 1915.

Whitman articles in *American Literature,* Vol. VI:

BAKER, PORTIA. "Walt Whitman and the *Atlantic Monthly.*"

CAMPBELL, KILLIS. "The Evaluation of Whitman as Artist."

MYERS, HENRY A. "Whitman's Conception of the Spiritual Democracy."

[*Bibliography*]

HOLLOWAY, EMORY, and SAUNDERS, H. S. Cambridge History of American Literature, Vol. II, pp. 551–581.

SHAY, FRANK. The Bibliography of Walt Whitman. 1920.

TRIGGS, OSCAR L. "Bibliography." Complete Writings of Whitman, Vol. X, pp. 139–233.

WELLS, CAROLYN, and GOLDSMITH, ALFRED F. A Concise Bibliography of the Works of Walt Whitman. 1922.

BOHEMIANS AND KNICKERBOCKERS

General

FOERSTER, NORMAN. "Later Poets." Cambridge History of American Literature, Vol. III, Part II.

HOWELLS, WILLIAM DEAN. Literary Friends and Acquaintance. 1900.

MABIE, HAMILTON W. The Writers of Knickerbocker New York. 1912.

WENDELL, BARRETT. "The Knickerbocker School." Literary History of America. 1901.

WINTER, WILLIAM. Old Friends; Being Literary Recollections of Other Days. 1909.

Individual Writers

THOMAS BAILEY ALDRICH. Chief titles: Poems, 1863; The Story of a Bad Boy, 1870; Marjorie Daw and Other People, 1873; The Stillwater Tragedy, 1880; Two Bites at a Cherry, 1894; Later Lyrics, 1896.

[*Available Editions*]

Poems. Household Edition. Best one-volume collection. 1918.

The Writings of Thomas Bailey Aldrich. Riverside Edition. 9 vols. Vols. I–II, Poems; Vols. III–IX, Prose. 1907.

[*Biography and Criticism*]

ALDRICH, LILIAN W. Crowding Memories. 1920.

ALDRICH, THOMAS BAILEY. The Story of a Bad Boy. 1870.

BOYNTON, H. W. "Thomas Bailey Aldrich," *Putnam's*, Vol. II, pp. 259–266.

GRATTAN, C. HARTLEY. "Thomas Bailey Aldrich," *American Mercury*, Vol. V, pp. 41–45.

GREENSLET, FERRIS. The Life of Thomas Bailey Aldrich. A. M. L. Series. 1908. New edition. 1928.

MORE, PAUL ELMER. Shelburne Essays. Seventh series. 1910.

PERRY, BLISS. Park Street Papers. 1908.

[*Bibliography*]

NORTH, E. "A Bibliography of Thomas Bailey Aldrich," *Book Buyer*, Vol. XXII, pp. 296–303. 1901.

"Bibliography." Life, by Greenslet, pp. 261–292.

RICHARD WATSON GILDER. Chief works: The New Day: a Poem in Songs and Sonnets, 1876; Lyrics, 1878; Poems and Inscriptions, 1901; A Christmas Wreath, 1903.

[*Available Editions*]

Complete Poems. 1910.
The Letters of Richard Watson Gilder, edited by Rosamond Gilder. 1916.
Poems of Richard Watson Gilder. Household Edition. 1908.

[*Biography and Criticism*]

DOWNEY, DAVID G. Modern Poets and Christian Teaching. 1906.
MATTHEWS, BRANDER. "Richard Watson Gilder," *North American Review*, Vol. CXCI, pp. 39–48.
WOODBERRY, GEORGE E., and others. "Richard Watson Gilder," *Century*, Vol. LVII, pp. 622–637. (Tributes at the time of Gilder's death.)

EDMUND CLARENCE STEDMAN. Chief works: Poems, Lyrical and Idyllic, 1860; Alice of Monmouth, an Idyl of the Great War, with Other Poems, 1864; The Blameless Prince, and Other Poems, 1869; Poetical Works, 1873; Victorian Poets, 1876; Poets of America, 1885; A Victorian Anthology, 1895; An American Anthology, 1900.

[*Available Editions*]

Poetical Works of Edmund Clarence Stedman. Household Edition. 1885. Other editions to 1901.

[*Biography and Criticism*]

BOYNTON, H. W. "Edmund Clarence Stedman," *Putnam's*, Vol. IV, pp. 357–361.
FULLER, MARGARET. A New England Childhood. 1916.
PIATT, JAMES J. "Mr. Stedman's Poetry," *Atlantic*, Vol. XLI, pp. 313–319.
PRITCHARD, JOHN P. "Stedman and Horatian Criticism," *American Literature*, Vol. V, pp. 166–169.
STEDMAN, LAURA, and GOULD, GEORGE M. The Life and Letters of Edmund Clarence Stedman. 2 vols. 1910.
TINKER, CHAUNCEY B. "Pan in Wall Street," *Saturday Review of Literature*, Vol. X, pp. 365–366.

[*Bibliography*]

STEDMAN, LAURA, and GOULD, G. M. The Life and Letters of Edmund Clarence Stedman. Bibliography in Vol. II, pp. 613–654.

RICHARD HENRY STODDARD. Chief titles: Songs of Summer, 1857; The King's Bell, 1862; Abraham Lincoln: an Horatian Ode, 1865; The Book of the East, and Other Poems, 1871.

[*Available Edition*]

Poems of Richard Henry Stoddard. Complete Edition. 1880.

[*Biography and Criticism*]

STODDARD, RICHARD HENRY. Recollections Personal and Literary, edited by Ripley Hitchcock. 1903.
VEDDER, HENRY C. American Writers of Today. 1894.

BAYARD TAYLOR. Chief works: Views-a-Foot: or, Europe Seen with Knapsack and Staff (2 vols.), 1846; Eldorado: or, Adventures in the Path of

Empire (2 vols.), 1850; Poems of the Orient, 1855; The Story of Kennett, 1866; The Picture of St. John, 1866; Lars: a Pastoral of Norway, 1873; The National Ode, 1877; Critical Essays and Literary Notes, 1880.

[*Available Editions*]

The Dramatic Works of Bayard Taylor, edited by Marie Hansen-Taylor. 1900.

The Works of Bayard Taylor. Household Edition. 14 vols. 1870.

[*Biography and Criticism*]

BEATTY, RICHARD C. "Bayard Taylor and G. H. Boker," *American Literature*, Vol. VI, pp. 316–327.

SMYTH, ALBERT HENRY. Bayard Taylor. 1896.

TAYLOR, MARIE H., and SCUDDER, H. E. Life and Letters of Bayard Taylor. 2 vols. 1884.

TAYLOR, MARIE H. and LILLIAN B. On Two Continents. 1905.

VINCENT, LEON H. "Life, Character, and Work of Bayard Taylor." American Literary Masters. 1906.

[*Anthologies*]

BOYNTON, PERCY H. American Poetry. 1918.

FOERSTER, NORMAN. American Poetry and Prose (rev. ed.). 1934.

KREYMBORG, ALFRED. Lyric America. 1930.

PRESCOTT and SANDERS. An Introduction to American Poetry. 1932.

STEDMAN and HUTCHINSON. Library of American Literature, Vols. VIII, IX, X.

WANN, LOUIS. The Rise of Realism. 1933.

CHAPTER X

New England — Right Wing

Nathaniel Hawthorne

AMONG the manuscripts left by Hawthorne at his death was an almost completed draft of the last story he wrote, "Septimius Felton."[1] It came at the end of a career that had won its substantial rewards of fame and fortune. There had been an extraordinarily long period of preparation in lonely obscurity, ten years of public life, and four years of comparative withdrawal. Then in valedictory he wrote this tale of a Concord youth who was irredeemably isolated. In 1837 when Longfellow, his college acquaintance, had congratulated him on the appearance of "Twice-Told Tales," he had written that he lived in a dungeon and was afraid to come out; that he could think of no fate more horrible than to have no share in the world's joys and sorrows.[2] A quarter of a century later he reverted to his early self in his latest full-length portrait:

> As for Septimius, let him alone a moment or two, and then they would see him, with his head bent down, brooding, brooding, his eyes fixed on some chip, some stone, some common plant, any commonest thing, as if it were the clew and index to some mystery; and when, by chance startled out of these meditations, he lifted his eyes, there would be a kind of perplexity, a dissatisfied, foiled look in them, as if of his speculations he found no end.[3]

---

[1] References are to the Standard Library Edition of "Hawthorne's Works," in 15 volumes, of which two are the biography "Nathaniel Hawthorne and His Wife," by his son, 1882–1891.

[2] Quoted in George E. Woodberry's "Nathaniel Hawthorne" (A. M. L. Series, p. 73), a long letter from Hawthorne to Longfellow after the publication of "Twice-Told Tales."

[3] Hawthorne, "Septimius Felton," in "Works," Vol. XI, p. 232.

> Septimius went into his house, and sat in his study for some hours in that unpleasant state of feeling which a man of brooding thought is apt to experience when the world around him is in a state of intense action, which he finds it impossible to sympathize with. There seemed to be a stream rushing past him, by which, even if he plunged into the midst of it, he could not be wet. He felt himself strangely ajar with the human race, and would have given much either to be in full accord with it, or to be separated from it forever.[1]

It may seem almost too easy to account for the manner of man he was. The early loss of his father; the extreme fashion of mourning that shrouded the household in his boyhood; an accident when he was nine that cut him off from active play for the next three years; a period of out-of-door solitude in his teens; and, after a college life that could not quite offset his boyhood background, twelve years in Salem, where, though it was his birthplace, he declared he was so retired that not a score of its inhabitants were even aware of his existence — these seem reasons enough for his being ajar with the social order, unrelated to it as he was except through his mother, his sisters, his adoring wife, his daughters and one little son.

Almost every contact that he made with people sent him back upon himself. Political friendships secured him a post in the Boston custom service, but he rejoiced in his escape from it. He made a try at being a Brook Farmer, and found the experience partly ridiculous, partly offensive. Concord, in his first residence, brought him no close friendships, filled him with disgust for the flotsam and jetsam of amateur philosophers who infested it as pilgrims to Emerson's door.[2] The Salem custom house years bore fruit in the bitter pages which preface "The Scarlet Letter." With Herman Melville whether in the Berkshires or in Liverpool, he was silent and unresponsive. When he went to England he found it little to his liking. Italy was better; but his greatest satisfaction —

---

[1] Hawthorne, op. cit. p. 250.

[2] Hawthorne, "The Old Manse," in "Mosses from an Old Manse," "Works," Vol. II, pp. 41–42.

in Florence — was that he was away from America. As to Liverpool: "I first got acquainted with my own countrymen there. At Rome, too, it was not much better. But here in Florence . . . I have escaped out of all my old tracks, and am really remote."[1]

His detachment rose almost to resentment, even at mere places. Of Salem he wrote that he was "invariably happiest elsewhere"[2]; his feeling for the town was the "mere sensuous sympathy of dust for dust."[3] The Concord River was indolent, sluggish, torpid; from its black mud "the yellow lily sucks its obscene life and noisome odor."[4] Having said this he cautioned the reader not to dislike the stream, which reflected heaven's blue; and then recalled that any mud puddle could do the same. Yet on the whole he enjoyed life at the Old Manse, within doors and in the garden and in the orchard.

Recalled to Salem by the necessity of making a livelihood, he found that he felt the same combined attraction and repulsion to past as well as to present.

> I seem to have a stronger claim to a residence here on account of this grave, bearded, sable-cloaked and steeple-crowned progenitor . . . than for myself, whose name is seldom heard and my face hardly known. He was a soldier, legislator, judge; he was a ruler in the Church; he had all the Puritanic traits, both good and evil.[5]

It is a grim fact of history that the old Puritan was on the bench at the time of the Salem witchcraft hysteria and acted aggressively as prosecuting attorney, jury, and judge.

> I know not whether these ancestors of mine bethought themselves to repent, and ask pardon of Heaven for their cruelties; or whether they are now groaning under the heavy consequences of them, in another state of being. At all events, I, the present writer, as their representative, hereby take shame upon myself for their sakes, and pray that any curse incurred by them — as I have heard, and as the

---

[1] Quoted in Woodberry's "Nathaniel Hawthorne," p. 265.
[2] Hawthorne, "Scarlet Letter," in "Works," Vol. V, p. 23.
[3] Ibid. p. 24.
[4] Hawthorne, "Mosses from an Old Manse," in "Works," Vol. II, p. 15.
[5] Hawthorne, "Scarlet Letter," p. 24.

dreary and unprosperous condition of the race, for many a long year back, would argue to exist — may be now and henceforth removed.[1]

This oppressive persistence of the past into the present rides him like an Old Man of the Sea. In "The House of the Seven Gables" he bursts into caustic invective. It is Holgrave, the photographer, who is speaking, and speaking fruitlessly to Phoebe, the placid compound of conservatism and inertia:

"Just think a moment, and it will startle you to see what slaves we are to bygone times — to Death, if we give the matter the right word!"

"But I do not see it," observed Phoebe.

"For example, then," continued Holgrave: "a dead man, if he happen to have made a will, disposes of wealth no longer his own; or, if he die intestate, it is distributed in accordance with the notions of men much longer dead than he. A dead man sits on all our judgment-seats; and living judges do but search out and repeat his decisions. We read in dead men's books! We laugh at dead men's jokes, and cry at dead men's pathos! We are sick of dead men's diseases, physical and moral, and die of the same remedies with which dead doctors killed their patients! We worship the living Deity according to dead men's forms and creeds. Whatever we seek to do, of our own free motion, a dead man's icy hand obstructs us! Turn our eyes to what point we may, a dead man's white, immitigable face encounters them, and freezes our very heart! And we must be dead ourselves before we can begin to have our proper influence on our own world, which will then be no longer our world, but the world of another generation, with which we shall have no shadow of a right to interfere. I ought to have said, too, that we live in dead men's houses; as, for instance, in this of the Seven Gables!"

"And why not," said Phoebe, "as long as we can be comfortable in them?"[2]

His life as a writer during the twelve years following graduation from college reinforced him in his habits of withdrawal from people into himself. The household he returned to was utterly unsocial. The young author neither gave nor received open sympathy. His writing was not read to the family. If

[1] Hawthorne, "Scarlet Letter," p. 25.

[2] Hawthorne, "Works," Vol. III, pp. 219–220.

he left the house during sunlight hours, it was to take long, lone walks in the country. He swam in the near-by sea before the town was stirring; he walked the streets in the evening shadows. His vital energy was drawn from reading and vented in brooding and writing.

Although he found some market for his tales and sketches, he won no stimulation from public applause; for he disguised himself not under one but under several pen names. Of his first novel, "Fanshawe" (1828), published at his own expense, he destroyed all the copies he could recover. From 1829 to 1836 "The Token," a Boston annual, was his main outlet, accepting in these years about twenty-five contributions. Through S. G. Goodrich, the editor, he also found a channel in the *New England Magazine*, and toward the end of the period in the *American Monthly Magazine* and *The Knickerbocker*, both of New York. The lack of wholesome, human contacts, either personal or public, told inevitably on Hawthorne's nerves and temper, and no doubt resulted in the touch of querulousness that crops out in his letters and self-descriptions.

Thus his themes are rooted in his negative experience. In his aloofness Hawthorne was increasingly sensitive to surrounding social forces and pressures and responses. He needed to fill his purse, and he was hungry for encouragement. He could not endure either being ignored or being hustled about. So he stands at the center of each of his major romances and of many of his tales and sketches in the person of a hypersensitive character confronted by a brute incarnation of the outer world. For Hester and for Arthur Dimmesdale, for Hepzibah and Clifford Pyncheon, for Priscilla, and for Donatello, complete isolation is impossible. Every deed that involves them involves the future and the surrounding world. Always there is the knocking at the gate, invasion from without; and this invasion is the harsher as it is the less deserved. Chillingworth's revenge on Dimmesdale is malign but not undeserved; but Priscilla, Donatello, and the two pitiful Pyncheons are innocent victims. Hepzibah and Clifford are hounded out of life by a bland representative of the law and the church. Priscilla falls in love with a reformer, one of the type, Thoreau complained, who pursued and pawed him with their "dirty institutions" and tried to constrain him into their "desperate, odd-fellow society"; she wilts at his touch. Donatello, innocent happiness in the flesh, is enmeshed in the web of society and destroyed by the fell spirit at its center. Hawthorne could not and would not have played his variations on this theme so insistently if any other had seemed as real.

Much of the remainder of his work had its source in his Puritan inheritance. None of the ultra-modern, anti-Puritan anti-New Englanders has drawn a more blasting indictment of decadent Puritanism than Hawthorne did generations before their pictures were offered as indictments of Puritanism as a whole. He recoiled from their theology with its acceptance of sin as a devil's wile to be atoned for only through the sufferings of a mediator or the tortures of hell. At which point he was at one with the Transcendentalists in substituting a hope for a dread. But his indictment of Puritanism gone to seed was more acrid than his reaction to the creed. Their intolerance, their arid bleakness of life, their pharisaism, and their hypocrisy furnished him with an abundance of resentments. So he was at once a product of his ancestry and a living protest against it.

But Hawthorne was an apostate against more than Puritanism. He was in accord with the rising individualism of his day and inclined to dissent from, if not to repudiate, the coercive enthusiasms of the social reformers. Of his interest in politics as a young man his sister wrote that it was so slight that "nothing would have kept it alive but my contentious spirit."[1] He felt a daily decreasing respect for "clerical people, as such, and . . . the utility of their office." His son could not remember that he ever went to church. As to education, though he was neighbor to Bronson Alcott of Temple School

---

[1] Julian Hawthorne, "Hawthorne and His Wife," Vol. I, p. 125.

fame, brother-in-law of Elizabeth Peabody (coworker with Alcott) and of Horace Mann, one looks in vain through stories, letters, and recorded conversations for any allusions to schools and schooling. The world of finance was unknown to him. As to slavery, his son has written, the risk of white blood for the liberation of the Negroes was in his opinion "utter sentimental nonsense." Nor, until war psychology had wrought on him, did he think the Union worth fighting for; not even then, in fact, for he hoped to give the Southerners "a terrible thrashing, and then kick them out." It was his wife's opinion that his soul was "too fresh with Heaven to take the world's point of view about anything." Which gives pertinence to the fact that Julian Hawthorne's life of his father is entitled not "Hawthorne and His Times" but "Hawthorne and His Wife."

It has been said — as if there were something vaguely or positively derogatory in the recital of such facts as these, and as if they deserved some rebuttal — that in actuality he was not timid, milk-and-watery, a sentimental young lady, or a bloodless sage. He was, in fact, physically robust, with more the look of a Webster than of a Charles Lamb. But his own preface to the "Twice-Told Tales" reprinted in 1851 not only refers to his reputation as "mild, shy, gentle, melancholic, exceedingly sensitive, and not very forcible," but questions whether his later writings had not some of them been influenced "by a natural desire to fill up so amiable an outline."

In the flush of success the author of "The Scarlet Letter" felt that he had proceeded "out of the Dreamland of his youth" into a "pleasant pathway among realities." But twelve years later, and with barely a twelvemonth to live, he acknowledged in the preface to "Our Old Home" that reality had offered anything but a pleasant pathway. "The Present, the Immediate, the Actual, has proved too potent for me. It takes away not only my scanty faculty, but even my desire for imaginative composition, and leaves me sadly content to scatter a thousand peaceful fantasies upon the hurricane that is sweeping us all along with it." Hawthorne the husband

and the villager may have been stalwart and robust, a good skater, even (in the right company) a convivial companion, but as an author he was none of these. His life in these two roles was like that Wayside house in Concord which still stands as an extraordinary evidence of his inability to harmonize past and present. Part of it, and the only attractive part, is an old New England cottage, low-studded, puncheon-floored, a bit of colonial Concord. The addition is largely Victorian English, with inordinately high ceilings and strange, semi-mortuary woodwork. And the whole is surmounted by a turret, for which he found the suggestion in Italy, though there is nothing Italian about its wooden awkwardness but its height. To find the actual, vital Hawthorne one must turn away from his actual, present world. He never belonged to it, though few men tried harder. He was never more remote from it than after the ten years of success, including the seven of foreign residence which offered him the familiar acquaintance with reality that did not belong to his art. In those last, neglected works that followed "The Marble Faun" there is in the highest degree a "kind of perplexity, a dissatisfied, foiled look . . . as if of his speculation he found no end."

Alone in busy Salem in the after-college years he made ready for his long-delayed career, writing in his Note-Books, as Emerson and Thoreau were doing, collecting themes and materials, making historical entries, jotting down detailed studies of odd characters, saving names, phrases, similes, and epigrams. "Miss Asphyxia Davis," "A lament for life's wasted sunshine," "A scold and a blockhead, — brimstone and wood, — a good match." "Men of cold passions have quick eyes." There are recurrent collections of ideas to be worked up. There seem to have been days when he was fertile in them; and many can easily be identified: "To make one's own reflection in a mirror the subject of a story." "A snake taken into a man's stomach and nourished there from fifteen years to thirty-five, tormenting him most horribly. A type of envy or some other evil passion." "A person to be in possession of something as perfect as mortal man has a right to demand; he tries to make it better and ruins it entirely." "Some very famous jewel or other thing, much talked of all over the world. Some person to meet with it, and get possession of it in some unexpected manner, amid homely circumstances." "The influence of a peculiar mind, in close communion with another, to drive the latter to insanity." "Pandora's box for a child's story." "A person to be the death of his beloved in trying to raise her to more than mortal perfection; yet this should be a comfort to him for having aimed so highly and holily." "To make a story out of a scarecrow, giving it odd attributes . . ." "A phantom of the old royal governors, or some such shadowy pageant, on the night of the evacuation of Boston by the British."[1] What Hawthorne attempted was essentially what Coleridge did in "The Ancient Mariner": to make an everyday application from anything but everyday material.

And yet at times he attempted what Wordsworth did in his larger share in the "Lyrical Ballads": to lift the material of everyday life out of the realm of the commonplace. It was one of his marked gifts to shroud with a kind of unreality characters and backgrounds that were drawn from close observation. His interpretation made them his own, though they were derived from the life about him. This process is in utter contrast with the invention of Poe. There were never such individuals as Arthur Gordon Pym or Monsieur Dupin or Fortunato or Roderick Usher. But Arthur Dimmesdale, Jaffrey Pyncheon, Hollingsworth and Kenyon, Hester, Phoebe, Zenobia and Miriam, were portraits made in the likeness of people who had walked the streets familiar to Hawthorne. Poe's settings are convincingly real. One can visualize details of the City in the Sea or the ghoul-haunted woodland of Weir, though one realizes that they never existed in fact. But Boston, Salem, Brook Farm, and Rome supplied actual backgrounds for Hawthorne. If the Puritans had

[1] These jottings may be found in the "American Note-Books," in "Works," Vol. IX, pp. 207 ff., 279 ff. The edition of the notebooks by Randall Stewart (1932) is important because of the restoration of many excisions by Mrs. Hawthorne.

builded as securely as the Romans, "The Scarlet Letter," "The Blithedale Romance," and "The House of the Seven Gables" could be illustrated — as "The Marble Faun" often has been — from photographs of surviving structures; and one of the surviving structures from Hawthorne's American novels is the most sought show spot in Salem to this day. Again, these actual scenes and people were put into stories for which there were historical bases, and the symbols around which they were woven — like the letter of scarlet and the many-gabled house — had been seen and touched by the author. The Maypole of Merry Mount once stood on the Wollaston hilltop, the great stone face is not yet weathered beyond all recognition, and the legends of Province House are amply documented.

In the preface to "The House of the Seven Gables," Hawthorne discussed his method of utilizing materials at hand to convey essential truths — not as the realist does, but in circumstances of his own choosing and with a "slight, delicate, and evanescent flavor" of the marvelous. And this shadowy unreality, he pointed out, comes from connecting "a bygone time with the very present that is flitting away from us. It is a legend prolonging itself, from an epoch now gray in the distance, down into our own broad daylight, and bringing along with it some of its legendary mist."[1] It is a cue to every one of the longer tales and to most of the shorter ones. Always plucking at the garments of the present is the outreaching hand of the past, the tradition of an elder day or the consequence of a deed committed before the opening of the story.

In a foreword to "Rappaccini's Daughter," which he describes as "from the writings of Aubépine," Hawthorne offers an estimate on his prose up to this time (1846) and, indeed, up to the year of "The Scarlet Letter," — 1850, — whether published before that date or not. It is so acute and complete that it leaves little if anything to be said for this period of inordinately prolonged literary apprenticeship:

---

[1] "Works," Vol. III, p. 14.

> As a writer, he seems to occupy an unfortunate position between the Transcendentalists (who, under one name or another, have their share in all the current literature of the world) and the great body of pen-and-ink men who address the intellect and sympathies of the multitude. If not too refined, at all events too remote, too shadowy, and unsubstantial in his modes of development to suit the tastes of the latter class, and yet too popular to satisfy the spiritual or metaphysical requisitions of the former, he must necessarily find himself without an audience, except here and there an individual or possibly an isolated clique.[1]

This accounts well enough for his position or lack of one; and the appraisal that follows is equally sound:

> His writings, to do them justice, are not altogether destitute of fancy and originality; they might have won him greater reputation but for an inveterate love of allegory, which is apt to invest his plots and characters with the aspect of scenery and people in the clouds, and to steal away the human warmth out of his conceptions. His fictions are sometimes historical, sometimes of the present day, and sometimes, so far as can be discovered, have little or no reference either to time or space. In any case, he generally contents himself with a very slight embroidery of outward manners, — the faintest possible counterfeit of real life, — and endeavors to create an interest by some less obvious peculiarity of the subject. Occasionally a breath of Nature, a raindrop of pathos and tenderness, or a gleam of humor, will find its way into the midst of his fantastic imagery, and make us feel as if, after all, we were yet within the limits of our native earth. We will only add to this very cursory notice that M. de l'Aubépine's productions, if the reader chance to take them in precisely the proper point of view, may amuse a leisure hour as well as those of a brighter man; if otherwise, they can hardly fail to look excessively like nonsense.[2]

His use of history, his resort to fantasy, his weakness for allegory, his unreality, his coldness or lack of passion, his faint yet unspontaneous humor, his rather labored forcing of the pen in the cross-section surveys of human experience and of daily life, his own vital inexperience that pushes him back

---

[1] "Mosses from an Old Manse," in "Works," Vol. II, p. 107.

[2] Ibid. pp. 107–108.

on vague generalization, and the resultant thinness of the tales and sketches, to all of these he properly pleads guilty before any indictment has been drawn against him.

His stipulation that the reader take "precisely the proper point of view" in order to find amusement in these tales and sketches for a leisure hour is altogether pertinent. And it is pertinent in connection with the reading of anything that comes from the past. Time is wasted on older literature if one refuses to consider the literary style and the general presumptions about life that prevailed when it was written. The present may be more remote from any genuine norm than the past was. Often one must go farther and accept an author in his departure from his own age as well as in his difference from the present; but Hawthorne's departure in these effusions of his Salem solitude was in the direction of the false conventions of the annuals — of boudoir literature composed for the delectation of the fair sex in their hours of ease. M. de l'Aubépine, said Hawthorne, contented himself "with a very slight embroidery of outward manners."

Up to 1846, then, Hawthorne's work was, of a truth, comparable to the embroidery of the samplers of those days, those pathetic marvels of needlework wrought with who knows what tears and travail by the little girls. The elaborate border pattern, the alphabet, the central design or semblance of a conventionalized picture, the inevitable moral sentiment, noble and oppressive, the date, the name, and the tender age of the precocious needlewoman. And when such a sampler was done, there was an end to it. It was an evidence of forced endeavor to no other end than its own artificial self. If it survives today, it is a curio to be preserved on the wall under glass. Childhood is no longer condemned to this sort of moralistic discipline which bore fruit in neither use nor beauty. Hester Prynne may have been forced to the perpetration of such before she was forced into wedlock with Roger Chillingworth, but when later she began to turn her needle to account she applied it to the beautifying of life; and it was in just this kind of vital significance that Hawthorne came to his own when, after due contact with men and women, he wrote the story of Hester Prynne.

In "The Scarlet Letter" Hawthorne wrote the first of his major romances and the best of them all. For the nearly four years of his headship at the Salem custom house his pen had lain unused. With the loss of his post it was released, with a store of energy and a store of material. The resultant novel was a recognizable "Hawthorne," but a "Hawthorne" with a difference. It had his characteristic economy of characters, — four central figures, — but they were no longer shadowy. Hester is an imperial figure, but an empress whose fine dignity and splendid endurance are offset by humanizing impulses and fallibilities. One can understand her love of Dimmesdale and her fear and hate of Chillingworth, for the men have substance, too. Hawthorne utilized the historic background to which he had often resorted, but made it the setting for dramatic tableaux that cling in the memory; and, in the way of the earlier stories, he obeyed the law of poetic justice in the contrasting overthrows of the two men, in the spiritual triumph of the heroine, and in the regeneration, and even financial enrichment, of little Pearl.

In method there was less change from his earlier writing than in either material or inner significance. Though the people live and act memorably and visibly, the book is a study in subjective analysis. One could properly borrow from the title of the eleventh chapter for a subtitle to the whole work: "or, The Interiors of Three Hearts." Like many of the bits from the apprentice period and like the other of the major novels, the story is dominated by a symbol; the scarlet letter shares significance with the recurrent scaffold and the continual interplay of sun and shadow. And true to form, Hawthorne could not escape from his habit of moralistic application and explication. It would have been a happy act of revision if he could have omitted the final chapter of "Conclusion" with its pedantic utterance: "Among many morals which press upon us from the poor minister's miserable experience, we put only this into a sentence: 'Be true! Be true! Be true! Show freely to the world, if not your worst, yet some trait whereby the worst may be inferred.'"

Yet as a moralist Hawthorne revealed a distinct change. The habit of drawing ethical conclusions was unaltered, but not so the kind of conclusions. In "John Inglefield's Thanksgiving," reprinted in "The Snow-Image and Other Twice-Told Tales" from "the musty and mouse-nibbled leaves" of an old periodical, Hawthorne subscribed to the Calvinistic doctrines of natural depravity and of unforgivable sin. Sin put one in the grasp of the devil; one might repent but not recover, for the devil, once his claws had reached an errant mortal "would snatch a guilty soul from the gate of heaven, and make its sin and its punishment alike eternal."[1] The offense of Prudence Inglefield was also Hester Prynne's; but in "The Scarlet Letter" Hawthorne wavered and then came to a new moral conclusion. Through the first half chastity is presented as an end-all and be-all, and the violation of it as the unforgivable sin, the verdict of Hester's townswomen; but as the tale progresses Hester triumphs, regains her position in the community, still cherishes her love, plans to fly with him unrebuked by the author-moralist. And the unforgivable sin becomes not the lovers' momentary surrender to passion, but the minister's prolonged and cowardly violation of his own integrity.

Moreover the devil disappears from the story, and fate, to which Hawthorne had often reverted in the early sketches, fights out the battle with free will. "By thy first step awry didst thou plant the germ of evil," says Chillingworth to Hester; "but since that moment, it has all been a dark necessity. Ye that have wronged me are not sinful, save in a kind of typical illusion; neither am I fiend-like, who have snatched a fiend's office from his hands. It is our fate. Let the black flower blossom as it may!"[2] The enduring quality of "The Scarlet Letter" rests in the fact that even though Hawthorne is incorrigible in his homiletic expoundings and

[1] Hawthorne, "Works," Vol. III, p. 590.
[2] Hawthorne, "Scarlet Letter," p. 210.

explainings, the truth is inherent in the story, the central figure is altogether convincing, and the two men are at least credible. It contains more flesh and blood, less embroidery, less allegory, than any other of his works.

In comparison "The House of the Seven Gables" is slight, confused and inconclusive. Hawthorne wrote this in the autumn after the publication of "The Scarlet Letter" while the publishers were eagerly waiting for a book to follow up the recent success. For his theme he chose the fateful blooming of the black flower that sprang from the dark necessity of Chillingworth's describing. But the tale was not itself the bloom of any necessity for artistic expression as the previous one had been; it was rather the boiling of a pot over a forced fire, with bookmakers and booksellers pumping at the bellows. In the preface Hawthorne told of his intent to present the truths of the human heart in romantic circumstances of his own choosing, interweaving a bygone legend with the "very present."

To achieve the effect he desired was the most subtly difficult of artistic ventures, and in the "Seven Gables" it is relatively unsuccessful. The two are not interwoven. The past is first presented in a conscientious and laborious introductory chapter, and it is later recalled by the quite mechanical device of endowing Holgrave, the photographer, with gifts as a writer and permitting him to read aloud one of his effusions in an interpolated chapter. The legend is more genuinely prolonged in the character of Jaffrey Pyncheon, the villain of the piece, than in any other element; but the judge is the major character whom Hawthorne least understood and least wanted to understand. The past in "The Scarlet Letter" is a background for real people; in the "Seven Gables" it is only the seedtime for a plot that comes to fruitage in a period which confuses and annoys him with the annoyance that he has already recorded in the ill-natured and somewhat petulant "Old Manse" and "Custom House" sketches. Holgrave, who is offered as a linking character, is in effect one of the past's posterity but no real heir, and a type of contemporary liberal on whom the author looked with conscious and self-approving tolerance. Hawthorne subscribed to Holgrave's invective against the domination of the past, at the moment of writing it, but later dismissed him with a wink as the kind of man who can entertain liberal principles only as long as they do not become inconvenient. Hepzibah Pyncheon is the genuine creation (Hawthorne's women are always superior to his men), and she is done in broad daylight. There is far less of legendary mist in the romance than there is of artistic irresolution.

The applause that followed stimulated Hawthorne during the next winter to carry through "The Blithedale Romance," the third full-length story within two years. In these years he was burdened also with seeing three books of collected short tales through the press. The pace was too fast and resulted in a slackening of his powers. Again he attempted to deal with the very present that was flitting away from him. He treated it this time not as a post-Puritan period, but as an age of miscellaneous "philanthropists," a designation of scorn which he visited in the story on the head of Hollingsworth. According to his own confession he groped "for human emotions in the dark corners of the heart" and never brought them out into daylight. Nor is the story suffused with mist; it is simply undeveloped. The necessary data about the histories of Zenobia and Priscilla are not evolved, but interpolated in the anecdote of Zenobia and the summarized explanation of their father. And this itself is left in vaguest terms, like the first faintest ideas for plot or scenario. The material is unassimilated — perhaps like the elements of American life, certainly like the unrelated figures in the summer revelry at Blithedale, where a group included "a Bavarian broom-girl, a negro of the Jim Crow order, one or two foresters of the Middle Ages, a Kentucky woodsman . . . and a Shaker elder."[1] He called the time "a chaos of human struggle" and declared that he saw in it no cause a sane man would die for. For better or for worse, it is Hawthorne's

[1] Hawthorne, "Works," Vol. V, p. 557.

last attempt to come to grips with his America. His gift was to deal with the human spirit in conflict with its own weaknesses; and when he tried to set this conflict against a background of existing life, he lost his way between the dreamland of allegory and the everyday scenes of circumstance.

Seven years of circumstantial life abroad intervened before he undertook the last of the major romances. Life had ceased to be cruel to him, but it still seemed hatefully coarse. America was no home for the artist; Liverpool certainly not; and Rome not quite, for it was a resort for expatriates where they tarried as aliens from their own land in an alien land. And an artists' colony is something less than a home: it is an asylum. The consequence was that Hawthorne, who could not feel at home under the shadow of St. Peter's nor in the neighborhood, however remote, of the Salem custom house, was driven to the only other haven of refuge he could think of — back to the shadowy past, from which he had so complacently emerged when he thought he was taking his place in the world of reality.

It was by the way of "The Marble Faun" that he made this retreat, the book which, in fact, is most specifically overloaded with photographic backgrounds. He located this meditation on the nature, the genesis, and the effect of sin away from his own land for the same reason alleged by Cooper — that the new country lacked the elements and the setting for romance; this despite their own narrative proofs to the contrary. He put it in Rome, therefore, and then filled it with scores of pages of nothing more than high-class guidebook writing about streets and piazzas and parks, churches, galleries and studios, and specific works of art, ancient and modern. This he did, he admitted, because he enjoyed doing it regardless of its value to the story.[1] In a less degree he was distracted by the period as well as by the place. Rome was a wicked city, he felt, and an unhealthy one, and its sanitation was no worse than the morals of its priesthood.

---

[1] See preface to "Marble Faun," in "Works," Vol. VI, pp. 15–16.

So he retreated from this picture that any tourist could confirm with his own eyes and his own prejudices, and went back in thought to the old New England of his youth and ancestry, back of Blithedale and the Salem of the Pyncheons, back to the view of life that he propounded in the early pages of "The Scarlet Letter." Life is sin-ridden as it was in John Inglefield's day. Man is naturally depraved, yet a sin once committed allows no earthly atonement; there is no redemption possible for the Hester Prynnes. Donatello is inevitably lost through his contact with sinful man. A Hilda can remain innocent, immaculate, uncontaminated by perpetration of evil; but "while there is a single guilty person in the universe," it is an innocence that is "tortured by that guilt."

It is in truth an instance of the past prolonging itself down into Hawthorne's very present, a strange subsidence by the author into a theology for which he felt an instinctive repugnance. He sank with hardly a struggle into the pessimism which threatened him in "The Blithedale Romance"; into the blackness of Calvinism that denied all joy, all strength, demanded lifelong self-abnegation, and thought of the afterlife as an escape from the mortal vale of tears.

"The Marble Faun" was Hawthorne's last full-length story published during his lifetime. In its insistence upon a theological interpretation of life it was not alone in the middle of the nineteenth century. Charles Reade, George Eliot, Anthony Trollope, each in an individual way, did the same thing. Mrs. Stowe as a New Englander did it from a point of view nearer to Hawthorne's. In the history of the American mind it was a long-persistent and often dominant way of thinking, and Hawthorne was its most eminent recorder. But the book is peculiarly Hawthorne's in its attempt to interweave fancy and reality, past and present; and in Hawthorne's output it is peculiarly significant in the unresolved conflict between the elements of fact and fancy and in the triumph in him, after indications of modernism, of the seventeenth century over the nineteenth.

As a piece of narrative writing also it harks back to the apprentice period. It is encumbered by irrelevant and dispensable description of Rome, which is the only Roman element in the romance. For Donatello, count of Monte Beni, and Miriam, with the mixed blood of English, Jewish, and Italian, wear the faintest of disguises over their New England Puritanism. Hilda is a complacent pharisee, and Kenyon an angular, detached dispenser of morals. Nothing in all Hawthorne is farther from credibility than the passage (Chap. XXXV) in which Kenyon offers Miriam and Donatello his intrusive exposition of their bonds and barriers and in which they listen with grateful deference. In its later editions the tale is followed with an appended set of explanations of "such incidents and passages as may have been left too much in the dark," an acknowledgment both of his failure and of his unwillingness to stand by it.

It is a striking paradox in Hawthorne's mature work that, after long building, he launched it with a tale of Puritan New England in which the author was freed from his narrow surroundings and fused emotion into life; but that he concluded it with a tale, ostensibly of modern Rome, which was cribbed and confined within the dogma of the old New England Puritans. The uncompleted romances he left behind him as the ungarnered fruit of his declining years round out the circle of his authorship. They are mist-shrouded, elusive, artificial, attenuated, continually at play with a favorite idea of his youth — the magic potion. Hawthorne was back in Concord, living in that strange conjunction of old and new into which he had converted his dwelling, as isolated from his neighbors as he had been in his Salem days. The war was on, and he was out of sympathy with it; out of sympathy with life.

Septimius went into his house, and sat in his study for some hours, in that unpleasant state of feeling which a man of brooding thought is apt to experience when the world around him is in a state of intense action, which he finds it impossible to sympathize with. There seemed to be a stream rushing past him, by which, even if he plunged into the midst of it, he could not be wet. He felt himself strangely ajar with the human race, and would have given much either to be in full accord with it, or to be separated from it forever.

Soon after he described this dilemma the escape came with his death.

The Cambridge Group

In the twenty years after the outbreak of the World War New England was assessed by the critics and historians the full price for a century of national prestige. From the outset this province was communicative and assertive. Encouragement of popular education and the establishment of printing created and supplied a little reading public, greatest of incentives to authorship. Up to the time of the Revolution the bulk of the interesting writings — not all, but most — came from the northern seaboard between New Haven and Boston. After the war the Connecticut Wits were overshadowed by some Philadelphians and some more emergent New Yorkers; but by the middle of the nineteenth century two men associated with Concord — Hawthorne and Emerson — and three identified with Cambridge and Harvard — Longfellow, Holmes, and Lowell — were generally yielded the palm. Thoreau and Whittier were on the way to reputation; but such writers as Poe, Whitman, and Melville, who had achieved before the Civil War, were all to wait long for belated national attention, which came in fullest measure after their deaths.

In the meanwhile the leading New Englanders enjoyed their successes. Their output made a Boston publishing house the most distinguished in the country[1]; marked it as the most desirable for a young Southerner like Henry Timrod, a young New Yorker like Edmund Clarence Stedman, a young Westerner like William Dean Howells. And the Boston group lent long life and prosperity to periodicals like the *North American Review*, the *Atlantic Monthly*, *The Congregationalist*, and the *Youth's Companion*. The doings at the Saturday

[1] The publishing house of Ticknor and Fields is a vital part of New England literary activity. See Bliss Perry's "Park Street Papers."

Club and the Radical Club[1] were cited on the literary pages of faraway daily papers; for the widespread sons and daughters of New England never flagged in interest, following the news as they could and, when they could, sending their sons on the back trail to Harvard and Yale, to Dartmouth and Bowdoin and Amherst and Williams.

The upcoming of New England historians — the elder Holmes and Sparks, Bancroft and Parkman — did not lead to understatement of New England's part in the political annals of America. What New England had done, New England recorded; and two of the early historians of American literature — Richardson at Dartmouth and Wendell at Harvard — gave full, if not fulsome, credit to what New England had thought and written. New England's natural bent for complacency became fixed withal, accepted for a half-century whatever the rest of the country granted it, claimed somewhat more. Mrs. Stowe wrote, rather as reminder of an obvious fact, that "New England was the seedbed of this great American Republic, and of all that is likely to come of it"[2]; the biographer of Edward Rowland Sill started with "Like most American men of letters the author of 'Opportunity' and 'The Fool's Prayer' was born in New England."[3] Holmes described a youth in the "Brahmin Caste" of his region as one whose "eye is bright and quick, — his lips play over the thought he utters as a pianist's fingers dance over their music."[4] He thanked God for the republicanism of nature which could develop a Lincoln, but he expected more of a Chauncy or an Ellery or an Edwards; and with a partially redeeming sense of humor he acknowledged that the Bostonian regarded his own town as the Hub of the Universe.

Two natural consequences followed. The picture thus drawn had to be corrected by alien observers. In literature

---

1 The records of these two social-literary clubs are to be found in E. W. Emerson's "Early Years of the Saturday Club," 1918; and Mrs. J. T. Sargent's "Sketches and Reminiscences of the Radical Club," 1880.

2 Mrs. Stowe, "Old Town Folks" (author's preface).

3 William B. Parker, "Edward Rowland Sill," p. 11.

4 Holmes, "Elsie Venner," p. 16.

figures ignored by New England had to be introduced into the tableau; figures unduly magnified had to be reduced. In the political and economic history the country had to be reviewed as from other points than Beacon Hill: by the propounders of the significance of the frontier, from the West; by the students of Spanish occupation the map had to be surveyed, with surprising effect, from the bottom upward. This was all in the nature of correcting and supplementing a defective and incomplete bird's-eye view of the United States.

But resentment has followed hard on correction in this reappraisal of national values. New Yorker, Southerner, and Westerner have somewhat suddenly burst into post-Victorian reproach at some of the worst aspects of Puritanism gone to seed, have written of these as if they were all of Puritanism, and have written of New England as if it were nothing but an embodiment of these. And of late another group of assailants, moved by a hostility that seems to have its roots in the Far West, have taken to gibing at New England because it was the seat of a colonial aristocracy (as every original colony was) and because the traditions of good breeding and conservative culture were still quietly persistent in Longfellow and his fellow townsmen. The "tie-wig school" and the "genteel tradition"[1] are perhaps legitimate labels to apply to these and men of their kind; but too often by the men who apply them they are used not only as labels but as badges of opprobrium, as though there were no legitimate place in American history for any but shirt-sleeved Charlemagnes of the new empire. The leader of this special assault revealed his bias triumphantly when he concluded his chapter on the "Tie-Wigs" with a picture of Robert Treat Paine drubbed by an indignant political opponent: "and so we leave him in the dust of the street, ignobly laid low by the strength of that vulgar democracy which was to bring down so many things held dear by Boston Tories."[2] And when he came on to the

---

[1] See V. L. Parrington's discussion of these New England writers in "Main Currents in American Thought," Vol. I, Book III, Parts I, IV.

[2] Parrington, "Romantic Revolution in America," pp. 294–295.

"Genteel" he betrayed himself again by the surprising retrospect of the same man in different perspective:

> Gone were the franker days of Robert Treat Paine when a wit might find his choicest *bon mots* in the bottom of his cups. Coarseness had given way to refinement. It was the romanticism of Brahmin culture, with all Falstaffian vulgarity deleted, and every smutch of the natural man bleached out in the pure sunshine of manners.[1]

This glorification of vulgarity as something commendable in itself is recurrent in latter-day criticism. It is interesting only with reference to the critics who indulge in it; and when it is resorted to in the neighborhood of Portland, Oregon, at the expense of the neighbors of Portland, Maine, it becomes no more than a quaint expression of provincial antipathy. The whole reaction is a reversal of Wordsworth's definition of poetry, now transposed into tranquillity recollected with emotion. In the study of the evolving American character there is no more reason for a historian's taking sides with the characters, groups, or regions than there is for a chemist's showing an emotional partiality for one of the elements. Paine sprawled in that Boston street more than a century ago. Democratic control has met with successes and with frustrations. All the way along there has been the interplay of entrenched tradition and aggressive revolt. All the way along it has been recorded in changing arts and social institutions.

The aristocratic tradition[2] was firmly established in colonial days, and of course more strongly, or more frankly, in the Southern settlements than in the Northern. Yet in Pennsylvania the Quaker lordlings were in control; in New York the great landlords ruled the day; in New England the royal governors and the merchant princes held the reins. Suffrage was not universal among adult males; far from it. And the distinction between "gentlefolk" and "simple men"

---

[1] Parrington, "Romantic Revolution in America," p. 436.

[2] See A. M. Schlesinger's "New Viewpoints in American History," Chap. IV, "The Decline of Aristocracy"; and D. R. Fox's "Decline of Aristocracy in the Politics of New York."

was marked not only by voting power but by dress, by seating in church, by classification in college catalogues. The members of the lower classes were seldom allowed to forget their status for long.

Membership in the privileged group inevitably brings its results. It is a status, and it is a point of view. It enjoys its own superiority and exclusiveness. It fights for its own privileges. It is marked by its own manners, its own education, its own enjoyment — consciously indulged — in the arts. Anything that suggests a stirring in the under strata of society suggests the possibility of change, and any suggestion of this sort is productive of alarm. The War of the Revolution was largely fought by believers in centralized and limited government. The Federalists who adopted the Constitution of 1787 were quite willing to forget the Declaration of 1776; and the children and grandchildren of that generation were a surviving and amiable element in American cultural life throughout the nineteenth century. Longfellow, Holmes, and Lowell belonged to it; so did hundreds of other men in the older Eastern cities. There is nothing peculiar to their district in their attitude toward life. It was general in their class and in their day. They simply happened to be spokesmen for it. But however general their attitude was, they naturally expressed it in terms of their region, and all three oscillated between Boston and Cambridge, the suburb across the Charles River.

The Boston which was the center of their intellectual life was both a stronghold of the old social order and the seat of an eager interest in arts and letters. On the slope of Beacon Hill was the Athenaeum Library, celebrated long after by Amy Lowell.[1] Just below were the Old Corner Book Store and the little shop maintained by the Peabodys. The theaters were rising at its foot. Music was being fostered under the wise persistence of John S. Dwight, Washington Allston was doing the best of his painting, and young

[1] See, in Amy Lowell's "Dome of Many-Coloured Glass," "The Boston Athenaeum."

Horatio Greenough was making his start as a sculptor. At the corner of the common across from the State House was the mansion of George Ticknor, historian of Spanish literature, hospitable in the offer of his rich library to the new generation of scholars. Bancroft, Parkman, Prescott, Motley, were lending new distinction to the pursuit of history in America whether or not on American themes. Elizabeth Peabody was a radioactive agent in all sorts of enterprises and enthusiasms: the Pestalozzian "Temple School," the "round table" conversations on history, the bookshop with its special yield of foreign publications, and the temporary publishing of *The Dial*. Francis H. Underwood was the untiring champion of the project which, with perfect unselfishness, he handed over to the abler founders of the *Atlantic Monthly*.[1] And scores of others with less definite fruits of perhaps less definite but no less zestful interest in life talked well and listened well and wrote well for the passing reader of the day.

To the miscellaneous reforms and miscellaneous speculations on the ways of the social order the Concordians were more hospitable, the Cantabrigians less susceptible. Almost everyone who was not actively involved in one or another of the uplift and reform projects was either alarmed or amused at the prevalence of them. Cooper's last caution in his closing work, "The Ways of the Hour," was an admonition against the liberalisms. Irving was not even alarmed. Emerson wrote Carlyle of the prevalence of men with schemes for ideal communities in their vest pockets, and confessed that he himself was "gently mad." He wrote a celebrated passage on the Chardon Street Convention of 1840:

> Madmen, madwomen, men with beards, Dunkers, Muggletonians, Come-Outers, Groaners, Agrarians, Seventh-day Baptists, Quakers, Abolitionists, Calvinists, Unitarians, and Philosophers, — all came successively to the top, and seized their moment, if not their hour, wherein to chide, or pray, or preach, or protest.[2]

---

[1] For an account of the founding of the *Atlantic Monthly* see Bliss Perry's "Park Street Papers," 1908.

[2] Emerson, "Works," Vol. X, p. 374.

Lowell was only writing in the same vein, but rather more brilliantly, in the opening of his essay on Thoreau, which is often cited as evidence of his genteel, tie-wig propensities. Such propensities he undoubtedly had; so did Longfellow; so did Holmes. They were more nearly the norm than the exception among educated Americans of their generation, and they had their parallels in contemporary England. It is because they represented aspects of American life and thought that each of them exerted his peculiar appeal.

Henry Wadsworth Longfellow

There is no possibility of debate as to Longfellow's immense popularity. The evidence of the number of editions in English and in other languages, the number of works in criticism, the number of titles in the British Museum catalogue, the number of poems included in scores of "Household" and "Fireside" collections, and the confidence with which booksellers stock up in anticipation of continued sales tell the story.[1] There is a parallel between his nearly twenty years as professor of modern languages and literatures at Harvard and his achievement as a poet of the people. As a teacher it was his task to instruct in the elements of the modern languages and to make a start at acquainting Americans with the song and story of the Old World. As a poet he was largely a reteller of old tales. He had no great inventive genius; he was a man of talent, applying the same industry to his writing that he did to a somewhat impressive mastery of foreign tongues, with twenty of which he was more or less familiar. With an ambition for something less than primary eminence, he had the honesty and good sense not to pretend to inspiration. On the contrary, he was continually projecting poems and continually sitting down not to write what he had thought, but to think what he should write. He was an avid

[1] Citations of Longfellow are to the Cambridge Edition of his "Works" (1886), 11 vols. Biographical studies are by Samuel Longfellow, "The Life of Henry Wadsworth Longfellow" (1886), 3 vols., and by T. W. Higginson, "Henry Wadsworth Longfellow."

but acquiescent reader, and what his reading yielded him was literary material rather than vital ideas. He accepted and reflected the ways of his time, not modifying them in any degree. But he touched the imagination of America with his twice-told tales and he mildly stirred its milder emotions.

With such an endowment and such an ambition, he undertook early in his career to write a succession of what he called "psalms" for the people. They were brief and homely counsels of courage, faith, resolution, aspiration, industry, fidelity, human sympathy. "And thou, too, whosoe'er thou art," he wrote in "The Light of Stars,"

> That readest this brief psalm,
> As one by one thy hopes depart,
> Be resolute and calm.[1]

"The Psalm of Life," the most celebrated of these, is memorable for its fourth stanza:

> Art is long and Time is fleeting,
> And our hearts, though stout and brave,
> Still, like muffled drums, are beating
> Funeral marches to the grave;[2]

but it is remembered more for the subsequent staccato appeals to ambition with its prosaic but challenging lines, "Be not like dumb, driven cattle," "Act, — act in the living present," and "Let us, then, be up and doing." "Excelsior," which is balladlike in content and psalmlike in its "moral," is another homily on aspiration, vividly presented but unhappily destined to be coupled with an uproarious melody chiefly associated with high times rather than lofty sentiments. "The Village Blacksmith" is introduced at work and at worship, commended for his simple goodness, and applauded in an appended stanza for being so obviously good that he serves as an example for the villager and for the reader. "The Bridge," in sentimental vein, develops the theme of the multitudes of sorrow-stricken who have crossed it, and the other

---

[1] Longfellow, "Works," Vol. I, p. 25.

[2] Ibid. p. 21.

multitudes who can see in the moonlit water a wavering symbol of divine love. As he wrote these simple lyrics, which offer little of stimulus or comfort to the modern intellectual, Longfellow was speaking as the voice of his generation in the idiom of his generation when the phrases of orthodox religion and the ethics of daily life rang true for a people who had been bred in the iteration of their cadences.

In this period of psalm-writing Longfellow as a translator was choosing sober and improving themes. The "Coplas de Manrique" is a transparently veiled Spanish homily on the vanity of human wishes; there are themes from the Spanish on "The Good Shepherd" and "The Image of God," and from Dante on "The Celestial Pilot" and "The Terrestrial Paradise." There is an Anglo-Saxon passage on "The Grave," and a German ballad in which a ribald discussion on "The Happiest Land" meets with pious reproof. In the course of this sort of writing, however, there comes "My Lady Sleeps," the serenade in "The Spanish Student," which is as simply effective and as fortunate in its musical setting as Shelley's "Indian Serenade" or Bayard Taylor's "Bedouin Love Song." This preoccupation with other literatures inevitably had its effect on Longfellow's treatment of native themes, as in "The Bridge," in which he likened the moonlight on the Charles River to a golden goblet falling into the water, a simile obviously drawn from Schiller's "König in Thule." It is an inclination, or a practice, that Longfellow admitted when, in "Seaweed," he explained

> So when storms of wild emotion
> Strike the ocean
> Of the poet's soul, erelong
> From each cave and rocky fastness,
> In its vastness,
> Floats some fragment of a song.[1]

As Longfellow came into his period of greatest productiveness, between 1845 and 1865, the play of rival interest in

[1] Longfellow, op. cit. p. 259.

foreign and native themes never led him to extended treatment of his contemporary America. A story to him was a story from the past, the sources of which were in print; a ballad was what a ballad was to Bishop Percy, either a "relique" or a new tale from the past told in what purported to be the old manner. Though the prime figure in his literary vista had written "De Vulgari Eloquentia," the fund of genuine folk material, the literature of the vulgar tongue in the United States, was of no interest to him. He was not exceptional in his disregard; perhaps it is because Longfellow's present is our past that the songs and ballads of the nineteenth century are now subjects of general attention. He was certainly an orthodox member in a community of relatively high culture in America when at one and the same time he fostered thoughts of national balladry and declared that "as our character and modes of thought do not differ essentially from those of England, our literature cannot."[1] He was right in his statement; his only error was in identifying the culture on the slopes of Beacon Hill with the culture of the whole country.

The "Tales of a Wayside Inn" in scheme, content, and literary implications are fairly representative of Longfellow and his circle. Attributing a succession of tales to a group of congenial acquaintances was an accepted device; but Chaucer and Boccaccio assembled homogeneous groups of Englishmen and Italians. Longfellow, in a land of polyglot derivations, gathered at the inn three American devotees of the past, a theologian, a scholar-bibliophile, and a poet, and with them a Norwegian musician, a Sicilian, and a Spanish Jew. Over the tales as a whole hangs an atmosphere of virtuosity such as the booklover of Bostonia might breathe in the Athenaeum Library, aware of the burying ground below and the Park Street Church beyond. It is apparent in "Robert of Sicily" and in "Sir Federigo's Falcon" — virtuosity applied to moralism. But there is a touch of cosmopolitanism in the Wayside Tales, too. "The Monk of Casal-Maggiore" is

---

[1] Samuel Longfellow, "Life," Vol. II, p. 20.

almost Boccaccian, on the safe side of ribaldry, but on its brink. And "The Rhyme of Sir Christopher" and his golden-haired mistress is offered without any strictures on the moral unregeneracy of the pair. "The Birds of Killingworth," also, is the work of a New Englander who could look upon the Puritan past with critical detachment.

The steps toward this detachment are apparent in the four major narratives from the American past which preceded "Tales of a Wayside Inn": "Evangeline" (1847), "Hiawatha" (1855), "Miles Standish" (1858), and "The New England Tragedies" (first form, 1860). The first two were the work of the scholar-poet, industrious in the collection of his data, eruditely experimental in the adoption of his measures, quite as "The Saga of King Olaf" was. Yet they marked in a high degree the skill in combining erudition with popular effectiveness which earned him his immense vogue. The immediate success of "Evangeline," of which five thousand copies were sold within two months, is easy to understand. The material was fresh and the story was sentimentally appealing. The pastoral prospect at the start, the dramatic episode of the separation, the long vista of American scenes presented in Evangeline's vain search, and the final rounding out of the plot, all belong to a "best seller"; and, as it happened, there was in 1847 no widely popular novelist in the United States. The local field belonged to the author of "Evangeline" as it belonged to the authors of "Marmion" and "Don Juan" a half-century earlier on the other side of the Atlantic. He was so free from dangerous rivalry that even his laborious employment of the exotic dactylic hexameters cost him nothing in popular esteem.

In 1854, the year of his withdrawal from Harvard, the scholar-poet hit on another American theme which drew him still farther from his own present. "I have at length hit upon a plan for a poem on the American Indians, which seems to me the right one and the only."[1] It was again a scholar's

[1] Samuel Longfellow, op. cit. Vol. II, pp. 247–248.

idea: to do with the traditions of the red man what Malory had done with the Arthurian story and what Tennyson was soon to be reweaving into the "Idylls of the King." Schoolcraft's Indian researches put the material into his hands, and the Finnish epic "Kalevala" supplied the appropriate measure. "Hiawatha" appeared in 1855 and was demanded by the public in repeated reprintings.

This work of the scholar has also the elements of enduring art: a fine surface and a firm substance. It appeals to the immature as a succession of picturesque stories. Its lack of plot is no defect to the youthful reader — nothing could be more plotless than the tales of Gulliver's sojourns with the Lilliputians or the Brobdingnagians. The episodes are as vivid and circumstantial as those in "Gulliver's Travels" or "Pilgrim's Progress." But they also deal with human types that belong to all romantic legend and all folklore: Hiawatha, the hero; Minnehaha, the spotless heroine; Chibiabos, the sweet singer, or artist; Kwasind, the strong man, or primitive force; Pau-Puk-Keewis, the mischief maker, or comic spirit. Any child will recognize them in Robin Hood, Maid Marian, Alan-a-Dale, Will Scarlet, and Friar Tuck. Again these human types are represented in the animal world of the folk tales, and natural forces are used as instruments in a supernaturally directed series of events.

Moreover, the epic note is insistent. A peace is declared among the warring tribes; Hiawatha is sent back by Mudjekeewis to live and toil among his people; he is commended by Mondamin because he prays "for advantage of the nations"; he fights the pestilence to save the people; he divides his trophies of battle with them; and he departs when the advent of the white man marks the doom of his race. So the ordering of the parts is ethnic, tracing the Indian chronicle through the stages that all peoples have traversed, from the nomad life of hunting and fishing to primitive agriculture and community life; thence to song and festival, a common religion, and a common fund of legend; and finally, in the tragic history of an oppressed people, to the decline of strength (the death of Kwasind), the passing of song (with Chibiabos), and the departure of national heroism as Hiawatha disappears into the sunset.

No other poem of Longfellow is so well harmonized in form and content. The fact of first importance is not that he derived the measure from a Finnish epic, but that this primitive epic form is the natural, unstudied way of telling a primitive story. The forms of literature that could survive only through oral transmission are simple in rhythm and built of parallel units. It was Longfellow's nice achievement to conjoin as poet and scholar,

Legends and traditions
With the odors of the forest,
With the dew and damp of meadows,
With the curling smoke of wigwams,
With the rushing of great rivers,
With their frequent repetitions
And their wild reverberations,
As of thunder in the mountains.[1]

With "The Courtship of Miles Standish" Longfellow returned to New England, telling his first long story of his own district and people. Both "Evangeline" and "Hiawatha" were narratives that ended with themselves. The glory of the Acadians and of the Indians had departed. But "Miles Standish" was like the following "New England Tragedies" in being very much alive. For the early Puritan, Longfellow felt a respect not untinged with both repugnance and humor. For his self-righteousness, his stridency, and his arid lack of feeling for beauty he displayed an amused contempt, but for his fighting powers and his self-control he felt a good deal of admiration. Miles Standish, he explained, was stalwart, practical, even magnanimous; but he was one of the prosy, unlovable kind who banished the birds from Killingworth with costly results. The more amiable character, John Alden, one of the poet's ancestors,

[1] Longfellow, "Works," Vol. II, p. 113.

was like the preceptor of Killingworth in his feeling for beauty in nature and in song. "Miles Standish" is his most kindly picture of the Puritans. In "The New England Tragedies" Governor Endicott's death comes in retribution for his ways as a persecutor, and Giles Corey's sacrifice to the witchcraft fanatics is a harsh indictment of unbridled bigotry.

For the last twenty years of his life Longfellow's main pursuit was in sustained narrative and translation. His rendering of Dante is a scholar-poet's pre-eminent piece of American translation, at once more poetic and more scholarly than Bryant's "Iliad" or Bayard Taylor's "Faust." It was a labor of devotion, extending over many years; the fruit of his teaching as well as of his study; and, in its final form, the result of nightly counsels with his learned neighbors, Charles Eliot Norton, James Russell Lowell, and others. Age, fame, and the affectionate respect of choicest friends protected him and perhaps insulated him from the events of the day. Yet little psalms and ballads no longer contented him. Life had become an outreaching drama to which he made an approach in his cyclic "Christus; a Mystery."

Once more his precedent was supplied him from the past. The first section, "The Divine Tragedy," was a reworking in dramatic form of Biblical themes in the structural sequence of the medieval mystery plays. Part Two, "The Golden Legend," used the name of the "Legenda Aurea," traditionally employed for the lives of the saints, which were later dramatized as miracle plays; and it introduced into a medieval setting an actual miracle cycle of nine units. Part Three dramatized two episodes from colonial New England. It was a monumental venture, but not a successful one. The first section is rather perfunctory. The second, medieval section is more convincing and effective; it was again the work of the scholar-poet. But the ambitious scheme was dependent upon the concluding section; and the concluding section, if it were to lead to anything definitive, demanded analysis of the modern world and an assertion of modern faith which should show that the course of Christianity had not ended in irresolution and confusion. Yet it is to irresolution and confusion that Longfellow brought it; not because it was his intention to do so, but because it was his fate. He shrank from the attempt to dramatize his own present. He really did not want to look at it. The nearest dramatic material for the culmination of his history was the tragic fanaticism of decadent Puritanism; and the best conclusion he could devise was, as a dramatist, to present it, and, as a Christian optimist, to repudiate it. The result was complete anticlimax for the chronicle as a whole, though the "New England Tragedies" in themselves are among the most vigorous of his writings.

He regarded the fragmentary and inconclusive "Christus" as a completed work. He described the completed "Michael Angelo" as "a fragment." This again is full of vitality, filled with portraits which are speaking likenesses of Renascence characters. They are confirmable and documentable, but they are also indubitably alive. The fourth act, with its great final utterance from the title character, is deeply moving. And as one reads it one can see that, in Michael Angelo, Longfellow presented his own doubts, which resulted in his own incapacity to bring the "Christus" to any definitive conclusion:

Who knows? who knows?
There are great truths that pitch their shining tents
Outside our walls, and though but dimly seen
In the gray dawn, they will be manifest
When the light widens into perfect day.
A certain man, Copernicus by name,
Sometime professor here in Rome, has whispered
It is the earth, and not the sun, that moves.
What I beheld was only in a dream,
Yet dreams sometimes anticipate events,
Being unsubstantial images of things
As yet unseen.[1]

---

[1] Longfellow, "Works," Vol. VI, p. 152.

Writing more consciously, Longfellow continued in his latest sonnets and in his valedictory "Bells of San Blas" to assert the "serene faith" that has been ascribed to him. This is the poet who was the people's favorite. The thousands who never heard of Dante and Michelangelo and never opened his learned "Christus" selected and loved the poems they could understand and could respond to as good, wholesome, uncritical, unthinking, optimistic Americans. Then they turned to Tennyson, just as the same sort of Englishmen in the same period turned from Tennyson to Longfellow.

James Russell Lowell

Longfellow was a New England romanticist, a teller of tales and a singer of songs who happened to live in America and was glad of it, because life was good to him there. Holmes was more of a rationalist and interpreter, but little of a critic. James Russell Lowell shared with Longfellow his literary erudition and his romantic feeling; with Holmes, his rationalism and his facility of expression. He was more muscular and more passionate than either and in much closer contact with his times.

He belonged to a family of perhaps a little more prestige than Holmes's and certainly than Longfellow's, and could look immediately to a father and two uncles who enjoyed distinction in commerce, the church, and law. Until graduation from Harvard he seemed to stand among the conservatives; but he was soon after swept into the ranks of what his generation were wont to call the radicals. It was a mild word during the middle half of the nineteenth century, used to classify the amiably tolerant and the benignantly progressive as well as every more emphatic or aggressive type of liberal. For some years young Mr. Lowell was allied with the more aggressive. He was a junior in college when Emerson delivered his address on "The American Scholar," and he must have heard echoes of it, as of the address to the theological students in the year he wrote his own class poem.

Before long he was deploring the "baby arrows" in this outburst with which he "dared assail the woundless Truth!" and throughout his career he was appealing to the truth as insistently as Emerson. During the 40's he became involved in the reform movements, at which he took a derisive fling in his essay on Thoreau,[1] coming out for the so-called temperance cause and against slavery. But his most substantial writing was in three appeals to the better nature of America: "Prometheus," "A Glance behind the Curtain" (on Cromwell), and "Columbus." In a letter on the first of these he wrote a friend:

> I have made it *radical*, and I believe that no poet in this age can write much that is good unless he gives himself up to this tendency.... So much of its spirit as poets in former ages have attained ... was by instinct rather than reason. It has never till now been seen to be one of the two great wings that upbear the universe.[2]

In these poems on his hopes and fears for America he coupled faith in the processes of the rationalist with faith in the intuitions of the Transcendentalist. Truth was never born of brute power; truth was not the offspring of chance; high impulse led toward truth. And when he came down to a definite issue in "The Present Crisis," he composed another ode to truth: it was an ethical impulsion, its home was in the future, it ennobled him who espoused it, it was the unflinching foe of falsehood; but it was also allied with reason:

> New occasions teach new duties; Time makes ancient good uncouth;
> They must upward still, and onward, who would keep abreast of Truth.[3]

Truth to Lowell was not the intellectual end of inquiry that for Emerson resulted in an understanding of the mysteries;

---

[1] For Lowell's own characterization of his youthful radicalism see the opening passage of the essay on "Thoreau," and the "Letters of James Russell Lowell" (edited by Charles E. Norton), Vol. II, p. 302. References to Lowell's writings are to the Standard Library Edition of his "Works" (11 vols.), 1890.

[2] Lowell, "Letters," Vol. I, p. 72.

[3] Lowell, "Works," Vol. VII, p. 184.

it was not even so rational a matter as he was to describe in "The Cathedral" of 1870, when he declared that "Nothing that keeps thought out is safe from thought." [1] It was always allied to a righteousness that was in peril and in need of champions. In these years he could be as vehement as Emerson or Thoreau. One of Holmes's friendly critics has called attention to the fact that the Autocrat's admirations were reserved for such temperate men as Everett, Webster, Bryant, Agassiz, Parkman. In Lowell's fiery years he was praising Garrison, Kossuth, Phillips, Torrey (the antislavery martyr), Palgrave (the political apostate).

While the fine recklessness possessed him it came to fulfillment in the first series of "Biglow Papers." In these nine bits of verse anent the Mexican War, the limitation of slave territory, and the checking of slave power, Lowell forgot himself more completely than he was ever to do again, and wrote simply, compactly, concretely, unlearnedly. They seemed, he wrote ten years later, like the work of someone else.

> This has helped to persuade me that the book was a genuine growth and not a manufacture. . . . All I can say is that the book was *thar* — how it came is more than I can tell. . . . And as for an historical preface, I find that quite as hard after now twelve years of more cloistered interests and studies that have alienated me very much from contemporary politics.[2]

Up to his thirtieth year Lowell, who was the same age as Whitman and only two years behind Thoreau, had developed quite rapidly and more nearly in the direction these men were to take than in the ways of his older neighbors in Cambridge. He was full of enthusiasm for life and for democratic life. He was close enough to passing events to be something of a realist about political and social conditions, but certain of the soundness of democratic principles and eager to fight for them. He was a zealous nationalist and an aggressive moralist, and he was as sure as any colonial Puritan

---

[1] Lowell, "Works," Vol. X, p. 50.

[2] Lowell, "Letters," Vol. I, pp. 295–296.

that he could not be mistaken about either the right or the truth — that God had no patience with anyone who disagreed with him; this despite the fact that though truth is eternal,

> her effluence,
> With endless change, is fitted to the hour.[1]

But the "cloistered interests and studies" that were to alienate him from politics were already beginning to allure him. He was a mercurial man who needed to oscillate between the library and the platform. He found that reform could not take up the whole of him, because the time had come for a change. He withdrew among his books, coming out to lecture and to teach, fulfilling the part of him that had composed the bookish "Vision of Sir Launfal" and the journalistic "Fable for Critics" in the year just following his excited activities as a citizen. As, however, every experience was an adventure for him and as he had a boylike superabundance of energy and the habit of exercising it indiscriminately, he poured the same amount of vigor into narratives, lyrics, and essays that he did into his protests against slavery and secession; and as there was no emotional need for this vivacity, it often took itself out in the self-indulgences of uncontrolled communicativeness: digression, irrelevancy, redundancy, pedantic posturing, sheer verbosity. Thus when he returned to the device of the "Biglow Papers" in the second series, his contributions averaged almost twice as long as in the first, and when he put them out in book form he almost smothered them in successive foreword, preface, prologue, introduction, interpolated explanation, and postscript. One of the letters in the second series was written in versified hog Latin.[2] It is natural that as he looked back on them he wondered how he could have written anything so forthright and simple as the first crisp utterances of Hosea Biglow.

---

[1] Lowell, "Works," Vol. VII, p. 138.
[2] Lowell, "Biglow Papers," second series, No. VIII.

This change in Lowell's manner of thought and literary style seems to have been more than an accident. It was related to his attitude toward the public, which for a moment he had addressed with such popular success. Lowell was not a man of the crowd. He sympathized with the Negro at long range; but he referred to the Irish as "paddies." He wrote in the conventional way of the dignity of labor; but he revealed no understanding or consciousness of the laborers who populated the near-by mill town that carried his family name. He grew fearful of the mob, skeptical about it, self-conscious and embarrassed at winning its approval. He was inclined toward the New England Brahmins; happy in his associations with the members of the Saturday Club and the faculty of Harvard College, and the group that founded *The Atlantic*, as why should he not have been? But the result was that more and more he inclined to write for this group, who liked good talk as a sort of intellectual steeplechase and who enjoyed a recondite allusion for their consciousness that it was caviar to the general. Writing for this audience, which was very much less than a reading public, brought Lowell to the pass of composing such an effusion as "Fitz-Adams' Story," three quarters of which is a rambling preliminary before the story comes with its own further generous introduction. All too often his essays and longer poems meander along like the "argymunt" supplied for Hosea Biglow's valedictory speech:

> Interducshin, w'ich may be skipt. . . . Spring interdooced with a few approput flours. Speach finally begins . . . subjick staited; expanded; delayted; extended. Pump lively. Subjick staited ag'in so's to avide all mistaiks. Ginnle remarks; continooed; kerried on; pushed furder; kind o' gin out. Subjick restaited; dielooted; stirred up permiscoous. Pump ag'in. Gits back to where he sot out. Can't seem to stay thair, etc., etc.[1]

It is almost all good, with the casual sequence of after-dinner talk uttered in the challenging presence of Oliver Wendell Holmes and his brother John and Tom Appleton and Tom

---

[1] Lowell, "Works," Vol. VIII, p. 377.

Aldrich, who have a long evening ahead of them and do not care where the talk drifts, so long as it contains plenty of "good things." So he fills his pages with quips and oddities like the gifts and favors at old-time children's parties—hidden all over the house and just as likely to defy search as to turn up under a napkin or in the umbrella of a departing guest.

Yet this habit of mind neither gives expression to certainty of convictions nor contributes to them; and the young "radical" of the 1840's, sure of his democracy, found increasing difficulty in reconciling the "manifest destiny" with the obvious facts. From 1820 on, Irving, Cooper, Bryant, and their followers had protested more and more frequently[1] on the perennial subject of the certain condescension in foreigners to which Lowell addressed himself in his essay of 1869. Yet none of these men so evidently played up to this condescension or so stimulated it by the petulance of their protests. Lowell, though loyal, was more and more apologetic, less and less confident of his countrymen. He outdid the average cultured American of his day in his reluctance to contemplate the incarnation of America. He knew that Uncle Sam was too mature for it; he feared that it was like Tom Sawyer; he did what he could to mold it into the image of Little Lord Fauntleroy; and he apologized for Whitman. When Mark Twain visited William Dean Howells in Cambridge in 1871, they were both young sojourners from what was to Cambridge an undiscriminated West. Young Mr. Clemens did not care at all; and young Mr. Howells did not care as far as he was concerned, though he cared a great deal in behalf of his friend, who was incorrigibly Western. And in recording his anxiety he recorded a striking fact about that generation: that polite America was afraid of the rough-and-ready Americans whom Europe was applauding. Mr. Howells did not care, he said of Mr. Clemens, to expose him "to the critical edge of that Cambridge acquaintance

---

[1] See pages 210, 211, 214, 226, 227.

which might not have appreciated him at, say, his transatlantic value. In America his popularity was as instant as it was vast. But it must be acknowledged that here for a much longer time than in England polite learning hesitated his praise. . . . I went with him to see Longfellow, but I do not think Longfellow made much of him, and Lowell made less."[1]

Mark Twain was too near the portrait of the "shirt-sleeved Charlemagne of empires new" that Lowell had already drawn. He once again aroused the doubt that had long been disturbing as to the democracy of which such a character was a typical product. This had cropped out in the essay on Thoreau, apropos of Emerson: "If it was ever questionable whether democracy could develop a gentleman, the problem has been affirmatively solved at last."[2] It had come up in the Lincoln essay: "Mr. Lincoln has also been reproached with Americanism by some not unfriendly British critics; but with all deference we cannot say that we like him any the worse for it."[3] In the ode on Agassiz he heaved a sigh of relief that the great Swiss naturalist was willing to put up with conditions in a country which offered him the career Europe had denied him. Even in the Harvard "Commemoration Ode"[4] he broke out suddenly with,

Who now shall sneer?
Who dare again to say we trace
Our lines to a plebeian race?

And when near the end of his life he delivered in England his address on "Democracy" he was uncomfortably aware of the English comments on the recent Haymarket riot in Chicago, and more disturbed at these than at the conditions which had produced the disorder or than at the miscarriage of justice toward which events were tending. It was the effect of a general habit as well as of a specific instance that made him approach his subject with a smile of half-apology: "I shall

---

[1] W. D. Howells, "My Mark Twain," p. 46.
[2] Lowell, "Works," Vol. I, pp. 367–368.
[3] Ibid. Vol. V, p. 192.
[4] Ibid. Vol. X, p. 28.

address myself to a single point only in the long list of offences of which we are more or less gravely accused, because that really includes all the rest."[1]

This shifting insecurity in Lowell is apparent in his experience as literary critic. He started with his eye on his own period, and in "A Fable for Critics" revealed at twenty-nine a remarkable sense for what was significant and enduring in the writers of his day. But he turned from his contemporaries in a succession of essays and rambling commentaries on the major English writers, looking aside to Dante, whom he was studying with Longfellow and Norton. These were long, readable, suggestive. They show that he was saturated in his subject matter and in much that was loosely relevant; but they have the looseness of structure that goes with reverie rather than with directed thinking. The best that was in them was in the summarizing, often introductory, passages, which had the excellence of the brief, unelaborated estimates in the "Fable." As far as his critical work had direction, it moved toward classicism, the direction of his life as a whole. But it is impossible to discover abiding convictions as to the function of literature or the function of criticism, or clear shifts from one conviction to another. One can find in him about what one wants. The new humanists laid claim to him, for he offered them ammunition; but so could the disciples of almost any school of criticism if they searched patiently and quoted as aptly as Lowell himself could quote. His criticism is to be read for stimulating and often brilliant passages of appreciation, not for a consistent body of reactions to literature, consistently conceived and methodically stated. Lowell was too much of a lyrist for that.

It was no doubt his gift for casual, extempore utterance, together with his easy grace of delivery, that won him his unprecedented success as minister to England, where, as one admiring Londoner put it, he found the Britons all

[1] Lowell, "Works," Vol. VI, p. 12.

strangers and left them all cousins. In diplomatic circles his tact modified his firmness, leading to detractions from some of his countrymen because he never defied or blustered. And in his important appearance as representative of the United States at all manner of social occasions he charmed his hosts by the facile pertinence of his public speech. It was, according to William Crary Brownell,

> the happiest, easiest, most graceful conceivable, with just the right proportion of play to seriousness, the ideal combination of ingredients for a post-prandial confection. . . . He was pithy without baldness and full without prolixity. He never said too much, or said what he had to say with too much gravity. His manner, in short, was perfection, but the real substance that his felicity of presentation clothed counted for still more. . . . And in England his unexampled popularity was very largely due to this gift.[1]

It was evidently as rhetorician, in the ancient sense, that Lowell reached his highest level of artistry. And it was as cosmopolitan among cosmopolitans, the American who was equally at home in London, in Rome, and in Madrid.

It was with similar consciousness of self-adjustment that he commended, with a touch of patronage, the free-and-easy Western American and the Hosea Biglow type of Yankee, in whom there was least trace of European heritage. So he faltered between the Old World and the New just as he faltered between the faith of the Middle Ages and the science that was both an avenue to the truth of change and a menace to the truth of stability. In "The Cathedral" he established a balance for himself; but it was not a secure one, for the fact was that he was afraid of his own conclusions, seeing no way out of paying lip service to freedom of inquiry and freedom of thought, yet finding no comfort in a complete emancipation from authority. It was the dilemma of his generation, and he stood irresolute before it. In "The Cathedral"[2] he wrote:

---

[1] W. C. Brownell, "American Prose Masters," pp. 271–272.
[2] Lowell, "Works," Vol. X, p. 50.

Science was Faith once; Faith were Science now. . . .
Shall we treat Him as if He were a child
That knew not his own purpose? nor dare trust
The Rock of Ages to their chemic tests,
Lest some day the all-sustaining base divine
Should fall from under us, dissolved in gas?

Yet later, in a letter, he wrote of the evolutionary theory, "Such a mush seems to me a poor substitute for the Rock of Ages — by which I understand a certain set of higher instincts which mankind have found solid under their feet in all weathers." The test of truth was become its palatability now, as it continued to be when he wrote "I am a conservative (warranted to wash) and keep on the safe side — with God as against Evolution." Or when he finally declared, "I continue to shut my eyes resolutely in certain speculative directions."[1]

These comments and confessions were expressed in personal letters not published till long after his death. During his lifetime he made no public declaration that he was faltering between the faith of Tennyson and the doubt of Arnold. But it is contained in a posthumous poem published soon after the deaths of Tennyson and Arnold. In the radicalism based on reason, on which he relied when he wrote "Columbus," he had no surviving confidence. Intellectual endeavor had left him "fumbling in a doubt." The only recourse was back to the instinct that as a young man had failed to satisfy him, and this instinct was in his mind the substructure of sound tradition. He had had his adventures early. Whether in economic or social or religious thought, as an aging man he returned to the comfort of an armchair by the fireside. New occasions no longer taught new duties.

[1] Lowell, "Letters," Vol. II, pp. 245, 325, 168.

Oliver Wendell Holmes

In this pageant of spokesmen for New England, all but one of whom lived under the shadow of the Massachusetts State House, Oliver Wendell Holmes, latest to survive, was at once the most old-fashioned and the most up-to-date. For he was a compound of two elements. As he acknowledged frequently and illustrated throughout the whole range of his writing career, he was a product of the eighteenth century, a conservative in tastes, and an ultra-conservative in social inclinations. Commenting in old age upon his Phi Beta Kappa "Poetry" of 1836, he alluded to himself as a "young person trained after the schools of classical English verse as represented by Pope, Goldsmith, and Campbell, with whose lines his memory was early stocked."[1] When he was not writing verse like Pope's, he was writing in the manner of Pryor and Gay and Akenside. When he turned from verse to the essay, he was Addisonian; and when he turned to the novel, there was more than a touch of Goldsmith in his method. He was intellectually of the eighteenth century too in his contempt for the whole breed of "dunces," in his distrust of the mob for its susceptibility to the religious charlatan and the political demagogue. Yet he was liberal in his reactions to theology, an active participant in the scientific movement of his day, an early contributor to medical knowledge, and a lifelong teacher of medical students. He was a product of the interplay between his instinctive tastes and social prejudices and his conscious interest in the intellectual developments of his day.

He seldom forgot his birth and breeding. His father, one of the early historians of the American Revolution, was a pulpit expositor of the old orthodoxy and the old breeding. He was an inheritor of the blood of the Bradstreet, Phillips, Hancock, Quincy, and Wendell families, and a natural champion of the Brahmin Caste,[2] to which he was recurrently allu-

---

[1] Holmes, prefatory note to "Works" (University Edition, 12 vols., 1891), Vol. XII, p. 35.

[2] Holmes, "Elsie Venner," Chap. I.

sive. One turns no further than the first installment in "The Autocrat of the Breakfast Table" to find him making consciously generous acknowledgments of the self-made man, but alleging his own preference for men of family, people with generations of the gentry behind them, preferably governmental and professional — heirs to portraits, slowly accumulated libraries, old silver, colonial furniture, and the manners that accompany these. He did not stop, however, with the preferences of the Autocrat. The Professor, who succeeded him, returned to the discussion in the fifth and sixth installments of his series: "I go politically for equality, — I said, — and socially for *the* quality."[1] Challenged to define his terms, he repeated the earlier statement with a new stress on wealth and with the almost incredible comment that money is the most permanent thing that a man could leave. "A man's learning dies with him; even his virtues fade out of remembrance, but the dividends on the stocks he bequeaths to his children live and keep his memory green."[2] Writing in 1859 with uncomfortable premonitions as to the coming political campaign, he insisted upon the need for gentility in the White House — a sentiment which, following the election of Lincoln, he somewhat begrudgingly modified in "Elsie Venner." The recurrence of this theme in Holmes's writing, together with the confirmation of his sentiments in his daily experience, stamps him as given to a social conservatism which those who care to may fairly brand as snobbery.

But it was something more than this. Cooper shared the same feeling of social complacency, and from time to time reasserted his superiority to the rank and file while he was inviting the sting of popular disapproval and receiving it and smarting from it.[3] On the other hand, Holmes, who kept off from politics and away from bitterly controversial subjects, was undisturbed either by the general course of events or by his own relations with the public; for his public was demon-

---

[1] Holmes, "The Professor," p. 331. [2] Ibid. p. 151. [3] See pages 257–262.

stratively friendly. It encouraged him to write from a slightly elevated vantage point with a slight degree of condescension in a tone of mild satire faintly flavored with cynicism.

He was amused at the sentimental ballad, as the orthodox eighteenth-century wit was, and he parodied it in "The Ballad of the Oysterman." He saw the futility in the miseducation of the American girl in the old-line "finishing" school, as John Trumbull had seen it before the War of the Revolution,[1] and he derided it in his verses on "My Aunt" and in the chapter on "The Apollinean Institute," interpolated in "Elsie Venner." He was entertained by the busy solicitudes of the Seventh-Day Adventists and the comet-invoked predictions of the end of the world, and had his say in "Latter-Day Warnings" as to the distance from the millennium indicated by the lawmakers, preachers, doctors, publishers, and vendors of all sorts of commodities. He listened with a gleam in his eye to the praises of the simple life, as doubtless stimulated by the appearance of "Walden," and wrote "Contentment" in proof that he could rub along with something short of the resources of Midas. In the centennial year of Jonathan Edwards's death he wrote a bit more cryptically than usual his "logical story" of the breakdown of that theological vehicle of Calvinistic faith, "The Deacon's Masterpiece, or The Wonderful 'One-Hoss Shay.'" In the meanwhile he was the unfailing occasional poet for his college class and for Harvard College on major anniversaries, and he was always ready with a salvo of verse for any other personal anniversary, arrival, departure, or otherwise sufficiently significant event to attract his attention and social endorsement.

A position of this sort in any community eventually raises the holder to the level of a local sage and assesses him the penalty which attends a diet on adulation — a form of intellectual flatulency. He becomes oracular without becoming profound, and he becomes overcommunicative and repeti-

[1] John Trumbull, "The Progress of Dulness," Part III, "The Adventures of Miss Harriet Simper." See above, p. 131.

tious, secure in his hearers' indulgence.[1] It is a danger that faces the teacher, the lay preacher, the local laureate; and Holmes was all three. His limitations as an observer of the ways of the world have been cited: he was a contented beneficiary of the prevailing order, willing to accept himself as witness to its beneficence. And he was also a literary conservative: "a little jealous of certain tendencies in our own American literature, which led one of the severest and most outspoken of our satirical fellow-countrymen . . . to say, in a moment of bitterness, that the mission of America was to vulgarize mankind."[2] He deplored the European tendency to applaud "the most lawless freaks of New World literature,"[3] and his only comment on Walt Whitman was to belittle him by extended and supercilious comparison with Lord Timothy Dexter, the colonial eccentric.[4]

Under the surface of his apparently complacent amiability, however, there was an independence of judgment which was twice foretold in his youth and which was a constant throughout his long life. The first time was on the occasion of an issue in his father's church when the son was forced to agree with the liberal majority, who literally took the pastor's pulpit away from him so that he had to re-establish himself in North Cambridge. Conflict between loyalty to conviction and loyalty to family interests and prides furnished a stout test. The other sign of independence was in Holmes's choice of a profession. He was socially predestined to some kind of intellectual life. From the outset he rejected the ministry as his "calling." He shrank from the formal complexities of the law as he did from the logic of the theologians. The thought of teaching seems not to have entered his mind at the time of his choosing. Literature could not assure him a livelihood. By elimination, outside of politics, only medicine was left;

[1] Thus, humorist though he was, he was capable of soberly drawing an analogy between the second volume of the "Autocrat" series and "Paradise Regained" and the second part of "Faust." See the preface to the revised edition of "The Professor at the Breakfast Table," p. v.

[2] Holmes, "Over the Teacups," p. 110.

[3] Ibid.

[4] Ibid. pp. 235–236.

but medicine was in his day not an accredited profession, for medical science was of the scantest, and the practice of "physic" was largely distributed between the barber, the bloodletter, the veterinary, the midwife, the "yarb doctor," and the miscellaneous quack. It was no small matter for this young Brahmin to disregard the exclamations and lifted eyebrows of his compeers and to seize the opening to contribute to the progress of a budding science. It was a decision that colored much of his writing and clarified his thinking, as he was inevitably involved in the growing conflict between the empirical procedure of his own profession and the traditionalism of his father's.

He was wide awake to change because he was so aware of the conflict. He noted it in the shifts in thinking that followed the findings of the biological sciences, and in the, as always, quicker responses in daily life to the inventions that made living more comfortable and less laborious.[1] As the years passed he could refer with amusement to the angry feelings and harsh laughter that greeted opinions of his "as if they were the utterances of a nihilist incendiary"[2] though twenty-five years later the opinions were the commonplaces of the time. As a rule he kept his temper, though he came nearer to abusiveness in his lines on "The Moral Bully" than ever again, and more extendedly insistent on the need of open discussion, the fear of which implied "feebleness of inner conviction,"[3] than his suavity ordinarily permitted him to be.[4] And he expressed complete satisfaction in his portrait of the stuffy Reverend Joseph Bellamy Stoker, affirming that he was drawn to less than lifelikeness, and that he would not stain his pages with more obnoxious realism.

His idea of freedom of conscience carried no mental reservations: "The very aim and end of our institutions is just

---

[1] Note the 1882 and 1891 prefaces to "The Autocrat of the Breakfast Table," pp. vi, ix; and the characteristic linking of past and present in "The Broomstick Train" in "Over the Teacups," pp. 226 ff.

[2] Holmes, "The Professor at the Breakfast Table," p. vi.

[3] Ibid. p. 109.

[4] Holmes, "The Guardian Angel" (preface), p. x.

this: that we may think what we like and say what we think."[1] This is familiar enough as a doctrine, and Holmes pursued it in familiar ways, which were pertinent and needful when he was doing it. In retrospect it is clear that in two particulars he was something more than just another recruit in the campaign for liberalism. As a medical scientist he had special knowledge and a special fund of illustration. This resource he perfectly characterized in his preface to "Elsie Venner"[2]: "My poor heroine found her origin not in fable or romance, but in a physiological conception fertilized by a theological dogma." He pressed his points throughout the trio of novels which he freely admitted were "medicated," and openly asserted were offered as narrative commentaries on the moot problems aroused by the impact of science on New England orthodoxy. He harked back to them in the long course of the "Breakfast Table" series. He played with the same themes in much of his light verse. And he capped all this with his volume of medical essays.

Holmes's other contribution to the subject, more literary in quality, is the succession of genuinely incisive observations that savor of the twentieth century far more than of the nineteenth. In 1873 he wrote:

All paraphrases are more or less perfect depolarizations. But I tell you this: the faith of our Christian community is not robust enough to bear the turning of our most sacred language into its depolarized equivalents. You have only to look back to Dr. Channing's famous Baltimore discourse[3] and remember the shrieks of blasphemy with which it was greeted, to satisfy yourself on this point."[4]

And at the very end of his life he returned to the theme:

"Faith" is the most precious of possessions, and it dislikes being meddled with. It means, of course, self-trust, — that is, a belief in

---

1 "Holmes, The Professor at the Breakfast Table," p. 118.

2 Page x.

3 "Unitarian Christianity" (discourse at the ordination of the Reverend Jared Sparks, Baltimore, 1819), in "Works," first American edition, Vol. III, pp. 59–103.

4 Holmes, "The Professor," p. 117.

the value of our own opinion of a doctrine, of a church, of a religion, of a Being, a belief quite independent of any evidence. . . . Its roots are thus inextricably entangled with those of self-love and bleed as mandrakes were said to, when pulled up as weeds.[1]

Such sentiments as these, and many to match them, had not been unexpressed before Holmes propounded them. They belong, in fact, to the orthodoxy of liberalism. But they did not belong to the orthodoxy of Holmes's Bostonia or of the widening circle of ex-New Englanders who belonged to his audience. It was because they would listen to him that his subscription to liberal thought, however limited, was important in his day.

Book List

Individual Authors

NATHANIEL HAWTHORNE. The chief works appeared as follows: Fanshawe, a Tale, 1828; Twice-Told Tales, 1837; Grandfather's Chair: a History for Youth, 1841; Famous Old People: Being the Second Epoch of Grandfather's Chair, 1841; Mosses from an Old Manse (2 vols.), 1846; The Scarlet Letter: a Romance, 1850; The House of the Seven Gables, a Romance, 1851; True Stories from History and Biography, 1851; The Snow-Image and Other Twice-Told Tales, 1852; The Blithedale Romance, 1852; A Wonder-Book for Girls and Boys, 1852; Tanglewood Tales for Girls and Boys: Being a Second Wonder-Book, 1853; The Marble Faun: or The Romance of Monte Beni (2 vols.), 1860; Our Old Home: a Series of English Sketches, 1863.

[*Available Editions*]

The American Notebooks. Based upon the original manuscripts in the Pierpont Morgan Library and edited by Randall Stewart. 1932.

Complete Works of Nathaniel Hawthorne. With introductory notes by George Parsons Lathrop. Riverside Edition. 12 vols. [1883]–1902.

Complete Works of Nathaniel Hawthorne. Wayside Edition. 24 vols. 1884.

The Heart of Hawthorne's Journals, edited by Newton Arvin. 1929.

The Yarn of a Yankee Privateer, edited by Nathaniel Hawthorne. Introduction by Clifford Smith. 1926.

The novels and tales are variously edited for school use. See especially American Authors Series, Modern Student's Library, American Writers Series, in current printings.

---

[1] Holmes, "The Professor" (preface), p. x.

[*Biography and Criticism*]

ALCOTT, A. BRONSON. Concord Days. 1872.

ARVIN, NEWTON. Hawthorne. 1929.

BEERS, HENRY A. "Fifty Years of Hawthorne." Four Americans. 1919.

BRIDGE, HORATIO. Personal Recollections of Nathaniel Hawthorne. 1893.

BROWN, E. K. "Hawthorne, Melville, and 'Ethan Brand,'" *American Literature,* Vol. III, pp. 72–75.

BROWNELL, WILLIAM CRARY. American Prose Masters. 1909.

CLARKE, HELEN A. Hawthorne's Country. 1910.

CURL, VEGA. Pasteboard Masks: Fact as a Symbol in the Novels of Hawthorne and Melville. 1931.

ERSKINE, JOHN. "Hawthorne." Cambridge History of American Literature, Vol. II.

FIELDS, JAMES T. Yesterdays with Authors. 1901.

FULLER, FREDERICK T. "Hawthorne and Margaret Fuller Ossoli," *Literary World,* January 10, 1885.

GATES, LEWIS E. Studies and Appreciations. 1900.

GORMAN, HERBERT. Hawthorne: a Study in Solitude. 1927.

HAWTHORNE, HILDEGARDE. Romantic Rebel, the Story of Nathaniel Hawthorne. 1932.

HAWTHORNE, JULIAN. Hawthorne and His Wife; a Biography. 1885.

HAWTHORNE, JULIAN. "The Making of 'The Scarlet Letter,'" *Bookman,* Vol. LXXIV, pp. 401–411.

HAWTHORNE, JULIAN. "The Salem of Hawthorne," *Century,* Vol. XXVIII, pp. 3–17.

HAWTHORNE, JULIAN. "Scenes of Hawthorne's Romances," *Century,* Vol. XXVIII, pp. 380–397.

HUNGERFORD, E. B. "Hawthorne Gossips about Salem," *New England Quarterly,* Vol. VI, pp. 445–469.

JAMES, HENRY. Hawthorne. E. M. L. Series. 1879.

LAWTON, WILLIAM C. "Hawthorne." The New England Poets. 1898.

LEWISOHN, LUDWIG. Expression in America. 1932.

MICHAUD, REGIS. "How Nathaniel Hawthorne Exorcised Hester Prynne." The American Novel of Today. 1928.

MORE, PAUL ELMER. "Hawthorne: Looking Before and After." Shelburne Essays, second series. 1905.

MORE, PAUL ELMER. "The Origins of Hawthorne and Poe." Shelburne Essays, first series. 1904.

MORRIS, LLOYD. The Rebellious Puritan: Portrait of Mr. Hawthorne. 1927.

MUMFORD, LEWIS. The Golden Day. 1926.

ORIANS, G. HARRISON. "The Angel of Hadley in Fiction: a Study of the Sources of Hawthorne's 'The Grey Champion,'" *American Literature,* Vol. IV, pp. 257–269.

PATTEE, FRED LEWIS. "Nathaniel Hawthorne." Development of the American Short Story. 1923.

POE, EDGAR ALLAN. "Tale-Writing: Nathaniel Hawthorne," *Godey's Lady's Book,* Vol. XXXV, pp. 252–256.

SCHNEIDER, HERBERT W. The Puritan Mind. 1930.

SHERMAN, STUART P. "Hawthorne: a Puritan Critic of Puritanism." Americans. 1922.

STEPHEN, LESLIE. Hours in a Library. 1892.

STEWART, RANDALL. "Hawthorne in England: the Patriotic Motive in the Note-Books," *New England Quarterly*, Vol. VIII, pp. 3–13.

STEWART, RANDALL. "Hawthorne and 'The Fairie Queene,'" *Philological Quarterly*, Vol. XII, pp. 196–206.

STEWART, RANDALL. "Hawthorne's Contributions to the *Salem Advertiser*," *American Literature*, Vol. V, pp. 327–341.

TICKNOR, CAROLINE. Hawthorne and His Publisher. 1913.

VAN DOREN, CARL. "Nathaniel Hawthorne." The American Novel. 1921.

WOODBERRY GEORGE E. Nathaniel Hawthorne. A. M. L. Series. 1902.

[*Bibliography*]

BROWNE, NINA E. A Bibliography of Nathaniel Hawthorne. 1905.

CATHCART, WALLACE H. A Bibliography of the Works of Nathaniel Hawthorne. 1905.

CHAMBERLAIN, JACOB C. First Editions of the Works of Nathaniel Hawthorne, together with Some Manuscript Letters, etc. 1904.

O'CONNOR, EVA M. An Analytical Index to the Works of Nathaniel Hawthorne. 1882.

Cambridge History of American Literature, Vol. II, pp. 415-424.

HENRY WADSWORTH LONGFELLOW. Chief works appeared originally as follows: Outre-Mer: a Pilgrimage Beyond the Sea, 1833–1834; Voices of the Night, 1839; Ballads and Other Poems, 1842; Evangeline, a Tale of Acadie, 1847; The Golden Legend, 1851; The Song of Hiawatha, 1855; The Courtship of Miles Standish, and Other Poems, 1858; Tales of a Wayside Inn, 1863.

[*Available Editions*]

Complete Writings. Craigie Edition. 11 vols. 1933.

Poetical Works. With bibliographical and critical notes by Horace E. Scudder. 6 vols. 1886.

Poetical Works. Household Edition. 1 vol. 1906.

The Works of Henry Wadsworth Longfellow. With bibliographical and critical notes and a Life, edited by Samuel Longfellow. 14 vols. 1891.

Separate poems and selections for classroom use appear in various editions. See especially American Writers Series.

[*Biography and Criticism*]

CARPENTER, G. R. Henry Wadsworth Longfellow. 1901.

COLTON, ARTHUR. "Longfellow: an Essay in Reputations," *Bookman*, Vol. LXXVI, pp. 128–133.

ELLIOTT, GEORGE R. "The Gentle Shades of Longfellow." The Cycle of Modern Poetry. 1929.

GORMAN, HERBERT S. "Longfellow's Golden Years," *Bookman* (November, 1926), Vol. LXIV, pp. 320–329.

GORMAN, HERBERT S. A Victorian American: Henry Wadsworth Longfellow. 1926.

HATFIELD, J. T. New Light on Longfellow. With special reference to his relations to Germany. 1933.

HIGGINSON, T. W. Henry Wadsworth Longfellow. A. M. L. Series. 1902.

HOWELLS, W. D. "The White Mr. Longfellow." My Literary Friends and Acquaintance. 1900.

JONES, HOWARD M. "Longfellow." American Writers on American Literature, edited by John Macy. 1931.
LONGFELLOW, SAMUEL. Final Memorials of Henry Wadsworth Longfellow. 1887.
LONGFELLOW, SAMUEL. The Life of Henry Wadsworth Longfellow. 2 vols. 1886.
MORE, PAUL ELMER. "The Centenary of Longfellow." Shelburne Essays, fifth series. 1908.
NORTON, CHARLES ELIOT. Henry Wadsworth Longfellow: a Sketch of His Life. 1906.
PERRY, BLISS. "The Centenary of Longfellow." Park Street Papers. 1908.
POE, E. A. The Literati: Some Honest Opinions. 1850.
PRITCHARD, JOHN PAUL. "The Horatian Influence upon Longfellow," *American Literature,* Vol. IV, pp. 22–38.
SAUER, LILLIAN B. The True Story of Evangeline. 1930.
SCHRAMM, WILBUR L. "Hiawatha and Its Predecessors," *Philological Quarterly,* Vol. XI, pp. 321–343.
STEDMAN, E. C. "Longfellow." Poets of America, Chap. VI. 1885.
TRENT, WILLIAM P. Longfellow and Other Essays. 1910.
WHITMAN, IRIS L. Longfellow and Spain. 1927.
WHITTIER, JOHN GREENLEAF. "Evangeline." Prose Works, Vol. II, pp. 63–71.

[*Bibliography*]

LIVINGSTON, LUTHER S. A Bibliography of the First Editions in Book Form of the Writings of Henry Wadsworth Longfellow. 1908.
Cambridge History of American Literature, Vol. II, pp. 425–436.

OLIVER WENDELL HOLMES. Chief works appeared as follows: Poems, 1836; The Autocrat of the Breakfast Table, 1858; The Professor at the Breakfast Table: with the Story of Iris, 1860; Elsie Venner: a Romance of Destiny (2 vols.), 1861; Songs in Many Keys, 1862; The Poet at the Breakfast Table: His Talks with His Fellow-Boarders, 1872; Songs of Many Seasons, 1862–1874; Over the Teacups, 1891.

[*Available Editions*]

Autocrat Edition. 13 vols. 1904. Best single-volume edition, the Cambridge Edition. 1895.
Riverside Edition. 13 vols. Prose, Vols. I–IX; Poetry, Vols. XI–XIII. 1891–1895.
Standard Library Edition. 15 vols. 1896. Last two volumes, "The Life and Letters of Oliver Wendell Holmes," by John T. Morse.

[*Biography and Criticism*]

The standard life is by J. T. Morse. 2 vols. 1896.
COOKE, GEORGE WILLIS. "Dr. Holmes at Fourscore," *New England Magazine,* October, 1889.
CURTIS, GEORGE WILLIAM. Literary and Social Essays. 1895.
DWIGHT, THOMAS. "Reminiscences of Dr. Holmes as Professor of Anatomy," *Scribner's,* January, 1895.
FIELDS, ANNIE. Authors and Friends. 1896.
GILDER, JEANNETTE. "The Genial 'Autocrat,'" *Critic,* May 9, 1896.

HIGGINSON, THOMAS WENTWORTH. Contemporaries. 1899.
HIGGINSON, THOMAS WENTWORTH. Old Cambridge. 1900.
HOWELLS, WILLIAM DEAN. My Literary Friends and Acquaintance. 1900.
HOWELLS, WILLIAM DEAN. "Oliver Wendell Holmes," *Harper's*, December, 1896.
KENNEDY, WILLIAM S. Oliver Wendell Holmes: Poet, Litterateur, Scientist. 1883.
KNICKERBOCKER, W. S. "His Own Boswell," *Sewanee Review*, Vol. XLI, pp. 454–466.
LANG, ANDREW. Adventures among Books. 1905.
LOWELL, JAMES RUSSELL. A Fable for Critics. 1848.
MATTHEWS, BRANDER. "Oliver Wendell Holmes." Cambridge History of American Literature, Vol. II.
MEYNELL, ALICE. The Rhythm of Life and Other Essays. 1897.
RICHARDSON, CHARLES F. American Literature. 1889.
STEDMAN, EDMUND CLARENCE. Poets of America. 1885.
WITHINGTON, ROBERT. "Religio Duorum Medicorum," *International Journal of Ethics*, Vol. XLIII, pp. 413–428.
WOODBERRY, GEORGE E. "Oliver Wendell Holmes," *Nation*, October 11, 1894.

[*Bibliography*]

IVES, GEORGE B. A Bibliography of Oliver Wendell Holmes. 1907.
Cambridge History of American Literature, Vol. II, pp. 540–543.

JAMES RUSSELL LOWELL. Chief works appeared in book form as follows: A Year's Life, 1841; Poems, 1844; Conversations on Some of the Old Poets, 1845; A Fable for Critics, 1848; Meliboeus-Hipponax. The Biglow Papers, edited with introduction, notes, glossary, and index, 1848; The Vision of Sir Launfal, 1848; Ode Recited at the Commemoration of the Living and Dead Soldiers of Harvard, 1865; Biglow Papers, second series, 1867; Under the Willows and Other Poems, 1869; Among My Books, 1870; The Cathedral, 1870; My Study Windows, 1871; Among My Books, second series, 1876; Democracy and Other Addresses, 1887; Political Essays, 1888.

[*Available Editions*]

Complete Poetical Works, edited by Horace E. Scudder. Cambridge Edition. 1897.
Letters to James Russell Lowell and Others, edited by William Roscoe Thayer. 1917.
Letters of James Russell Lowell, edited by Charles Eliot Norton. 2 vols. 1894.
New Letters of James Russell Lowell, edited by M. A. De Wolfe Howe. 1932.
Works. Elmwood Edition. 16 vols. 1904. (Contains an added volume of essays and of poetry and three volumes of letters.)
Works of James Russell Lowell. Riverside Edition. 11 vols. 1892.
Individual poems and selections appear in various editions for class use.

[*Biography and Criticism*]

The standard life is by Horace E. Scudder. 2 vols. 1901.
CLARK, HARRY H. "Lowell — Humanitarian, Nationalist, or Humanist?" *Studies in Philology*, Vol. XXVII, pp. 411–441.

CURTIS, GEORGE WILLIAM. James Russell Lowell. 1892.

FOERSTER, NORMAN. American Criticism. 1928.

FOERSTER, NORMAN. "The Creed of Lowell as Critic," *Studies in Philology*, Vol. XXIV, pp. 454–473.

GOLANN, ETHEL. "A Lowell Autobiography," *New England Quarterly*, Vol. VII, pp. 356–364.

GREENSLET, FERRIS. Lowell: His Life and Work. 1905.

HALE, EDWARD EVERETT. Lowell and His Friends. 1898.

HIGGINSON, THOMAS W. Old Cambridge. 1899.

HOWELLS, WILLIAM DEAN. My Literary Friends and Acquaintance. 1900.

HOWELLS, WILLIAM DEAN. "A Personal Retrospect of James Russell Lowell," *Scribner's*, September, 1900.

JAMES, HENRY. Essays in London. 1893.

MEYNELL, ALICE. The Rhythm of Life and Other Essays. 1893.

NORTON, CHARLES ELIOT. "James Russell Lowell," *Harper's*, May, 1893.

NORTON, CHARLES ELIOT. "Letters of Lowell," *Harper's*, September, 1893.

PARKER, CLIFFORD S. "Professor Lowell: a Study of the Poet as Teacher," *Colonnade*, Vol. XII (1919), No. 5.

POLLAK, GUSTAV. International Perspective in Criticism. 1914.

PRITCHARD, JOHN PAUL. "Lowell's Debt to Horace's 'Ars Poetica,'" *American Literature*, Vol. III, pp. 259–276.

REILLY, JOSEPH J. James Russell Lowell as Critic. 1915.

SCUDDER, HORACE E. "Mr. Lowell as a Teacher," *Scribner's*, November, 1891.

STODDARD, RICHARD H. Recollections Personal and Literary. 1903.

THORNDIKE, ASHLEY H. "Lowell." Cambridge History of American Literature, Vol. II, Book II.

UNDERWOOD, FRANCIS H. Lowell; a Biographical Sketch. 1882.

WARREN, A. "Lowell on Thoreau," *Studies in Philology*, Vol. XXVII, pp. 442–461.

WENDELL, BARRETT. Stelligeri and Other Essays. 1893.

[*Bibliography*]

COOKE, GEORGE WILLIS. A Bibliography of James Russell Lowell. 1906.

LIVINGSTON, LUTHER S. A Bibliography of the First Editions in Book Form of the Writings of James Russell Lowell. 1914.

Cambridge History of American Literature, Vol. II, pp. 544–550.

CHAPTER XI

Southward and Westward

Reconstruction and the South

OF THE Southern pair of poets Timrod and Hayne, somewhat as in the case of Halleck and Drake, Timrod, the more promising, died early. As a youth he was given to the introspective seriousness and grave extravagances of the growing poet, and he succumbed readily to the sentimentalism of his region. Yet even his earlier work proved that he could be a voice as well as an echo. In 1859 his first volume was published under the coveted imprint of Ticknor and Fields of Boston. It had much of the Byronic strain that had infected the whole temper of literary America a generation earlier and had nearly disappeared from the North long before; and it was tinged with the Spenserian influence that Byron communicated to his imitators. But Timrod was a regional poet in a much more specific way than this. He was engulfed in the war, like all his contemporaries. One of the sonnets (probably written before 1862) — "I know not why, but all this weary day" — is filled with ominous despair:

> Now it has been a vessel losing way,
> Rounding a stormy headland; now a gray
> Dull waste of clouds above a wintry main;
> And then, a banner, drooping in the rain,
> And meadows beaten into bloody clay.[1]

He had been something of a local laureate on local occasions; now he was a challenger to arms. He celebrated the birth of the Confederacy with high enthusiasm in "Ethnogenesis." And, as war poets are measured, he wrote less abusively than

[1] Timrod, "Poems" (1873), p. 202.

many of his allies, no more recriminatively than the average poets of the North or such admired ones as Whittier and Lowell. He shared in the reasoning of his district, exulted in the beneficent part the triumphant Confederacy was to play in history, flouted the fanatical foes of slavery who dared

> to teach,
> What Christ and Paul refrained to preach,[1]

and resorted freely to the vocabulary of the liberty lover when writing of the Northern invaders. He was bound to see red at times, although his first inclination was to stress his hopes for the South above his hatred of the North. No one of his compeers rose to the level he reached in "The Cotton Boll" and "Ethnogenesis." The newly federated South was to send out from its white fields an idealized harvest that "only bounds its blessings by mankind." The labors of the planter were to strengthen the sinews of the world. But across this mood struck the acrid thought of the war, and in a moment Timrod was both vilifying "the Goth" and resolving to be merciful. As an individual he endured without flinching. As a Confederate patriot he dreamed

> Not only for the glories which the years
> Shall bring us; not for lands from sea to sea,
> And wealth, and power, and peace, though these shall be;
> But for the distant peoples we shall bless,
> And the hushed murmurs of a world's distress.[2]

It was the optimist's perennial justification for war and appeal to a tribal god. The idealists on both sides were resorting to it — always resort to it. And when the war was over, in his "Address to the Old Year" (1866), like the idealists on both sides, he was all for complete and speedy reconciliation. In the approach toward this millennial conclusion Timrod was spared the blunders of Reconstruction days, for he died within the next twelvemonth, serene in his hopes.

---

[1] Timrod, op. cit. p. 102.

[2] Ibid. p. 104.

The more one encounters Timrod's friend and exact contemporary, Paul Hamilton Hayne, the more pathetic a figure he seems in the history of the artist; for he was an absolute devotee of the Muses, without gifts to match his devotion. He was the obviously willing and capable young man to do the editorial chores. If *Russell's* could have survived, Hayne might have had a happily useful career and have achieved the degree of self-criticism that Aldrich and Gilder gained. But he was forced to live by his pen at the worst of times and places; and the result is apparent in the only kind of poetry that industry and good intentions can produce.

Much of it was for special occasions. Hayne wrote on demand for everything, from art exhibits to cotton expositions — always conscientiously, without any special lightness, depth, or felicity. He fell into the contemporary convention of writing on romantic subjects that he knew only through other men's poetry. Better work sprang more directly from his experience; and he did his quota as a versifying journalist. Some of his war lyrics are stirring, though not up to Timrod's best. Some of his post-war protests are spirited and quite justified by the stupid clumsiness of Northern domination. "South Carolina to the States of the North" and "The Stricken South to the North" suggest in verse what Tourgée's "Fool's Errand" and Page's "Red Rock" present in extended prose fiction. Hayne's tributes to other poets, particularly to Longfellow and Whittier, are full of generous admiration; many of his nature poems ring true. Most of all, the Southern pine fascinated him by its perennial grace and strength and its mysterious voice; a pine-tree anthology could be culled from his verse. In the years after the war Hayne lived in a picturesque poverty, making out of necessity a virtue for which he has been too fulsomely applauded. The fact is that he was neither man of action nor intellectually equipped to lead the contemplative life. Rather he was an amiable and dignified gentleman who was quite as baffled by the turn of the religious and philosophic tide as he was by Sherman's march to the sea. In a patient and long-suffering sort of way he clung to the courtly traditions of a past that he had accepted but never studied; and he seemed to believe that faith in God would be justified by a restoration of the old order to which, as a "Southron," he was committed.

Sidney Lanier, a dozen years or so younger than Hayne and Timrod, was still a pre-war school and college boy, and old enough to be a participant in the fighting. The South claimed him in action; and in heritage he was a son of Southern traditions, tracing the Lanier ancestry to a court musician of the Stuarts, and beyond to a conjectured past in France. His mother sang and played in the home, and his father, a courtly lawyer, was a gentle reader of the Old School. Macon, Georgia, his boyhood home, was a town of extreme nonconformist orthodoxy where "the only burning issues were sprinkling versus immersion, freewill versus predestination."[1] Out of these elements Lanier was compounded: a derivative of Calvinistic theology and Cavalier culture, a lover of literature and music, a virtuoso in both, a student of the aesthetics of both, supersensitive and highly emotional as an artist, driven by stern ethical compulsions as a child of God, and characteristically expressing himself in "chaste bacchanalia"; serving the Lord like Longstreet and Cooke, fervent in spirit as Poe and Chivers.

A promising student, he found his chief zest in wide reading and in flute-playing. He was convinced that his talents were in music, but was ethically impelled to check them because he could not satisfactorily assure himself as to "the province of music in the economy of the world."[2] Appointed tutor in Oglethorpe University, he decided to be a teacher and to round out his preparation by two years at Heidelberg. When this plan was blocked at the outbreak of the war, he seemed well started on the path trod by Longfellow and Lowell. Four years later he came home with health permanently impaired

[1] Edwin Mims, "Life of Lanier" (A. M. L. Series), p. 23. [2] Ibid. p. 39.

by hardships in camp and prison. An energetic soul, always happier when in action, and happiest when projecting some expansive plan, he took refuge in grinding work — taught, drudged at the law, and was almost submerged as an artist when the friendships of Hayne and Bayard Taylor buoyed him up. The last decade of his life was an exciting preface toward poetic fame and fortune, but he died in his fortieth year. In the retreating tableaux of the past he appears as emotionalist, moralist, technician.

By 1870 the call for a new literature and a new criticism in the South was recurrent and insistent. Short-lived magazines again sprang up and were flooded with copy before their early deaths. Most of the writing was ostentatiously sectional in tone, but some approached the standard set by Joel Chandler Harris in his appeal for an almost millennial literature that should be "intensely local in feeling, but utterly unprejudiced and unpartisan as to opinions, tradition, and sentiment."[1] Equally in the interest of the South was Hayne's demand for criticism that would put a quietus on the scribblers who had nothing to say and said it badly. "No foreign ridicule" (the adjective was significant), he wrote in the *Southern Magazine* (1874), "can stop this growing evil, until our own scholars and thinkers have the manliness and honesty to discourage instead of applauding such manifestations of artistic weakness and artistic platitudes as have hitherto been foisted on us by persons uncalled and unchosen of any of the muses."

At the same time a combination of generosity and enterprise led several Northern magazine editors to solicit contributions from the South. In 1873 *Scribner's Monthly* projected a widely advertised series on "the great South." *Harper's* published another. *The Atlantic*, with Howells as editor, followed conservatively; and *The Independent* opened its columns to men whom it had been blasting a dozen years earlier. Most important to Lanier was *Lippincott's*, in which

---

[1] Mims, op. cit. p. 284.

"Corn," "The Symphony," and "The Psalm of the West," with certain shorter poems, were published in 1875, 1876, and 1877 — poems by which his reputation was much widened. The 70's were propitious years for new Southern writers, and, with the possible exception of George W. Cable, none profited more from the shifting of the wind than Lanier did.

The development of the Peabody Symphony Orchestra in Baltimore was a further sign of the reawakening of artistic life in the South. Music had gained a new hold on Lanier during an enforced health trip to Texas in the winter of 1872–1873. He had reveled in concerts in New York, but in San Antonio he fell in with a group of musicians as a fellow player. Without formal instruction he had become a flute virtuoso. In the following autumn he played for the director of the Peabody Conservatory of Music, Baltimore, and in December went in triumph to his initial rehearsal as first flutist in the newly organized orchestra. For the rest of his life music was his surest means of support, a source of pleasure that amounted to little less than dissipation, and a not always happily modifying influence on his poetry. As a performer he played in a kind of ecstasy. As an auditor his appreciation was controllingly sensuous, an experience of raptures, thrills, and swooning joys.

> Divine lamentations, far-off blowings of great winds, flutterings of tree and flower leaves and airs troubled with wing-beats of birds or spirits; floatings hither and thither of strange incenses and odors and essences; warm floods of sunlight, cool gleams of moonlight, faint enchantments of twilight; delirious dances, noble marches, processional chants, hymns of joy and grief: Ah, midst of all these I lived last night, in the first chair next to Theodore Thomas' orchestra.[1]

From such a parade of his "sensibilities," one is prepared for his frequent references to the modern composers, few to Bach and Beethoven, and his omission of Brahms. One is helped to understand how he could have indulged in his gushing dictum that "music is love in search of a word." Music was of

[1] "Letters of Sidney Lanier, 1866–1881," p. 69.

prime importance to Lanier, a field of emotional revelry. The kind that he enjoyed and the kind of enjoyment he found in it account for him as a poet — the more clearly when compared with what music meant to Browning, who was no less of a connoisseur but rugged and muscular withal. To Lanier the temptation was always imminent to express in poetry the flutterings and floatings, the odors, incenses, and essences, the cool gleams and faint enchantments, that were his characteristic translations of music, his attempts to supply it with the words he alleged it was in search of.

But attempts in this direction inevitably led to a certain tenuosity, a certain deficiency in direct communication. To make one art a prolonged set of analogies to another is to subtract from one and not to reach the other. And the flutist, in his light soprano register, failed too often to express in poetry anything other than light soprano sentiments in light soprano tones. He was a florid soprano at that (with a few notable exceptions, to which we shall come), with a generous measure of self-pity. He wrote in "To Bayard Taylor" of "the endless grief of art," identifying — not unnaturally, perhaps — the apparently endless grief of post-bellum days in the South and the depressions of his own depleted health with the essential experience of the artist in normal times and in full vigor. Once he referred to the "poetic region" as "serene and sunny," [1] but for years, while he was struggling to get his feet under him, he wrote like an invalid lady, or like the invalid he was, who thought in feminine imagery. The Southern hills became outraged breasts with rumpled draperies, stains that the ravisher would not let be washed, and so on, and so on. The trees were embraced by "long-armed woman vines," and the arms were "languid." The leaves that brushed against one in a wood caressed like women's hands. Poem after poem is filled with saccharin amorosities. "Sweet" is a recurrent adjective applied in every sort of connection. The flute tones, moreover, with a

---

[1] Letters, op. cit. p. 168.

kind of airy melancholy, decorate the theme of life in elaborated overtones of extended metaphor. In "June Dreams, in January," for example, Noon is a pulsing-hearted being who throbs,

> while the fervent hours exhale
> As kisses faint-blown from their finger-tips
> Up to the sun.

"Tender darkness" ensues, and with it faint odors and dim sighs, and then a full stream of alternative metaphors. The dreamer regards his outburst as possibly extravagant; but, as an appended narrative relates, a "room-fellow" slips it into the mail, and a receptive editor turns "the fleeting song to very bread."

In these earlier utterances too were the romantic formulas of chivalry. Lanier compiled a "Boys' Froissart," "King Arthur," "Mabinogion," "Percy." His longest youthful effort "The Jacquerie," which, like Pinkney's "Rodolph" and Poe's "Politian," never became more than a fragment, leaps in the second line "on the conquered ramparts of the night" and never descends from the setting of chivalry or discards its trappings through that long and verbose effusion. In 1862 while in camp he likened the Civil War to a tournament, revising and refining on it in a lyric for the "Psalm of the West" in 1876. In "The Revenge of Hamish," as in "The Jacquerie," he revolted from the harshnesses of feudalism, but he celebrated the beauties of courtliness and courtly love and expressed himself in their idioms.

Lanier was a real reader and a good deal of a student; but he was not free, as the profound student is, from the showy preciosity that belonged to some of his fellow Southerners and to the period of his boyhood. It appeared and it survived in "The Crystal" and "Clover," two poems of his latter years. Both introduce "the course of things" and both play with the idea that in its progress, though art may endure, no single artist may. In "The Crystal" he calls the roll — Homer, Socrates, Buddha, Dante, Milton, Aeschylus, Lucretius, a dozen more — and condones their shortcomings, forgiving each in turn, as though he himself were the course of things and something of a spiritual pharisee at that. In "Clover" this same course is become a consuming ox which champs and chews Dante, Keats, Chopin, Raphael, Lucretius, Omar, Angelo, Beethoven, Chaucer, Schubert, Shakespeare, Bach, and Buddha — he enumerates them twice, and, doing so, permits himself to parade his favorite poets and composers, ephemeral though they were, and indulges in that regional extravagance of imagery and elaboration of poetical dainty devices which was a major defect in the poets of the South.

He was, withal, the moralist who came honestly by his moral purposefulness in his Presbyterian heritage. He struggled long over the problem of dedicating himself to any of the arts. Having finally decided that "the province of music in the economy of the world" could be defended, largely because it appealed to him so irresistibly, he moved more easily to the moral defense of poesy, putting the poet on a plane with prophet and seer. It was a traditional line of reasoning. In "Corn" the poet

> leads the vanward of his timid time
> And sings up cowards with commanding rhyme.[1]

In "The Bee" he will fertilize the "worldflower" as a pollen bearer. In "The Marshes of Glynn" he is

> the catholic man who hath mightily won
> God out of knowledge and good out of infinite pain.[2]

The poet's judgments, he held, are certain to surpass those of his age, certain to reap a harvest of derision and abuse, certain to approach the right because they are made in the light of eternity rather than in the shadow of any passing day. Lanier was a poet; but he was a Presbyterian, an evangelist astride of Pegasus.

Like a good evangelist, he was very much aware of certain disturbing tendencies in the age. The prevalence of doubt distressed him. In "Acknowledgment" he deplored an age

[1] Lanier, "Poems" (edited by his wife, 1884), p. 54. [2] Ibid. p. 17.

that half believed its half-beliefs and was no more thorough in its doubting, and he took refuge by the fireside with a devoted wife. In "Remonstrance" he imagined the loss of even this refuge, belabored "opinion" with hard names, and ended in a burst of somewhat petty irritation as other evangelists have been known to do. The incursions of trade in a country that had once placed religion above it moved him with somewhat the same result. "Corn" is a versified protest at the economic dependence of the planter — gamester's catspaw and banker's slave; and "The Symphony" is an arraignment of the whole industrial system:

> If business is battle, name it so:
> War crimes less will shame it so,
> And widows less will blame it so.[1]

Lanier had not lacked contact with life: in the war, in the ensuing hardships, in comparative freedom of movement about the country, in professional activities; yet he gives the impression of one who had not established contacts with the life he had touched. Though more amiable, he reminds one of the Lady in "Comus" who is encased in innocence, irreproachable because unapproachable, but not beyond uttering reproaches which are none the more palatable for their asperity. Even when based on truth they are hardly more effective than the shrill outcries of a little child at a mastiff.

In the modest volume of Lanier's collected work, mainly written during his last eight years, there is a marked variety of poems showing literary influence, and a culminating work which is peculiarly his own. "The Revenge of Hamish" is an unusually successful attempt to emulate the heroic tale, the better for restoring the spirit of the elder day without imitating the manner. "How Love Looked for Hell" is obviously pre-Raphaelite in tone. D. G. Rossetti might have written it. In "The Stirrup-Cup" there is an Elizabethan note. "Night and Day" and "The Marsh Song — at Sunset" are frankly built on Shakespearean allusion. These and their like

[1] Lanier, op. cit. p. 61.

give token of Lanier's versatility, just as the "Song of the Chattahoochee" displays his command of certain obvious devices of diction and rhythm. But the poems most distinctive of Lanier are the longer meditations already mentioned and, in particular, "Sunrise" and "The Marshes of Glynn."

These two, written in an order reverse to the sequence as they stand, are virtually a sustained poem in two sections, the records of one day's spiritual experience. A clearer title would be "The Marshes of Glynn" for the whole and "Sunrise" and "Sunset" for the parts. They are personal utterances of the poet in form, in sensuous opulence, in social sympathies, in religious conviction. Written at about the time of Bryant's death and in the structural sequence of Bryant's "Thanatopsis," they mark the long stride taken in the religious thought of the orthodox nonconformist, a stride actually taken by Lanier between boyhood and manhood. In "Thanatopsis" the various language that nature speaks is expounded in general terms before "Thoughts of the last bitter hour" lead to the monody on death and the resolve so to live that death shall have no fears. Bryant had made slight progress from Anne Bradstreet in her "Contemplations." Lanier's poems differentiate the tones of nature, lingering in the cloistral depths of the woods during the June heat. In the cool and quiet of coming evening the poet's

> heart is at ease from men, and the wearisome sound of the stroke
> Of the scythe of time and the trowel of trade is low,
> And belief overmasters doubt.[1]

So, toward sunset, he leaves the protected green colonnades and goes out unafraid to face the expanse of "a world of marsh that borders a world of sea." Here he is filled with a great exhilaration, like that which he felt at the approach of dawn.

> Oh, what is abroad in the marsh and the terminal sea?
> Somehow my soul seems suddenly free
> From the weighing of fate and the sad discussion of sin,
> By the length and the breadth and the sweep of the marshes of Glynn.[2]

---

[1] Lanier, op. cit. p. 15.

[2] Ibid. p. 16.

From them, in this still sin-ridden, theologically minded region and period, he learns the emancipating lesson of life — the power of aspiration and the sustaining strength of faith. "Thanatopsis" ends with a nobly stated but restraining admonition; "The Marshes," with a song of liberty:

As the marsh-hen secretly builds on the watery sod,
Behold I will build me a nest on the greatness of God:
I will fly in the greatness of God as the marsh-hen flies
In the freedom that fills all the space 'twixt the marsh and the skies:
By so many roots as the marsh-grass sends in the sod
I will heartily lay me a-hold on the greatness of God.[1]

Lanier is even yet pursuing a metaphor, but no longer with languor. He writes in the positive mood and measure of Browning's "Saul." Both poems celebrate the throwing off of paralyzing restraints and the substitution of hope for dread that resulted from the religious struggles in nineteenth-century Christendom.

Lanier went farther than any of his Southern contemporaries toward answering the appeal of Joel Chandler Harris and representing the South by writing as a citizen of the world. He was "intensely local" in his sentiments and convictions, but "unpartisan" in his conscious expression of them. He was an aggressive thinker, though not an original one. Apparently the gentleness of his manner offset the vigor of his social criticisms. He was a lover of beauty, a man of stylisms and mannerisms, rather than a consistent creator. He may not be ranked with the great; but at his best he is not out of place in company with Bryant and Lowell and Morris and Arnold.

Against the background of the controversy that led up to the Civil War, the development of a sectional literature inevitable with such a war, the scars left by the fighting, the impoverishment following the destruction of property, and the effects of the policies of the victors during the carpet-

[1] "Poems," p. 17.

bagger days, Joel Chandler Harris, born in 1848, stands out for his balance, his wisdom, his achievements as a journalist, and his indubitable gifts as a tale-teller.

From the beginning of his long career in journalism his bent for satire expressed itself in comments on the life around him which could not have been made by a rabid sectionalist. At moments when he was writing on his negligible novels he could lapse — as in "Gabriel Tolliver," "Sister Jane," or the four tales in "The Making of a Statesman" — into the sugary conventions of the Southern romanticist. These were composed in the easy days of achieved reputation when the distant echoes of the war were dying. But as editor, critic, and creator of "Uncle Remus" he was of another mind.

> We do not regard [he wrote in 1879] this question of sectionalism as at all political in the usual acceptance of the term. We look upon it as a disaster of the most deadly aspect — a disease that slays the social instincts of the people and destroys commercial enterprise and national progress. We have protested against it, not as Georgians nor as Southerners, but as Americans.[1]

He applied the generalization in an editorial on literature in the South:

> The very spice and essence of all literature, the very marrow and essence of all literary art is its localism. No literary artist can lack for materials in this section. . . . Where is the magician who will catch them and store them? You may be sure that the man who does it will not care one copper whether he is developing and building up Southern or Northern literature, and he will feel that his work is considerably belittled if it be claimed by either on the score of sectionalism. . . . The sectionalism that is the most marked feature of our modern politics, can never intrude into literature. Its intrusion is fatal, and it is this fatality that has pursued and overtaken and destroyed literary effort in the South. The truth might as well be told. We have no Southern literature worthy of the name, because an attempt has been made to give it the peculiarities of sectionalism, rather than to impart to it the flavor of localism.[2]

---

[1] "An Important Admission," *Atlanta Constitution*, December 6, 1879.
[2] "Provinciality in Literature," *Atlanta Constitution*, November 30, 1879.

But it was impossible even for this most temperate of Southerners to free himself from the bane of sectionalism. The most that he could do was to try to curb his neighbors in their excesses of feeling and to try to persuade the Northern press not to goad the ex-Confederates by consistent misrepresentation. He asked that the North should send an observer to see the South as it was and report honestly, suggesting that ex-President Grant be the visitor. He appealed to the *New York Times* in a series of editorials[1] not to "pursue the people and the society of the South." The defects in Southern attitude, he maintained, were human rather than sectional, or, if they were sectional, the South had been driven to them by the tactics of the North. He visited New England to prove to himself that there was no fundamental difference and, of course, found what he was looking for:[2] the same poverty, provincialism, and blindness to their own defects, and, on the whole, less generosity to the Negro and no understanding of him.

As to the Negro problem, Harris offered the old defense that there never would have been one if the North had not imposed it on the slave states and reimposed it in the early days of Reconstruction. In behalf of his section he reiterated that the abuses of slavery should not have been identified with slavery as a whole, that most masters had been kind and most slaves happy; and he returned frequently to a favorite contention, that Mrs. Stowe's inherent genius had actually transformed "Uncle Tom's Cabin" from the indictment she tried to make it into "a defence of American slavery as she found it in Kentucky."[3] As to the Negro of the closing years of the century, Harris looked confidently on his increasing prosperity, his growing information, and the promise held out for the race by such a leader as Booker Washington. In all this he was, patently, a political section-

[1] *Atlanta Constitution*, January 4, 16, 17, 20, 29, 1880.

[2] The above quotations and citations are made available in "Joel Chandler Harris: Editor and Essayist," edited by Julia Collier Harris. University of North Carolina Press.

[3] Ibid. p. 116.

alist though not a bitter one, which makes it the more notable that he was what he tried to be, a literary expositor of local rather than sectional characteristics.

Harris as a writer of local stories was extraordinarily voluminous for a man who had to do his work on the run either in the course of his job as newspaperman or in stolen intervals. For a quarter of a century he averaged more than a volume a year. And in this output he did the work that distinguishes him only on the theme of Uncle Remus and in the realm of Negro folklore. The other material is interesting to the delver, but it fails because it had no singleness of conception and no consistency in treatment. It oscillated between the literary-sentimental local-colorism that swept the country between 1870 and 1890 and the unvarnished tale-telling that transcribed the life of the tellers with the least interposition of artifice; and the oscillation occurred within the limits of single stories, irreparably confusing the effect. Thus a favorite character in Harris's roster was the girl of mixed heritage who rose to varying levels of high refinement in total disregard of all surrounding influences. Such a character is unconvincing whether she is the abducted princess of the fairy tale, Harte's M'liss, Cooke's Peony, or Harris's Pud Hon Bivins, Sis Poteet, or Zepherine Dion. All these provincial folk of the sequence, from "The Luck of Roaring Camp" to "Main-Travelled Roads," were presented by observers who looked with sympathetic patronage on them. The authors were unusual in their time in giving serious attention to the people on the soil, people who had been reserved for use as comedy types in a kind of post-Shakespearean tradition. Harris was interested and pleased at this. He was up-to-date in his reading and, like a good journalist, he was quick to respond to the taste of the times. But he also reflected this taste. It is impossible not to see his liking for the cracker-box philosophers, for E. W. Howe and for G. W. Cable, but also for Bret Harte, Helen Hunt Jackson, and Thomas Nelson Page; and it is impossible not to see what an odd compound fiction might and did become from a man who was letting his "other-fellow" self take charge of him and direct his pen without interference from his more conscious and potentially critical self. Harris did not take this writing seriously, and there is not much reason why anyone else should.

He persisted in declaring that his success with Uncle Remus was wholly an accident. This was merely a way of saying that his telling of these tales was uncalculating and spontaneous, and that even after many of them had been printed in the *Atlanta Constitution* and copied in the *New York Evening Post* he had no idea of their eventual popularity and their title to permanence. But modesty and mock modesty are easily confusable — the latter may persist as a mannerism; so that when Harris later referred to "the accidental success of the 'Remus' trash," he meant that the success was surprising, and he knew that it was not trash. The real accident was that of a miner who stumbles on a rich lode and is not sure of his find until it has been assayed. Harris had known the tales for long without thought of transcribing them; and he really knew them because he knew the Negroes. He wrote the first of them at the request of his newspaper chief. He collected some of them into a book at the request of a New York publisher. He was bewildered at the applause they received and amused to find that he had become a folklorist.[1]

It was the genuineness of the material, and the natural, unstudied gifts of a man who could transcribe the idiom and the spirit of it, which made the combination into a classic. Nothing could have been more natural than Mark Twain's immediate response to it, or Harris's delight in Mark Twain's enthusiasm. They were two of a kind. The consequence of "Uncle Remus's" reception was equally natural. The author did systematically what he had at first done accidentally: he held to his intimate knowledge and his homely and perfect manner, but unearthed new material, accepted versions and variants that poured in on him, and enjoyed

[1] See author's introduction to the new edition of 1903.

the fact that scholarly experts were studying, collating, and comparing his tales with others from the American plains, from the West Indies, from Brazil, from various regions in Africa, and from India. And the superiority of this story anthology to anything else that Harris wrote shows that his peculiar and rare gift was to transcribe rather than to invent or interpret.

Though he lived until 1908 and was widely known only after 1880, and although as editor and essayist he worked to free his generation from "the worn ruts of a period that was soul-destroying in its narrowness,"[1] he was consistently retrospective as a writer of narrative. The ruts he wanted to obliterate were worn in the Reconstruction period. His way of escape was in a return to the past. The echoes of the war were faintly audible in his stories about the proprietors of the South; his Negro was a plantation survival; and his crowning literary achievement was in perpetuating through Uncle Remus the faithful servitor of the old plantation who had learned his master's language, but who in his own quaint dialect handed on to his master's children the immemorial lore of the primitive African. Harris the journalist was a post-bellum American. The transcriber for Uncle Remus took refuge in the recesses of the past.

The Mid-Century Frontier

The frontier, what was written about it, and its expression of itself, is of course insistently recurrent in the chronicles of American thought as it has already been in this study; but about 1830 the more newly settled regions began to supply so much material that it demands attention by itself. No discussion of the theme can go far without an acknowledgment that Frederick J. Turner gave the impulse for its general contemporary study.[2] The inquisitive may easily find plenty

[1] "Harris: Editor and Essayist," p. 36.

[2] F. J. Turner, "The Frontier in American History" (containing his essay of 1893), 1920.

of vague predecessors; but he must search long to find one better than Nathaniel Ames, the almanac-maker,[1] who included in his issue for 1758 "A THOUGHT *upon the* past, present, *and* future State *of* North America." After a two-hundred word disposal of the past, Ames proceeded:

II. Secondly, The Present State of North America. — A Writer upon this present Time says "The Parts of *North America* which may be claimed by *Great Britain* or *France* are as of much Worth as either Kingdom. — That fertile Country to the West of the Appalachian Mountains (a String of 8 or 900 Miles in Length) between Canada and the Mississippi, is of larger extent than all *France, Germany* and *Poland*; and all well provided with Rivers, a very fine wholesome Air, a rich Soil, capable of producing Food and Physick, and all Things necessary for the Conveniency and Delight in Life: in fine, 'the Garden of the World!'" Time was we might have been possess'd of it: At this Time two mighty Kings contend for this inestimable Prize. . . . If we do not join Heart and Hand in the common Cause against our exulting Foes, but fall to disputing among ourselves, . . . "We shall have no Priviledge to dispute about, nor Country to dispute in."

III. Thirdly, of the Future State of North America. . . . The Curious have observ'd, that the Progress of Humane Literature (like the Sun) is from the East to the West; thus has it travelled thro' *Asia* and *Europe*, and now is arrived at the Eastern Shore of *America*. As the Coelestial Light of the Gospel was directed here by the Finger of G O D, it will, doubtless, finally drive the long! long! Night of Heathenish Darkness from *America*; — So Arts and Sciences will change the Face of Nature in their Tour from Hence over the Appalachian Mountains to the Western Ocean. . . .

Events moved faster and farther than the almanac-maker dreamed. Four generations later an American historian was citing an American census report which celebrated the passing of the frontier line and the closing of a great historic movement. It was because the chapter was closed but the pages were still legible as those of Nathaniel Ames that Turner urged the study of the Western advance, the men

[1] See pages 95–96.

who grew up under it, and the varied results in the community. Turner could not interpret the significance of the frontier without first defining it; and the definition developed a series of meanings like a series of interfitting Japanese boxes. Simplest is the use employed by the superintendent of the census for 1890: the line, somewhere toward the west, of territory owned by the United States on the sunset side of which the population was less than two to the square mile. A second, with deep implications, is that in its westering progress the frontier line always lay just east of free lands; a third, that it was the boundary between savagery and civilization; a fourth, that with variations determined by the nature of the regions, pioneering progressed in the regular order of exploring, trapping and trading, ranching, farming or mining, and, at last, the full-fledged industrial community.

The historical approach to the literary significances of the frontier demands acquaintance with certain obvious constants in the equation that are familiar to the student of history: what the American physical frontier has been; what the processes have been; and what have been the political, social, and cultural fruits of frontier experience.

1. The physical frontier began naturally with the Atlantic coast, on which at the end of a century there was a string of more or less isolated settlements from Massachusetts to Georgia. Then the mountains became the frontier, a zone of escape and a buffer from the Indians. Over these the settlers began to spread before the Revolutionary War. The discomforts of the War of 1812 revived the westward impulse. Kentucky, Tennessee, and Ohio were already in the Union; between 1816 and 1821 five more states were admitted: Indiana, Mississippi, Illinois, Alabama, Missouri. By 1837 the desirable Indian reservations were engulfed, the Mississippi Valley on both sides of the river was white man's country, and the frontier was creeping toward the Rockies. With the discovery of gold the creep became a rush. Overland and by water the fortune seekers made their ways, leaving the frontier line still far to the eastward with a vast

reach of unoccupied land (much of it desert) in the interval. Then in the 50's prospectors working back found traces of gold in Colorado; and in the years of the Civil War the last stretch of prairie was overswept, mineral resources were discovered on the high plains between the Rockies and the Sierras, and settlement spread into the mountain regions. In the meanwhile Texas had been annexed, and the territories of New Mexico and Arizona made the connecting link to California. Between 1865 and 1890 the lands were thrown open to settlers, and the free areas subject to government grants were all dispensed to schools and colleges, to railroads, and to individual homesteaders. By 1890 the call of free land was over; the last rush into Oklahoma was a memory; the story of the frontier was awaiting its chroniclers, and the significance of the frontier its interpreters.

2. There was a regular procedure in this westering progress. After the explorers, trappers, traders, who served as the cutting edge of civilization, came settlers with their first problems of breaking land and housing themselves, and their next ones of establishing working relationships. They brought techniques of settlement which had to be adapted to the regions they entered, shifting from wooded country to prairie and from prairie to high plains; and they brought social traditions — some satisfactory, some needing modification or abandonment. When farms were operable, neighborhoods were established and town organization was in force; roads, schools, churches, courts, and the printing press followed; and the district was no longer in the foremost zone. It was a passageway to the extreme frontier, supplying also some of the youth and some of the incorrigibly restless elders who were impelled to follow the sun. Further changes ensued. For a while this secondary frontier shared the temper of the zone beyond it, depending on the country eastward for fresh recruits, basic supplies, financial backing, and the market at which to recoup its fortunes. But in time it was left too far behind for this. As it fell back a new tide began to overflow it, the tide of industrialism. It became a middle-

man's region and, on the whole, a creditor's region. As its memories of the frontier receded, it looked backward to a recent heritage, but it looked around on anything but frontier conditions. It was, perhaps, located in an agricultural area, but it was become a city of merchants, manufacturers, and bankers. It read the crop reports, but it followed the stock exchange too. Today it steers for financial security between the Scylla of farm mortgages and the Charybdis of broker's loans. The post-frontier cherishes a sentimental regard for the wheat field, but it listens with respectful deference to the opinions of Wall Street.

3. From the frontier regions and the frontier processes the historian went on to his main theme: the significance of the frontier in American history. From the beginning to the end of pioneer days the movement was impelled by poverty, manned by youth, buoyed by hope, and maintained by hard and unremitting labor. Assets of these kinds were not open to quantitative measurement. They were equalitarian in essence; for each pioneer could have as much of any of them as his own nature would afford. They did not depend on any theory of democracy, but they produced democracy in fact — a democracy which felt impatient resentment at any assumption of superiority whether on the frontier or in the older country. And whatever traits were demanded of the frontier recruits were reinforced by the actual frontier life. Those who lacked courage and persistence stopped on the way or returned. Those who could not endure the hardships died. Primitive conditions subjected humankind to the brutal tests of survival through selection and adaptation, and the survivors naturally retained in heightened degrees the qualities that the frontier demanded and begot.

Men and women of this stock believed in social progress and in their own power to contribute to it by mastering the land and enriching themselves at the scene of their conquest. The successful few were assured that life had taught them things about their needs and rights that the older country must be convinced of. By the provisions of the Constitution they were being reluctantly accepted not as colonials, but as members in a federation, with full prerogatives and well-developed vocal powers. An ignorant, complacent, provincial East could not be left in ignorance and complacency. The West was aware of clear sectional differences; the East, conscious of encroachments, spoke of the pioneers as idle, shiftless, prodigal, passionate, impatient of restraint, and feared their influence on national policies as their representation was increasing in Congress. It might well do so; for the frontier was developing a new type of American with an aggressive approach to national problems. These people who had been unified by common successes, hardships, and needs were confident in their optimism but relentless and incessant in their demands that the government help in the development of the West. National policies as to land, tariff, and internal improvements all originated in frontier needs. So did foreign policies during the period of territorial expansion. So, too, did the actual promotion of democratic ideas and, whether for better or for worse, of democratic social experiment. This is the gospel according to Turner.

Early Ventures in Formal Literature

The chief deduction to be drawn from the best literary study of the frontier when it was yet east of the Mississippi[1] is that, with the rarest exceptions, literature about the frontier by travelers is likely to be more genuinely authentic than the early attempts of the frontier to put itself into print. The reason is easy to find. Pioneers from the outset swap yarns and sing songs; but when the frontier begins to put itself on paper, it has ceased to be the habitat of the pioneer. It is becoming back country. It is self-consciously taking its pen in hand to address the gentle reader. The district may be satisfied with being rough and ready; but the element in it that wants to read and write wants also to be polite and quiet, to mind its *p's* and *q's*. And so it was up to a hundred years ago in the Middle West.

[1] R. L. Rusk, "The Literature of the Middle Western Frontier." 2 vols, 1925.

Mrs. Trollope[1] bore testimony to this polite quality in the current journalism when she wrote:

> Every American newspaper is more or less a magazine, wherein the merchant may scan, while he holds out his hand for an invoice, "Stanzas by Mrs. Hemans" or a garbled extract from "Moore's Life of Byron"; the lawyer may study his brief faithfully, and yet contrive to pick up the valuable dictum of some American critic that "Bulwer's novels are decidedly superior to Sir Walter Scott's."

Thus *The Microscope* in Louisville in 1824 looked to Sterne for precedent, and reflected Addison and Goldsmith too. As for the more ambitious monthlies and quarterlies, chasteness and elegance were their long suits. Like their Eastern models, they borrowed or stole in the name of culture. *The Western Review* (Lexington, 1819) printed not only translations and imitations from Europe, but poems in foreign tongues. *The Western Monthly Magazine* (Vandalia, 1830) planned to devote itself, in addition to statistics of Illinois, to essays, tales, "literary intelligence, fugitive poetry, . . . notices of the fine and useful arts." So did *The Hesperian, The Literary Focus, The Transylvanian*; and so, more futile than many another in the descending scale, did the *Rose of the Valley*. The exceptions, like the *Western Monthly Review* and the *Illinois Monthly Magazine*, one of which tried to be local enough to deserve the attention of the future historian and the other to make the West aware of itself, served only to mark the general rule. And the *Western Messenger*, which from 1830 on was the pre-eminent monthly, was the project of a number of Bostonians, many of them only temporary sojourners, whose comings and goings reduced Cincinnati to an intellectual suburb of the "Hub," not a typical frontier town, and a near-frontier town more in location than in spirit.

The story of the early fiction in the region was similar. Timothy Flint, the first novelist, wrote a great deal that was picturesque and exact about the Western country, but not in

[1] Frances Trollope, "Domestic Manners of the Americans," in Rusk, "Literature of the Middle Western Frontier," Vol. I, p. 131.

his novels. These, from one who knew his material as Flint did, were almost incredibly far-fetched and unreal. He evidently agreed with Cooper's dictum that the New World was barren of material for the creative artist. The tales of James Hall, mostly short stories, came a little nearer to reality. He intended, he said, to make fidelity the chief claim for merit in his narratives; they were to be of, by, and for the West. But he still could allow an old trapper to exclaim at a critical moment, "Let us creep to yon log. . . . Be cool — my dear young friend, be cool"; and Hall turned his back and shot in the opposite direction when he wrote of the scandalously riotous camp meetings: "So close is the union between good taste and religious feeling . . . the mind, elevated by the pursuit of a high object, becomes enlarged and refined." [1] There are realistic touches in the stories of both Flint and Hall, but in their romantic temper these men are far nearer to Rousseau and Cooper than to Rölvaag and Cather. With the notable exception of Mrs. Kirkland's "New Home — Who'll Follow? or, Glimpses of Western Life" (1839), there was little before Eggleston's work of a generation later to mark the day of genuine realism in Western fiction.

In its verse again the frontier was true to type in ignoring frontier possibilities. There was a native tone in such adopted songs as have survived, but in little else. There was satire, as in the colonial near-frontier, but satire of the town and the townsman; a few passable lyrics which show that the love of beauty is never quite extinguishable; and epics! Let Dwight and Humphreys and Barlow share doubtful honors with Genin and Emmons. Genin, with his "Napolead," can easily cope with Dwight and Humphreys; and as for Emmons, his "Fredoniad: or, Independence Preserved, an Epic Poem on the Late War of 1812" (forty cantos in four volumes) will amply outweigh Barlow's "Vision of Columbus" and "The Columbiad," to which it was twenty years later expanded.

---

[1] James Hall, "Tales of the West" (1853 edition, pp. 34 and 10).

Finally, the characteristics of Middle-Western frontier stage and drama drive the point home. Seven thousand productions which have been pursued to their footlights were like any other seven thousand in the history of the American stage before 1840. The English tradition was overwhelming. The repertory was not only not western, it was not American. When, in Cincinnati in 1801,

> The laughing muse here for the first time sate
> And kindly deigned to cheer our infant state,

she did so in English idiom and mainly in the idiom of the eighteenth century. Anything further than this was the fashion of New York, itself a reflection of later London modes.

The popular reading of the day was just as attentive to the East and to England. The appetite of Cincinnati and Lexington and Louisville was for dishes prepared in the old publishing centers. There was a certain earnest protestation of interest in the high dignitaries of literature. Shakespeare was a name to conjure with, and Milton, and Pope. The migratory New England Brahmins on the banks of the Ohio responded to Emerson's championship of Carlyle and spoke respectfully of Wordsworth and Coleridge and Emerson himself. Cooper and Irving had no strong vogue — very likely because they had both experimented with Western subject matter. The Americans dear to the hearts of the Ohio valley were Fitz-Greene Halleck, James G. Percival, and Nathaniel Parker Willis. Of the English, the contemporaries everyone doted on were Mrs. Hemans, "L. E. L.," Miss Porter, Hannah More, and, of course, the twin giants of the day, Scott and Byron. All their works were reviewed, most of them pirated, many of them dramatized, many parodied. They provided a background of common allusion and even romantic names for the steamers plying on the rivers: *Lady of the Lake, Ellen Douglas, Marmion, Corsair, Mazeppa, Medora.*

As the frontier pushed out across the prairie, the findings on the printed literature here[1] reinforce the findings from the

---

[1] D. A. Dondore, "The Prairie and the Making of Middle America," 1926.

Ohio valley. All the early writing about it and most of the early writings done on the spot are "hifalutin" stuff. Sentimentalism was the order of the day. The prairie in these books is about as convincing as conventional backdrops by scene painters who have spent their lives in town. The love scenes are clumsily coy; the hero, if he is not a prig transferred to the open spaces, is the type of villain who is capable of every offense in the sight of God and man, but who is instantaneously redeemable at mention of his grieving mother or the appearance of a defenseless and immaculate maiden. The Saxon inclination to moralizing was given full sway; observance of poetic justice made the tales improving to the highest degree; and style fitted substance in its stilted smugness.

The Western tales by immigrant writers were tinctured with romantic unreality. The archetype is Gilbert Imlay's "Emigrants" of 1793. It is a book with a thesis: that England was politically corrupt and that American innocence was bliss. Every character, said the author, was drawn from a model; but every one can be found in the pages of Frances Burney. These people, the best of them ruined in fortune and forced "to seek an asylum in America," find the asylum rather turbulent; but after a rough experience crossing the Alleghenies, following the Ohio as far as Louisville, and encountering the grandeurs of nature and the magnanimities of the noble red man, the heroine "perfects her prospect of happiness," and the hero's understanding has not only been regenerated, but his person has already become so robust that he has now more "the appearance of an Ancient Briton" than of the London dandy in the opening chapters. Imlay has performed the office of moral instructor. Gustave Aimard, Frenchman, entertained perhaps an equally high purpose, but wrote pattern blood-and-thunder tales with all the preconceptions of Chateaubriand and all the devices of the Beadle dime novels; and his total irresponsibility about the simple facts almost rivals Munchausen's. Though the Germans were, as one would expect, a shade more scrupulous,

Möllhausen was too prolific to be careful in any respect, Gerstäcker was fascinated by what today is dignified as "organized crime" and did well by it in its border activities, and Sealsfield (Karl Postl) leaned to poetic pictures of nature and deserved Longfellow's commendation for this feature of his prolific output.

The prevailing falseness of the picture is easy to account for. The early writer on the frontier was bound by the preconceptions of the stay-at-home who furnished his public. He set his reader's imagination free in a fertile land, full of game, with just enough risk and hardship to offer thrill and delay success. For every reader who was tempted to convert fiction into fact, a hundred or a thousand settled more snugly by the fireside. The frontier served its purpose for a multitude of absentee landlords, soothed by the narcotic of unveracious fiction, and it supplied a salable formula for the writer of popular romance. Moreover, he fell before an insidious temptation; for he hankered after a happy ending quite as eagerly as his readers, though he knew that for the average pioneer the frontier was dreary and the ending was drab. Natural kindliness made it hard for the story-teller to follow the grim course of events. To reinforce his tenderheartedness he could fall back on the propriety of poetic justice. So he played Providence in a sentimental religiosity, and in his closing chapters paid his favorite characters in cash the rewards which a compassionate theology postponed a stage farther but finally bestowed as the unearned increment laid up in heaven.

Fact about the frontier could be converted into fictional truth only by the novelist who was both an actual pioneer and an honest artist. That is why only two or three have approached high success and why these belong to a later day.

Popular Story and Song

No forms of American literature are more complexly interrelated than the tales, fables, and ballads that about a hundred years ago began to find their way from oral transmission to the permanency of print. They reach back to Old World tradition, tarry on the Atlantic coast, and follow the shifting frontier; they are inevitably connected with the elusive subject of American humor, and, in the field of humor, to satire, burlesque, parody, fantasy; they are inseparable from the history of realism in America, but they are hardly less so from the annals of sentimentalism; they impinge on folklore; they ornament biography; they are borrowed and modified in poetic narrative, prose fiction, and drama. There is a great mass of material at hand for the student of the subject; more is being brought to light from year to year; still more is within reach. How far classification of facts and deductions from them can be carried is an open question. It is clear that the most to be done now is to recognize certain broad features of the subject and refrain from trying to force all the facts into inclusive patterns. Here and there events seem to fall into reasonable sequences; here and there one is emboldened to speak of causes and effects. But the great array of material is like the frontier along which it developed: sprawling, shifting, various in aspect, multifarious in expression, and genially defiant of discipline.

The prime distinction of all this literature is that it came into being without the aid of pen or printing press, and that it kept alive for years or generations before it was set down in black and white. In America, as in the British Isles, it existed in the ruder country while polite literature was reigning in the cities, and it served as campfire accompaniment in the winning of the West. But as the story-telling side of it was occupied largely with local scenes and regional types, and as these literary materials were coming into vogue while the reading public widened, there is need, by way of preface to an account of literature of the people, for a word on the early literature about the commoner written for the educated reader, and tales and sketches for the commoner written by educated authors.

There was, for example, a substantial body of writing about the commoner from the late eighteenth century on. In fiction H. H. Brackenridge used Teague O'Regan in the successive installments of "Modern Chivalry"[1] as a caricature of the American democrat in a satire on American democracy. The homespun Yankee appeared on the stage as early as Tyler's "Contrast"[2] in fulfillment of the Yankee Doodle, or New England bumpkin, of Revolutionary ballad.[3] Barker introduced a Nathan Yank in his "Tears and Smiles" of 1807; and the type, after many recurrences, came to popular success with Jonathan Ploughboy in Woodworth's "Forest Rose" of 1825. Moreover, all these characters led to the breeding of special comic interpreters, until one of the early Jeffersons, the earlier Hackett, "Yankee" Hill, Dan Marble, and J. S. Silsbee owed their reputations in whole or in part to their gifts in Yankee impersonation. The stage, finding a box-office attraction, was not slow to follow up the Yankee with the backwoodsman as soon as this type made its way into popular consciousness. N. M. Ludlow ruefully recorded his boredom at having to sing "The Hunters of Kentucky" in costume on every pertinent and inappropriate occasion until he wished that the idea for this too popular entr'acte feature had never occurred to him.[4]

As these pictures of the native American were displayed to the reader and theatergoer, there was something of a progression from caricature to representation. O'Regan was a comic-strip feature, a grotesque who was related to reality only as a departure from reality. He was chiefly interesting to his creator not for himself, but for the extraordinary fact

---

[1] See pages 174–176.

[2] See page 185.

[3] A. H. Quinn, "The American Drama from the Beginning to the Civil War," Chap. XI, "American Comedy Types," 1825–1860.

[4] N. M. Ludlow, "Dramatic Life as I Found It" (1880), pp. 237, 238, 241.

that creatures only less extraordinary, like Cooper's Aristabulus Bragg,[1] could thrust themselves into the forefront of the American scene. Soon, however, to the men who portrayed them and the people who read of them or saw them on the stage, they became interesting because they were more and more verifiable, though still quaint figures from a lower social stratum. This was a reason why London applauded Hill's and Silsbee's impersonations; but it was also a reason for their vogue with the gallery gods in American cities and with the patrons of the little stock companies all over the country. They were comedy figures rather than comic figures, and the type quickly developed differentiations. On the one hand was the teller of anecdotes — stories that smacked of the soil and of the loafing place; on the other was the cracker-box philosopher, a commentator on the ways of the hour and the affairs of the nation.

Though no hard and fast line may be drawn between writings about the common man and writings for him, the distinction in emphasis is clear as soon as the almanac is cited. This went into the home of the countryman and the villager and, as surviving perforated copies show, was regularly hung on the wall for daily reference. Franklin's introduction of interpolated wit and humor, promptly adopted by the two Nathaniel Ameses,[2] was a universal feature before the end of the eighteenth century; and poetical selections, saws, and jocosities about the weather were regularly supplemented with anecdotes that savored more of the barnyard than of the library, of the barroom than of the drawing-room. The humor of the regular almanacs was native to the people and less forced than the humor of the later comic almanacs, which were in great vogue between 1830 and 1860.

In this attempt to market humor in bulk the jest book preceded the comic almanac. It was a hodgepodge for the

---

[1] See page 261.

[2] Nathaniel Ames (father and son), "The Essays, Humor and Poems of Nathaniel Ames, Father and Son . . . from their Almanacks," 1726–1775. See pages 96 and 591 above.

undeveloped mind, confessedly "culled from every source of wit and humor accessible to the compiler," if the editor of "The Chaplet of Comus"[1] was a representative of his kind in 1811. He is worth citing only on account of two matters on which he plumed himself: he admitted to his pages nothing that could "crimson the cheek of modesty, or call for the animadversions of the most severe moralist," and he included an unprecedented amount of American humor. This must mean that, in contrast with the almanacs, previous jest books were utterly devoid of native humor; for "The Chaplet" itself did not offer one entry in ten that is not recognizably drawn from some foreign source. As to its "moral" qualities, it seems to have been no less exceptional than "The American Jest Book" of 1833;[2] for this was subtitled "A chaste . . . collection . . . for the amusement of the young and old of both sexes," and was alleged to be the first of its kind in its regard for the proprieties. Note its address to the reader:

> The *point* of a large majority of the anecdotes and bon mots, hitherto offered to the public, in such compilations, rests merely upon oaths, upon indelicate and indecent allusions; upon a man being at one time transformed into the hackneyed character of a goose or an ass; the domestic and professional relations of life, also, have been, for centuries, a standing jest; the husband is generally embellished with a pair of horns, the wife arrayed in a pair of breeches; the doctor is in league with the undertaker, the attorney with the devil; the clergyman is looking after his tythe-pig, and the taylor after his cabbage. Indeed not a single volume, in the form of a Jest Book has ever been published, that was fit to be read by any female without a blush, nor by young persons, of either sex, without some injury to their morals.

These observations are worthy quotation not only for the summary of traditional printed humor but also for the evi-

[1] "The Chaplet of Comus; or Feast of Sentiment, and Festival of Wit," 1811.

[2] "The American Jest Book," being A Chaste Collection of Anecdotes, Bon Mots, and Epigrams, original and selected, for the Amusement of the Young and Old of Both Sexes: by the Author of the American Chesterfield, 1833.

dence they offer that at the very time when the homely humor of native types was coming into wide circulation and high popularity, there was an active solicitude for all who were capable of blushing — young people and females of all ages.

Propriety was deferred to especially in the sentimental annuals,[1] which sprang up just before 1830 and were in their heyday until the approach of the Civil War. The first in the United States was published in 1829; there were hundreds of issues, for there were over forty annuals, most of them running in series. They were secular and religious, for young and old. They too were embellished — it was a favorite word of that day — with engravings of extraordinary unreality.

> Those steel-engraved beauties . . . that Highland Chieftain, that Young Buccaneer, that Bandit's Child, all in smoothest *mezzotint*, — what kind of world did they masquerade in? It was a needlework world, a world in which there was always moonlight on the lake and twilight in the vale; where drooped the willow and bloomed the eglantine, and the jessamine embowered the cot of the village maid . . . a world in which there were fairy isles, enchanted grottoes, peris, gondolas and gazelles.[2]

Diction and metaphor were as artificial as the contents and the letterpress and the embellishments. Yet it is worth repeating: at the moment when realism and sincere art and honest satire and the homely rudeness of the folk types were becoming familiar in print, they had to make their way against this current of prudishness and sentimentalism, which itself was emphatically a literature for the people and fondly welcomed by them. The purists of both letters and morals were violently opposed to the free and easy qualities of this familiar literature. A polite school which could strenuously

---

[1] H. A. Beers, "Life of N. P. Willis" (1885), pp. 77–82; Littell's *Living Age* (1844), Vol. III, p. 361; *Atlantic Monthly* (1893), Vol. LXXI, p. 138; *North American Review* (1834), Vol. XXXVIII, p. 198; S. G. Goodrich, "Recollections of a Lifetime" (1857), Vol. II, pp. 259–278, 537.

[2] H. A. Beers, "N. P. Willis," p. 78.

protest at Webster's introductions of Americanisms into a dictionary[1] was sure to cry out against the American idioms of speech and action that were tincturing the prose and verse of the day. Thus the *American Whig Review* (June, 1845) deplored the influence of writers like Haliburton and Seba Smith, "who degrade and vulgarize the tongue and taste of the country"; and Edmund Clarence Stedman was hardly more than an echo of Joseph Dennie, when, a half-century later, he wrote to Bayard Taylor, "The whole country, owing to the *contagion* of our American newspaper 'exchange' system, is flooded, deluged, swamped beneath a muddy tide of slang, vulgarity, inartistic bathos, impertinence and buffoonery that is not wit."[2] Yet floods and deluges are beyond human control; and this one left fertile the ground over which it swept.

Native Types in Popular Tales

The sources of this flood were in the life of the newly settled regions; its substance was the flow of anecdote current among the new settlers, born of their experiences and developed in the telling, as tale-tellers and listeners worked together or loafed together on the levees, in the taverns, and around campfires in the forests, on the prairies, or at the mines. Most of these tales probably came into being as isolated yarns, but it is apparently the nature of the anecdote to be centripetal. It prefers to belong to a group or to be attached to a name. Well-known characters attracted to themselves type stories from all sorts of obscure sources, and certain pattern tales were applied and reapplied to various heroes.

John Henry, one of the latest heroic figures to have emerged, is a nice example of a myth in the making.[3] He is

[1] See pages 206, 207.

[2] "Life and Letters," Vol. I, p. 477.

[3] Guy B. Johnson, "John Henry: Tracking down a Negro Legend," 1929, and Louis W. Chappell, "John Henry: a Folk-Lore Study," 1933. A collection of John Henry songs is appended.

still in the process of fusion from the various tales related about him. Apparently a little over a half-century ago a group of Negro laborers were brought up from the lower Mississippi to work on the Chesapeake and Ohio Railroad. While construction was going on certain labor-saving machinery was offered for sale to the engineers. They were skeptical, as experts always are about innovations, and the report spread that John Henry, finest of the workmen, killed himself trying to prove a foreman's boast that he could outdo a steam drill. But John Henry was a Negro; so a similar tale was told along the river that he met his death competing with a steam crane loading cotton on a river boat. At any rate he was a gigantic Negro who met his death in tragic competition with a machine; and a cycle of stories grew to fit the case of such a creature, whether roustabout or railroad hand. Thus a legend grows.

The most distinctive kind of anecdote, the "tall tale,"[1] was largely based on exaggeration, as with the backwoodsman, for example. He had an almost ritualized self-introduction. He was gamecock of the wilderness. He could whip his weight in wildcats with a panther thrown in. He could outfight, outwrestle, outjump, outboast, any other braggart in the Western Hemisphere. And he ended his recital with a whoop, a cockcrow, and a winglike flapping of his elbows. A paragon of hardihood, he was also a paragon of ugliness. He could fell a coon from its perch by grinning at it; he could grin the bark off a tree. And he was not satisfied with small game. The Big Bear of Arkansaw was a Moby Dick on dry land. When finally killed, his skin covered a mattress, with several feet to spare on each side.

Everything in the world of this tale-teller was hyperbolical. Even when he was frightened his hair stood out so straight that he couldn't get his head within six inches of the pillow. He lived in the midst of a nature on the same heroic scale. He had a farm where the beets and potatoes grew so fast that

[1] "Tall Tales of the Southwest" (edited by F. J. Meine); "Folk-Say, a Regional Miscellany" (1930) (edited by B. A. Botkin), pp. 48–60.

they quarreled for room underground, and a stranger mistook the beets for cedar stumps, and the potato hills for Indian mounds. A pig lay down at night on a grain of corn and was killed before morning by the percussion as it shot up. The squash vines flourished so that one of them chased a drove of hogs a half-mile and made mincemeat of a shoat that stubbed its toe and fell in front of its pursuer. And the wind! It could drive a shingle into a tree stump, mortise two boards together into a perfect carpenter's job, run along a barbed-wire fence and roll it up in a neat spool. It could blow the breath of life into a corpse; blow him, revived, onto the side of a barn from which his wife had to scrape him off; and blow the collected pieces into shape again. In such a world local prides lived up to the extraordinary stimulation of their environments. From Virginia to Texas, from Indiana to Arkansas, local complacency rivaled that of the Arizonan who alleged that the only improvements his country needed were cooler climate and better company and who was unabashed at the rejoinder that these were the chief deficiencies of hell. Naturally in a country where the humor was so broad, it expressed itself in practical jokes and in detailed accounts of the jokers' exploits.

The twentieth-century reader must remember that he can be acquainted with these tall tales only because something artificial has happened to them — they were transcribed; and the transcription was possible for only two types of writer: the man who was so uncontaminated by books that he could naturally set down the informal speech of the storyteller, or the artist who had such control of his medium that he could reproduce the tale in spite of all the traditions of polite literature. The stories as we have them in print do not represent "a symbolism shaped by some mystical pattern in the folk mind, but the conscientious work of writers, frequently intelligent and sometimes very talented, who knew quite well what they were doing."[1]

---

[1] Bernard De Voto, "Mark Twain's America," p. 243.

But here "the plot thickens." If the tall tale fortunately survived in something like its original form, it escaped, as certain other tales and sketches of the frontier failed to do; and two kinds of these must be mentioned in a sort of extended parenthesis. One of these is the character sketch, frequently carried into full-length portraiture by repeated employment of the same individual.[1] Thus, for example, William T. Thompson originated Major Jones of Georgia and pursued him through five volumes of sketches. Johnson J. Hooper developed Simon Suggs of Alabama, not at quite such length but with equal vividness. George W. Harris created Sut Lovingood of Tennessee. These and others represent the frontier character caricaturing itself. The sketches are less spontaneous, more calculated than the tales, pictures of the frontier instead of stories that came from it. The region was posing before the camera rather than unconsciously revealing itself in its own yarn-spinning.

The other type character of the more artificial sort was the popular commentator on political, social, cultural events.[2] He emerged in the person of Seba Smith's Jack Downing; and the fate of Jack Downing is illustrative of the artifice that lay behind his characterization. For Jack was actually kidnaped by other writers, one of whom made more of him than his own literary parent had done. There was a long procession of shrewd critics of the Downing type. There is no question as to their effectiveness and their popular appeal; but James Russell Lowell, creator of the best of them all, serves also as the best proof that they belong to the library rather than to the corner grocery store. These extended portraits, then, and these political critics were by-products of the literature of the people. They were related to the simpler story very much as the so-called frontier town was related to the actual frontier, which had passed farther westward. They have their place in social and cultural history on account of both subject matter and popular appeal; but they taper

[1] "Some American Humorists," edited by Napier Wilt, 1929.

[2] J. R. Tandy, "Crackerbox Philosophers," 1925.

off through the newspaper columnists into less and less effective newspaper humor. In contrast with them the tall tales loom up in impressive epic magnitude. Let us return to them.

They center around a succession of regional characters,[1] and the growth of each cycle or legend is likely to have followed about the same course. The tales were started with actual events in the lives of actual people, events that are remarkable but credible. Their virtue lay not in their verity but in their appeal to the hearer, and as spoken tales they depended in total effect more on the manner of their telling than on firmness of structure or neatness of conclusion. The teller, however, in improving on his original facts and in attributing a current tale to a named type character, made him stronger and craftier, and bettered his achievements in the telling. From a man he was enlarged to the dimensions of a superman. And then, in many instances after his death, the man who started in fact passed from the level of the superman to the realm of pure fantasy.

The simple Yankee, for example, once made "notions" and sold them. It was the day of the peddler. All Yankeeland could not peddle to itself; but the Connecticut man could slip down between the end of the Berkshire Range and Long Island Sound, making his way into New York State and thence to the South. His salesmanship was of a higher grade than his goods. If "he had a mind to" he could sell shoestrings to the barefooted and paper parasols to the Eskimos.

> Abreast of the frontier . . . tramped this long-legged wizard, decade by decade. . . . The farther he receded from view the more completely he changed into a sly, thin ogre, something greater than human size. He was a myth, a fantasy. Many hands had joined to fashion his figure, from the South, from the West, even from New England. . . . By the end of the eighteenth century the shrewd image had grown secure.[2]

---

[1] Constance Rourke, "American Humor," Chaps. I, II.

[2] Ibid. p. 5.

R. M. Bird celebrates the growing reputation of the type in his "Sheppard Lee" of 1836. "With that the rascal began to sing a song; of which all that I recollect is that it related to the joys of a travelling tinman, tricks, rogueries and all— that it began somewhat in the following fashion:

When I was a driving along Down East,
I met old Deacon Dobbs on his beast;
The beast was fat, and the man was thin—
'I'll cheat Deacon Dobbs,' says I, 'to the skin—'"[1]

It is the same character who boasts in verses that could be sung to "Yankee Doodle":[2]

I've pencils without any lead
  They're reckoned much more proper—
Sealing wax, black, white and red,
  And gold rings made of copper.[3]

The backwoodsman has already been mentioned. David Crockett stands for the type in fighting, hunting, or matching wits. After his death, according to the tale-tellers, the bears, alligators, and rattlesnakes took fresh courage. In retrospect he became juggler of comet tails, wielder of the lightning. He could strike sparks from his knuckles. One morning when it was so cold that "the daybreak froze fast as it was trying to dawn," he beat a bear against the ice until the oil ran, squeezed it on the earth's "axes," whistled "Push along, keep moving,"[4] and started the day on its course. Listen to a Crockett ballad:

Now I'll tel you 'bout a fite I had wid Davy Crockett,
Dat haff hoss, haff kune, an haff sky rocket:
I met him one day as I go out a gunnin,
I axe him whar he guine, an he say he guine a kunein.

[1] "Sheppard Lee," Vol. II, p. 132.

[2] The Yankee peddler is variously recurrent in tales of the American countryside; as, for example, in W. G. Simms's "Guy Rivers" (Jared Bunce) and "Border Beagles" (Watson); in Woodworth's play "Foundling of the Sea" (Zachariah Dickerwell) and one of "Yankee" Hill's roles, "Hiram Dodge, the Yankee Peddler." See also the characterization in Timothy Dwight's "Travels in New England and New York," Vol. II, pp. 54, 55.

[3] "Early Songs of Uncle Sam" (edited by G. S. Jackson), p. 49.

[4] Rourke, "American Humor," pp. 58, 59.

Let us take another tale:

Never do you mind,
  Just follow after Davy,
And he'll pretty quick show you
  How to grin a coon crazy.

He grinned away a while,
  And he never 'peared to mind it;
Eatin' away at sheep sorrel,
  And never looked behind it.

And Uncle Davy said,
  "I think it must be dead;
I saw the bark fly
  All around the thing's head."

. . . .

Then we locked arms,
  I thought my breath was gone;
I never was squz so,
  Since the hour that I was born.

And then we did agree
  To let each other be,
For I was too hard for him,
  And so was he for me.

And when we came to look,
  Both of our heads was missin';
He'd bit off my head,
  And I swallered his'n.[1]

Mike Fink, king of the keelboatmen,[2] traveled like these others, from the East through the Mississippi Valley to the plains, but not quite so far toward the status of demigod. Now and again in his later years he was downed in a free fight. Toward the end he was more like Achilles sulking in his tent than Patroclus raging on the battlefield; and his

[1] "Folk Songs of the South" (edited by J. H. Cox), pp. 499, 500.

[2] Walter Blair and F. J. Meine, "Mike Fink, the King of the Keelboatmen," 1933. The one extended literary treatment of Mike Fink is in "The Song of Three Friends," by John G. Neihardt, 1919.

death was ignoble. But in mid-career his was a name to conjure with. A Pennsylvania backwoodsman, born before the Revolutionary War, he was drafted as boatman when the Ohio became a highway from Pittsburgh to the westward and southward. No man could fight or drink or shoot or handle a boat like Fink. No man hated the steamboat more. Possibly it was because the course of events drove him from the river in disgust, so that his life ended in anticlimax, that the Fink legend also sagged instead of lifting him into the conventional apotheosis of mythical heroes. There seems to have been little minstrelsy about Fink; but a few fragments of song are attributed to him by the writers who celebrate him as the last and best of the keelboatmen:

Hard upon the beech oar! —
She moves too slow! —
All the way to Shawneetown,
Long while ago.[1]

Or again,

The boatman is a lucky man,
No one can do as the boatman can,
The boatmen dance and the boatmen sing,
The boatman is up to everything.

Hi-O, away we go,
Floating down the river on the O-hi-o.[2]

These legendary figures, in certain respects similar in their evolutions, are reassuringly different. There was no one myth-forge from which they were all stamped with simple changes of die. Thus Paul Bunyan, archetype of the lumbermen,[3] has no such solid original as Crockett and Fink. He is

[1] Morgan Neville, "The Last of the Boatmen," in "Western Souvenir," n. d. (1829), p. 114.

[2] Blair and Meine, "Mike Fink," p. 156.

[3] E. R. Jones, "Bunyan's Progress"; H. Langerock, "The Wonderful Life and Deeds of Paul Bunyan"; E. S. Shepherd, "Paul Bunyan, His Camp and Life"; James Stevens, "Paul Bunyan"; booklet of Red River Lumber Company, "Paul Bunyan and His Blue Ox." By 1935 Paul was featured in the annual circus of the Chicago Boy Scouts, together with Sour Dough Sam and the Blue Ox, marking the passage of folklore to a rising urban generation.

more like the characters of the Welsh "Mabinogion" or like Crockett, the demigod. He is now cloudlike, and now mountainous. And the humor of his exploits is hardly the humor of campfire reminiscence, to be put in homely idiom between shiftings of the quid. It is more bardic, more susceptible of declamation, even if the declaimer is garbed in motley. Paul is more magnificent than Davy or Mike, less human; and as the lumberman is a still surviving type, Paul's saga, only lately reduced to print, includes recent events and inventions. These other characters lend themselves to the portraiture of the woodcut. Bunyan, more ornate, calls for a large canvas, or a fresco in a Western state capitol — or a northwestern one; for he has his own habitat, not in South or West but in the north woods.

In all the accounts of the real figures of the frontier in South and Southwest the point is in one respect utterly different from that of the older North and East. The conscious literature was consciously edifying; it was not only polite but also moral. The Saxon insistence on ethical motivation was seldom relaxed at any section of the Atlantic seaboard. But the unconscious, or unliterary, literature of the backwoodsman, plainsman, riverman, was frankly unethical, amoral. The prevailing practice is summed up in Simon Suggs's favorite saw, "'It is good to be shifty in a new country' — which means that it is right and proper that one should live as merrily and comfortably as possible at the expense of others." Crockett boasted of his shiftiness as proudly as of his shooting prowess. Ovid Bolus is presented at great length and with the utmost gusto in Baldwin's "Flush Times" as a natural liar who was moved by "the irresistible promptings of instinct, and a disinterested love of art." Lane's tale of the two Wilkinses, father and son, who were cheated out of their cotton by a thimblerigging middleman, appends for its moral the advice not to be so gullible as they.[1] If it is pertinent to refer to these tales as

[1] For the preceding allusions see F. J. Meine's "Tall Tales," pp. 34, 47, 72, 73, and 373.

savoring of folk literature, it is pertinent to suggest that guile prevails in all of it, and that Reynard the Fox and Brer Rabbit move on the same plane with Simon Suggs. On the open, fluid frontier the ethics implicit in these stories is the ethics of success, in which the chief difference between the older and the newer country is that in the newer, rapacity is frank and undisguised.

Yet the Western "bad man" is witness that in the early days of settlement social needs demanded social codes, and that, though the word "morality" may not have been invoked, the violator of the code got short shrift at the hands of his captors. From Murrell, of Andrew Jackson's day, to William Bonney ("Billy the Kid") of two generations later, the Western outlaw did his work and developed his legend. Billy, who met his death in 1881, was a kind of literary survival of the old superman type; like the earlier examples in the growth of his story, but unlike them in the lack of records in the vernacular.[1] He was reputed to be an amiable, gentle, smiling, ruthless murderer. His enshrinement in the printed page is a fulfillment of the sentiments of one of his survivors, that "a fellow that raised as much hell as he did deserves some kind of monument." Billy met his death at the gun of Sheriff Pat Garrett, not because he was a deadly gunman but because he was a gunman in a cause that was immoral in his widespread community. He was an outlaw, and that was bad; but he was also a "rustler," or cattle thief, and that was worse because it put him in active defiance of the code of the country as well as of the laws. Along all the frontiers it was understood that the role of energy and enterprise might be played on no higher a level than Benjamin Franklin's — that honesty was the best policy; and that in point of petty chicanery a man might select his own

---

1 According to Maurice Fulton in "Folk-Say," for 1930, three printed accounts of his life appeared before the Garret-Upson version a year after his death. The contemporary reader can know him through the admirable full-length chronicles of Stanley Vestal and Walter Noble Burns, both of which, however, are the work of talented literary artists.

policy if he thought that minor dishonesty were a better one. But this freedom extended only to a line on which it did not defy the interests of a whole community. No trapper was free to tamper with other men's traps; no riverman to make away with another's boat or cargo; no miner to invade another's claim.

Thus as the frontier moved out over the plains there developed the legends of the rustler-villain and of the ranger-hero. The ranger had his special role. In the old days of open ranges and free grass no cattleman could keep track of his wandering property. Any large herd might include dozens of brands. Collecting all one's own strays was impossible; returning them impracticable. The dishonest had every inducement for large-scale thievery, and the honest built up a complicated system of marketing and accounting for the various brands that depended on the highest type of organized fair play. The ranch owner was a kind of feudal lord over his domain; but his fortunes depended on an employee who was anything but a serf — "a proud rider, skilled, observant, alert, resourceful, unyielding, daring, punctilious in a code peculiar to his occupation."[1] The man who aspired to be a ranger must have all these traits or acquire them; and as a dynamic, romantic type this chevalier of the plains became the theme of countless pages — pages of both prose and verse.

Out on the range he sang to himself: sometimes to beguile his loneliness, sometimes in the night to quiet his herd. He made no boast of his endurance or his courage, though he now and then recited his hardships. He was a sentimentalist, and his melodies were as plaintive as the burden of his songs. Down from the days of the long annual drive from Texas to the northern feeding grounds comes his most characteristic song:

Early in the spring we round up the dogies,
Mark and brand and bob off their tails;

[1] J. F. Dobie, "A Vaquero of the Brush Country," p. xii.

Round up our horses, load up the chuck-wagon,
Then throw the dogies upon the trail.

It's whooping and yelling and driving the dogies;
Oh how I wish you would go on;
It's whooping and punching and go on little dogies,
For you know Wyoming will be your new home.

Whoopee ti yi yo, git along, little dogies,
It's your misfortune, and none of my own.
Whoopee ti yi yo, git along, little dogies,
For you know Wyoming will be your new home.[1]

Again there is need of a parenthesis. The cowboy evidently belongs in the roster of frontier types. But as a type in printed literature he is distinct from wandering Yankee, backwoodsman, riverman, in not taking shape in local anecdote and coming into print through the homely medium of the local newspaper. It is only in balladry (of which more later) that he took his place in oral literature. He appeared in the history of the Southwest when the attention of the scribes and publishers was turned in that direction and when they promptly recognized his possibilities for exploitation. The result was that the cowboy — the most peculiarly American of frontier types and the upholder of a unique code — was at once seized upon as the subject of innumerable cheaply conventionalized "thrillers."

In this wild-West fiction, which shares popularity with the detective story and has an equally impressive news-stand array of magazines, the cowboy and the Indian fighter developed together; and the latter, exemplified by "Buffalo Bill," was the last vivid figure from what was once the frontier. It is a far cry from David Crockett to William F. Cody. Both were genuine characters from the West; both were picturesque individuals; both were writers of personal reminiscence. But Crockett was an outstanding example of a fresh type who had a hand in opening up the West, and Cody

[1] "Cowboy Songs" (edited by J. A. Lomax), p. 87.

was a showy survival of a declining type who witnessed the closing of the frontier. Crockett was edited and published and conventionalized and finally expanded into a legendary figure; but he was an untamable figure and died with his boots on. Cody, on the other hand, was a willing captive of civilization and capitalized his career. Crockett had his parallel in Daniel Boone, and met a spectacular death at the Alamo. Buffalo Bill took his cue from P. T. Barnum, and lingers in the memory of the aging as a rival showman to that Paine who combined history and fireworks in the illuminated "Fall of Pompeii." Paul Bunyan, to be sure, was actually discovered by the public after the passing of Buffalo Bill; but Paul had happily become a legendary character before he attracted the attention of the reading public. Colonel Cody, in contrast, met the fate to be expected for a wild-West type who emerged late enough not only to be written up like a cowboy but also to be exhibited like a buffalo. And that was because the West was no longer wild.

Ballads, Imported and Native

Songs and ballads have had their frequent mention already;[1] so often as to deserve certain generalizations in connection with the literature of the people.[2] There is a body of balladry to be found among all the folk who live away from the main-traveled roads. The oldest type, the English and Scotch, is an evident survival of colonial culture in the regions isolated enough to have resisted the transforming influences of the nineteenth and twentieth centuries. In the fast-accumulating body of material being collected in out-of-the-way places there is always a fraction that goes back

---

[1] See above, pp. 118–123, 389–391, 400–402.

[2] "American Ballads and Songs," edited by Louise Pound; "Minstrelsy of Maine, Folk-Songs and Ballads of the Woods and the Coast," edited by F. H. Eckstorm and M. W. Smyth; "Songs and Ballads of the Maine Lumberjacks with Other Songs from Maine," edited by R. P. Gray; "Mountain Minstrelsy of Pennsylvania," edited by H. W. Shoemaker; "Folk-Songs of the South," edited by J. H. Cox; "Cowboy Songs," edited by J. A. Lomax; "American Ballads and Folk Songs," ed. J. A. and Alan Lomax; "American Songbag," ed. Carl Sandburg.

to Child's great collection.[1] There is also a further sizable fraction of local ballads composed in the form and spirit of these originals: comparable accounts of love and of marriage, of death and disaster, of conflict and adventure, of faithfulness and of perfidy, as a rule seriously sentimental, sometimes humorous. There is another fraction yet of ballads in these keys and tempos drawn from other countries or other parts of America than the ones where they are sung.

In spite of this heavy obligation to traditional song and ballad, this material is like the pioneers who drew upon it in being modified by the new surroundings to which it has been brought. Thus when the cowboy sings of Albon and Amanda on the Western plains, he does so in the oldest of measures. Yet he sings of campfires and canoes and native shores and tyrants' chains and catamounts in an irresponsible combination that could only result from the fusing of an ancient theme with new local idioms. The song as it stands belongs to nowhere because it belongs to so many places; but the cowboy has his indubitable share in it. When he sings "O bury me not on the lone prairie," he does not know that he has simply transplanted "Ocean Burial," for which a Saunders and an Allen composed the words and music. But when he opens up with "I Want to be a Cowboy," he is more likely to be aware that he is crooning or bawling a parody of the gospel hymn "I Want to be an Angel." Certainly if he does not realize this he loses a good deal of the point and of the ungodly pleasurableness of the last stanza:

And when my work is over to Cheyenne then I'll head,
Fill up on beer and whiskey and paint the damn town red,
I'll gallop through the front streets with many a frightful yell;
I'll rope the slant old heathen and yank them back to hell.[2]

[1] For example, in the recent "Ballads and Sea Songs of Newfoundland," edited by E. B. Greenleaf and G. Y. Mansfield, nineteen are referred back to the classic source book, F. J. Child's "English and Scottish Ballads," and all but one of these are cited from one to a dozen times in anthologies drawn from other widely separated regions.

[2] "American Ballads" (edited by Louise Pound), p. 173.

There are more purely local lyrics of which the heritage is not so clear. Possibly if one knew enough, a genealogy could be devised for any of them, though it might demand the ingenuity of the devisers of coats of arms for the newly rich. The song of the little dogies, already cited, is a sentimental piece with an entirely new theme for which any analogy would be pretty far-fetched. And the ironical "Starving to Death on a Government Claim" has its own variants and is planted in various localities; but it is of its own sort, for the government claim is peculiar to the American frontier, and its hardships are peculiar to the settler there:

Tom Hight is my name, an old bachelor I am,
You'll find me out West in the country of fame,
You'll find me out West on an elegant plain,
And starving to death on my government claim.

Hurrah for Greer county!
The land of the free,
The land of the bed-bug,
Grasshopper and flea;
I'll sing of its praises
And tell of its fame,
While starving to death
On my government claim.[1]

The American Western bad man is an easy translation of the English outlaw; but the American lumberman is again without a precedent as a "shantyman," though his hardships, his grievances, his tragedies, and his high jinks and extravagances when he comes to town with a full purse are no more than paraphrases of these features in the lives of sailors, miners, and plainsmen. He has an alphabet song that begins,

A's for the Axe, as we very well know,
And B's for the Boys that can use them also;
C's for Choppings we soon can begin,
And D's for the Danger we often stand in.[2]

---

[1] "Cowboy Ballads" (edited by J. A. Lomax), p. 278.
[2] "Minstrelsy of Maine" (edited by Eckstorm and Smyth), p. 31.

The Danger is mostly with R, the River, and with log drives on it; and the lumberman's song of widest reach seems to have been anent of it, "The Jam on Gerry's Rock":

Come all you loyal shanty boys, wherever you may be,
I would have you give attention and listen unto me,
Concerning six brave shanty boys, so loyal, true and brave,
Who broke the jam on Gerry's Rock and met a watery grave.[1]

Inevitably in a new country there are songs of the homesick wanderer wherever he goes: the runaway boy, the fugitive from justice, or the lonely nomad as he comes to the end of his trail. There are songs of dying sailors, dying cowboys, dying rangers, dying hoboes, dying Californians, and of the deaths of named men of every type. And there are standardized catastrophe songs of flood, fire, train, and shipwreck. These are built to pattern, as are the burial songs of the deep blue sea, or of the lonely prairie, or of wherever else the vagrant has drawn his parting breath. And they are not confined to the regions from which they sprang. The cowboy sings of the sailor; the sailor, of the lumberman; the lumberman, of the ranger; and the songs seem to have passed as readily from the West to the East as from the old settlements to the new.

The strictures often passed upon Bret Harte and his successors for their conventional-romantic pictures of Western life are fair with reference to the total impression given by these authors. They tell the truth, but they tell far from the whole truth; their characterizations are not false but one-sided. For the striking difference between the rough-and-ready tone of the tall tale and the sentimental tone of most of the lyrics shows of the so-called "wild Westerner" that when his emotions were touched he was a sentimentalist of the first order. Whatever his language or his behavior when the sun was high or the barroom lights were gleaming, in his meditative hours he was all for a simplified, idealized

[1] "Minstrelsy of Maine," op. cit. p. 87.

set of theorems about life. In his actual experience men were bundles of attributes in every sort of combination; in his ballads the most satisfactory heroes were unblemished, the heroines immaculate and irreproachable, and the villains blameless. The only repentance that counted was the edifying repentance of the deathbed. The lover was eternally true, or faithless from the start. Not always, of course; for there were songs of humor and satire as well as songs of sentiment. But the evident liking of the frontiersman for this sort of formula, as shown in his fondness for song that expressed it, is a partial explanation for some of the softer traits given him by Harte and others. If the artificial fictioneers sentimentalized about the men who were "Men in the Open Spaces," these men did something of the same kind when they sang their ballads of "Fair Fannie Moore" and "Utah Carroll" and "The Dying Ranger" and "Young Charlotte."

On the basis of his song and story, what may safely be said of the American villager, woodsman, plainsman, mountaineer, in distinguishing his multiple self from the multiple self of the town or city dweller? Has anyone given a better answer than Wordsworth did in another age and in another connection?

> Humble and rustic life was generally chosen [he wrote of his contributions to "The Lyrical Ballads"] because, in that condition, the essential passions of the heart find a better soil in which they can attain their maturity, are less under restraint, and speak a plainer and more emphatic language; because in that condition of life our elementary feelings coexist in a state of greater simplicity and, consequently, may be more accurately contemplated, and more forcibly communicated; because the manners of rural life germinate from those elementary feelings, and, from the necessary character of rural occupations, are more easily comprehended, and are more durable.

Freedom from restraint, freedom from reticence, freedom from overrefinement and oversubtlety, are the basic qualities of these songs and stories and of the folk who for generations found their amusement in telling and singing them. They are far enough from the ruling characteristics of the polite literature which prevailed in America during these same generations.

For side by side with the ballads that hark back to older models is a varied anthology of more recent songs with more recently composed melodies that have become familiar over the whole country. They are common currency from the mountain cabin to the country-club terrace. But this kind of song, however popular, takes one away from frontier, frontier types, and the passage of ballads from one singer to another, and brings one back to village, town, or city, and to the printed "Songster" which rivaled almanac and joke book in circulation among the literate but unliterary.[1]

The songbooks, widely current in the middle half of the nineteenth century in the United States, included echoes of the older song, but were valuable to their purchasers also because they were up-to-date in their contents. There was a profession of this in their title pages: they offered what had never before been presented in book form, they contained songs as sung by popular actors then on the stage, and they included a fine miscellany, like that in the "Rosebud Songster": "A choice collection of Patriotic, Comic, Irish, Negro and Sentimental Songs" which were properly "embellished with 60 engravings."[2] They borrowed from Shakespeare, Byron, Burns, Shelley, Scott, and Moore, from Bryant and Longfellow; all of which confirms the popular taste of the times as revealed in various other quarters.

They also reflected the ways of the hour in allusions to what was going on. A single jingle with eight stanzas and seven more "encore verses" sums up its own era with its references to the railroad, the balloon, the "electric telegraph," mesmerism, shorthand, the daguerreotype, socialism, "laughing gas," prohibition, repudiation of public debt, pat-

---

[1] See, for an example of this type of song in contrast to the folk balladry, G. S. Jackson's "Early Songs of Uncle Sam," a running commentary with abundant quotations. Boston, 1933.

[2] Jackson, "Early Songs," pp. 17, 18.

ent medicines, and women's bustles. Most ditties were not so inclusive; there were whole songs on many of these themes. There were topical songs in large numbers, and songs of "the boys" — humorous and complacent in a mild sophistication that came to the border line of producing the blush that all respectable editors of the time wanted not to inspire.

In addition to the songs that people sang for fun, there were several kinds that were sung on occasion and for a purpose. One of these was the antislavery song, discussed in connection with that movement.[1] Another that persisted as long as people went to "rallies" and whipped up enthusiasm with singing was the temperance lyric. They were collected in separate volumes, many of them; they were introduced into temperance plays; and in time they inspired mirthful lyric replies from the incorrigibles. Another kind was the political lyric, a type which reached its height in the campaign of 1840, when Harrison and Tyler were sung into the White House, past the retreating figure of the luxurious Van Buren, on a log-cabin and hard-cider platform; and in 1844, when "the Clay Minstrel" had it out with "the Democratic Lute" in the battle which made a president out of James K. Polk.[2] Campaign songs and temperance ditties belong to a distant past. Prohibition succumbed in 1933 without a strain of melody in its defense; the last campaign song was raised in the Progressive uprising and downfall of 1912. But two other types of song are perennial, and in their history of a century and a half reveal much as to the direction of popular taste in that interval. They deserve a brief section to themselves.

Patriotic Songs; Hymns

As a gloss on culture history, patriotic songs are variously significant: the melodies, for their origins and their place in music; the words, for the circumstances that inspired them, their combination with the melodies, their first success, their vitality, their reflection of popular taste.

---

[1] See pages 389–391, 400–402. [2] See Jackson, "Early Songs," Chaps. IV, VIII.

"Yankee Doodle," for example, is full of surprises, inconsistencies, paradoxes. Today it is only a military-band tune which no adult group ever sings. The stanza known to everyone is not a part of the Revolutionary ballad. The music is unheroic; the title is derogatory to the people who adopted it. The melody had been familiar in England for years; the familiar quatrain was current in England before the Stamp Act. Variants multiplied; and one, a broadside, attests in the title to its currency before April, 1775: "Yankee Doodle; or (as now christened by the Saints of New England) the Lexington March. N.B. The words to be sung throu' the Nose, & in the West Country drawl and dialect." The stanzas of elaboration and those in reply gave ground by 1787 for the remark of Jonathan in Tyler's "Contrast," that he could not sing but a hundred and ninety verses of it. In time, however, the words lost interest for all but antiquarians, so that the stanza in "The Songster's Museum" was already true by 1826:

> Yankee Doodle is the *tune*
> Americans delight in.
> 'Twill do to whistle, sing, or play,
> And just the thing for fighting.

The story of "Hail Columbia" is quite different except for the fact that music preceded words. "The President's March," a band tune, was popular in 1794 within a year of its production in Philadelphia. In 1798 Joseph Hopkinson, on request, composed the words as an appeal for a unified country at a moment when party claims between Federalists and Democrats were broadening a dangerous rift through conflicting sympathies with England and with France. "Hail Columbia," as sung at a benefit performance by the actor Gilbert Fox, was popular from the start. It was promptly repeated at other theaters; it was twice printed within a few days. "Soon no public entertainment was considered satisfactory without it," and it has survived without change.

We owe "The Star-Spangled Banner" to the existence of a popular melody and the inspiration of a dramatic event — the British attack on Fort McHenry in 1814. Words and music of "To Anacreon in Heaven," constitutional song of the Anacreontic Society in London, were published in 1771. They were such favorites of convivial souls that the words were reprinted in at least twenty-one magazines and song collections in England between 1780 and 1804, and the melody, with original or adapted words, was printed thirty times in America between 1796 and 1813. In the thrill of discovery that "the flag was still there"[1] after a night of bombardment, Francis Scott Key began his version of the song "in the dawn's early light," sketched out the remainder on his way to land, copied it on arrival at his Baltimore hotel, and saw it in circulation as a broadside the next day. At the outset it met with only moderate popularity, being omitted, as a universal favorite could not have been, from many important songbooks during the next twenty years. It was not widely accepted as a national anthem until the Civil War; and then came two more paraphrases with George Tucker's attempt to requisition it for the Confederacy in "The Southern Cross," and with Oliver Wendell Holmes's added stanza.

Here are three types, the common factor being that music offered the pattern for the words. "Yankee Doodle" was a sort of ballad, loaded on a music vehicle which has rolled through the decades without its burden. "Hail Columbia," adapted to a march tune, was made public in propitious circumstances and achieved an immediate vogue, but is rarely sung today except to fill out a formal program. "The Star-Spangled Banner," set to an old convivial tune, with a range that demands the exhilaration of the cup, has been granted long life on account of its official recognition, though it defies vocal assault by any casual group. And "America,"

[1] O. G. Sonneck, "The Star-Spangled Banner, Hail Columbia, America, Yankee Doodle"; Victor Weybright, "Spangled Banner, the Story of Francis Scott Key" (1935), Chaps. IV–IX.

the fourth permanently national song, casually written in 1832 by the youthful S. F. Smith, was set to an English tune of ninety years' standing encountered in a German songbook lent him by Lowell Mason. This, therefore, was no more indigenous than "Yankee Doodle" or "The Star-Spangled Banner."

In recognition of all this an attempt was made in 1861 to inspire a national hymn by organizing public competition for a substantial prize.[1] The committee of award accepted their appointment with misgivings, reluctant "to assume the function of deciding for their fellow citizens a question which it seemed to them could really be settled only by general consent and the lapse of time." Their fears were realized when they exercised their right to make no award. In the meanwhile general consent was being given to a song and to a hymn which are abidingly popular with the lapse of time. These are "Dixie" and "The Battle Hymn of the Republic." The original "Dixie" was composed, words and music, in 1859 by Dan D. Emmett, then under contract as composer of "Negro melodies and plantation walk-arounds" with a New York minstrel company. On a bleak northern Sunday he knocked out this rush order around the traveling showman's autumnal saying, "I wish I was in Dixie." The rollicking measure won every audience, and the sentiment reinforced its appeal in the South. Sung early in 1861 in New Orleans, it made a sensational hit, and soon all the Confederate states rang with it. A few months later Albert B. Pike tried to fit heroic Southern words to it, but he was no more successful than Fanny J. Crosby was in her attempt to recapture the melody for the North. All the variants from either section died away; but Emmett's original words and music still bring Southerners to their feet as no other song in America brings any audience. They stand in deference to the tradition of "The Star-Spangled Banner," but they rise to "Dixie" itself.

---

[1] Richard G. White, "National Hymns — How They are Written, and How They are Not Written," 1861.

"The Battle Hymn of the Republic" had perhaps the most varied career of all American songs of patriotism. Originally a Southern camp-meeting tune, it was introduced into a Massachusetts mobilization camp in 1861. The first secular words were half applied to a gangling Scotch recruit named John Brown. When it became a regimental song, the officers tried in vain to apply it to Ellsworth, first Northern commissioned officer to fall in the war. Inevitably new versions were written applying to John Brown of Ossawatomie, by H. H. Brownell, Edna Dean Proctor, Charles Sprague Hall, and anonymous writers; and variants from these developed beyond recall. The hymn had become a resounding war ballad; but the ballad was to be rehabilitated as a hymn again. This happened when Julia Ward Howe, one of a party to visit the Army of the Potomac in 1861, was urged to dignify the chant with adequate words. Her attempt was christened by James T. Fields and appeared in the *Atlantic Monthly* early in 1862. "John Brown's Body" belonged to the marching soldiers; "Mine eyes have seen the glory of the coming of the Lord," to the religious enthusiast reliant upon a tribal god. And they were equally popular.

Popular consent and the lapse of time elected to preserve from the Civil War a few other melodies, and incidentally the words attached to them unless these were displaced by others. George F. Root's "Battle Cry of Freedom" and "Tramp, Tramp, Tramp, the Boys are Marching," Henry Clay Work's "Marching through Georgia," and Patrick S. Gilmore's "When Johnny Comes Marching Home" are examples of original words and music; and James R. Randall's "Maryland," of the successful setting of new words to an old melody — this time the German "Tannenbaum." "Maryland" belongs, of course, only to a single state; the others, widely played by parading bands, are occasionally resorted to at "patriotic exercises," but are kept alive as melodies chiefly through their adoption by schools, college fraternities, and other social groups. Since the Civil War there has been no significant addition to the anthology of patriotic song.

There is a definite suggestiveness in the qualities of the passing American favorite of the World War — "Over There." It does not contain great music or any kind of poetry. It does meet, however, certain requirements of the fruitless competition of 1861: it is "of the simplest form and most marked rhythm, the words easy to be retained by the popular memory, and the melody and harmony such as may be readily sung by ordinary voices." In this respect George M. Cohan met the situation as Root and Work and Gilmore did fifty years before, and, like them, he wrote music of the day. It belonged to the same public that was delighting in O. Henry, Walt Mason, Irvin Cobb, and Will Irwin, all in the main sane and obvious people. It came from Broadway, and it represented Broadway — purveyor of the nation's amusements — in the twentieth century.

But "The Star-Spangled Banner" and "Hail Columbia" belonged to the public of Francis and Joseph Hopkinson and John Copley and Gilbert Stuart. The artistic work of that day was neatly turned and graceful; poetry and music lent themselves to dashes of magniloquent heroism and tender sentiment. The gallant traditions of manly strength, feminine grace, the cheering influence of the social glass, and a traditionally aristocratic point of view were all implicit in the first national lyrics. They may not have represented the tendency, but they did represent the taste of the day. John Howard Payne's patron would say that "the desolating effects of democracy" were registered in the loss of these echoed gentilities. So would James Fenimore Cooper, and Washington Irving would not dissent. "Over There," "There'll be a Hot Time in the Old Town Tonight," and "Hail, Hail, the Gang's All Here" seem to be among the prices of democracy. And what has been paid in terms of songs of patriotism has also been paid in hymns of worship.

For various reasons no selection of American hymns can quite compare in certainty with the choice of patriotic songs, but the outstanding types and the drift of development are quite comparable. Three hymns of Timothy Dwight, Ray Palmer, and Oliver Wendell Holmes are signs of the times up to 1860. Dwight's contribution, "I Love Thy Kingdom, Lord," belongs to the period of "Hail Columbia" and is involved in the theology of Jonathan Edwards, Dwight's grandfather. In spite of some confusions of imagery and the mortuary tone of one stanza, it maintains a tone of solemn and hopeful self-dedication; and set to the eighteenth-century tune "St. Thomas," it becomes an austere but not unlovely choral. Palmer's "My Faith Looks Up to Thee" (1830) is orthodox in its theology, representing life as a period of durance before an ultimate ransom, and in its way it has reinforced the faith of millions who were equally indebted to its sentiments and to Lowell Mason's sentimental "Olivet," which he composed for it and which perfectly fits it. Holmes's "Sun-Day Hymn" (1859), known often by its opening line, "Lord of all being, throned afar," is properly described by one hymnologist as "always a favorite in gatherings of different denominations and creeds." The liberal Professor at the Breakfast Table wrote with this intent, prefacing it with the hope that men would "forget for the moment the difference in the hues of truth we look at through our human prisms, and join in singing . . . this hymn to the source of the light we all need to lead us, and the warmth which alone can make us all brothers." His hope was fulfilled; for the hymn in finding its adequate melody transformed "Louvan" from the saccharin thing it was when set to Bowring's "How sweetly flows the gospel sound." The "Sun-Day Hymn" belongs to the slender anthology of sacred songs that are indubitably poetry.

The theme of "My Faith Looks Up to Thee" is the theme of Phoebe Cary's "One Sweetly Solemn Thought" (1825), which deserves less attention than it has received, as Mrs. Stowe's beautiful "Still, Still with Thee, when Purple Morning Breaketh" (1855) deserves more. Shaking off the spell of the graveyard, Mrs. Stowe was concerned with a living faith. This faith is the burden, too, of Whittier's

"Our Master" (1866), a devotional poem from which several hymns have been excerpted, of which the best-known includes the stanzas beginning "We may not climb the heavenly steeps."

A new set of composers arrived with this mid-century group — Barnby and Bradbury and Dykes, whose music represents a departure from the sturdy processional rhythms of Mason's "Laban" or "Uxbridge" or "Hamburg." Their melodies tend to the use of three-four and six-four measures and to consequent sweetness rather than vigor. They are better attuned to the emotional appeals of the nonconformist pulpit than to the stately traditions of Rome or England. They mark the difference between Longfellow and Newman; between Calkins's "Waltham" (for Bishop Doane's "Fling out the Banner") and Sherwin's "Chautauqua" (for Mary A. Lathbury's "Day is Dying in the West"), each a high example of its kind in the 70's. In other words, the new hymns were at one with the theology and the secular poetry of the day — confident, aspiring, fervent to the point of sentimentalism. The period could produce such triumphant songs as "Fling out the Banner" or "Onward, Christian Soldiers" (the latter, of course, English) and such hymns of tenderness and serenity as those of Whittier and Miss Lathbury; but the pursuit of these inclinations led to the verge of a precipice.

For the attempt to unite the breadth and dignity of older song with the warmth and color of the later led on from sentimental ornateness to tawdry sensationalism. The decline in hymn-writing from Bernard of Clairvaux by way of the Wesleys to Phoebe Cary and, in musical composition, from the Gregorian chants via Mason and Bradbury to P. P. Bliss (of "Hold the Fort" and "Pull for the Shore") reached the popular *descensus Averno* in the Moody and Sankey "gospel hymns." The banalities of evangelistic song paralleled the banalities of secular song. There is little to choose between "Rescue the Perishing" and "The Long, Long Way to Tipperary" or between "Hold the Fort" and "A Hot Time in the Old Town." Folk song had its beauties; so did the song of the gentry bred in the school of Handel and Haydn. But the songs of the city streets or of the gospel rally had little to redeem them. They were both democratized and vulgarized.

Mark Twain

Mark Twain probably touched American life at more points than any other author of his generation. The first half of his story has been written into his books, and the whole has been told, with his help, in one of the best of American biographies.[1] It involves directly his Virginia parentage and the pioneer experiences of his father and mother — John and Jane (Lampton) Clemens — in the Tennessee mountains; his own residence in the Mississippi Valley and on both seacoasts; his activities as printer, river pilot, journalist, lecturer, publisher, author; his friendships with all sorts and conditions of men from California miners to crowned heads; the joys and sorrows of family life; the making and losing of several fortunes; and an old age crowned with honors, fortune, and immense popularity, yet overshadowed by clouds of doubt and grief.

The symbol of that life is supplied in the log raft on which Huckleberry Finn floated down the Mississippi, a raft without directive power of its own on a full stream with a shifting channel. Mark Twain was born in a river town on the way to Eldorado, of parents whose hearts were somewhere else. Hannibal, Missouri, his boyhood home, was at a mid-point on the waterway of traffic between North and South and in the line of travel between East and West. It was a typical station in the near-frontier; it passed on supplies and it caught the returning news. It shared the temper of the zone beyond it, depending, like the still newer regions, on the country eastward for fresh recruits, for basic supplies, for financial support, and for the market in which to regain the

[1] By Albert Bigelow Paine.

dollars it had already borrowed and spent. And it was due to be replaced by another secondary frontier as it fell back in spirit and in circumstances to the third or fourth or fifth stage in the development of the West. Such a drifting raft could supply diversion and excitement, and food for thought; but, essentially unstable, it could afford no basis of security, no point of departure, for departure implies at least momentary anchorage.

There was no security to be found in his parents; the mother was high-spirited and disappointed; the father, consistently unsuccessful. Nine years as journeyman printer, capped by fifteen months of drifting to the East and back, helped to make a nomad of the younger Clemens. As a river pilot he was raised to a dizzy, histrionic eminence only to be pulled down by the coming of the war. At this central point in the country there was not even a secure sectionalism on which he could rely. When he tried to find what was right in terms of other people, he found that the highly respectable Missourians were perplexingly on both sides. Being a Confederate recruit for three months in the petty guerrilla skirmishings of the region was a meaningless experience for him.[1] And when he set out for Nevada he dodged an issue on which he had no convictions, and he caught up once more with the frontier that had flowed beyond him in his boyhood. He knew too much about it to entertain any illusions. His picture of the claim jumpers and prospectors in the mining regions is the honest record of a few fabulous strikes and a myriad of blasted hopes. His summary of frontier evolution is mordantly, ironically realistic:

> How solemn and beautiful is the thought that the earliest pioneer of civilization, the van-leader of civilization, is never the steamboat, never the railroad, never the newspaper, never the Sabbath-school, never the missionary, — but always whiskey! Such is the case. Look history over; you will see. The missionary comes after the whiskey — I mean he arrives after the whiskey has arrived; next

---

[1] See "Private History of a Campaign that Failed."

comes the poor immigrant, with axe and hoe and rifle; next, the trader; next, the miscellaneous rush; next, the gambler, the desperado, the highwayman, and all their kindred in sin of both sexes; and next, the smart chap who has bought up an old grant that covers all the land; this brings in the lawyer tribe; the vigilance committee brings the undertaker. All these interests bring the newspaper; the newspaper starts up politics and a railroad; all hands turn to and build a church and a jail — and behold! civilization is established forever in the land.[1]

Into this turbulent life Mark Twain was not to merge himself. Journalistic success brought him to the East, gave him opportunities for travel and for seeing other civilizations with no standards to judge them by. He was looking at the Louvre from a merry-go-round. Marriage plunged him into ultra-conventional surroundings which only served to unsettle him the more. A comet-like rise in prestige and popularity, a meteoric business downfall and a quick recovery, and a succession of personal bereavements helped offset and overcome the one most steadfast factor in his life — the social and religious traditions which his wife brought to bear on him, traditions that he encountered too late either completely to accept or completely to repudiate.

His writing was an immediate reflection of his external life, starting from the West, progressing to a consciousness of contrasting American and European cultures, and thence to speculative inquiry as to the end and aim of human existence. Although if one were talking "periods," "The Innocents Abroad" of 1869, which preceded the first, would need to be argued over into the second, it is clear enough that for the first fifteen years of his great vogue Mark Twain was writing chiefly about the West, in which he had grown up; and that, read in the order of their relation to his career, "The Gilded Age," "Tom Sawyer," "Huckleberry Finn," "Sketches New and Old," "Life on the Mississippi," and "Roughing It" carry him up to the point of his pilgrimage to the Holy Land.

[1] "Life on the Mississippi" (Harper, 1911), pp. 428–429.

It was in the years described and chronicled therein that his mood and manners were determined, his observation was trained, his spirit of inquiry was roused, and his incapacity to satisfy his own questionings was bred in him.

As he moved away from his first habitat, never to forget it but never to return except as a sojourner, observation and inquiry combined to interpret his own country in the light of foreign cultures, as in "The Innocents Abroad," "A Tramp Abroad," and "Following the Equator." The purpose of the first and most famous of these, he explained in the preface, was to stress the observer rather than the thing observed. How would the reader "be likely to see Europe and the East if he looked at them with his own eyes"? And in "The Prince and the Pauper," "The Connecticut Yankee," and "Joan of Arc" he simply reversed the lens and interpreted the past in the very aggressive light of the present. With something of the inclination of James Branch Cabell, but with nothing of his manner or his intention, he took his reader to distant times and places but incessantly jogged his elbow with reminders of immediacy.

He was glad of escape from the past, from kingship and serfdom, and scornful of the romanticism which gilded over the oppression and squalor. But deep in his heart he was scornful too of the disingenuousness that gilded over the prosperous sanctimonies of his democracy. Past and present seemed more and more alike to him; Europe and America; despotism and democracy; Christianity and paganism. Science overthrew the Christian mythology for him, reduced the world to a "little floating mote," reduced mankind to a biological genus, reduced him to a philosophy of pessimism. From "The Man that Corrupted Hadleyburg" and "Following the Equator" to "Captain Stormfield's Visit to Heaven" and "The Mysterious Stranger" Mark Twain identified all humankind with human nature, and human nature with naturalism rather than with humanism. He established his fame as a Westerner writing of the West, and it is this part of his work that will endure; yet as he became involved in problems and overloaded his books with purposes he grew so typical of his generation that his career became almost equally significant with his works, and his biography as important in history as "Huckleberry Finn" is in literature.

Mark Twain, then, drifting along on the current of American life, was swept from the West on the tributary stream of popular humor into that back reach on the river which lay between the rapids of the Civil War and the whirlpools of the new industrialism. He came to his maturity at an auspicious moment, when the journalism of the country was coming out in recklessly fresh, informal jocularity which was related to the old American humor, but a great departure from its recent manifestations. It belonged to the people and was journalistic because it found no natural outlet in the more elegant publications. The men who were indulging in it were unconscious of making any contribution to national literature. They could not have won the attention of Irving's readers, perusers of the old Annuals, admirers of Knickerbocker courtliness. They wrote for the world of Horace Greeley and for armies of readers who never heard of Greeley's metropolitan newspaper. Regardless of polite literary tradition, they were bringing to the surface a tradition as long as history and as wide as the continent. The native American comic characters had long existed in popular consciousness and had sometimes approached the outer fringes of polite letters, but only on temporary sufferance, like entertainers in the mansions of the gentry. There was the Yankee with his drawl, his habit of understatement, his picturesque and unexpected figure of speech, and his sober utterance of extreme exaggeration. There were the backwoodsman and the river-boatman with their bragging, whooping tall talk. The Yankee turned the Englishman and the townsman to contempt; the backwoodsman discredited the Yankee. The plainsman or the miner combined the two and turned his scorn on any kind of "tenderfoot." And all of them were endless raconteurs, yarn-swappers on street corners, in taverns, around campfires, dependent for audiences on the skill of their telling and to a great degree on the tallness of their tales.[1]

Very much of the frontier humor as it became identified with definite names was set down by Easterners who had their predecessors at home and had developed the knack there. Artemus Ward, who learned the West as a tramp printer, came from Maine; Petroleum V. Nasby, who edited country papers in Ohio, from New York; Josh Billings, Ohio deck-hand, farmer, and auctioneer, from Massachusetts; John Phoenix, Western explorer and surveyor, from the Bay State, too. And more often than not New York, Boston, and Philadelphia were the first to put the newspaper jocosities between covers and purvey to an eager East the rough stuff of the West. It was a flood that threw up on its waves a few real treasures, the rarest of which was Mark Twain.

If there had been no journalistic side stream he might still have gone on his way; but these other men put the public into a humor for him. One difference at the outset was his — that he was pre-eminently the voice of the West rather than a voice about the West. This was the main difference too between him and most of the actual frontier writers. For, as a rule, when the frontier began to put itself on paper, it took its pen in hand to address the gentle reader in terms that would not be offensive. The district might be satisfied with actually being rough and ready, but the element in it that wanted to read and write wanted also to be polite and sophisticated.

Not so Mark Twain. He began as the other tale-tellers did, allowing an undercurrent of seriousness to appear now and then in the flow of his extravagance; depending, like the schooled yarn-spinner, on his manner for much of his effect; and keeping a sober face, Yankee-fashion, while he played, Western-fashion, with the burlesque and the hoax, the preposterous and the absurd. By the time he was ready to start eastward he had learned on river levee and steamboat deck,

---

[1] See pages 606–618.

in the camp and on the lecture platform, what the most effective methods were.

All Tully's rules and all Quintilian's too,
He by the light of listening faces knew,
And his rapt audience all unconscious lent
Their own roused force to make him eloquent.[1]

He was quite deliberate and calculating. His essay on "How to Tell a Story" is evidence.

> The humorous story is American, the comic story is English, the witty story is French. The humorous story depends for its effect upon the *manner* of the telling; the comic story and the witty story upon the *matter*. . . . The humorous story is told gravely; the teller does his best to conceal the fact that he even dimly suspects that there is anything funny about it. . . . The humorous story is strictly a work of art — high and delicate art — and only an artist can tell it.[2]

His letter to a London editor[3] is only the best of many passages which reveal his scrupulous regard for diction. He had (to paraphrase his own words) a singularly fine and aristocratic respect for homely and unpretending English, he did not indulge in the vagaries of spelling common with the journalistic humorists, and he treated punctuation as a "delicate art."

This editorial attitude toward his manuscript was doubtless reflected from his years of discipline in handling type. A similar attitude toward his humor reflected the discipline of his marriage. Mrs. Clemens firmly assisted him in drawing a line between his publications and his private speech and correspondence. He had, according to William Dean Howells, a Southwestern, Lincolnian, Elizabethan breadth of parlance, which Howells could not call coarse without calling himself prudish. As a result Howells was always hiding away in odd pigeonholes certain of Mark Twain's more startling letters; not wanting either to reread them or to destroy them.[4]

---

[1] Lowell, "Agassiz," Vol. II, lines 52–55.

[2] "Works" (Harper), Vol. XXIV, pp. 263–264.

[3] Paine's "Life," pp. 1091–1093.

[4] "My Mark Twain," pp. 3–4.

Mark Twain's humor relied on his never-failing and extravagant use of the incongruous and irrelevant. Often this appeared in similes and metaphors: "A jay hasn't got any more principle than a Congressman";[1] "His lectures on Mont Blanc . . . made people as anxious to see it as if it owed them money."[2] It emerged in his impertinent personalities, as on his remark on first meeting Grant: "General, I seem to be a little embarrassed. Are you?"[3] Or as in his reply on being asked why he carried a cotton umbrella in London, that it was the only kind that would not be stolen there. It appeared too in his sober misapplication of familiar historical facts; and it was developed most elaborately in the favorite literary "gag" of the period — the printed hoax, such as "The Empire City Massacre,"[4] "The Petrified Man," or the autumn scene and the solitary esophagus in the midst of "The Double-Barrelled Detective Story."

A particular charm attached to his work among his big public in the apparent spontaneity of what he wrote and spoke. It seemed to be for his own delectation, the casual improvising of the moment. At times, of course, he must have improvised — with the art of a musician whose technique has been painstakingly acquired before it can be freely employed; but often the utterance his hearers took for extempore was composed to the last syllable and delivered with an art that concealed the artifice.[5] For the multitudes who bought up the editions of "The Innocents Abroad" the salient feature was its jovial extravagance. The first feeling of the public was that he had out-Phoenixed "Phoenix" and beaten "Petroleum Nasby" at his own game. Beyond question he literally enjoyed himself when giving hilarious enjoyment to others; the free play of his antic fancy was a kind of self-indulgence. But it was also a habit from which he could not refrain. All his works

---

[1] "A Tramp Abroad" (Harper), Vol. I, p. 17.
[2] Ibid. Vol. II, p. 173.
[3] "Life" (Harper), Vol. I, p. 360.
[4] "Life" (Harper), Vol. III, Appendix C, p. 1597.
[5] As expounded by Mark Twain in "How to Tell a Story."

were written in the spirit of the Western raconteur; beyond the short unit he had no controlling sense of structure; and he capitalized his deficiency. The account of how he salvaged the story of "Those Extraordinary Twins" from out of the story of "Puddn'head Wilson" is as entertaining as either of the stories. He suffered a sort of claustrophobia that resented any narrative restriction. Thus "Joan of Arc," a late work, is approached, pursued, and concluded in a spirit of admiration often amounting to reverence. Yet in the character of "The Paladin" and in Joan's uncles the historian reverted to his broadest jocosities. There are interpolated pages of pure farce, companion pieces with portions of "The Man that Corrupted Hadleyburg." Near the close of his life he declared "Joan" to be the best of all his books; and, naturally, for in mood it was the utterance of a cynic, a discouraged old man in a metropolitan library, but in tone it was recurrently free and easy, casual, discursive, laugh-provoking, Western.

"The Innocents Abroad" was the voice of the West of which "Joan of Arc" was an echo. To make that historic voyage to the Holy Land, Mark Twain went from the Pacific coast via New York City to the Old World as an accredited correspondent of a California newspaper. He shared the contempt of the West for the Eastern tenderfoot and the distrust of both East and West for the corruptions of Europe. America had been preening itself on its superior morals and manliness for the better part of a century. The America for which he spoke and to which he wrote knew little about history and nothing about art and literature. Ignorance confronted with history and art and literature may confess to itself. If it does not, it may sound a barbaric yawp and wear its hat indoors, like Whitman; or it may bluster and laugh, like Mark Twain. Every honest Californian would agree that the average European was a scamp, that the ancestral European had been a bully or a cringer, that ancient art was the hocus-pocus of the dilettante, that Raphael was a joke, that the Arno was a barnyard creek, that the honest

American was the noblest work of God, and that the American pretender to European culture was a traitor to his kind. At one point, however, this Westerner displayed the profoundest respect. Against the background of his new section of a new land genuine antiquity seemed awe-inspiring. There was a solemnity in the evidence of the passing centuries. He gibed at the "old masters"; but he entered a cathedral with respect, walked in reverent silence among the ruins of the Holy Land, and acknowledged in the Alps the presence of the Most High. For the near half-century since "The Sketch Book" America had been hearing of Europe from American travelers. Now American travel was beginning to be more than the exception. America was not going to be Europeanized if Mark Twain knew it. He did his best to correct the tendency; and a million Americans shouted with laughter, threw up their hats, and sang "He's a jolly good fellow."

This nationwide applause gave him the kind of self-confidence that heightens mannerisms, and his chief mannerism became an elaborate jocosity which borders on clownishness. It was the slapstick of the old comedy, the custard-pie-throwing of the comic film. It was both extravagant and prolonged. Occasionally, and with fit material, it was and still is amusing — as with his prefatory explanation of the use of the well in disposing of superfluous characters in "Those Extraordinary Twins"; more often, as the years went on, it was forced and ineffectual, even abysmally so — as with the unhappy speech at the *Atlantic Monthly* dinner of 1877. But the popular applause also gave a chance to the burlesquer, the practical joker, the hoaxer, to lure the mind of the public across the continent. Cooper had looked westward; so had Longfellow; so did Horace Greeley; Lincoln had drawn men's eyes in that direction. Mark Twain in volume after volume treated the Mississippi not as a western boundary but as the central artery of the United States. And with his Eastern collaborator, Charles Dudley Warner, in "The Gilded Age" he bound East and West together.

As long as he tarried in this Western home of his imagination he was, in the words of the old rhetorics, clear, simple, and effective. But now he was living in the East, married to a conservative Easterner, a sort of equator for him, the incarnation of an imaginary line that he never ignored but was always tempted to cross. He was in Hartford, most conservative of towns; hobnobbing with Warner; fraternizing with the Reverend Joseph Twichell, professional alumnus of Yale College; giving surprise parties to Harriet Beecher Stowe; lecturing to the assembled clergymen on their Monday day of rest. If the West had been able to hold him, he might have gone on in his jocosities oblivious to the new science and the old theologies and the rising conflict between them. In the East he could not escape this; he became completely immersed in it, and he was utterly unprepared for it. As the submergence in this quicksand proceeded, Mark Twain the gay, mocking Western tale-teller was transformed into Mark Twain the bewildered and sardonic amateur philosopher.

Susan Clemens, born in 1872, wrote in her journal in the 1880's: "He is known to the public as a humorist, but he has much more in him that is earnest than that is humorous. . . . He is as much of a philosopher as anything, I think." And, further, "I think he could have done a great deal in this direction if he had studied while young, for he seems to have enjoyed reasoning out things, no matter what."[1] "If he had studied while young," Mark Twain might have gained a knowledge of philosophic thought that would have steadied him in his own thinking. Yet possibly not; for his thinking was at the same time all his own and quite in the current of nineteenth-century thought.

With an initial distrust of all authority he made his analysis of the views prevailing in Christendom. His reason was alert to challenge theology wherever it was at odds with science. He found nothing in the Bible to question that man was the

[1] Quoted in the "Life" (Harper), Vol. III, p. 844.

crowning achievement in creation, but everything in the doctrines of evolutionary thought to suggest that man was only a link in a far-evolving succession of higher forms. He found a God in the Old Testament who was "an irascible, vindictive, fierce, and ever-fickle and changeful master,"[1] though in the ordering of the universe he appeared to be steadfast and fair. Reason unseated his faith in a literal reading of the Scriptures and his confidence in creeds founded on them. He lost the God of the Hebrews, but, for a while, found his own "in the presence of the benignant serenity of the Alps."[2]

For the afterlife he could find no such assurance. For many men of his generation the solution was to take refuge in the authority of the dogmas they had challenged; many of the most radical came back with relief to the protection of the Roman Catholic faith; but he could not make his way into the harbor. There is a pathos in the many passages of which the following is an example: "I would gladly change my unbelief for Neligan's faith, and let him make the conditions as hard as he pleased."[3] His most clearly formulated profession of faith was in reality a profession of doubts:

> I believe in God the Almighty. . . . I think the goodness, the justice, and the mercy of God are manifested in His works; I perceive that they are manifested toward me in this life; the logical conclusion is that they will be manifested toward me in the life to come, if there should be one.[4]

As in his discrimination between "antiques" and antiquity, Mark Twain held to the distinction between what Emerson called "historical Christianity" and the ideals from which its adherents have fallen away, for a long while keeping clear from a desperate cynicism. He judged the religion of his countrymen by its personal and national fruits and was filled

---

[1] "Life" (Harper), Vol. II, p. 412.
[2] "A Tramp Abroad" (Harper, 1911), Vol. II, p. 51.
[3] "Innocents Abroad" (Harper, 1911), Vol. I, p. 376.
[4] Quoted in the "Life" (Harper), Vol. IV, p. 1583.

with wrath at the indignity of an Episcopal rector's refusal to perform the burial service of the unconfirmed actor George Holland, and at the extortionate demand of the American Board of Foreign Missions for indemnities after the Boxer Rebellion in China.[1] They affected him as did the sanctimonious cruelty of the pilgrims he accompanied to Jerusalem.

On the national ideals of Christendom he spoke in bitter prophecy in 1908:

> The gospel of peace is always making a deal of noise, always rejoicing in its progress but always neglecting to furnish statistics. There are no peaceful nations now. All Christendom is a soldier-camp. The poor have been taxed in some nations to the starvation point to support the giant armaments which Christian nations have built up, each to protect itself from the rest of the Christian brotherhood, and incidentally to snatch any scrap of real estate left exposed by a weaker owner. King Leopold II of Belgium, the most intensely Christian monarch, except Alexander VI, that has escaped hell thus far, has stolen an entire kingdom in Africa, and in fourteen years of Christian endeavor there has reduced the population from thirty millions to fifteen by murder and mutilation and overwork, confiscating the labor of the helpless natives, and giving them nothing in return but salvation and a home in heaven, furnished at the last moment by the Christian priest.
>
> Within the last generation each Christian power has turned the bulk of its attention to finding out newer and still newer and more and more effective ways of killing Christians, and, incidentally, a pagan now and then; and the surest way to get rich quickly in Christ's earthly kingdom is to invent a kind of gun that can kill more Christians at one shot than any other existing kind. All the Christian nations are at it. The more advanced they are, the bigger and more destructive engines of war they create.[2]

With his religious belief, never strong, unsettled by the theories of a mechanistic philosophy, and his fears as to humankind reinforced by the brute facts, Mark Twain came finally to the crisis in which he had no creed to appeal to and could only rely on a pattern of behavior. On this ethical side

---

[1] Paine, "Life" (Harper), Appendix J, pp. 1128–1130.

[2] Quoted in the "Life" (Harper), Vol. IV, pp. 1467–1468.

of his philosophy he had his feet on solid ground; he had no doubts about morality or moral obligations. He was the sort of man characterized by Dreiser, who "deliberately and of choice holds fast to many, many simple and human things, and rounds out life, or would, in a natural, normal, courageous, healthy way."[1] He had formulated his rule of conduct for the Hartford neighbors: "Diligently train your ideals upward, and still upward, toward a summit where you will find your chiefest pleasure, in conduct which, while contenting you, will be sure to confer benefits upon your neighbor and the community."[2] It determined his own behavior and his critical reactions. And it was because he eventually was convinced of what the Calvinists used to call "natural depravity" and what the moderns call naturalism that he came at last habitually to think and speak of the "damned human race," and that he wrote his bitter indictment of it in "The Mysterious Stranger."

Years of marriage, of prosperity, of associations in a world where Howells was his literary sponsor and H. H. Rogers his financial guide, had brought him to the point where, if he had chosen to shuffle and hedge, he might have contended that keeping silence was one way of conferring the benefit of contentment on his nearest neighbors. But he was honest with himself, and admitted that to speak what he felt about the ways of the world would cost him too much in the way of lost friendships and lost admirers. He continued to write, but said that someone else might begin plain speaking if he chose,[3] and he left behind him manuscripts which have been issued in volume after volume posthumously, with "The Mysterious Stranger" as the egregious example of what he chose not to utter in the flesh. It was an unheroic conclusion to a career; a decline from recklessness to prudence, if not to timidity. He had led a life of perplexities, doubts, inde-

---

[1] "Twelve Men," p. 1.

[2] Quoted in the "Life" (Harper), Vol. II, p. 744.

[3] Van Wyck Brooks, "The Ordeal of Mark Twain," Chap. X, "Let Somebody Else Begin."

cisions. His most admiring friend put it in kindliest terms when he ended a tribute with a reference to "the intensity with which he pierced to the heart of life, and the breadth of vision with which he compassed the whole world, and tried for the reason of things, and then left trying."[1]

In matters religious during Mark Twain's lifetime, and particularly the first two thirds of it, intellectual and emotional inertia, greatest of stabilizers, kept the vast majority contentedly in line. Mark Twain, however, was peculiarly susceptible to the lure of novelty, whether in an invention, a nostrum, or a new idea. Not subject to Christian dogma as a finality of thought or a controlling force, he was ready and eager to substitute the certainties of observational science for the certainties of speculative religion. He was satisfied with the assertion of the man in the laboratory that we can know only what we can measure, and satisfied that life could be reduced to tangibles subject to mensuration. He was far from satisfied with the conclusions of science as to the nature and destiny of man, but he saw no escape from them; for he was so convinced that the scientist was in command of his facts that he "left trying" for the substance of things hoped for and the evidence of things not seen. Had the scientists of his day become the metaphysicians that they are today, — with their frank speculations on the nature of matter, and their doubts as to whether the atom is an electric generator, a miniature solar system, or an undulation of probabilities, — he would very likely have taken refuge in the certainties of speculative philosophy as over against the honest uncertainties of science. But he swapped horses in midstream; he had no other choice; and he was swept under. His later works were the flounderings of a drowning man.

Yet slowly, in this period, critical America came to the conclusion that popular America for once was right: that Mark Twain, the Mark Twain of the West, was worth reading. His use of the American scene, his resort to American

---

[1] Howells, "My Mark Twain," p. 100.

humor, his exercise of an American mind developed by essentially American experiences, and his insistence on an American point of view, his gifts and his limitations, made him a national figure. His courage may have waned and his powers may have become confused, but his honesty was unassailable; his manner was all his own; and, beyond any man of his kind, he knew "how to tell a story."

To and From the Gold Coast

Pioneer evolution in the California days of the gold rush was so speeded up that one can see it take place as in the moving pictures that present the blooming of a flower. Earlier exploring and settlement had been relatively deliberate. But with the discovery of gold on the coast, the pot at the end of the rainbow was too alluring for the slow progression of former years. Once reached, this coast, unlike all the other westward stretches, was on the way to nowhere else. Life could not be thinned out by seepage further toward the sunset. Enterprise was not drained away. The defeated and the dissatisfied retreated along the back trail, and those who remained were indeed magnificently isolated by the Sierras and the desert or by the sea. Here the Saxon and the Latin met the Oriental and the Mexican: Europe, as always, overcoming the rest of the world, and Saxon, as always, dominating in the end. But here the Saxon learned to play from the Spaniard, as he learned from the Frenchman in New Orleans. He exchanged the political rally and the camp meeting for the cabaret and the theater; held out golden baits for the Booths and the Barretts, the Boucicaults and the Barrymores; and opened the door for the long apprenticeship of young David Belasco.[1]

The army of gold-seekers had their camp followers of every established type, including representatives of the press and writers for the journals. Joaquin Miller had come ahead of

[1] Constance Rourke, "Troupers of the Gold Coast."

the rush. Mark Twain was there not long after; so were Bret Harte and Artemus Ward and "Orpheus C. Kerr." Forthwith there developed in regular frontier fashion two types of self-expression in print. One is the echo of what is said and sung — anecdote and ballad. (Now at last a belated echo comes also in a printed collection of diaries.) The other is the sentimentalized account of what the frontier liked to think itself, and more especially what it wanted to be thought. The far reverberations of the song-and-story echo reached the East and stirred the hearts of the stay-at-homes, coloring music-hall and Negro-minstrel programs. Stories of personal adventure, not so honest as the leaves from surviving notebooks, were seized on by Eastern readers. And soon (prepared for special consumption) a narrative convention was established, a bevy of Western magazines sprang up as preternaturally as the theaters had before them, and the tales were published first in the West and later for readers along the Atlantic coast.

Bret Harte was the most successful purveyor of these meretricious sentimentalities, turning coast pioneers into good copy for distant romantic readers: dealing with mining camps in which no one ever worked; mines that men sought for, found, and gambled with; miners who behaved like opera choruses; women freezing in snowdrifts with never a mention of the cold; Mother Shipton comfortably starving to death in ten days and departing life with an epigram; M'liss, shaggy as a Shetland colt and sleek-souled as Little Eva. Almost all the Western tales, and all of hundreds of others about the West, were built, like sham folklore, from combinations of a few pat themes and motifs that were soon as outworn as the tritest poetic diction. They rang the changes on the miraculous reforms unconsciously achieved by women and babies, the redeeming grace of loyalty between "pardners," the dramatic effect of recognition scenes between long-separated lovers. And they were ridden with type characters: the last man in the deserted camp, the learned recluse, the adopted Indian child or the white child adopted by

Indians, the woman disguised as a man, the gallant gambler. Even the Plautine *miles gloriosus*, the coward braggart, was translated into the idiom of the mining camp. Harte, who was a drifter without stability or ideas of any kind, for a while applied to this material a neat craftsmanship which was consciously Dickensian in detail and mannerism. In the 1870's he drifted first to New York City and then abroad. His contact with the coast, though fairly long and quite varied, was very tenuous. He was like a feature reporter whose job was to write human-interest stories which, if possible, should be both moving and improving. He was not related to his material as Joaquin Miller was, and as Mark Twain loomed above him he shrank to the dimensions of a trinket shop at the foot of Pike's Peak.

Miller's cradle was a covered wagon going West; and he died within sight of the Golden Gate. Most of his work was true to frontier type in its literary, bookish style; but he had more than the average perception of his region in seeing the implications of pioneering. Both traits are illustrated in his tribute to the early settlers:

> O bearded, stalwart, westmost men,
> So tower-like, so Gothic built!
> A kingdom won without the guilt
> Of studied battle, that hath been
> Your blood's inheritance. . . . Your heirs
> Know not your tombs: The great plough-shares
> Cleave softly through the mellow loam
> Where you have made eternal home,
> And set no sign. Your epitaphs
> Are writ in furrows.[1]

His series of primitive experiences and primitive hardships among the Indians and his various vocations, including those of express messenger, newspaper editor, and petty judge, gave him a schooling more valuable than what he received in a

---

[1] "Westward Ho" (Harr Wagner), second stanza.

pseudo university in Oregon. He belonged to the region, but the region did not care for his first volume of verse as it did for Mark Twain's and Bret Harte's first tales of about the same date. It was too literary even for a frontier which likes to hark back to kingdoms and battles and heirs and towers and tombs.

In a fit of impatience which he deplored later he set out for Italy, whence he wrote "Vale! America."[1] Unable to find a publisher, he printed and distributed for review a hundred copies of "Pacific Poems," and was quickly lionized in London, received as a peer of Dean Stanley, Lord Houghton, Robert Browning, and all the pre-Raphaelite brotherhood. They liked his boots, velveteens, and sombrero; they enjoyed his subject matter and did not at all object to his evident respect for English models. For a dozen or more years of oscillating between the big cities on both shores of the Atlantic, Miller continued to write on frontier themes. His most characteristic poems were stories of thrilling experiences in the open. In "My Own Story," "Life amongst the Modocs," "Paquita," and "My Life among the Indians" he employed the same material in prose. In other poems, particularly in "Isles of the Amazons" and "The Baroness of New York," he returned to the romantic formula of contrasting forest and town; and in "A Song of the South" he attempted unsuccessfully to relate a poem to the Mississippi as he had often done with the mountains and the high plains.

In the writing of this middle period the dominant feature is his praise of elemental force. Nature was dynamic for him. Sea and forest at rest suggested latent powers. His best scenes deal with storm, flood, and fire; and when occasionally, as in the departure scene of "The Last Taschastas," he painted a reposeful background, the burnished beauty of the scene set forth the violence of the episode. In

[1] See note on this poem in the Bear Edition, Vol. IV, p. 42: "I do not like this bit of impatience. . . . It is an example of almost an entire book written in Italy."

his characters he most admired primitive strength. Man coping with nature thrilled him, and woman coping with man. His feminine characters were sunburned, heavy-maned, Amazonian, a singularly consistent type, almost a recurrence of a single model. In the judgment of Whitman, whom he encountered in Washington, he fell from grace in the treatment of love. If he did not vie (to paraphrase John Burroughs) "with the lascivious poets in painting it as the forbidden" passion, he did compete with the fleshly school in depicting its charms. Yet in his strange concluding romance, "Light," he struggled to overcome the sensual element with the spiritual.

Although Miller was related to his material, evidently knew it from experience, he was not identified with it. He had none of the humor of the frontier tall talker, none of the hilarity or the burlesque spirit. He had the ceremoniousness of the Indian, the Mexican, the Spaniard. The sole trait which he shared with the time and place was its vast sentimentalism; and in his middle period he was a complete example of the literary self-consciousness that prevails among the average of writing post-frontiersmen. His verses have little delicacy of appeal to the ear. They blare at the readers like brasses in an orchestral fortissimo; clamor with the strident regularity of a Sousa march. The measure accords well with the rude subject matter: the tramp of the pioneer, the plod of oxen hauling a prairie schooner, the roar of prairie fire or forest wind, and (with a difference) the hoofbeat of galloping horses or stampeding buffalo. While it expresses the rhetorical magniloquence that befits a country of magnificent distances, it finds its parallels in the narrative rhythms of Scott, Byron, and Coleridge, by which he was often and evidently affected. Until well past mid-career he was boyishly open to direct literary influences. He had no theory of prosody; his originality was inherent in his genuine liking for primitive material; so he tried his hand at writing in the manner of this, that, and the other man.

In his latter years he showed that he knew better, and emended himself in his revisions. Thus, for example, "The Baroness of New York" of 1877 is a sea-island Amazon, presented in the manner of Scott, who invades New York, in the fashion of Byron; included in the collected poems of 1897, the Byronic portion is dropped, and the rest, reduced to less than half, is greatly simplified. His later poetic tales were supplemented with more and more frequent short lyrics, and his style became more direct and homely. In 1902 he wrote:

> Will we ever have an American literature? Yes, when we leave sound and words to the winds. American science has swept time and space aside. American science dashes along at fifty, sixty miles an hour; but American literature still lumbers along in the old-fashioned stage-coach at ten miles an hour; and sometimes with a red-coated outrider blowing a horn. We must leave all this behind us. We have not time for words. A man who uses a great, sounding word, when a short one will do, is to that extent a robber of time. A jewel that depends greatly on its setting is not a great jewel. When the Messiah of American literature comes, he will come singing, so far as may be, in words of one syllable.[1]

From now on Miller atoned for his former imitativeness, but he abandoned his former material too. For him the frontier became a retreating memory. Still, however, he retained his sentimentalism in his new and obvious ambition to become the Messiah of whom he dreamed. In this he was led out of his own orbit quite as completely as Mark Twain was, and in somewhat the same direction:

> Could I but sing one song and slay
> Grim Doubt; I then would go my way
> In tranquil silence, glad, serene,
> And satisfied, from off the scene.
> But ah, this disbelief, this doubt,
> This doubt of God, this doubt of good, —
> The damned spot will not out.[2]

---

[1] In "Poems" (Harr Wagner), Vol. I, p. 183.
[2] "Adios," in "Poems" (Harr Wagner), Vol. V, p. 190.

So while this doubt, which belonged to the age, was being deepened at close range across San Francisco Bay by Ambrose Bierce and Jack London, Miller built his "hillside Bohemia" on the heights above Oakland and tried, by an association that suggests the old Greek academy, to point a way for the younger generation of poets. No lessons were taught; but he insisted on the assumptions of certain "tenets or principles of life" that in their sentimentalism antedate the sentimentalism of the frontier and the sentimentalism of the Declaration of Independence, reverting to the eighteenth-century philosophers who propounded the theories of natural goodness, natural rights, and natural equality: that there is nothing ugly in nature; that there is no waste in nature; that man should learn the lesson of economy; that man is good; that man is immortal. Miller passed on, and the doubt remained; realism and another type of naturalism were too much for him; but in his buoyant optimism he was a natural aftermath of pioneering days.

Although the effect of Edward Rowland Sill's thirteen years of residence in California was largely negative, his career is typical as a piece of American cultural history. He was an expatriate from that part of the Connecticut valley to which Mark Twain resorted; he was an alien in the mining regions where Mark Twain had been at home. He did not belong to any literary group. Because of a certain artistic timidity he never made literary friendships even with literary neighbors. In his attempts to find himself and his proper work he lived on both coasts and in the Middle West and contributed to the leading monthlies, *The Atlantic* and *The Overland.*

A student at Yale, he was impatient with the intellectual lethargy of a college with a dull curriculum little redeemed by vital teaching or reference to current thought. He picked up what crumbs he could from miscellaneous reading, was "rusticated" for neglect of his studies, wrote Carlylesque essays of discontent, and accepted his diploma with a sense of protest at what he supposed was the world. "Morning" and "The Clocks of Gnoster Town" are the chief poetical fruits of the experience. California, where he lived from 1861 to 1865, offered him a relief, but too much of a relief. The license of a frontier mining country did not supply him the kind of freedom that he had yearned for in New Haven; so he took refuge in the companionship of an intellectual and music-loving Yale family out there. His revolt from the world and his return to it, motivated in "The Hermitage" by the charms of a lovely blonde, had a deeper cause in the trials of his spiritual adolescence. He wanted to enter a profession and fell back on teaching as a Hobson's choice. Only after he had left California did he acknowledge its charm in his verse. Though he was later to write in sardonic comment on the dry season,

> Come where my stubbly hillside slowly dries,
> And fond adhesive tarweeds gently fade,[1]

he had a real feeling for the open vistas, the gentle climate, and the Californians' "independence of judgment; their carelessness of what a barbarian might think, so long as he came from beyond the border; their apparent freedom in choosing what manner of men they should be; their ready and confident speech."[2] "Christmas in California," "Among the Redwoods," and "The Departure of the Pilot" are examples of much California verse and the spirit of many of his letters. It was pleasant, friendly, and detached. He was not of the West; he could not quite return to the tidy complacency of Windsor or Hartford or New Haven. He spent his last five years in a suburb of Cleveland, Ohio.

Sill died the year after Emily Dickinson and at the age when Hawthorne at last came into public favor with the publication of "The Scarlet Letter." Something of a resemblance to them both is apparent in his incapacity to cope

---

[1] Parker, "Life of Sill" (Houghton Mifflin), p. 189.

[2] Josiah Royce, "Race Questions," p. 205.

with external life, his shyness, his gentleness, the slight asperity of his resentments, his refuge in anonymity. Life at Yale was barely tolerable for him; it was no better on the Pacific coast nor on his two returns to the East; and he left the University of California because the "position had become intolerable for certain reasons that are not for pen and ink." He published only one volume of poems during his lifetime, "The Hermitage"; "The Venus of Milo, and Other Poems" was privately printed. When Thomas Bailey Aldrich opened the pages of *The Atlantic* to him, he hid his frequent contributions under the pen name Andrew Hedbrook.

He had no more interest in the Civil War than these other shy poets did.

> What is the grandeur of serving a state whose tail
> Is stinging its head to death like a scorpion?[1]

Like these others, hungry for life and repelled by it, he took refuge under his own rooftree, in his own broodings, and in his own slight mockeries.

> For my part I long to "fall in" with somebody. This picket duty is monotonous. I hanker after a shoulder on this side and the other. I can't agree in belief (or expressed belief — Lord knows what the villains really think, at home) with the "Christian" people, nor in spirit with the Radicals. . . . Many, here and there, must be living the right way, doing their best, hearty souls, and I'd like to go 'round the world for the next year and take tea with them in succession.[2]

Instead he acknowledged his defeat in his two widely known lyrics, "Opportunity" and the "Fool's Prayer"; he paid his disrespects to the perplexities of the philosophers and theologians in "Five Lives"; and in his latter days he lent himself to the shadowy, half-suppressed, understated kind of humor that becomes the Yankee gentry: "Her Explanation," "Momentous Words," "The Agile Sonneteer." He was in retreat, in either sense, when he died at what is called the prime of life. He had seen far more of the great, sprawling country

[1] Parker, op. cit. pp. 34–35.

[2] Ibid. pp. 129–130.

than most of his fellow countrymen. It was still the country described by Crèvecœur before the Revolutionary War:

> As Christians, religion curbs them not in their opinions; the general indulgence leaves everyone to think for themselves in spiritual matters; the laws inspect our actions, our thoughts are left to God. . . . Exclusive of these general characteristics, each province has its own, founded on the government, climate, mode of husbandry, customs and peculiarity of circumstances. . . . Whoever traverses the continent must easily observe these strong differences.[1]

It was the last moment before the engine and the dynamo began to pull the far-flung country together. The clumsy work of Reconstruction was still being bungled. In spite of all his contacts Sill knew hardly more than if he had stayed in Connecticut. Life was a riddle, the United States a picture puzzle; he looked at them both, and with a faint smile of amusement he gave them up.

Book List

RECONSTRUCTION AND THE SOUTH

General

BASKERVILL, WILLIAM M. Southern Writers: Biographical and Critical Studies. 1898–1907.

HOLLIDAY, CARL. A History of Southern Literature. 1906.

HUBNER, CHARLES W. Representative Southern Poets. 1906.

LINK, S. A. Pioneers of Southern Literature. 2 vols. 1903.

MANLY, LOUISE. Southern Literature. 1895.

MOSES, MONTROSE J. The Literature of the South. 1910.

ORGAIN, KATE A. Southern Authors in Poetry and Prose. 1908.

PAINTER, F. V. N. Poets of the South. 1903.

SMITH, C. ALPHONSO. "Possibilities of Southern Literature," *Sewanee Review*, Vol. VI, pp. 298–305.

SNYDER, H. N. "The Matter of Southern Literature," *Sewanee Review*, Vol. XV, pp. 218–226.

TRENT, WILLIAM P. William Gilmore Simms. 1892.

WAUCHOPE, G. A. Writers of South Carolina. 1910.

WOODBERRY, GEORGE E. "The South in American Letters," *Harper's*, Vol. CVII, pp. 735–741.

[1] "Letters from an American Farmer" (Everyman Edition), pp. 46, 47, 48.

Individual Authors

HENRY TIMROD. Poems, 1873; Katie, 1884.

[*Available Editions*]

Complete Poems, edited by Paul Hamilton Hayne. 1873.
Poems. Memorial Edition. 1901.

[*Biography and Criticism*]

AUSTIN, HENRY. "Henry Timrod," *International Review*, September, 1880.
CARDWELL, G. A., JR. "The Date of Henry Timrod's Birth," *American Literature*, Vol. VII, pp. 207–208.
HAYNE, PAUL HAMILTON. Sketch of Timrod (1873 edition of the Poems).
ROUTH, J. S. "Some Fugitive Poems of Timrod," *South Atlantic Review*, January, 1903.
SHEPERD, HENRY T. "Henry Timrod: a Literary Estimate." Publications of the Southern History Association, Vol. III, pp. 267–280.
THOMPSON, HENRY T. Henry Timrod, Laureate of the Confederacy. 1929.
VOIGT, G. P. "New Light on Timrod's 'Memorial Ode,'" *American Literature*, Vol. IV, pp. 395–396.
VOIGT, G. P. "Timrod's Essays in Literary Criticism," *American Literature*, Vol. VI, pp. 163–167.
WAUCHOPE, G. A. "Henry Timrod, Laureate of the Confederacy," *North Carolina Review*, May 5, 1912.
WAUCHOPE, G. A. Henry Timrod, Man and Poet. 1915.

PAUL HAMILTON HAYNE. Poems, 1855; Sonnets and Other Poems, 1857; Legends and Lyrics, 1872.

[*Available Edition*]

Poems of Paul Hamilton Hayne. Complete Edition (his own selections). 1882.

[*Biography and Criticism*]

BROWN, J. T., JR. "Paul Hamilton Hayne," *Sewanee Review*, April, 1906.
HAYNE, W. H. "Paul Hamilton Hayne's Methods of Composition," *Lippincott's*, December, 1892.
HUBBELL, JAY B. "George Henry Boker, Paul Hamilton Hayne, and Charles Warren Stoddard: Some Unpublished Letters," *American Literature*, Vol. V, pp. 146–165.
PRESTON, MARGARET JUNKIN. Introduction to the 1882 edition of the Poems.
See, also, Edwin Mims's introduction to the Hayne selections in the Library of Southern Literature, Vol. V, pp. 2265–2271.

SIDNEY LANIER. Chief works: Tiger-Lilies, a Novel, 1867; Poems, 1877; The Science of English Verse, 1880; The English Novel, 1883.

[*Available Editions*]

Poems of Sidney Lanier, edited by his wife, with a memorial by William Hayes Ward. New edition. 1924.
The Select Poems of Sidney Lanier, edited by Morgan Callaway. 1895.

[*Biography and Criticism*]

CLARKE, G. H. Some Reminiscences and Early Letters of Sidney Lanier. 1907.

GOSSE, EDMUND. Questions at Issue. 1893.

GRAHAM, PHILIP. "Lanier and Science," *American Literature*, Vol. IV, pp. 288–292.

HIGGINSON, THOMAS W. Contemporaries. 1899.

KENT, CHARLES W. "A Study of Lanier's Poems," *PMLA*, Vol. VII, pp. 33–63.

MIMS, EDWIN. Sidney Lanier. A. M. L. Series. 1905.

NORTHRUP, M. H. "Sidney Lanier: Recollections and Letters," *Lippincott's*, March, 1905.

STARKE, AUBREY H. "Lanier's Appreciation of Whitman," *American Scholar*, Vol. II, pp. 398–408.

STARKE, AUBREY H. Sidney Lanier: a Biographical and Critical Study. 1933.

STARKE, AUBREY H. "Sidney Lanier: Man of Science in the Field of Letters," *American Scholar*, Vol. II, pp. 389–397.

WARREN, ROBERT P. "The Blind Poet: Sidney Lanier," *American Literature*, Vol. II, pp. 27–45.

WAYLAND, JOHN W. Sidney Lanier at Rockingham Springs. Where and How "The Science of English Verse" was Written. 1912.

[*Bibliography*]

CALLAWAY, MORGAN. Bibliography, appended to "The Select Poems of Sidney Lanier." 1895.

STARKE, AUBREY H. Bibliography, in "Sidney Lanier," pp. 455–473. 1933.

WILLS, G. S. Bibliography of Lanier. Prepared for the Southern History Association. 1901.

Cambridge History of American Literature, Vol. II, pp. 600–603.

JOEL CHANDLER HARRIS. Chief works: Uncle Remus, His Songs and His Sayings, 1880; Mingo and Other Sketches in Black and White, 1884; Uncle Remus and His Friends, 1892.

[*Biography and Criticism*]

BASKERVILL, WILLIAM M. Southern Writers. 1898.

COUSINS, P. "The Debt of Joel Chandler Harris to Joseph Addison Turner," *Chimes*, Vol. XLII, pp. 3–10.

HARRIS, JULIA C. (Ed.). Joel Chandler Harris: Editor and Essayist. 1931.

HARRIS, JULIA C. The Life and Letters of Joel Chandler Harris. 1918.

WADE, JOHN D. "Profits and Losses in the Life of Joel Chandler Harris," *American Review*, Vol. I, pp. 17–35.

WIGGINS, ROBERT L. The Life of Joel Chandler Harris. With Stories and Other Literary Work not Hitherto Published. 1918.

[*Bibliography*]

WOOTEN, KATHERINE H. Bibliography of the Works of Joel Chandler Harris. Monthly Bulletin of the Carnegie Library of Atlanta, June, 1907.

[*Anthologies*]

ALDERMAN, E. A., and others. Library of Southern Literature, Vols. V, VII, XII.
CLARKE, JENNIE T. Songs of the South. 1913.
FOERSTER, NORMAN. American Poetry and Prose (rev. ed.). 1934.
FULTON, MAURICE G. Southern Life in Southern Literature. 1917.
KREYMBORG, ALFRED. Lyric America. 1930.
STEDMAN and HUTCHINSON. Library of American Literature, Vol. X.
TRENT, W. P. Southern Writers. Selections in Prose and Verse. 1905.
WANN, LOUIS. The Rise of Realism. 1933.

THE MID-CENTURY FRONTIER

History and Criticism

BOYNTON, PERCY H. The Rediscovery of the Frontier. 1931.
COGGESHALL, WILLIAM T. The Poets and Poetry of the West. 1860.
DONDORE, DOROTHY A. The Prairie and the Making of Middle America. 1926.
FOREMAN, GRANT. Advancing the Frontier, 1830–1860. 1933.
HAZARD, LUCY L. The Frontier in American Literature. 1927.
HOUGH, EMERSON. The Passing of the Frontier. 1921.
RUSK, RALPH L. The Literature of the Middle Western Frontier. 2 vols. 1925.
TURNER, FREDERICK J. The Frontier in American History. 1920.
WILLARD, JAMES F., and GOODYKOONTZ, C. B. (Eds.). The Trans-Mississippi West. Papers read at a conference held at the University of Colorado, June 18–June 21, 1929. 1930.

Representative Frontier Writings

BRACKENRIDGE, HENRY M. Journal of a Voyage up the River Missouri. Second edition. 1904.
BRACKENRIDGE, HENRY M. Recollections of Persons and Places in the West. 1834.
DRAKE, BENJAMIN. The Life and Adventures of Black Hawk: with Sketches of Keokuk, the Sac and Fox Indians, etc. 1838.
DRAKE, DANIEL. Pioneer Life in Kentucky. 1870.
FLINT, TIMOTHY. Recollections of the Last Ten Years. 1826. Edited, with introduction, by C. Hartley Grattan. 1932.
HALL, JAMES. Legends of the West. 1832.
HALL, JAMES. Letters from the West. 1828.
HALL, JAMES. Sketches of the History, Life, and Manners in the West. 1835.
HOFFMAN, CHARLES FENNO. A Winter in the West. 1835.
JOHNSON, THOMAS. The Kentucky Miscellany (4th ed.). 1821.
KIRKLAND, CAROLINE M. A New Home — Who'll Follow? or, Glimpses of Western Life. 1839.
LUDLOW, NOAH M. Dramatic Life as I Found It. 1880.
PIKE, ZEBULON M. An Account of Expeditions. 1810.

ROYCE, SARAH. A Frontier Lady; Recollections of the Gold Rush and Early California, edited by Ralph H. Gabriel. 1932.

SMITH, SOLOMON. Theatrical Apprenticeship and Anecdotal Record. 1846.

SMITH, SOLOMON. Theatrical Management in the West and South. 1868.

Collections

COGGESHALL, WILLIAM T. The Poets and Poetry of the West. An anthology with biographical sketches. 1860.

COLEMAN, RUFUS A. Western Prose and Poetry. 1932.

FRENCH, JOSEPH L. The Pioneer West (narratives). 1923.

GALLAGHER, WILLIAM D. Selections from the Poetical Literature of the West. 1841.

MCCLUNG, JOHN A. Sketches of Western Adventure. 1832.

MEINE, FRANKLIN J. Tall Tales of the Southwest. 1930.

POPULAR SONG AND STORY

General

ALLEN, JULES V. Cowboy Lore. 1933.

BARR, JAMES. The Humor of America. 1909.

BECK, E. C. "Lumberjack Ballads and Songs," *English Journal*, Vol. XXI, pp. 52–58.

BLAIR, WALTER. "Burlesques in Nineteenth Century American Humor," *American Literature*, Vol. II, pp. 236–247.

BLAIR, WALTER. "The Popularity of Nineteenth-Century American Humorists," *American Literature*, Vol. III, pp. 175–195.

BRANCH, DOUGLAS. The Cowboy and His Interpreters. 1926.

CLEMENS, CYRIL. Josh Billings: Yankee Humorist. 1932.

DE VOTO, BERNARD. "The Big Bear of Arkansas." Mark Twain's America. 1932.

DOBIE, J. FRANK. A Vaquero of the Brush Country. 1929.

DONDORE, DOROTHY. "Big Talk! The Flyting, the Gabe, and the Frontier Boast," *American Speech*, Vol. VI, pp. 45–55.

FAXON, F. W. Literary Annuals and Gift-Books: a Bibliography, with a Descriptive Introduction. 1912.

HOWARD, JOHN TASKER. Stephen Foster, America's Troubadour. 1934.

JACKSON, GEORGE P. White Spirituals in the Southern Highlands. 1933.

MOTT, FRANK L. "Exponents of the Pioneers," *Palimpsest*, Vol. XI, pp. 61–66.

QUINN, ARTHUR H. "American Comedy Types." American Drama from the Beginnings to the Civil War. 1923.

RICE, GAITHER. "New Steamboatin' Days on Our Rivers," *New York Times Magazine* (November 10, 1929), pp. 4–5, 20.

ROURKE, CONSTANCE. American Humor. 1931.

TANDY, J. R. Crackerbox Philosophers. 1925.

Special Types

Buffalo Bill, the Indian Fighter

Anonymous. "The Legend of Buffalo Bill," *London Times Literary Supplement*, October 17, 1929.
CODY, WILLIAM F. The Adventures of Buffalo Bill. 1904.
CODY, WILLIAM F. An Autobiography. Illustrated by N. C. Wyeth. 1920.
CODY, WILLIAM F. True Tales of the Plains, by Buffalo Bill. 1908.
WALSH, RICHARD J., and SALSBURY, MILTON S. The Making of Buffalo Bill: a Study in Heroics. 1928.
WETMORE, HELEN CODY. The Last of the Great Scouts; the Life Story of Colonel William F. Cody . . . As Told by His Sister. 1899.

Paul Bunyan, Lumberman

ALVORD, THOMAS G. Paul Bunyan and Resinous Rhymes of the North Woods. 1934.
BOWMAN, JAMES C. The Adventures of Paul Bunyan. 1927.
BROOKS, JOHN LEE "Paul Bunyan; Oil Man." Publications of the Texas Folk-Lore Society, No. 7. 1928.
FINGER, CHARLES J. A Paul Bunyan Geography. 1931.
JONES, EDWARD R. Bunyan's Progress. A Volume of Verse on Paul Bunyan Up to Date. 1929.
LANGEROCK, H. "The Wonderful Life and Deeds of Paul Bunyan," *Century*, May, 1923.
LAUGHEAD, W. B. The Marvelous Exploits of Paul Bunyan, as told in Camps of Lumbermen. 1924.
SHEPHARD, ESTHER S. Paul Bunyan, His Camp and Life. 1924.
SHERMAN, STUART P. "Paul Bunyan and the Blue Ox." The Main Stream. 1927.
STEVENS, JAMES. Paul Bunyan. 1925.
STEVENS, JAMES. The Saginaw Paul Bunyan. 1932.
TURNEY, IDA V. Paul Bunyan Comes West. 1928.
WADSWORTH, WALLACE. Paul Bunyan and His Great Blue Ox. 1926.

David Crockett, Backwoodsman

ADAM, G. M. The Life of David Crockett . . . An Autobiography . . . with an Introduction. 1903.
CROCKETT, DAVID. An Account of Colonel Crockett's Tour to the North and Down East. 1835.
CROCKETT, DAVID. Colonel Crockett's Exploits and Adventures in Texas. 1836.
CROCKETT, DAVID. A Narrative of the Life of David Crockett . . . Written by Himself. 1834.
HOUGH, EMERSON. The Way to the West . . . Lives of Three Early Americans: Boone, Crockett, and Carson. 1903.
MCNEIL, EVERETT. In Texas with Davy Crockett. 1908.
ROCHE, JAMES J. The Story of the Filibusters. 1891.
ROURKE, CONSTANCE. Davy Crockett. 1934.
THOMASON, JOHN W., JR. The Adventures of Davy Crockett, Told Mostly by Himself. With illustrations. 1934.

Mike Fink, River-boatman

Anonymous. "Mike Fink: the Last of the Boatmen," *Western Monthly Review*, July, 1829.

Blair, Walter, and Meine, F. J. Mike Fink, King of Mississippi Keelboatmen. 1933. (Valuable bibliography.)

Field, J. M. "The Death of Mike Fink," *St. Louis Reveille*, October 21, 1844; June 14 and 21, 1847.

Neville, Morgan. "The Last of the Boatmen." The Western Souvenir, a Christmas and New Year's Gift for 1829, edited by James Hall. 1829.

Porter, William. "Mike Fink's Death," *Spirit of the Times*, July 9, 1842.

Spotts, C. B. "Mike Fink in Missouri," *Missouri Historical Review*, Vol. XXVIII, pp. 3–8.

Prose Collections

The American Jest Book, a Chaste Collection of Anecdotes, Bon Mots and Epigrams. 1833.

The Chaplet of Comus; or, Feast of Sentiment and Festival of Wit. 1811.

Coronado's Children: Tales of Lost Miners and Buried Treasures of the Southwest, edited by J. Frank Dobie. 1930.

Folk-Say; a Regional Miscellany, edited by Ben A. Botkin. 1929– .

New England Joke Lore, edited by Arthur G. Crandall. 1922.

Our American Humorists, edited by Thomas L. Masson. New edition. 1931.

Sixty Years of American Humor, edited by Joseph L. French. 1924.

Some American Humorists, edited by Napier Wilt. 1929.

Stagecoach and Tavern Tales of the Old Northwest, edited by Harry E. Cole. 1930.

Tall Tales of the Kentucky Mountains, edited by Percy MacKaye. 1926.

Tall Tales of the Southwest, edited by Franklin J. Meine. 1930.

Tall Tales from Texas, edited by Mody C. Boatright. 1934.

Verse and Ballad Collections

American Ballads and Folk Songs, edited by John A. and Alan Lomax. 1934.

American Ballads and Songs, edited by Louise Pound. 1922.

The American Songbag, edited by Carl Sandburg. 1927.

Ballads and Songs of the Shanty-Boy, edited by Franz Rickaby. 1926.

British Ballads from Maine, edited by Barry, Eckstorm, and Smyth. 1929.

Cowboy Songs and Other Frontier Ballads, edited by John A. Lomax. Last edition, 1934.

Early Songs of Uncle Sam, edited by George S. Jackson. 1933.

English Folk Songs from the Southern Appalachians, edited by Olive D. Campbell and Cecil J. Sharp. 1917.

Folk-Songs of the South, edited by John H. Cox. 1925.

Frontier Ballads, edited by Charles J. Finger. 1927.

Mountain Minstrelsy of Pennsylvania, edited by Henry W. Shoemaker. 1931.

Roll and Go: Songs of American Sailormen, edited by J. R. Cokard. 1924.

Slave Songs of the United States, edited by Allen, Ware, and Garrison. 1929.

Songs and Ballads of the Maine Lumberjacks . . . etc., edited by Roland P. Gray. 1924.

South Carolina Ballads, edited by Reed Smith. 1928.

Traditional Ballads of Virginia, edited by Arthur K. Davis. 1929.

Vermont Folk Songs and Ballads, edited by Flanders and Brown. 1931.

Voices of the Southwest, edited by Hilton R. Greer. 1923.

Weep Some More, My Lady, edited by Sigmund Spaeth. 1927.

Patriotic Songs

BROWNE, C. A. The Story of Our National Ballads. 1919.

ELSON, LOUIS C. The National Music of America. 1915.

KOBBE, GUSTAV. Famous American Songs. 1906.

NASON, ELIAS. Our National Song, a Monogram. 1869.

SMITH, NICHOLAS. Stories of Great National Songs. 1899.

SONNECK, OSCAR G. Miscellaneous Studies in the History of Music. 1921.

WHITE, RICHARD G. National Hymns — How They are Written, and How They are Not Written. 1861.

American Hymns

Anonymous. "America's Contribution to English Hymnody," *Theological Monthly*, Vol. I, p. 35. 1889.

ALLEN, E. A. "Old Hymns and New Creeds," *Nation* (1911), Vol. XCIII, p. 443.

BREED, DAVID R. The History and Use of Hymns and Hymn-Tunes. 1903.

DICKINSON, EDWARD. Music in the History of the Western Church. 1902.

GOULD, NATHANIEL D. History of Church Music in America. 1853.

METCALF, FRANK J. American Psalmody, 1721–1820. 1917.

METCALF, FRANK J. American Writers and Compilers of Sacred Music. 1925.

METCALF, FRANK J. Stories of Hymn Tunes. 1928.

STEVENSON, W. F. "Biography of Certain Hymns," *Good Words*, Vol. III, p. 641. Reprinted in *Living Age*, Vol. LXXVI, pp. 609–613.

TILLETT, WILBUR F. Our Hymns and Their Writers. 1892.

TO AND FROM THE GOLD COAST

General

FOERSTER, NORMAN. "Lesser Poets." Cambridge History of American Literature, Vol. III.

KREYMBORG, ALFRED. "Mid-Western and Far-Western Frontiers." Our Singing Strength. 1929.

PATTEE, FRED L. The Development of the American Short Story. 1923.

PATTEE, FRED L. A History of American Literature since 1870. 1915.

ROURKE, CONSTANCE. Troupers of the Gold Coast. 1928.

Individual Authors

FRANCIS BRET HARTE. Chief volumes are: The Luck of Roaring Camp and Other Sketches, 1870; Plain Language from Truthful James ("The Heathen Chinee"), 1870; Poems, 1871; Gabriel Conroy, 1876; Stories in Light and Shadow, 1898.

[*Available Editions*]

The Lectures of Bret Harte, compiled by Charles M. Kozlay. 1909.

The Letters of Bret Harte, assembled and edited by Geoffrey Bret Harte. 1926.

Sketches of the Sixties, by Bret Harte and Mark Twain. Forgotten material now collected for the first time from *The Californian*, 1864–1867. Compiled by John Howell. 1926.

Writings of Bret Harte. Standard Edition, with introductions and glossary. 19 vols. 1896–1903. Vol. XIX has an index to characters in the stories and romances.

[*Biography and Criticism*]

BEASLEY, THOMAS D. A Tramp through the Bret Harte Country. 1914.

BOYNTON, HENRY W. Bret Harte. Contemporary Men of Letters Series. 1903.

CANBY, HENRY S. "Bret Harte's Tragedy," *Saturday Review of Literature*, Vol. VIII, pp. 485, 488.

CANBY, HENRY S. "The Luck of Bret Harte," *Saturday Review of Literature*, Vol. II, pp. 717–718.

CHESTERTON, GILBERT K. "The Genius of Bret Harte." Varied Types. 1909.

JONES, IDWAL. "The Bret Harte Country," *American Mercury*, Vol. VII, pp. 147–153.

MERWIN, HENRY C. The Life of Bret Harte. 1911.

PEMBERTON, T. EDGAR. Bret Harte; a Treatise and a Tribute. 1900.

STEWART, GEORGE R., JR. Bret Harte, Argonaut and Exile. 1931.

STODDARD, CHARLES WARREN. "Early Recollections of Bret Harte," *Atlantic*, Vol. LXXVIII, pp. 673–678.

[*Bibliography*]

STEWART, GEORGE R., JR. A Bibliography of the Writings of Bret Harte in the magazines and newspapers of California, 1857–1871. 1933.

JOAQUIN MILLER. Chief volumes appeared as: Songs of the Sierras, 1871; Songs of the Mexican Seas, 1887; Songs of the Soul, 1896; Complete Poetical Works (rev. ed.), 1902.

[*Available Editions*]

Poems, collected and edited by the author. 5 vols. 1908.

Poems. De Luxe Edition. [illegible] vols. 1909.

Poetical Works of Joaquin Miller, edited, with introduction, by Stuart P. Sherman. 1923.

Works of Joaquin Miller. Bear Edition. 6 vols. With autobiographical sketch. 1909–1910.

[*Biography and Criticism*]

BEEBE, BEATRICE B. (Ed.). "Joaquin Miller and His Family-Letters," *Frontier*, Vol. XII, pp. 344–347.

BEEBE, BEATRICE B. (Ed.). "Letters of Joaquin Miller to His Brother," *Frontier*, Vol. XII, pp. 121–124.

BEEBE, BEATRICE B. (Ed.). "More Letters of Joaquin Miller," *Frontier*, Vol. XII, pp. 223–228.

MILLER, JOAQUIN. Overland in a Covered Wagon; an Autobiography, edited by Sidney G. Firman. 1930.

PETERSON, MARTIN S. "The Border Days of Joaquin Miller," *Frontier*, Vol. XI, pp. 362–375.

PETERSON, MARTIN S. "Joaquin Miller: an Introductory Sketch," *Revue Anglo-Américaine*, December, 1930.

READE, FRANK R. Cincinnatus Hiner Miller. A Critical Biography. In press. 1934.

SHERMAN, STUART P. Sketch, introduction to the Poetical Works. 1923.

STERLING, GEORGE. "Joaquin Miller," *American Mercury*, Vol. VII, pp. 220–229.

WAGNER, HARR. Joaquin Miller and His Other Self. 1929.

EDWARD ROWLAND SILL. Chief volumes: The Hermitage and Other Poems, 1868; Poems, 1888.

[*Available Editions*]

Poetical Works of Edward Rowland Sill. Household Edition. 1906.

The Prose of Edward Rowland Sill, with an Introduction comprising some Familiar Letters. 1900.

[*Biography and Criticism*]

ARVIN, NEWTON. "The Failure of Edward Rowland Sill," *Bookman*, Vol. LXXII, pp. 581–589.

DOWNEY, DAVID. Modern Poets and Christian Teaching. 1906.

PARKER, WILLIAM B. Edward Rowland Sill: His Life and Work. 1915.

[*Anthologies*]

FOERSTER, NORMAN. American Poetry and Prose (rev. ed.). 1934.

STEDMAN and HUTCHINSON. Library of American Literature, Vol. X.

WANN, LOUIS. The Rise of Realism. 1933.

MARK TWAIN. Chief works appeared as follows: The Celebrated Jumping Frog of Calaveras County, and Other Sketches, 1867; The Innocents Abroad; or, the New Pilgrim's Progress, 1869; Roughing It, 1872; The Gilded Age: a Tale of Today, 1874; The Adventures of Tom Sawyer, 1876; A Tramp Abroad, 1880; The Prince and the Pauper: a Tale for Young People of All Ages, 1882; Life on the Mississippi, 1883; The Adventures of Huckleberry Finn, 1885; A Connecticut Yankee at King Arthur's Court, 1889; The Tragedy of Pudd'nhead Wilson, and the Comedy, "Those Extraordinary Twins," 1894; Personal Recollections of Joan of Arc, 1896; The Man that Corrupted Hadleyburg, 1900; The Mysterious Stranger, 1916; What is Man, and Other Essays, 1917.

[*Available Editions*]

Letters of Mark Twain, edited by Albert Bigelow Paine. 1917.
Mark Twain Anecdotes, edited by Cyril Clemens. 1929.
Mark Twain: Selections, edited by F. L. Pattee. 1935.
Mark Twain: Wit and Wisdom, edited by Cyril Clemens. 1935.
Mark Twain's Autobiography, with introduction by A. B. Paine. 1924.
Mark Twain's Speeches, with introduction by William Dean Howells. 1923.
The Writings of Mark Twain. Author's National Edition. 25 vols. 1869–1922. (Several editions from this type.)
The Connecticut Yankee, Huckleberry Finn, Tom Sawyer, and Life on the Mississippi have been variously edited for student use.

[*Biography and Criticism*]

BRASHEAR, MINNIE M. Mark Twain, Son of Missouri. 1934.
BROOKS, VAN WYCK. The Ordeal of Mark Twain (rev. ed.). 1933.
CLEMENS, CLARA. My Father: Mark Twain. 1931.
CLEMENS, CYRIL (Ed.). Mark Twain the Letter Writer. 1932.
DE VOTO, BERNARD. Mark Twain's America. 1932.
GILLIS, WILLIAM R. Gold Rush Days with Mark Twain. With an introduction by Cyril Clemens. 1930.
GILLIS, WILLIAM R. Memories of Mark Twain and Steve Gillis. 1924.
HENDERSON, ARCHIBALD. Mark Twain. 1912.
HOWELLS, WILLIAM DEAN. My Mark Twain. 1910.
LAWTON, MARY. A Lifetime with Mark Twain; the Memories of Katy Leary, his Servant. 1925.
LEACOCK, STEPHEN. Mark Twain. 1933.
MABBOTT, THOMAS O. "Mark Twain's Artillery; a Mark Twain Legend," *Missouri Historical Review*, Vol. XXV (1930), No. 1.
MATTHEWS, BRANDER. Inquiries and Opinions. 1907.
PAINE, ALBERT BIGELOW (Ed.). Mark Twain's Notebooks. 1935.
SEDGWICK, HENRY D. The New American Type. 1908.
SHERMAN, STUART P. "The Democracy of Mark Twain." On Contemporary Literature. 1917.
SHERMAN, STUART P. "Mark Twain." Cambridge History of American Literature, Vol. III, Book III.
WAGENKNECHT, EDWARD. Mark Twain: the Man and His Work. 1935.
WALLACE, ELIZABETH. Mark Twain and the Happy Island. 1913.
WEST, VICTOR R. "Folklore in the Works of Mark Twain." University of Nebraska Studies in Language, No. 10. 1930.
The definitive life is Mark Twain, a Biography; the Personal and Literary Life of Samuel Langhorne Clemens, by A. B. Paine. 3 vols. 1912.

[*Bibliography*]

HENDERSON, ARCHIBALD. Mark Twain: a Bibliography of Books, Essays, and Articles Dealing with Mark Twain, 1869–1910. 1912.
JOHNSON, MERLE. A Bibliography of the Works of Mark Twain. A List of First Editions in Book Form and of the first printings in Periodicals of his Varied Literary Activities. 1910.
PAINE, ALBERT B. "A Chronological List of Mark Twain's Writings, Published and Otherwise, from 1851 to 1910." Life, Vol. III.
RINAKER, CLARISSA. Mark Twain Bibliography. Cambridge History of American Literature, Vol. IV, Part III.

PART III

The Recent Past

CHAPTER XII

Deferred Reputations

Ambrose Bierce

THERE is nothing in common between Ambrose Bierce and these preceding figures except the accident of their residence in California. Contrasts or comparisons between them in some way connected with the frontier have no sound basis. Bierce was nothing of the pioneer or explorer, despite his last mysterious journey. He was a cosmopolitan character who enjoyed the cosmopolitan atmosphere of San Francisco. But he resisted every influence that dominated the town or the region, and as journalist, critic, artist he might have done his work anywhere else. Yet the major part of it was done here; his immediate effect was strongest here.

He once wrote that literary criticism was hopelessly obscured by the introduction of personal facts. His own reputation has recently been confounded by a great multiplication of such data. In a section subtitled "Bits of Autobiography," and casually elsewhere in his pages, perhaps enough emerges: that he was a youthful Northern combatant in the Civil War,[1] a journalist abroad, at home whether in Washington or in San Francisco; and that, like one of his own characters, he succeeded in seeking "obscurity in the writing and publishing of books," finally disappearing in the wilds of Central America in an oblivion from which his ghost was long and late in emerging.[2]

---

[1] Napier Wilt, "Ambrose Bierce and the Civil War," in *American Literature*, Vol. I, pp. 260–285.

[2] ". . . his final jest with death in Mexico" (McWilliams, "Ambrose Bierce," p. 64). Neale, in the "Life of Ambrose Bierce," presents several ideas that have been favored (Chap. XXVI), with his own conclusion that Bierce selected a "trysting-place with Death" somewhere along the Grand Canyon of the Colorado. De Castro, in "Portrait of Ambrose Bierce," insists that he joined himself to the forces of Villa in Mexico. Vincent Starrett, "Ambrose Bierce," Chap. III, accepts the fact that he went into Mexico.

He was a voluminous critic and satirist, born to the manner of "The Devil's Dictionary," a collection of sardonic definitions addressed to "the 'enlightened souls' who prefer dry wines to sweet, sense to sentiment, wit to humor, and clean English to slang." These are the elected audience too for his "Fantastic Fables," an Aesopian collection applied to a nineteenth-century world of economics and politics, as well as for the several volumes of his satirical verse, mostly occasional. From these smaller units the reader may follow along an ascending series of more substantial and more explicit social criticism: "Kings of Beasts," designed in pure whimsy, but rifted through with satire; "The Land beyond the Blow," eleven sketches after the manner of Swift; "Two Administrations," prose and verse dialogues attributed to members of the McKinley and Roosevelt cabinets; "Antepenultimata," essays on civilization, law, politics, religion, labor, and woman; and, finally, "Ashes of the Beacon," "an historical monograph written in 4930 . . . on the lamentable failure of 'self-government' in ancient America,"[1] and "The Shadow on the Dial," on the kindred but less hopeless thesis that "our civilization, being the natural outgrowth of our moral and intellectual natures, is open to criticism and subject to revision."[2] Besides all this, Bierce wrote the less than four volumes that are the work of artist rather than critic; and in both criticism and artistry he was more nearly in tune with the 1920's, which reacknowledged him, than with the 1890's, which chose to ignore him in his prime.

As a mature commentator on life Bierce wrote in a mood of conscious and dreary disillusionment. At rare moments he would permit himself a burst of wistful sentiment:

> Oh days when all the world was beautiful and strange; when unfamiliar constellations burned in the Southern midnights, and the mocking bird poured out his heart in the moon-gilded magnolia; when there was something new under a new sun; will your fine, far

[1] "The Collected Works of Ambrose Bierce" (12 vols.), Vol. I, p. 17. Neale Publishing Co., 1909–1912.

[2] "Works," Vol. XI, p. 27.

memories ever cease to lay contrasting pictures athwart the harsher features of the later world, accentuating the ugliness of the longer and tamer life? . . . Ah, Youth, there is no such wizard as thou! Give me but one touch of thine artist hand upon the dull canvas of the Present; gild for but one moment the drear and somber scenes of today, and I will willingly surrender another life than the one that I should have thrown away at Shiloh.[1]

But for the most part he lived in the thought of his contempt for the majority and their disapproval of him:

> I dreamed, and in my dream came one who said, . . .
> "Because thou hearest in the People's voice
> Naught but the mandate of an idiot will
> Clamoring in the wilderness, but what
> Or why it knoweth not; because all this
> And much besides is true, I come."[2]

The democratic experiment as he saw it was dubious if not doomed. It was devised by "dupes of hope purveying to sons of greed," the rule of the majority being only a disguised way of redeclaring that might makes right. In the United States it was saddled with an absurd trial-by-jury system, and consequent criminal immunity for women; with corruption by predatory wealth, which fostered a malign insurance business and a murderous network of railways; and with a high protective tariff provocative of inevitable and imminent labor conflict. Nor could he see anything to be hoped for from extension of suffrage to women or from the organization of the workingmen, for he could not believe in either the honesty or the intelligence of the populace. Naturally he believed that no statesmanship could develop in such a soil; politics was the rank weed to be expected from it. An elected officer assumed his duties in face of a vote of non-confidence on the part of half, or more, of the electorate. He stood for nothing, since, said Bierce, long before it was a current saying, the leading parties were indistinguishable except in name. The

---

[1] "Works," Vol. I, p. 269.

[2] "Land of the Pilgrims' Pride," in "Works," Vol. IV, p. 78.

gullible "pol patriot," with his "deplorable habit of saying what you have got tired of hearin,"[1] aggravated the case. He had his early say, too, on the machinery of justice, returning often to the attack on the perversion of law through the intricacies of legal procedure and the skill of experts trained in the arts of evasion.

These untoward conditions did not rouse in him the zest of the reformer. He was not concerned lest one good custom or a multitude of bad customs should corrupt the world. He was pretty well convinced that the social order was beyond redemption. With the rest of his generation he had quite evidently read the Darwins and Herbert Spencer. He responded to the genetic findings of the biologists with the pessimism that the first encounter with science is likely for a while to stimulate in all active minds. Life was a hard and hazardous battle against overwhelming natural forces. "Civilization is the daughter of discontent, and worthy of its mother; . . . Contentment is a virtue which at present seems to be confined mainly to the wise and the infamous."[2] The reward was something neither to be relished when gained nor missed when lost. To cap all, as a forlorn compensation "we have set up fantastic faiths of an aftertime in a better world from which no confirming whisper has ever reached us across the void. Heaven is a prophecy uttered by the lips of despair, but Hell is an experience from analogy."[3]

Yet beneath his negativism Bierce seemed to feel misgivings about his misgivings — doubt of his doubt. Spencer's omniscience was annoying, the more so that his conclusions were not easy to gainsay:

> I know too well
> What Herbert Spencer, if he didn't tell
> (I know not if he did) yet might have told. . . .[4]

---

[1] "Works," Vol. XII, p. 163. (The passage is dialectal.)
[2] Ibid. Vol. IX, p. 184.
[3] Ibid. Vol. XI, p. 149.
[4] "An Unmerry Christmas," in "Works," Vol. IV, p. 155.

Bierce's invective against the laws carried with it a subscription to the law as a body of agreement on social behavior. And he believed rationally in morality as a commendable and desirable set of habits and controls. He was altogether scornful of liberty set up in denial of social obligation, and he abhorred the tyrannies of revolution equally with the tyrannies of despotism.

He came round in the end, not surprisingly, to his "ultimate and determining test of right — 'What in the circumstances would Jesus have done?' — the Jesus of the New Testament and not the Jesus of the commentators, theologians, priests, and parsons."[1] He was not, he was careful to explain, a Christian in any ecclesiastical sense, but he was a wholehearted admirer of Jesus, who was pre-eminent to him as "a moral lightning calculator." In the way of thoughtful doubters Bierce was out of tune with any set of extremists. To religious orthodoxy of the sort that associates doubt with vice, anarchy, and atheism, he was, of course, anathema, and quite ready to return objurgation with objurgation. To the amoralist and apostle of liberty he was an old fogy because he still believed in a code, even though the code was to be derived from life and not imposed on it; and he could meet contempt with contempt. And he was of no particular comfort to himself, for unrelieved disillusionment hums a sad burden in a minor key.

Yet along the blind alley of circumstance, and above and around it, life still afforded Bierce mystery and beauty. The mystery lay in the spirit world, in the indeterminable connection between that and the world of matter, and in the very marvels of intellectual and emotional happenings. The beauty lay in the chance of finding just the right words with which to narrate the adventures of the spirit. His best-known volume contains a series of remarkably vivid pictures. Once read they are cut deep into the memory by the vigor of the etching and the momentous narrative significance.

---

[1] "Works," Vol. XI, p. 225.

"An Occurrence at Owl Creek Bridge," though not above the level of Bierce's more effective writing, is most often cited because of its ingenious construction and its surprise ending: the discovery that the prolonged account of an escape by a condemned spy has been imagined in the moment between the drop of the hangman's trap and the fall to the end of the rope. "A Son of the Gods — a Study in the Present Tense" reveals in its subtitle Bierce's conscious enjoyment of a technique, as he develops in sharpest detail a long suspense passage, leading to the splendid and inevitable death of a lone reconnoiterer watched by thousands of his fellow soldiers.

The constant factor in the book is extreme emotional tension. Sometimes the characters are pathological and the situations abnormal. The people and the events are barely within the reach of credibility. Bierce thus often turned naturally to war episodes, because, though actual, they were farthest from the even tenor of normal life. In these it was the rarest occurrence for him to reveal a sense of humankind in general. The mass, the herd, the crowd, served as a dim background for one man living at the highest pitch and often enough dying of the tension; and the individual himself was less a character than a piece of susceptibility played on by overwhelming emotions. So he wrote of the unbalancing effect on a man of accepting and serving a penal sentence for burglary in order to protect his mistress from exposure; of death following great expectations protracted for five years by the terms of an eccentric will; of madness induced by night solitude with a corpse, by isolation in the dark with what proves to be only a stuffed snake, by reading a ghost story "in suitable surroundings."

Bierce passes on toward the farther end of no man's land in "Can Such Things Be?" a collection of tales in which he resorts to the horrors of the werewolf and malign specter very much as they appear and reappear in the Japanese redactions of Lafcadio Hearn. But between the products of the two men there is the obvious difference between the familiar and the exotic. Hearn's tales of shadowed offenses to visitants from the spirit-land and the terrors of spectral revenge are matched by Bierce's use of Occidental brute facts, the more horrible because of their daily recurrence in the newspapers. The attendant spirit of a loving wife is a possibility in "Kotto" or "Kwaidan," but the murder of a loving wife under false suspicion of infidelity belongs to "Can Such Things Be?" — and so too the tracks, the footprints, the wild screams, the traces of struggle, the mutilated remains of the bogeys' victims. Bierce seemed dedicated to the rousing of "pity and terror"; and then, in the midst of the volume, the more conspicuous for its isolation, is a little allegory called "Haiti the Shepherd" on the theme that "happiness may come if not sought for, but if looked for will never be seen" — very pretty, very moralistic, very unlike its author.

Quite at the apex of the narratives included in Bierce's collected works is "The Monk and the Hangman's Daughter." It has been the subject of much controversy and recrimination. It both was his work and was not. In a circumstantial foreword he attributes the original to a German who pretends to derive it from an old manuscript, and the first English version to a faithful but uninspired translation. His own version, he says, is a free rendition of this. This leaves out of account an insistent claimant, but the claimant does not dispose of the fact that Bierce had a hand in casting it into final form. On aesthetic grounds the source of the plot and even the original development are of secondary moment. In its present form it is an evidence of what Bierce could contribute to and could wish to ascribe to himself. Its pre-eminence among his writings also proves his indebtedness to his sources, partly acknowledged and, apparently, partly withheld.

His gifts as an artist lay in differing and conflicting powers. On the intellectual side he was a sardonic wit and a humorist. The special endowment of the wit is a capacity for acute and often acrid wording of nice discriminations. He sees a discrepancy or incongruity and brands it with a phrase or a sentence. It is what Aesop did with his "sour grapes" or what Sydney Smith did to the suppressors of blasphemy when he said of one offender that he was capable of speaking disrespectfully of the equator. Wit imposes a sentence and offers a challenge. In the subject of wit there is little to laugh at, though its turn of expression may provoke a smile. It is directed at culprits who are both fallible and responsible, and hence is always turned on humankind. Though the high-hanging grape and the oblivious equator may figure in witty observations, they are never the objects of them. What Bierce had to say in the vein of the wit is to be found in the "Dictionary," in the "Fables," and in a fair share of his verses; and it was consciously addressed to those who prefer wit to humor.

His humor was again intellectual and again, in its casual play, largely dependent on his gift for phrase. It emerges now and then in his more serious volumes, as in the passing comment on a nondescript building, that it was "a somewhat dull-looking edifice of the Early Comatose order, and appears to have been designed by an architect who shrank from publicity, and although unable to conceal his work . . . did what he honestly could to ensure it against a second look."[1] And in a consciously literary way it was frequently aimed at the specious and hifalutin styles of the fine-writing and eloquent-speaking schools. Throughout "Kings of Beasts," his gayest series, he fell foul of the dealers in rhetorical bromides, and often most happily. Vide the passage on the "mush rat," which runs in part,

> When he throws his eyes upon a tree the doom of that monarch of the forest primeval is sealed its caroar is at a end and its name a by word in the mouths of men, for he ganaws it down while you wait, and as it thunders to earth he raises the song of triump and lashes the air to foam! His house is fathoms five under the glad waters of the deep blue sea, and the steam boats pass above him as he pursues the evil tenor of his way, in maiden meditation, fancy free.[2]

In the fashion of Thackeray and Holmes and Bret Harte, Bierce tried his hand at parody, and he succeeded perhaps as

[1] "Works," Vol. II, p. 281.

[2] "Works," Vol. XII, p. 14.

well as they, which was only moderately well. For he was satirist rather than parodist; he quite lacked the flexibility of the latter. Nothing of this sort by Bierce can approach the best of Untermeyer or Carolyn Wells or J. C. Squire, or the average of Max Beerbohm, whose "Christmas Garland" is the best of the genre since the "Rejected Addresses" of 1812. Always, whether as wit or as humorist, Bierce was taking the offensive against sentimentalism. He was more than a little suspicious of faith, hope, and charity. Feelings of any sort except distrust, scorn, and wrath seemed rather dangerous to him. The intellect must be a strong fortress against them all.

Yet sense was in the balance against sensibility, for Bierce was essentially a man of feeling. So on the aesthetic side he added the delicate perceptions of the portrait painter to the caustic judgments of the cartoonist. The attitude and the utterance of the two are in complete contrast. The intellectual Bierce was always on the offensive, always ready to express himself in brilliant brevities; but the Bierce who wrote of the mysteries and thrills of individual experience was receptive, deliberate, and deliberative, ready to surrender to a mood in wise passiveness, willing to court in the shadows the shy thoughts that would not come out into the sunlight.

His shorter narratives suggest Poe, and can be comfortably laid on the Procrustean bed made ready in "The Philosophy of Composition." In scale, determination of tone, establishment of background, and the rest of it, they submit to the same tests as "The Cask of Amontillado" and "The Fall of the House of Usher." But Bierce very naturally resented the common report that he was a disciple of Poe. The tonal resemblance of their stories is clear, and it is clearly the result of their resemblances in mind and temper; but in the most insistent feature of Bierce's workmanship — the elaboration of a single point of time for its subjective values — his tales are more imperatively suggestive of Victor Hugo's before him or of Stephen Crane's that were to come. One cannot read "The Red Badge of Courage" or "The Open Boat" without feeling that Crane may have learned a lesson or two — and learned them very well — from "Bits of Autobiography" and "In the Midst of Life."

Bierce's normal audience should have been his between 1890 and 1910. His thinking, though not markedly original, was independent and aggressive and today seems provocative. He saw straight when he looked at actual conditions, and he came out plainly with what he saw. But he met with no general response. Much of what he had to say was implicit in Bellamy's "Looking Backward," which fascinated the multitude with its explicit picture of a communized Boston before communism had become a pariah in the public mind. It was rather more than suggested in Howells's "Traveler from Altruria," with its flavor of sugar-coated socialism. But Bierce's criticisms were more drastic and his opinions less hopeful. He did not believe in Arcadias or Utopias or Altrurias or Platonic republics. He rejected communism and socialism, and he was as devastating in his assaults on them as the plain-spoken objectors in the Platonic dialogues who are set up for the not always convincing rebuttals of Socrates.

But no one took the trouble to rebut Bierce. The reading public of those years was almost beyond the reach of the iconoclast, for it did not bestir itself to analyze critical thinking. It was easier to dismiss disturbing thought without analysis. It liked Lanier's prettiness without noting the thorn-stemmed roses among the lilies in the Lanier anthology. It contented itself with the nuances of Howells's humor and disposed of his Tolstoyan leanings as odd but harmless. It considered "Looking Backward" to be amusing fantasy. So Bierce said his say on the way of the world; and the world ignored him, an exhorter at the gateway to Vanity Fair.

It is not quite so easy to understand the almost total ignoring of his tales as well as his criticisms. The upcoming of the *Yellow Book* and the *Chap-book*, Baudelaire's enthusiasm for Poe and the decadents' discovery of Baudelaire, the developing vogue of Zola, the beginnings of an active Russian influence, the emergence of Ibsen, Hauptmann, Sudermann, Shaw, attention to the sterner voice of Hardy, it would seem, might all have developed an audience for Bierce. But they did not. Or it would not be easy to understand, if Thomas Beer had not reminded us in "The Mauve Decade," that in the 90's the American magazines, natural channels for American short stories, were charily discreet,[1] printing outspoken things from across the Atlantic but rejecting and deleting from American authors the circumstantial, the realistic, the grim. It was on this last account, he declares, that Bierce's "Killed at Resaca" and "An Occurrence at Owl Creek Bridge" were refused, and that most of his stories might be still unprinted if grimness were universally accepted as due ground for refusal. So it was that newspapers, literary supplements, and newly established weeklies became the refuge for sterner stuff if the authors were alert enough to find them; and, once printed in these, in the manner of refugees the grim tales disappeared from public view.

A generation later, if Bierce had been writing, he would have had his audience. His social theses would not have attracted much attention, no longer being fresh or startling, but they would have been either condemned or approved. And the best of his narratives, equal in bulk to the best of Poe's, would be read, let us say, by the readers of Aldous Huxley, Arthur Machen, Sherwood Anderson, and Ernest Hemingway.

Lafcadio Hearn

Hearn, like Melville, Bierce, and Emily Dickinson, failed to win his real audience during his lifetime. During his latter years, in the 90's, a few people read his books and bought them, actually enough to bring him modest literary returns before his death. He was writing about Japan at the time; but the public was interested in the new Japan that was

[1] Thomas Beer, in "The Mauve Decade," "The American Magazines," pp. 211–242.

whipping China and Russia, and he was writing about the old one; so the vogue did not spread far. Yet some of Hearn's readers followed his work because they wanted to understand a part of the Orient as seen by one who loved it. And others continued because they felt that he had the soul of a poet and wrote a beautiful prose. One little volume after another came out and had its little posthumous day, for the writer died early in the new century. Until at last, with a weariness for an Occidental civilization that had come to its logical climax in the World War, a larger public, who turned away from daily circumstance with Hudson and Conrad and O'Brien and Maugham, rediscovered Hearn and encouraged the publishers to bestow on him the distinction of a mortuary monument in sixteen volumes and a de-luxe edition.

Hearn's birth, wanderings, and physical handicaps made him as tempting a subject as Poe, and resulted in like biographical distortions. Specifications: an Irish father, surgeon in the British army, and a Greek mother; loss of both parents in early childhood; upbringing under the bony and featherless wing of a prosperous Victorian great-aunt; schooling in French Roman-Catholic seminaries; college in American newspaper offices, first in a transplanted New England town on the banks of the Ohio and then in a Gulf port where the last traditions of the Creoles were waning before the makers of the New South; at thirty-seven three years of travel or foreign sojourn, mostly in the French West Indies; and, finally, fourteen years of writing and teaching in Japan, and death at the age of fifty-four. These experiences, imposed on a little, half-blind, supersensitive man from Greece, Ireland, England, France, the Middle West, the isles of tropic seas, and a Japan invaded but not yet transformed by alien influences, made him a striking composite of cultures and gave point to his comments on the culture of Great Britain and the United States.

For the gossip-monger there is much to gloat over in the first two thirds of Hearn's career and a little in the remainder.

He was undersized, homely, and extremely near sighted; he was fickle, irritable, and sometimes ungrateful; but he was egregiously the artist. The gap between his art and his life was rather greater than in the case of Poe; and what Griswold did to befoul Poe has been quite equaled by the inquiries and opinions about Hearn circulated by Gould and Tinker. Gazing on him with myopic eyes, they lost sight of his mind and of the depths of life and heights of beauty that his mind's eye revealed. The essential truth about Hearn is that he was a romanticist who found his double impulsion in a distrust of the Christian creed under which he was brought up and of the sordid life into which he was thrust, who leaned for philosophical support on the teachings of Herbert Spencer, and who strove for release in a lifelong search for beauty.

His earliest memories of baby boyhood were of a discipline that nightly condemned him to fearful darkness. Ghosts came, and he was forbidden to talk of them because they did not exist. But as his elders invoked the Holy Ghost, he inquired about the Godhead and was rewarded with hideous information about a malevolent deity who was chiefly god of hell. Then came the revelation, through some illustrated books on art, of the splendid, virile, and lovely deities of Greek mythology. It was a thrilling delight; but it was assailed as soon as his pagan leanings were discovered, and Christian propriety expurgated the pictures. Finally an honest confessional admission that he had wanted the devil to come to him in the form of a beautiful woman was met with such dire admonitions that he was filled with hope that the temptation might be realized. It was the final confirmation of his paganism. To the end of his life he never forgave Christianity. In his youth, incapable of speculative philosophy, he applied the practical test and rejected the religion on the scriptural ground of judging it by such fruits as he knew. Schooling in Roman Catholic seminaries did not bring him back to the arms of the church; and disinheritance by his well-to-do relatives and the poverty of his later boyhood introduced him to the grimmest realities of a Christian civilization — the slum and the workhouse. He had solid grounds for his later "inclination to believe that Romanticism itself was engendered by religious conservatism."[1]

The revolt begun against dogma was reinflamed by circumstance. For years he lived from hand to mouth, suffering penury and hunger, seeing much that was horrible, writing about some of it. His newspaper report of the "Tanyard Murder" displayed his powers and shocked certain of his later critics. He had simply come to the point of such emotional numbness that only a violent stimulus could stir him. He described himself at the time as "the sensational reporter"; but as an extremist, and an amusing one to his observing self, he believed not only in the "revoltingly horrible" but also in the "excruciatingly beautiful." More soberly he wrote a friend, ten years after this, that a man must specialize in order to succeed and that he was pledging himself "to the worship of the Odd, the Queer, the Strange, the Exotic, the Monstrous. It quite suits my temperament."[2] Yet before long he came to a change of heart, possibly through the experience of feeling more certainty as to his next meal. The fascinations of French realism waned, and he somewhat suddenly became conscious of reviving Saxon inhibitions. With a reaction which was no less violent than unpredictable he went over to the opposing camp. He protested at the "raw and bloody pessimism of Zola," who was "the idealist of the Horrible, the Foul, the Brutal, the Abominable."[3] It was an indication to Hearn of national degeneracy. Even the French language encountered his wrath: it was peculiarly adapted for enshrouding the most awful forms of human depravity with exquisite art. With the unction of a recent convert he thanked his stars that literary conservatism still reigned in England and the United States. He was grateful for the "brawny moral tone" that

[1] "The Writings of Lafcadio Hearn" (16 vols.), Vol. XIII, p. 199. Houghton Mifflin, 1922. Quotations by permission of the publishers.

[2] Vol. XIII, p. 322. [3] Vol. XVI, p. 21.

prevailed in the pages of Dickens and Thackeray; the power of self-control among English and American authors; the retention of the primal purpose of fiction, which was to recreate minds that were weary of the toil and strife of the world. The sensational reporter who had anticipated the *fin de siècle* decadents in pursuit of the horrible and the monstrous was become an ethical romanticist.

In this reaction against the professingly Christian world, the world of actual circumstance, and the realms of realism and naturalism, Hearn continued to the end. In the life that surrounded him as a journalist he saw no more to admire in New York than in London, or in Cincinnati than in New York. Even in New Orleans the human city was buried under a lava flood of sordid chicane. The golden sunlight of eternal summer shone for him on a charnel house of corruption. He was ready to abandon himself to cynical skepticism; was, in fact, abandoned to it when he found himself under the spell of Herbert Spencer, thenceforth his literary superman.

The overpowering influence of Spencer is common in the literary history of the period, but in Hearn's case it was an experience with a difference. Often the effect was to deprive the young believer of a comfortable faith. The "Data of Ethics" and "First Principles," said Theodore Dreiser, for example, stripped him of all that he deemed substantial — "I was completely thrown down in my conceptions or non-conceptions of life"; supplied him only with "the definite conviction that one got nowhere."[1] But for Hearn, who was deep in the center of indifference, the effect was positive redemption. "I . . . learned what an absurd thing positive skepticism is. I also found unspeakable comfort in the sudden and, for me, eternal reopening of the Great Doubt, which renders pessimism ridiculous, and teaches a new reverence for all forms of faith."[2] What Hearn derived from Spencer

[1] "A Book about Myself," pp. 457–458. [2] "Writings," Vol. XIII, p. 371.

was an approach to the study of human experience and a stimulus to pursue the study for himself.

What he came to was a form of romantic moral idealism. The mind, he maintained, wearied by toil and strife, could be recreated only in escape from reality; the escape should be to an ideal world, sensuously, but, above all, morally beautiful. Because the morals of the present were avenues to fulfillment of human possibilities, the common sense of the mass condemned attempts to overthrow the moral code. But for the educated the new teaching of ethics should substitute a rational for an emotional morality, though with the masses the old emotional reactions should preserve the moral balance of the world. In the ideal world, however, such a balance would be preserved through inherent instinct; and only in a world where it prevailed could the consciousness of the code be permitted to sleep. Short of this millennium, therefore, Hearn concluded, moral idealism must be sought and practiced because of its necessity as a regulating force.

Spencer might have seemed near-infallible to his disciple if Hearn had lived out his life in America; but when he found in Japanese culture a multitude of confirmations for what Spencer had derived from other sources, the influence was doubled. Hearn's whole volume "Japan: an Attempt at an Interpretation" is interspersed with references to Spencer's generalizations and the parallel facts in Japanese life. Near the beginning is the acknowledgment that "the evolutional history of ancestor-worship has been very much the same in all countries; and that of the Japanese cult offers remarkable evidence in support of Herbert Spencer's exposition of the law of religious development."[1] There are citations of Spencer in reference to the spirits of the dead, the longevity of religious dynasties, the intensity of patriotism in militant societies, the vague character of the Shinto hierarchy, the theory that the greater gods of a people represent the later forms of ancestor worship, even the thesis that

[1] "Writings," Vol. XII, p. 23.

elaborate pronominal distinctions prevail where subjection is extreme. The chapter on "The Higher Buddhism" is a running commentary on Spencerian doctrines, the book is appended with Spencer's advice to the Japanese nation on the proper policy toward Occidental intruders, and the last reference to him in the text calls him "the wisest man in the world."[1]

Hearn's sex philosophy, if it deserve so formal a name, was not unrelated to Spencerian influence and was interwoven with his Japanese experience. Until late maturity his impulse led him to shroud every phase of sexual feeling in deep reticence; not because the subject was holy, nor because it was unholy, but because it was intimately personal. Just this reticence he met with in Japan, finding himself under the need of explaining at length to his students the difference between Eastern and Western attitudes when he faced the theme of romantic love in English literature; and his explanation was semi-apologetic. To these boys he was less outspoken than he was to one of his old New Orleans friends: "We live in the murky atmosphere of desire in the West; — an erotic perfume emanates from all that artificial life of ours; . . . It now seems, even to me, almost disgusting."[2] He inclined toward satisfaction with the Japanese mode, in which the social order belonged to the dominant male whose interests were divided between the worship of his ancestors and the perpetuation of his line. As there was no economic barrier to marriage he mated early, knew no suppressed desires, enjoyed the devoted subjection of his wife, and wanted no intimacy of companionship. Everything was done decently according to the code, though the code tacitly allowed the two notable exceptions of the geisha girl in life and the romantic love of folk and fairy tale in literature. Yet, withal, Hearn felt that the golden mean was somewhere between the East and the West. In the Western life that he almost abhorred there was something of himself. There

---

[1] "Writings," Vol. XII, p. 444. [2] Vol. XIV, p. 228.

was something deficient in the impassively regulated life of the East. An overstimulated sense of sex "cultivates one aesthetic faculty at the expense of all the rest. And yet — perhaps its working is divine behind all that veil of vulgarity and lustfulness. It is cultivating also, beyond any question, a capacity for tenderness the Orient knows nothing of."[1]

Deep in disgust with a self-righteous Western civilization which in his later years was choosing to blast him as "an atheist, a debauchee, a disreputable ex-reporter,"[2] he analyzed himself as Spencer might have done:

> My dear friend, the first necessity for success in life is to be a good animal. As an animal you don't work well at all. Furthermore you are out of harmony mentally and morally with the life of society: you represent broken-down tissue. There is some good in the ghostly part of you, but it would never have been developed under comfortable circumstances. Hard knocks and intellectual starvation have brought your miserable little animula into some sort of shape. It will never have full opportunity to express itself, doubtless; but perhaps that is better. It might otherwise make too many mistakes: and it has not sufficient original force to move the sea of human mind to any storm of aspiration. Perhaps in some future state of . . .

Here the voice of Spencer ceased and Hearn took up the theme in his own person:

> I think civilization is a fraud, because I don't like the hopeless struggle. If I were very rich I should perhaps think quite differently — or, what would be still more rational, try not to think at all about it. . . . I am already deemed the "moral plague-spot" of Japan by the dear missionaries. Next week I'll try them with an article on "The Abomination of Civilization!" . . . But I have at home a little world of about eleven people, to whom I am Love and Light and Food. It is a very gentle world. It is only happy when I am happy. If I even look tired, it is silent, and walks on tiptoe. It is a moral force. I dare not fret about anything when I can help it — for others would fret more. So I try to keep right.[3]

[1] "Writings," Vol. XIV, p. 229. [2] Ibid. p. 214.

[3] Ibid. pp. 214–216. One gains the impression that Hearn's desire for self-control was far from fulfilled, from his son's "Father and I," by Kazuo Koizumi, pp. 17, 129–150.

Throughout his later career Hearn was self-disciplined as an artist. From his work as journalist he brought none of the illusions of the lazy-inspired. He must fill his mind and plan his work and lay out ambitious programs and submit to the "foul Fiend Routine." In his newspaper writings there was a measure of scrupulous translation from the French and an element of leaves from strange literatures — Egyptian, Persian, Indian, Chinese, Finnish. There was erudition in some of the articles. His liking for the recondite cropped out all along his career, sometimes as in the charming chronicle of Père Labat, the Martinique pioneer, and sometimes as in the perfunctory literary and entomological summaries for which a Japanese student did the preliminary drudging. But the best of his writing, the part that is beyond confusion with anyone else's, is the writing in which out of his vivid experience or out of his delicately sympathetic interpretation, he preserved the evanescent charm of scenes and episodes that provided him escapes from Anglo-Saxondom.

For, from the time when Hearn went to New Orleans as an aged young man to the end of his short pilgrimage, his life was a succession of infatuations with places and peoples. The spirit of the quest was in it, but it sprang superficially from restless discontent. The Creole life of the Gulf port first stirred him as woodland and stream stirred the boy Wordsworth, needing no aid unborrowed from the eye. Then the sensuous experience fulfilled itself, and he hungered for new scenes. Somewhere else he must feel the thrill of fresh sensation. "Whenever I go down to the wharves, I look at the white-winged ships. O ye messengers, swift Hermae of Traffic, ghosts of the infinite ocean, whither will ye bear me?"[1] And again, "If I could only become a Consul at Bagdad, Algiers, Ispahan, Benares, Samarkand, Nippo, Bangkok, Ninh-Binh — or any part of the world where ordinary Christians do not like to go! Here is the nook in which my romanticism still hides."[2]

---

[1] "Writings," Vol. XIII, p. 172. [2] Ibid. p. 289.

When the choice came, a ship bore him to Martinique, where the opulent exuberance of life enthralled him for a little. After the subtle reticences of the vanishing Creole tradition, this island in the West Indies confronted him like an extravagant whimsy of nature. There was an ostentatiousness as of a *nouveau riche* among staid aristocrats. But the excess of stimulant drugged his imagination; the color display numbed his senses; the myriad rush of impressions dulled him to any particular one; the heat served as a narcotic; concentration was impossible. Yet retreat to the farthest possible contrast did not relieve him. In New York there was no emotion recollected in tranquillity, because there could be no tranquillity for him in Babylon. He was so horrified by the confusion worse confounded that he was in no mood for happy memories. He had written that he needed new vitality after two years in the tropics. He found it, and with it a newly vitalized vocabulary: "I want to get back among the monkeys and the parrots. . . . This is frightful, nightmarish, devilish! Civilization is a hideous thing. Blessed is savagery! . . . I am sorry not to see you — but since you live in hell what can I do?"[1]

By a happy accident he went to another hemisphere; sent there to prepare "copy" to accompany some illustrations for *Harper's Magazine*. Hearn was never to leave Japan; for he found there all the best that had charmed him in New Orleans and Martinique: the fine manners of a seasoned culture filled with speechless dignities, loveliness of sky and sea and vegetation, freedom as yet from the brute massiveness of Occidental life. Once more, however, though not so quickly as in the West Indies, the first fervor of enthusiasm waned. To begin, the quiet gray-and-blue beauty of these gentler islands stilled and soothed him. The people were simple, charming, kindly; their games, dances, legends, superstitions, immemorially old. But, all too soon, he found that in the gentleness of the folk there was a baffling effacement of individu-

---

[1] "Writings," Vol. XIV, pp. 70, 71.

ality; that the charm of their half-lights and half-shadows was bought at the price of brilliancy; that the immemorial customs had begotten insuperable reservations; and that where there were no angers there were no hilarities — only the blue-and-gray levels of highly developed amenity and decorum.

This absence of shadow in Japanese life was not to last.

> The West [he wrote indignantly] burst into their Buddhist peace, and . . . Japan paid to learn how to see shadows in nature, in life, and in thought. . . . Then Japan wondered at the shadows of machinery and chimneys and telegraph-poles; and at the shadows of mines and of factories, and the shadows in the hearts of those who worked there. . . . Whereat Japan became rather serious, and refused to study any more silhouettes. . . . But some of the shadows still clung to her life; and she cannot possibly get rid of them. Never again can the world seem to her quite so beautiful as it did before.[1]

And never observer wrote more truly.

Nowhere in life did Hearn find abundance of beauty and the conditions for abundance of creative energy also. Everywhere life was compounded of unequal values. In his home in the Japan not yet transformed by Occidental influences, he came to a temporary anchorage; but not for long. If only to see Japan from a distance, he decided to return for a while to the civilization he shrank from but could not resist. He was buoyed by this prospect when he died. The oft-repeated charges against the peculiar insufficiencies of America for the artist's life break down in face of such a cosmopolitan experience. The insufficiencies belonged not to a country but to a machine age, the menace of which he saw before his generation did. He was spared the spectacle of Japan's surrender to it. If he had lived he could have continued his retreat before it to "Bangkok, Ninh-Binh," and the few remaining points "where ordinary Christians do not like to go."

Naturally enough Hearn did not achieve his audience until the day when the machines of peace and war had developed far enough to give clearer pertinence to his observations.

---

[1] "Writings," Vol. VII, pp. 124, 125.

Emily Dickinson

Emily Dickinson was the latest but not the least distinguished American of the nineteenth century to achieve full recognition in the twentieth. She was uninterested in gaining a contemporary audience, not wanting to be a celebrity and disdaining the idea of selling her poems.[1] Between 1890 (four years after her death) and 1896 three series were published in many American and English printings, and by the turn of the century over fifteen thousand copies of her works had been circulated. But this generous recognition came in the decade when literary experiment was briefly popular. From 1897 to 1909 there seems to have been no mention of her in print.[2] In 1912 Miss Dickinson was one of the trio discussed in an article on "Three Forgotten Poetesses." In 1914 less than six hundred copies of her notable volume "The Single Hound" were ventured by the publishers, with a second printing less than half as great. In 1921 the total sales of all the series of her poems barely exceeded two hundred copies. If there was anything to be judged from public verdicts, the implication of more than twenty years of neglect seemed beyond debate: Miss Dickinson had had her little day.

But the awarding of posthumous fames has proved that popular opinion, whether positive or negative, needs a longer confirmation than twenty years. By 1924 the time had come for a reversal of the verdict. The "Life and Letters" then published went into several large printings in America and England. A fresh demand arose for her writings on both sides of the Atlantic: more than five thousand volumes of a new and "complete" edition were disposed of within a few months; the "Further Poems" appeared in 1929, and the stage was set for the centenary year and the

---

[1] See the "Poems" of Emily Dickinson (1930), pp. 15, 223, 278–279.

[2] See bibliographies by A. L. Hampson (1930) and by G. F. Whicher (1930). Also A. M. Wells's "Early Criticism of Emily Dickinson," in *American Literature*, Vol. I, pp. 243–259.

flood of books and articles which attested to the fact that Emily Dickinson was unforgettable.

The essential facts about her as an individual are clearly that she was born and bred in the Calvinist tradition; that she was a mild, and sometimes mildly irreverent, apostate from Calvinism and steadfast in the Christian faith; that she belonged to a region, thought "New Englandly," and felt herself to be no more provincial than any queen; that from childhood she was extremely devoted to house and home; that in early womanhood she met, loved, and parted from a man she could not marry; that for the rest of her life she withdrew into the seclusion of her village home; that here she was constantly writing little lyrics, sharing her lyric self mainly with her brother's wife, who lived next door; that she also sought and enjoyed the stimulating friendship of three well-known literary men who could have introduced her to a public had she wanted; that she chose the narrow circle which she set for herself; that the world of her imagination was wide as time and space; and that though she was sobered by the frustration of a love to which she was always constant, she was nevertheless constantly revealing herself as gay, playful, whimsical, vivacious, wise in a wisdom that was enriched by a sense of humor. An unfortunate fact attending her celebrity is that inquisitive biographers have chosen to make a mystery of her personal life, rejecting the straightforward and perfectly credible story accepted by those who knew her best, with the result that a succession of conflicting romances has been fabricated which may best be regarded as fundamentally unimportant and mutually destructive. They cancel out like the factors in multiplication of improper fractions, and arrive at a product of minus one. The vital fact is that she survived an overpowering but not devastating experience which determined her daily course of life, colored all her writing, and inspired the best of it.

It is doubtful whether the influence of Susan Gilbert Dickinson, her sister-in-law, can be overestimated. It is one matter to be indifferent to a public, and another, which offers no paradox, to be dependent on some sympathetic response. Miss Dickinson's family were normally concerned with daily routine, village affairs, the commonplaces of an amiably conventional life. They were probably more than normally tolerant, if not sympathetic, with the daughter-sister who preferred them to the rest of the world and who often preferred solitude to the family circle. Respecting her individual choice and cherishing her as a member of the family, they gave her neither help nor hindrance as a poet. But her beloved new friend, "a hedge away," was new enough and distant enough to be the recipient of a multitude of messages which were addressed to her as a public of one, which were intimately personal as missives, but from which the poet sought some oral response as well as reply. Miss Dickinson conceived of poetry as communication; without doubt many of her verses seem cryptic simply because the occasion for them was too clear to herself and her auditor to need the redundancy of explication; and letter after letter addressed to Susan Dickinson during her absences from the village express in the most extravagant terms a need for the nearness of her congenial spirit, a nearness that may often have inspired a lyric which was never confided to her.

The simplest, the most obvious, and the least impressive of Miss Dickinson's poems are on the themes suggested by the local scene in the garden, in the fields and farms, and on the surrounding hills. They are simple and natural, not deeply interpretative, frequently in the nature of poetic conceits. The one most often quoted is neither seasonal nor pastoral, but on the theme of the new marvel in the valley — the railway train.[1] It could hardly have been written without thought of a reader, sharable like a smile or a gentle jocosity. And so it is with most of the poems assembled under the title of "Nature" in the collected works.

But the case is quite different with the other three divisions as classified by her original editors: Life, Love, Time and

---

[1] "Poems" (1930), p. 22.

Eternity. It is impracticable to pigeonhole such utterances finally; no two assorters would divide them alike; but as classifications go these will serve as they stand. A reading of the group entitled "Life" discloses a poet who, leaving all "conceits" behind, faced life with tragic bravery. Far the most insistent theme is that of life unfulfilled, the sense of the value of that which is withheld.[1] Success is sweetest to the unsuccessful; heaven eludes us as the bee does the schoolboy; the fallen soldier wins the emperor's victory; distance lends enchantment; complete happiness would be unendurable; spare the starving the mention of food, the captive, of freedom; spare the hungering even a plenitude of viands; forbidden fruit is sweetest; an open door closed to the wanderer redoubles his loneliness. The motif recurs relentlessly, yet not in mawkishness or self-pity. Steadily the notes of self-reliance, courage, steadfastness, and faith accompany it:[2]

> For the one ship that struts the shore
> Many's the gallant overwhelmed creature
> Nodding in navies nevermore.[3]

These lyrics on life, too, are not too Olympian to withhold the poetess, though she has no time for hate, from outbursts of scorn[4] at the preacher who talked so much of breadth that he proved his narrowness; at the man with a face so hard that a stone would feel at ease with him; and at the brittle gentlewomen with "dimity convictions" and a refined horror of "freckled human nature." And she scorned the platitudes that life refutes by a single honest test.

Perhaps the poems included under "Nature" were her more youthful ones — there is practically no way of dating most of them except by the changes in handwriting, and there is always the chance that an early one was transcribed later; or possibly they represented the sensibilities of the

---

[1] "Poems" (1930), pp. 3, 16, 18, 23, 25, 28, 31, 34, 36, 40, 42, 45, 51, 54.
[2] Ibid. (1930), pp. 3, 6, 8, 10, 11, 13, 17, 24, 32, 41, 46, etc.
[3] Ibid. (1930), p. 52.
[4] Ibid. pp. 31, 46, 58.

early editors, who seem to have been less confident about surrendering the poet to posterity than her subsequent one,[1] who also has her reservations. At any rate, in the remainder of the work there is more of gaiety and gladness and far more of challenge or even insolent defiance of accepted values than is discoverable in the "Nature" group or than is hinted in the section entitled "Life." Love, it appears, is the supreme experience;[2] not as a figure of speech, but as a literal absolute. What it does not include is nothing; what it does include is all affections, aspirations, loyalties, faiths. The face of the lover outshines the face of the Saviour; the belief in him is the only way of expressing belief in God; the desire for him makes nothing of time and space. Heaven is in the nearest room if he is there; if he is away no space can really divide, no time is too long to wait. He justifies the belief in immortality and supplies the substance for faith in it. She brushes aside the formulas of courts and altars as she would "brush a summer by" if he were coming in the fall. It is the very ecstasy of love's madness, but it is not a fleeting one, and under its recurrent possession Miss Dickinson wrote unsurpassably.

So possessed, she becomes understandable in her quiet nineteenth-century New England village a knight's move down the street from the church and within sound of the chapel bell of the orthodox college for which grandfather, father, and brother had long wrought. Except for an occasional flash of contempt for the "unco guid" she was not impatient with these: her own people were too closely allied with them; but she rejected the cornerstone and the keystones of their temple not without amusement.[3] The Bible was an ancient book "written by faded men." It needed the touch of a troubadour throughout. Heaven, with its accouterments of

---

[1] The poems published in 1890 and 1892 were "edited by two of her friends, T. W. Higginson and Mabel Loomis Todd"; the poems of 1896, by Mrs. Todd; the subsequent collections of 1914 and 1929, by Miss Dickinson's niece, Martha Dickinson Bianchi.

[2] "Poems" (1930), Part Three, pp. 126–154, etc.

[3] Ibid. (1930), pp. 20, 175, 255, 259, 296, etc.

robes and crowns, appealed to her as little as it did to Mark Twain. She was glad she did not believe in it, but she was also glad that those she loved took comfort in the prospect of it. Prayer for whatsoever she might desire was a mockery. She had tried it and had been ignored or derided. The God who looked like Michelangelo's, a bearded old man on a throne, could be gently twitted as her father could when she asked him, as he came in from the lower meadow, if the frogs had been deferential. She addressed the Most High as "Papa above," and deplored the fact that he was always in heaven — never made a visit, never took a nap. This can be over-analyzed, but it may be said that she came by her gay irreverence naturally. It was the New England whimsy, covertly expressed, that Sarah Kemble Knight confided to her diary; it was the very-diluted bold badness that the Amherst College boys indulged in when they roared the gospel vulgarized, or Negro spirituals as taught them by the melodious black, "George-Henry" Davis. It was the skepticism of Mark Twain offset by the faith Mark Twain yearned for. It was the contempt of Thoreau when he said of this theological deity that men had "somewhat hastily concluded" that it was their chief end to glorify God and enjoy him forever. Yet these were rejections of the trappings and tropes of religion. Her mind, bred as she was, was saturated with the phrases of Biblical and theological speech. Phrases thus taught become as ineradicable as vocal dialect. They cannot be rejected; they can only be preserved or modified. Miss Dickinson in her soberer moments implied these modifications in scores of her lyrics on faith, hope, immortality, God;[1] but she summed them up in one which is utterly unorthodox and profoundly religious. In this, on first thought, she ranks poets first, and after them the sun, summer, and heaven; but, on second thought, she decides that to write "Poets" is "to comprehend the whole."[2]

---

[1] "Poems" (1930), pp. 20, 37, 167, 170, 174, 182, 195, 207, 217, 293, 305, 330, etc.

[2] Ibid. (1930), p. 280.

This poem is suggestive of Emerson in both form and tone, which is natural on every count. By temperament she must have been susceptible to his influence and, by experience, sympathetic to this other and more spectacular apostate from Calvinism. His volume of poems was given to her when she was nineteen; in that same year the book containing "Nature," "The American Scholar," and the "Divinity School Address" was published; and her brother and his wife, in the house at the other end of the path, were eager readers of the man who was more than once a guest there when he came lecturing to Amherst. Comparison of these two compounds of convention and revolt shows that she played on a wider keyboard than Emerson did in his published poems; at times she was more piquantly irreverent, and in her reverential moods she was more content to use the locutions of the Calvinists. But a fair comparison would liken the unrestraint in Miss Dickinson's poems with the unrestraint of Emerson's journals. Emerson's comments on his reverend grandfather's prayer for rain, on eugenics among the Brook Farmers, on the prosperous Unitarian tone of "In Memoriam," prove to be quite in Miss Dickinson's mocking vein, and many a passage on life, death, and immortality to be as acceptable to the users of orthodoxy's set phrases.

The likeness extends to matters of style also. How many fairly discriminating readers might be puzzled if asked to tell which of the poets wrote the following quatrains?

He who has no hands
Perforce must use his tongue;
Foxes are so cunning
Because they are not strong.

Ever the Rock of Ages melts
Into the mineral air,
To be the quarry whence to build
Thought and its mansions fair.

They are, in fact, both Emerson's; but it is doubtful if any but Emersoniacs and Emilists could be certain in their ascriptions, and even then the answer would depend more on recognition than on judgment. There is no need to infer from this resemblance that the younger poet was an imitator of the older or that she was an unconscious reflection of him. Genuinely creative artists usually go their own ways. A Van Gogh may be warped out of his orbit by successive discipleships; but they cease to govern him, and he comes back to his own ways. Yet an influence may be effective in reinforcing what "the candidate preliminary was." In the few cases when Miss Dickinson put herself in the way of receiving advice she rejected all suggestions as to form, sending Colonel Higginson more of the same kind with the bland query "Are these more orderly?" She may well have thought of Emerson as an ally when she did it, for she sent Mrs. Higginson "Representative Men," "a little granite book for you to lean on." The one recorded instance of accepted criticism was her two revisions, for "Sister Sue," of the later stanzas of "Safe in their alabaster chambers"; but these were not revisions of prosody.

Rather more than enough has been written about her versification. There is slight ground for either praise or blame for her departures from complete regularity. The outstanding facts about it are simple and obvious. She was primarily interested in what she had to say. She was not an experimenter in the modern sense. For her sententious verse she chose a few simple forms and was chiefly attentive to rhythms and stanzaic patterns. She inclined to employ rhymes, but to make no sacrifice for them and not very much exertion; and when the rhyming word did not occur she almost always used an assonant or alliterative word as a substitute. These are facts that statistically minded prosodists may confirm. There is also in the case a certain speculative factor which has been introduced by more than one discriminating critic. Perhaps the consciousness of not writing for immediate publication may often have relaxed her attention to minor details of form. Judged by her finest utterances she seems too much of an artist to have been equally content with these and with many of the notes and fragments that she left behind her. For the artist is keenly aware of the difference between a sketch and a finished painting, a poem and a note for a poem. Of course details of poetic technique can never raise more than secondary questions. Even the much objurgated Colonel Higginson was more interested in what she had to say than in the way she said it and, repeatedly asked to criticize, limited his criticisms to the surface, accepting the essence.

What one responds to in Miss Dickinson's pages is the indefinable, of which she spoke with her mentor in her natural poetic hyperbole: "If I read a book and it makes my whole body so cold no fire can ever warm me, I know *that* is poetry. If I feel physically as if the top of my head were taken off, I know *that* is poetry." [1] She herself communicates the thrills she was alluding to; but she does other things: she sets the imagination afloat in moods of quiet contemplation, and she produces a sheerly intellectual effect in the satisfaction caused by her deftness with words. Combined with her other gifts, the gift for epigram draws the mind back from flights of the imagination and complements feeling with thought:

Time is a test of trouble,
  But not a remedy.

Too much of proof affronts Belief.

  To fill a gap —
Insert the thing that caused it.

A load is first impossible
When we have put it down.[2]

Miss Dickinson was a believer in the theory of compensation. Her intensities of pain were measurable by her capacity for pleasure. "I find ecstasy in living," she said; "the mere sense of living is joy enough." She cannot tell how glad she is; she's a "tippler leaning against the sun." Childhood, sunlight, hope, laughter, are the things she believes in. There's a childlikeness in her like that of the youthful Wordsworth,

---

[1] "Letters," Vol. II, p. 315. [2] "Poems" (1930), pp. 196, 300, 321, 342.

when stream and forest were all-satisfying; but she is child and adult in one, temporarily sobered by thoughts of the being whose dwelling is the light of setting suns, the ocean, the air, and the mind of man.

Her place in literature seems secure. The reason for the oscillations of her popular repute lies in the superficial oscillations of popular taste. When she was first introduced to the public, she rode on a wave of literary virtuosity. "Triolets, villanelles, rondels, rondeaus," were in the air, and she was accepted with the writers of these dainty devices and forgotten with them. The volume of 1914 came out when poetry was ceasing to be a parlor accomplishment in the United States; but no volume of poems by a forgotten poet could be heard over the noise of the World War. In the following years, while readers were being educated steadily to enjoy poetry as poetry, there was a resurgence of experiment in poetic forms, in art forms of every kind. So the barriers were removed, and Miss Dickinson passed into her second and permanent reputation.

Henry Adams

Brooks Adams, brother of a famous brother, began a rambling essay on the heritage of Henry[1] with a precautionary set of warnings:

> I must admit frankly that Henry had certain intellectual peculiarities without allowing for which I deem it impossible to fully appreciate either the work he did or his way of doing it.
>
> And, to begin with, Henry was never, I fear, quite frank with himself or with others. . . . Also he dearly loved paradox, and nothing amused him more than propounding something which he knew would startle his guests or rouse in them the spirit of contradiction. . . . He knew perfectly well what he wished to imply and the response he sought to elicit, but to have explained himself would have spoiled his fun. . . . But I think in his "Education" he has carried his joke, at times, perhaps a little too far for his own fame.

---

[1] Brooks Adams, "The Heritage of Henry Adams," in "The Degradation of the Democratic Dogma," pp. 1–122.

For instance, he poses, more or less throughout his book, as having been a failure and a disappointed man. He was neither the one nor the other, as he knew well. He was not a failure, for he succeeded brilliantly in whatever he undertook, where success was possible; and he was not disappointed, for the world gave him everything he would take.[1]

Henry Adams would have said, in one of his favorite locutions, that "no one with the intelligence of an average monkey" could fail to detect these traits and allow for them. They are apparent from a reading of his biography and his autobiography and his voluminous correspondence; but his brother's warning is justified for the average monkey who will not study these thousand octavo pages.

Great-grandson and grandson of two presidents of the United States, son and secretary of the minister to England during the Civil War, his roots were planted in the eighteenth century, his education bridged the middle of the nineteenth, and his maturity carried him over the vast gap away from these and into the twentieth. Family-conscious and highly endowed, he was an intellectual aristocrat and something of a social snob. His inheritance of a competence and marriage to a fortune comfortably buttressed his independence of mind, made it possible for him to court unpopularity, write anonymously, print privately, and leave his greatest work for posthumous publication. It would have surpassed all his other paradoxes if he had been widely acclaimed in his own day. It is altogether reasonable that he has now emerged as a vital critic of American life and a searching inquirer into the whys and wherefores of human affairs.

The personal, picturesque, and paradoxical aspects of the man lead off into anecdotal paths away from literary history. Underlying these the essential Henry Adams was a contemplative man who progressively withdrew from the activities of diplomacy, journalism, and teaching to the life of the historian-philosopher, but who lived almost invisibly in the

---

[1] Ibid. pp. 1–6, passim. By permission of The Macmillan Company, publishers.

midst of things. He had a rare mind and great capacities as a scholar; somehow he contrived to maintain the scholar's calm and to refrain from hurry and hurriedness. Yet he was in constant contact with the most various sorts of people. He enjoyed polite society in the conventionally polite ways, while expressing polite scorn for it. Quietly unaggressive, he made it his business to become acquainted and to stay acquainted with such intellectual men as attracted him. He was an intimate of two of the pre-eminent American artists of his day. Through his connections with the key men he was from early young manhood better posted on what was going on at the national capitol than all but the rarest office-holders. And in the course of the years he piled up an immense mileage of travel: in western Europe; in the Near East; in Central America and North America; and, before the end, in the Far East and the islands of the Pacific, always in search of man as a social being and of some principle of control in his history. His knowledge of documents, which was vast, was built on the wide foundation of what he knew at first hand.

He began his background work for social history and criticism with a series of letters from London to Boston and New York papers which ended with his indiscretion in writing as an independent observer while he was secretary to the minister to England. Writing was resumed six years later with essays on history, finance, and American politics published in American and English reviews; it was continued during his editorship of the *North American Review*, at the period of his Harvard professorship, and was completed with his nine volumes of history of the administrations of Jefferson and Madison. He was past his fiftieth year; he had written thousands of pages of history in detail; he was ready to look for some controlling principles that could be interpreted in terms of cause and effect, that could explain the past and anticipate the directions in which society was moving. For many years, he wrote, he had lost himself in studying what the world had ceased to care for;

he must attempt now to find out what the mass of men did care for, and why. For himself, since "susceptibility to the highest force is the highest genius; selection between them is the highest science; their mass is the highest educator,"[1] his work was cut out to determine what these highest forces were and to see how, eventually, their mass became, or failed to become, operative on the mass of mankind. Was there in the field of history any principle to be evolved and applied that would affect society as basically as the philosophy of Rousseau had, or the teachings of Adam Smith, or the theories of Darwin?

I ask myself, What shape can be given to any science of history that will not shake to its foundation some prodigious interest? The world is made up of a few immense forces, each with an organization that corresponds with its strength. The church stands first; and at the outset we must assume that the church will not and cannot accept any science of history, because science, by its definition, must exclude the idea of an active and personal providence. The state stands next; and the hostility of the state would be assured toward any system or science that might not strengthen its arm. Property is growing more and more timid and looks with extreme jealousy on any new idea that may weaken vested rights. Labor is growing more and more self-confident and looks with contempt on all theories that do not support its own. Yet we cannot conceive of a science of history that would not, directly or indirectly, affect all these vast social forces.[2]

If "prodigious interests" and "vast social forces" could be unsettled, they could be only by showing something more prodigious and more vast of which these lesser interests and forces were merely manifestations. In his latter years Henry Adams, professional student of the Middle Ages and historian of his own country, confessed his ignorance in the possession of hoards of unrelated fact and set himself to find out what dominant force or succession of forces set them in motion and what direction had been given and would be

[1] "The Education of Henry Adams" (Houghton Mifflin), pp. 351, 352, 475.

[2] "Degradation of the Democratic Dogma," pp. 128–129. By permission of The Macmillan Company, publishers.

followed in human affairs. Setting himself to the task, he undertook the book which we know as

> "Mont-Saint-Michel and Chartres: a Study of Thirteenth-Century Unity." From that point he proposed to fix a position for himself, which he could label: "The Education of Henry Adams: a Study of Twentieth-Century Multiplicity." With the help of these two points of relation, he hoped to project his lines forward and backward indefinitely, subject to correction from anyone who should know better.[1]

Reduced to lowest terms his conclusions amounted to something like this: The curve of thought coincides with the accepted values of men.[2] Man behaves in accordance with his deep-seated presuppositions about life. By the thirteenth century Europe was committed to a Christian religion which dominated life, in which the concept of the Virgin, the Holy Mother, was pre-eminent. She was a goddess because she was a force; "she was reproduction — the greatest and most mysterious of all energies."[3] Being this she was the inspiration of man's highest art; and in the religion of which she was the dominant figure, and in the life controlled by that religion, she was evidence of a divine will which gave unity to all life and the illimitable hopes of approach toward perfectibility here and salvation hereafter. However, the Christian faith, Henry Adams saw, had been slowly surrendering ground to another force — the powers inherent in nature and slowly coming under human command, of which the dynamo could be taken as a symbol. The transformation performed by this new force was not merely material. All life had been readjusted to it until the factory and the skyscraper superseded the cathedral, and economics usurped the place of religion. The supernatural forces of the older day had been unseated by the natural forces of the present. Yet up to 1900 the thirteenth and nineteenth centuries fell back on one common assumption: physics taught what religion had — that the universe was a

---

[1] "Education" p. 435.
[2] "Democratic Dogma," p. 288.
[3] "Education," p. 384.

cosmos, ruled by laws of nature, an evidence of design. Then, quite suddenly, physics surrendered. Adams

> found himself in a land where no one had ever penetrated before; where order was an accidental relation obnoxious to nature; artificial compulsion imposed on motion; against which every free energy of the universe revolted; and which, being merely occasional, resolved itself back into anarchy at last. He could not deny that the law of the new multiverse explained much that had been most obscure, especially the persistently fiendish treatment of man by man; the perpetual effort of society to establish law, and the perpetual revolt of society against the law it had established; the perpetual building up of authority by force, and the perpetual appeal to force to overthrow it; the perpetual symbolism of a higher law, and the perpetual relapse to a lower one; the perpetual victory of the principles of freedom, and their perpetual reversion into principles of power; but the staggering problem was the outlook ahead into the despotism of artificial order which nature abhorred. The physicists had a phrase for it, unintelligible to the vulgar: "All that we win is a battle — lost in advance — with the irreversible phenomena in the background of nature." [1]

Adams was continually declaring of his work as a historian that he was not concerned with the correctness of scientific findings, but only with their direction along the paths of human thought. The same may be said of his inferences from them. Given the directions of science, the direction of the inferences from them was what Adams indicated. He himself was the proof; but he was also proof of the deep and incorrigible human repugnance to such inferences. He was unwilling to give up to them; he refused to admit that the universe could teach him nothing beyond the Pythagorean proposition. Self-respect demanded that he find something more fundamental and more satisfying. On this search he set forth in his old age, seeking "A Dynamic Theory of History," attempting to develop "A Law of Acceleration." [2] He came as far as to propound them, but had

[1] "Education," pp. 457, 458.

[2] "Education," Chaps. XXXIII, XXXIV; "Democratic Dogma," Chap. III.

to stop short of demonstration. The rest must be silence. It was time to go. Perhaps on his centenary, in 1938, he might return and then "for the first time since man began his education among the carnivores . . . find a world that sensitive and timid natures could regard without a shudder."[1] It is equally probable that he would not find such a world and that he would still refuse to surrender his hope.

In seeking his conclusions he proceeded as an erudite and patient investigator. He was tireless in pursuit of any path that offered a chance for reaching his goal. But in the statement of his conclusions he revealed the defects of his temperament. A philosophic study of the direction and the outcome of the human experiment does not happily lend itself to irony and paradox, as his apologist, Brooks Adams, was eager to explain; nor to a prevailing looseness in the use of terms which may be permitted the conversationalist — the continual exposition of chaos in terms of law, the idioms of evolution at off times when he was not repudiating the theory of evolution. Yet it is likely enough that the mood of disillusion and the tone of disillusion were both in part accountable for the wide acclaim which greeted his best-known book, "The Education," when it was first offered to the public in 1918 while the echoes of the World War were freshly reverberating. America found the war foreshadowed there and a confirmation of the prophecy. America ignored a foreshadowing of the economic collapse, preferring to reread Adams's political satire on a "Democracy" which was safely in the past.[2] And with that selective attention which makes any generation applaud what it agrees with, — a segment in the 1920's on the "curve of thought," to which Adams gave his latest study, — the public assented to his deep distrust of the tendencies of his time and, failing to read between the lines, overlooked his deeper distrust of the pessimism which to the end overshadowed him but never quite succeeded in overwhelming him.

---

[1] "Education," p. 505.

[2] See pages 740–742.

Book List

Individual Authors

AMBROSE GWINETT BIERCE. Chief published works appeared as follows: Tales of Soldiers and Civilians (later called "In the Midst of Life"), 1891; Can Such Things Be? 1893.

[*Available Editions*]

Battle Sketches by Ambrose Bierce, with engravings on wood by Thomas Derrick. 1930.

The Collected Works of Ambrose Bierce. 12 vols. 1909–1912.

Letters of Ambrose Bierce, edited by Bertha Clark Pope, with a memoir by George Sterling. 1922.

Ten Tales by Ambrose Bierce, with introduction by A. J. A. Symons. 1925.

Twenty-one Letters of Ambrose Bierce, edited, with a note, by Samuel Loveman. 1922.

[*Biography and Criticism*]

Anonymous. "A Collection of Bierce Letters," *University of California Chronicle,* Vol. XXXIV, pp. 30–48.

BOYNTON, PERCY H. More Contemporary Americans. 1927.

BROOKS, VAN WYCK. Emerson and Others. 1927.

DE CASTRO, ADOLPHE D. Portrait of Ambrose Bierce. 1929.

GRATTAN, C. HARTLEY. Bitter Bierce: a Mystery of American Letters. 1929.

MCWILLIAMS, CAREY. Ambrose Bierce: a Biography. 1929.

MCWILLIAMS, CAREY. "Ambrose Bierce and his First Love; an Idyl of the Civil War," *Bookman,* Vol. LXXV, pp. 254–259.

MENCKEN, H. L. "Ambrose Bierce." Prejudices, sixth series. 1927.

MILLER, ARTHUR M. "The Influence of Edgar Allan Poe on Ambrose Bierce," *American Literature,* Vol. IV, pp. 130–150.

MONAGHAN, FRANK. "Ambrose Bierce and the Authorship of 'The Monk and the Hangman's Daughter,'" *American Literature,* Vol. II, pp. 337–349.

NATHAN, G. J. "Ambrose Light," *American Spectator,* Vol. II, p. 2.

NATHAN, G. J. "Critical Presumptions — General." Passing Judgments. 1935.

NEALE, WALTER. Life of Ambrose Bierce. 1929.

PATTEE, FRED LEWIS. The Development of the American Short Story. 1923.

POLLARD, PERCIVAL. Their Day in Court. 1909.

STARRETT, VINCENT. Ambrose Bierce. 1920.

STERLING, GEORGE. "The Shadow Maker," *American Mercury,* Vol. VI, pp. 10–19.

WILT, NAPIER. "Ambrose Bierce and the Civil War," *American Literature,* Vol. I, pp. 260–285.

[*Bibliography*]

GAER, JOSEPH. Ambrose Gwinett Bierce: Bibliography and Biographical Data. 1935.

STARRETT, VINCENT. Ambrose Bierce: a Bibliography. 1929.

LAFCADIO HEARN. Chief works published as follows: Stray Leaves from Strange Literature, 1884; Some Chinese Ghosts, 1887; Chita: a Memory of Last Island, 1889; Youma, the Story of a West-Indian Slave, 1890; Glimpses of Unfamiliar Japan (2 vols.), 1894.

[*Available Editions*]

An American Miscellany. Criticisms and Stories now First Collected. Edited by Albert Mordell. 2 vols. 1924.

Appreciations of Poetry, selected and edited, with introduction, by John Erskine. 1916.

Books and Habits: from the Lectures of Lafcadio Hearn, selected and edited, with an introduction, by John Erskine. 1921.

Editorials by Lafcadio Hearn, edited by Charles W. Hutton. 1926.

Interpretations of Literature, selected and edited by John Erskine. 2 vols. 1915.

Kwaidan; Stories and Studies of Strange Things, with introduction by Oscar Lewis. 1932.

Life and Literature. Selections from Hearn. Edited by John Erskine. 1917.

Occidental Gleanings. Sketches and Essays now First Collected. Edited by Albert Mordell. 2 vols. 1925.

Pre-Raphaelite and Other Poets. Lectures by Lafcadio Hearn. Selected and edited by John Erskine. 1922.

Some New Letters and Writings of Lafcadio Hearn, collected and edited by Sanki Ichikawa. 1925.

Talks to Writers. From the Writings of Hearn. Edited by John Erskine. 1920.

The Writings of Lafcadio Hearn. 16 vols. 1922. (Of this set the last four volumes contain Hearn's Life and Letters, edited by Elizabeth Bisland).

[*Biography and Criticism*]

BAREL, LÉONA Q. The Idyl; My Personal Recollections of Lafcadio Hearn. 1933.

BECK, E. C. "Letters of Lafcadio Hearn to His Brother," *American Literature,* Vol. IV, pp. 167–173.

BISLAND, ELIZABETH (Ed.). Life and Letters of Lafcadio Hearn. 2 vols. 1906.

BOYNTON, PERCY H. More Contemporary Americans. 1927.

GOULD, GEORGE M. Concerning Lafcadio Hearn. 1908.

KENNARD, NINA. Lafcadio Hearn. 1912.

KOIZUMI, KAZUO. Father and I; Memories of Lafcadio Hearn. 1935.

LEWIS, OSCAR. Hearn and His Biographers. 1930.

NOGUCHI, YONE. Lafcadio Hearn in Japan. 1910.

TEMPLE, JEAN. Blue Ghost: a Study of Lafcadio Hearn. 1931.

THOMAS, EDWARD. Lafcadio Hearn. 1912.

TINKER, EDWARD. Lafcadio Hearn's American Days. 1924.

[*Bibliography*]

PERKINS, P. D. and IONE. Lafcadio Hearn: a Bibliography of his Writings, with introduction by Sanki Ichikawa. 1934.

SISSON, MARTHA H. Lafcadio Hearn: a Bibliography. 1933.

STEDMAN, LAURA. Bibliography. Arranged for the Life of Hearn by G. M. Gould. 1908.

EMILY DICKINSON. Chief volumes, all posthumous: Poems, 1890; Poems (second series), 1892; Poems (third series), 1896.

[*Recent Editions*]

The Complete Poems of Emily Dickinson, with introduction by Martha Dickinson Bianchi. 1924.

Emily Dickinson Face to Face: Unpublished Letters, with Notes and Reminiscences, edited by Martha D. Bianchi. 1932.

Further Poems of Emily Dickinson, edited by Martha D. Bianchi. 1929.

Letters of Emily Dickinson, edited by Mabel Loomis Todd. 2 vols. 1894, 1931.

Poems of Emily Dickinson, edited by Martha D. Bianchi and Alfred L. Hampson. 1930.

Selected Poems of Emily Dickinson, edited by Conrad Aiken. 1924.

The Single Hound; Poems of a Lifetime, with introduction by Martha D. Bianchi. 1914.

"Unpublished Poems of Emily Dickinson," *New England Quarterly*, Vol. V, pp. 217–220. (Six poems collected by Margaret H. Barney and Frederic I. Carpenter.)

[*Biography and Criticism*]

AIKEN, CONRAD. "Emily Dickinson," *Dial*, Vol. LXXVI, pp. 301–308.

BIANCHI, MARTHA D. The Life and Letters of Emily Dickinson. 1924.

BLOOM, MARGARET. "Emily Dickinson and Dr. Holland." *University of California Chronicle*, Vol. XXXV, pp. 96–103.

BLUNDEN, EDMUND. "Emily Dickinson," *Nation and Athenaeum*, Vol. XLVI, p. 863.

BROWN, ROLLO W. "A Sublimated Puritan," *Saturday Review of Literature*, Vol. V, pp. 186–187.

CHADWICK, HELEN. "Emily Dickinson: a Study," *Personalist*, Vol. X, pp. 256–269.

HIGGINSON, THOMAS WENTWORTH. "Emily Dickinson." Carlyle's Laugh, and Other Surprises. 1909.

JENKINS, MACGREGOR. Emily Dickinson, Friend and Neighbor. 1930.

KELEHER, JULIA. "The Enigma of Emily Dickinson," *New Mexico Quarterly*, Vol. II, pp. 326–332.

KREYMBORG, ALFRED. "The Tippler against the Sun." Our Singing Strength. 1929.

MCLEAN, SYDNEY R. "Emily Dickinson at Mt. Holyoke," *New England Quarterly*, Vol. VI, pp. 25–42.

MILES, SUSAN. "The Irregularities of Emily Dickinson," *London Mercury*, February, 1926.

MORAN, HELEN. "Queens Now," *London Mercury*, June, 1932.

POHL, F. J. "The Emily Dickinson Controversy," *Sewanee Review*, Vol. XLI, pp. 467–482.

POLLITT, JOSEPHINE. Emily Dickinson; the Human Background of Her Poetry. 1930.

SAPIR, EDWARD. "Emily Dickinson, a Primitive," *Poetry*, Vol. XXVI, pp. 97–105.

SCHAPPES, MORRIS U. "Errors in Mrs. Bianchi's Edition of Emily Dickinson's Letters," *American Literature*, Vol. IV, pp. 369–384.

TAGGARD, GENEVIEVE. The Life and Mind of Emily Dickinson. 1930.

TODD, MABEL LOOMIS. "Emily Dickinson's Literary Debut," *Harper's*, Vol. CLX, pp. 403–471.

UNTERMEYER, LOUIS. "Emily Dickinson," *Saturday Review of Literature*, Vol. VI, pp. 1169–1171.

UNTERMEYER, LOUIS. "Thoughts after a Centenary," *Saturday Review of Literature*, Vol. VII, pp. 905–906.

WELLS, ANNA. "Early Criticism of Emily Dickinson," *American Literature*, Vol. I, pp. 243–259.

WHICHER, GEORGE F. "A Chronological Grouping of Some of Emily Dickinson's Poems," *Colophon*, March, 1934.

WHICHER, GEORGE F. "Emily Dickinson's Earliest Friend," *American Literature*, Vol. VI, pp. 3–18.

[*Bibliography*]

HAMPSON, ALFRED L. Emily Dickinson; a Bibliography. 1930.

WHICHER, GEORGE F. Foreword to "Emily Dickinson; a Bibliography." 1930.

HENRY ADAMS. Chief titles: Democracy, an American Novel, 1880; Historical Essays, 1891; Mont-Saint-Michel and Chartres, 1904; The Education of Henry Adams, 1918; The Degradation of the Democratic Dogma, 1919.

[*Biography and Criticism*]

ADAMS, HENRY. The Education of Henry Adams. 1918. (Autobiography.)

ADAMS, JAMES TRUSLOW. The Adams Family. 1930.

ADAMS, JAMES TRUSLOW. Henry Adams. 1933.

ADAMS, JAMES TRUSLOW. "Henry Adams and the New Physics," *Yale Review*, Vol. XIX, pp. 283–302.

BEACH, JOSEPH WARREN. The Outlook for American Prose. 1926.

BECKER, CARL. "Henry Adams Once More," *Saturday Review of Literature*, Vol. IX, pp. 521, 524.

FORD, WORTHINGTON C. (Ed.). A Cycle of Adams Letters. 1920.

FORD, WORTHINGTON C. (Ed.). Letters of Henry Adams; 1858–1891. 1930.

HOWE, M. A. DE WOLFE. "The Elusive Henry Adams," *Saturday Review of Literature*, Vol. VII, pp. 237–239.

MORE, PAUL ELMER. Commemorative Tribute to Henry Adams. 1922.

[*Bibliography*]

ADAMS, JAMES TRUSLOW. Henry Adams, pp. 213–229. 1930.

[*Anthologies*]

CARGILL, OSCAR. The Social Revolt. 1933.

FOERSTER, NORMAN. American Poetry and Prose (rev. ed.). 1934.

KREYMBORG, ALFRED. Lyric America. 1930.

STEDMAN and HUTCHINSON. Library of American Literature, Vol. XI.

UNTERMEYER, LOUIS. Modern American Poetry. 1913–1930.

WANN, LOUIS. The Rise of Realism. 1933.

CHAPTER XIII

Democracy and the Dynamo

The Temper of the 1890's

IT MAY have been an accident in time or it may have sprung from a consciousness that a century was ending, but the 1890's, like several other tenth decades, were more than averagely eventful and provocative. In the literary stratum of the English-speaking world the passing of a generation of writers was enough to give one pause. Within a few years of 1890 came the deaths of Arnold, Ruskin, Morris, Carlyle, Tennyson, Browning, as well as Emerson, Longfellow, Melville, Lowell, Whitman, Whittier, Holmes, Mrs. Stowe. The readers of poetry in English were recalling Emerson's "Terminus," Longfellow's "Ultima Thule," Whitman's "Good-Bye, My Fancy," Whittier's "Lifetime," Tennyson's "Crossing the Bar," Browning's "Asolando." Hamlin Garland, young Western upstart, might discredit the torchbearers in his essay on "Crumbling Idols," but the public could see no evident successors nor any clear promise of them. The leaders of the next generation were either silent or unheard; and in the meanwhile, though some of the elders had sounded their alarms, what most men remembered were the faith in the established order of Tennyson and Longfellow, the ultimate optimism of Emerson and Whitman. It was not yet orthodox to question the refrain that Pippa sang as she passed, and there seemed to be only minor occasions for justifying the ways of man to God. On the whole, in Anglo-Saxondom the assumption stood that the moral order prevailed.

What really prevailed, however, in both England and America was a set of idioms of speech which had the most superficial of relations to the actions they accompanied. Men were not ready to admit the implications of what the findings of science were doing to philosophy and Protestant orthodoxy, or of what the applications of science were doing to social life. Yet, as society surrenders more readily to the inventor than to the philosopher, Maxwell and Marconi and the Wright brothers and the maker of the gasoline engine were on the way toward a victory in an America which was still well intrenched in the church and the market place against Darwin and Marx. So the fortune makers, indebted to the machine for their wealth, were bulwarks of the political order under which they had made it, and also bulwarks of the church, and ostentatious in the new fashion of expiatory benevolence.

The measure of value in a generation is indicated in the measure of its pre-eminently enviable man. He may be not what the generation would advertise as its ideal, but rather the tacit formula of what youth would like to become and of what elders covet for their children, better embodied than put into words. It is fairly clear that in seventeenth-century New England, Cotton Mather was such a figure; in eighteenth-century Virginia, William Byrd, gentleman; in Revolutionary days, Benjamin Franklin, journalist, inventor, legislator, diplomat, commoner; in pre-war nineteenth century, John Jacob Astor, empire builder. At the turn of the century Theodore Roosevelt played this role.

He was proud citizen in a land where a secure economic system was conserved against all foes by the Republican party, and he was reinforced in his conviction by pulpit and press.[1] A Brooklyn clergyman declaimed that the Democratic platform of 1896 was composed in hell. *The New York Tribune* explained after election that Bryan had been defeated because right was right, and God was God. But the situation was confusing; there were abuses within the system, and even

[1] For the following passage see Henry F. Pringle's "Theodore Roosevelt, a Biography" (a lavishly documented volume), pp. 162–511, passim.

the men Roosevelt chose to describe as "malefactors of great wealth" were appealing to God. It was proper enough for President McKinley to "pray for light and guidance" before evolving a Rooseveltian imperialistic program; but it was embarrassing when Baer, the mine operator, defied Roosevelt and the public with the declaration that God in his infinite wisdom had given control of the property interests of the country into the right hands. The problem for Roosevelt, in the formula acceptable to his day, was to wage a moral warfare in behalf of the existing order, carrying it in two directions: he must fight malefactors from within, and he must overwhelm "all the lunatics, all the idiots, all the knaves, all the cowards, all the honest people who are slow-witted" — all the people of every stripe who condemned themselves by voting opposition tickets. Business and righteousness were in alliance; if they were not, they ought to be; at any rate, he was the Conscience of Big Business. Equipped with a confessed ignorance of economic fact or theory and a wavering policy, but with an assertive sense of righteousness and fine dramatic instinct, he became a moral champion of popular causes. He borrowed liberal doctrines from those whom he abused; but no Republican could surpass him in fear of ultra-liberal doctrines or in his power of vilifying those who espoused them. His tactics were popular. Each generation has its abusive epithet for the liberals and a way of identifying it with everything villainous. It was what the Federalists did a hundred years earlier when they damned a man by calling him a republican. Roosevelt stood like a Colossus, fending off the wrong people on the right wing and all the people on the left wing with the same salvo of abuse for both. It was spectacularly effective.

As the years passed he appealed more and more successfully to the Anglo-Saxon love of a moral principle identified with material interests. He was champion of the square deal, dispenser of substantial justice, trust buster; political knight-errant against naughty rich men, malignant poor men, despoilers of the national honor, foreign aggressors; excoriator of muckrakers, nature fakers, members of the Ananias Club. He was sportsman, hunter, soldier. He left the White House for the wilds of Africa and came back to "stand at Armageddon and battle for the Lord." He smashed the now wicked Republican party, singing "Onward, Christian Soldiers." And Americans idolized him because he was so essentially their man. He was the first President who had not been enveloped in official dignities, the only one for whom a nursery toy was ever named. Americans reveled in a blend of strenuosity and moral fervor whom John Morley in one mood could describe as a combination of St. Vitus and St. Paul and in another could compare to Niagara Falls. They shared his satisfaction with the general economic situation and his solicitudes for it. They had just been aroused by the war with Spain, and shared his militant nationalism. They could understand his explosive talk. "I have to use bromides in my business," he explained in confidence. And they swarmed to support him as crusader, wielder of the sword of the Lord.

A more or less comfortable conservatism supplied the background for the national picture. Religiously the country was still what it was when Emerson commented on a people who assumed that divine revelation was ended "as if God were dead," and when Thoreau deplored a ministry who could not bear all kinds of opinions. The disinclination for solid discussion on any solid theme and the desire to hush up disturbing argument, sometimes charged to the repressive influence of Puritanism, was merely the perennial first defense of conservatism. Naturally and unfortunately the healthy English practice of heckling was frowned down. All public speakers were privileged; challengers were hissed or, if persistent, were hustled out as disturbers of the peace. Yet it was not easy for the liberal to get a hearing from the respectable. Women speakers, half feared and half respected, were regarded as socially not quite desirable. One could never tell when and how they might break out. Marked liberals were contemptuously disposed of as cranks.

In New England — at the "Hub" — the mildly inquiring organizations of an earlier day were in a decline. The old Town and Gown Club was a thing of the past; so was the Radical Club, whose name belies it, but whose informal programs for fifteen years after the Civil War had ventilated the intellectual atmosphere; and the Concord School of Philosophy had crept into Bronson Alcott's grave. The South, reconstructed but unregenerate,[1] was even less adventurous of mind. It looked back with pride on an old culture, with yearning to a departed social order, with solicitude on the invasions of industrialism, and in Southern Methodism and Hard-Shell Baptistry it supplied the final strongholds for decadent Puritanism. The West, not yet clearly articulate, partook of its Eastern heritage.

Yet there were signs that the country was waking up and that the kind of criticism which Cooper and Hawthorne, Emerson and Thoreau, Lowell and Melville, had uttered, which Whitman and Mark Twain had partly uttered and partly suppressed,[2] and which the country had agreed to ignore or deride, was soon to receive a hearing. The lazy assumption that a manifest destiny for America absolved the average citizen from civic responsibility was up for challenge; and the magnificent isolation theory, which freed the United States from participation in world affairs and all obligation for world welfare, was upset before the decade was over by the rude fact of the war with Spain. An awakened national self-consciousness made America consider its ways and look to its relationships, and the literature of the day reflects these changes.

As to the domestic sentiments in the country during the decade, all the basic institutions were touched. The respectable citizen began to realize that government did not run itself, and that, particularly in the large cities, it could be no better than the machinery of a government which was com-

[1] See the first essay, by John Crowe Ransom, in "I'll Take My Stand, the South and Agrarian Tradition," by Twelve Southerners.

[2] See pages 403, 404, and 645.

posed of men with the apt title of "practical politicians." The politicians had been led to be practical by the persuasive ways of capital, which, since the days of John Jacob Astor, had seen that it was easier to buy political action than to bother with the details. Frederick Townsend Martin, traitor to his class, stated the case simply and blandly:

> The class I represent care nothing for politics . . . we are the rich; we own America; we got it, God knows how, but we intend to keep it if we can by throwing all the tremendous weight of our support . . . against any legislature, any political platform, any presidential campaign that threatens the integrity of our estate.[1]

Naturally civil service reform was aimed at the active corruptionists; and legislation aimed at wealth, the large employer, and "the bloated bondholder" followed. While this house cleaning was in its early stages liberalism was arising in the Protestant churches, and a resultant series of heresy trials marked the same conflict between orthodoxy and modernism that was to rise once more in the 1920's with the activities of the so-called Fundamentalists. Again, with the continued agitation for equal suffrage that had been mooted since the 1840's, the shift in the political and economic status of woman at last began an effective challenge to the archaic theory of the home, in which man was master and wife was subject and chattel. And at the same time a thoroughgoing change in the attitude toward the child, in home and school, led through kindergarten and elementary grades on the long trail that wound later to the high school and finally to the college, proceeding all the way on the assumption that youngsters should be not schooled chiefly in docility but stimulated to independence of thought and action.

It was only fresh beginnings that were being made in these directions, but they were enough to disturb the complacent American who was grown used to regarding himself as the norm of the universe. In spite of his resistance, it became increasingly safe to inquire of him as to the infallibility of

[1] C. A. and M. R. Beard, "The Rise of American Civilization," Vol. II, p. 303.

the scriptures, Biblical or constitutional, or democratic equality in America as tested by the facts, or the possibility of error among the fathers of American history; or even to ask quite respectfully exactly what was meant by the nobility of womanhood as contrasted with any other nobility, or what was peculiarly dignified in the dignity of labor.

Awakening Nationalism

Thus the acknowledgment was being variously made during these years that Americans could not continue a life of romantic evasions while a world of facts was staring them in the face. In his unexcited way Henry Adams threw out a challenge to the historians that Turner and Beard and Nevins and Schlesinger and Dodd were to accept before long. "What shape," he asked, "can be given to any science of history that will not shake to its foundations some prodigious interest?"[1] His answer was that any but the most uncritical was bound to come into conflict with the intrenched forms of government, church, organized wealth, or organized labor. Already Bryce's "American Commonwealth" had presented the American democracy as it was instead of as Crèvecœur predicted or Barlow dreamed. Ostrogorski's "Democracy and the Organization of Political Parties" carried the investigation a step farther. Thorstein Veblen, in his "Theory of the Leisure Class," mocked the old-fashioned economists who were eager defenders of capitalism. The memory of Edward Bellamy's "Looking Backward" was recent and vivid; and the conversion of Howells to Tolstoyan doctrines, attested in "A Traveler from Altruria" and "The Eye of a Needle," gave fresh point to a realism which had seemed lackadaisical to many an impatient critic. The self-consciousness that leads to introspection was on the rise in the country when the war broke with Spain.

But this, like all appeals to arms, put an end for the moment to any popular feeling but perfervid and militant

[1] "Democratic Dogma," p. 128.

patriotism. Weir Mitchell had already written "Hugh Wynne" before the hostilities began. Published serially, it boomed the circulation of *Scribner's* and ran through many a book edition in the following year. Mary Johnston's "To Have and to Hold" and Paul Leicester Ford's "Janice Meredith" were equally popular; and Winston Churchill's series, "Richard Carvel," "The Crisis," and "The Crossing," met with a total circulation that few novelists of substance have ever rivaled. No doubt the mood of national glorification stimulated the writing of historical novels as well as the market for them. It was no time for popular realism. The days of the founders were remote, picturesque, and fruitful in heroic legend. It was pleasant to look back on them and, in the latter days of imminent imperialism, to feel that the manifest destiny was being wrought out in a fashion worthy of the forefathers.

This is what throws Churchill into relief against the buoyant patriotism of the moment. He wrote most and was read most in the heyday of the historical romancers. He did not employ the past, as Hovey did, in order to treat of a perennial human problem without the distraction of incidental modernisms; and he did not employ it as Shaw and Cabell and Moeller and Hagedorn and Untermeyer and Erskine were to do in order to bring the ancients down to date. He was content to follow the example of Walter Scott in using speech, manners, and actions of the past while he told good stories of the past. He was quite uncritical of what he found there — less than Scott was, but no more so than his public or than his contemporaries who were doing the same thing.

A deliberate workman and a good deal of a student, he succeeded in re-creating the aspects of the past that interested him — the landscapes, houses, costumes, speech, manners, episodes, of his periods. A certain courtliness prevails in his works, even in "The Crossing," whose setting is far from the court, and in "The Crisis," in which courtly ways are survivals from a receding past. But if he liked good manners, he also admired sturdy character and believed in it as a constant in American life. Richard Carvel, forthright democrat, put to shame the fops and roués of the Old World; David Ritchie, bold and steady, was an ideal frontiersman; Stephen Brice, sturdy young Yankee, held his own among the rebels in St. Louis. Churchill assumed that American history had been made by men who were moved like these men, by high principle; and that their descendants would be the safeguards of the future. It was easy for him to go on to the further assumption that a country filled with simple, upright citizens would automatically enjoy a simple, upright government. He was soon to learn, however, that passive respectability, which regards itself as its own excuse for being, is anything but a political asset, and to show what he had learned in his next tale, "Coniston"; but that is transitional both in the period of American history it deals with and in its whole tone and temper, belonging with the fiction on "the square deal."[1]

The novel was not the only literary vehicle for militant nationalism at the time, nor Winston Churchill the only author sensitive to shifting currents of national feeling. Richard Hovey was far more susceptible to influence and far more emphatic in response. He was the most picturesque, histrionic, emotional American poet of his period, hardly rivaled in these respects since then by anyone except Jack London. Gayest of college students, most sentimental of Dartmouth alumni, Hovey was prince of good fellows, most engaging of talkers. Naturally he became lyrist for his college, odist for his fraternity. For a while a crowd of good fellows and a stein on the table represented the glory of life for him. Then the love of the road seized him. He reveled in the thought of vagabondage, wrote three volumes anent it with Bliss Carman, and indulged in very little of it, contenting himself with the idea. He decided to become a high-church priest; studied Hebrew; affected, as always, the extremest of dress; observed all the offices of monastic worship; and left the seminary to become a newspaper reporter.

---

[1] See pages 754–762.

Then for a little while he was an actor. He read papers at the summer sessions of Thomas Davidson's school at Farmington, Connecticut, translated Maeterlinck and Mallarmé, espoused Delsartism, everywhere the center of a tableau, everywhere talking good talk, everywhere posturing in the costumes that were necessary to his dramatic daily life.

With the outbreak of the war with Spain he became a thoroughgoing jingo. In the excited self-righteousness after the sinking of the battleship *Maine* he published in the *New York World* "The Word of the Lord from Havana" and helped to inflame the country by circulating the slogan for revenge:

Ye who remembered the Alamo,
Remember the Maine!
Ye who unfettered the slave,
Break a free people's chain! [1]

Two months later, excited beyond measure by the immediate issue, he nationalized God and deified war, not only justifying America against Spain, but, regardless of the lessons of history, declaring that the race could develop only through the repetition of past experience:

By strife as well as loving — strife,
The law of Life, —
In brute and man the climbing has been done
And shall be done hereafter. Since man was,
No upward-climbing cause
Without the sword has ever yet been won.[2]

He joined all the chauvinists of that springtime of 1898 in idealizing war in order to defend what he regarded as the national altruism behind the war with a decadent European power; and he anticipated the various types of determinists in his declaration that humankind are in subjection to established and invariable modes of behavior.

But this was not his philosophy. He believed quite otherwise, being merely more than normally subject to the power

---

[1] "Along the Trail" (Dodd, Mead), pp. 4, 5.

[2] Ibid. p. 15.

of war psychology. He was at work at the time on his "Guenevere, a Poem in Dramas," an ambitious cycle never to be completed; and in *The Bookman* of December, 1898, he was quoted as saying:

> My next work of considerable extent — it won't be begun for several years — will elaborate in a similar way, certain aspects of politics; and I presume that my old age will be devoted to a series of poetical works in which the religious thought will be the central theme.

Two years later he died.

It is one of the many distinctions of William Vaughn Moody that he was able to withstand war hysteria as few poets have done. Though the total impression from Moody's poems is one of more than epic breadth, he did not maintain his wider sympathies at the cost of turning his back on his own time and land. In a clear, objective way he loved his mother's prairie country of Indiana, both for its rich expanse and for the harvests with which it could "feed a universe at need." Before the vogue of civic celebrations had developed he marshaled, in the memorable third stanza of the "Ode in Time of Hesitation," the most splendid pageant of America that has yet been imagined. In that vernal lyric he compacted into a few lines all his confident hopes for his country's future. Cape Ann children seeking arbutus, hill lads of Tennessee harking to the wild geese on their northern flight, were one with the youthfulness of Chicago, the renewing green of the Western wheat fields, the unrolling of the rivers down the white Sierras, the downward creep of Alaskan glaciers, the perennial palm crown of Hawaii. It was, in truth,

> the eagle nation Milton saw
> Mewing its mighty youth.[1]

But his love for America was more than rhetorical. He felt the perils that threatened its youth. Within its boundaries he flinched at the economic dangers that menaced it. "Gloucester Moors" admits his solicitude if not his fear at

---

[1] William Vaughn Moody, "Poems" (Houghton Mifflin, 1900), p. 23.

the "sounds from the noisome hold" in the ship of America, which was aimless on the high seas. There is no hope in this poem — only speculation and distress; but in "The Brute," whether it was a new-found confidence or only a different lyric mood, there is a sweeping optimism. As a nation among nations he felt that America was a land to rejoice in only when it was right. He was full of concern while the country was being swept into excited jingoism in the first intoxication of imperial outreach. He was never more proud than when in "The Quarry" he recorded Secretary Hay's frustration of the plans for partitioning China among the European powers, yet never more indignant than when he began to suspect that the defense of downtrodden subjects was advanced only as a subterfuge for seizing sugar plantations and naval bases. He never wrote in support of the war. While its echoes were still reverberating he challenged its motives — not those alleged, but the motives of the money-changers who traduced the soldiery to "cheat and scramble in the market place of war." He lamented the passing of Whitman's strong spirit and Whittier's yearning wrath, though he had kept his head better than they. He hoped that the soldier fallen in the Philippines might

> never dream that his bullet's scream went wide of its island mark,
> Home to the heart of his darling land where she stumbled and sinned in the dark.[1]

And he threatened the men in Washington that if they actually "put to hire" the conquest bought with blood and life,

> on your guiltier head
> Shall our intolerable self-disdain
> Wreak suddenly its anger and its pain;
> For manifest in that disastrous light
> We shall discern the right
> And do it, tardily. — O ye who lead,
> Take heed!
> Blindness we may forgive, but baseness we will smite.[2]

[1] Moody, op. cit. p. 30. [2] Ibid. p. 25.

Conscious Cosmopolitanism

This militant self-consciousness of the United States was stimulated by an increasing awareness of Europe as a seat of ancient cultures that were bearing new fruits in the present. Until toward the end of the century American literary education had been almost exclusively rooted in the classics. The superstition still survived in all its confusedness that the employment of Latin and Greek grammar as an instrument of discipline for schoolboys, and the employment of classical literature as something for boys to construe at so many pages of prose or so many lines of verse per day, combined in the performance of some cultural miracle. Modest excursions had been made in the use of modern languages and literatures in the early decades of the nineteenth century, and at Harvard in 1818 George Ticknor had begun the work that was to be followed for sixty years in a limited way by himself and Longfellow and Lowell. Yet at the close of the century it was still a rare American who could read or speak a foreign language unless he was born to it, or who had even so tenuous an acquaintance with any recent masterpieces as he had with certain of the Greek and Latin classics. The end of the century brought with it a kind of rediscovery of modern Europe that gained something of a hearing for several representative critics of the day. Of these none was more substantial or enduring than William Crary Brownell.

Brownell was in his way expositor of the critical philosophy that forty years later came to be described as the New Humanism and that forty years earlier had been extensively propounded by Arnold and less explicitly by Lowell. So similar in doctrine was this American to his English predecessor that one might easily attribute to Brownell the definition of criticism that Arnold formulated: "Of the literature of France and Germany, as of the intellect of Europe in general, the main effort, for now many years, has been a critical effort; the endeavor, in all branches of knowledge, theology, philosophy, history, art, science, to see the object as in itself it really is."[1] And with a simple change of the national adjective he might have added, as Arnold did, that "owing to the operation in [American] literature of certain causes, almost the last thing for which one would come to [American] literature is just that very thing which now Europe most desires — criticism."

It was Brownell's endowment, as his one-time disciple, Stuart Sherman, acknowledged of him,[2] to be "more abundantly supplied with those general ideas in which the permanent value of critical writing largely resides" than almost any of his contemporaries. It was his gift to write solidly and trenchantly. It was his fortune to be living in a day when an increasing audience was developing and to enjoy at the very end of his career a reputation that he had been deserving for thirty years.

His especial work in the 90's was to lead the way toward a fresh evaluation of American life and character by setting up a comparison with the French. His writing began with "French Traits" (1889) and "French Art" (1892); it was carried on in four volumes of specifically literary criticism — "Victorian Prose Masters" (1901), "American Prose Masters" (1909), "Criticism" (1914), and "The Genius of Style" (1924); and it was rounded out, with discussion of general ideas and permanent values, in "Standards" (1917) and his valedictory volumes of 1927 — "Democratic Distinction in America" and "The Spirit of Society."

The spirit and purpose of his entire doctrine was foreshadowed in his first book, an analysis of French culture as an index to French character and a determinant of it. It is sound enough in its judgments to have stood the test of forty years. In its concluding chapter, or postlude, "New York after Paris," is a comparison for the reader who may not have made it, of the two national characters as symbolized in their leading cities. Brownell did not achieve wide popularity. His writing was too austere, too rigorously intellectual. Although

[1] "Essays in Criticism" (New York, 1883), p. 1.
[2] Stuart P. Sherman, "Points of View," p. 90.

he contributed to the rediscovery of Europe by the America of the 90's, he did not write in the spirit of the discoverer or of the exhorter. To some of his contemporaries the culture of western Europe was a novel and exciting phenomenon that encouraged them to the abandonment of critical standards. To Brownell it was neither new nor exciting, and it served to reinforce him in his belief in standards. He became and remained a distinguished spokesman for the Party of Culture in the ensuing controversy with the Party of Nature, always uttering what he had to say in the light of his declaration that the end of a critic's effort "is a true estimate of the data encountered in the search for that beauty which from Plato to Keats has been virtually identified with truth, and the highest service of criticism is to secure that the true and the beautiful, and not the ugly and the false, may in wider and wider circles of appreciation be esteemed to be the good."[1]

This was not the substance nor the tone by which to attract popular attention in the early 90's. It was uncalculated and unqualified to stir the group of Americans who were giving their "Hear, hears" to Garland's "Crumbling Idols" or chuckling at the sprightly essays of Harry Thurston Peck, the critical N. P. Willis of this latter day. Peck's writings have sunk to oblivion, but the discussion of his influence by the author of "The Mauve Decade" reminds us of his temporary importance. In those years when the up-to-date were acquiring merit by their gains in literary sophistication, Peck and others, says Thomas Beer, "did what they could, in varying ways, for the European continent in letters."[2] This was largely to display an ostentatious familiarity with obscure Continental authors. A glance at Peck's pages, sprinkled with names of minor luminaries, many of which have escaped even the cyclopedias, makes it easy to understand why he was described as having a mind like a goldfish, "everlastingly drawn by some bright object to the glass of its tank." And

[1] Brownell, "Criticism," p. 85.

[2] "The Mauve Decade," p. 197. Reprinted by permission of, and special arrangement with, Alfred A. Knopf, Inc., authorized publishers.

there is further significance in the paragraph with which Beer follows this metaphor, for it appears that the mind of the sophomoric critic was continually "swirling off in fright to shelter in weeds."[1] Nietzsche startled him, Ingersoll scared him, George Moore annoyed him. "He wanted to be mundane, and . . . honestly strove to be liberal," but he was beset by "the Puritan ghost."[2] He was indeterminate and vacillating because in his emancipation he found himself, in contrast with Brownell, without any basic belief. So there could be no defined issue between them, Peck's courage failing him at the very point of challenging the standards to which Brownell was committed.

James Gibbons Huneker, a man whose star was rising as Peck's waned, was a critic of far higher specific gravity. Huneker began publishing just before the turn of the century, and for many years was a sort of general guide to Continental culture. Possibly his Roman Catholic upbringing accounts for his quick responsiveness to much that was European, his liking for religious ceremonial, his consistent deference to the writings of Cardinal Newman. He was schooled in music, versed in pictorial and plastic art, theatergoer and playreader, facile and energetic writer. The number of subjects on which he could pronounce with some expertness was impressive; the extent of his reading and allusive power was wide and varied. His "Iconoclasts, a Book of Dramatists" was the first substantial work by an American on any drama later than the Elizabethan; his books on music — "Mezzotints," "Overtones," "Melomaniacs" — and the studies of "Chopin" and "Liszt" were equally solid; no less so, "Promenades of an Impressionist," mainly on painting, or his "New Cosmopolis," on modern capital cities, or his various autobiographical volumes.

Yet he was under such incessant journalistic pressure to make copy (thousands of words a week) that his comments on the seven arts were almost invariably in the nature of

---

[1] "The Mauve Decade," p. 191. [2] Ibid. p. 197.

specific evaluations, almost never in the broad, and his allusions were limited to specific artists and works of art. He said that a critic should have an artistic credo; but he never had time to state his own, and as he was no dogmatist it is hardly possible to deduce one from his effusions. He impresses one always as having had the technical knowledge requisite for criticism, but of having gained it on the run and of having never taken the time to meditate on what he had seen or to set it against a background of generalizations or constants. Vivacious and informative as his pages are, they become the pages of the connoisseur rather than of the critic.

He had, however, the double superiority to Peck of knowing what he was talking about and of expressing himself without fear or favor, and the advantage over Brownell of an infectious enthusiasm.

> That gusto of his is two-thirds of his story. It is unquenchable, contagious, inflammatory. . . . One feels, reading him, that he is charmed by the men and women he writes about, and that their ideas, even when he rejects them, give him an agreeable stimulation. And to the charm that he thus finds and exhibits in others, he adds the very positive charm of his own personality. He seems a man who has found the world fascinating, if perhaps not perfect; a friendly and good-humored fellow; no frigid scholiast, but something of an epicure, in brief the reverse of the customary maker of books about books."[1]

It is a gusto that led him into crazy-boy extravagances of speech and that made him interminably sing the praises of Pilsner; but it won him many readers when a roster of contemporary European writers was being translated from unknown names in the United States to household words in the homes of the reading public. No single man had more to do with bringing about this change.

One of the early fruits of literary self-consciousness in the country in the 90's — it deserves hardly more than a paren-

---

[1] Reprinted from H. L. Mencken's "Book of Prefaces," pp. 159, 160, by permission of, and special arrangement with, Alfred A. Knopf, Inc., authorized publishers.

thesis — was the epidemic of little precious periodicals, of which *The Chap Book* (1893–1897) was the most distinguished, and *The Philistine* (1897–1916) the longest-lived. In the winter of 1896–1897 they sprang up and died like midges, extending across the country, from *Truth in Boston* to San Francisco's *Lark.* They harked back to Poe via Baudelaire; they emulated the French poets with their "triolets, villanelles, rondels, rondeaus" that Petit the Poet was to contemn in the "Spoon River Anthology." They were adorned with descriptions that they called vignettes, and abounding in pastels in prose. Nothing definite from them clings in the memory except one quatrain on "The Purple Cow," by Gelett Burgess, and his later literary substantives — blurb, bromide. There was a spirit of mild revolt in them, or secession, the idea being that escape from Americanism as it was faultily expressing itself was to be found not in the resort to any truly American substance or style but in flight to the all-embracing Latin Quarter.

The so-called international novel was a good deal more significant than the artiness of the fly-by-night periodicals. Howells's early tales and sketches against Italian backgrounds had appeared so long before that the 90's could have forgotten them. Henry James had begun Americo-European stories of distinction with "The American" of 1873. The rich vein of contrasting cultures had been opened a century earlier with Tyler's "Contrast" and had been worked from time to time ever since. Mrs. Wharton was soon to reopen it with "The Valley of Decision" and to rework the theme of "The American" in the last episode of "The Custom of the Country." In 1890 Clyde Fitch opened his career characteristically with a trial piece for Richard Mansfield, "Beau Brummel," finding his way to New York only after this youthful excursion to London and Paris. Ten years later Booth Tarkington did very much the same thing in beginning with "Monsieur Beaucaire," continuing with "The Gentleman from Indiana," and not settling into Hoosierdom until, like the central character in "His Own People," he discovered that he was not by nature a consistent cosmopolitan and that for him John Howard Payne had said the final word about home. The various fictional essays of this sort are minor symptoms of the fresh awareness of Europe. Only one new author in this field was to produce anything more than a casual and negligible expression of a passing mood.

This was Henry B. Fuller, who dedicated his first book to Charles Eliot Norton, critic and historian, and whom Huneker cited as "the one felicitous example of cosmopolitanism" in the United States to be classed with Henry James. A Middle Westerner of Eastern parentage, he followed schooling in Chicago with a brief business experience, and topped his domestic education with a full year in Europe in 1879–1880, returning for five more leisurely visits between then and 1896.

In the eleven-year period from 1890 on, Fuller published eight volumes. He started with two exotic, tenuously constructed romances of Italian life, deftly phrased, subtly expressive of the subtle play of flickering emotion, full of the preciosity of men and women whose chief satisfaction lay in nice discrimination, past masters in suppressions and controlled implications. They were remarkable creations for a young Chicagoan in their fragile vitality and their complete disjunction from the life of the Windy City. Fuller seemed to recognize, however, that he must either peter out or turn back to the life he belonged to. So he moved from the life of "The Chevalier of Pensieri-Vani" and "The Chatelaine of La Trinité" to "The Cliff-Dwellers" and "With the Procession," realistic pictures of his own crude and crudely growing metropolis. With "The Other Side," "Stories of Transatlantic Travel," and "The Last Refuge" he crossed the ocean again, but in the company of American characters; and in "Under the Skylights" he returned to Chicago, where he was to find his material until his extraordinary last winter in 1928–1929.

Fuller's later career has its roots so deeply set in this period that the mention of it belongs here logically in spite of the chronology. Life in his home city absorbed him and then silenced him. He helped to shape the book-review section of the *Chicago Evening Post*, in which he had a hand in 1901 and 1902, following this with a somewhat slighter connection with the *Chicago Herald* as editorial writer. From the establishment of *Poetry* to his death he was on the advisory committee of the magazine, reading copy, writing reviews, and frequently helping in the routine of publication. With the turn of the century the world seems to have been too much with him in political getting and spending. The events of the Spanish-American War and the outreach of American imperialism horrified him. In 1899, unable to secure a publisher, he privately printed a violent attack on President McKinley and his policies — "The New Flag." His narrative volume of 1901, "Under the Skylights," was on the enervating influence of Philistinism on the potential arts of Chicago, "The Downfall of Abner Joyce" specifically applying to Garland. After a long interval "Waldo Trench and Others" was a series of mocking satires on negligible Americans abroad; and in 1917 his "Lines Long and Short," biographical sketches, had none of his earlier suavity of tone, was as mordant as "Spoon River," which it followed, and was directed by name at various public figures in America.

From the entrance of the United States into the World War, Fuller led the life of a semi-recluse in his metropolis, frequently seen, generous in friendly services to a chosen few, at home to no one. Then in the first half of 1929 he made a kind of literary recapitulation of himself. Stimulated by some of his friends he resumed the thread of his first novel, in one month writing and transcribing "Gardens of This World," reviving some of his earlier characters, and introducing, in his own words, "a lot of new folks." In February he swung, as he had done after "The Chevalier," to Chicago, and between then and April completed another full novel, "Not on the Screen," a social picture and a satire on moving-picture scenario-writing. Stimulated rather than exhausted by this double effort, he projected at once "a great big poultice of a thing . . . a mass 100,000. People love 'language.'" But fatal illness followed while one of the other two books was still in press. In his oscillation between a kind of Old World nostalgia and defeated hopes for the New World Fuller was uncontent to retreat and courageous enough to fight, but not quite effectively robust in his realism. Yet his artistry was deft and fine, and his work has more distinction than that of many a more muscular contemporary.

It is at this point only that Henry James can be adduced in connection with any general relationship to his country or countrymen. Born in New York of literary parentage, educated in the university towns of Europe, resident most of his life abroad, an English citizen in his later years, he developed quite naturally into the most persistent of international novelists, chiefly concerned with the play of highly schooled intellects and emotions among the people who neither toiled nor spun. In the peculiar and increasingly complex intricacy of his technique he offers nice problems for the technical reader; so nice, in fact, that no narrative technician can resist the lure of him, an inevitable object of attention to the connoisseur — an object on which, in the minds of many, connoisseurship hinges. He has thus become the subject of a cult and has been written about almost as voluminously and complexly as he himself has written about his small corner of life. There is little reason for contributing further to this side of the discussion of James. The question still remains as to the intrinsic substance of his novels, to illustrate which one book will serve about as well as another.

Against backgrounds almost always intercontinental or transatlantic move characters from both sides of the Atlantic, or from the eastern side, who belong to the leisure class. The episodes, where they exist, are adventures of the mind, as all episodes are, to be sure, but unstimulated by action and unaccompanied by dramatic event. In the earlier novels, such as "The American" and "Roderick Hudson," the plots are more definitive and the style more lucid than in the later ones. In these, after "The Tragic Muse" (the last to involve much real vitality of character or vigor of action), the novels past "The Awkward Age" to "The Golden Bowl" and beyond become mild revels in complexity. Every motion of the hand, every lift of the eyebrow, demands motivation. Every question of motivation becomes a problem in motivation, with alternative answers. Words fail of exactness and are cumulatively qualified. In the end James crosses the line short of which he is mainly concerned in what he is communicating, to the place where his dominant interest is in how he is expressing himself. There are passages in his prose, plenty of them, that are fairly comparable to passages in Gertrude Stein's. Doubtless time cannot change nor custom dull the infinite variety of art; yet in the realms of high art the maximum of effect is produced with the minimum of apparent effort, a characterization that could never be made of any of James's later work.

The maximum of effect, furthermore, cannot be gained in his stories because of the tenuosity of his material. "The Awkward Age," for example, centers about the marriage and non-marriage of two London girls. Nothing objective happens. The tale is told in ten long conversations, each entitled for one of the chief participants in the story. They all talk with circuitous elusiveness except when one of the girls is twice presented as a complete ingénue. At the end one's only feeling is of wonder that the author could have made so much out of so little — such slight matter, such little people. In his attitude toward these people James put himself in a somewhat equivocal position. For their general social and spiritual insufficiency it is impossible that he could have had much regard. They represent the world of "The Newcomes" and "Vanity Fair" done down to date. Yet he betrayed a lurking admiration for them, their ways, their attitude toward life. They were, in his conception, "civilized," by which he meant that civilization had done its work in lifting them to a plane on which they could be oblivious to what was going on in the human substrata. He made it their privilege "to sit there . . . with the curtains drawn, keeping out the cold, the darkness, all the big, terrible, cruel world — sit there and listen forever to Schubert and Mendelssohn."[1] An old Spanish-leather chair, drawn curtains, Schubert and Mendelssohn — the picture is complete.

James's fiction thus conceived of is Swiss carving on ivory. It has the same minuteness of detail, the same inutility, the same remote and attenuated relationship to any deep emotional experience or vigorous human endeavor. One cannot appreciate the expenditure of so much technical skill on such fragile substance, and substance in which so little of either truth or beauty is inherent. In his narrowly limited field as a novelist James was a master. For more than forty years and in more than thirty volumes he did the thing he chose to do with no concession to popular taste. Yet, admire him as they may, most readers turn with relief to the literature of activity and of the normal, healthy beings who are seldom to be encountered in his pages.

There is rather more than the usual difference between the novels of James and his critical theory about novels that one expects between theory and practice in artists who indulge in both. For there is a boldness in James the critic. The novel in English, he asserted often, had fallen on evil days. It was equivocal, mushy, untruthful. He had no patience with the sweetly romantic, the pretty-pretty, or the happy-ending schools of fiction. There was little being written in English, he said, that was truthful and courageous. The author should be free in his choice of method and in his selection of matter. As freedom in both respects was being practiced in France, James's doctrine of liberty found its illustrations across the Channel. Thus he wrote of Maupassant:

> Hard and fast rules, a priori restrictions, mere interdictions (you shall not speak of this, you shall not look at that) have surely served their time, and will in the nature of the case never strike an energetic talent as anything but arbitrary. A healthy, living and growing art,

---

[1] "The Bostonians."

full of curiosity and full of exercise, has an indefeasible mistrust of rigid prohibitions. Let us then leave this magnificent art of the novelist to itself and to its perfect freedom, in the faith that one example is as good as another.[1]

He wrote to Howells in 1884 that he had been seeing Daudet, Goncourt, and Zola; that they interested him more than anything else and were writing the only fiction that he could respect. And with Howells, James was first to take up the cudgels for Zola in the United States at a time when the French naturalist was being vilified on all sides.[2] What is more: James not only entered the conflict, but he and Howells won the battle for a freedom which neither of them elected to exercise in the fashion of the Continental authors whose cause they were championing. It marked, with James, that social and national rootlessness from which he suffered all his life. He elected, he said, as a mark of "civilization," to write so that one could not tell whether he were American writing of England, or English writing of America. He was born in America, bred on the Continent, and died a naturalized Englishman. He chose to applaud the freedom in choice of subject of the French naturalists, but he chose to exercise the reticence of the most cautious of Victorians. And, on the whole, he failed to meet his one test for the novel — that it should be interesting; for after his early period his novels became interesting only as museum pieces.

James from time to time expressed his apologia, and from time to time his apology, over his predilection for literary orchids. His life of William Wetmore Story, Americo-Italian sculptor, is generously self-explanatory. So is his critical study of Hawthorne and his accounting for the "provincialism" of the author of "The Scarlet Letter." The "moral is that the flower of art blooms only where the soil is deep, that it takes a great deal of history to produce a little literature, that it needs a complex social machinery to set a writer in

[1] *Fortnightly Review*, March, 1888. Also in "Partial Portraits."

[2] Herbert Edwards, "Zola and the American Critics," in *American Literature*, Vol. IV, pp. 114–129.

motion."[1] Cooper, temporarily under the same spell, had said the same thing fifty years before.[2] But James, in a letter written in the year the Hawthorne volume was published, wrote deprecatively of his own "charming little standard . . . of wit, of grace, of good manners, of vivacity, of urbanity, of intelligence"; and at another time of his lack of "grasping imagination," which proved him less than the master who could write worthily of American matters. The admirer of James who gives his case away by writing as his defender[3] contends that James was most profoundly American in his nostalgia for Europe, citing that his followers today are many, and all are expatriates. As a matter of fact every country has its alienated souls. Artists as a genre cannot be cited anywhere for their cozy domesticity or comfortable neighborliness. The sturdier ones usually fight out the issue with themselves on the home ground. The expatriate, whether he come from Idaho, Arkansas, Wisconsin, or New York, proves nothing save that in the dilemma which creative artists have faced from the beginning of history, in all times and all lands, the path of retreat has proved the easier for him, and that he has gained nothing in happiness by choosing it.

Two of the poets who showed most promise toward the turn of the century, Hovey and Moody, died before reaching middle age. Their reactions to militant nationalism have already been cited.[4] It was only in this connection that either of them wrote explicitly on American themes. Both seemed to move on the assumption that poetry as poetry could be expressed only in purely lyric form or in terms of traditional literary material drawn from the Old World. Hovey's most ambitious project, "Guenevere, a Poem in Dramas," was

---

[1] "Nathaniel Hawthorne," p. 3.

[2] See page 262.

[3] Matthew Josephson, "Portrait of Artist as American," pp. 70–138, 265–288. In this work, in which James is inevitably the major figure, the author elaborates a thesis already frequently advanced by Van Wyck Brooks, that the United States is peculiarly inhospitable to the artist spirit.

[4] See pages 718–720.

projected as a trilogy of trilogies, employing the Arthurian theme for a study of the rival claims of individual freedom and social obligation. The four completed units form a dim and expansive tapestry background of romance, quite the natural one for a translator of Maeterlinck and Mallarmé. According to the exposition of his friend Bliss Carman,[1] Hovey was not interested in "Arthurian legends . . . for their historic and picturesque value as poetic material," but because they afforded him "a modern instance stripped of modern dress." It was natural for a man who saw everything in drama and in costume drama at the time, and it was characteristic of his period. It was also evidence of deficiency in the imaginative grasp which could make him master of the materials nearer at hand.

The case with Moody was comparable but distinctly different. It is true in his case also that his chief work was projected as a dramatic trilogy, expressed this time in a fusion of Hebrew, Greek, and Roman legend; that "Old Pourquoi" challenges the scheme of creation from beneath a Norman sky, that "A Dialogue in Purgatory" is Dantesque, and that his whole output is saturated with influence from the romance literatures. Yet Moody had not only saturated himself in other literatures; he had assimilated them. And he was able in his prose dramas to write of the American Western theme or of the interplay of sectional characters. What Moody did in "The Great Divide" and "The Faith Healer," and the cogent sanity that he showed in his occasional poems, already referred to, lift him above the level of the bookishness of such contemporaries as Sterling, Scollard, F. D. Sherman, Johnson, who were always writing as from a library alcove. Moody did write imitative verse — examples can be culled from the magazines in which they were printed; but he excluded them from the single volume of poetry which he was willing on second thought to submit to the public.

---

[1] "The Holy Grail and Other Fragments," a posthumous volume, with introductory material about the plan of the drama-cycle, by Bliss Carman and Mrs. Hovey.

Aside from the explicit poems of time and place, Moody's verse may be regarded as related and preliminary to the trio of poetic dramas which was just short of completion at his death. The shorter poems contain the elemental ideas in the plays — harbingers confirmed and fulfilled by the event. It is a sequence composed by a Puritan, if you will, but a paganized Puritan, containing Moody's concept of the entire "scheme of salvation." It is on the theme of the union between God and man and the consequent incompleteness of either. The unity is threatened by God's uncontent with peaceful inactivity and man's endowment with a divine restlessness. So the tragic conclusion of "The Fire-Bringer" is that at the moment when Pandora is singing her wonderful lyric of union between God and his creatures, man has won freedom at the awful cost of disunion following Prometheus's gift of fire from the heavens. In "The Masque of Judgment," second stage of the epic, man "wanton, unteachable, intolerable," frustrates God's hope to woo him back to obedience. Drooping, "white and pitiful," on his throne, he sees no recourse but to doom to destruction this very part of himself. He executes his judgment, therefore, "with suicidal hand," since

> Man's violence was earnest of his strength,
> His sin a heady overflow, dynamic
> Unto all lovely uses, to be curbed
> And sweetened, never broken with the rod![1]

The final stage was projected in "The Death of Eve." It was to contain the reconciliation through the voluntary return to him of Eve, Hebrew counterpart of Prometheus, seeker for knowledge and power that should lift mankind above the brutes, consequent breeder of discord between man and his creator. The trilogy was to culminate with a song of Eve which, in its peaceful harmony, was to stand in double contrast with the conflict between Pandora's song and the young men's chorus at the end of the first play, and with the

[1] William Vaughn Moody, "Poems and Poetic Dramas" (Houghton Mifflin), p. 358.

chaotic destruction described in the dialogue between Uriel and Raphael which concludes the second. Toward this lyrical climax Moody had made two studies, both of which failed to meet his desire for this final chord, both of which are included in his published poems, and neither of which is quite intelligible apart from the design of the trilogy. The earlier attempt was the wild and defiant "I am the Woman." Though this opens with

> I am the Woman, ark of the law and its breaker,

it progresses to the point of urging obedience on man, revises the self-description to

> ark of the law and sacred arm to upbear it,

and concludes,

> Open to me, O sleeping mother. The gate is heavy and strong.
> Open to me, I am come at last: be wroth with thy child no more.[1]

Yet this lyric was on the wrong note; for there was a militant defiance in it of a spirit still tameless and only reduced to the acquiescence of spiritual exhaustion.

A second study — the dramatic poem with the same title, "The Death of Eve" — covers, in the rapid narrative of its first ninety lines, the action of the dramatic fragment and goes on to a new song, perhaps the song with which the play might have ended. For in this, although there is still a tone of Promethean defiance, is the glad challenge of the lover who will not be gainsaid:

> Far off, rebelliously, yet for thy sake,
> She gathered them, O Thou who lovest to break
> A thousand souls, and shake
> Their dust along the wind, but sleeplessly
> Searchest the Bride fulfilled in limb and feature,
> Ready and boon to be fulfilled of Thee,
> Thine ample, tameless creature, —
> Against Thy will and word, behold, Lord, this is She.[2]

---

[1] Moody, op. cit. pp. 127, 132, 132.

[2] Ibid. p. 142.

The trilogy is both the result of conscious preliminaries and the summation of fundamental convictions elsewhere recorded without reference to the monumental work. The fusion of pagan and Christian tradition occurs in the pair of poems (which Moody characteristically does not present as a pair) "Good Friday Night" and "Second Coming." The undercurrent of evolutionary thought is another constant, the aspiring impulse which makes life rise not through struggle against outer forces so much as through the innate impulse to develop. In the sardonic "Menagerie" the idea is ironically put:

Survival of the fittest, adaptation,
And all their other evolution terms,
Seem to omit one small consideration,

which is no less than the existence of souls:

restless, plagued, impatient things,
All dream and unaccountable desire. . . .
Mystical hanker after something higher.[1]

These souls are all expression of the universal soul which finds its own salvation in ceaseless "groping, testing, passing on," — the creative struggle described by Raphael in "The Masque of Judgment" as

The strife of ripening suns and withering moons,
Marching of ice-floes, and the nameless wars
Of monster races laboring to be man.[2]

His treatment of woman, traditional yet modern, was again a constant in his poetry. She was the dominant influence in history. Eve and Prometheus were one, but Prometheus was a poor, defeated character by compare; for Moody, in Eve and Pandora, presented woman not only as donor and fulfiller of love but as final agent in the reconciliation of human and divine. In this scheme there is more

---

[1] Moody, op. cit. p. 65.

[2] Ibid. p. 282.

than a hint of Μήτηρ θεῶν, the mother of the gods, when Eve cries out at the last,

Yea, she whose arm was round the neck of the morning star at song,
Is she who kneeleth now in the dust and cries at the secret door,
"Open to me, O sleeping mother."[1]

From this archaic tradition both the poems of Eve progress through the ages when woman is molded by man's conception of her, and in both she re-emerges as the Promethean spirit who in the end was to fulfill the plan which in the beginning she had endangered. No reference to any woman in any of Moody's poems is out of harmony with this dominant idea.

For various reasons Moody's poetry is not easy to read, undestined to wide popularity. He was not interested in composing simple lyrics or narratives for the multitude. He seldom aids the reader by means of even an implied narrative thread. The verse inspired by contemporary history is neither self-explanatory nor footnoted. Moody consistently employed events, actual or imagined, as avenues of approach to emotional and spiritual experiences, demanding a contribution from the resourceful imagination of the reader. It is because the whole implication is not laid out on the surface of his poems that Moody has become largely a poets' poet. Their instinctive grasp of the deeper figurative meanings, their immediate response to elusive metaphor, and their understanding of his vigorous, exact, but sometimes recondite diction, make them his best audience. For they too can most nearly appreciate the distinguished beauties of his work — his wide and intimate knowledge of world literature, the opulence of his style, the firmness of his structure, the scrupulousness of his detail. Through the rising and risen poets of the generation Moody's influence is exerted on many who acknowledge it and on many who are unconscious of it and unacquainted with him at first hand.

---

[1] Moody, op. cit. p. 132.

Democracy and the Common Man

The variously expressed national self-consciousness of post-Civil War days had left its chief literary record in the exposition of local types, in a fulfillment of Crèvecœur's forecast of 1780: "Each province has its characteristics founded on the government, climate, mode of husbandry, customs and peculiarity of circumstances. . . . Whoever traverses the continent, must observe these strong differences, which will grow more evident in time." The aftermath was still being harvested in the 90's. Cable and Harris, Page and Mrs. Deland, Miss Murfree and Mrs. Ward, were still writing. Fox and Allen, Garland, and Miss Wilkins were continuing with provincial tales of rural life, and Davis, Matthews, and Fuller were presenting urban pictures. But the frontier was closed, standardizing effects of railroad, telegraph, and national advertising were soon to be felt, and later to be augmented by automobile, moving picture, sound recorder, and radio. The study of provincial types was to be superseded until its restoration with the rise of a retrospective treatment of the frontier in the 1920's and the new regionalistic movement of still later.

With the airing of the sinister alliance of politics and "big business" during the Grant regime and the progressive organization of labor in the last quarter of the century, there was an increasing inclination in the country to discuss the effect of this alliance on the practical workings of democracy and, in this discussion, to utilize fiction as a vehicle for social criticism. Henry Adams and John Hay were among the earliest forerunners with their two anonymous novels, "Democracy" and "The Breadwinners." Both were members of the privileged class, cosmopolitans, close to the heart of government, believers in the theory of democracy, aristocrats in fact. Both felt that the writing of popular fiction was a little undignified, were unwilling to take the personal consequences of signing their stories, yet could not resist the impulse to write mildly startling criticism of American life. And both enjoyed the satisfaction of raising a little hue and cry, the temporary thrill of eluding the curiosity of the public and the amusement of each being suspected of writing the other's story.[1]

Henry Adams wrote his novel on the strength of first impressions as a resident at the national capital. He saw Washington against the contrasting background of the London in which he had served as private secretary to his father, American minister to England during the Civil War, and he analyzed the play of politics and statesmanship there in the light of his broad knowledge as historian.[2] The President in the novel is a demagogue and a weakling. The dominant character, a Western senator, is no better than the President, though stronger. Senators as a group are vainglorious, self-seeking, unscrupulous; other congressmen not so intelligent and no more honest. The foreign diplomats are altogether more sophisticated but no more trustworthy; and an elusive member of the upper house from Massachusetts, representative of the old aristocracy in the new order, disillusioned and world-weary, clings to the forlorn doctrine that defective though democracy may be, all the other experiments have been tried, and all are somewhat less preferable. As the story goes on, there are shady doings just around the corner and scandals in the near background. Adams had no gifts as a novelist. His characters are lay figures, his conversation stiff, his episodes devoid of dramatic action. But the book was startling because it was written by an author of evident worldly experience and because its tone was so coldly and dispassionately caustic. It was as damaging in 1879 as the altogether different exposure of Washington life in 1921, "Revelry," by the altogether different namesake, Samuel Hopkins Adams. The greater vulgarity in the picture of the Harding administration represents difference of taste in the authors more than difference of characteristics in the periods. Henry Adams's novel, how-

---

[1] "Letters of Henry Adams," pp. 336–354.

[2] See pages 701–703.

ever, with the exception of the Washington episodes in the Mark Twain-Warner "Gilded Age," was the first to deal so critically of national politics and its manipulators.

The popular success of "Democracy" no doubt stimulated John Hay to follow with his tale of industrial life four years later. "The Breadwinners" was a circulation breeder as a serial for *The Century*, before it sold widely in book form. Hay proved hardly more skillful at description and narration than Adams, and he was far less of an observer or critic; but he sounded a popular conservative note — the note of alarm at the steadily spreading organization of labor. The National Labor Union had faded out in 1872 after six years of faltering existence, but the Knights of Labor had grown steadily since 1869, and the American Federation of Labor had entered on its long life in 1881. The movement held out a definite threat of class struggle that was to head up shortly in the Homestead and Pullman strikes. Property holders resented the movement without wishing to understand it, and John Hay was their anonymous spokesman. His fictive hero was a gentleman "whose hands had the firm hard symmetry which showed they had done no work." His slight contact with corrupt municipal politics disgusted him. Turned back one day in the course of a horseback ride, he meditated on "ruffians with theories in their heads and revolvers in their hands neither of which they knew how to use." There is not an implication in the whole story that labor had the slightest real cause for discontent or any justification for seeking methods of collective bargaining; the capitalists are represented as quite properly resorting to espionage and armed mercenaries. "The Breadwinners" is an interesting book largely because it is so bad a book. If a writer as intelligent as John Hay could completely fail to understand the drift of industrial life, the reading public could hardly be expected to do better. His one achievement was to call to attention the fact that something was happening. He was to be followed in time by a number of men who were not so blind as he.

No public change can take place except as it represents an aggregate of individuals. William Dean Howells both marked the change toward a prevailing critical realism and was changed by the pervasive influences of the day. For the quarter-century preceding 1889 Howells had been the thoroughly conventional novelist, gaining satisfaction and giving pleasure through the exercise of his admirable technique. In this period he wrote always, to borrow an expression first applied to Tennyson, as if a staid matron had just left the room, a matron nurtured on the reading which gave rise to his own literary passions — Goldsmith, Cervantes, Irving, Longfellow, Scott, Pope, Mrs. Stowe, Dickens, and Macaulay; a matron, in short, who was the Lady of the Aroostook at forty-five, the mother of a numerous family, aggressively concerned that no book which fell into her daughters' hands should cause the blush of shame to rise upon the maiden cheek. Howells wrote not only on an early experience in the life of this lady, but on "A Modern Instance," "A Woman's Reasons," "Indian Summer," and, best of all, "The Rise of Silas Lapham." He was giving ground for Samuel Crothers's pale-gray pleasure as a reader when, he confessed:

> I turned eagerly to some neutral-tinted person who never had any adventure greater than missing the train to Dedham, and I . . . analyzed his character, and agitated myself in the attempt to get at his feelings, and I . . . verified his story by a careful reference to the railroad guide. I . . . treated that neutral-tinted person as a problem, and I . . . noted all the delicate shades in the futility of his conduct. When, on any occasion that called for action he did not know his own mind, I . . . admired him for his resemblance to so many of my acquaintances who do not know their own minds. After studying the problem until I came to the last chapter . . . I suddenly [gave] it up, and agreed with the writer that it had no solution.[1]

If nothing had occurred to break the sequence, Howells was on the way to wasting his energies, as James did, "in describing human rarities, or cases that are common enough only in

[1] S. M. Crothers, "The Gentle Reader" (Houghton Mifflin), pp. 111, 112.

the abnormal groups of men and women living on the fringe of the great society of active, healthy human beings."[1]

Howells's books of this period, in other words, were the work of a well-trained, unprejudiced observer whose ambition was to make contributions to the slice-of-life school of fiction, selecting his slices off the top and serving them daintily. "Venetian Life" and "Italian Journeys" were the first logical expression of his desire and his capacities — books of the same sort as "Bracebridge Hall" and "Outre-Mer" and "Views Afoot" and "Our Old Home" and all their kind. "A Foregone Conclusion" and "A Fearful Responsibility" simply crossed the narrow bridge between exposition and fiction, employing the same point of view and the same technique. Howells was interested in American characters and in the nice distinctions between different levels of savoir faire and genuine culture. In "Silas Lapham," the peak of his performance before 1890, the blunt Vermonter is set in contrast with the frayed aristocracy of Boston. He amasses a fortune, becomes involved in speculation, in business injustice, and in ruin. But whatever Howells had to say then of social and economic forces, he said of powers as impersonal as gravitation. Business was business, and the man subjected to it was subjected to influences as capricious but as inevitable as the climate of New England.

More and more as a realist he became absorbed in carrying out a theory of fiction, the presentation of character at the expense of plot. "The art of fiction," he wrote in his essay on Henry James in 1882, "has become a finer art in our day than it was with Dickens or Thackeray. We could not suffer the confidential attitude of the latter now nor the mannerism of the former any more than we could endure the prolixity of Richardson or the coarseness of Fielding. These great men are of the past — they and their methods and interests; even Trollope and Reade are not of the present." He dismissed moving accidents and dire catastrophes from the field of the

---

[1] Romain Rolland, "Jean-Christophe," Vol. III, p. 54.

new novel, substituting for fire and flood the slow smolder of resentment and a burst of feminine tears. With "April Hopes" of 1887 he deliberately composed an unfinished story, following two young and evidently incompatible people to the marriage altar, but leaving their subsequent sacrifice to the imagination of the reader, who must imagine his own sequel or go without.

But when he was past fifty he underwent a social conversion, and when he wrote his next book about a familiar couple, the Marches, he and they together risked "A Hazard of New Fortunes." No longer willing to play at life where the safety of life was completely insured, he and they went down into New York from the comparative security of Boston, competed with strange and uncouth people, and learned something about poverty and something about the workings of injustice. In fact, they learned what went into "Annie Kilburn," and "The Quality of Mercy" and "The World of Chance" and "A Traveler from Altruria" and "The Eye of a Needle," learning it all through the refreshed vision gained from a belated reading of Tolstoi. Writing from his heart of this conversion, Howells avowed, in "My Literary Passions":

> It is as if the best wine of this high feast, where I have sat so long, had been kept for the last, and I need not deny a miracle in it in order to attest to my skill in judging vintages. In fact I prefer to believe that my life has been full of miracles, and that the good has always come to me at the right time, so that I could profit most by it. I believe that if I had not turned my fiftieth year, when I first knew Tolstoi, I should not have been able to know him as fully as I did. He has been to me that final consciousness, which he speaks of so wisely in his essay on Life. I came in it to the knowledge of myself in ways that I had not dreamt of before, and began at last to discern my relations to the race, without which we are nothing. The supreme art in literature had its highest effect in making me set art forever below humanity, and it is with the wish to offer the greatest homage to his heart and mind which any man can pay another, that I close this record with the name of Lyof Tolstoi.[1]

[1] "My Literary Passions," last paragraph.

This passage is quite as important as Howells tried to make it; not in terms of Russia, however, but in terms of America. For it attests that the admiring young friend of Longfellow and Lowell, while the latter was still living, had shifted allegiance and was making reverent acknowledgment not to the splendors of an ancient civilization but to the newest iconoclast in the Old World.

There was no startling change in the materials of his fiction and hardly any change in the method. It was simply enriched — or complicated — by a new purpose. To his former portrayal of the individual, Howells added a criticism of the role he was playing, and was permitted to play, in society. He added an interpretation of the institutions of which the individual was always the creator, sometimes the beneficiary, and all too often the victim. In his maturity he kept his balance, in distinction to many younger authors of similar purposes and convictions. He wrote nothing so extreme as London's "Iron Heel" or as Sinclair's "Jungle," "Oil," and "100%," all explicitly propagandist novels; nothing so insistent as Norris's "Octopus," Whitlock's "Turn of the Balance," Poole's "Harbor"; nothing so clumsily moralistic as Page's "John Marvel, Assistant"; nothing so evidently the fruit of painstaking study in an unfamiliar field as Churchill's "Dwelling Place of Light." His later novels were written out of an experience in which he had found that life was infinitely complex, with some redeeming and some unintelligent and baffling good in it.

By 1894 Howells came to a point at which he wanted to present his social thesis as a thesis, doing so in "A Traveler from Altruria," a series of conversations on the nature of American life. Following an old literary device, Mr. Homos from Altruria (Mr. Man from Elsewhere) gains his first impression of America through a visit to a conservatively minded novelist, Mr. Twelvemough, at a summer resort in which the hotel furnishes "a sort of microcosm of the American republic." Here, in addition to the host, are an enlightened banker, a complacent manufacturer, an intolerant and dogmatic professor of economics, a lawyer, a minister, and a society woman, who "as a cultivated American woman . . . was necessarily quite ignorant of her own country, geographically, politically and historically"; and here also are the hotel-keeper, the baggage porter, a set of college-girl waitresses, and a surrounding population of "natives," as the summer resorter invidiously dubs the inhabitants whom he wisely does not venture to call peasants. In the earlier part of the essay the social cleavages are embarrassingly revealed — the ignominy of being a manual laborer or, worse still, a domestic servant, and the consequent struggle to escape from toil and all the conditions that surround it. This leads promptly to a study of the economic situation in a republic where every man is for himself.

Pinned by insistent questions from the visitor, the defenders of the American faith take refuge behind what they regard as the static quality of human nature, only to be further embarrassed by the Altrurian's innocent surprise at their tactics. He does not understand that it is in human nature for the first-comer to demand first service, or for every man to be for himself, or for a man "to squeeze his brother man when he gets him in his grip," or for employers to take it out on objecting employees in any way they can. To Mr. Twelvemough it becomes a matter of doubt as to whether the traveler is naïve or ironical in his implication that human nature is capable of development.

The latter two-thirds of the treatise, in its engaging conversational disguise, forms an indictment of a system that permits slavery in all but name, and that extols the rights of the individual only when they apply to the property holder. It culminates with an address by the Altrurian — an "account of his own country, which," according to his host, "grew more and more incredible as he went on, and implied every insulting criticism of ours." The book concludes,

We parted friends; I even offered him some introductions; but his acquaintance had become more and more difficult, and I was not sorry to part with him. That taste of his for low company was incurable, and I was glad that I was not to be responsible any longer for whatever strange things he might do next. I think he remained very popular with the classes he most affected; a throng of natives, construction hands and table-girls saw him off on his train; and he left large numbers of such admirers in our house and neighborhood, devout in the faith that there was such a country as Altruria, and that he was really an Altrurian. As for the more cultivated people who had met him, they continued of two minds upon both points.[1]

The challenges of the Altrurian prevail in all Howells's later works. On the whole it is significant that novels of so liberal a tone drew down so little criticism from the conservative. Seldom has an iconoclast been received with such unintelligent tolerance. The suavity of his manner; the continuing appearance of his books of observation and travel; the recurrence — as in "The Kentons" — of his old type of work, or the resort — as in the long-unpublished "Leatherwood God" — to fresh woods and pastures new; and all the while the amusing presentation of his favorite characters, particularly the bumptious young business man and the whimsically incoherent American woman, beguiled his old readers into a blind and bland assumption as to Howells's harmlessness. Yet novel after novel on the same subversive themes from younger, less skillful hands excited the criticism and opposition which prove that the truth struck home. Howells's widest influence has been exerted through his followers. His lack of sensationalism and sentimentalism debarred him from the "best-seller" class; but for fifty years he was followed by the best-reading class, and though there have been far and ostentatious departures from the social groups on which he chose to focus his realism, few novelists of the later generation have been unconscious of his work or have written more veraciously about the subject matter of their choosing.

There is a logical as well as chronological relationship between the early career of Hamlin Garland and the later phase of Howells. In the 90's their interests were similar. Howells

[1] Howells, "A Traveler from Altruria," pp. 317–318.

left his Ohio-valley near-frontier about 1860, the year of Garland's birth in the remoter Middle West of Wisconsin. Garland went East in his twenties as Howells had done and was befriended by the elder man, who was now comfortably established as a comfortable novelist; for he was always friendly to young authors, and he could see that Garland had brought with him a rich fund of literary material.

Hard experience had taught this Middle Westerner the truth of pioneering days. In one way they were highly romantic for the instinctive and incorrigibly hopeful frontiersmen. The Garlands and the McClintocks, his mother's family, were enlisted by nature in the conquest of the prairie. They were "clarion voiced and tireless." Like children, they made a game of reaping, a race of husking, a "bee" of threshing, and, like children, they were unstable and incurably restless for change. Their favorite song was

> Then o'er the hills in legions, boys,
> Fair freedom's star
> Points to the sunset regions, boys,
> Ha, ha, ha-ha!

It was the rallying song of the pioneer, "a directing force in the lives of at least three generations of my pioneering race."[1] So for the Garlands it was from Wisconsin to Minnesota to Iowa, from farm to village and back again, from Iowa to Dakota; for the McClintocks no final repose till the Pacific stopped the western progress; for the Garlands, none till they returned in poverty and defeat to Wisconsin.

This was the realistic side of pioneering days: their restlessness, the grim tribute of grinding labor they exacted, the heart-rending sacrifices of the women and children who had no choice but to follow the men and slave for them, the unrewarded lives of the rank and file in the conquering pioneer hosts, and the repugnance to it all that was climaxed in an escape to the East. When after six years' absence Garland went back for a visit, he saw that the "Song of Emigration

[1] Garland, "Son of the Middle Border," p. 46.

had been, in effect, the hymn of fugitives."[1] Nature was as alluring as ever in its beauties, but men and women had suffered in their struggle to possess an acreage and wrest a living from it. Every home he visited had its half-hidden evidence of striving and despair. Girls had wasted from beauty to premature old age. Shoulders were bent and eyes were dimmed. Age had found no reward worth seeking, and youth was looking, furtively or openly, for some way of escape. The whole enterprise of pioneering had been extravagant of energy and wasteful of human life.

So in the early 90's Garland pictured that life in "Main-Travelled Roads" and "Prairie Folk" with a fidelity that startled and offended both East and West — the West because it was grimly true; the East, because it discredited a pleasant myth. In "A Member of the Third Estate" and "The Spoil of Office" he went on to present the hopelessness of the farmer as an economic and political catspaw, and in "Rose of Dutcher's Coolly" to indicate the aridity of life on the plains for the thirster after truth and beauty. Like many in his generation Garland was greatly stimulated by the social theses of Herbert Spencer and the economic theories of Henry George — they were major prophets for the young liberals; and for a while he was all aflame in behalf of his people. But he had never chosen the pioneer life, he did not feel committed to the land, and as he stayed away his ardor cooled and his vigor waned.[2]

The Rise of the "Muckrakers"

At the time "The Breadwinners" was published in *The Century*, this monthly and three others, *The Atlantic*, *Harper's*, and *Scribner's*, shared the honors among American periodicals. *The North American Review* was older but had passed its prime. *The Outlook* and *The Independent* appealed to a more churchly constituency. Various others were more specifically literary or political, or specialized in some other direction.

---

[1] Garland, op. cit. p. 368.

[2] See pages 845–848.

A foreigner, hoping to find somewhere in print a cross section of American life might have expected to see it in these four publications. But he would have been misled, getting only a sitting-room-table literature that could not disturb the serenity of a comfortably prosperous family as it gathered of an evening about the duplex burner. All four were conservative in subject and taste, consciously inoffensive, definitely committed to the avoidance of controversial subjects. There were tabooed words, short and simple ones, and tabooed suggestions that seem prudish to the twentieth century. Ambrose Bierce and Stephen Crane had to look elsewhere for publishers because their stories were too grim or too frank, though the editors would accept from Du Maurier or Hardy or Meredith what they would reject from an American pen, apparently feeling that England and France must be responsible for their own errors but that the editors must censor everything American.

A glance at the contents of the four in the year when *McClure's* set out on its startling program offers evidence enough. *Scribner's*, in a department of contemporary comment, indexed articles on "Birds, Bonnets, and the Audubon Society," "The Knell of the Theatre Hat," and "Are we to have the Metric System?" It published a serial by James Barrie and opened an article on "The New York Working Girl" by stating that shirt-making is "a burden she takes up lightly and gladly." *Harper's*, in its current events section, commented on national tennis, intercollegiate athletics, tornadoes in the South, heat in New York, a mine disaster, and a railroad wreck. Its one suggestive title, "The Dominant Idea in American Democracy," raised the real question of the impersonal power of organized wealth, but concluded comfortably that it need only be mentioned to be held in check. It printed no serial stories, but included a harmless bit from John Kendrick Bangs in two installments and two installments from Mark Twain's potboiler, "Tom Sawyer, Detective." *The Century* had articles on Africa, Alaska, Guiana; an article on the gold standard, about which there was unanimity of opinion among its readers; confined "Politics and Political Reform" to a series of brief and discreet editorials; and put its main weight on three serials — biographies of Lincoln and Napoleon and a novel by Mrs. Humphry Ward. *The Atlantic* printed a series of filial articles on Hawthorne by one of his children, strongly reinforced with numerous other literary reminiscences; discussed immigration, a timely subject on which all conservative *Atlantic* readers might feel alarm; and contained a series on "Presidential Possibilities" (it was an election year), none of whom was even nominated. All four periodicals were clearly edited with an eye on the "nobody" from whom, according to Frank R. Stockton, a single note of protest could raise more stir in the office than ten letters from intelligent people. There was nothing to challenge America in its prosperous complacency, and the price of these magazines, as well as their contents, was determined with the prosperous in mind.

Three new editors, Walker of *The Cosmopolitan*, Munsey of *The Argosy* and *Munsey's*, and McClure of *McClure's*, started a new chapter in magazine-publishing when in 1893 they set record-making prices of fifteen, twelve and a half, and ten cents an issue. They were all trying to build up circulations among the public untouched by the "big four." Munsey gained his idea from analyzing the older periodicals, comparing these with the Sunday newspapers, and deciding that their editors were editing for themselves and not for their subscribers; that, living in an artificial literary world, they put out publications which woefully lacked human interest. McClure earned his knowledge of the average American mind by peddling for three summers in the Middle West. Both decided that big subscription lists could be attracted first of all by intimate, personal accounts of famous people. While the formal Lincoln and Napoleon revivals were in full swing, Ida Tarbell's simply written lives won more readers for McClure than the scholastic serials in *The Century*, on whose staff he had served. In the meanwhile he and Munsey were running "Plain Talks to the People," "Real

Conversations," "Human Documents." Through his newspaper syndicating scheme he created publics for Conan Doyle and for Kipling, who had been consistently rejected by *Harper's*. Then he organized his issues round the series written by trained journalists like Lincoln Steffens, Ray Stannard Baker, and Ida Tarbell, employing them for as long as they needed, to compose careful studies in contemporary history, accurate, condensed, and convincing — the kind of studies which could not be flattering to an imperfect social life.

People were becoming more and more interested in great business combinations, powers that they thought of uneasily as trusts or monopolies. Instead of printing general articles on economic tendencies, McClure engaged Miss Tarbell to spend five years on the fifteen installments of the Standard Oil series. At the same time he gave Steffens a commission not to theorize on corruption in politics but to undertake a series on the government of American cities. He did not rely on uninformed writers nor on experts who could not write: he employed expert writers and gave them all the time they needed. By January, 1903, his program came to a natural climax, with the publication of contributions by his three leading writers, on "Standard Oil," "The Shame of Minneapolis," and "The Right to Work" (the coal strike of 1902). "Thus," McClure wrote in his autobiography, "the origin of what was later called the 'muckraking' movement was accidental. It came from no formulated plan to attack existing institutions, but was the result of merely taking up in the magazine some of the problems that were beginning to interest people a little before the newspapers and the other magazines took them up."[1] But it was so popular a development that within the decade the total magazine circulation was increased tenfold; and though it is true that the magazine and the newspaper became all-sufficient for most of the people represented in this increase, every thousand added to the magazine-buying public added something to the book-reading element.

[1] S. S. McClure, "My Autobiography," p. 246.

Appeals for the "Square Deal"

Stephen Crane defies classification, yet defies omission. He stands out in his period in the manner of "the red sun . . . pasted in the sky like a wafer," to which he alluded in his most celebrated book.[1] His connections with current literary history were as varied as his personal relations, which ran from the newshawks in Park Row past Howells and Garland to neighborliness in England with Henry James and Joseph Conrad. He wrote as a naturalist, akin to Zola, anticipating a phase of Norris and London and Dreiser and their successors. He wrote as an impressionist, very likely unaware of just what he was doing, yet at times with striking consistency. He shocked the magazine editors as successfully as Ambrose Bierce was doing and as successfully debarred himself from their pages. His sentiments were as unorthodox in America as his literary methods. He enjoyed one sensational success, "The Red Badge of Courage"; and he met a fourfold response from it: wide reading from the public which pays for best-sellers; prompt invitations from newspaper editors who saw in him the makings of a special reporter; continued disapproval from the literary magazine people; and cordial endorsement from the novelists mentioned above. It was not until the middle 1920's that his collected works were considered worth publishing, at about the time that re-recognition was being given Melville, Hearn, Bierce, and Emily Dickinson. This is quite understandable. Crane was an innovator, but not in one line nor repeatedly enough in any one line to make himself felt. He was an iconoclast, but not a very damaging one. He had a slow beginning, writing at first some most insipid stuff; and he had an early end, abroad, at a time when other vivid men of his age were able to reap what he had sown. He had sown energy, but without any such purposefulness as the American public was wanting. He had no ambition to be either prophet or evangelist.

---

[1] "The Red Badge of Courage," in "The Works of Stephen Crane" (edited by Wilson Follett), Vol. I, p. 69.

Not so, however, with such other spokesmen for the people as Frank Norris, Jack London, and Upton Sinclair, as a few dates and titles between 1901 and 1907 attest. Norris's "Octopus" appeared in 1901 and "The Pit" in 1903; London's "People of the Abyss" in 1903, his "War of the Classes" in 1905; Sinclair's "Jungle" in 1906 and London's "Iron Heel" in 1907 — a sixfold attack (that could easily be multiplied sixfold) on the exploitation of the public by organized wealth.

Frank Norris (1870–1902), fulfilling the promise of his earlier efforts, "Vandover and the Brute" and "McTeague," projected a "trilogy of the wheat," in which he undertook to give an imaginative and poetic conception of wheat-raising and a realistic treatment of the trafficking in the crop on which no man could long venture with impunity. In these novels "The Octopus" is the railroad combine which oppresses the wheatgrower, and "The Pit" is the symbol of the speculator who is equally regardless of farmer or consumer. "The Wolf," never written, was to have dealt with the relief of a famine in the Old World. Norris aspired like his own character Presley, the poet: "He strove for the diapason, the great song which should embrace in itself a whole epoch, a complete era, the voice of an entire people."[1] He conceived of the wheat as an enormous, primitive force:

> The Wheat that had killed Cressler, that had engulfed Jadwin's fortune and all but unseated reason itself; the Wheat that had intervened like a great torrent to drag her husband from her side and drown him in the roaring vortices of the Pit, had passed on, resistless, along its predetermined course from West to East, like a vast Titanic flood, had passed leaving Death and Ruin in its wake, but bearing Life and Prosperity to the crowded cities and centres of Europe.[2]

Norris's companion stories are combinations of hard fact and sentimental optimism. He saw a situation through the farmer's eyes. Between his tilled fields and the market lay a

[1] "The Octopus" (1922), p. 9.

[2] "The Pit," p. 402. Copyright, 1903, Doubleday, Doran & Company, Inc.

steel highway, owned in the distant East, controlled by an impersonal corporation, inhuman and greedy. Against this organization of capital any unprejudiced study will show that the frontier had a deep and genuine grievance and that the farmer had brooded over it until he was ready to blame it for all that it deserved and for a good deal more besides. Norris's picture of the slaughter of a herd of sheep by an onrushing train through a cut in the hills implies that the railroad corporation was not merely heartless: that it was deliberately malevolent. Yet Norris corrects this impression, which belongs to the farmer and not to himself. To him the whole cruel story is only a phase in an evolutionary process at the back of which is essential righteousness. In an afterword he declares, "The larger view always and through all shams, all wickedness, discovers the Truth that will, in the end, prevail, and all things, surely, inevitably, resistlessly work together for good."[1] It is a conviction which the author had a perfect right to hold, but it is clearly imposed on the story rather than derived from it.

Jack London (1876–1916) preached revolution instead of depending on evolution. His extraordinary energy dissipated itself in a life of adventure that found its record in a long series of stories, of which "The Call of the Wild" and "The Sea Wolf" are best known, and in a life of violent social protest that found its vent in part in a succession of violent books. In his writing career of sixteen years he wrote fifty volumes, an extraordinary performance in mass production but reason enough for the comparative lack of distinction in his output. Oyster pirate, common seaman, tramp, Klondike gold-seeker, he studied a little while at the University of California, and he evidently read a good deal in economics. But his most definite piece of study was in his life in the East End of London, which combined adventure with a search for information about the life of the unemployed, and bore fruit in "The People of the Abyss." He concluded rather eagerly

---

[1] "The Pit," closing passage.

not only that there was much hardship and injustice in the most enlightened nations, but that this was the result of a cold malice in the controlling classes. He did not believe with such observers as H. G. Wells that wealth was neither malicious enough nor skillful enough to create and maintain the worst of existing conditions. "The Iron Heel" maintains quite the opposite thesis, and "Revolution" offers London's program of redress. His death in 1916 removed him from the scene just before war influences and post-war methods of repression partially fulfilled his picture of conservative tactics. In the next few years his books of social protest could hardly have been circulated. In his own day their author was too evidently excited to be successfully exciting. Norris was more artistic; Sinclair, more gifted as a writer and more substantial as a critic.

Upton Sinclair until he wrote "The Jungle" in 1906 gave little sign of being the child who is father to the present man of that name. His earliest works were thin, shallow, sugary. There was a good deal of Byron's self-pity in them, none of his vigor, and certainly none of his humor. Then his intense seriousness seems suddenly to have been diverted from himself into the paths followed by Norris and London and by every serious student of the social order for the last century and a half. In "The Jungle," which subordinated art to argument, he showed the great gifts for developing character and narrating dramatic action which make him a compelling story-teller. In this novel and in his succeeding work were all his special traits: the sense of the trained journalist for selection of the timely topic; an intense desire for social justice, heightened as the years have passed by the consciousness of injustice to himself; an ability to use documents, whether in direct controversy or woven into narrative; a readiness to employ the vehemence as well as the logic of the prosecuting attorney; and a belief in human perfectibility which encourages him to carry on the campaign with amazing energy and persistence.

"The Jungle," dedicated to the workingmen of America, is a novel of the stockyards, involving the tragic career of a

Lithuanian immigrant. The first half of the story traces the experience of the man and his family, the circumstances of their employment, their housing, their mishaps at the hands of sharpers, police, and politicians. The account suggests the Russian novelists in its fidelity. It passes judgment on the unscrupulousness of the employer as to the quality of his goods, the treatment of his hirelings, his chafferings with the men who are responsible for governmental inspection and control. It pictures, in contrast, the central figure as forced into criminality by surrounding circumstances and then brutally mistreated by the whole legal system, in which the underlings — police, detectives, and jail staffs — become open enemies of offenders who are not protected by influence. The victim, transformed from an eager, honest laborer into an enemy of society, loses wife, child, and family in a series of outrageous miscarriages of justice. But the skill of the earlier part of the tale is lost as the author goes on into explicit socialist propaganda. Sinclair wanted to save society and was unwilling to sacrifice his immigrant. At the end of the story the logic of events is suspended. Jurgis has a job and is vaguely expectant of a social millennium in the very near future.

Nevertheless the story gave two promises, both of which have been fulfilled: that Sinclair could write narratives as few Americans can, and that he was permanently enlisted in a running campaign against the economic system. Projected under the title of "The Dead Hand" (though he abandoned its use), Sinclair's discussions of the influence of wealth on the leading institutions became an imposing series: "The Profits of Religion," "The Brass Check" (journalism), "The Goose Step" (the colleges), "The Goslings" (the schools), "Money Writes" (the publishers). All tend to extremes and often make the worse appear the better argument; but they cannot be dismissed as baseless. Some of Sinclair's later novels — "100%," a story of debased pseudo patriotism, "Oil," and "Boston," an intimate picture of the Sacco-Vanzetti case — offer equal claims to attention as journalism, history, and literature.

Norris and London and Sinclair were the shock troops in the fictional assault on organized wealth from 1901 on. A second wave of less violence followed hard after them. The writers are neither so vigorous nor so constant. Some of them, like Thomas Nelson Page, William Allen White, and Winston Churchill,[1] seem to have adopted this theme because it was in the air. Used to other sorts of subjects, they took a turn at this one in the spirit of the journalist, like a McClure or a Bok on the lookout for timely topics. Others, such as Brand Whitlock, Ernest Poole, and Sherwood Anderson, enlisted in the campaign with a good deal of zest, but tired of the role of crusader and turned to other less militant undertakings. None had the energy or the conviction of the original trio.

Brand Whitlock, an avowed follower of Howells, prefaced his "Turn of the Balance" in 1907 with a quotation from the older man, ending significantly: "In fact it seems best to be very careful how we try to do justice in this world, and mostly to leave retribution of all kinds to God, who really knows about things." The story is the evident work of a man who knew much at first hand about crime and legalism and who did not regard the law as the word of the Lord. He showed how erratic is the balance of justice and how resourceful the lawyer can be in swinging it against poverty and in favor of wealth. The same contrast between human and divine justice prevails in William Allen White's "A Certain Rich Man" of two years later. White, after describing the rise to imperial power of John Barclay, brought him to the bar of public opinion, which is impervious to the influences that play on ordinary courts; for this public opinion is "God moving among men. . . . Through the centuries, amid the storm and stress of time, often muffled, often strangled, often incoherent, often raucous and inarticulate with anguish, but always in the end triumphant, the voice of the people is indeed the voice of God!"[2] And White was unwilling to allow poetic

[1] Notably in "Coniston."

[2] W. A. White, op. cit. p. 326.

justice to prevail only in the distant future; he contrived, as Norris did, to square accounts within the limits of his novel, leaving the thoughtful reader dubious as to whether his scrip will be redeemable on the Day of Judgment.

Page's "John Marvel, Assistant" (1909) is both less and more of an achievement than these others. It is a pleasantly ending romance in which a rather lightweight gentleman becomes a serious citizen and is rewarded with both an heiress and the gratitude of his fellow townsmen. But it is also a vehicle for a series of theses which involve an acknowledgment to the Jewish race, the recognition of socialism as a factor to be reckoned with in modern life, the viciousness of unscrupulous finance coupled with rotten politics, specious philanthropy, and truckling ecclesiasticism. The book is clumsily and carelessly written, but it used and apparently popularized a formula — a variant on the wise and foolish virgins — which reappeared often in social novels of the next few years. This is the formula of the frivolous college boy with a long purse and the serious college student who is earning his way — Silver Spoon and Baggy Trousers. They meet and part in freshman year; Silver Spoon is a general favorite; Baggy Trousers disappears into the obscurity reserved for good scholarship. Years after, they encounter each other in an industrial dispute, when Baggy Trousers as a champion of labor opens the social eyes of Silver Spoon and makes a sadder and a wiser man of him.

This reoccurs in Ernest Poole's "Harbor" (1915), though Poole in this, his first mature work, writes with a far more intimate knowledge of the industrial world and with a far better sense of the mutual interdependence of the capitalist, the engineer, and the laborer. He sees that the laborer is not receiving his dues, but he catches a glimpse of the technician who dreams, for example, of a great harbor which will be not the chaos of New York but a harmonious and smooth-working unity that only the great planner and the daring capitalist can achieve with the help of the workingman. The formula occurs again, not impressively, in Churchill's "Far

Country" (1915), and somewhat vaguely in "The Dwelling Place of Light" (1917), as Churchill turned from history and politics and religion to the urgent subject of industry, and displayed the same conscientious desire to prepare himself carefully and to write improvingly on a pressing problem in modern American life.

Sherwood Anderson, in "Windy McPherson's Son" (1916) and "Marching Men" (1917), saw the situation from a less partisan viewpoint. He saw the laborer reduced to the status of machine tender and pieceworker. He thought of him, therefore, not as a victim of capitalism, but as a puppet in an evolutionary process that neither workman nor capitalist can control. He allowed two young village fortune hunters to get within reach of the game and decide it is hardly worth the shooting. Instead of brooding over the wrongs of the laborer, they dream of a social millennium that will be reached through a restoration of the "rhythm of life" symbolized in the tramp of marching men. Anderson's enthusiasm carried him off his feet. One reads a passage like this and is not stirred:

> Chicago is one vast gulf of disorder. Here is the passion for gain, the very spirit of the bourgeoisie gone drunk with desire. The result is something terrible. Chicago is leaderless, purposeless, slovenly, down at the heels. And back of Chicago lie the long cornfields, that are not disorderly. There is hope in the corn. Spring comes and the corn is green.[1]

Evidently the writer was stirred, but it was by listening to his own street-corner diatribe against the social order, capped with a fairy-tale nature that plants and tills the orderly cornfields without the help of the farmer. It is a far cry from this sort of writing to the kind that the hero of "Marching Men" aspired to: "He wanted his true note as an individual to ring out above the hubbub of voices and then he wanted to use the strength and virility in himself to carry his word far." Fervent as he was in his early work, Anderson did not

---

[1] "Marching Men" (Dodd, Mead), p. 156.

hit on this true note of his own until he passed from thinking of men and women as slaves to the industrialism from which he himself had escaped, and had come to think of them as living in a world of primary experiences so vital that their inciting causes faded into insignificance.

"The Revolt from the Village"[1]

Interest in the common man was not confined to the realists in the years after the turn of the century. The romantic and idealistic writers had long been enjoying their innings and had built up a convention of the idyllic village: Sweet Auburn, as Goldsmith recollected it; Cranford, as Mrs. Gaskell had re-created it. It stood in the same hall of good repute with the Old-School Southern gentleman, the wild Westerner, the American bad boy, whose badness was so mildly mischievous, the American tired business man, the gaily approachable but irreproachable American girl. It is a late post-Victorian revival in fiction; but it still marks a current concern with the commoner and, like most post-Victorian survivals, it serves as a point of departure toward something more modern and more lifelike.

There had been two traditions about the average American village. One was that it was the undisturbed abode of all that was reputable, homely, amiable, altruistic, the last secure haven of "friendship, honesty, and sweet-clean marriageable girls." In one story after another the American boy went away from this perfect community; had his fling; sobered down; turned his back on the wickedness of Europe and the American big city; and in the last chapter came home to the village street, the white picket fence, the faithful family dog, the lilacs, the moonlight, the waiting lady love, and happiness ever after. It was the loveliest village of the plain, but it was not America. Always the town was described with benevolence rather than with detachment or with anything like critical honesty.

[1] A phrase of Carl Van Doren's. See his discussion of it in "Contemporary American Novelists."

Thus it stands in Mrs. Deland's "Old Chester Tales." Such people as Mrs. Deland described have certainly lived. Such wisdom as she gives to old Dr. Lavender is certainly a redeeming feature in many a town where it manages to survive in solitude. But there is nothing in Old Chester to suggest that the whole story of the town is not told, and that there is any trace of viciousness or malignity even in the unchronicled stories of the folks in the background. There is not even a defeated villain to disturb the serenity. Old Chester is the stronghold of intrenched and usually petty conservatism, against which the sane wisdom of Dr. Lavender stands out in pleasant relief. Mrs. Deland's own interest in the town was that of the absentee landlord. For nearly thirty years she made literary visits back to the quaint old place, recording them in short stories; but her more substantial novels drew her out of the backwater into the current of life. Helena Ritchie is awakened. Mrs. Maitland, the iron woman, holds her own in the driving business world. The titles of "The Rising Tide" and "The Vehement Flame" carry their own implications.

Zona Gale, like Mrs. Deland, seems to have come down into the world by way of a hamlet that finally surfeited her with its sweetness. Friendship Village was apparently in Wisconsin, but, in the words of one of her friendly critics, "it actually stood . . . upon the confectionery shelf of the fiction shop, preserved in a thick syrup and set up where a tender light could strike across it at all hours."[1] She prefaced the latest of her volumes of short stories culled from there (they ran from 1908 to 1919) with a quotation from a fictive visitor to Russia in the first days after the revolution: "It was a dazzling revelation of the deep, deep powers for brotherhood and friendliness that lie buried in mankind. . . . There is no end to what men can do — for there is no limit to their good will, if only they can be shown the way."[2] But in a fore-

[1] Carl Van Doren, "Contemporary American Novelists," p. 164.

[2] Quoted from Ernest Poole's "Village." By permission of The Macmillan Company, publishers.

word to the third tale in this volume there is a hint of self-consciousness: "When stories are told of American gentleness, childlike faith, sensitiveness to duty, love of freedom, I do not remember to have heard anyone rejoin: 'Yes, but Americans are not all like that.'"[1] It is exactly the kind of remark that was being made, and the kind that Miss Gale herself was soon to justify in "Miss Lulu Bett," of the very next year.

Booth Tarkington also contributed to the general contentment at the interpretation of the American village as a happy and innocent community. According to some of his critics he was culpable for concentrating not so much on goodness as on amiable stupidity — on people who ought, perhaps, to be bored by their lots, but who enjoy life because they don't know enough to be unhappy. Tarkington has a special gift for the delineation of such men and women because they are children in all but years, and he has a natural aptitude for drawing children. Yet he is bigger than his characters, even when he is treating them most indulgently. His sympathy with them is usually tinged with irony; he understands them but never identifies himself with them; he is affectionate but detached. So too with the town of his boyhood and his boyhood itself. It has the passive respectability of William Sylvanus Baxter's uncle. It is observant but untroubled by convictions.

For this Mr. Baxter the United States is a residential district. He does not think of it in terms of either militant or civic patriotism. It does not hold his allegiance any more than does the church, a multiplex institution with a series of meeting houses among which the town is socially distributed. The family is the family, unchallengeable as the Ohio River, a placid stream rippling to eternity without falls or rapids, unruffled even by transverse winds. As an observer Mr. Baxter feels that life is well enough if only people will let it alone; but as they do not, he is made a little uneasy by the activi-

[1] "Peace in Friendship Village," p. 45. By permission of The Macmillan Company, publishers.

ties of the sordid and unwashed politician and the ruthless captain of finance. On the whole, dear old Indiana is good enough for Mr. Baxter; what is good enough for him ought to be good enough for the coming generation. From these sentiments Tarkington long showed no inclination to demur. Crowns and thrones might perish, kingdoms rise and wane, but old Indiana constant would remain. And Indiana was, to all intents and purposes, one big, sprawling village. Then at last there came a change in his attitude toward life and his representation of it. It is risky business attributing causes. Even the author himself might be puzzled on going back into the history of his shifting attitudes. Perhaps it is enough to say that very shortly after the close of the war, and a little after the rising of the "revolt from the village," Tarkington came closer to the changing life of his day and the changing point of view, just as Mrs. Deland had done during the war and as Miss Gale did while its echoes were still ringing. "Miss Lulu Bett" (Gale, 1920), "Alice Adams" (Tarkington, 1921), and "The Vehement Flame" (Deland, 1922) carry common implications as to what was happening to the old idylists of the village.

What caused the change in these chief chroniclers of the idyllic village was a definite movement with definite writers at the forefront. Yet these were not without precedents. As far back as 1868 Whittier, in his prelude to "Among the Hills," writing of the New England of a half-century before that time, pictured the thwarted, narrow, pinched results of village life in the "Shrill, querulous women, sour and sullen men" whom he could remember from his boyhood.[1] In 1883 E. W. Howe offered in vain to the leading publishers in the East the manuscript for "The Story of a Country Town." It was not the kind of thing that they thought readers wanted. He printed it himself, and on its success was able to select, from the many that applied, the house which should publish it. He was outspoken to confess in a novel that the romance

---

[1] See page 212.

of pioneer life did not result in heroic types in the ex-frontier towns; that the frontiersman who had retired, whether in success or failure, was more likely to be slack, shabby, gossipy, unimaginative, and bibulous. Yet no tide of similar realism set in. Mark Twain, to whom Howe sent a copy, wrote: "Your picture of the arid village life is vivid, and, what is more, true. I know, for I have seen and lived it all." But it was not till sixteen years later that Mark Twain published "The Man that Corrupted Hadleyburg," which contained a truth, offered not as realism but in the spirit of bitter farce-comedy. And it was another sixteen years before "the revolt" actually set in with the startling appearance not of a novel but of a volume of fragments in free verse, which, like Howe's story, is said to have gone the rounds of the publishers' offices before one of them had the astuteness and the good fortune to accept it.

This was Edgar Lee Masters's "Spoon River Anthology." The most valuable single passage on this much discussed work is Masters's own compact preface for "Toward the Gulf," with its inscription to William Marion Reedy. It was on this editor's suggestion that Masters rather casually struck off the first five Spoon River epitaphs. They were a more than casual "resuscitation of the Greek epigrams, ironical and tender, satirical and sympathetic," assembled into a collection — later variously supplemented — of nearly two hundred and fifty brief units, each a self-inscribed epitaph by one of the Spoon River townsfolk. These represent the various types in an American country town and represent the line of cleavage not so much between the good and the bad as between those who wish to be considered respectable and those who do not care — the former class including idealists and hypocrites, and the latter conscientious radicals and confirmed reprobates.

The "Anthology" was violently assailed as a wicked and cynical production, largely by the people who did not read the book through or did not understand it. Almost no one noticed that the characters were introduced in a progressive series, and that the most impressive element in the roster, and the one that bulks largest in the last quarter, is the element composed of idealists. There is Davis Matlock, who decided to live life out like a god, sure of immortality. There is Tennessee Claflin Shope, who asserted the sovereignty of his own soul, resolving to live freely and finely; and the Village Atheist, who knew that only those who strove mightily could attain eternal life; and Lydia Humphrey, who in her church found the vision of the poets. In spite of the protests of readers who were so offended by the Inferno of the earlier pages that they never read on to the concluding Paradiso, the book achieved its great circulation (fifty thousand copies within three years) among a partly tolerant and partly curious public and gained enviable applause from the most discriminating critics. The enemy had entered the gates of the town, and it was in for a pretty rough experience at the hands of the invaders.

There is a danger in this village metaphor, however tempting it may appear. The essential matter to keep in mind is that in this first quarter of the twentieth century there was a growing tendency to try to see things as they were. This tendency arose in western Europe and the United States apparently as one consequence of the World War. It expressed itself in terms of all kinds of life, individual and social; among these the small town naturally came in for its share of attention, and the novelists came to town, as it were, by various routes. Thus E. W. Howe reached it by the route of general disillusionment with life as he traveled it on the frontier; and when he followed Masters's lead with "The Anthology of Another Town," he wrote a series of anecdotes from the point of view of the honest pessimist. "Trying to live a spiritual life in a material world is the greatest folly I know anything about." And, again, "Pessimism is always nearer the truth than optimism." He had no grievance against life but entertained no ideals about it.

Sherwood Anderson came to "Winesburg, Ohio" along quite a different highway — the road of industrial protest.

In his earlier books, and particularly in "Marching Men," he was preoccupied with the problems of the laborers' world and with a sense of responsibility for setting it right. Society was chaos, the workingmen were a wronged body, and a restoration of the rhythm of life was needed to set all things right in a sentimental millennium. In his hopes and fears he was everything that Howe was not. The thought of the machine was almost overwhelming, as it ironed the workmen out to one size and thickness; and as they lost feeling for materials and zest in the use of their tools, grossness and lewdness and profanity became the pitiable outlets of their thwarted selves. For a while Anderson wrote as an evangelist; but in 1919, with "Winesburg," he left the workingman, as he became more interested in what was going on in the minds of people than in what was going on outside their bodies. They were the same people, surrounded by similar conditions, but they were no longer mainly significant to him because they were creatures of circumstance. Standardization, which when achieved brings the outward evidence of inward dullness, was gaining ground on the public; but there was still a chance for individual life and thrill and emotional adventure. So Anderson escaped from the prison camp of an industrialized society into a jungle where self-expression runs free. "Winesburg," therefore, though it is always cited between "Spoon River" and "Main Street," marks less of a revolt from the village than of a revolt from social control. It is an aspect of a town instead of a whole town like Howe's, and it concentrates on the scandal which features only the first third of "Spoon River." Anderson saw in Winesburg what Freud would have looked for and found in Friendship Village or Old Chester or Cranford or Sweet Auburn.

All these expositors of the town have seen it from some slant or bias that interfered with their sense of perspective. But Anderson was more of an artist than most of them. Sitting once before the Cathedral of Chartres, he came to know what the old craftsmen felt who had built themselves into the fabric of it. He saw that he could not be content to stay there dreaming endlessly of old days. He must do as they did, living in the moment in his own country, taking part in its growth, working honestly in the rough material of Middle Western village life, and chiseling it into form with the words which were his tools. He wanted to carve out figures inherent in the stones that lay on every side. He wanted to carve in full respect for fine craftsmanship, but not to be enslaved by the conventions of the craft. When in the reality of his people he recognized an element that the story-tellers just before his day had avoided, this served as a challenge to him rather than a warning. The Victorians on both sides of the Atlantic had been reluctant to acknowledge the persistence of sex feeling. Swinging toward the other extreme, he harped on the subliminal sex feelings, sometimes so persistently as to remind one of Thoreau with his chanticleering from the roost to wake his neighbors, or of Whitman sounding his barbaric yawp over the roofs of the world. There are other writers for such as are not interested in Anderson's raw material, but in his treatment of it Anderson has written always with sincerity and often with distinction.

Sinclair Lewis stands in direct contrast with Sherwood Anderson in his treatment of the community. Anderson takes his characters as relatively free agents and employs the town simply for stage setting. Lewis comes to the point from which Anderson set out and regards the town as an active menace which threatens the freedom of the individual. The climax of civilization, says Lewis, is the town of today that "thinks not in hoss-swapping but in cheap motor-cars, telephones, ready-made clothes, silos, alfalfa, kodaks, phonographs, leather-upholstered Morris chairs, bridge prizes, oil-stocks, motion-pictures, land-deals, unread sets of Mark Twain, and a chaste version of national politics."[1] This provincial town, with its standardization of mediocrity, might be let alone, if it were merely passive; but

[1] Lewis, "Main Street" (Harcourt, Brace), p. 264.

it has become a force seeking to dominate the earth, to drain the hills and the sea of color. . . . Its conception of a community ideal is not the grand manner, the noble aspiration, the fine aristocratic pride, but cheap labor for the kitchen and rapid increase in the price of land. . . . If all the provincials were kindly . . . there would be no reason for desiring the town to seek great traditions. It is . . . the small busy men, crushingly powerful in their common purpose, viewing themselves as men of the world but keeping themselves men of the cash-register and the comic film, who make the town a sterile oligarchy.[1]

As an indictment this is clear enough, and there is plenty of evidence on which to establish it, particularly as it takes issue with the obnoxious stupidity which is quite another thing from stupid kindliness. Excellence in a thesis novel, however, requires excellence in the novel as well as in the thesis; and it requires incomparably good story-telling to carry the double pack. Lewis admits great admiration for Dickens, praising him for his creation of character but condemning him for pages on pages of "lying hypocrisy." Lewis neither offends nor achieves with Dickens. "Main Street" pretty largely makes its case as a case, but leaves in the memory no imperative episode and no unforgettable person. One comes with a touch of surprise to a passage that alludes to Champ Parry and Sam Clark as kindly and to Harry Haydock, Dave Dyer, and Jackson Elder as the malignants in the social group. To look back over the story is to confirm the statement; but, without the reminder and the review, they all belong to one indistinguishably vulgar and stupid crowd. The few people that one remembers are not essentially Main Streeters. Carol is a woman-out-of-business, a foil and complement to Una Golden of "The Job." Doc Kennicott perhaps represents Gopher Prairie; but in the story he is used only to "play up to" the leading lady, though he is bigger than his role. One has vague memories of others, but cannot recall their names.

The creation of character is, of course, what Lewis did

[1] Lewis, op. cit. p. 267.

achieve in "Babbitt," though the success of George F. as an artistic creation lies in the fact that he is not the caricature he is usually said to be. His failure as an individual lies in the pathetic fact that he struggles to save his own soul and to free himself from the web of circumstance. Always around him, overwhelming all but the last vestige of protest in him, is the overgrown village which is known as the city of Zenith. The material side of it he likes; he rebels feebly against the standardization of thought; and in the end, irredeemably Babbitt, he still yearns for better luck for his son. "Arrowsmith" repeats the indictment against the community, but extends it to the biggest city. "Elmer Gantry" returns to it with the charge that the community which frustrates the good man rewards the charlatan; but by this time Lewis has extended his indictment from the village to include the American people as a whole.

For Book List see pages 852–855.

CHAPTER XIV

The Contemporary Scene

CRITICISM REVITALIZED

THIS prevailing tendency to re-estimate the values of American life led before long to a new chapter of American criticism. In 1913 John Macy published a modest volume, "The Spirit of American Literature," in which for the first time an American looked over the whole field of national letters without assuming at the start that he was bound to make out good cases for the best-known writers and writings. He concluded that American literature was still a province of the British and quite markedly provincial at that. Two years later Van Wyck Brooks, in "America's Coming of Age," charged the country not only with unorganized, undirected, immature vitality but with a lack of defined issues and recognizable divisions of opinion. Both critics, in the questions they put and their challenging way of putting them, recall the two major contentions in Matthew Arnold's essay on "The Function of Criticism": that for the creation of a master work of literature two powers must concur — "the power of the man and the power of the moment, and the man is not enough without the moment"; and that there must be "Criticism first: a time of true creative activity, perhaps hereafter, when criticism has done its work."

It need hardly be said again that America had had its cogent but largely unheard critics in the past. It is perhaps worth noting that these men had lacked their moments because they had been forced to address a typical American, brought up "in a sort of orgy of lofty examples, moralized poems, national anthems, and baccalaureate sermons; until he is charged with all manner of ideal purities, ideal honorabilities, ideal femininities"[1] but never taught that making a living should be incidental to something higher, and always encouraged to believe that life is a free-for-all scramble for material things, with highest rewards reserved for the most rapacious.

For these later critics people's minds had been prepared in ways that we have just been noting. The sense of America's involuntary importance in international affairs, awakened by the Spanish War, was now reaffirmed by the greatest war in history. And, capping all the rest, new educational methods based on stimulating the child rather than on checking him at every turn had aroused the spirit of challenge in the liveliest members of the generation just out of school and college and now confronted them with an unparalleled array of conditions that called for challenge. Aware that they were not living in the best of all possible times in the best of all possible worlds, they were forced to place the responsibility on the elder generations and in large degree on the generation just ahead of them. These were the conditions that developed an early and eloquent spokesman for the younger generation in the brilliant and ill-fated Randolph Bourne.

Brooks's call for debate, therefore, came at a timely moment. As he looked about his country he felt that America's long need to concentrate on occupying a continent and building up its industries had sacrificed the free individual to material ends, and that the first revolt of youth was in a new individualism that had no objective beyond a self-expression without an inner meaning. So quite in the sense of Arnold, Brooks was for creating the "moment" by defining the objectives of American youth and American life. The old American faith was limited and outworn. To build up, he declared, a "programme for the conservation of our spiritual resources" was the task of American criticism.[2]

---

[1] Brooks, "America's Coming of Age," p. 17.

[2] Brooks, "The Critics and Young America," in "Criticism in America," pp. 150–151.

Free discussion was the first step; then would come a knowledge of what was to be sought and the ways of seeking it. There was to be no lack of critical discussion in the years that followed.

In the stimulating of debate and the defining of issues, H. L. Mencken deserves a generous share of credit; for, beginning with his "Book of Prefaces" (1917), he carried on for years a general assault along the whole battle line of established tradition. He stimulated followers, stirred up opponents; he was praised to the skies, mocked at, and derided; and, by the timidly respectable, who did not read him, he was put into the category with Machiavelli, Voltaire, and Tom Paine, whom also they had not read. In fact, while he has some of the qualities of Voltaire and more of Tom Paine, he is more nearly comparable to Poe. Unlike Poe, he emerged in a period which was ready for him and for the general ideas that are at the basis of all serious discussion. Like Poe, he made his widest appeal to the reading public as a critic in spite of his output in verse, fiction, and drama. Like Poe, his ambition was to own and conduct a critical magazine with a national circulation. Unlike Poe, he was enormously industrious, methodical, businesslike; and he succeeded in a generation which offered ample rewards for these qualities.

In their literary style they are much alike. Mencken wrote of Poe what Poe might have written of Mencken: "He could never quite throw off a congenital vulgarity of taste, so painfully visible in the struttings of his style." But both could go much farther than this.[1] Mencken, writing on the level to which the author of "The Literati" often dropped, stated that in William Allen White's earliest fiction "there was a flavor of chewing gum and marshmallows," that Vachel Lindsay, "alas, has done his own burlesque," and that Hamlin Garland "has no more feeling for the intrinsic dignity of beauty . . . than a policeman." Poe fell foul of public

---

[1] See page 425.

opinion in the United States by saying that Hawthorne was "scarcely recognized by the press or the public, and when noticed at all . . . merely to be damned by faint praise." Mencken did the like with "What these fellows say is almost always nonsense, but it is at least the sort of nonsense that the American people yearn to cherish and believe in — it somehow fills their need."

In both Mencken and Poe is a contempt for the mob, both writing as intellectual aristocrats. Poe, however, fostered a rancor that was born of resentment and confined himself mainly to discussion of literary technique; but Mencken, prosperous and popular, assailed, with jovial truculence, the ways of the lawmakers and judges, preachers and teachers, Puritans and reformers, optimists and idealists. In fact, he spent so much of his energy in belittling ideas and institutions that it is hard to lay hold of his positive convictions. More nearly than anywhere else he seems to have summed them up in the points of belief he credited with emphatic approval to E. W. Howe. These propound intelligent self-interest as the "only real human motive"; commend money-getting as a means of self-interest, an evidence of good citizenship, and a measure of efficiency; discredit all claimants to disinterested public spirit; and lay the blame for public abuses on the "credulity, emotionalism, and imbecility" of the people. Yet these tenets are supplemented by the statement that Howe is the voice of the better sort of American people, "the people who discern the eternal realities in the mass of rumble-bumble," a description not easy to reconcile with the Philistinism of the mere money-grubber, and an admission of the existence of "eternal realities" that leaves the nature of them still undefined.

For all his bad-man braggadocio Mencken can be accounted for only by some such formula as he applies to Howe, who believes in the homely virtues. Mencken's incessant bombardment of stupidity, ignorance, ugliness, hypocrisy, bigotry, injustice, can rise from nothing but a desire to overthrow them. The more one reads him, the clearer it becomes that he is an incipient "Puritan" who feels the call of duty and spends much of his time repudiating it. He has said bookfuls of savage things about other people. The worst to be said of him — from his own alleged viewpoint — is that he has quite evidently been working in and out of season to be of service to the American people. Not otherwise could he have written in an unguarded moment:

> [Criticism] accomplishes two important effects. On the one hand, it exposes all the cruder fallacies to hostile examination, and so disposes of many of them. And on the other hand, it melodramatizes the business of the critic, and so convinces thousands of bystanders, otherwise quite inert, that criticism is an amusing and instructive art, and that the problems it deals with are important. What men will fight for seems to be worth looking into.[1]

What was needed for the debate was a spokesman for the conservers of tradition to uphold the need for authority while acknowledging the law of change. Of the men in the field who might have played the role, Brownell was too austere in manner to gain a wide hearing; Irving Babbitt and Paul Elmer More, too eclectic. A younger, more militant man, Stuart Sherman, took up the gage. The battle, a perennial one, was on anew: in the field of art, as to what conventions were settled and how far the artist might experiment; in the field of learning, as to whether there was any "ultimate"; in the field of conduct, as to whether society was profiting from present conditions in state, church, school, market, and family, and whether the individual should wholly accept, or redefine, or abandon the ancient codes of morals and ethics, and the standards of truth and beauty.

Sherman, to use his own phrases, became a spokesman for the school of Culture as opposed to the school of Nature. The Puritans were favorite objects of attack; they were charged with surviving as joint heirs to the smugness of Cotton Mather, the austerity of Jonathan Edwards, the strident angularity of Shaw's Mrs. Dudgeon, and the zest for censor-

[1] "Criticism in America" (Harcourt, Brace), p. 286.

ship typified in Anthony Comstock. Sherman, ignoring this straw man, contended that the actual Puritan was essentially the insurgent and that his chief bequest to America was a sturdy integrity of character. The school of Nature upheld the "natural man," and Sherman assailed him as found in the pages of Theodore Dreiser with a ferocity that was more natural than cultured. In the debate on patriotism as a magic force chiefly to be invoked in war times, Sherman became pretty much of a fire-eater and very much of an Anglo-Saxon patriot with a kind of jealous ungenerosity to Americans of recent European extraction. Sherman hated the hatred of what he called the "monoptic school of naturalistic critics and novelists" because of their unfairness as well as their unsoundness. But they goaded him into a badness of manners and loss of temper which resulted in loss of effectiveness in controversy.

However, after standing the brunt of the battle for several years, Sherman developed an unexpected tolerance and in his latest utterances gradually relaxed in austerity, condoning the ways of the younger generation, granting absolution to much modern fiction on the ground that it was no worse than the fiction of the past, and actually meting out praise to Dreiser's "American Tragedy," which contains all the features he had been inveighing against not long before. Sherman had written in consistent admiration of such older critics as Brownell and Paul Elmer More, but toward the end they regarded him as an apostate from the cause. "I do not like to see a man of your ability," wrote More, "take up the job of whitewasher"; and, "Yours is but a sickly sort of democracy at bottom, and needs a doctor." Yet in the critical movement of the day Sherman had contributed so effectively to a defining of the issues that his own defection from the ranks of the idealists is a matter of minor import.

One reason for the change may have been the very vehemence with which he wrote between the time when he entered the fray as professor in a Midwestern state university and his move to New York City as literary editor of a metropolitan journal. A hazard of new fortunes comes from a disposition to change, and a long practice as attorney for the defense leads one to say things for the sake of the argument that have no ground in either sound principle or sober judgment. No doubt Mencken goaded Sherman to sterner passion and Sherman stimulated Mencken in the wielding of the goad. At the outset they occupied abstract positions: Mencken contending that America had fallen into the lowest of low estates, that the worst in American life and art was due to its culture and the best to a miraculous bloom from no known seed and with no perceivable promise; Sherman, that there had been many virtues in the past, and that there was much hope for the future provided the current corrupting tendencies could be checked. But when the argument became confused with the personalities which Sherman was the first to use, Sherman became a hater and Mencken a mocker. Sherman tended to interpret life as finely poetic and tinged with tragedy; Mencken, as a bitterly amusing comedy. To Mencken, in his anti-Messianic, egocentric zest for life, it was a cascade of events with abundance of pleasurable possibilities; to Sherman it was an ordered cosmos, a pathway paved with service and hedged with abnegations. But Mencken took daily delight in badgering "right-thinkers" and "forward-lookers," and Sherman poured out the vials of his contempt at the corrupting influence of the naturalists and nihilists. By the time they were frankly calling names the argument had turned into a performance, and the debaters into exhibitionists. It became a game of which, being men of resource and imagination, they both naturally tired.

The kind of discussion carried on by Sherman and Mencken could not be kept alive in the midst of a vast silence. It is only because they were the clearest and most insistent voices in a chorus that they are audible at this distance. The choral was fugal, with now this set of voices and now that making its variation on the common theme of American culture, past, present, and future. As a sign of the times a succession of symposia in the 1920's is worth noting. The solidest, "Criticism in America," is the most substantial because it is an anthology rather than a symposium, a collection of utterances written independently, not only free of any common formula but free in all sorts of tangential divergences, a sort of Roman candle in the bibliography of criticism. The contributors apply to themselves and to each other various tags and epithets which are more or less disingenuous, and, with certain rare and honorable exceptions, do not keep above the plane of personalities. The marked feature is that the contributing critics are sure of the dignity of their calling. Says T. S. Eliot, "Criticism is the . . . development of sensibility; . . . and as sensibility is rare, unpopular and desirable, it is to be expected that the critic and the creative artist should frequently be the same person."[1] Says Mencken, the critic "makes the work of art live for the spectator; he makes the spectator live for the work of art. Out of the process come understanding, appreciation, intelligent enjoyment — and that is precisely what the artist tried to produce."[2] And Spingarn goes equally far in his contention that "aesthetic judgment and artistic creation are instinct with the same vital life."[3]

The symposia reveal the states of mind of the authors more truly than the conditions in America. Thus "Civilization in the United States" is an index to the temper of a group who were especially repugnant to the Brownell-More-Sherman cohorts on account of their declared belief that the worst in American life came from its traditions and that the best was accidental. Thirty authors of like mind started from the prefatorial assumptions that there was little but "dichotomy" between preaching and practice in America, that it was by no means an Anglo-Saxon country, and that it was emotionally starved. Significantly, though avowed foes of Puritanism

---

[1] "Criticism in America," pp. 209–210. [2] Ibid. p. 190. [3] Ibid. p. 44.

they omitted any formal discussion of religion from the collection. Resolved to write soberly, fearlessly, and urbanely, all but two or three of the more experienced wrote in the fear of each other, afraid of being caught approving of anything, and in tones that alternated from truculence to specious levity. Yet it was significant that so large a group should be of this mind; and their insistence on the need for restudying the past in the United States and for re-examining the present was altogether to the point.

The twelve contributors to "The Taming of the Frontier" were even more resolutely pessimistic. They announced as their thesis that "the gods of individualism . . . have been thrown down to make way for the gods of standardization," a thesis which was novel at the time only in their offering the anarchy of the old frontier towns as the ground for their belief. With anarchy, their interest in the frontier seemed to end; they turned to it in evident repugnance for a present from which any escape was welcome — even a contemplation of the bad old days of the Western past. The book was more of a post-war document than an American treatise. The authors were one with the Englishmen then described by Beverley Nichols as feeling that they were born only to suffer, that all life was futile, that the best they could do was to harden their hearts, and to whom Middleton Murry was attributing an exaggerated cynicism and an appetite for sensationalism, whether crude or refined.

The contributors to "Recent Gains in American Civilization" were men of a different temper — more mature, long experienced in active fighting for liberal causes, for freedom of speech and of research, for freedom of the press and in the pulpit. No body of men knew more directly than they the powers that were seeking to obstruct change and to repress the advocates of change. But none was better versed in the history of American life and the nature of the American people. There was a humor in the volunteering of these protestants against the existing order to give testimony to the recent improvements in that order; and there was a convincing quality in their evidence, for no one could discount it as sentimental optimism. And the burden of their findings was that there had actually been substantial gains all along the line, with valid hope for further definite progress; this from men like Beard in history, Chase in economics, Thomas in politics, Fosdick and Ward in religion, Dewey in philosophy, and others of their caliber.

By 1929 matters were ripe for an intellectual catalysis, a precipitation of the critical discussion; and it came in the outburst of talk and writing on the subject of the so-called New Humanism. Although Sherman had been for a while the chief spokesman for the party of Culture and tradition, he had had three telling defects: he was not the first of the party in time, he was not the first in real authority, and he was not constant in his position. The real contemporary leaders, W. C. Brownell,[1] Irving Babbitt, and Paul Elmer More, all less dynamic in style, all relatively overlooked in the years since the World War, were now called to the front. Babbitt had adopted his theme with "Literature and the American College" in 1908, contending for standards and balances in estimating values; had continued in the same vein with "The New Laokoön" in 1910; in 1919 had attacked Rousseau as undisciplined, uncultured, deficient in sense of proportion; and in "Masters of French Criticism" and "Democracy and Leadership" in 1924 had continued the plea for standards in ethics, art, and criticism. Paul Elmer More had begun even earlier (in 1904) with the first of his series of "Shelburne Essays." In a long editorship of *The Nation* he had exerted a strong conservative influence on contributors as well as readers; and after relinquishing his post he wrote repeatedly and at length on the relation of Greek philosophy to Christian thought.

The humanism to which these men subscribed (and more particularly their suddenly acquired disciples marshaled by Norman Foerster) was not new, though it was newly em-

---

[1] See pages 722–723.

phasized. It represented a middle ground on which the pattern for man was "the something in his nature that sets him apart simply as a man from other animals and that Cicero defines as 'a sense of order and decorum and measure in deeds and words.'"[1] In the conflicting beliefs of the day it stood between the supernaturalism of the churchman and the naturalism of the biochemical determinists; in literary criticism, between romanticism and the naturalism of the ultra-realists. Unfortunately for the clarity of the debate that ensued, no definition of humanism proved satisfactory to many of its proponents or to any of them very long. The authors of the symposium "Humanism and America" were in open and complicated disagreement, and were reduced thereby largely to discussion compounded of disapproval of their allies and objurgations of their opponents. Tested by their literary judgments,[2] they proved to be equally captious; there are no masterpieces nor master authors in the history of world literature for whom there was any accord of approval. The champions of standards were bowing down before a set of undefined abstractions, and the counterblast, "A Critique of Humanism," had as its common factor a dissent from these abstractions without a counter-doctrine. The desirable goal of a definition of issues was no nearer at the end of the discussion than at the beginning, and the discussion waned because the magazine editors who played it up for more than a year could no longer harp on that string. Yet the hue and cry over the New Humanism had two results: the presentation of a somewhat blurred point of view from which life, literature, and the other arts could be evaluated; and the attraction, by its vehemence, of a popular attention to these problems which was unprecedented in the United States. That so many people were paying attention to something of the kind was in its way more significant than just what they were paying attention to.

---

[1] Irving Babbitt, in "Humanism and America," p. 28.

[2] E. Bernbaum, "The Practical Results of the Humanistic Theories," *English Journal,* Vol. XX, pp. 103–109.

The inclination among the malcontents to discredit American culture as the source of American commercialism and to belaud European culture without acknowledging its fruits in European chaos was offset in the 1920's by a handful of wiser studies which admitted the cleavage of the new country from the Continental past, saw the futility of imitation, and looked for independent growth. They supplemented and, in the main, confirmed the observations of such foreign commentators as André Siegfried and Bernard Faÿ. Siegfried's "America Comes of Age" (1927) carried in its title a fulfillment of Brooks's book of a dozen years earlier. And Faÿ's "American Experiment" (1929) emphasized anew the difference in national temperaments and behavior, — a typical commentary from the Old World on the New; age and tradition facing youth and boundless energy; Ambassador Claudel regarding Colonel Lindbergh. "Amazing! I never lost his restless energy. I never had it." And what that energy was to accomplish, the French critic was willing to leave to the future.

Three American estimates written with this perspective may be cited as typical of many more: Lewis Mumford's "Sticks and Stones" (1924), Waldo Frank's "Rediscovery of America" (1929), and Frederic L. Paxson's "When the West is Gone" (1930).

Mumford's study is made in terms of architecture, starting with colonial America as an heir to European ways; showing how the earliest towns were almost immediately forced to meet problems of town-planning and housebuilding in terms of new conditions; following to the evolution of the big city and the development of the "imperial façade" of boulevards and parks flanked by public buildings behind which discomfort and squalor were blanketed much as in ancient and imperial Rome; proceeding to the domination of the machine, which, with the disappearance of the craftsman, dictated that home, office building, or factory be an assembling of mill and foundry products; and concluding, much as Brooks had done in "America's Coming of Age," with an appeal for a unification of American life which might enable Americans to live and work and play and worship in something other than an unregulated miscellany of structures derived from everywhere but home.

Waldo Frank, influenced, like Mumford, by Spengler's "Decline of the West," opened with a listing of the chief convictions dominant in the medieval world, and declared that they were interesting only because they had been abandoned. He traced the confusion in an America floundering between lost beliefs, vague ideals, and actual conditions, noted the development of the power-man demanded in the opening centuries and his succession by the comfort-seeker, product of prosperity. Yet he concluded, American-wise, in spite of his depressing picture, in the optimistic conviction that the country was "capturable"; that the people of America were capable of entertaining ideals without which they would perish.

Paxson soberly followed the deduction to be drawn from the history of the frontier, that dramatic series of departures from precedent which were the destiny of the pioneer. He showed how Washington, representing the West of his day, led the way to national independence; how Jefferson, appealing to the men of the back country, overthrew Federalism and established a broader democracy; how Jackson of the Mississippi Valley was the next insurgent leader; and how Lincoln of Illinois fought for new issues at the head of a new and triumphant party. With the defeat, for the first time, of the fifth challenge of the West, by the Populists, the historian showed how Eastern industrialism at last became strong enough to cope with insurgent Western liberalism. And he concluded with a speculation as to whether the America of the future would sink back toward the old European order from which it had sprung or would continue to reach for its own solution of its new problems, thus ending, like the others, with a hope that was almost confidence.

Personality and Fate in Fiction

From the date of Howells's conversion to Tolstoyan doctrines,[1] his influence, combined with the spirit of the times, tended to convert the novel into a vehicle for criticism. But the world of institutional life cannot usurp an art to the exclusion of the individual, who is the chief subject of all literature. There is an imposing body of fiction written in the United States since 1890 in which fate, in the form of personality, is the theme, and in which circumstance, as determined by such mechanisms as state and market and court and church and school, has only incidental place.

With the death of Howells in 1920, Edith Wharton was left as the connecting medium in American fiction between his generation and the group who took the center of the picture after the War. One could begin to define later tendencies among American novelists by saying that they reveal influences to which she was long or always impervious. She belonged to the privileged class into which James was born and Howells gravitated; and this class composed her world. The men in her novels not infrequently disappear into a vague realm of business; the single introduction of labor and labor problems is used merely to aggravate a marital misunderstanding. Her characters ignore the machinery of institutionalized life and, almost equally, the whole field of institutionalized art — the theater, the opera house, the art gallery, the library. They dissent from the crowd because, being the crowd, it must be vulgarly wrong. They are full of refinements and keenly aware of the dictates of good form, which make them live in continual fear of one another's faint disapproval, faintly but damningly expressed. Her characters are almost uniformly dominated not by the law but by a code which is stronger than any law.

To this code Mrs. Wharton gives the name of "The Custom of the Country" in a novel which is a key to much of

---

[1] See page 745.

her writing. Undine Spragg, beautiful, ambitious, and none too scrupulous, defies or ignores the code successively in Rocky Mountain Apex, in New York City, and in France. Everywhere she is stronger than the individuals she encounters, and nowhere strong enough to contend with the custom of the country. It is as impersonal as gravitation and as incessant in its pressure. In "Ethan Frome," unusual for Mrs. Wharton in dealing with rural characters, Ethan and Mattie try to take life into their own hands. They meet their nemesis in lifelong dependency on the woman who has thwarted them, but to whom, in terms of the code, they would have played traitor. Lily Bart, in "The House of Mirth," is trained in incompetency by the code that rules at her social level, and, left impoverished on the death of her father, is too much of a lady and too little of anything else to cope with the situation by making a good "catch." The only things she can do well are to procrastinate and equivocate; and, so doing, she comes to a miserable end.

Mrs. Wharton never did better in writing of this world than in one of her later books, "The Age of Innocence." It is a novel about the early 70's in New York, contrasting the rigid complacency of the Old School generation with the Bohemianism of the outer world of arts and letters, with the startling encroachments of the vulgar rich, with the dry rot of some among the elect who only pretend to concur (and whom their friends pretend not to detect), and with the honestly decent who were half smothered by the unventilation of the exclusive best houses in New York. The three leading characters are all victims of Mrs. Grundy, who, by and large, is the dominant character in Mrs. Wharton's book; and this not because the novelist approves of the old lady, but because she acknowledges her power over all who wish to survive in the limited world where the duenna queens it.

Mrs. Wharton's manner belongs to this world. It is keen, brilliant, clever in the way of the social dictator who has a highly developed sense of form, a sharp eye, and a sharper tongue. The dialogue gleams and glimmers, seldom falling to the level of actual conversation. It is attenuated, like the people whom it characterizes; it is doubtless quite fair to them; it has a distinction like their own and like Mrs. Wharton's descriptions of them. They are a part of America today; but the reader can take them only as the author usually does, with a slight measure of compassionate amusement. Spiritually they have the kind of phosphorescence that is caused in some organic matter by decay. Howells turned away from them in mid-career. James and Mrs. Wharton remained faithful to them and demonstrated what distinction of artistry can do with undistinction of subject matter.

Willa Cather, who, like Mrs. Wharton, believes that the primary element in fiction is the development of character rather than the analysis of social life, deals mostly with more primary types. The dedication of her first book of distinction, "O Pioneers!" to a lady and author of the Old School, Sarah Orne Jewett, is an indication only of her progress away from the happy enjoyment of self-realization to the harrowing struggle toward that end. Mrs. Wharton's characters are never vigorous enough for success; they flinch and fail in the face of circumstance; they incline to peter out. Miss Cather's more notable characters achieve some permanent satisfaction in life. Whether this success is won in studio or study, or whether it is won on the plains, it seems to be the result of a primitive, driving impulse which is more controlling than controlled and which is related to natural, primitive experience. Alexandra Bergson's actions smack of the soil; so do Antonia Shimerda's. Thea Kronberg, on the way to fame, flees tumultuous Chicago to regain her poise in a sun-flooded Arizona canyon.

The trio with which Miss Cather established her literary standing, "O Pioneers," "My Antonia," and "The Song of the Lark," are all chronicles of hard, dreary beginnings and ultimate success — the development not only of individual character but of a new social order by passionate souls expiating their mistakes in bewildered pain as the struggle goes on. In the first of the stories looms the splendid figure of Alexandra, masterful, too magnanimous to be understood, doomed to spiritual solitude among her own people, but indomitable. In the second appears Thea, equally single-minded and equally poised, who succeeds on the stage as Alexandra succeeds on the soil. Through the two Miss Cather identifies the spirit of the pioneer with the spirit of the creative artist, ignoring the lesser figures in the epic of the frontier, just as she ignores orchestra, chorus, and stage-hands in the triumph of the prima donna. But from the last of the three stories emerges Antonia, apotheosis of the pioneer working-woman; Martha, glorified on the frontier, a rich spring of life, suffused at the end in a sunset gleam against the background of field and furrow.

Yet Miss Cather falls short of perfect fidelity to her material for a twofold reason: she is a Nebrasko-Virginian writing of immigrant folk. That means, for one thing, that she knows her people only as well as they can be known through sympathetic observation. They are idealized, interpreted as creative personalities, vested with the characteristics of the artist whom Miss Cather knows by nature as well as by observation. And it means, for another thing, that since she knows her immigrants through sympathetic observation, when sympathy and observation fall into conflict, sympathy wins. She has the kindliness of an indulgent literary parent; she is unwilling to resign them to their fates — as she consents to do with the "lost lady," for whom she has no respect or affection. She does not, therefore, record the sacrifice of the individual pioneer as the pioneer army conquers the plain, though she allows her fictive offspring to stray into the very last ditches of defeat before she serves as leader of relief parties in a series of unconvincing rescues.

For a while, perhaps under the disrupting influences of the World War, Miss Cather seemed to be warped out of her orbit on such flights as "One of Ours" and "The Lost Lady." Yet as one thinks of these in conjunction with the next two, "The Professor's House" and "My Mortal Enemy," and these with the foregoing novels and the pair that succeeded them, a pattern emerges which is so nicely consistent that one suspects it, fearful of having fashioned it out of less than substance. The early group, up to "My Antonia," deals with creative energies in the studio and on the plains, artists and pioneers struggling for self-fulfillment and, by grace of their own natures and the assistance of the author, achieving it. After an interval of four years this post-bellum quartet is concerned with weaker personalities — native Americans subjected to American contemporary life, baffled, frustrated, defeated by it.

Finally, "Death Comes for the Archbishop" and "Shadows on the Rock" turn from the Anglo-Saxon Protestant American scene to the regions of Spanish-American and French colonial culture and find security in the most substantially enduring tradition in the modern Occident — the authority of the Church of Rome. It is a cycle with epic implications which, happily, are left as implications and not advanced as a thesis. It affirms the dramatic past, with its wealth of opportunity for action and for triumph. It denies the fruitfulness of the present, with its material pressures which have proved too strong for the individual. And it finds its repose in a tranquil culture, a life of unity and order, resting on authority and an established mode of living and believing. "What is any art," Miss Cather has asked, "but an effort to make a sheath, a mould in which to imprison for a moment the shining, elusive element which is life itself, — life hurrying past us and running away, too strong to stop, too sweet to lose?"[1]

•

The novels of Theodore Dreiser, by focusing attention on his literary naturalism, helped to lead the way to the humanistic controversy. In 1900 his "Sister Carrie" was published and promptly withdrawn, the same year in which Zola's "Fecundity" was widely circulated in the United States. We were not used then in America, Dreiser commented later,

---

[1] "Song of the Lark," p. 304.

to calling spades spades, particularly in books. We had great admiration for Tolstoi and Flaubert and Balzac and De Maupassant at a distance, but mostly we had been accustomed to that refined company of English sentimental realists who told us something about life, but not too much. The book was withdrawn by the publishers. Eleven years after "Sister Carrie," "Jennie Gerhardt" appeared and caused a sensation, reviving the earlier novel; other stories followed, and the controversy was on. Sherman declared that Dreiser had told just two things about his favorite character, Cowperwood: that he had a rapacious appetite for wealth and for women. The books about him, he wrote, were in effect huge sandwiches, "composed of slices of business alternating with erotic episodes." Mencken retorted on "the critical imbecility which detects naught save a tom-cat in Frank Cowperwood." A third critic, who was more interested in understanding Dreiser than in fighting, said that he was a mystic who employed the gestures of a realist.

Anyone who has had Dreiser held up to him as a morbid anatomist of souls might well begin a direct acquaintance with him by reading "Twelve Men." Almost every subject of these dozen portraits, to use Dreiser's own formula, "deliberately and of choice holds fast to many, many simple and human things, and rounds out life, or would, in a natural, normal, courageous, healthy way."[1] As portraits these men are merely set against picturesque backgrounds; but in the six novels that represent the author's most ambitious attempt to present life men and women are put in the midst of a multitudinous world, subject to forces to which they cannot adjust themselves and which they cannot in the least control. Whether the central characters are externally successful or not, success is not an end or even a resting point for them. It is a wave crest on a turbulent stream.

For Dreiser, starting with a conviction that life was ordained on just and orderly lines, was forced into surrender

[1] Dreiser, op. cit. p. 1.

of this position. It was the reading of Herbert Spencer's "Data of Ethics" and "First Principles"[1] that set him on his uncharted course. He felt the rhythm of life, but the central fact to him was that the whole thing was unknowable, incomprehensible. He went into the depths and was not sure that he ever got entirely out of them. He has made, more or less explicitly, many admissions that he is not resigned to agnosticism. Again and again he rejects the existence of justice or morality even as abstract standards; yet he never stops groping for what he calls "the equation inevitable." Life, he says, knows no law but the law of the jungle; but he falls back, after all, on another law in an Emersonian resort to compensation: In the end, he has often asserted, a balance was invariably struck wherein the mass subdued the individual or the individual the mass — for the time being. For the sea was ever dancing or raging. In the meantime there had sprung up social words and phrases expressing a need of balance — of equation. These were right, justice, truth, morality, an honest mind, a pure heart — all words meaning a balance must be struck. These social words, repudiate them as he may, are the nearest substitute for the Rock of Ages that he can find, and he continually clambers back to them as the sea dances and rages.

In the "painful kingdom of time and place" Dreiser is doing a work as massive and hard-wrought as the statues of Rodin. The failure of most of his characters to "round out life in a natural, normal, courageous, healthy way" is because he feels it his artistic duty to write of the actual world. Possibly it is the disorder of the world that is finally responsible for the clumsy maladroitness of his novel structure and most of his prose and for the occasional surprising occurrence of a passage of surprising beauty. His literary offenses are as obvious as the harsh ugliness of the life he describes; yet he can write such passages as this and relieve his novels by such moments:

---

[1] See "A Book about Myself," pp. 457–458; "A Hoosier Holiday," pp. 343–344, 368; "Hey Rub-a-Dub-Dub," p. 174; etc., etc.

What has impressed me most about life, always, is the freshness and newness of everything, the perennial upwelling of life in every form; the manner in which, as age steals on for some, youth, new, innocent, inexperienced, believing, takes charge, its eyes alight with aspiration, its body ablaze with desire. . . . Does the bit of thread or pattern that we see here now show the least evidence of wear or tear? Is not the race as new, as fresh as ever? We rise betimes and the ancient sunlight streams fresh and strong and *new* into our passing window — the window, which, in a few years, will be as forgotten and as unrecoverable as we ourselves shall be.[1]

Sherwood Anderson, though he has made his contributions to the chronicles of passionate love, has turned to this as one of many themes. In individual stories he has stressed it out of normal proportion, but it does not hold the central place in his work as a whole. In "A Story Teller's Story" is a passage in which he admits a boylike wish to be not only loved but to be dreaded and feared. And he indulged the desire to figure as bold and bad in some aspects of "Winesburg, Ohio," carrying it to excess in "Many Marriages." He is, in fact, a sensitive artist and sensitive to most hostile comment. He could be hurt by the criticism that any of his characters are not worth putting into fiction; but the charge that he is a wicked man with a wicked mind could not disturb him. At times he has been over-insistent on the imperativeness of sex, too conscious to be impressive. The truth about this phase of him lies somewhere between the loudest outcries of his most hostile critics and the prevailing implications of his most erotic pages: he is not so morbid as his accusers insist, and the problem does not loom so large as he suggests.

The real object of self-expression is revealed in a subordinate figure of "Dark Laughter," Sponge Martin. It is the self-fulfillment that comes with competency to do something well, the doctrine of John Ruskin and William Morris. Sponge is just one more man in a factory, inactive, unprotesting, contented; but he is a capable workman whose

---

[1] "Hey Rub-a-Dub-Dub" (Liveright Publishing Corporation), p. 201.

hands have become so skilled that he does not need to pay attention to them as his mind runs on in vague reverie and his tongue in rambling talk.

> Bruce decided that the old man was not necessarily self-satisfied. With him being satisfied or not satisfied did not count . . . he liked the skill of his own hands. That gave him something to rest on in life. . . . He rested in that fact and his wife rested in him. The man and woman had stayed within the limits of their powers, had moved freely within a small but clear circle of life.[1]

A greater problem for Anderson, judging from its recurrence, is the problem of surmounting or overthrowing the walls that isolate one person from another. The metaphor, once noted, recurs insistently throughout the stories. Only now and again do humans come into each other's spiritual presences. Partners, plotters, husbands and wives, are all held apart by impalpable barriers. In a sketch called "The Man's Story" Anderson expounds this in prose and puts it into a poem which ends:

> Do you see this hand? Suppose it held a knife that could cut down through all the falseness in you? Suppose it could cut down through the sides of buildings and houses where thousands of people now lie asleep.
>
> It would be something worth thinking about if the fingers of this hand gripped a knife that could cut and rip through all the ugly husks in which millions of lives are enclosed.[2]

Anderson finds self-expression for himself as a "word-fellow" in working for "the tale of perfect balance, all the elements of the tale understood, the power of self-criticism fully at work." As a result of this the reader closes a book of his, feeling that on the whole he has been reading poetry. His medium is fitted to the American life in which he was born and to which he is devoting himself. It is a part of America whose fineness is crudely articulated and not given to nice nuances of manner. In his treatment of it Anderson

---

[1] Anderson, "Dark Laughter" (Liveright Publishing Corporation), p. 117.
[2] "Horses and Men" (Viking Press), p. 296.

is fulfilling his hope to make his "true note as an individual ring out above the hubbub of voices . . . and to use the strength and virility within himself to carry his word far."

To the attentive reader Joseph Hergesheimer has given the key to his interpretation in the book called "From an Old House." He has installed himself in a homestead that prolongs the quiet of an early American pastoral in the midst of a tumultuous present. It promotes the spirit of the patriot, as this roots itself in love of the land; depresses him with a sense of the social disintegration now in process; and reawakens the faith of the Federalist who is skeptical about the democratic experiment that is substituting bungalows and apartment houses for homesteads which stand foursquare against the winds of innovation. He himself is a Presbyterian child of the kind of aristocratic past that Linda Condon, born of the Lowries, returned to when she became Linda Hallet. What he cherishes from this past is not its religious belief, but a capacity for enjoyment and an independence of mind and action that belong to the well-intrenched aristocrat. He misses just these traits in the present; and as for himself, he would not, except for the capacity for work, he admits, have chosen his own character, with its lack of calmness, fidelity, hardness of body, resolution in bearing and mind.

Admiring these virtues, he makes them live in the novels which earned him his reputation: "Java Head," "The Three Black Pennys," "Linda Condon," and "Balisand." And he adds to these a highly developed formality coupled with the independence that is the heritage of the nonconformist aristocrat. It belongs to all the "black" Pennys, but no less to Isabel Penny, a product of super-cultivation yet resilient as a Damascus blade. It belongs to Linda Hallet, who, like Isabel, could with unraised pulse defy her husband in behalf of palpitant youth. It is a part of Richard Bale, who on the morning of a duel to the death can tell his wife only by indirections of his sentiment too deep for words. It is a part, and the larger part, of Taou Yuen, who comes to Java Head, in

New England, from a Chinese civilization measured by millenniums and whose implicit but unmistakable vitality is never betrayed into outward expression. Dealing with characters like these, Hergesheimer, after the fashion of Hawthorne, has "connected a bygone time with the very present that is flitting away from us," and has seldom forgotten that the present is escaping into a later past. A minor key prevails throughout his pages — the key sounded on the entrance of Jasper Penny, "conscious of the invidious beginning weariness of accumulating years," and, similarly, on the entrances of Richard Bale and Govett Bradier. To them all a renewal of youth is offered and mockingly withheld. The hand of the past is upon them as the present slips away.

But there is another aspect of the picture. As Hergesheimer went on in his career the hand of the present exerted an increasingly disconcerting pressure. He became self-conscious in behalf of Dower House, aware that it was a conspicuous survival from the past. Near by was a golf club house from which could be heard in the dance music "a confusion of forms very like the age . . . the assault of a persuasive discontent."[1] These phrases may be applied to the trend of such later novels as "Cytherea," "Tampico," "The Bright Shawl," and "The Party Dress." "Cytherea," the book, for example, is a confusion of forms just as Cytherea, the doll symbol, is the assault of a persuasive discontent. And the course of the central figures, Lee Random and Savina Grove, is the course of the club-house vulgarians, impossible for the aristocrats of "Java Head" or "Balisand." The book starts with a gross violation of hospitality, slips off into a furtive elopement, and culminates in a fateful orgy of sexual excess. Such things happen; but they do not happen in these ways to the people of tradition and fine feeling with whom Hergesheimer first consorted in his novels. If the story had been true to them he would not have needed to follow it with so much labored explanation.

[1] "From an Old House," p. 156.

In his first fine fervor for the old homestead he once resolved never to lapse from its mood in his writings or to depart from the traditions of its builders. But, never conspicuous for fidelity, as he confesses, he again ignored this resolution when he wrote "Tampico" and returned to the humid sensuousness of Central America. It is a novel of disintegration which carries with it the suggestion that it is more than a novel — that it is a document in artistic history. All these earlier works, drawn from American history and written in the mood of the Dower House, seem vitally different from the latest ones partly because they are so similar. The central characters are men and women of distinction, measurably self-controlled, but ungovernable by outer control. They behave and misbehave like "quality," dominated by a set of convictions about personal honor, sex chivalry, and class loyalty that they are willing to die for. These convictions are rather primitive and not very noble, but they are nevertheless ennobling because they stimulate positive faith and positive action. But the later stories chronicle neither distinction of character nor distinction of action nor even distinction of manners. There is little left in them but occasional reminiscent gleams of gentility. Their vulgarities would disgust a Linda Condon or a Richard Bale. And if Richard Bale would lift an eyebrow and shrug a shoulder at Govett Bradier, so would Howat Penny at the Hergesheimer who opened a magazine essay with the salute, "I am getting damned tired of art." With most novelists who have written notably the earliest works could well be spared. The reverse is true of Joseph Hergesheimer.

James Branch Cabell in the years just after 1920 was the most aggressive and most discussed romantic novelist in the United States. Probably no American author since Cooper was more roundly abused or more fulsomely praised. The discussion of his literary ways and works was augmented by his recurrent comments on himself, for, in the persons of certain story-spokesmen, notably Manuel and Jurgen,

Robert Townsend, Felix Kennaston, and John Charteris, he has stated his case in scores of passages. He has had little patience for the methods of the realist:

> No one on the preferable side of Bedlam wishes to be reminded of what we are in actuality, even if it were possible, by any disastrous miracle, ever to dispel the mist which romance has evoked about all human doings.[1]

Says Charteris:

> If ever I were to attempt a tale of Litchfield, I would not write a romance, but a tragedy. I think I would call my tragedy "Futility," for it would mirror the life of Litchfield with unengaging candor; and, as a consequence, people would complain that my tragedy lacked sustained interest, and that its participants were inconsistent; that it had no ordered plot, no startling incidents, no high endeavors, and no special aim; and that it was equally deficient in all time-hallowed provocatives of either laughter or tears.[2]

In his discontent with the land of fact he invents a land of romance — Storisende, "which is bounded by Avalon and Phaeacia and sea-coast Bohemia, and the contiguous forests of Arden and Broceliande, and on the west of course by the Hesperides."[3] It is an ancient realm where the code of chivalry still prevails, and a man serves God, honor, and his lady to the fullest. For the adoption of this code the seeker of romantic relief must strip himself of every vestige of New-Worldliness and lend himself to the Coleridgian "willing suspension of disbelief" which is needed for the far journey.

This is the more of a problem for a Cabell, since he sets out to the land of Chivalry from the modern land of Gallantry, where the code has been abandoned but where the manners have been in part retained: a somewhat elevated formality of speech, an inclination to talk as from the rostrum, a brave show of deference to beauty and womanhood, a vocal insistence on honor and chivalry, and the stagey insincerity

---

[1] "Beyond Life" (McBride), p. 43.

[2] "The Rivet in Grandfather's Neck" (McBride), pp. 160, 161.

[3] "The Cream of the Jest" (McBride), p. 42.

that follows hard on any conventionalized and outworn forms. Gallantry is Chivalry with its tongue in its cheek, and it is perfectly expressed in "Cords of Vanity, a Comedy of Shirking."

Mr. Cabell's approach to life is not so direct that it may be summed up either in woman-worship, which is chivalry in perfection, as in "Domnei," or in shirking, which is chivalry degenerate, as in "Cords of Vanity." The greater part of his writings lie in the no man's land between. Of the stories of Poictesme, his ancient world, most are written with an ill-concealed smile, if not, as in the case of "Jurgen," with a smirk. They are romances of two worlds, ostensibly about an ancient one, though always seen with modern eyes. Thus the "epistle dedicatory" of "The Line of Love" is addressed to Mrs. Grundy, a lady whom Dreiser ignores but whom Cabell likes to annoy. Knowing that it would be useless to poison her soup, he seldom misses a chance to spoil her appetite.

One book marks the balancing of the two worlds — "The Cream of the Jest," in which Felix Kennaston, author, lives in the body in a twentieth-century world, acquires two motor cars, has money in four banks, an enlarged waistband, and a yearning for the romance that he finds nowhere about him. By means of a magic charm he is enabled to make off nightly to a world of dreams and idyllic adventure. Everywhere he sees men and women scurrying through a jungle of confused circumstance, "like feeble-minded ants," where he and he only can see the awe-inspiring design. Thrilled with the sense of beauty and order to which he is blinded in Litchfield, he is buoyed through days of unimportant tasks and tedious, useless little habits. So, returning to daily life, he smiles with the sophistication of a contemporary Virginian, but carries through the days enough of the chivalric code to be true to his love, — disavowing loyalty even while he practices it, — and to his Christian God, and, between the two, quite incidentally, to his own honor.

It is the approach (but the successful approach, one cannot help noting) of Hergesheimer in his "Cytherea." Cabell achieves his romance by flights from Litchfield to Storisende, but always finds something in Storisende to reconcile him to Litchfield. The unattainable is actually unattainable; the near approach to any object of desire dissolves the dream and recalls the present, but casts over the present the aura of the faraway.

Cabell's avowed intention, much quoted, is "to write perfectly about beautiful happenings." Doing this, for him, does not mean acquiring a perfect technique and employing it spontaneously. He is a laborious pleasure hunter. His style is like his use of geography and genealogy and his partly actual and partly invented authorities. It is wrought out by hard craftsmanship, no step in which is easier for any taken before. He writes of revision:

> I wrote and rewrote, shifted and polished and adorned until it seemed I would never have done. . . . Then you dip into an Unabridged, and change every word that has been written, for a better one, and do it leisurely, rolling in the mouth, as it were, the flavour of every possible word, before decision.[1]

Such processes do not lead to spontaneity of effect, and one does not find this in Cabell's pages. But he has many times anticipated criticism, as in his comments on Felix Kennaston, one of his many fictional counterparts:

> His high-pitched voice in talking, to begin with, was irritating; you knew it was not his natural voice, and found it so entirely senseless for him to speak thus. Then, too, the nervous and trivial grin with which he prefaced almost all his trivial remarks . . . was peculiarly uningratiating.[2]

His own style is indubitably established, consciously dependent on archaism, but dependent for relief on marked and homely modernisms. On the whole it is attractive, and sometimes it is charming. But it is pedantic in phrasing and in dispensable detail. Knowing that fancy is more important

---

[1] "The Cords of Vanity" (2d ed.; McBride), pp. 178, 180.
[2] "The Cream of the Jest" (McBride), p. 46.

than fact in the tales, the reader is annoyed and distracted by circumstantial matters of chronology and genealogy that delay action and throw no light on motivation.

The notable fact about Cabell in the modern pageant has been his persistence in playing his own role until through ability and the coöperation of the censors he achieved a wide hearing. He ought to be taken as seriously as he takes himself, which is not very seriously, for his tongue as a rule is ostentatiously in his cheek. If he had clung to his declared intention of withdrawing from authorship when he reached the age of fifty, he would have closed a picturesque performance with an altogether characteristic gesture; but few farewell tours unensured by old age have ever proved to be bona fide.

The New Era in Poetry and Drama

In 1896 Edwin Arlington Robinson privately printed a little pamphlet of poems in an edition so small that a copy is now a collector's item of a value many times the cost of the original issue. In the next year was published "The Children of the Night." People opening it — and casually closing it again — could see from the table of contents that it included some quatrains, a couple of ballades, a villanelle, and several sonnets. This was in the fashion of the 90's. There were also verses on Thomas Hood and George Crabbe, subjects which, barely listed, would hardly startle a potential reader into sudden interest. But there was a sonnet entitled "Zola," which was addressed not to the novelist but to the censorious, who were carrying on their

squeamish and emasculate crusade
Against the grim dominion of his art.[1]

And there was another sonnet shaft aimed at the biographer-gossips who, "like long-clawed scavengers," had reveled in riotous facts about Verlaine, bidding them be content with his

[1] Edwin Arlington Robinson, "Poems" (1920), p. 85. By permission of The Macmillan Company, publishers.

verse, to "let the dead flesh be dead, and let the worms be its biographers."[1] Furthermore, there were the sixteen lines about "Richard Cory," perfect antithesis to Verlaine, incomparable aristocrat, with grace and gold and imperial manners and so little satisfaction in life that he put a bullet in his head one summer night.

Except for these altogether incidental verse forms which Robinson resorted to in his first bow to the public he is impossible to "date." He is modern, but a proof that modernity in art does not depend on strangeness or newness. He writes no word of modern movement or up-to-date inventions. Like the best of provincials, he finds all that he needs to write about in his village, which he calls Tilbury. The qualities that make his townsmen alive are constants in human life. Change a few allusions, and you may put them as far back in history as you choose. On the other hand, read his Arthurian episodes, and you will see that he felt no interest in "reconstructing the past," turning to the past because he found vivid people there whom he could contemplate free from the distractions of a circumstantial present.

Few constants in Robinson's poems are more insistently recurrent than his disregard for the world of getting and spending, and his contempt for the usual measures of success. In his salutatory to "Dear Friends" he assures them that if the shame he wins for singing is all his own, the gold he misses for dreaming is all theirs. The voice of "Cassandra" is heard early in his second volume warning the dollar worshipers that they are paying for what they gain with all they are, and mocking them for having the ages as their guide and lacking the wisdom to be led. "Flammonde," with his firm address, cosmopolitan air, impeccable taste, Prince of Castaways, borrowed what he needed, strengthening his credit when he bowed, soothing the disgruntled into munificence. "Captain Craig," otherwise insolvent, bequeathed to his quartet of friends God's universe. Avon, Matthias, Talifer, on the

---

[1] Robinson, op. cit. p. 96.

other hand, are neither better nor worse off for their riches.[1] And, strangely enough, Shakespeare, living in "a phantom world he sounded and found wanting," was just perversely paradoxical enough to be a materially thrifty soul with an interest in things that had "equivalence in . . . shillings"![2]

Yet Robinson's contempt for the rewards of success is not a contempt for life or a disillusionment. The passages that suggest this are the sentiments of the men and women to whom they are ascribed. Nothing could be more devastating than Shakespeare's exposition that "It's all Nothing":

Your fly will serve as well as anybody,
And what's his hour? He flies, and flies, and flies,
And in his fly's mind has a brave appearance;
And then your spider gets him in her net,
And eats him out, and hangs him up to dry.
That's Nature, the kind mother of us all.
And then your slattern housemaid swings her broom,
And where's your spider? And that's Nature, also.
It's Nature, and it's Nothing. It's all Nothing.[3]

But in the title poem of the volume which contains this dramatic soliloquy, "Ben Jonson Entertains a Man from Stratford," after all the doubts and queries raised by the sight of the man silhouetted against the sky, he doubts the doubt and reasserts the belief in strength and courage, already asserted in "Captain Craig." He does so because

a sure music fills him and he knows
What he may say thereafter to few men, —
The touch of ages having wrought
An echo and a glimpse of what he thought
A phantom or a legend until then.[4]

Of course all is not well in Robinson's world. The "Tilbury tune," which is the tune of the Philistines, has a false note in it:

A note that able-bodied men might sound
Hosannas on while Captain Craig lay quiet.[5]

---

[1] Robinson, op. cit. pp. 84, 12, 3, 149.
[2] Ibid. p. 31.
[3] Ibid. p. 28.
[4] Ibid. p. 60.
[5] Ibid. p. 114.

Harder to bear in this world, however, than a moral squint in the blundering crowd is the fact that man is born to trouble as the sparks fly upward. Nevertheless he does not despair in the face of evil.

> Because one half of humankind
> Lives here in hell, shall not the other half
> Do any more than just for conscience' sake
> Be miserable? Is this the way for us
> To lead these creatures up to find the light, —
> Or to be drawn down surely to the dark
> Again?[1]

"Captain Craig," despite the slight esteem in which most critics hold it, remains the key poem to Robinson's philosophy. It is a series of monologues, rifted with childhood, sunlight, laughter, and hope, declaimed by an indomitable old vagabond of eternity who is invincible in death and is fittingly borne to the grave while at his request the trombones of the Tilbury band blare the "Dead March in Saul." The captain is the poet let loose, stripped of all verbal restraint. Men of his type are never restrained; they are extravagant of time, of gesture, of vocal and rhetorical emphasis, of words. Out of the abundance of their hearts their mouths speak all sorts of irresponsible, whimsical, exalted, splendid speculation. Captain Craig is self-expression in very being, and condemns in joyous scorn the man who believes that life is best fulfilled through discipline and renunciation. Instead he offers this:

> It is the flesh
> That ails us, for the spirit knows no qualm,
> No failure, no down-falling; so climb high
> And having set your steps regard not much
> The downward laughter clinging at your feet,
> Nor overmuch the warning.[2]

This is the prevalent Robinsonian note. His disbelief in negativism leads him often to be impatient and caustic and leads the cloudy-minded to either eager acceptance or timid

[1] Robinson, op. cit. pp. 126, 127.

[2] Ibid. p. 151.

deprecation of what they think is his cynicism, not knowing the difference between this and irony. Robinson is not cynical about the things that are more excellent. He is only protesting at mistaken ideas as to what is more excellent; trying to substitute light for shadow, laughter for gloom; saying, with Larry Scammon in his prose play "The Porcupine":

> Stop me if I am too cheerful; but at the same time, if I can instil the fertile essence of Hope into this happy household, for God's sake let me do it. . . . You had better — all of you — begin to get yourselves out of your own light, and cease to torment your long-bedevilled heads with the dark doings of bogies that have no real existence.[1]

This latter passage implies that Robinson was in conscious revolt against the repressive qualities in New England ways, — Puritanism, so called, — and the other citations suggest that at heart he was one of the so-called Puritans, conscious of the controlling powers of ethical standards, aware of a Power behind them, inclined to indulgence in homily and exhortation; in all of which there is some truth, but very much less than the whole truth about the man.

For he is neither the spokesman for a region or a clan, nor the proponent of a dogma. Essentially he is an artist who has some of the qualities of his region and who believes in the enfranchising parts of its traditions.

His artistry has much of the Yankee in it: on the one hand, its laconic, word-sparing quality and its tendency to understatement; on the other, its gift for circumlocution when this device will either conceal or veil what the Yankee has in mind or what is in his mood. Shakespeare, as Ben Jonson expounded him to the man from Stratford, was no Yankee when the zest for talk was on him, no more than Captain Craig; and he elicited a perfect Yankee reaction:

> Talk? He was an eldritch at it; and we listened —
> Thereby acquiring much we knew before
> About ourselves, and hitherto had held
> Irrelevant, or not prime to the purpose.[2]

---

[1] "The Porcupine," p. 104.

[2] "Poems" (1920), p. 25.

Moreover, it is this trait of expressing by indirection that makes Robinson seem more exclusively intellectual than he actually is. The man who does not wear his heart on his sleeve is not therefore heartless, but he is bound sometimes to produce that impression. And the man who on occasion talks by indirection or, on occasion, so curtly that "he throws away everything but the meaning — and keeps that to himself," does not always suffer from a tertian ague of tongue-tiedness and verbosity. These are parts of his lyric self. He can be frozen like John Gorham, or he can be melted in paternal love and sympathy like King Howel in the unsurpassable concluding lines of "Tristram."

Robinson stands out so clearly among the poets writing in English today because he wore his Americanism as easily as he wielded his poetic powers. He invented no new measures and departed from no old ones. After a few youthful adventures in virtuosity he abandoned all that sort of thing, and developed within the limits of old prosody a style which is indubitably his own. And it is quite as much of a fact to record of the American reading public as it is of the poet, that though he was practically ignored for fifteen years, during which one of his most important volumes was published, the appearance of a new work by the Robinson of later years eventually became a literary event of prime importance. He is the best of answers to the Jeremiahs who insist that America is hostile to creative art, blighting it in the bud.

Robert Frost is another case in point. He has been persistently and cheerfully single-minded about what he wanted life to yield him, but common-sensible and almost hard-headed too. To think of the poet who wrote for twenty years on an average literary income of ten dollars as stalking through the world with a somber eye fixed on achievement and fame would be quite to misconceive him. Various pulls swerved him from the direct path. Until the public came belatedly to know him, it was the need of daily bread. Since then it has been the desire of publishers and college presidents to thrust bread on him in distracting circumstances. And now that daily bread can be secured with less sweat of brow than formerly, he reverts to his old desire to live relaxed and unhurried, leaning against life until it stings him into utterance.

> Well, if I have to choose one or the other,
> I choose to be a plain New Hampshire farmer
> With an income in cash of say a thousand
> (From say a publisher in New York City.) [1]

The fact that his first three volumes, two of them quite slender, held all he cared to preserve from nearly a quarter-century of writing, and that it was seven years before a fourth was added, and six more to the fifth, proves his freedom from inward or outward pressure. In the meanwhile he has remained steadfast in the rocky hill country north of Boston; and being self-sufficient, he has found life good there, that being what he has made it.

In its broadest divisions Frost's work falls into lyrics and sketches — the records of moments of feeling and moments of observation. "A Boy's Will" is wholly of the first type; "North of Boston," "Mountain Interval," and "New Hampshire," largely of the second; "West Running Brook," once more of the first. The little songs in "A Boy's Will" tell by implication something of a poet's experience in deciding what life owes him and what he owes the world. Sill attempted the same thing in his consecutive account of "The Hermitage," as did Bynner in "The New World"; Frost, in a succession of lyrics. Each of Frost's sequence was written for itself; they would not have been genuine, the poet has said, if they had been written as a conscious sequence; and they are separate and independent, beautifully so. Yet the unity is there, as he once discovered and as he has revealed in his annotated table of contents; so they may be read together for their total truth. The poet and his bride withdraw into the happy seclusion of the countryside; and here, without

---

[1] "New Hampshire" (Holt), p. 16.

ecstasizing or sentimentalizing over it, they enjoy its quiet and peace and beauty. But they find that care cannot be wantonly banished by happiness, and in the end they come down the hills and into the world again.

> Out through the fields and the woods
>   And over the walls I have wended;
> I have climbed the hills of view
>   And looked at the world, and descended;
> I have come by the highway home,
>   And lo, it is ended.[1]

"North of Boston" and "Mountain Interval," except for the memorable forewords and afterwords, contain few of these brief lyrics. They, in turn, without being too mechanically grouped, may be separated into poems largely on men and women in the presence of nature, and poems largely on men and women in relation to each other. "Mending Wall," "The Woodpile," and "The Mountain" are of the former sort. Two country neighbors meet each other in early spring to repair the stone walls upset by winter frosts, spring thaws, and the hunters. One, the poet, speculates on the fact that every year nature overthrows man's artifice; the other sturdily labors to restore his own handiwork because "Good fences make good neighbors." The situation is presented without comment. A pile of wood stands deserted and exposed out in the winter snows. A prop has fallen and vines have covered it in the years since it was laboriously stacked there. Where has the builder gone who stored the fuel that is now wasting "with the slow, smokeless burning of decay"? Again it is the mystery of nature and the transitoriness of man. Imagination lingers where the poem ends. The Mountain spreads so wide that on its lower slopes and the fringe of land around it there are only sixty voters in the township. It looms in their midst, dominating and limiting life; few have time to go to the top, and fewer still, a surviving curiosity.

---

[1] "A Boy's Will" (Holt), p. 62.

There is a rigor in the earth north of Boston. Winter is insistent. It frightens the colt, who is unused to snow, discourages the early northward-flying birds, lets death descend on the autumn, breaks the birches with its ice storms, overthrows the walls, reluctantly succumbs to spring. Spring marks rather the departure of the ice king than the coming of plenty. Enjoyment of summer is delegated to the city vacationists. So the characters presented by Frost are products of duress and adversity. They live in a country which has come to old age on arid tradition. They are unacquainted with mirth or song or play. Their human contacts have been few and monotonous; for they are off the main-traveled roads, and the summer visitors do not understand them and are fended off by them. With little to alleviate life, they have lost the traits of Pauline charity. Hard pride and grim endurance have lined their faces, labor has bowed their backs, and inbreeding has done the rest. They are, in short, the same people Whittier characterized in his foreword to "Among the Hills."[1] And they are to be found not only in New England. Similar conditions produce the same type anywhere in Protestant Anglo-Saxondom. Frost has fixed them in his pictures with the idioms of speech and action peculiar to his region.

Frost is no more concerned with the world of institutions than Robinson, treating them with blithe scorn in "New Hampshire," ignoring them elsewhere. He has no reforms to advocate or social theories to advance. He does not even propound a philosophy of life. If we are to deduce one from his collected work, it is a common or garden philosophy that a cheerful, persistent man might be expected to have. He does not want to be a sentimentalist, and certainly he does not want to be a vitriolic sensationalist. He hates all sorts of "gang talk" uttered for effect. His convictions have grown not so much from what he has thought as from what he has felt; and because they are the fruit of his temperament

---

[1] See page 212.

rather than the children of his mind, he has very little to say about them *in extenso* — always excepting his one indulgence of this sort: "New Hampshire." He feels that though this is not the best of all possible worlds, it is the best he knows, and that as far as his life is concerned it is pretty much a world of his own making. If he has misgivings at the actual ugliness of life, he admits them and records them, but he is reassured by its actual and potential beauties. Of all that life has to give he finds nothing to rival sympathetic companionship: between neighbors, friends, parents and children, husbands and wives.

Though averse to drawing open analogies from nature or writing openly about himself, he did both in the last stanza of "Birches," going far toward an explanation of his reticent optimism:

> I'd like to get away from earth awhile
> And then come back to it and begin over.
> May no fate wilfully misunderstand me
> And half grant what I wish and snatch me away
> Not to return. Earth 's the right place for love;
> I don't know where it's likely to go better.
> I'd like to go by climbing a birch tree
> And climb black branches up a snow-white trunk
> *Toward* heaven, till the tree could bear no more,
> But dipped its top and set me down again.
> That would be good both going and coming back.
> One could do worse than be a swinger of birches.[1]

Among the artists who were miscellaneously called "these modern poets" when they were becoming known, Frost, like Robinson, has confined himself to established poetic rhythms and verse patterns; has mastered them; and, particularly in the use of the iambic pentameter, has achieved a manner which is more than a mannerism. It is his distinction to have attained the high level of technique at which the maximum of technical effect is reached and held with the least apparent effort. Thus "The Road Not Taken," prefatory to "Moun-

[1] "Mountain Interval" (Holt), pp. 39, 40.

tain Interval," the account of a dilemma resolved by chance, has the effect of being almost as casual in form as the decision it tells about; but it is composed of a set of five-line stanzas with far from the simplest of rhyme schemes and complete fidelity to the pattern. "Stopping by Woods on a Snowy Evening," one of the "grace notes" in "New Hampshire," again reads smoothly, but again the verse pattern parallels the indecision of the poetic moment. The scheme carries the second rhyme of each stanza into the next — obviously either an endless pattern or an uncompleted one unless the poet finds a way out; and he does, not by escape but by the one apt step.

Whose woods these are I think I know.
His house is in the village though;
He will not see me stopping here
To watch his woods fill up with snow.

My little horse must think it queer
To stop without a farmhouse near
Between the woods and the frozen lake
The darkest evening of the year.

He gives his harness bells a shake
To ask if there is some mistake.
The only other sound's the sweep
Of easy wind and downy flake.

The woods are lovely, dark and deep.
But I have promises to keep,
And miles to go before I sleep,
And miles to go before I sleep.[1]

Similarly, in such a poem as "The Runaway" the rhyme seems to be quite casual; but if one chooses to give a second or third glance, the twenty-one lines fall into three groups each of which has too nice a symmetry to have found it by accident:

a b a c b c; a b c c a b c; a a b c c b d d

---

[1] "New Hampshire" (Holt), p. 87.

As to verse stresses, Frost contends that there are two rival factors: the absolute rhythm demanded by the pattern adopted, and the flexible rhythm demanded by the ways words are pronounced and by their relative emphasis. Neither, he says, should be subordinated to the other. In what is called iambic pentameter, most of the units should be iambic, and most of the lines should have five stresses; but in cases of departure from the pattern, there is nothing to explain away or condone; the rhythm will return to it. There is nothing new in this, except among prosodists. But in his acknowledgment of it Frost practices the informality of the well-bred man who is so sure of his *p's* and *q's* that he does not have to "mind" them every moment of the time. More exactly, he does not need to seem to "mind" them. It is doubtful if Frost often built wiser than he knew, even though at times he may have been happily affected by a sudden flash. There is no doubt that after life has stung him to utterance, and after he has weighed and considered what he has uttered until he is ready to repeat it out loud, the effect is, in the modern colloquialism, that he has said something that time. "Sometimes," he once wrote, "I have my doubts of words altogether, and I ask myself what is the place of them. They are worse than nothing unless they do something; unless they amount to deeds as in ultimatums or battle-cries."[1] In most of what he has released to the public he has met his own challenge; and the public has responded to him, for out of his homely material and in his homely way he deals with the substance of life.

"The most energetic and unflagging experimenter, Miss Lowell's versatility became amazing. She has wielded a controversial cudgel with one hand, and with the other she has written Chaucerian stanzas, polyphonic prose, monologues in her native New England dialect, irregular vers libre, conservative couplets, translations from the French, echoes

[1] Quoted by Louis Untermeyer in "The New Era in American Poetry," p. 30.

from the Japanese, even primitive re-creations of Indian folklore." This by one of her most friendly and admiring critics — who elsewhere called her "a female Roosevelt among the Parnassians" — explains why Amy Lowell claims attention as much for her part in the experimental tendencies of the second dozen years in the century as for her intrinsic values.

At an age when Keats's and Shelley's careers were over, Miss Lowell decided to become a poet. For eight years she devoted herself to study, and at an age when Byron had died she first published a poem. It is a normal progression in literary history for authors first to fall into the fashions of the day and then to transfer interest from style to substance. Miss Lowell approached writing with the usual deference for form; but, arriving with one of the periodic waves of interest about modes and manners in all the arts, she never graduated from this youthful phase. She developed into a theorist who occasionally wrote poetry and often what was a little less than poetry, rather than into an indubitable poet like Robinson or Frost. She had joined something which for want of a better name may be called a movement, and she was always audible toward the forefront of it.[1]

Her first volume, "A Dome of Many-Coloured Glass," was no more than what one might have expected from an averagely gifted but more than averagely studious and persistent follower of the Muse. The form was tight and the manner was tame. The influence of Tennyson was apparent and that of Keats was very strong. Much of it sounded like Emily Dickinson. The longest unit was on the Athenaeum Library, where Miss Lowell had passed a large part of the preceding years. It included speculations on the nature of poetry, a little picture likening the poet to a diver poised for a plunge into a pool of mysterious new experience, and a fragment comparing him to that most painstaking and unimpassioned of craftsmen — a worker in stained glass. If Miss

[1] Alfred Kreymborg, "Our Singing Strength," Chap. XX, "The Free Verse Revolt."

Lowell had been content to continue in this vein, publishers and public would probably have been content to ignore her after another volume.

But with "Sword Blades and Poppy Seed" she joined forces with the experimenters. This was in 1914, when Ezra Pound issued a collection of imagist poems just before bidding farewell to the school, the year before Miss Lowell was to avow herself as one of the imagists and to stimulate the publishing of their three annual volumes. Naturally, then, there were already some examples of the type in "Sword Blades." In spite of the fact that the imagists declared their principles to be "the essentials of all great poetry," their six tenets were eyed askance as though they were strangely new. They were well enough as far as they went; but they failed to include all poetry, and much of the greatest, while they did include a good deal of eloquent prose.[1] Here are two chill night pictures, both in good imagist style:

And while the moon
Swings low across the sky,
Athwart a waving pine tree,
And soon
Tips all the needles there
With silver sparkles, bitterly
He gazes. . . .[2]

While the earth has slumbered,
All the air has been alive
With feathery flakes descending,
As if some northern Ceres reigned,
Showering her silvery grain
Over all the fields.[3]

Each is marked (1) by common diction exactly used (except for "athwart"), (2) by varied rhythms, (3) by freedom in choice of subject, (4) by images, (5) by hard and clear effects,

[1] See the good-humored essay on George Meredith, entitled "An Unacknowledged Imagist," by John L. Lowes in *The Nation*, February 24, 1916.
[2] Amy Lowell, "A Dome of Many-Coloured Glass" (Houghton Mifflin), pp. 3, 4.
[3] Thoreau, "Excursions," p. 162.

and (6) by concentration. One was published as verse by Miss Lowell in 1914; the other, as prose by Thoreau in "Walden," 1854; and the novelty of free verse was anticipated in Whitman's "Leaves of Grass" the year after "Walden" appeared.

A further experiment in style, used exclusively in "Can Grande's Castle" in 1918 and supposed to be in a quite new set of harmonics, was heralded as "polyphonic," or many-voiced, prose, the voices being "meter, vers libre, assonance, alliteration, rhyme and return." It was immensely self-conscious, the effects as flagrantly calculated as in the most painstaking of program music. The reader was assaulted by decorative effects of the old "North German Lloyd" or the modern moving-picture-palace obviousness. Polyphonism made less of a ripple than imagism; both soon lisped into silence on the shores of oblivion. And Miss Lowell's experiments in innovation came to a fortunate end before they reached the extremes of Kreymborg and the rest of the "Others," as they described themselves in their joint volume. Yet her enthusiasm for the bizarre led her into an ambush when she seriously reviewed "Spectra," not realizing that Emanuel Morgan and Anne Knish were Witter Bynner and Arthur Davison Ficke cutting poetic capers in disguise.

Form still pre-empted her interest, as adoptions of Chinese and Japanese stanzaic patterns came to the fore with her. But the significant thing was that her allusions to the poet and to herself were to the self-conscious craftsman continually sitting down to think what he should write, instead of to write what he had thought.

> The cat and I
> Together on this sultry night
> Waited.
> He greatly desired a mouse;
> I, an idea.
> Neither ambition was gratified.[1]

---

[1] "Pictures of the Floating World" (Houghton Mifflin), p. 197.

When on other nights ideas did offer themselves, she was likely to pounce on them and worry them to death. It is not the way in which lasting poetry takes form. It does not remind one so much of her favorite poet, Keats, as it does of Pope spending a summer at Twickenham polishing the life out of a sonnet.

The poems of Amy Lowell are crowded with sense impressions. For the most part the pictures are of limited and sophisticated subjects: gardens, studios, bookshops, museums, streets. The gamut of emotions is limited. Skepticism bans reverence and love of country; there is no fear, nor hate, nor gaiety; and in the realm of love, only the love that is directly interfused with passion. The lyrics are often written as if by a man lover, dazzled by the beauty of his mistress; ravished by the thought of what her costume conceals and her continence withholds. There is energy in every page, but usually the energy of fidgets rather than of power. Yet at long intervals the real fervor of creation arose, as in "Patterns," "Guns as Keys," "The Dinner Party," "The Bronze Horses," and "Lilacs," in which is revealed, uniquely in Miss Lowell's pages, a genuine regional affection. These and their like represent her finest moments.

Behind her freshness and independence of style is a foundation of old-fashioned literary formalism. Literature was something to be stored away in museums or shelved in libraries. It belonged to "the republic of letters," that most select of aristocracies. If Miss Lowell had been docile and acquiescent, she might have contented herself with this compound of literary conventions. If she had enjoyed the serene independence of Frost and Robinson, she might have gone on her way without expressed dissent from literary tradition. If she had had the social convictions of Masters or Sandburg, she might have joined the chorus of protest at the ways of the world. Instead she enlisted in an innocuous revolt within the republic of letters. All that she gained from it was the éclat of a drum major in a passing procession.

With the years just following the World's Fair of 1893, Chicago,

> gigantic, wilful, young . . .
> With restless violent hands and casual tongue
> Moulding her mighty fates,[1]

became vocal in a new way. The city had never been voiceless; but up to this time the country had heard little from it beyond the tumult from political conventions, the shouts from the wheat pits, and the uproar of the recent Haymarket riot. Long after Far West and Gulf and Tidewater and Southern-mountain regions had been heard from in poetry and fiction, Chicago had not a memorable story, song, or picture to its credit. Now the Columbian Exposition supplied a fresh stimulus. W. M. R. French and the new art institute, Theodore Thomas and the new orchestra, William R. Harper and the new university, furnished rallying points and attracted the support of local millions. Young authors, artists, sculptors, came to town and were patronized, not always for their own good, by the wealth that was unsettling individuals while it was establishing beneficent institutions. Certain collegians in the East, rebellious at the domination of the Victorians and the passing generation of New Englanders, decided to "put Chicago on the map." Stone and Kimball set up as publishers; *The Chap Book* ran its four-year course; *The Dial* continued on its modest way; orchestra, art museum, and university flourished; Moody and Masters came to town; Fuller began writing. Eugene Field had been journalizing there for some time, but it was in those days that Chicago had its modest literary renascence. And when it became of age — about 1914 — Masters's voice had changed, and he and Carl Sandburg and Sherwood Anderson and Floyd Dell and a dozen others began to speak so loud and clear that all the country had to listen.

Masters's "Spoon River Anthology," on its publication in 1915, was the most read and most talked of book of

---

[1] Moody, "Poems" (1901), p. 13.

poems in America. Coming out in installments over a long period in a distinguished but obscure weekly, William Marion Reedy's *Mirror*, the collected poems were offered to several publishers before one ventured to accept them. Then their circulation was rapid from the first. People who knew their classics were interested and amused at the combination of an old Greek form with the doings of an Illinois town. People who were allured but disappointed by the glitter and hollowness of much of the new verse were refreshed by the grim substance of this book. People who had never read poetry took up the volume because they heard it had "punch." Villagers read it to protest,[1] as later they were to protest at "Winesburg, Ohio" and at "Main Street"; and the literary procession was joined, of course, by the novelty hunters and the "shocker" hunters, and the tasters who want a spoonful of what everybody is reading.

There were the same two insistent notes in the chorus of comment that greeted "Leaves of Grass" sixty years earlier: that it was queer and that it was morbid; and there was reason for both charges. The "Anthology" was different from the norm at the time, though its novelty lay in the return to a classical convention. It was also disturbing to the sensitive because it acknowledged and expatiated on the presence of hypocrisy, hate, greed, and lust in American life. In their attention to the romantic formulas, almost everyone failed to see that in Masters's mind these elements, though existent, were not the most important in Spoon River; for he acknowledged the saving grace of love, loyalty, spiritual strength, and toward the end of the collection massed the idealists and the conquerors of circumstance.

In his treatment of sex he displayed a certain adolescent preoccupation with the theme, which belonged to a good many Americans of the day. They apparently felt that to indicate freedom to choose what they would, they must be bold and bad. They have been followed by a group who feel the

---

[1] See pages 766–767.

necessity of being tough. Masters's "Dialogue at Perko's," "Victor Rafolski on Art," "The Widow La Rue," startling when they appeared, show how far the public has become accustomed to, or atrophied by, discussion of explicit sex experience. From a modernist with the frankness of Whitman, the analytical gifts of Browning, and the bias of Freud, they were inevitable. But the bias led to the usual over-emphasis, a point which is nicely illustrated by comparison of Masters's tercentenary Shakespeare poem with Robinson's. Robinson touched on the bard's susceptibility to women, but dismissed it to dilate on his superhuman wisdom. Masters devoted the last two thirds of Shakespeare's monologue on the night of his last carousal to sex confessions. Robinson's passage is a few lines in length, ending with the admission that there's no reason for going into it and little is known about it. Masters's is nearly two hundred and fifty lines long, beginning with "The thing is sex" and ending with common brothel profanity.

It is in this weakness for running off on tangents, and an increasing tendency to force realistic matter to support prepossessions and prejudices, that the curve of Masters's career descends as definitely from "Spoon River" as it rose toward it. Only in the titles of a succession of later volumes do we find anything in the way of a synthesis in his output; and there it is implied but left unfulfilled in "The Great Valley," "Toward the Gulf," and "The Open Sea." Masters proceeds like an unacknowledged agnostic. For a while he struggles to assure himself that reason and the will of God prevail. Life is an inextricable confusion. It is hard to tell strength from weakness, honesty from duplicity, the ennobling from the debasing. But there are such traits as strength, honesty, and nobility, and there is a controlling design in human life.

In this there is something of the Greek tradition which regarded man as beset by the fatefulness of his own character. But there is in Masters quite as much of another point of view which regards man as beset by society. Spoon River, as human as Robinson's Tilbury or Frost's grim countryside, is more definitely touched by the tide of namable event. He writes of Lincoln, Altgeld, Theodore Roosevelt, Bryan; of Chicago with named streets and buildings and offices where high finance and low politics are manipulated. As time goes on his work becomes more frankly prosaic and more prolix. "Children of the Market Place" is a really illuminating study of Stephen Douglas; "Mitch Miller" is a tedious elaboration of what might have been a neat sketch of a boy whose imagination was dominated by "Tom Sawyer"; the book on Lincoln is a hundredfold worse than the verses on Shakespeare because it is a hundred times as long. One comes to think of Masters in the past tense. It turns out that he lost his way in total irresolution. He was neither classicist nor modernist, lawyer nor poet, poet nor prose writer, novelist nor biographer, Chicagoan nor New Yorker. His one success was an adroit application of a historic method to contemporary material. It was timely, popular, influential. It will serve as a milestone in American literature. That is a good deal for Masters to have set up. But that was all.

Vachel Lindsay, another Illinoisan, had much the same experience for parallel reasons. At just about the time of "Spoon River" (1913 to 1917) he published two volumes of prose and three of verse that marked him as an individual and engaging voice from the Middle West. He came from Springfield, Illinois, and proclaimed quite rationally that "the things most worth while are one's own hearth and neighborhood." Circulating from here he preached the gospel of beauty as a pedestrian on three leisurely tramps through South, Northeast, and Middle West; and he wrote them up in "Adventures while Preaching the Gospel of Beauty" and "A Handy Guide for Beggars." Dovetailed in with these were three books of verse: "General William Booth Enters into Heaven," "The Congo," and "The Chinese Nightingale."

Apparently he was something of a modern troubadour and apparently he had succeeded not only in trading his rhymes for bread but in making them interesting in the homes by the roadside. And in the three volumes of poetry he had successively reached through the minds of Salvation Army "heeler," river-levee Negro, and Chinese laundryman to far vistas of religious vision, primitive savagery, and Oriental romance. In these books Lindsay was a provincial, almost parochial, character with a liberating imagination. Unhappily he took on more and more completely the role of eccentric minstrel. He posted poems on billboards, recited them from soapboxes and on the vaudeville stage, became addicted to lyceum audiences. He chanted his verses with awkwardly convincing effectiveness, but gradually was converted from poet to entertainer and exhibitionist. Moreover, he abandoned his own home and neighborhood for a succession of others in the South and West, and, with his vogue gone, was attempting a literal and figurative "comeback" at the time of his death.

Both Masters and Lindsay seem to have had something in them of the migrant, adventuresome West. Both drew attention to themselves at an auspicious moment when the American reading public was waking up to the values of an indigenous literature. Both went off on various literary tangents and deserted the life in terms of which they had expressed themselves while winning their audiences. The casual observer would be led toward generalizing that the new country could beget only vagrants and back-trailers if the thought of Carl Sandburg did not give him pause.

For there is nothing of vacillation in Sandburg. Born in one of the towns where Lincoln and Douglas debated, schooled in miscellaneous odd-jobbing, in Lombard College, and in soldiering, commercial writing, and newspaper work, he learned his region not as a member of one of the professions nor as professional wanderer but as laboring proletarian. He was like Frost and Robinson and Masters and Hergesheimer in one respect only: that in 1903 he put out a little publication which was completely ignored, and that by 1914 he faced a public which had grown up toward him in the meanwhile. His first real hearing came through the good offices of Harriet Monroe, who published a group of his verse in *Poetry*, that remarkable achievement of hers which for a full quarter of a century has been so uniquely and so inconspicuously important. One of these, "Chicago," won the enviable Levinson prize, and served as title poem for his "Chicago Poems" of 1916.

The opening line in this volume, "Hog Butcher for the World," stirred the hue and cry that he intended it to. Chicago, it appears as the poem goes on, is a tall bold slugger set in contrast with the little soft cities. This is no more than a colloquial elaboration of the lines already written by Moody.[1] The address farther on "To a Contemporary Bunkshooter" is the challenge of a common man, capable of vulgar talk, who resents vulgar treatment of hallowed themes. He sneers, "Where do you get that stuff? . . . Go ahead and bust all the chairs you want to."[2] Poetry has always shaken the lance at shams and charlatans. The objection is not to the poetic material, then, but to the poetic license which treats of a brute subject in brutal language. It is the old question as to the rival claims of the literary tongue and the vernacular; the question that Dante and Chaucer and Wordsworth and Whitman all settled in favor of the simpler, more colloquial diction. When Sandburg writes of "The Sins of Kalamazoo" he blackguards the town in the words of a "loafer lagging along"; when he arraigns political thievery he does it by listening to the braggadocio of the thief:

Nothin' ever sticks to my fingers, nah, nah, nothin' like that,
But there ain't no law we got to wear mittens — huh — is there?[3]

But this is not Sandburg's only diction. The second entry in "Chicago Poems" begins:

The shadows of the ships
Rock on the crest
In the low blue lustre
Of the soft inrolling tide.[4]

---

[1] See page 816.
[2] "Chicago Poems" (Holt), p. 62.
[3] "Smoke and Steel" (Harcourt), p. 45.
[4] "Chicago Poems" (Holt), p. 5.

The words again fit the theme. And the third poem in the same volume ends with,

> And then one day I got a true look at the Poor, millions of the Poor, patient and toiling; more patient than crags, tides and stars; innumerable, patient as the darkness of night—and all broken, humble ruins of nations.[1]

Obviously the poet does not sing one tune alone or in one key; speaking in character as lyrist or novelist or dramatist does, paying his readers the compliment of omitting quotation marks. Perhaps only those who have heard Sandburg's voice in conversation, in ballad-singing, and in the reading of his poems can quite respond to his artistry; for it is a voice of melodious rhythms, full of depth and tenderness, free from vehemence, simply used without a touch of elocution, but with a flexible command of tone effects and the nicest feeling for the retard and the half-pause. It is a voice for quiet ironies rather than noisy invectives, and pre-eminently for the expression of sympathies rather than antipathies.

In the changing world in which Sandburg finds himself and which he knows from the bottom up, he has a feeling for social injustice and protests against it; but as one of the people he is upheld by confidence in the power of the people to protect themselves.

> When I, the People, learn to remember, when I, the People, use the lessons of yesterday and no longer forget who robbed me last year, who played me for a fool — then there will be no speaker in all the world to say the name: "The People," with any fleck of a sneer in his voice or any far-off smile of derision.[2]

It is the pathos rather than the tragedy of the mob that moves him. It is pathetic that toilers toil all day and all year with no prospect but toil and dirt and poverty; that the city turns to dross the fresh gold of life poured into it; that the fish crier and the little shopkeeper, and the immigrant laborer on a picnic with his family, with so little to rejoice

---

[1] Sandburg, "Chicago Poems" (Holt), p. 6. [2] Ibid. p. 172.

in, still ascend the hills of happiness. But it is pathetic too that wealth in its pride builds temporary corporations and mausoleums, and fences to fend off the poor, forgetting that at the end are only cool tombs, and that nothing can fend off death and the rain and tomorrow.

Escaping from the town he finds reassurance in the broader expanses of time and space. He does not need, like Masters, to make fluent demonstrations of his familiarity with the latest speculations of science. The time and space of yesterday are long enough and wide enough to give play for his imagination:

> O prairie mother I am one of your boys. . . .
> I speak of new cities and new people,
> I tell you the past is a bucket of ashes.
> I tell you yesterday is a wind gone down,
> a sun dropped in the west,
> I tell you there is nothing in the world
> only an ocean of tomorrows,
> a sky of tomorrows.[1]

The prairie nourishes the living and houses the dead, symbol of eternity. Across it lie the railroads, slender ribbons of steel connecting the transitory towns. Yet the careless take the towns more seriously than the stretches between and the reaches of time beyond all living towns:

> I am riding on a limited express, one of the crack trains of the nation.
> Hurtling across the prairies into blue haze and dark air go fifteen all-steel coaches holding a thousand people.
> (All the coaches shall be scrap and rust and all the men and women laughing in the diners and sleepers shall pass to ashes.)
> I ask a man in the smoker where he is going and he answers: "Omaha." [2]

In his "Smoke and Steel," which followed "Chicago Poems" and "Cornhuskers," Sandburg left the streets and the plains for the factory and the laborer; but as he still kept alive his sense of time and space he did not write as a re-

[1] "Cornhuskers" (Holt), p. 11.
[2] "Chicago Poems" (Holt), p. 40.

former. If Huntington, railroad president, and Blithery, wage earner, were destined to the same goal, class struggles were hardly more important than Presidential administrations or ward politics. He saw in the Western prairies vast expanses across which men strayed or struggled but in which they were soon buried. He saw in a machine world a process of creation which dealt death and destruction, but which made things only slightly less ephemeral than human life. The grass needed only a few years to obliterate battlefields so that passengers would ask where they were, from conductors on trains soon to be scrapped. Even the rusty gun of the buck private would be among the "wished-to-be-forgotten things," useful only as a home for spiders.

So as a poet he lives in the great spaces, but in the presence of beauty too, finding it on every side — in the manifold moods of earth and sky and sea, in the innocence of childhood, in honest love and honest labor, in homely ways and places. Sandburg treats life frankly and without bitterness because on the whole he likes it and believes in it. He believes in being happy, but not in being "doubled-up, doggone, happy-happy" because people of that brand of happiness "bust hard . . . when they bust." He does not want to dodge issues; but to him life with all its ugliness is touched with beauty and filled with solemnity. That is what he has found in the life and character of Abraham Lincoln, whose biographer he has become. "It is altogether fitting and proper" that he should have. For he belongs to the region, as the martyr-President did, shares his realism, his sense of humor his sober faith, his patience with life, his gift of phrase.

The years between the Civil War and the end of the century offer more to the historian of the American theater than to the chronicler of the drama. The theater serves as an index, like magazine and newspaper, of popular taste that was content with mediocrity; and it marked an ebb tide in the history of American drama. There were Steele MacKaye and William Gillette, to be sure, and James A. Herne and

Bronson Howard; and Thomas and Fitch were to come with the 90's. Their output as a whole, and certainly that of the older quartet, was artificial and untrue. Barrett Clark has fairly summarized the period:

> It is not the quaintness of the language and the labored style of these plays that has caused them to be forgotten, it is the fundamental fact that they are the products of superficial writers, of men who could say and believe that "plays are not written but rewritten," an epigram appropriately attributed to Boucicault, Bronson Howard, Augustin Daly, Augustus Thomas, and a dozen other able playmakers. The kind of plays these men wrote were indeed rewritten: they had to be. But here "rewritten" means picked apart, built up, "lifted," like a dowager's face, put on a diet, painted, and rouged.[1]

If this seem too severe an indictment, Bronson Howard supplied complete confirmation in his "Autobiography of a Play" with its meretricious laws of dramatic construction, which were merely rules for Broadway salesmanship, and with his insistence on "subjects of universal interest," so faithfully developed in "The Banker's Daughter" that he could triumphantly assert the play was "successful in Chicago!"

With the turn of the century and thereafter, playwrights began to appear who for the first time in America knew drama in its relation to the other arts (with Dunlap and the elder MacKaye perhaps honorable exceptions), and who wrote plays out of the fullness of their experience, not indifferent to the box office, but not chiefly concerned with it. The movement started in England and on the Continent and, as we can now see, in the United States as well; but the traditional American neglect of American literature still led the first alert critics on this side the Atlantic to lay all their emphasis on foreign writers. Thus in 1905 Huneker's "Iconoclasts" dealt with Norwegian, French, German, Italian, Russian, Belgian, and English dramatists, and Hale's "Dramatists of Today" was of the same complexion. But by 1910 the drift was indicated in Eaton's "At the New Theater and Others,"

---

[1] "An Hour of American Drama" (Lippincott), p. 20.

about half of which was devoted to American themes; and Eaton's dedication is significant in its tribute to a "leader in the movement for a better appreciation among educated men of the art of the practical theater."

To an art that is totally dependent for fruition on some sort of patronage, the development of an intelligently appreciative audience is of first importance. Among the agencies active over the land the most dynamic are the thousand little, or neighborhood, or workshop, or community, or school and college theaters from Provincetown to Pasadena. From their own constituencies they have supplied much of the transient patronage that is vital to the New York theater. Broadway has watched their experiments in production, too, has adopted new methods of staging, has hired and richly rewarded the men and women who proved that they had something fine which also paid. The clear consequences are that the upper level of Broadway plays produced during the 1920's had more than before to offer the discriminating playgoer, that the proportion, as well as the number, of such offerings rose, and that an immense incentive was held out to the men and women who think of playwriting as an art.

An attendant fact is the displacement in the mind of such a playgoer of the theatrical craftsman by the dramatic artist and of the star actor by the play. To a marked degree the playwrights of distinction have changed from writing for the stage to regarding the stage as an avenue for their writings. These are broad statements and open to rejoinders, but behind them is an impressive list of performances which utterly repudiate the claptrappy dramatic laws of Bronson Howard and his ilk. Percy MacKaye's most interesting products all dared and drew the scorn of the orthodox. Eugene O'Neill has never conceded to current stage tradition, but has repeatedly challenged it and with incredible success. George Kelly disowns all formulas and insists only on presenting character. Sidney Howard, not an innovator, is nevertheless absorbed in what he is doing and not in the way he does it. Stallings and Anderson created their joint success, "What Price Glory," not because they wrote a startlingly realistic war play but because they presented a genuine struggle between genuine characters. On the other hand, Kaufman and Connelly, in their collaborated fantasy, "Beggar on Horseback," lifted the stage to the level of a dream world, displaying the same command over their medium that one of them has since shown in the folk religion of "Green Pastures," and the other in the satiric extravaganza of "Once in a Lifetime."

A passage in a letter from O'Neill shows the immense difference between the independent present and the cheaply conventional generation that preceded it, even though the independence offers a substitution of conventions — old Greek for modern Continental.

> Where I set most store by myself [is] as a bit of a poet, who has labored with the spoken word to evolve original rhythms of beauty where beauty apparently isn't — *Jones, Ape, God's Chillun, Desire,* etc. — and to see the transfiguring nobility of tragedy, in as near the Greek sense as one can grasp it, in seemingly the most ignoble, debased lives. And just here is where I am a most confirmed mystic, too, for I'm always, always trying to interpret Life in terms of lives, never just lives in terms of character. I'm always acutely conscious of the Force behind. . . . And my profound conviction is that this is the only subject worth writing about and that it is possible — or can be — to develop a tragic expression in terms of transfigured modern values and symbols in the theater which may to some degree bring home to members of a modern audience their ennobling identity with the tragic figures on the stage. Of course, this is very much of a dream, but where the theater is concerned, one must have a dream, and the Greek dream in tragedy is the noblest ever."[1]

O'Neill is going his own way. Fortunately the other good playwrights are going their ways too. But he is not a closet dramatist. His way leads across the stage, and his audiences make their ways by the thousands past the box offices to see his plays. Often — probably always — he falls short of

[1] Quoted in A. H. Quinn's "History of the American Drama from the Civil War to the Present," Vol. II, p. 199.

what he is attempting. To symbolize lofty ideas with lowly characters and to reveal truth without expounding, demands super-actors and super-audiences and demands more control of the sermonizing impulse than O'Neill sometimes exhibits. But the impressive fact remains that he continues to dream the Greek dream in modern terms and that Americans continue to share the dream as paying auditors. Until these latter years it could not have been done.

Time would fail to tell of Gideon and Barak. The list of individual and independent playwrights is enlarged each season. They can venture to do things in their own ways, with a chance for a hearing. Stage history in recent years has once more refuted the charge that the United States is hostile to the artist. On the contrary, it is so hospitable that charlatan and faddist are continually pushing to claim squatter's rights on land that has been cleared by honest settlers. Perhaps it is better so. Good soil is good for weeds as well as for flowers; and while the hot-house is still nursing its seedlings, the theater soil of the present is fallowed at last for a healthy native growth.

The Rediscovery of the Frontier

Early census returns in the spring of 1930 announced that Oklahoma City had a population of one hundred and eighty-four thousand. Miss Ferber's "Cimarron," a best seller of that season, looked back only forty years on the transformation of Indian Territory into Oklahoma. Both the census and the novel served as reminders that the opening of this district marked the closing of the frontier. Yet this reminder could be given only to such as already knew that the frontier had always been significant in American life, and never more so than in its disappearance. Most of the country is still indifferent to the fact. Millions of ostensibly educated Easterners lump everything beyond Pittsburgh and Buffalo into an indeterminate West which they are aware of only as a region of recurrent, vague, and harmless political unrest.

But there is something about the West more popularly intriguing than its politics. It is immensely, romantically picturesque, and its human picturesqueness, which has been real and really American, has been very recent. After the World War and the general revival of American self-examination, a wave of interest in the frontier and the post-frontier was registered in the publication of a great number of books. The United States, in the mood of John Milton on arriving at the age of twenty-three, was startled by the fact of suddenly achieved maturity. The semblance might deceive the truth; but time, the subtle thief, had stolen on the country, and the discovery that its youth was gone turned it to retrospection, introspection, circumspection.

There is a great mass of printed material — not to call it all literature — about the frontier and the pioneer, most of which appeared before this outburst. Of the matter contemporary with the event, some that was unconscious and genuinely revealing appeared in unliterary publications and only subsequently came in for critical attention. In its day the polite ignored it or apologized for it. The conscious literature of frontier days was of two main kinds: what was written from the frontier — almost invariably affected, revealing little but the wish of the writers to compose the kind of thing approved by tradition; and what was written about the frontier by more or less careless and more or less unscrupulous sojourners who put into writing sentimentalized and rapidly conventionalized accounts to be marketed in the older country.

All this early output furnished the subject for one class of later books — the studies of the literature of the frontier, some richly informative, others inclining to such neat interpretations that they became in the manner of their kind formulas imposed on the past rather than deductions drawn from it. Another voluminous group is composed of retrospective studies and portraits, usually interesting, usually misleading when written to prove something, and at their best when limited to facts from which the derivable theories are left to the reader. The best material and, of course, the nearest to pure literature is the later narrative: the novels of the native pioneer, truly told; the novels of the immigrant pioneer; and the supplementary biographies which emphasize how little there is to choose between fact and fiction, — these carry along an epic cycle that is concluded with the fact and fiction of the "back-trailers," who seek in return to the older settlements the contentment in life which their forebears had hoped for in the West.

Following Paxson's "History of the Frontier" in 1924 and the literary studies by Rusk, Dondore, and Hazard of the three succeeding years,[1] scores of books appeared on the West which were neither narrative, formal history, nor explicit criticism. Taken as a whole, however, they are significant both as records and as interpretations; and they are particularly interesting when read in the light of Turner's original and reiterated thesis as to the formative influence of the frontier on the pioneer. It is safe to say that the less didactic the authors of these books were the better they serve as supporters of Turner's contention. For many of them were world-weary and war-weary, turning to the West to celebrate the passage of a heroic age and applauding in that remote setting men and events that could be duplicated in every dramatic detail by the gangsters of the nearest big city. Most of them enjoyed the fellowship of kindred mind with Thomas Beer when, in 1926, they read a reminiscent passage:

> The Dalton gang was out of business after five years of graceful, even endearing performance. . . . They were amiable and rather mannerly bandits, on the whole, and yet no ballad bears their name. The great tradition of Sturdevant, Murrel of the "mystic clan" in Andrew Jackson's reign, Boone Helm, Billy the Kid and Jesse James ended here in an alley on the crackling sound of Carey Seaman's shotgun.[2]

Of this mind were the group-authors of "The Taming of the Frontier," already referred to.[3]

---

[1] See pages 595–600. [2] "The Mauve Decade," p. 69. [3] See page 780.

The authors of "The Taming of the Frontier" looked back to it as to a lost estate, a state of primitive freedom never to be regained. The chroniclers of the cow country recorded a passing phase of civilization and held no special thesis for it. A third point of view emerges in Mrs. Gerould's "Aristocratic West" — very Eastern and very consciously magnanimous. In the early days of the Far West, she asserted, there sprang up a more vital and romantic code than any in America since colonial days. This code was "liberally inherited, carefully cherished," and beyond question generously bequeathed from the East. "By so much as it still shapes and colors the Far Western attitude to life, is the Far Western attitude admirable, interesting, superior."[1] She endorsed the Grand Canyon, as it were, and patted the Rockies on the back. This unequivocal code was ascribed by Mrs. Gerould to the same people whom the authors of "The Taming of the Frontier" looked back on as cheerful blackguards and happy bandits. To her the only West worth saving was an orderly West which was being swept into modern chaos. To them the only West worth lamenting was a gay anarchy which was being subjected to modern standardization. In the middle ground the writers who were not struggling with a literary proposition showed how the lion of lawlessness lay down with the lamb of courtliness, and made no attempt to account for the twentieth-century West as a progeny of their begetting.

It would be quite misleading to imply that in these fruitful years, 1925 to 1927, the American interest in the frontier or surviving frontier traits was limited to historians, literary critics, social theorists, and their readers. Bill Hart and Tom Mix reached a hundred through the film for every one reached through print; Will Rogers came into his own in these years; in these years the rodeo was brought East, horrifying some spectators, delighting others, thrilling all. And a somewhat less than casual glance at book and maga-

---

[1] K. F. Gerould, "The Aristocratic West," p. 5.

zine publication for the 1920's shows that there was a culmination of attention to all sorts of matters relating to the Men who were being Men in the Open Spaces. The guides to books and magazines tell the same story. Of collections wholly or largely of frontier songs and ballads, six in all, four were published in 1927. Of the fourteen books on the cowboy, three belong to 1926 and four to 1927. Paul Bunyan, Munchausenized performer of prodigies in the lumber camps, had his little vogue from 1922 to 1925. Magazine articles on the cowboy rose from an annual average of two in 1919–1921 to an average of nine in 1925–1927, and articles and stories of frontier life from three a year in the earlier period to twenty-four a year in the latter. One of the greatest moving-picture successes of these years was "The Covered Wagon." While the memories of the frontier were receding and the characteristics fading, the 1920's were collecting them, like ship's clocks or Windsor chairs.

Naturally the most momentous record was in the pages of the novelists; the foregoing has been only a preface; all the rest of the story is theirs. It is the story of American-born pioneers, of immigrant pioneers, and, finally, of the back-trailers.

In sober truthfulness about the American pioneer, author and public really came together in the 1920's[1] with Herbert Quick's "Vandemark's Folly" and "The Hawkeye." Quick had written attractive whimsies in the early years of the century, things that were neither sober nor true. While he was doing them Frank Norris, thrilled with the responsibilities of the novelist, had propounded his poeticized economic thesis, and William Allen White had advanced another with his "A Certain Rich Man," all interesting documents, all chapters in the exploitation of the West, all just short of excellence as works of art and too early to profit from the rediscovery of the frontier. Quick, however, had lived

[1] For earlier treatments or mentions by Crèvecœur, the Ameses, Cooper, Irving, Mark Twain, Miller, Norris, Garland, Cather, and others see Index under the entry "Frontier."

through a frontiering experience, shared in the conquest of the open country, witnessed the paying of a heavy price in human sacrifice, fought exploiters in behalf of his fellows, and shouldered his way into leadership. He had learned to write as a journalist, and at sixty he was mellow, unembittered, sympathetic, ready for his crowning work. Events conspired for him; the subject was ripe, and the public was ripe for it. He wrote authentically of the middle of the century in Iowa: home-finding, ground-breaking, town-building, developing into a solid community. There is no lack of hardship; yet withal it is a story of victory.

The implication is that life spares the deserving and punishes the wicked. Life had in fact dealt kindly with Herbert Quick, and he fell into the error of regarding his case as typical. That is the implication in the title of his autobiography, "One Man's Life." "I feel sure," he writes therein, "that I have heard the same individual bird change from the rather thin and tweedling song of the east to the bold and liquid sweetness of the west." It is a theory springing from success gained and held in the new country. It could be reinforced by the reminder that Harte and Mark Twain and Garland, who returned to the East, all showed a tendency to "tweedle" in their latter years. It is not born of ignorance — anything but that in Quick. Yet it could have been developed only by ignoring the grim experience of the majority, not so strong nor so brave as this chronicler, who apparently was resolved to deal as kindly with life as life had dealt with him.

There is a notable paucity in both bulk and significance of fiction that presents the native frontiersman in the first stages of pioneering — actually in contact with the earth. It remains for the chroniclers of the immigrants to do best with this; and we shall come to them. The American farmer was promptly carried on by the novelists into the Gilded Age, though it was not for him to enjoy its glitter. It was the drabbest of periods for the homesteader who had become the prairie townsman. When prosperity or failure brought a frontier farmer back to town, the odds were against him, for he had never learned to be a social creature. Caution in dealing with nature had grown side by side with suspicion in dealing with human nature, breeding a conservatism that was equally leery of committing itself to a new farm machine, a new political doctrine, or a new interpretation of the book of Genesis. Relieved of the urgency of field and flock, he might substitute busyness for activity, but he was much more likely to subside into inertia. In a town which was beginning to be mechanized, moreover, prosperity seemed to be reserved for the factory and to be withheld from the field. He was offered sterile hours of leisure in an alien world with nothing to do in them, no family habits of crafts or games or songs to resort to, these playing little part in the American countryside.

E. W. Howe has said that the vigilance of the gossip is the safeguard of morals in such a town. To judge from his own epoch-marking "Story of a Country Town" and some thousands of pages of later testimony, he has done too much honor to Mrs. Grundy's efficacy. Yet gossip holds a whip over the villager, inducing a guarded existence, bridling life with caution. The one note of general protest direct from this life shows that the only articulate community consciousness in the broad region has been the perennial awareness, perennially justified in America, that bank and factory were allied against farm, and that the farm was the hindmost with the devil holding the mortgage — four billions' worth in 1920. Though the prairie states started abortive, rival, self-defeating movements, the natural fear of taking chances held them in political line, and they floundered hopelessly in the attempt to find for themselves any happy springs of enjoyment, any undrained sources of vital interest. For the ex-frontiersmen of the prairie states, the evenings of their lives were like the evenings of their days of labor: they were too tired to feel, to think, or to dream, and the town to which they gave character, though urban in the census report, was rural in essential traits.

The worst human fruits of such an era are to be found in the first half of the "Spoon River Anthology"; the average, in "Main Street"; E. W. Howe is one of the best. He has quoted with evident pleasure in his autobiography, "Plain People," H. L. Mencken's summary of his beliefs: that intelligent self-interest is the only vital human motive; that it is a virtue to get money; that, "barring acts of God," people fail and succeed according to their deserts; that reformers are all charlatans; and that public abuses must be laid to "the credulity, emotionalism, and imbecility" of the public. If Mencken and Howe had not regarded this as a fair statement, the one would not have made it nor the other have quoted it. Yet it is the law of the jungle; it disregards even the small subscription to religion or to "moral perfection" conceded by Benjamin Franklin, and the merciful doctrine of moral imperfection propounded by Clarence Darrow; it shows the deference for property inherent in the Constitution before the addition of the Bill of Rights; and at a half-dozen points the "plain propositions" are in conflict. Yet even in its self-contradictions it is doubtless a fair statement of Howe's philosophy, and a partial statement of the views of the post-frontier for which he was so long a spokesman.

Thus spake Atchison, Kansas; but Emporia, Kansas, made reply, William Allen White, tender-minded and more cosmopolitan, retorting to "Ed" Howe, the tough-minded provincial. On most of the theses laid down by Mencken they disagree. White holds that altruism is gradually replacing self-interest in social practice; that self-interest leads to demands for special privilege and vicious corporate practices; that these latter are good for neither winners nor losers; that cranks and reformers teach social wisdom; that many of the incapable and irresponsible are more sinned against than sinning. On two points only do the eminent Kansans concur: that the man of talents and industry can make a decent living, and that the voice of the people is anything but the voice of God.

Both speak for Kansas and the corn belt, but as from watchtowers commanding different vistas. Howe is old enough to be reminiscent of actual frontier days. He recalls Indian fights, buffalo hunts, the last of the Jameses, the reign of fanatical orthodoxy, antislavery agitation and the Civil War, the coming of the railroads, land speculation, financial wildcatting, scurrilous newspaper feuds. Then — with the changing of the town from the eastern outpost of the cattle trails to the western goal of the barnstormer — the coming of Beecher and Ingersoll, Oscar Wilde, Fanny Davenport and Minnie Hauk, and the onset of worldliness. His wedding had in it a simulation of the grandeur of palaces, courts, and cathedrals, though it occurred in a story-and-a-half house in a country town. Yet he finally achieved for himself a house with steam heat and "the best bedroom in Kansas, with a private bath," — and tried to compensate for his grandeur by calling his place Potato Hill. Howe's chronicle is a recital of all sorts of facts and opinions tinged by a latent sentimentalism reeling helpless in the face of overwhelming fact. He favors the doctrine of predestination, "somewhat liberalized"; but he believes that the people who have gone wrong ought to have behaved. And always this modernized Franklin of the prairie couples industry and thrift with good behavior and success.

William Allen White is less static a character. His selection of editorial articles in "The Editor and his People" contains a section headed "The Decay of a Conservative," a semi-centennial article on Emporia tracing his own growth from dreamy romanticism over a town that existed in fancy to a recognition of the town in fact. But he does not allege that his people have kept pace with him. In the volume of the next year (1925), "In Our Town," there is no evidence that they regard themselves as heirs to a heroic age, that they are aware of having shared in an epic movement, or that they are inclined to self-criticism. Kansas becomes something of a mystery to him. He describes the state as fair and fat with prosperity; and yet:

> Kansas is the Mother Shipton, the Madame Thebes, the Witch of Endor, and the low barometer of the nation. When anything is going to happen in this country, it happens first in Kansas. Abolition, Prohibition, Populism, the Bull Moose, the exit of the roller towel, the appearance of the bank guarantee, the blue-sky law, the adjudication of industrial dispute as distinguished from the arbitration of industrial differences — these things came popping out of Kansas like bats out of hell. Sooner or later, other states take up these things, and then Kansas goes on breeding other troubles. Why, no one seems to know.[1]

The springs of abolition and prohibition were in New England Puritanism. The issues were moralistic; the will to power, the desire to dictate, and the fighting spirit have a clear genealogy through Plymouth and Massachusetts Bay by way of the English Commonwealth to the Reformation. The springs of Populism and Progressivism were in the West, in a vague discontent; but the will to power and the fighting spirit were in decline. A low barometer is not the cause of anything: it is only the indicator of a symptom. The editor did not seem to realize that the ex-frontier has become a seat of infection rather than a seat of power, with just enough recurrent energy to send occasional scattered insurgents to Congress, but not enough courage or solidarity to stand fast in their support.

In his interpretation of the Mississippi Valley ex-frontier, Sinclair Lewis leads the way in critical sagacity. "Main Street" opens with a rebellious girl, spirit of the bewildered Middle West, looking out from a Minnesota hillside crossed not long ago by Indians and fur traders. She is a student in a sectarian college, eager to know and to live, unaware of the world's capacity for dullness or its gift for casual cruelty. She has been bred in a Minnesota-New England town which has a firmer anchorage in the past than most of the surrounding communities. She wonders whether its people feel free to challenge the "sanctified lies" and the "ancient stale inequalities."

[1] "The Editor and his People," p. 174. By permission of The Macmillan Company, publishers.

When, after marriage, she moves to Gopher Prairie, she discovers that her new neighbors do not know what conversation is, and that they have lost the power for impersonal thought and the mood for spontaneous play. She finds that the early autocracy of Yankee professional men has passed to the merchants, but that the tribal rulers of the town, in their observance of the accepted morals and accepted chicaneries, are hypocrites to the core. She is told that the spirit of the place is sound, wholesome but afraid; it gives vocal subscription to sweetness and not too much light. In short, except for freedom from a squirearchy, Gopher Prairie is like all villages in Anglo-Saxondom that are neither rural nor urban, that have lost the smell of the soil and have not acquired the scent of patchouli. She finds dignity and greatness only in the awful and limitless plains, some invisible barrier excluding these qualities from the town. It has its own credo:

> The Baptist church . . . is the perfect, the divinely ordained standard in music, oratory, philanthropy and ethics. . . .
>
> The Republican Party, the Grand Old Party of Blaine and McKinley, is the agent of the Lord and of the Baptist Church in temporal affairs.
>
> All socialists ought to be hanged. . . .
>
> People who make more than ten thousand a year or less than eight hundred are wicked.
>
> Europeans are still wickeder.
>
> It doesn't hurt anyone to drink a glass of beer on a warm day, but anybody who touches wine is headed straight for hell. . . .
>
> The farmers want too much for their wheat.
>
> The owners of the elevator-company expect too much for the salaries they pay.
>
> There would be no more trouble or discontent in the world if everybody worked as hard as Pa did when he cleared our first farm.[1]

The defenders of this orthodoxy look with suspicion and fear on any who inquire into its articles, disregard them, or look beyond them. Carol Kennicott finally succumbs, for she is only an averagely bold and energetic idealist.

---

[1] "Main Street" (Harcourt, Brace), pp. 152, 153.

Gopher Prairie greatly magnified becomes the Middle-Western city of Zenith. According to Lewis the difference between the two is only a matter of size; but the bigger community is harder for the average man to resist. George F. Babbitt has probably less initiative than Carol began with. His fight is less open and prolonged, so much less so that it is hardly a fight at all, and could be disguised like an official report of a military retreat as successive assumptions of more strategic positions. His tactics are cautiously military too, in being always pursued with primary attention to the base of supplies. Yet until he is overwhelmed by the town, Babbitt dreams and yearns. Even when he has married the wife he has not aspired to and thriven in the business he did not elect, he distrusts the hullabaloo of busyness in which he is involved. He has secret leanings toward Seneca Doane, the radical lawyer, and knows in his heart that Doane is correct in his contempt for good, clean, domestically sound, throat-cutting pirates who shout good fellowship and hesitate at nothing that makes for success. He slips away from the crowd to think things over, but is sucked back so far into the maelstrom that he becomes a minor prophet of the gospel of efficiency and a dispenser of ominous threats to the un-American skeptics who ask how the ship of state became transformed into a national band wagon and want to know where it is going as it thunders along Prosperity Boulevard. Yet the solidest satisfaction he gains in the whole story is in his son's combined impudence and recklessness in having a mind of his own and going his own gait.

The theme of "Main Street" and "Babbitt" becomes the theme of "Arrowsmith" and "Elmer Gantry": that the atmosphere of the Middle West is stifling to the scientist and ozone for the charlatan and demagogue. As documents the two books are significant. They confirm Howe and White. They have been impressively confirmed by the careers of Billy Sunday and W. J. Bryan. As novels they are in a trough between the wave peaks of "Main Street" and "Dodsworth"; but "Dodsworth" belongs later in the discussion.

The experience of the immigrant pioneer is notably different from that of the American moving from one part of the country to another. Miss Cather, of the contemporaries, has made her significant contribution,[1] and she has been supplemented by Ruth Suckow and Martha Ostenso. But these all have lacked in some degree complete fidelity to their material, willingness to follow the data where it led, and a perfect understanding of the immigrant experience. "The more . . . an author," writes Glenway Wescott in one of his prefatory passages, "has in common with his characters the better; typical trivialities surpass in significance the noblest feelings; an immediate report is more valuable than reminiscences, the rest is lyricism. . . . No judicious novelist, however prosaic, will strive to outdistance life; he will choose problems which only seem insoluble, which in some corner of society, in some small illustrative scale, have been solved."[2] Wescott's passage might have been written explicitly about the Norwegian-American Ole Edvart Rölvaag.

The various national migrations to the United States have, of course, been widely varied in kind and have been variously recorded. No other has come to so fine a literary flowering in recent years as the Norwegian; and in its deepest essentials it may probably be taken as representative of them all, or at least of all who came into the West. At the census of 1920 more than a million born in Norway or of Norwegian parentage lived in the six north-central states; and as three fourths of these have followed rural lives, they have been peculiarly free to foster the language and traditions of the homeland. A literate people, they became prolific in authorship, publishing in their own tongue for their own people on both sides of the Atlantic. Prevailing in their writings is the consciousness of the pilgrim and the sojourner. Almost without exception the two lands are linked in the stories: a poor boy comes to America, thrives, and returns to claim his sweetheart and to wreak vengeance on a Norwegian oppres-

---

[1] See pages 787–789. [2] "Good-Bye Wisconsin" (Harper's), pp. 36, 37.

sor; a poor boy comes to America, sends back for his sweetheart, and reaches the high goal of the pulpit; a poor boy comes to America and has a daughter who rebels at the sordidness of Jonasville, another Gopher Prairie, and goes to Chicago, where she marries one Miles Standish Ward; a poor boy comes to America and makes his fortune, but sinks into spiritual bankruptcy; another develops into solid, courageous citizenship, bent on contributing the best of Norwegian character to the land of his adoption; a Norwegian sculptor strives to find his place in the American scene.

To this tide of fiction from O. A. Buslett, Peer Stromme, Waldemar Ager, Simon Johnson, and H. A. Foss, Rölvaag had been contributing his "Letters from America," "The Forgotten Path," "Two Fools," "The Ship of Longing." Yet to give them these English names is misleading, for they were published in Norwegian and in Norway. Then came throughout the reading world a new vogue for the novel of the soil, accelerated by Knut Hamsun's influence; then also, in the United States, the fresh zest for frontier tales; and then, finally, the announcement that Johan Bojer was planning to treat the theme of the Norwegian immigrant on the American prairie. It was an unconscious challenge to Rölvaag which he at once accepted. In 1924, within a month, the two novelists published. In 1927 "Giants in the Earth," Rölvaag's tale, was issued in an English version which within a twelvemonth ran to forty-four printings. "Peder Victorious" followed two years later, and the trilogy was completed with "Their Father's God."

An exceptional man, Rölvaag compressed great breadth and variety into his career. Not content with mastering two languages and blending two cultures, he progressed from the life of the toiler to the life of the scholar and thence to the life of the artist. He is what Nathaniel Bumppo Cooper or Antonia Shimerda Cather might have been. He not only saw all he wrote about; it was all in the warp of his emotional experience. When he wrote, therefore, he was not the frontiersman trying to handle a pen with his trigger finger, or a

Joaquin Miller in sombrero and boots at a London salon. He was the only kind of novelist who could vie with Johan Bojer and surpass him; for he was the primitive subject of Bojer's "Emigrants" and also Bojer's peer as creative writer.

The fundamental difference in the approaches of the two novelists is apparent at a glance. Bojer wrote as a Norwegian about emigrants; Rölvaag, as an American about immigrants. Rölvaag's participation in the experience gave his work an emotional depth that could not be reached by a mere observer. The narrative undertaking to which he set himself was to present through event and circumstance the double ordeal of the alien of another country and another speech. He must not only break the kinship of the soul with the soil in which it has grown — the pioneer from the East or the British Isles had done that; he must cope with a new language. Yet genuinely to acquire a new speech demands a "spiritual readjustment which is forever beyond the power of the average man because it requires a remaking of soul. He cannot give up the old, because that would mean death to him, and he cannot master the new — the process is simply beyond his powers."[1] This is a phase of national assimilation that any American or any Norwegian can grasp intellectually, but only the Norwegian-American who has survived the struggle can grasp and present it in its emotional verity. The physical conquest of a wilderness leaves no time for language study, and acquiring a language means much more than building up a workaday vocabulary. The complete transition from one land to the other can come only with so intimate a mastery of the new tongue that the emotional life can find spontaneous expression in it. And that is the miracle of acquiring a new soul that only one in ten thousand may achieve. It is the tragedy inherent in this situation which leads to the conquest of the pioneer — to Turner's brief statement that the wilderness masters the colonist. The immigrant pioneer in particular is confronted by peril upon

[1] Letter from O. E. Rölvaag to the author.

peril: first of physical defeat while he and his kind are transforming the surface of the earth; then, when the community closes around him and assimilates his children as it cannot assimilate him, of social submergence without inner adjustment; then, in the midst of small-town Philistinism, of the ostracism which follows independence or the surrender to Mammon which follows material success; and further, the new problem, now transferred to his offspring, of adjustment to rival aliens as well as to the native stock. One can trace these ordeals as they are visited on the figures in the extended Rölvaag chronicle.

The tale of the second immigrant generation on the verge of its adult career has been told also by Martha Ostenso in "Wild Geese"; but her treatment differs as markedly from Rölvaag's as Bojer's does from that of the earlier stages. For she represents youth, and Rölvaag speaks for both age and youth. He is tolerant of the young and compassionate for their elders; she is the voice of intolerant rebellion. Her Caleb Gare, fearful product of pioneering days, is a merciless archfiend with an insatiable lust for land and power and no grand desires to redeem his greed. He is a spiritual counterpart of the land, as harsh and as tyrannous. The planting and tilling season is a "terrific, prolonged passion," oblivious at its height, like every great passion, to anything beyond itself, forgetful of any aim, regardless of every obstacle. Miss Ostenso has not been quite able to convey her meaning through direct narrative. Her two young lovers stop to expound her thesis in the midst of the story:

> Life here at Oeland, even, may seem a negation but it is only a reflection from so few exterior natural objects that it has the semblance of negation. These people are thrown inward upon themselves, their passions stored up, they are intensified figures of life with no outward expression — no releasing gesture.

"Yes," says the other, "there's no feeling left after the soil and the live stock have taken their share."[1] And they talk

[1] "Wild Geese," pp. 105, 106.

about books. Not only that, but they find their own solution, not in any victory over these conditions, but in escape from them; and as the author sends them back to urban conditions from which she has brought them as transient observers of the actual pioneer stock, she kills off the villain of the piece by trapping him in a bottomless swamp while a brush fire sweeps out of control and destroys his finest, unreaped crop.

One thinks back to Crèvecœur's unfulfilled prophecy of a new race, fused from the nations of the Old World: new men acting on new principles, entertaining new opinions, forming new opinions. It is true, as the rhapsodist predicted, that the American who was to come has caused great changes in the world. The rest may be true some day short of the millennium. In the meanwhile the fusing process is still on, and the crucible proves to be anything but a bed of roses. That is why the honest teller of frontier tales, who undertakes neither to idealize nor to prophesy, is bound to be a somber recorder of somber vicissitudes.

So on the land that we choose to think of as permanent, because any other thought is too uncomfortable, the social order shifts in spite of the beneficiaries who like to think of it as established, because any other thought is intolerable to them. Some succeed in the new country and stay where they have scored their successes. Many succeed and go East to spend their fortunes. For the rest there is a new word, "maladjustment." It is an excuse and explanation for the harsher word "failure." It accounts also for people who have felt that they were in the wrong region, whose repugnance to it would probably have led to defeat, and who have sought safety and happiness in retreat to the older country. The term "back-trailer," as Hamlin Garland gave it to us, applies especially to those of the second generation whose distaste for the frontier is coupled with the memory that they themselves never chose to brave it. Howells left the Middle West and looked back on it with friendly interest; John Hay, on the other hand, was almost hostile. He left it in spirit when he went to college in Rhode Island as a boy of seventeen. He was embarrassed and half ashamed at the vogue of his "Pike County Ballads"; asked Stedman to omit "Little Breeches" from his anthology, disowning it as a "hopeless fluke" with an "odious name"; omitted from his poetical works all but three poems with any reference to the West; urged his friends to read "Castilian Days"; published a series of letters from Illinois and called them "A Poet in Exile." Soon after, he emerged in a letter from young Major Thomas Wentworth Higginson. A picnic outside of Washington was "got up for a young Mr. Hay," who spent the afternoon "laboring not to appear new-mown" and not to appear as Western as Abraham Lincoln, whose secretary's secretary he was. As the years went on he succeeded in outliving every suggestion of field and farm so that a President from Ohio, McKinley, referred to him in almost envious admiration as a conservatory product, a fine flower of civilization.

It is quite evident that the richest material relative to the frontier has been on the shock troopers of the earlier phases of pioneering; and it has been abundantly used. The sober and negative experience of the back-trailer has been so far left for only one or two. This is not for lack of authors who have known the story at first hand. Most of the writers who came out to the Mississippi Valley and beyond, and very many who were born there, have not been content to remain. Howells and Hay, Eggleston and Mark Twain and Bret Harte, Markham and Masters, Ezra Pound, John Gould Fletcher, T. S. Eliot, only begin the list. In fact, the expatriates have been almost all recruited from the ex-frontier. Writers who could have dealt with the theme have been numerous enough; but the story is not an easy one to tell, for it must be composed in a minor key, with no big crescendos, and can be hardly more than sustained anticlimax. Wescott, near the beginning of his career, and Garland, toward the end of his, have dealt most effectively with it.

Garland prepared the ground for it in "A Son of the Middle Border," began the actual chronicle in the second volume of it (which his publishers prevailed on him to misname "A Daughter"), and concluded it explicitly in the final installment, "Back-Trailers from the Middle Border." The man on the post-frontier at the passing of the century, especially if he were the son of a pioneer, was likely to have various misgivings. On the one hand was his open dissatisfaction with conditions in a district where the first heroic campaign was over, where the heroes of the campaign were passing into dependent old age, and where there was no fresh enthusiasm for life or for vigorous performance. The little towns were drab and ugly; there was no desire to beautify them or to beautify life in them. In the midst of such circumstances the alien immigrant had no choice; he had made an irrevocable one; but the American found that this very choice was forcing him into a new dilemma — that of being an alien among aliens, a stranger on American soil, or, pioneering now over, of taking the back trail.

If, then, he felt as Garland did, that he had tastes which could be better gratified in the older settlements and powers that could be better spent there, he might join the centripetal movement of the day and justify himself by saying that he belonged as much to the present as his father had to the past. He could point to all the other men of his kind who had preceded him in the same migration. Yet when he pulled up stakes the West continued to tug at his heart-strings. He found himself softening for lack of exercise; chafing at dust and soot and noise; pining for the roominess of the country, an acreage instead of a fire escape, for the sound of wind in the trees, the odor of new-mown hay and burning leaves. More poignant was the sense of vague disloyalty to his ancestry, the men of power from whom he had sprung. Ought he to have left the region and its labors? He begged the question by arguing that "there *must* be people who still love to farm, to milk cows, to pick fruit, and to dig potatoes — how else could we go on eating?"[1]

[1] "Back-Trailers," p. 301.

He convinced himself thus, humanly searching for a principle after reaching a decision; but there came new complications into the changing life. On the frontier one was all for simplicity, making a virtue of necessity. There were days, still vividly rememberable, when Garland scorned a dress suit as "the livery of privilege" worn only by the predatory rich and their servants. Ultimately he sits at Carnegie's table undistinguishable in dress both from the other guests and from the waiters. Evening clothes have become a symbol of democracy. Nor is this all: wealth, hated and distrusted from the viewpoint of the debtor frontier, became amiable at close range, turning out to have ennobling qualities. He not only came to approve it in general, but dropped the condemnation of intangible wealth and happily invested the proceeds from the sale of his Oklahoma land. The ex-frontiersman clipped his coupons with quiet joy and expanded with confidence in his emancipation from "the tyranny of the sky." Fear of the weather died; the hot winds of Dakota and the blizzards of Oklahoma sank into dim memories of a danger-ridden past.

Then he came to the heart of the matter. The back-trailer turned to the East because it was the avenue to the past. He summered in London once and again, and reveled in ancient dignities. He had none of Mark Twain's insistence that the American should not defer, or pretend to defer, to everything European. He was quite as reverent as Mark Twain among the ruins at Karnak or in the presence of the pyramids; but he was more easily satisfied; any pageant is a symbol of antiquity, and antiquity is something to revere. The Connecticut Yankee jeering at King Arthur's court was a blasphemer. The elder days should never be stripped of the glamour of romance. The back-trailer, completing the circuit, found his El Dorado in the lands from which the first pioneers set out in search of theirs. It was the return of the prodigal son, sure of his food and cured of his restless discontent. The older regions offered beauty and the peaceful gratification of the senses. The son of the power-man was become the complacent comfort-seeker. This is some distance from fulfillment of Howells's wish of 1894:

> Garland is taking on the world ingenuously and interestingly; he will never be sophisticated, and I hope he won't lose the simplicity of his ideal, such as it was when he had his "Main-Traveled Roads" under his feet, and throbbed with his fine, angry sympathy for "the familiar and the low."

Glenway Wescott supplements fiction on the back-trailer with observations that have more to do with establishing a state of mind and less to do with immediate circumstance. To Garland life is an objective experience. He plowed and milked and sweated as a husky boy. He journeyed East over memorable miles, studied and starved in chill rooms in Boston, traveled and wrote and went in and out of editorial offices, and hobnobbed with innumerable people in all kinds of picturesque settings. To think of his books is to think of definite events happening in definite settings and to recall definite aspirations that were always connected with specific conditions of living. It is the experience of the materialist.

Wescott, in "The Grandmothers," recounts the experience of the romanticist. A young Westerner of the third generation finds himself looking back at life in the same Wisconsin where Garland was born and bred. He is grown up, as the saying goes; but that means nothing to him. He wonders what he has grown up to and what he has grown up from. From his own heritage he cannot escape. It fascinates him; he is an incarnation, and he dwells on the lives of his forebears in a kind of extended introspection. From the region, however, he may free himself. Its past, "a wilderness of history and hearsay," need not be his; it is merely the studio in which the family portraits were painted and still hang. He will never participate in the active life there. He has neither the build nor the will for hard labor, and necessity has not driven him to it. He knows that he could not have endured the comfortless glory of his grandparents. Money that one of the Towers married made schooling possible for him, and early escape to Chicago. Yet he is a Tower himself; and he realizes, as none of them could have, that what he has inherited from them are the traits that doomed them to non-success on the frontier.

They were slight of body. They were sensitive and unassertive, and scrupulous in ways that withheld them from entrance into a fierce free-for-all. Churlish, clumsy men had shouldered them aside. They cherished a grievance against this common clay and felt superior in defeat. Into their young artistic descendant have passed creative vanity that brought forth little, and fruitless pride that fed upon itself. What chance for the fringe of aristocracy on the fringe of civilization? There had been so little hope that its fulfillment was little indeed. Now the changed conditions confront him with a question. What is his place, what his obligations? His people were pioneers because their dispositions unfitted them for anything else without fitting them for this desperate alternative. His own alternatives are hardly less desperate. He goes abroad, and one day comes back for Christmas in the home town. It is a new town, newer than the surrounding farms. The houses — wooden tents — are not anchored to the earth. Things are unsettled: the manners of the people, the church, the little college. Men who want things done are pulled between the challenges of the younger generation and the conservatisms of the elder. A normal situation, it is aggravated here by the lack of either settled traditions or articulate desires. The whole Middle West seems to him to suffer from the nervousness of vagabonds who have no native land left. "There is no Middle West. It is a certain climate, a certain landscape; and beyond that, a state of mind of people born where they do not like to live."[1]

In a few days he turns back to the East, headed, sooner or later, for Europe. He says "Good-Bye Wisconsin" in a book filled with the yearnings and defeats of this region, which, in the life of the nation, represents neither age nor

---

[1] "Good-Bye Wisconsin" (Harper's), p. 39.

youth. It is melancholy to leave; for he knows that democracy is coming to some sort of climax and that his generation, those whose birthrights have set them more to doing than thinking, will soon be claiming the powers and rewards of the lords of the earth. For himself, however, he wishes that he could write a book about ideal people living in ideal circumstances, where outer harmony and beauty prevail and where only the ineluctable trials of the spirit can intrude. And he would like so to write it that he and his origins and his prejudices and his Wisconsin will all disappear. When he has done this he will ask himself whether he has chosen the way of the courageous, and he will stand self-condemned. Wisconsin is too much for him, America is too much for him, and he seeks his El Dorado in Europe. It is the final word in reaction against the life that the pioneers left as their legacy. Vague optimism accepts it; militant energy converts it into something finer; the ways of the back-trailer are followed to their ultimate resort in the life of the expatriate. Of this Glenway Wescott is the interpreter.

The last phase of the cycle appears in those heirs to the labors of the pioneer who will not accept their heritage. It is a tale that is told, a round completed. History and literature have recorded its stages; but there remains the question of the sequel. The westering movement gave life to much that is most truly American. It held out the promise of peace and plenty. Beyond the horizon, and ever beyond, it offered happy contentment. It ravished the dreamer with the hope of an earthly paradise, reviving his youth, lending him fresh vigor to reach what seemed so nearly within his grasp, enriching him in the prospect of what lay beneath the sunset gilded by its splendor. The promise was not fulfilled. What the pioneer found was less than what he sought; he was fettered by the old Adam in himself; his past pursued him. But at his best he was stronger for the ordeal. He had learned to endure, to attempt the impossible, and never to lose hope. In him and his sterner offspring is the capacity for new vision and for finding a new America within himself.

It is this which is suggested in the Western character from Sinclair Lewis's "Dodsworth." After sacrificing a Babbitt and an Arrowsmith to Western philistinism and frustrating a Carol Kennicott, Lewis presents in Sam Dodsworth a man who is strong enough to succeed and also to withstand success. A complete product of new America, he resolves to put his energy and money into his own way of doing what he thinks is worth while. This is not establishing an art museum or subsidizing an orchestra, but making motor cars that owners can enjoy themselves in and go slow in, and building suburbs that are authentically American, as different as can be from the crazy agglomerations of architectural odds and ends that surround most of our cities. Instead of representing in Dodsworth merely the energy of the frontiersman put to work toward ends he has never understood, or of admiring in him an insatiable desire for activity as implicitly as the sentimentalists used to admire "sensibility" as an end in itself, Lewis makes this big cub a dreamer who at fifty decides to continue his education, and find out what he is involved in, and keep on dreaming. He is Babbitt undefeated, Arrowsmith with a stiffened backbone; for he is big enough to resist the silly coerciveness of men who are littler than he, and to learn from the men who are bigger. So when Elon Richards, cosmopolite and financial magnate, advises him after his retirement to return to the American adventure, "because it is an adventure that we have here — the greatest in the world — and not a certainty of manners in an uncertainty of the future, like all of Europe," he assents. Richards, he concludes, is right: "Our adventure is going to be the bigger because we *do* feel that Europe has a lot we need. We're no longer satisfied with the log cabin and the corn pone. We want everything that Europe has. We'll take it."[1] Dodsworth has already graduated from the school that could mistake the "everything" of Richards's remark for material belongings. He confesses to his inexperience and sets out to

---

[1] "Dodsworth" (Harcourt, Brace), p. 172.

learn from Europe, and to keep on growing in wisdom as well as in stature. In doing so he keeps alive the spirit of the frontier and holds out a promise for the future in America.

Book List

THE RECENT PAST

This past is so recent and the multiplicity of material so great that only general books on the period and general and special discussions of the literature are listed here.

The indispensable bibliography for the period as a whole is "Contemporary American Literature," by John Matthews Manly and Edith Rickert, with introduction and revision by Fred B. Millett. 1929.

General Works on the Period and the Literature

I. The Period

ADAMS, JAMES TRUSLOW. The March of Democracy, Vol. II. 1933.
ADAMS, JAMES TRUSLOW. Our Business Civilization. 1929.
ALLEN, FREDERICK L. Only Yesterday. 1931.
BEER, THOMAS. The Mauve Decade. 1926.
BROWNELL, W. C. Democratic Distinction in America. 1927.
BURROUGHS, JOHN. Accepting the Universe. 1920.
CALVERTON, V. F. The Newer Spirit; a Sociological Criticism of Literature. 1925.
CHAMBERLAIN, JOHN. Farewell to Reform. 1932.
CHASE, STUART. Prosperity: Fact or Myth. 1929.
CHASE, STUART. The Tragedy of Waste. 1929.
EDMAN, IRWIN. The Contemporary and his Soul. 1931.
FAŸ, BERNARD. The American Experiment. 1929.
FRANK, WALDO. The Re-discovery of America. 1929.
HAYS, ARTHUR GARFIELD. Let Freedom Ring. 1928.
LEWIS, WYNDHAM. Time and Western Man. 1928.
LIPPMANN, WALTER. A Preface to Morals. 1929.
LIPPMANN, WALTER. A Program for Freedom. 1934.
ORTON, WILLIAM A. America in Search of Culture. 1933.
PAGE, KIRBY (Ed.). A New Economic Order. 1930.
PAGE, KIRBY (Ed.). Recent Gains in American Civilization. 1928.
PAXSON, FREDERIC L. When the West is Gone. 1930.
PRINGLE, HENRY F. Theodore Roosevelt, a Biography. 1931.
SANTAYANA, GEORGE. Character and Opinion in the United States. 1934.
SIEGFRIED, ANDRÉ. America Comes of Age. 1927.

STEARNS, HAROLD E. (Ed.). Civilization in the United States. 1922.
STEFFENS, LINCOLN. Autobiography. 1931.
SULLIVAN, MARK. Our Times: the Turn of the Century. 1926.
SULLIVAN, MARK. Our Times: America Finding Herself. 1927.
SULLIVAN, MARK. Our Times: Pre-War America. 1930.
SULLIVAN, MARK. Our Times: the War Begins, 1909–1914. 1932.
SULLIVAN, MARK. Our Times: Over Here, 1914–1918. 1933.
SULLIVAN, MARK. Our Times: the Twenties. 1935.
VEBLEN, THORSTEIN. The Theory of the Leisure Class. 1899.
WHITEHEAD, ALFRED N. Science and the Modern World. 1926.

II. The Literature

BEACH, JOSEPH WARREN. The Outlook for American Prose. 1926.
BECHHOFER, C. E. The Literary Renaissance in America. 1923.
BOYNTON, PERCY H. More Contemporary Americans. 1927.
CALVERTON, V. F. The Liberation of American Literature. 1932.
FOERSTER, NORMAN (Ed.). The Reinterpretation of American Literature. 1928.
HICKS, GRANVILLE. The Great Tradition. 1933.
LEWISOHN, LUDWIG. Expression in America. 1932.
PARRINGTON, V. L. Main Currents in American Thought, Vol. III. 1930.
PATTEE, FRED LEWIS. The New American Literature. 1930.
SQUIRE, J. C., and others. Contemporary American Authors. 1928.

[*Fiction*]

ADAMS, S. H., AUSTIN, MARY, and others. The Novel of Tomorrow and the Scope of Fiction, by Twelve American Novelists. 1922.
AMES, VAN METER. The Aesthetics of the Novel. 1928.
DU BREUIL, ALICE J. The Novel of Democracy in America. 1923.
EDGAR, PELHAM. The Art of the Novel. 1933.
FOLLETT, H. T. and W. Some Modern Novelists. 1918.
FOLLETT, WILSON. The Modern Novel. 1918, 1923.
FORSTER, E. M. Aspects of the Novel. 1927.
HALL, ERNEST. The Satirical Element in the American Novel. 1922.
HARTWICK, HARRY. The Foreground of American Fiction. 1934. (Bibliography.)
MICHAUD, REGIS. The American Novel To-day. 1928.
O'BRIEN, EDWARD J. The Advance of the American Short Story. 1923.
PATTEE, FRED L. The Development of the American Short Story. 1923.
VAN DOREN, CARL. The American Novel. 1921.
VAN DOREN, CARL. Contemporary American Novelists. 1922.
WHARTON, EDITH. The Writing of Fiction. 1925.
WHEELER, H. L. "Contemporary Novels and Novelists: a List of References to Biographical and Critical Material," *University of Missouri Bulletin*, Vol. XII, No. 3. 1921.
WILKINSON, HAZEL. "Social Thought in American Fiction (1910–1917)," *University of Southern California Studies in Sociology*, Vol. III, No. 10. 1918.
WILLIAMS, BLANCHE C. Our Short Story Writers. 1920.

[*Drama*]

BAKER, GEORGE P. Dramatic Technique. 1919.
BURLEIGH, LOUISE. The Community Theater in Theory and Practice. 1917. (Bibliography.)
CHENEY, SHELDON. The New Movement in the Theater. 1914.
DICKINSON, THOMAS H. Playwrights of the New American Theater. 1925.
CLARK, BARRETT H. An Hour of American Drama. 1930.
EATON, WALTER PRICHARD. At the New Theater and Others. 1910.
GOLDBERG, ISAAC. The Drama of Transition. 1922.
HAMILTON, CLAYTON. Conversations on Contemporary Drama. 1924.
LEWISOHN, LUDWIG. The Drama and the Stage. 1922.
MACGOWAN, KENNETH. The Theatre of Tomorrow. 1921.
MACKAYE, Percy. Community Drama. 1917.
MACKAYE, PERCY. The Playhouse and the Play. 1909.
MODERWELL, HIRAM K. The Theatre of Today. 1914.
MOSES, MONTROSE J., and BROWN, JOHN MASON (Eds.). The American Theatre as Seen by its Critics, 1752–1934. 1934.
NATHAN, GEORGE JEAN. The Critic and the Drama. 1922.
QUINN, ARTHUR HOBSON. A History of the American Drama from the Civil War to the Present Day. 2 vols. 1927.

[*Poetry*]

AIKEN, CONRAD. Scepticisms. Notes on Contemporary Poetry. 1919.
AUSTIN, MARY. The American Rhythm. 1923.
EASTMAN, MAX. The Enjoyment of Poetry. 1913. Rev. ed. 1921.
EASTMAN, MAX. The Literary Mind. 1931.
KREYMBORG, ALFRED. Our Singing Strength, an Outline of American Poetry. 1929. (Last two thirds on "the recent past.")
LOWELL, AMY. A Critical Fable. 1922.
LOWELL, AMY. Tendencies in Modern American Poetry. 1917.
LOWES, JOHN LIVINGSTON. Convention and Revolt in Poetry. 1919.
MONROE, HARRIET. Poets and their Art. 1926.
NEILSON, WILLIAM ALLAN. The Essentials of Poetry. 1912.
UNTERMEYER, LOUIS. The New Era in American Poetry. 1919. Rev. ed. 1923, entitled American Poetry since 1900.
WILKINSON, MARGUERITE. New Voices. 1919. Rev. ed. 1928.
WILKINSON, MARGUERITE. The Way of the Makers. 1925.
WOOD, CLEMENT. Poets of America. 1925.

[*Criticism* (Titles not listed heretofore)]

BABBITT, IRVING. Democracy and Leadership. 1924.
BABBITT, IRVING. Literature and the American College. 1908.
BOURNE, RANDOLPH. Youth and Life. 1913.
BROOKS, VAN WYCK. Letters and Leadership. 1918.
BROWNELL, W. C. Criticism. 1914.
BROWNELL, W. C. French Traits. 1889.
BROWNELL, W. C. Standards. 1917.
CABELL, JAMES BRANCH. Beyond Life. 1919.
ELIOT, T. S. The Sacred Wood. 1920.
HUNEKER, JAMES GIBBONS. Bedouins. 1920.
HUNEKER, JAMES GIBBONS. Egoists. 1909.
HUNEKER, JAMES GIBBONS. Iconoclasts. 1905.

HUNEKER, JAMES GIBBONS. Unicorns. 1917.
MACY, JOHN. The Spirit of American Literature. 1913.
MENCKEN, H. L. A Book of Prefaces. 1917.
MENCKEN, H. L. Prejudices. 6 vols. 1919–1927.
MORE, PAUL ELMER. Shelburne Essays. 11 vols. 1904–1921.
SHERMAN, STUART P. The Genius of America. 1923.
SHERMAN, STUART P. The Main Stream. 1927.
SPINGARN, J. E. Creative Criticism. 1917.

[*Histories*]

DE MILLE, GEORGE E. Literary Criticism in America. 1931.
FOERSTER, NORMAN. American Criticism. 1928.

[*Collections*]

American Criticism. 1904.
Contemporary American Criticism. 1926.
Contemporary Opinion. 1933.
Criticism in America, its Function and Status. 1924.
A Critique of Humanism. 1930.
Humanism and America, Essays on the Outlook of Modern Civilization. 1930.

CHAPTER XV

Points of View

THE end of any such survey as this is the end of an open cornucopia. One of the childhood memories of anyone brought up in nineteenth-century New England must be the Thanksgiving celebrations in church, where the chief decoration and symbol was a horn of plenty. It was a gilded horn six feet high at the mouth, replacing the pulpit for the occasion and pouring out a colorful cascade of vegetables and fruits: "punkins" at the bottom, where they were supposed to have flowed, up to apples and grapes, with wheat sheaves and corn shocks in the background. It was a visible sign of abundance, and the hours were hours of thanksgiving and good cheer. That was in the 1890's, when the measure of a nation's wealth was riches for the rich and a full dinner pail for the man of low estate, and when national prosperity was accepted as an evidence of God's favor. Only a blind or foolhardy decoration committee would venture to stage such a feature nowadays. Values have changed, abundance is no more a common possession, and Heaven's beneficence is no more counted on.

Not only that, but the phrases of godliness and goodliness, which first expressed faith, then were used to keep faith alive, and then survived as empty echoes, are no longer universally received at face value. The horn of plenty and what it meant to the 1890's was the last expression of an old order of belief and behavior. Its dismissal to the realm of the obsolete is a step in the procedure of American thought: the domination of religious faith and ethical precept of the seventeenth century; the challenge of the eighteenth century to the altar by the shop till and the flag; the challenge of the nineteenth century to the flag by the treasure vault and the machine that it served; the twentieth-century breakdown of the money-changers after they had captured machine and flag and altar, undermining the old faiths and offering in exchange world chaos and universal distrust. That is why the cultural cornucopia opening toward the future pours out the indeterminate miscellany of the day. And that is why the outpouring is something more than an unrelated miscellany — the fruits not of confident abundance but of impoverishment and misgivings.

A history must stop; it can seldom conclude. The decade of the 1930's will serve as a broad stopping line, but it is a line across a fabric, not drawn but cut, and cutting both threads and pattern. Some of the threads, or tendencies, are clearer than others; some are spending themselves, in which fact there is significance. They shift and interlock and blend, but they are definite enough to be distinguishable. A pair of them are negative in tone and value: the output of the cryptic stylists and the output of the articulate apostles of defiance and despair. Another pair are positive but fractional and insufficient: the Marxists' attempt to commandeer literature in behalf of a new social order, and the regionalists' varying attempts to save the individual from the domination of society. Still another, largely expressed in terms of criticism, whether aesthetic or social, is a broader gospel of constructive optimism.

The once more recurrent rise of cryptic stylisms is distinctly a product of the times; for if anything in the arts is a sign of impoverishment it is the artistic movement which lays its stress on expression rather than on content. When, moreover, the movement emphasizes expression to the point of repudiating the need to communicate, and finds its leaders in artists from other lands and in expatriates, it offers complete evidence of bankruptcy. To be sure, one can think of no reason why people concerned with the arts should not run off on such a tangent if they choose to, or why they should not take themselves seriously if they choose to. But there is no reason, either, why they should be taken seriously by other people. Yet it is part of this kind of literary episode that the leaders of innovation in art are always taken with ultra-seriousness by a group of surrounding enthusiasts. The last half-century has seen a Whitman cult, late in development but all the more serious for that; a James cult; a Dickinson cult — one of their prophets calls them "Emilists"; a Joyce cult; even a Hart Crane and an Eliot cult. Sometimes, as in the cases of Whitman, Miss Dickinson, and, perhaps, Eliot, disciples have stressed form at the expense of substance when there was real and clear content to be reckoned with. Oftener the manner has been so arresting that it has received prime or exclusive attention; and the epidemics have taken form in abstract stylisms as more and less gifted amateurs have caught the successive infections of imagism, dadaism, symbolism, vorticism, cubism, or even the practical joke, spectrism.

When the most that could be said of such writing has been on its form, it has inevitably been exotic and ephemeral, inevitably an evasion of life, inevitably a riddle to all but its perpetrators. Alfred Kreymborg, who takes T. S. Eliot quite seriously, makes a typical record of "The Waste Land's" reception. "There was no middle-ground at the time, and there is scarcely any now. The detractors considered the thing an outrageous hoax, and even some of the devotees feared that the master was spoofing the enemy, and tempered their comments accordingly. Nearly everybody waited for somebody else to say the first word, secretly dreading the prospect of making an ass of himself."[1] Hart Crane, who took himself quite seriously, wrote sixteen lines entitled "At Melville's Tomb," which included the following:

And wrecks passed without sound of bells,
The calyx of death's bounty giving back
A scattered chapter, livid hieroglyph,
The portent wound in corridors of shells.[2]

---

[1] Kreymborg, "Our Singing Strength," p. 535.

[2] From "Collected Poems of Hart Crane" (Liveright Publishing Corporation), 1933.

And then he wrote to Harriet Monroe, who should understand modern poetry if anyone can, that "the calyx refers in a double ironic sense both to a cornucopia and the vortex made by a sinking vessel. As soon as the water has closed over a ship this whirlpool sends up broken spars, wreckage, etc., which can be alluded to as *livid hieroglyphs*, making a *scattered chapter* as far as any complete record of the recent ship and her crew is concerned."[1] Which two passages demonstrate, as Max Eastman remarks, both that Crane possessed poetic mind and feeling and that he was a master in the art of "talking to himself in public."[2]

Again Kreymborg, who may fairly be cited because he so cordially contributed to the experimentalism of the 1890's, recognizes now with a feeling of mingled amusement and nostalgia that the ventures of that day are as dead as Ezra Pound would be without his gestures; that they are dead because "a conquest over form, old or new, is never enough"[3]; and that this late "impulse toward free adventure, individualism, experiment, is virtually at an end, temporarily at least."[4] The poet-critic's final adverb is well added; for this ripple on the surface of literature, so clearly passing today, the third of its kind within forty years, is continually recurrent and always negligible in charting any long course.

Another group of negativists, the apostles of despair, are a natural product of the times. Once more let Kreymborg supply the text, not because he stated it newly or unusually but because he stated it at all:

> The influence of Whitman, the towering rebel, the multifarious liberties of the free verse brigade — these have had their day in the sun. The moon is now in the heavens, the moon of melancholia, of despair. . . . We are in an era of impersonality, of supposed imper-

---

[1] Quoted by Max Eastman in "The Literary Mind," pp. 94, 95.

[2] Ibid. p. 96.

[3] Kreymborg, "Our Singing Strength," p. 340. Reprinted by permission of Coward, McCann, Inc.

[4] Ibid. p. 524.

sonality. The lens of science, disclosing man not as a ruler of himself and his destiny, but as one of the atoms investing the cosmos, has destroyed or submerged the ego — apparently.[1]

The lens of science of the nineteenth century perched man on a floating mote in the cosmos; the science of the twentieth century reduced the cosmos to a series of vibrations; but the pressure of circumstance following the World War capped the climax with the result that some of the less hardy of the rising generation, brought up on the benevolent assumptions enumerated by Van Wyck Brooks[2] and with less than Job's endurance, were moved to curse God and live, because life was not as pleasant as they had expected it to be. Stephen Crane long anticipated them when he wrote:

> A man said to the universe:
> "Sir, I exist!"
> "However," replied the universe,
> "The fact has not created in me
> A sense of obligation."[3]

But Stephen Crane was relatively unsupported by exigent fact or current testimony. Now the scientists, inventors, and money-changers had brought about a sudden awareness of a slow change. So some of the younger writers became desperate, one sign of despair being a defiance of all the old hopes and all the old reticences.

This has expressed itself in every mood from grimness to gay impudence. In a Robinson Jeffers — who also has his cult — it has reached the most abysmal depths. Man is a puppet, passion-blown. Jeffers regards him with such disdain that one speculates on why he troubles to consider what he describes as "the animals Christ was rumored to have died for." He denies his subjects all nobility, he refuses them any sympathy, and he expends splendid powers in his fugal treatment of lust, hate, and despair. George Sterling, his ecstatic interpreter, founder of the Jeffers cult, did him no great

---

[1] Kreymborg, op. cit. p. 524. [2] See pages 772–773.

[3] "Works" (edited by Wilson Follett), Vol. VI, p. 131.

service in dramatizing him in his solitude on the Pacific coast, lodged on a crag beside a rough stone tower of his own building, with statistics on the years required to build it. This kind of theatrical glooming could be impressive at a glimpse, but it ceases to impress year after year. No admirer mentions Jeffers without mentioning the crag and the tower. His isolation in fact, coupled with his cynicism in mood, sets him in a role which he plays with the uncontrol of a Junius Brutus Booth as he struts his hour upon a specially constructed stage, where, he explains,

> I drew solitude over me, on the lone shore,
> By the hawk-perch stones.

In contrast, E. E. Cummings, the poetaster who abjures capital letters and distributes punctuation marks with a sprinkler, is gay-naughty, not wicked but tough, playing Apache at the literary soirée. According to a sympathetic interpreter his naughtiness starts in anti-Puritan reaction, his bent for eccentricity from the "Others" of 1916, his wide flights in it from revolt to what had become conventions of free verse; his fleshliness is related to Swinburne's, his popularity enhanced by the fact that his most risqué verse has had to be privately printed. "He is a brilliant compound of love, romance, idealism, antipathy, realism, slang, prohibition, booze, jazz, and more jazz."[1] There is nothing more to be said except that he is engagingly debonair, and clearly talented, and that he is typical of the tough poets and story-tellers, who are always youthful and usually young in their display of boldness, badness, and dirtiness — suggestive of the small boy who bends his arm in a strong-man pose and invites observers to feel his biceps, if they can. It is misanthropy and disillusion in motley; and Cummings's motley does much toward redeeming it, more than with many another who enjoys the bad-man mummery.

This same sense of protracted adolescence pervades the work of Ernest Hemingway. With excelling narrative gifts

---

[1] Alfred Kreymborg, "Our Singing Strength," p. 516.

he is always harping on two strings: his world-weariness and his connoisseurship. They are traits of a kind of youthful naïveté, cloaked in a disguise of disillusionment. Frederic Henry, in "A Farewell to Arms," explains that during the service at the front he was "embarrassed by the words sacred, glorious and sacrifice and the expression in vain. . . . Abstract words like glory, honor, courage or hallow were obscene beside the concrete names of villages, the numbers of roads, the names of rivers, the numbers of regiments and the dates."[1] This is self-description and doubtless explanation of Hemingway's counteracting introduction of such concrete details as his iterative allusions to the latrine. They take the taste of glory out of one's mouth. It may account also for his insistence on eating and drinking and vintages and the delights of the gourmet and the excesses of the carouser. It goes far to account also for his obsession with the bull-fight, in which he gains his vicarious enjoyment of gore and death while displaying his technical knowledge of an art unfamiliar to most peoples and unknown to Americans. There is no question as to his skill in narration; there is no question as to his conscious employment of it — his exhibitionism; and there is no doubt that in his choice of subject among the globe-trotters on alien soil he has so far lost contact with any substantial life that he has very little left for himself but the exercise of a nice but extremely self-conscious technique.

Hemingway leads along this route to William Faulkner, who has many features in common. He also was in the World War, and wrote his reactions into fiction — two novels. He also was encouraged to write by Sherwood Anderson, and felt the influence of Gertrude Stein. He also, therefore, naturally combines intense interest in narrative technique, structural and stylistic, with the tone of disillusionment expressed in terms of brutal naturalism. "Soldiers Pay" and "Sartoris" do what Dos Passos had done in "One Man's Initiation" and "Three Soldiers" and what Hemingway was to do in

[1] "Farewell to Arms," p. 196.

"A Farewell to Arms." Faulkner's "As I Lay Dying" and "The Sound and the Fury" out-Herod Hemingway and reach the abysses frequented by Jeffers. "Sanctuary" reaches deeper because of the author's sardonic employment of his powers to split the ears of the groundlings. In the same mood in which the art critic Wright played Proteus as S. S. Van Dine, Faulkner lured and caught his public with this doubly lawless tale of rape and lynching. It is cynicism raised to a high power. But it is also naturalism gone to seed. It does not mean anything. It is only picturesque, melodramatic glooming again. In the hands of the greater naturalists brute fact is interpretable into something beyond itself. In the hands of Faulkner, who both does not like what he sees and sees only what he likes to, brute fact leads only to folly and despair. One turns away from him and his kind to read of a life which, *in toto*, is not a sum of brutal and often pathological details.

There have been wise words said by other contemporaries about these Jaqueses and Jeremiahs. There is Robinson's observation on the passing character in "Captain Craig," who, shown a child or anything that laughs, forthwith begins

> to crunch his wormwood
> And then runs on with his "realities."
> What does he know about realities,
> Who sees the truth of things almost as well
> As Nero saw the Northern Lights? [1]

There is Robert Frost's dilemma, forced on him by a "New York alec," of choosing between being prude or puke; he likes neither option but particularly objects to being a puke, "mewling and puking in the public arms,"

> Who cares not what he does in company,
> And when he can't do anything, falls back
> On words, and tries his worst to make words speak
> Louder than actions, and sometimes achieves it.[2]

---

[1] E. A. Robinson, "Collected Poems," p. 129.
[2] Robert Frost, "New Hampshire," p. 16.

And there is Archibald MacLeish's

> Greatness they have forgotten and pride and the envy of
> Nobler lives than their own and the service of honor. . . .
> Virtue and nobleness: honor and love they laugh at!
> Their speech is irony: the whipped man's speech.[1]

Jeremiah, the original, however, was not an apostle of despair. He was not much interested in converting the habitual offender, accepting his behavior with the leopard's spots and the Ethiopian's skin. He could be as circumstantial too on the ways of the wicked as any ultra modern. Yet for the faithful he wrote, "Refrain thy voice from weeping and thine eyes from tears; for thy work shall be rewarded, saith the Lord . . . and there is hope for thy latter end, saith the Lord."

It is in his hope for the latter end that Dos Passos is distinguishable from these

> Prophetic, would-be-Delphic manger-snappers
> That always get replaced when they are gone.[2]

Sinclair Lewis, stirred by Dos Passos's "Manhattan Transfer," once told of the kind of novel that he would most like to write. Partly paraphrased, partly quoted, it comes to this:

The ideal novel — what may be the foundation of a whole school of novel-writing — will do what all novelists have frequently proved could not be done. It will give the panorama, the soul, of a whole community. It will be full of the passion for the beauty and stir of life — of people, of rivers, and little hills, and tall towers by dawn and furnace-kindled dusk. Many will call such a novel sordid. But it will not be. For even Keats felt no more passionate and sensitive reaction to beauty in her every guise than will inform it. Naturally it will be free of that sickly complex wherein one hates the lyrical, the charming, the demure aspect of beauty, and perversely proclaims ugliness alone as noble; that natural yet

[1] Archibald MacLeish, "Panic," p. 29.

[2] Robinson, op. cit. p. 129.

also puerile revulsion against the prettifying of the machine-made commercial tales. Yes, this novelist will be slated as sordid, a low fellow. He will not see life as necessarily approaching the ideals of a life-insurance agent. He will see it as a roaring, thundering, incalculable, obscene, magnificent glory.

The qualities applauded by Lewis in "Manhattan Transfer" are re-achieved in "42d Parallel" and "1919"; and in these latter what V. F. Calverton[1] calls Dos Passos's "leftness" in viewpoint has "crystallized into a challenge." Already in two plays, "The Garbage Man" and "Airways, Inc.," Dos Passos had pronounced his indictment of the ways of capitalism. And now in the two-thirds completed trilogy — and a trilogy always implies a certain programed purposefulness — he passed ahead of the mere iconoclasts, to answer questions as well as to ask them, and to provide a new order to replace an old one. They are clearly propagandist novels;[2] "yet their effectiveness both as fiction and as propaganda lies in the fact that their communistic sympathies are never more than implicit."[3] Thus the American Marxists point with pride to Dos Passos as their major prophet, their pre-eminent if not their sole representative whose convictions do not overwhelm his art. He implies their doctrines — or did imply them up to the 1930's — and fulfills their contention that revolutionary literature must be good as literature.

But as there is only one Dos Passos (Louis Adamic, who writes as well, is too dispassionate), and as their literary interests have to be vented mainly in criticism, the Marxists come off rather poorly on the whole. For they are confronted by a dilemma which is inherent in Marxism. It is the role of the critic to abide by his convictions, — aesthetic, so-

---

[1] V. F. Calverton, "The Liberation of American Literature," p. 462. See also pages 450–467 for a review of the present proletarian movement in American literature.

[2] For a characteristically sound discussion see Max Eastman's "Art and the Life of Action."

[3] Henry Hazlitt, in *The Nation*, Vol. CXXXIV, p. 344.

cial, philosophical, — but in his appraisal of writers and their writings to divest himself as far as he may of his emotions. The Marxist, however, has to play a double role. He must master the essentials of an intricate economic-social theory upbuilt on a system of Hegelian dialectic — an undertaking so difficult that few Marxists will admit that other Marxists are good Marxists; and then he must uphold his doctrine with all the fervor of an early New England Puritan. But as soon as a man thinks he has been put in possession of the ultimate truth, as soon as he is absolutely sure as to what is good for the world, he is disqualified to perform the functions of the critic, for he becomes a religious enthusiast who can and does deny intelligence and integrity to all who disagree. Under the sway of his emotions he suspends critical discrimination; and, somewhat schooled in dialectic, he displays a passionate ingenuity in using, disusing, or abusing the facts for the buttressing of his conclusions.[1] This for the moment may be stated regardless of the soundness of his convictions, and only with regard to the soundness of his criticism. But it explains why in the field of criticism a Calverton or a Hicks is so fallible and why in the field of creative art a Dos Passos or a Rivera is such a rare bird. Its pertinence here is in the positive fact that the proletarian writers have, like Tolstoi, put life above art and that they find something more stimulating to propound than a counsel of despair.

In the attempt at finding a pattern in life which admits of a program for it, the regionalists with their multifarious activity are at the far pole from the proletarian revolutionists. For the Marxists look toward "the creation of a new society which will embody, like Soviet Russia today, a social, instead of an individualistic ideal,"[2] and the regionalists are concerned with "direct contemplation of character and emotion, of all the ideas and desires that sustain character, and not

---

[1] For a critique of such criticism see the author's review of "The Great Tradition," by Granville Hicks, *International Journal of Ethics,* Vol. XLIV, pp. 471–474.

[2] Calverton, op. cit. pp. 461, 462.

social structure in itself."[1] In one of the best generalized discussions of the whole theme of regionalism yet published,[2] the editor of *Folk-Say* makes an initial discrimination between the four types of regionalism in the United States.

> The Localist (of the North-West) is the empiric, matter-of-fact regionalist, interested in developing local or native materials rooted in a specific soil. The Naturist (of the South-West) is the mystical, cosmic regionalist, with a philosophy of the land and the folk, of the Good Life and the indigenous, interested in developing native modes of expression mediating between man and the universe. The Traditionalist (of the Old South) is the humanist, creative regionalist, interested in a usable past as a source of personal symbols and values, aesthetic and ethical. The Culturist (of the metropolitan and cosmopolitan East) is the social, cosmopolitan regionalist, combining and transcending the other approaches, interested in shaping life as well as literature according to the needs and resources of interrelated regions.

As any region is largely rural, the characters savor of the soil and usually contribute to the not always short and simple annals of the poor as followed by regional expositors in all sections of the United States. At first glance this seems like no more than a revival of the local-color writing of the sort that spread in a kind of cyclonic curve from Bret Harte's California via Cable's New Orleans, Harris's Georgia, Miss Murfree's mountain counties, Page's Virginia, up to New England, out to the middle border of Garland, and back to the Ohio valley of Fox and Allen. But regionalism is more than this; if it is at all relevant to this earlier wave, it is only as a fulfillment of the promise made and unfulfilled by Garland in his first short stories and novels.

For the general trait of the earlier local-color output is that the superficial idioms of speech and modes of life which characterized the various districts were recorded therein, but

---

[1] Allen Tate, "Regionalism and Sectionalism," *New Republic*, December 23, 1932.

[2] B. A. Botkin, "We Talk about Regionalism — North, East, South, and West," *The Frontier*, May, 1933.

that the plots which carried these were made after a formula which involved the old romantic assumptions about rewards and punishments and the dispensing of poetic justice. Nature and the social order were nothing but accessories. A man might be sunburned or frostbitten, wear oilskins or homespun, say "I guess" or "Ah reck'n," but the story was bound to come out right unless the man was wrong. In contrast with this the best of the current plain tales, no less faithful to the surface facts, deal with life as it actually takes place, allow character and circumstance to lead to their natural conclusions, and, if the authors are sufficiently veracious, do not insist on either happy or tragic endings. Furthermore, in many of these novels the individual is implicitly accepted as more significant than society, and if he is at odds with society he is quite as likely to be treated as a victim as he is to be condemned as outlaw or traitor. Once again the regionalists, like Fenimore Cooper, look on the juggernaut of advancing civilization as inevitable but not necessarily desirable. They distrust the domination of the machine age as clearly as the proletarian writers do, or the defenders of an agrarian order.

Of the various regional groups the traditionalists of the old South have captured the center of the stage of late, expressing themselves in schools of local drama and poetry and expounding their position in a substantial symposium. As the Southern champions of anti-industrialism are also anti-Marxian in their assumption that "the responsibility of men is for their own welfare and that of their neighbors, not for the hypothetical welfare of some fabulous creature called society,"[1] they are for preserving in Dixie Land the best of an agrarian culture which is being rapidly overcome by the invading industrialism of the North. They are not trying to save America, but to save the South from America; and they are out of sympathy with the Southern element which hails the growth of the "New South," apologizes for Southern conservatism, deplores the survival of outworn tradition, sings

[1] "I'll Take My Stand," p. xviii.

the praises of progress, and celebrates this progress with eloquent commentary and more eloquent statistics on "Looms and Furnaces."[1] They hold a broad thesis against the ways of a capitalistic society which subsidizes science and the applications of science to the machine, and against the consequent campaign for unlimited saving of labor though to no defined end, with the resultant overproduction, underemployment, multiplication of needs, haste to gratify them, and development of the belief that "ideal living would consist in a series of good times unbroken by interludes of no place to go."[2]

They oppose to this industrialism an agrarian way of life, with the somewhat idyllic description of it as one "in which agriculture is the leading vocation, whether for wealth, for pleasure, or for prestige — a form of labor that is pursued with intelligence and leisure, and that becomes the model to which the other forms approach as well as they may."[3] The definition suggests the popular and sardonic distinction between an agriculturist and a farmer. The acme of the system is obviously the agriculturist living fully and richly in an old Kentucky home with its undeniable superiorities to a Park Avenue pent-house.

The cue to the temper of several of the essays in "I'll Take My Stand" is contained in the title to the first one, "Reconstructed but Unregenerate." Perhaps it is well for the non-Southerner to be reminded that hot resentment can survive for so long after the war that has so few survivors. The cue to their central theme, the need for the preservation of the best in Southern tradition, is effectively presented in a leisurely portrait sketch of "Cousin Lucius." Cousin Lucius, of slaveholding planter stock, born before the War, was sent to a Georgia Methodist college where he studied the classics, English literature, and Southern eloquence in the first years of Reconstruction. Hard Times met him on his return. He

---

[1] Edwin Mims, "The Advancing South," especially the introduction and Chapter IV.

[2] "I'll Take My Stand," p. 309.

[3] Ibid. p. xix.

could not beg; to labor on his father's farm he was ashamed; so he succeeded to the headship of a local academy, a gracious and benignant figure in a wide neighborhood, and the happy husband of Cousin Caroline, who had brought him, except for money, everything that a man might ask for in a wife. Yet even when he inherited the paternal farm, with its potential earnings, Hard Times still pursued.

Then, when he had reached middle age, someone found that Georgia had a new source of wealth in peaches and, by virtue of the refrigerator car, a new market in New York City. Before long Cousin Lucius was persuaded that "the master compromise had been achieved, that an agricultural community could fare well in a dance where the fiddles were all buzz-saws and the horns all steam-whistles."[1] Advertising and salesmanship brought him a share in a swimming pool, a waning interest in the church, an enlarged acreage, the presidency of a local bank, universal respect, the decline of the peach industry, and the reimpoverishment of a countryside that had been taught in boom times to mortgage its insecure future along with its tangible possessions. This was what progress had done as the industrial North had given a lesson to the agrarian South. It is the lesson that the contributors to "I'll Take My Stand" have taken to heart, and that is inherent in the creative writing of the later Ellen Glasgow, of Allen Tate, John Crowe Ransom, and the rest of their school. They attempt in it to make that "most luminous defence" of their point of view which is found in "its noble embodiment in persons."

The defect of this Southern traditionalism, apparent in both the thesis and the embodiment of the thesis, is that, after all, it is not markedly noble. Agriculture is pursued at such a distance that it does not involve doing a day's work, paying one's debts, or keeping sober. The doctrine inveighs against an invading industrialism, but does not present a self-sustaining agrarianism. It is like the gardens Southern

---

[1] "I'll Take My Stand," p. 284.

novelists revel in. Azaleas and camellias triumph above the weeds, and wisterias riot on high, the grandiloquent blooms of early spring; but there is a long, hot summer to follow, and a chill winter against which there is the most casual provision. The novels are often better than their thesis; in which respect they are like the best of regionalist fiction from whatever region. They are concerned with some indigenous phase of American life, and they present it with a high average of artistic veracity.

The approach of the philosopher-novelists and philosopher-critics is different from that of the Marxians and the Southern traditionalists in not offering a program even while it holds out hopes for the future. It is similar in basing itself on a recognition of what has happened to American culture in terms of economic evolution. In all cases the Americans who are looking ahead are in strong dissent from what they see as they look around. But the philosophic apostles of hope, though recognizing the economic background of the day, regard it more as a symptom than as a cause, and, so regarding it, are concerned not with programs for reform or for revolution in the organization of life but with the nature of the American of whom the organization of life is merely an expression. They are nearer to Emerson, Whitman, and Thoreau than to Henry George, Eugene Debs, and Upton Sinclair.

When, a few years ago, a deputation of representative Americans headed by John Dewey were officially welcomed to Russia, the theory and the workings of the Soviet Union were expounded and exhibited to them; and at place after place when the hosts had completed their part of the program the Americans were asked to explain American plans and objectives. They reported on their return that they were hard put to it for adequate answers. All they could reply, after contemplative chin-rubbing, was that the American temper would not submit to an imposed plan; that the much heralded doctrine of rugged individualism, submitted to the test, would be invoked by labor and the white-collar class as well as by captains of industry and finance, though with less emphasis on its ruggedness; that the United States, habituated to a century and a half of trial and error, was committed to this method of procedure, which was the procedure of scientific research; that the America of the prosperity era was markedly skeptical as to experiments, that it was at least averagely capable of error, but that it still had the energy and confidence of youth, and that in these were vague but great potentialities.

It is idle business to dismiss this attitude toward the American future as born of unwillingness to face the facts or incapacity to see them. By and large the verdict among the appraisers of life in the United States is a verdict of hope and expectation based on the experience and character of the nation. There is an irony in the fact that the most aggressively pessimistic talkers, who speak as evangels of modernism, emancipators from the trammels of the past, and prophets of despair, in freeing themselves from Victorianism — the code of the nineteenth century in England — and from Puritanism — the code of the seventeenth century in New England — have only returned to the English code of the eighteenth century — the code prevailing from Pope to Byron. Although none but Mr. Cabell is clear as to his genealogy, there is a reason; for at many points the America of today is like the England of two centuries ago. There is the same prevailing assault on dullness and sentimentalism, stimulated by the same activity of evangelist and demagogue. The people are asserting themselves now as they were then. What the revolutions of the eighteenth century began, the world confusion of the twentieth century is following up. And the dullness and sentimentalism of the former day were the seed ground of a fresh reassertion of the human spirit, developing a public to replace the patron and a citizenry to replace the yokelry, and leading to fresh and vital arts.

The more sober critics of broader culture, however anti-Puritan and however anti-Philistine they may be, hold fast to that which is good. I open, for example, Ludwig Lewisohn at random and find this[1]:

> He has been, so far, afraid of both greatness of theme and elevation of speech. Yet the theme is in his soul and in his very bones and he could without doubt write largely and nobly if he would let himself. And that courage toward large and noble work upon large and noble themes must be — unless we are to sink into a long period of futility — the next step in the process of creative speech in America.

In 1878 Ralph Waldo Emerson delivered in the Old South Church in Boston his address on "The Fortune of the Republic."[2] In view of the changes that have taken place since then it is extraordinarily up-to-date in tone and content, particularly as this was after his productive period and must have been written still earlier. After his brilliantly generalized exordium, he passed on by way of the struggles between dynasties to the struggles for liberation, and thence to the founding of the democratic experiment in America which in its time represented "the sentiment and the future of mankind." Then, with the honesty which was his, and the recurrent vehemence for which he does not receive due credit, he drew his indictment against a decadent United States. The Republican party was "drivelling and huckstering away, for views of party fear or advantage, every principle of humanity and the dearest hopes of mankind." The average voter, drunk with the national prosperity, was gambling away "all the prized charters of the human race . . . for a paltry, selfish gain." The masses had arrived at "a sloven plenty . . . an unbuttoned comfort." The young men lacked idealism. The country was a "riot of mediocrities and dishonesties and fudges." Nevertheless, in spite of institutional decadence, Emerson found in the capacities of the average man a promise of fulfillment; in his desire for justice an assurance of his power to maintain it. He could

[1] "Expression in America," p. 588. A passage on the poetry of Mark Van Doren.

[2] "The Works of Emerson," Centenary Edition, Vol. XI, pp. 511–544.

have wished that will and endeavor were more active; but he saw the light breaking, and he looked to the future with confidence.

Just fifty years after this address, John Dewey wrote "A Critique of American Civilization,"[1] which was in remarkable agreement with Emerson's estimate. His picture of the contemporary scene was no happier; but he too looked to the common man, whose security and comfort he wished for as steps toward participation in more ideal values. In the country he saw, as Emerson had seen, institutional activities that were lower in motive than private ones, an "inner tension" in the social order in which the upward pull was from unofficial forces. In the people he saw the correctives for the ills they suffered, and in the wide spread of self-criticism a guaranty that the scale of values in American life was tending to rise rather than decline. Since that critique was written America has been forced back on the finer realities that money cannot buy, learning through duress what prosperity could never teach. Sadder and wiser, perhaps, but neither bitter nor hopeless, it still has the energy of youth which greets the future confident in its own powers. That is the temper of the nation and the dominant temper of its literature today.

---

[1] In "Recent Gains in American Civilization" (edited by Kirby Page), pp. 255–276.

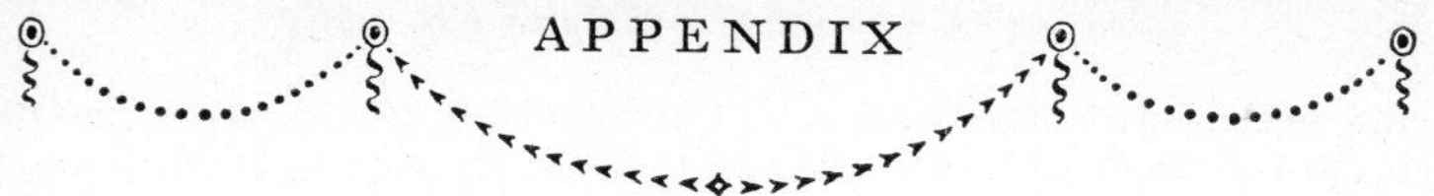

APPENDIX

Facts about Authors

These facts about dates, places, and events in the lives of the authors discussed above are assembled here because there has been no systematic presentation of them in the text. The more formal book lists accompany the history and criticism in the body of the work.

ALCOTT, (AMOS) BRONSON (1799–1888), b. Wolcott, Connecticut; son of farmer. Meager education; peddled in south-Atlantic states; taught school in Connecticut, in Boston (1828–1830), in Germantown, Pennsylvania (1831–1833); conducted "Temple School," Boston, with Elizabeth Peabody, 1834–1839. Visited England, 1842. Attempted to found community, "Fruitlands," 1844–1845. Moved to Concord, Massachusetts; superintendent of schools there, 1859. Later years peripatetic philosopher, holding "Conversations" in Boston and New York, lecturing widely but unprofitably. Family supported by efforts of wife and success of daughter Louisa May. Prime mover in Concord School of Philosophy, 1879–1888.

ALDRICH, THOMAS BAILEY (1836–1907), b. Portsmouth, N. H. Three years of boyhood in New Orleans. Clerk in New York City at sixteen. Returned to New England; younger member of Cambridge group, contacts with Longfellow, Lowell, Holmes, and English romanticists affecting him. Editorial positions with minor New York and Boston journals, 1855–1875; editor of *Atlantic*, 1881–1890. Wrote much lyric poetry, verse drama, and two better known prose works: the autobiographic "Story of a Bad Boy," 1869, and the volume of short stories "Marjorie Daw and Other People," 1873.

ANDERSON, SHERWOOD (1876–   ), b. Camden, Ohio, of mixed ancestry. Schooling irregular, ended at fourteen. Engaged at various jobs; at seventeen wandered to Chicago. Served in Spanish-American War. Manager of paint factory in Elyria, Ohio; revolted and turned to writing; became member of the Chicago group. After trip abroad (1921), lived for a while in New Orleans. Settled in Marion, Virginia, and edited two newspapers. Gained public through the *Little Review* and the *Dial*. Won *Dial* award, 1921. Writings include novels, short stories, poems, autobiography. Associated with *American Spectator*. Dramatized "Winesburg, Ohio" for Hedgerow Theater group, 1934.

BARKER, JAMES NELSON (1784–1858), b. Philadelphia, son of prominent politician and soldier. First theatrical success with "Tears and Smiles," 1807; prominent in political circles; captain in War of 1812. Alderman (Philadelphia), 1817; mayor, 1819. Supported Jackson, 1828. Collector of the port, 1829–1838; comptroller of the Treasury, 1838–1841; subsequently in office of chief clerk of the Treasury. Contributed light verse and occasional poems to various magazines in addition to his major work as dramatist.

BARLOW, JOEL (1754–1812), b. Redding, Connecticut. In Yale, 1774–1778; during vacation of 1776 participated in battle of Long Island. Read "Prospect of Peace" at public examination of senior class; chaplain in army, 1780. Taught school, managed a business, arranged new version of the Psalms, edited the *American Mercury*, 1784–1785; admitted to bar, 1786. Contributed to the "Anarchiad"; published "The Vision of Columbus," 1787 (worked on since 1779). In Europe, 1788, as agent for Scioto Land Company, which failed. Lived in London, 1790–1792; prominent in radical circles; put through publication of Paine's "Age of Reason." Wrote "Advice to the Privileged Orders," 1792; proscribed by English government; fled to France. Made money through investments. American consul in Algiers, 1795–1805. Friend of Robert Fulton; helped finance the steamboat. Revised "The Vision," published as "The Columbiad," 1807. Settled near Washington, 1805; a director of Bank of Washington; intimate with Jefferson. Sent as minister to France by Madison, 1811; sought Napoleon in Poland, where he died and is buried.

BELASCO, DAVID (1859–1931), b. San Francisco. Newsboy; graduated from West Coast "college," 1875. Stage debut, 1874, San Francisco; stage manager Baldwin's Grand Opera there. Toured with Hearn's "Hearts of Oak," 1880; for several years on theatrical "road." Stage manager Madison Square Theater, New York City; on staff of Lyceum Theater; owner of Belasco Theater. Wrote and adapted scores of plays. Inventive in stage mechanics; trainer of many actors.

BIERCE, AMBROSE (GWINETT) (1842–1914?), b. Ohio, of New England forebears. No formal education, but read voraciously. Served in Civil War with Ninth Indiana Infantry; later brevetted major. At end of war assisted General Hazen as inspector of northwestern army posts. To California, 1866, entering journalism with contributions to the *Argonaut* and the *News Letter*, which he later edited. *Overland Monthly* published his first story, 1871. To England, 1872; several years on staff of *Fun*; contributed to *Figaro* and *Hood's Comic Annual.* Back to America, 1876. Wrote again for the *Argonaut* and the *Wasp*; in 1887 began column "Prattle" for Hearst's *Examiner.* Next five years several volumes of collected stories. Became Washington correspondent for the *New York American*, 1896, and a force in shaping opinion on public issues. Disappeared into Mexico in 1913 and presumably died at hands of bandits.

BIRD, ROBERT MONTGOMERY (1806–1854), b. New Castle County, Delaware. Read widely; M.D., University of Pennsylvania, 1827; practiced only a year. Professor of materia medica, Pennsylvania Medical College, 1841. Wrote several plays; "The Gladiator," first to be produced, by Edwin Forrest, 1831. After a quarrel with Forrest, turned to writing novels; "Nick of the Woods" the most popular, reprinted ten times in London, four in Germany. In Philadelphia politics; editor and part owner of the *North American*, 1847.

BOKER, GEORGE HENRY (1823–1890), b. Philadelphia of well-to-do Quaker family. Graduated from Princeton, 1842; contributed to *Nassau Monthly*. Studied law. Traveled abroad. Abandoned law for literature. Published volume of poems, "A Lesson of Life"; wrote tragedy, "Calaynos," produced in America only after success in England. Other plays moderately successful. "Poems of the War," 1864. One of the founders of Union League. Minister to Turkey, 1871; to Russia, 1875. Returned to Philadelphia, 1878. Success of revival of "Francesca da Rimini," 1882 (first produced, 1855), inspired his last play, "Nydia."

BRACKENRIDGE, HUGH HENRY (1748–1816), b. Scotland. Family migrated to Pennsylvania, 1753. Self-educated; taught school in Maryland; in Princeton as student and tutor. Friend of Madison and of Freneau, with whom he wrote "The Rising Glory of America," 1771. Again taught school; studied divinity. Wrote plays on the Revolution; edited the *United States Magazine* in Philadelphia, 1779. Studied law in Annapolis. Settled in Pittsburgh, 1781; aided establishment there of first newspaper, bookstore, and academy. In state assembly, 1786–1787; championed Constitution. Justice of Supreme Court, Pa., 1799. Removed to Carlisle, 1801. "Modern Chivalry," his satirical novel, appeared in first form in 1792; revised and extended frequently to 1815.

BRADFORD, WILLIAM (1589(90)–1657), son of a Yorkshire yeoman. At age of twelve studied the Bible and attended nonconformist meetings. Joined separatist congregation at house of William Brewster in Scrooby, Nottinghamshire, in 1606; accompanied the group to Holland, 1609, where it became part of the church of John Robinson. Citizen of Leyden; described as fustian weaver (1613) and say worker (1620). One of leaders of migration to America. Governor of Plymouth, 1621, a post he held for all but five years until his death, much of the time without salary, exercising plenary powers and being chiefly responsible for the colony's decisions. His "History," finished about 1650, though known early in manuscript, not published until 1856.

BRADSTREET, ANNE (*c.* 1612–1672), daughter of Thomas Dudley, steward to the Earl of Lincoln. Good education. At sixteen married Simon Bradstreet; came to Massachusetts, 1630, with husband and father, the latter then deputy governor of the colony. At Ipswich until 1644; then at North Andover. Mother of eight children. Among her descendants, Richard Henry Dana, Wendell Phillips, Oliver Wendell Holmes. "The Tenth Muse," published, London, 1650, by friends; second edition (Boston, 1678) included, among additions, "Contemplations."

BROOKS, VAN WYCK (1886–   ), b. Plainfield, New Jersey. Graduated from Harvard, 1907. At once joined staff of Doubleday, Page & Company. First book in 1909. Instructor, Leland Stanford University, 1911–1913. On editorial staff of Century Co., 1915–1918. Associate editor of *Freeman*, 1920–1924. For time co-editor of the *American Caravan*. In 1923 awarded *Dial* prize for formulation of new critical point of view.

BROWN, CHARLES BROCKDEN (1771–1810), b. Philadelphia, Quaker family. Health frail. Wide reading; educated at private academy of Robert

Proud. Contributed papers, "The Rhapsodist," to the *Columbian Magazine*, 1789. Studied law and abandoned it in 1793 to be first in America to seek a living from authorship. In New York City, 1793, 1795, 1798–1801. In Friendly Society, of which William Dunlap was also member. Published "Alcuin," 1798, dialogues on equality of sexes; six novels between 1798 and 1801. Editor, *Monthly Magazine and American Review*, 1799–1800; *Literary Magazine*, and *American Register*, 1803–1807; *American Register*, 1807–1810.

BROWNELL, WILLIAM CRARY (1851–1928), b. New York City. Educated at private schools and Amherst College. Entered journalism in New York City. One of Century Club group of writers and artists. In France, 1881–1884. On staff of *Philadelphia Press*, 1884–1886. From 1888 on, editor and literary adviser for *Scribner's*. Writings confined to theory and practice of criticism.

BRYANT, WILLIAM CULLEN (1794–1878), b. Cummington, Massachusetts. Father country doctor and member of legislature. Educated by private tutors; precocious faculty for verse; wrote satire, "The Embargo," 1808, which his father published. In Williams College, 1810–1811; studied law; admitted to bar, 1815; practiced at Great Barrington, 1816–1825. Attracted attention by "Thanatopsis," written in 1811, published in the *North American Review*, 1817; "The Ages," Phi Beta Kappa poem at Harvard, 1821. To New York, 1825. Co-editor of the *New York Review*. Assistant editor of the *New York Evening Post*, 1826, editor, 1829–1878. Several trips to West and to Europe. Broke with Democratic party, 1848; supported Lincoln, whom he introduced at Cooper Union in 1860; supported Andrew Johnson. A pre-eminent citizen of New York till death.

BURROUGHS, JOHN (1837–1921), b. of New England stock in Roxbury, New York. Supplemented elementary education by teaching and put himself through Ashland Collegiate Institute; later attended Cooperstown Seminary. Early manhood divided between writing and teaching. First essay in *Atlantic Monthly*, 1860; contributor to *New York Leader*. Clerk in Treasury Department at Washington, 1863–1872. Knew Walt Whitman well. Last years of life largely at "Riverby," on west shore of Hudson, but traveled extensively. Writings attracted Roosevelt, with whom he led a campaign against destruction of wild life, 1903. Later scientific writing reveals interest in thesis of evolution.

BYRD, WILLIAM (1674–1744), b. Virginia. Educated in England; traveled on Continent. Returned to America, 1692; elected to House of Burgesses. Defended Sir Edmund Andros in England, 1697, and acted as colony's agent. Returned to Virginia. Inherited large estate. Made receiver-general, 1706; admitted to council of state, 1709. Defended successfully judicial powers of council against Governor Spotswood, again representing colony in England. Erected famous house at Westover; collected largest library in the South; 1728 and 1736, commissioner for surveys of colony's boundaries. President of council, 1743; Fellow of the Royal Society. Friend of Roger Boyle, earl of Orrery. Writings, records of the surveying expeditions, left in manuscript and published in 1841.

CABELL, JAMES BRANCH (1879–), b. Richmond, Virginia. Graduate of William and Mary College, 1898. Teaching French and Greek, 1896–1898. Newspaper work, 1899–1901. Writing since 1904. Genealogist, Virginia chapter of Sons of Revolution; president Virginia Writers' Club, 1918–1921. Has written poems; a play; eleven novels, revising or enlarging six of them; six volumes of short stories, revising four; besides miscellaneous essays and sketches and genealogical studies. Popular reputation greatly enhanced by the censoring of "Jurgen," 1919 and 1921, subsequently rescinded.

CABLE, GEORGE WASHINGTON (1844–1925), b. in South, of Virginia and New England parents. Served through the Civil War in Fourth Mississippi Cavalry; later surveyor. After period contributing to a feature column in 1869, on staff of the *New Orleans Picayune.* Ten years accountant for cotton firm, while writing his first sketches of Creole life, published in *Appleton's* and *Scribner's.* Devoted years to lecture-readings, part of time touring with Mark Twain. Moved to the North. Started Home-Culture Clubs, now the Northampton (Massachusetts) People's Institute. After 1885 interested in philanthropy, reform, and Bible study.

CALEF, ROBERT (1648–1719), b. probably in England. Settled as cloth merchant in Boston, Massachusetts, by 1688. Attacked Cotton Mather for attitude toward witchcraft, 1693. Wrote "More Wonders of the Invisible World," 1697, published in England, 1700. Copy burned by Increase Mather in Harvard yard.

CATHER, WILLA (SIBERT) (1876–), b. Winchester, Virginia. Graduated from University of Nebraska, 1895. Lived in Nebraska, where her family has settled. Pittsburgh *Daily Leader,* 1897–1901; with *McClure's Magazine,* 1906–1912. Travel extensive; long residence in the Southwest. Wide popularity won with "My Antonia," her fourth novel (1918). Pulitzer prize for "One of Ours," 1922.

CHILD, LYDIA MARIA (FRANCIS) (1802–1880), b. Medford, Massachusetts. Educated in public schools; one year at a seminary. First novel, 1824. Taught school, 1825–1828; edited *Juvenile Miscellany,* 1826–1834. Married, 1826. Published "Frugal Housewife," 1829 — twenty editions by 1836. Prominent in abolitionist circles, publishing "An Appeal in Favour of That Class of Americans Called Africans," 1833; edited *National Anti-Slavery Standard,* 1841–1849. Offered to nurse John Brown. Correspondence with a Virginia lady, Mrs. Mason, published, 1860; sold 300,000 copies.

CHIVERS, THOMAS HOLLEY (1809–1858), b. Washington, Georgia. Educated in private school and Transylvania University. M.D., 1830. Professional career prevented by ill-health. Enjoyed a sort of offensive-defensive alliance with Poe; strongest resemblances between some of their poems. Three plays and eight volumes of poetry reveal his interest in exotic material and varied verse forms.

CHURCHILL, WINSTON (1871–), b. St. Louis. Graduate of United States Naval Academy, 1894. First success with "Richard Carvel," 1899. Member New Hampshire legislature, 1903–1905; failed in anticorporation campaign for governorship in 1908; hence "Coniston," "Mr. Crewe's Career," and "A Far Country." Two plays; eleven novels. No fiction since 1917.

CLEMENS, SAMUEL LANGHORNE (1835–1910), b. Florida, Missouri, of Virginia stock. Supplemented scanty schooling by experience as printer and river pilot and varied life in the West and South. From 1862 to 1865 editor in Virginia City, Nevada, and San Francisco. In 1867 made a voyage which resulted in his first book, "Innocents Abroad," 1869. For a time edited a newspaper in Buffalo. After marriage (1870) settled in Hartford, Connecticut, for twenty years, following with ten years of travel and final residence in New York. Lost heavily through failure of a publishing house he founded, 1894. Repaid debts largely from earnings of round-the-world lecture tour. Triumphal visit to England, 1907; crowned by honorary Litt.D. from Oxford. Died at "Stormfield," Connecticut. Left quantities of manuscript, much of which has been posthumously published.

COOKE, JOHN ESTEN (1830–1886), b. Winchester, Virginia, of old Virginia family. Educated in public schools and law study; admitted to bar, 1851. Published in the *Southern Literary Messenger* and *Harper's*. At thirty had published poems, essays, short stories, and seven volumes of fiction. Biographer of Stonewall Jackson and Robert E. Lee. Later output historical tales of Virginia.

COOPER, JAMES FENIMORE (1789–1851), b. Burlington, New Jersey; son of large landowner in Otsego County, New York. Studied under tutor in Albany; at Yale, 1803; dismissed, 1806. Voyage to England and Spain as a sailor, 1806–1807; in navy, 1807–1811. Married daughter of a Tory, 1811. Lived as gentleman farmer. First novel, "Precaution," 1820, a failure; "The Spy," 1821, a success in England as well as in America. Moved to New York; founded the Bread and Cheese Club; M.A. from Columbia, 1824. In Europe, 1826–1833. Returned to Cooperstown. Wrote several works critical of America ("The Monikins," 1835; "Homeward Bound" and "Home as Found," 1838), which aroused hostility and involved him in constant literary warfare, aggravated by litigation with neighbors at Cooperstown. Attacked by the press, he responded with several libel suits, which he conducted and won. Wrote "History of the Navy of the United States," 1839. Weathered public hostility but never rewon his wide reading public.

COTTON, JOHN (1584–1652), b. Derbyshire. Educated at Trinity College, Cambridge — B.A., 1603; M.A., 1606; fellow of Emmanuel College. Took orders, 1610; received B.D., 1613. Vicar at Boston in Lincolnshire, 1612. Became a Puritan leader; preached farewell sermon to Winthrop's migration in 1630. Summoned before Court of High Commission, 1632; resigned his living, crossed to New England. Immediately chosen teacher of Boston church. A leading figure in religious and political life; official spokesman for the theocracy in all controversies, notably against Anne Hutchinson, Roger Williams, and critics in England.

CRANE, STEPHEN (1871–1900), b. Newark, New Jersey; son of clergyman. Went to Lafayette College and Syracuse University, beginning newspaper work while at college. In New York wrote intermittently for the *Herald* and the *Tribune*; in 1892 published first characteristic novel, "Maggie: A Girl of the Streets." In 1895 traveled as a reporter for Bacheller Syndicate in the Southwest. Won reputation with "The Red Badge of Courage," 1896. In 1897 correspondent for Greco-Turkish War, and the next year for the Spanish-American War. Last years alternately in New York City and England.

CRÈVECŒUR, MICHEL GUILLAUME JEAN DE (1735–1813), b. near Caen, Normandy. Part of education in England. Migrated to Canada; served under Montcalm; explored Great Lakes and Ohio River country. After 1759 traveled through New York, Pennsylvania, the Carolinas. Naturalized citizen, 1765. Married; settled in Orange County, New York, 1769. In France, 1780–1783; French consul in New York, 1783–1790. Friend of Jefferson and Franklin. Returned to France, 1790. "Letters from an American Farmer," 1782, represent his reactions to the democratic experiment in America. "Sketches of Eighteenth Century America" not published till 1925.

CROCKETT, DAVID (1786–1836), b. Tennessee. Ran away from father's farm to Baltimore, 1799; adventurer and vagrant. Six months of schooling, 1804. Served under Jackson in war with Creek Indians. State legislature, 1821, 1823; Congress, 1827–1831, 1833–1835. Alienated constituency by his honest independence. Set out in 1835 to find new home for his growing family. Became involved in Texan affairs; killed at the Alamo. Author, with assistance, of autobiographical works important in frontier literature.

DALY, (JOHN) AUGUSTIN (1838–1899), b. Plymouth, North Carolina. Moved as child to New York; at once attracted to theater. More interested in production than acting; soon became critic for a succession of New York papers. Made adaptations from French and German, dramatized novels, composed plays of city life. As producer, 1869–1899, in New York preeminent in discovering talent in playwrights and actors. In 1878 made first of several trips to England with his stock company, and in 1886 took the first English-speaking company to Germany since Shakespeare's day. Opened his own theater in London, 1893, with notable productions of Shakespeare, operating it, as well as the one in New York, till his death.

DELAND, MARGARET (MARGARETTA WADE) (1857–   ), b. Allegheny, Pennsylvania. Educated in private schools; studied drawing and design at Cooper Institute, New York City. Taught design in girls' school. Since 1880 has lived in Boston and Cambridge, Massachusetts, and Kennebunkport, Maine. Has written a volume of verse, ten novels, fourteen volumes of short stories, notably on Old Chester and Dr. Lavendar, and three of essays and sketches.

DENNIE, JOSEPH (1768–1812), b. Boston, Massachusetts. Father a loyalist; graduated, Harvard, 1790; admitted to bar, 1794. Friend of Royall Tyler. Edited *The Tablet*, 1795, and (at Walpole, New Hampshire) *Farmer's Weekly Museum*, 1796–1798. Secretary to Timothy Pickering, Philadelphia,

1799. Founded and edited *The Port Folio*, 1801–1812. His "Lay Preacher" best known of several series of Addisonian essays.

DERBY, GEORGE HORATIO (1823–1861), b. Dedham, Massachusetts. Graduated from West Point, 1846; served in Mexican War with gallantry; on duty in California. Reputation as a wit and eccentric; left by a friend in charge of *San Diego Herald*, 1853, made it conspicuous for humorous features. Contributed to *The Pioneer*, San Francisco, 1854. First volume of "Phoenixiana," 1855, a nationwide success. Transferred to East, 1856.

DICKINSON, EMILY (ELIZABETH) (1830–1886). Lived entire life in Amherst, Massachusetts. Father, lawyer, legislator; trustee and treasurer of Amherst College. Educated in local schools and one year in Mount Holyoke Female Seminary. Close friend of townswoman, Helen Hunt Jackson. A recluse most of mature life. Wrote continuously but not for public. Poems posthumously published.

DRAKE, JOSEPH RODMAN (1795–1820), b. New York City. After father's death reared by relatives at Hunt's Point on East River. Met Fitz-Greene Halleck, 1813. Studied medicine; M.D., 1816. Married; traveled in Europe; partner in pharmacy. Wrote "Croaker Papers" with Halleck, 1819. Died of consumption after trip to New Orleans. Chief poems published posthumously.

DREISER, THEODORE (1871–   ), b. Terre Haute, Indiana, of German-American parentage. Educated in public schools of Warsaw, Indiana, and at the state university. In newspaper work in Chicago and St. Louis, 1892–1895. Editor of *Every Month*, 1895–1898. Editorial positions on *McClure's*, *Century*, *Cosmopolitan*, and various other magazines; finally editor-in-chief of the Butterick publications (*Delineator*, *Designer*, *New Idea*, *English Delineator*), 1907–1910. Organized the National Child Rescue Campaign, 1907. Made official visit to Russia, 1927. Since 1900 published twenty volumes, the most notable of which are novels. First popular success, "An American Tragedy," 1925.

DUNLAP, WILLIAM (1766–1839), b. Perth Amboy, New Jersey; father, loyalist. Moved to New York. Studied under local painter; became professional portrait painter, 1782; in London, under Benjamin West, 1784–1787. Became interested in theater; first play to be performed, "The Father," 1789. Partner in father's business; then bought part interest in New York "Old American Company," 1796; sole owner, 1798; translated and adapted German and French successes; company failed, 1805. Resumed painting; again connected with theater, 1806–1811; again lived by painting. Edited the *Monthly Recorder*, 1813; assistant paymaster general for state militia, 1814–1816. A founder of The National Academy of Design, 1826. "History of American Theater," 1832; "A History of Arts of Design in America," 1834; a temperance novel, 1836; a history of New York, 1837, 1839; a biography of Brockden Brown; adapted or wrote about seventy plays.

DWIGHT, JOHN (SULLIVAN) (1813–1893), b. Boston. One of first members of Transcendental Club; leader at Brook Farm, teaching Latin and music.

Contributed articles on music to *The Harbinger* and lectured on musical appreciation. Edited *Daily Chronotype*, Boston, 1851. Published *Dwight's Journal of Music*, 1852–1858. Contributor on music to histories and cyclopedias. Largely responsible for professorship of music at Harvard.

DWIGHT, TIMOTHY (1752–1817), b. Northampton, Massachusetts. Graduated from Yale, 1769. Taught in New Haven school and in Yale six years. Chaplain in Continental Army; at Northampton, Massachusetts, 1779–1784; preacher, farmer, and two years state legislator. Political and social doctrines expressed in "Triumph of Infidelity," 1788. Contributed to post-war patriotic verse with "Greenfield Hill" and "Conquest of Canaan." Four volumes of "Travels in New England and New York" prepared as source book for future historians. A leader among the "Hartford Wits." Contributor to the "Anarchiad." President of Yale, 1795–1817.

EDWARDS, JONATHAN (1703–1758), b. East Windsor, Connecticut; father, clergyman; of eleven children the only son. Precocious in speculative and scientific thinking. Graduated from Yale, 1720; A.M., 1724; tutor till 1726. Colleague pastor with grandfather, Solomon Stoddard, Northampton, Massachusetts, 1727; sole pastor, 1729. Spokesman for rigid Calvinism; participated in Great Awakening, defending the revival in three controversial pamphlets. Offended congregation by attempting discipline of young people for immoral reading and attacking established practice of the "half-way covenant"; dismissed, 1750. Refusing calls from Virginia and Scotland, moved to Stockbridge, in western Massachusetts, as village pastor and missionary to Indians. Here wrote "The Freedom of the Will." Succeeded his son-in-law, Aaron Burr (Sr.), as president of College of New Jersey (now Princeton), 1757. Died after inoculation against smallpox.

ELIOT, JOHN (1604–1690), b. Hertfordshire. Graduated from Jesus College, Cambridge, 1622. Took orders; under influence of Thomas Hooker. Removed to Massachusetts, 1631; pastor at Roxbury. With Richard Mather and Thomas Weld prepared the "Bay Psalm Book," 1640, first book printed in New England. Dedicated life to conversion of Indians, studied their languages; translated the Bible and a catechism into dialect of the Massachusetts Indians; published an Indian grammar.

EMERSON, RALPH WALDO (1803–1882), b. Boston, Massachusetts; son of minister of First Church, ancestors for six generations including clergymen. Father died, 1811. Education superintended by mother and aunt, Mary Moody Emerson. Boston Latin School, 1817; graduated from Harvard, 1821; taught school; studied for ministry. Health poor; winter of 1826 in Florida. Installed, 1829, colleague pastor of Second Church of Boston; sole pastor, 1830; resigned, 1832, unwilling to conduct communion ceremony. Married, 1829; wife, Ellen Tucker, died, 1831. Traveled in Europe. Met Carlyle, Landor, Wordsworth. Settled at Concord; lectured on various subjects. Married Lydia Jackson, 1835. Edited Carlyle's "Sartor Resartus," and other volumes first published in United States; published "Nature," 1836; delivered "The American Scholar," 1837, to Phi Beta Kappa society at Cambridge; addressed senior class of Divinity College,

Harvard, 1838. Edited the *Dial*, 1842–1844. Europe, 1847–1848, lecturing. Refrained from active participation in Brook Farm and in abolitionist party, but spoke often in favor of latter's ideals, 1844–1862. Contributed to *Atlantic Monthly*. LL.D. from Harvard, 1866. House burned, 1872; friends contributed to rebuild it and to finance a trip to Europe. In last ten years increasingly a victim of aphasia.

FIELD, EUGENE (1850–1895), b. St. Louis, of New England parents. Attended Williams College, Knox College, University of Missouri. Held editorial positions on St. Joseph, Kansas City, St. Louis, and Denver newspapers; from 1883 till death columnist for Chicago *Morning News*. Toward end of life developed great interest in Horace and in book collecting. Writings consist chiefly of humorous and satirical skits and whimsical poems for children.

FIELDS, JAMES THOMAS (1817–1881), b. Portsmouth, New Hampshire. In 1831 went to Boston and at once made ties with young writers and book dealers. In 1838 junior partner in the publishing house later known as Ticknor and Fields, and after many changes as Houghton Mifflin Company. Friend and adviser to foremost writers of his day in America and England. In 1861 succeeded Lowell as editor of the *Atlantic Monthly* for nine years. In 1870 retired from business and spent his later years in lecturing and in reminiscent writing.

FITCH, WILLIAM CLYDE (1865–1909), b. Elmira, New York. Amherst College, A.B., 1886. Interested from childhood in drama, and at college in dramatic and operatic performances. Did hack work for several New York journals. During a residence on the Continent became part of the aesthetic movement and met many writers there and in England. On return began dramatic authorship in earnest, writing for Mansfield and later for English actors. By 1901 the leading name among American playwrights, with a list of fifty-six original plays and adaptations. Died abroad, 1909.

FOSTER, STEPHEN COLLINS (1826–1864), b. Pittsburgh, of Scotch-Irish parents. Entered academy, 1841, but educated chiefly under tutors. Tried bookkeeping, but popularity of early songs opened career in music. First songs published in minstrel collections, 1848, 1849, used by Christy and others. Later sold songs in manuscript. After 1860 lived in New York, writing freely, reiterating qualities of early and best songs. Some half-dozen of his songs written in 1850's permanently significant in folk music of America. Improvident, he died in abject poverty, though the most popular song writer in American history.

FRANKLIN, BENJAMIN (1706–1790), b. Boston, son of chandler and soap boiler. Grammar-school education. Apprenticed to father, 1716; then to brother James. Publisher of *New England Courant*, for which he wrote the "Dogood Papers." Ran away to Philadelphia, 1723. Governor Keith sent him to England, 1724, to get printing-press materials. Worked in London as journeyman printer; published pamphlet "Dissertation on Liberty and Necessity, Pleasure and Pain," 1725. Back to Philadelphia; established own press; purchased *Pennsylvania Gazette*, raised circulation to 10,000.

Began publication of "Poor Richard's Almanac," 1732, soon translated in Europe. Founded the "Junto," 1727. Public printer for Pennsylvania, 1730. Founded first circulating library. Became freemason, master of grand lodge of Pennsylvania, 1732; clerk of Assembly, 1736–1751. Formed first fire company in Philadelphia; postmaster, 1737. Branch printing offices in six cities; big income. Organized American Philosophical Society, 1743. Invented stove, 1742; proved identity of lightning and electricity, 1752; Member Royal Society, 1753. Received Copley medal; various other medals, diplomas. Retired from active business, 1749. Many public offices, state and national. Improved street lighting, paving; aided foundation of Academy (later University of Pennsylvania). To London as colony's agent, 1757; friends among statesmen and intellectuals; LL.D. from St. Andrews, 1759; D.C.L., Oxford, 1762. Pennsylvania again sent him to England, 1764. Wide travel, general popularity. Associate French Academy, 1772. Support of colonial interests forced him to leave England, 1774. Member Continental Congress, on ten committees; postmaster-general, 1775; on drafting committee of "Declaration of Independence." Commissioner to France, 1776–1785. Commissioner to negotiate treaty with England, 1781. President of Pennsylvania, 1785–1787; delegate Constitutional Convention, 1787. In last years published scientific pamphlets, papers against slavery. "Autobiography" begun in 1771, continued, at plea of friends, in 1784, 1788; published, 1791.

FRENEAU, PHILIP (1752–1832), b. New York. Father a wine merchant of Huguenot descent; family moved to New Jersey. Graduated from College of New Jersey, 1771. Commencement poem with his roommate, H. H. Brackenridge, "The Rising Glory of America." Taught school; studied law; became journalist in Philadelphia. Achieved fame as satirist, 1775. In West Indies, 1775–1778. Fresh outburst of war poems on return. Voyage to Azores, 1779. Built and sailed a privateer, 1780; captured by British and confined for two months on prison ship in New York Harbor. Occupied as journalist (edited *Freeman's Journal*, 1781–1784) and shipmaster to 1791; translator in State Department for Jefferson while editor of the anti-Federalist *National Gazette*. Retired to estate at Mount Pleasant, New Jersey, 1793. Edited *Jersey Chronicle*, 1793–1794. Again went to sea, voyaging as far as Calcutta. Settled finally at Mount Pleasant, 1807. Unproductive for last twenty years of his life.

FROST, ROBERT (LEE) (1875–   ), b. San Francisco, of New England parents. Returned to New England at ten years of age. Short term at Dartmouth in 1892. In 1897, two years after marriage, entered Harvard for two years. Farmed unsuccessfully one year; taught English at Derry, New Hampshire, 1900–1911, and psychology at Plymouth, 1911–1912, meantime writing poems publishers rejected. Sold farm and took family to England. Neighbor to several poets; continuing to write there till 1915. In 1913 and 1914 English publishers issued volumes of his verse, "A Boy's Will" and "North of Boston"; made reputation speedily. Back to America, settled on farm in New Hampshire. Taught English at Amherst College,

1916–1920, and since 1923. From 1921 to 1923 "poet in residence," University of Michigan, where he is still Fellow in Letters. Pulitzer prize for poetry, 1924 and 1931.

FULLER, HENRY BLAKE (1857–1929), b. Chicago. Educated in public schools there. For a time at a "classical academy" in Wisconsin. In Europe, 1879–1880, 1883, 1892, 1894, 1896–1897. Literary editor of the *Chicago Evening Post*, 1902; editorial writer for the *Chicago Record Herald*, 1911–1913. Last journalistic work, reviewer for the *New Republic*, the *Nation*, and other journals. From 1912 to his death on the advisory board of *Poetry: a Magazine of Verse*. His last two books written just before his death.

FULLER, MARGARET (1810–1850), b. Cambridgeport, Massachusetts; eldest of eight children of local lawyer and politician. Strenuous and precocious childhood; health injured by overapplication. Father died, 1835; supported her family by teaching in Boston and Providence. Intimate with leading Transcendentalists; edited the *Dial*, 1840–1842. Traveled on the Great Lakes, 1843. Literary critic for the *New York Tribune*, 1844–1846. In Europe, 1846; married Marquis Ossoli, 1847, by whom she had one child; participated in Italian revolution; fled Rome after its capture by the French; drowned in storm off Fire Island Beach, with husband and child, while on return to America. Critical articles, published by Horace Greeley, collected in three volumes after her death. Two earlier volumes appeared under own hand.

GARLAND, HAMLIN (1860–   ), b. near West Salem, Wisconsin, of Scotch and New England ancestry. Went with pioneer family to Iowa, Dakota, and back to Wisconsin. Schooling interrupted, finishing at Cedar Valley Seminary, Osage, Iowa. Taught, 1882–1883. Revolting from farm life, went East, studying in Boston Public Library and gaining interest of W. D. Howells. Visit to Middle West, 1887, motivated realistic studies of prairie life. Moved to Chicago, and after some years of conventional Western writing gravitated to New York City. American Academy of Arts and Letters, 1918; Pulitzer prize for biography, "Daughter of the Middle Border," 1921. Later works a long series of reminiscences.

GILDER, RICHARD WATSON (1844–1909), b. Bordentown, New Jersey. Father, schoolmaster. Went to local schools; for a while assistant to father. Brief service in Civil War. Paymaster, Camden and Amboy Railroad; 1869–1870 edited *Hours at Home*, following it, with J. G. Holland, when it was merged with *Scribner's Monthly*, and continuing with shift to the *Century*, of which he became editor. Chief authorship, lyric poetry. One of Century Club group, Society of American Artists, Authors' Club, American Academy. Active in civic work, especially on housing problems in slums.

GODFREY, THOMAS (1736–1763), b. Philadelphia, son of glazier. Fair education. Apprenticed to watchmaker. Lieutenant in provincial forces, 1758–1759; purchasing agent in North Carolina, where he wrote "Prince of Parthia" (1759), produced in Philadelphia, 1767. Contributed poetry to the *American Magazine* and published "Court of Fancy," modeled after

Chaucer's "House of Fame." Works, in one volume, published by Nathaniel Evans, 1767.

HALE, SARAH J. (JOSEPHA BUELL) (1788–1879), b. Newport, New Hampshire. Daughter of Revolutionary soldier. Education largely from mother, brother, and husband. Widow, 1822, with five children after nine years of marriage. Wrote verse and in 1827 the novel "Northwood, or Life North and South" (republished, 1852). Edited *Ladies' Magazine*, 1828–1837, and *Godey's Lady's Book*, 1837–1877. Prolific, both in her own columns and in many books, in writing for guidance, edification, and liberal education of women. A national influence.

HALLECK, FITZ-GREENE (1790–1867), b. Guilford, Connecticut. Clerk in New York City business house, 1811–1829. Met Joseph Rodman Drake, 1813, with whom he wrote the "Croaker Papers" for the New York *Evening Post*, 1819. Followed this with "Fanny," a social satire. Clerk under patronage of John Jacob Astor, 1832–1849, after whose death he retired to Guilford on a small pension. "Marco Bozzaris" a favorite declamation piece.

HAMMOND, JOHN (?–1707), author of "Leah and Rachel, or the Two Fruitful Sisters, Virginia and Maryland," 1656, represented himself as having lived nineteen years in Virginia and two in Maryland, whence he escaped a death sentence passed on him for having supported Governor Stone and the Lord Proprietor.

HARRIS, JOEL CHANDLER (1848–1908), b. Putnam County, Georgia. "Printer's devil" at fourteen on J. A. Turner's *Countryman*. For twenty-five years associated with the *Atlanta Constitution*, becoming editor in 1890. For this he contributed social and political satire, editorials, and his studies in Negro folklore, beginning with "Uncle Remus: his Songs and his Sayings," published in book form, 1880. Strong Southerner but vigorous anti-sectionalist. Friend of Theodore Roosevelt. American Academy of Arts and Letters.

HARTE, (FRANCIS) BRET (1836–1902), b. Albany, New York. Went with mother to California in 1854; express messenger, typesetter, teacher, clerk, secretary of California mint. First editor of the *Overland Monthly*, 1868–1871, jumping into national popularity with "Luck of Roaring Camp" in second number. Went East on invitation of the *Atlantic* for monthly contributions. Output disappointing. In 1878 went abroad to minor consular appointments, remaining there in obscurity till his death.

HAWTHORNE, NATHANIEL (1804–1864), b. Salem, Massachusetts, son of sea captain. Father died, 1808. Boyhood secluded. At Bowdoin, 1821–1825; friend of Longfellow and Franklin Pierce; lived retired life, wrote steadily, destroying much. Novel "Fanshawe," published anonymously, 1828; wrote for the *Token*, an annual, under pseudonyms. Edited *American Magazine of Useful and Entertaining Knowledge*, 1836–1838; compiled a "Universal History." "Twice-Told Tales" (1837) attracted but little attention. In custom house in Boston, 1839–1841. At Brook Farm, 1841–1842. Married Sophia Peabody; settled at "Old Manse," Concord, earning a small income by his pen. In customs service at Salem, 1846–1849; success with the

"Scarlet Letter," 1850. Lived in Lenox, Massachusetts, 1850, friend and neighbor of Melville; in West Newton; again in Concord. Campaign biography of Pierce rewarded with appointment as consul at Liverpool, 1853–1857; traveled on Continent, 1858–1860. Returned to Concord; contributed to the *Atlantic Monthly*. Latest novels, posthumously published, of little significance.

HAY, JOHN (MILTON) (1838–1905), b. Salem, Indiana. Graduated from Brown University, 1858. In the President's office under Lincoln, 1861–1865; secretary of legation at Paris, 1865–1867. Chargé d'affaires at Vienna, 1867–1868; at Madrid, 1869–1870. Returned to United States; became editorial writer and twice temporary editor for *New York Tribune*. Rest of life divided between diplomatic and literary activity. Ambassador to Great Britain, 1897; Secretary of State, 1899, with hand in more than fifty major treaties in American diplomacy. Wrote mass of diplomatic utterances and letters; a monumental "Life of Lincoln" with collaboration of J. G. Nicolay, with whom he edited the works of Lincoln; several volumes of poems; and a novel, "The Breadwinners," published anonymously, 1884. Charter member, American Academy of Arts and Letters.

HAYNE, PAUL HAMILTON (1830–1886), b. Charleston, South Carolina. Nephew of Governor Robert Y. Hayne. Educated at South Carolina College; studied law. Edited *Russell's Magazine*, 1857–1860, and *Charleston Literary Gazette*. Contributed to *Southern Literary Messenger*. First volume of poems, 1855. In Confederate Army on staff of General Pickens. Impoverished by war, lived near Augusta, Georgia, after 1865. Edited poems of Timrod, 1873; lives of Robert Y. Hayne and Hugh Swinton Legaré, 1878; five volumes of poems.

HEARN, LAFCADIO (1850–1904), son of a surgeon major in British army, of mixed English, Irish, and gypsy blood. Unhappy childhood in Ireland and St. Cuthbert's College. To America, 1869; job after job. Contributed articles to the *Cincinnati Enquirer*, and in 1874, reporter. Positions on the *Enquirer* and the *Cincinnati Commercial*. Ill-health and revolt led him to New Orleans, 1877, with commission to write up political conditions in Louisiana. Two years in West Indies; eked out editorial earnings by translations from French and Spanish, and several volumes of exotic sketches for New York journals. Next few years alternated between New York and the West Indies, writing. From 1889 to end of life lived in Japan, teaching in several native schools — finally, in the Imperial University at Tokyo — and writing interpretations of Japanese literature and culture. Married a Japanese and became naturalized.

HERGESHEIMER, JOSEPH (1880–   ), b. Philadelphia. Quaker school and Pennsylvania Academy of Fine Arts, followed by art study in Italy. Wrote several years without recognition. First published group of magazine articles, 1913. Won recognition with "The Three Black Pennys" (1917), "Java Head," and "Linda Condon," 1919. Has supplemented more than a dozen volumes of fiction with essays, travels, biography, and autobiography. Recurrent contributor to the *Saturday Evening Post*.

HOFFMAN, CHARLES FENNO (1806–1884), b. New York City. Attended Columbia; admitted to bar, 1827; practiced three years. Edited the *Knickerbocker Magazine*, 1833; edited successively the *American Monthly*, the *Mirror*, the *Literary World*. Traveled in West, searching for health. Became insane, 1849.

HOLMES, OLIVER WENDELL (1809–1894), b. Cambridge, Massachusetts. Son of leader of Calvinistic orthodoxy, historian of Revolutionary War. Educated at Phillips Andover Academy, 1825; Harvard, 1829. After trial at law study, undertook medicine, 1830–1833. Early researches in puerperal fevers important. Study in Europe, 1833–1835. Professor of Anatomy, Dartmouth, 1838–1840; at Harvard Medical School, 1847–1882. "Old Ironsides," 1830, won attention. Helped launch the *Atlantic Monthly*, 1857, with first of "Breakfast Table" series, continuing it in 1859, 1873, and 1890. A favorite lyceum lecturer, after-dinner speaker, and laureate for special occasions throughout his career.

HOOKER, THOMAS (1586?–1647), b. Leicestershire, England. M.A., Emmanuel College, Cambridge, 1611, where he was later Fellow. Minister at Esher in Surrey and lecturer at Chelmsford in Essex. Silenced by Laud, 1629, fled to Holland and emigrated to America, 1633. Pastor at Newtowne (Cambridge), Massachusetts. Criticized ecclesiastical qualification for suffrage; led settlement at Hartford, Connecticut, 1636. Famous preacher and apologist for Congregational system.

HOPKINSON, FRANCIS (1737–1791), b. Philadelphia; son of lawyer. Graduated from College of Philadelphia, 1757. Admitted to bar, 1761. Spent a year in England with his cousin, bishop of Worcester. Practiced law in Philadelphia. Active in learned societies; versatile in the arts. Signer of Declaration of Independence, aided the Revolution, and later supported fight for the Constitution. Judge of Admiralty for Pennsylvania, 1779–1789; district judge, 1790. Composed music, painted, wrote essays and verse after manners of Addison and Pope. His "Battle of the Kegs," "Pretty Story," and "The New Roof" important propaganda during the Revolutionary War and the critical period thereafter.

HOVEY, RICHARD (1864–1900), b. Normal, Illinois, of Eastern ancestry. Much of boyhood in Washington, D.C. Dartmouth, 1885; class poet, Phi Beta Kappa, and laureate of college and fraternity thereafter. Ventured study of theology, journalism, acting. Collaborated in three volumes with Bliss Carman. Lecturer at Barnard College (Columbia University) from 1898 to time of his death.

HOWE, ED (EDGAR WATSON) (1853–   ), b. Treaty, Indiana. Began newspaper career at twelve; at nineteen publisher of paper at Golden, Colorado; at twenty-four owner and editor of Atchison (Kansas) *Daily Globe*. Since 1911 publisher and editor of *Howe's Monthly*. His "Story of a Country Town," 1883, followed by some twenty-five other titles, chiefly stories and sketches, and by his autobiography, "Plain People."

HOWELLS, WILLIAM DEAN (1837–1920), b. Martins Ferry, Ohio. At fourteen compositor on father's newspaper; correspondent of *Cincinnati*

Gazette at nineteen, on *Ohio State Journal* at twenty-two; occasionally wrote poems which reached the *Atlantic Monthly*; finally brought out small volume of verse with J. J. Piatt. Campaign biography of Lincoln brought consulship to Venice, 1861–1865. Positions subsequently with leading New York journals. Sub-editor, 1866–1871, and editor-in-chief, 1871–1881, of the *Atlantic Monthly*. Between 1880 and 1890 wrote novels for the *Century Magazine*; from 1885 to 1916 published through Harpers; editor of the critic's department, "The Editor's Study," on *Harper's*, 1886–1892, and "The Easy Chair" from 1900 to the end of his life, 1920.

HUMPHREYS, DAVID (1752–1818), b. Derby (now Ansonia), Connecticut. Graduated from Yale, 1771. Captain in Continental Army, major, aide to General Putnam; secretary to Washington, 1780. Secretary of commission to Europe under Franklin, Adams, and Jefferson, 1784; in Connecticut legislature, 1786. Aided in suppression of Shays's rebellion. A "Hartford Wit," contributor to "The Anarchiad." Resided with Washington, 1788–1790; minister to Portugal, 1791–1796, to Spain, 1796–1801. Captain-general, War of 1812; F.R.S.

HUNEKER, JAMES GIBBONS (1860–1921), b. Philadelphia. Graduated from Roth's Military Academy; studied law. Studied piano at home and abroad; teacher, National Conservatory, New York City, 1886–1898; dramatic and music critic for several New York journals; dramatic and art editor for the New York *Sun*. Works include music, art and literary criticism, general essays, autobiography, and correspondence.

IRVING, WASHINGTON (1783–1859), b. New York. Studied in city schools; took up law. Contributed "Jonathan Oldstyle" papers to the *Morning Chronicle*, 1802. Health poor; in Europe, 1804–1806. Issued "Salmagundi" papers with his brother William and James K. Paulding, 1807–1808. "Knickerbocker History of New York" (1809) brought him reputation. Abandoned law; silent partner in brothers' business, which failed; on staff of Governor Tompkins during War of 1812; connected with *Analectic Magazine* of Philadelphia, 1813–1814. Well received in England, 1815; friend of Campbell, Jeffrey, Moore, and Scott, the latter influencing Murray to publish "The Sketch Book," 1820. Traveled on Continent; U. S. attaché, Spain, 1826–1829; secretary of United States legation in London, 1829–1831. Returned to New York, 1832; toured Western prairies. Minister at Madrid, 1842–1846.

JAMES, HENRY (1843–1916), b. New York City, son of Henry James, publicist; brother of William James, philosopher. In European schools from twelve to seventeen. Entered Harvard Law School, 1862. Returned to Europe, 1869. Began contributing articles to American magazines in 1865. Most eminent of American literary expatriates and one of the few from the East. In 1915 became a British subject; the following year decorated with the Order of Merit.

JOHNSON, EDWARD (1598–1672), b. Kent, England. Came to New England, 1630. One of the founders of the town of Woburn, which he represented in Court of Assistants till 1671. Published his "Wonder-Working Providence of Sion's Saviour in New England," London, 1652.

KENNEDY, JOHN PENDLETON (1795–1870), b. Baltimore. Graduated from Baltimore College, 1812; served in War of 1812. Admitted to bar, 1816; in Maryland legislature; in Congress, 1838–1845, a Whig leader. Secretary of the Navy, 1852–1853. Several trips to Europe; American Commissioner at Paris in Exposition of 1867. Supported North in Civil War. Befriended Poe; intimate with Thackeray, for whom he supplied local color in "The Virginians." "Swallow Barn" (1832), Addisonian in form, an early specimen of sympathetic Southern realism.

KNIGHT, (MRS.) SARAH KEMBLE (1666–1727), b. Boston, Massachusetts, daughter of merchant. Took over husband's affairs on his death. Made her celebrated journey to New York, 1704. Opened dame school, Boston, 1706; Benjamin Franklin and Samuel Mather among pupils. Moved to Norwich, Connecticut, 1714. Signature on over one hundred public papers from office of Recorder of Deeds. An able business woman. Journal of trip to New York first published, 1825.

LANIER, SIDNEY (1842–1881), b. Macon, Georgia, of Huguenot and Cavalier ancestry. Graduated from Oglethorpe University, 1860; tutor, 1860–1861; in Confederate army; health undermined after capture and imprisonment. In Alabama, 1865, clerk and teacher; returning to Macon, studied law and practiced with father, 1868–1872. In San Antonio, Texas, 1872; in Baltimore, first flutist, Peabody Symphony Orchestra; wrote words for Cantata Centennial Exposition, 1876. Lecturer on literature, Johns Hopkins, Baltimore, 1879 to death.

LEONARD, DANIEL (1740–1829), b. Norton, Massachusetts. Graduated from Harvard, 1760. In colonial legislature; pamphlet controversy with John Adams, "Novanglus," defending loyalist position as "Massachusettensis." Withdrew to England, 1776; property confiscated.

LEWIS, SINCLAIR (1885–   ), b. Sauk Center, Minnesota, son of physician. Graduated from Yale, 1907. For ten years newspaper man in Connecticut, Iowa, and California; magazine editor, Washington, D.C., and reader for several New York publishers. Traveled extensively in the United States and later abroad. Won recognition with sixth novel, "Main Street," 1920, maintaining popularity without a lapse. Declined Pulitzer prize for "Arrowsmith," 1926, as protest at conditions pertaining to award. First American to win Nobel prize for literature, 1930.

LINDSAY, (NICHOLAS) VACHEL (1879–1931), b. Springfield, Illinois. Educated, public schools; Hiram College, Ohio, 1897–1900; Art Institute, Chicago, 1900–1903; New York School of Art, 1904–1905. Lecturer for Y.M.C.A., 1905–1909; for the Anti-Saloon League in Illinois, 1909–1910. Between 1910 and 1913 made his walking tours, "preaching the gospel of beauty" and "trading his rhymes for bread." Later gave poem recitals throughout America. Won recognition with "The Congo," 1914.

LOCKE, DAVID ROSS (1833–1888), b. Vestal, New York. Journeyman printer and reporter on various Western papers; edited Findlay (Ohio) *Jeffersonian*, in which appeared the first of the "Petroleum V. Nasby" papers, 1861. Edited *Toledo Blade*, 1865; popular lecturer after 1871.

LONDON, JACK (1876–1916), b. San Francisco. Educated, public schools; newsboy, "boy socialist"; shipped before the mast; worked as itinerant laborer. Entered University of California, leaving to go to Klondike in the gold rush. Won recognition with "The Call of the Wild," 1903. In same year revealed radical sympathies with "The People of the Abyss." War correspondent in Russo-Japanese War. An aggressive socialist, yet subject to love of grandeur, he wrote himself to exhaustion, dying at forty on his ambitious country estate.

LONGFELLOW, HENRY WADSWORTH (1807–1882), b. Portland, Maine. Printed first verse in Portland *Gazette* at thirteen. Graduated from Bowdoin College, 1825; professor of modern languages there after three years abroad. Smith professor at Harvard, succeeding Ticknor and preceding Lowell, 1836–1854. Resigned to devote himself to writing. Period of strongest European influence, 1833–1847; period of major American narrative poems, 1847–1863; maturest fruits of scholarship and artistry, 1867–1882. Honors, Oxford and Cambridge, 1868–1869; bust in Westminster Abbey.

LONGSTREET, AUGUSTUS BALDWIN (1790–1870), b. Augusta, Georgia. Graduated from Yale, 1813. Practiced law; state legislature, 1821; district judge, 1822. Edited Augusta *Sentinel*, 1838. Entered Methodist ministry, 1838. President, Emory College, 1839; University of Mississippi, 1849; South Carolina College, 1856; again of University of Mississippi. Advocate of secession. Known in literature as author of "Georgia Scenes," published anonymously, 1835, and variously reprinted.

LOWELL, AMY (1874–1925), b. Brookline, Massachusetts; sister of President Lowell of Harvard and Percival Lowell, astronomer; distant relation of James Russell Lowell. Educated, private schools and travel. Adopted role of poet, preparing from 1902 to 1910. Ardent disciple and biographer of Keats. Critic of French and American poets; leader among experimentalists. Pulitzer prize (posthumous), 1926.

LOWELL, JAMES RUSSELL (1819–1891), b. Cambridge, Massachusetts, son of Unitarian clergyman. Graduated from Harvard, 1838; class poet. Abandoned law for literature. First volume of poems, 1841; edited the *Pioneer*, 1843. Succeeded Longfellow as Smith professor of modern languages and literatures, 1855–1877. Edited *The Atlantic*, 1857–1861; joint editor, *North American Review*, 1864–1872. Honors from Oxford and Cambridge, 1873 and 1874. Minister to Spain, 1877–1880; to England, 1880–1885.

MACKAYE, PERCY (1875–   ), b. New York City, son of Steele MacKaye, actor, playwright, stage designer. Graduated from Harvard, 1897. In Europe, 1898–1900. Taught, 1900–1904. Lectured on theater, 1906–1913, at Harvard, Yale, Columbia, and other universities. Fellow in poetry and drama, Miami University, Ohio, 1920–1928. Work divided between plays, social comedy, historical, regional; masques and pageants, opera librettos, and biography of his father, a chapter in theatrical history.

MASTERS, EDGAR LEE (1869–   ), b. Garnett, Kansas, of New England ancestry. Spent youth in Fulton County, Illinois, through which flows the Spoon River. Attended Knox College; studied law in father's office; admitted to bar, 1891, practicing in Chicago for over twenty years. Published verse since 1898, not attracting public attention until stimulated by William Marion Reedy, editor, *Reedy's Mirror*, St. Louis, to follow up a casual group of poems which eventually became the "Spoon River Anthology" (1915). Has continued to use Middle Western material in poems, novels, and biography.

MATHER, COTTON (1663–1728), b. Boston, son of Increase Mather; grandson of John Cotton. A.B., Harvard, 1678; M.A., 1681. Colleague pastor of North Church, 1685. Opposed Sir Edmund Andros, 1688–1689; influential in politics under Sir William Phips; 1690, fellow of Harvard; organized societies for the reform of manners. Lost political power under rule of Joseph Dudley; resigned office at Harvard, 1703, after his father was ousted from presidency. Well known abroad; elected to Royal Society, 1713; honorary degree University of Aberdeen, 1710. Knew many languages, including some Indian dialects; reading, encyclopedic. Advocated inoculation for smallpox, 1721. Published over four hundred and fifty titles, several on witchcraft, before and after persecutions at Salem; these show a belief in "possession" but skepticism about some findings in 1693. Outstanding conservative leader; became more tolerant, assisting at ordination of a Baptist minister, 1718, and admitting members of other denominations to communion in his church. Pastor of North Church, 1723–1728.

MATHER, INCREASE (1639–1723), b. Dorchester, Massachusetts, son of Richard Mather; A.B., Harvard, 1656; M.A., Trinity College, Dublin, 1658. Held several English livings; finally chaplain to English garrison at Isle of Guernsey. Returned to Boston, 1661, having lost his pulpit at the Restoration; pastor of North Church, 1664. Licenser of the press, 1674. Leader of conservative party; opposed "halfway covenant" and dominated synod of 1679–1680, which emphasized autocratic nature of the church system. President of Harvard, 1685–1701; colony's agent in England, 1688–1692, securing new charter of 1691 from William III. Ousted from Harvard by liberal opposition under Joseph Dudley, 1701. Formed scientific society, 1683; advocated inoculation for smallpox, 1721. Friend of Robert Boyle, the physicist, and of Richard Baxter. Published over one hundred and fifty works; "Cases of Conscience" (1693), though revealing belief in witchcraft, probably aided in ending convictions. In last years more tolerant, assisting at ordination of a Baptist minister, 1718.

MELVILLE, HERMAN (1819–1891), b. New York City. Educated, Albany Academy. Sailed before the mast to Liverpool, 1837; taught school; sailed on whaler, 1841, to South Seas; escaped the ship; lived among the islanders; rescued; adventured among Pacific islands; returned aboard naval ship, 1844. Published first narrative of own adventures in "Typee" (1846), achieving notice in England and America. Married a daughter of Chief Justice Lemuel Shaw of Massachusetts, 1847; lived in Pittsfield, friend of Hawthorne. European trips, 1849, 1856. Reputation waned after "Pierre," 1852. Moved to New York City, 1863; position in custom house, 1866–1885. Last published work "The Confidence Man," 1857; volume of poems on Civil War (1865) and three other privately printed volumes only literary output thereafter. Devoted energies to business and philosophical speculation. In last days wrote "Billy Budd," published in 1924.

MENCKEN, HENRY LOUIS (1880–), b. Baltimore of German ancestry. Educated, private schools and Baltimore Polytechnic. Entered journalism, and by 1903 was city editor of the Baltimore *Morning Herald.* Literary critic for *Smart Set* and co-editor with George Jean Nathan, 1914–1924. War correspondent, 1916–1917. Contributing editor of *The Nation* since 1921. Founded the *American Mercury* with Nathan (1924), retiring, 1933.

MILLER, "JOAQUIN" (CINCINNATUS HINER) (1839–1913), b. Indiana, 1839. Taken to Oregon in infancy. A runaway; lived for several years among miners and Indians. Graduated from Columbia College, Oregon, 1858. Between then and 1870 pony-express rider, adventurer, editor, lawyer, justice. Not taken seriously as writer on the coast, he left for London, where he won exotic popularity. Life from 1873 to 1887 a confused record of wanderings. Then returned to California, where he lived picturesquely on "The Hights" at Oakland until his death.

MITCHELL, SILAS WEIR (1829–1914), b. Philadelphia. Educated, University of Pennsylvania and Jefferson Medical College. Studied abroad. Surgeon in Union army during Civil War. Professor in Philadelphia Polyclinic College; forty years associated with Philadelphia Orthopaedic Hospital; aided in planning University of Pennsylvania Medical School. Wrote medical treatises, some poetry, several novels. Member American Academy of Arts and Sciences and National Academy of Science.

MOODY, WILLIAM VAUGHN (1869–1910), b. Spencer, Indiana, son of a river-boat captain. Prepared for Harvard by alternate study and teaching and completed work in three years, 1893. Remainder of short life marked by prolonged travels and eight years in English department, University of Chicago. Popular success with his prose play, "The Great Divide," 1906. Strongly influential over many younger poets of his day.

MORE, PAUL ELMER (1864–), b. St. Louis. Educated, Washington University and Harvard. Taught at Harvard and Bryn Mawr. Literary editor of *The Independent,* 1901–1903, the *New York Evening Post,* 1903–1909; edited *The Nation,* 1909–1914. Lectures at Princeton. Major work the series of "Shelburne Essays," 1904–1921; later series, 1928– .

MORTON, (MRS.) SARAH WENTWORTH (1759–1846), b. Boston, Massachusetts, of wealthy merchant family. Unusual education for the time. Married Perez Morton, brilliant and erratic. Contributed verse to the *Massachusetts Magazine, Columbian Centinel, Port Folio, Monthly Anthology.* Thirty years after her death her name was assigned to the novel "The Power of Sympathy," now ascribed to William Hill Brown.

MORTON, THOMAS (1590?–1647), lawyer of Clifford's Inn. In New England, 1622; again 1625, settling at Mount Wollaston (now Quincy), Massachusetts; assumed command; renamed it Merry-Mount, 1626. Erected Maypole; sold liquor and arms to Indians. Endicott raided post; banished Morton, 1628. He returned, was arrested, put into stocks, his house was burned, and he was sent in chains to England, 1630. Released; entered service of Sir Ferdinando Gorges. "The New English Canaan," 1637. Back to Plymouth, 1643; imprisoned a year; fined a hundred pounds; banished. Died in poverty at Agamenticus, Maine.

MOWATT, (MRS.) ANNA CORA (RITCHIE) (1819–1870), b. Bordeaux, France, daughter of New York merchant. Came to United States, 1826. Precocious. Married at fifteen; published the novel "Pelayo" at seventeen. Year and a half in Europe; aided husband in business reverses, giving dramatic readings. Wrote popular stories as "Helen Berkley." On stage, 1846–1854. Last years in Europe. Her play "Fashion" the best social comedy in United States since Royall Tyler's "Contrast," over fifty years earlier.

MUMFORD, LEWIS (1895–), b. Long Island. Wrote for technical magazines while still in high school. Studied at New York University, City College, Columbia, and New School for Social Research. Associate editor, *Fortnightly Dial*, 1919. Lecturer at New School for Social Research and at School of International Studies, Geneva. Critical volumes range from literary biography to social studies, arts, and architecture. Guggenheim Fellow, 1932–1933.

NEWELL, ROBERT HENRY (1836–1901), b. New York City. Literary editor, *Sunday Mercury*, 1858–1860; on staff of *New York World*, 1869–1874; edited *Hearth and Home*. "Orpheus C. Kerr" papers widely printed in newspapers; collected in three volumes, 1862–1865. Also wrote verse, novels, a play.

NOAH, MORDECAI MANUEL (1785–1851), b. Philadelphia, of Portuguese Jewish parentage. Self-educated; journalist, Charleston, South Carolina. Had responsible connections with six successive New York City dailies. Sheriff, surveyor, judge. Zionist leader. Consul to Tunis, 1813. Playwright, chiefly on themes from American history.

NORRIS, FRANK (1870–1902), b. Chicago. Studied at University of California and Harvard, after three years of art study in Paris. War correspondent in South Africa for *San Francisco Chronicle*, 1895–1896; associate editor of *The Wave*, San Francisco, 1896–1897; war correspondent in Cuba for McClure's syndicate, 1898. Known for tendency to naturalism in earlier stories and for two-thirds-completed "Epic of the Wheat." Several posthumous volumes, including essays, short stories, and his first novel, written at Harvard.

ODELL, JONATHAN (1737–1818), b. Newark, New Jersey. Graduated from College of New Jersey; studied medicine; surgeon in British army. Took orders, 1766; rector at Burlington, New Jersey. Loyalist, driven out of charge, removed to England. Later filled official positions in New Brunswick. Wrote vigorous loyalist verse during Revolution.

O'NEILL, EUGENE (GLADSTONE) (1888–), b. New York City; son of actor. Educated, Catholic schools and Betts Academy; part of 1906–1907 at Princeton. Globe-trotter and vagabond, 1909–1912; in sanatorium, 1912–1913; first playwriting, 1913–1914. A year at Harvard with "47

Workshop"; and 1916, first connection with the Provincetown Players, through whom much of his work was to be produced, subsequently often produced with marked success by the New York Theater Guild. Pulitzer prize for drama, for "Beyond the Horizon" (1920), "Anna Christie" (1922), "Strange Interlude" (1928). Popular with European audiences; works widely translated.

OTIS, JAMES (1725–1783), b. West Barnstable, Massachusetts. Brother of Mercy Otis Warren. Graduated from Harvard, 1743. Practiced law in Plymouth two years; then in Boston. Resigned office of advocate general to oppose "writs of assistance," 1761; became leader of patriotic party; published important declarations against Parliamentary taxation; proposed assembling of Stamp Act Congress, 1765. Injured in fray with commissioner of customs, 1769; suffered severe mental derangement. Participated in battle of Bunker Hill; retired to Andover.

PAINE, ROBERT TREAT (1773–1811), b. Taunton, Massachusetts. Christened Thomas Paine; changed to avoid confusion, painful to his family, with the author of "Common Sense." Graduated from Harvard, 1792. Unsuccessful in business. Edited *Federal Orrery*, 1794–1796. Became an enthusiast on drama and theater; married an actress; disowned by family. Practiced law in Boston. Died in destitution.

PAINE, THOMAS (1737–1809), b. Thetford, England. Quaker parentage. After various discreditable failures came to America, 1774. Wrote for the *Pennsylvania Magazine* year and a half. "Common Sense," January, 1776; "The Crisis," 1776–1783. Voted rewards by New York and Pennsylvania for war services, 1785. To Europe, 1787. French citizen and deputy to French Convention. Discredited among American conservatives for "Rights of Man," 1791–1792, and "Age of Reason," 1793. Returned to America, 1802. Last years in obscurity.

PARKER, THEODORE (1810–1860), b. Lexington, Massachusetts. Son of a farmer and mechanic. Worked with father while studying in district school; qualified for Harvard, 1830; followed full course by himself, but as he paid no tuition received no degree; given A.M. in 1840. In Divinity School, 1834; ordained pastor of West Roxbury (Unitarian) Church, 1837. Spokesman for radical religious thought, finally establishing a virtually independent congregation, the so-called Twenty-eighth Congregational Church of Boston (1845); conspicuous leader of abolitionists. Contributed to *Massachusetts Quarterly Review*, 1847–1850. Health broke down; died in Italy.

PAULDING, JAMES KIRKE (1778–1860), b. Dutchess County, New York. Meager education. Removed to New York; collaborated with brother-in-law, William Irving, and Washington Irving in "Salmagundi" papers, 1807. Defended America against British criticism during War of 1812 in "The Diverting History of John Bull and Brother Jonathan," and "United States and England"; as reward appointed secretary of board of navy commissioners by Madison. Navy agent in New York, 1825–1837; Secretary of the Navy, 1837–1841. Retired to native county; spent last years in writing.

PAYNE, JOHN HOWARD (1791–1852), b. New York. At fourteen, while clerk in a mercantile house, secretly edited the *Thespian Mirror*. First play, "Julia," performed in 1806. Studied at Union College. Became actor, 1809; made a success. In England, 1813. Wrote plays, adapted others from French and German; produced in all about sixty plays, one of which, "Clari, the Maid of Milan," contained "Home, Sweet Home." Friend of Irving, Coleridge, and Lamb. Returned to America, 1832. Espoused cause of Cherokee Indians, with whom he lived for a time. Consul at Tunis, 1842–1845, 1851–1852.

PECK, HARRY THURSTON (1856–1914), b. Stamford, Connecticut. Educated, private schools and Columbia, where he taught Latin and Sanskrit. Edited *The Bookman* at founding, 1895. Resigned, under pressure, from Columbia, 1910. Various editorial connections: with "International Cyclopedia" and "New International," with "Library of World's Best Literature," and, as literary editor, with the *Commercial Advertiser*. Writings ranged from children's stories, written under pseudonym "Rafford Pyke," to personal and critical essays.

PINKNEY, EDWARD COOTE (1802–1828), b. London. Son of William Pinkney, then United States Commissioner in England. After eight years in navy, admitted to Maryland bar. Edited *The Marylander*, 1827. Known for "Poems" (1825), praised by Poe.

POE, EDGAR ALLAN (1809–1849), b. Boston, son of actors. Father disappeared; mother died in Richmond, where Scotch tobacco merchant, John Allan, adopted him. Educated, Richmond and England, 1815–1820; in University of Virginia; compelled to leave in debt, 1826. Ran away to Boston, published "Tamerlane and Other Poems," "by a Bostonian"; entered army under assumed name. At Mrs. Allan's death, 1829, Allan helped him secure appointment to West Point; expelled, 1831. Taken in by aunt, Mrs. Clemm, Baltimore, whose daughter, Virginia, fourteen, he married, 1836. Published stories, 1832; prize-winning "MS. Found in a Bottle," 1833, led to editorship of the *Southern Literary Messenger*, 1835. Erratic conduct led to dismissal, 1837, as, again, in Philadelphia from *Burton's* and from *Graham's*, for each of which he had multiplied circulation. After 1844 eked out existence by journalistic work in New York. Projected several magazines of his own; for a time controlled the *Broadway Journal*. "The Raven" (1845) was a success; "The Literati," published in *Godey's Lady's Book*, 1846, attracted attention. Death of his wife (1847) threw him into melancholy and a succession of love affairs. Died in Baltimore, 1849.

QUICK, (JOHN) HERBERT (1861–1925), b. Iowa. Educated, country schools. Taught and studied law, 1882–1890. Practiced in Sioux City, 1890–1908. Edited *Farm and Fireside*, 1909–1916. Mayor, Sioux City, 1898–1900. Best writing done after 1920 in novels and autobiography, all dealing with early farming life in Iowa.

RIPLEY, GEORGE (1802–1880), b. Greenfield, Massachusetts. Graduated from Harvard, 1823; studied for ministry; ordained, 1826. Active in Transcendental group. One of defenders of Emerson against Andrews

Norton ("The Newest Form of Infidelity") after the Divinity School Address, 1838. Edited anthology, "Specimens of Foreign Standard Literature" (14 vols.), 1838–1842. Left pulpit, 1841; prime mover in Brook Farm undertaking. Settled in New York City, 1848, as staff writer for Horace Greeley's *Tribune*. Joint editor with C. A. Dana of "Appleton's New American Cyclopedia," 1857–1863.

ROBINSON, EDWIN ARLINGTON (1869–1935), b. Head Tide, Maine. School at Gardiner, Maine, the "Tilbury" of his poems. At Harvard, 1891–1893. To New York in 1897, working miscellaneously until he attracted the attention of Theodore Roosevelt, who secured him a post in the customs service. From 1911 member of Peterboro colony, New Hampshire. Pulitzer prize for "Collected Poems" (1922), "The Man who Died Twice" (1925), "Tristram" (1927).

ROGERS, ROBERT (1731–1795), b. Methuen, Massachusetts. Soldier in French and Indian War, 1756–1763. Governor of Mackinaw, 1766. From then to the end of his life involved in a succession of unsavory experiences in English military service. Probable author of "Ponteach, or the Savages of America," 1766, an indictment of English tactics with the Indians.

RÖLVAAG, OLE EDVART (1876–1931), b. Helgeland, Norway, of seafaring family. At twenty came to United States to work on uncle's farm in South Dakota. Educated, Augustana College, Iowa, 1899–1902; St. Olaf's College, Minnesota, 1902–1905; University of Oslo, Norway, 1905–1906. Professor at St. Olaf's from 1906 till his death, teaching Norwegian literature. American citizen, 1908. Secretary and president, Norwegian-American Historical Association. Wrote always in Norwegian, assisting in translation. First wide success with "Giants in the Earth," 1924; translated, 1927.

ROWSON, (MRS.) SUSANNA (1762–1824), b. England. Lived as child in Massachusetts until her father, a loyalist, was deported to England, 1778. Won reputation there as novelist, with "Charlotte," 1790. Married in London; husband bankrupted; returned as actress to America (1793), appearing often in her own plays, "The Volunteers" and "Americans in England." Conducted school for girls in Boston to 1822.

SANDBURG, CARL (1878–   ), b. Galesburg, Illinois, of Swedish immigrant parentage. Worked as boy in several Middle Western cities. Eight months in Puerto Rico, Spanish-American War, 1898. Worked way through Lombard College, Galesburg, 1898–1902. First writing in newspaper work in Milwaukee. Organizer for Socialist-Democrat party in Wisconsin and secretary to mayor of Milwaukee. After several newspaper connections in Chicago, joined staff of *Daily News*, which he served in various capacities from 1916 to 1933. Levinson prize for poetry, 1914. Shared prize of Poetry Society of America, 1918 and 1921. Phi Beta Kappa poet, Harvard, 1928. Lincoln student and biographer. Widely known as lecturer, reader, and ballad singer; compiler of "American Song-Bag."

SEWALL, SAMUEL (1652–1730), b. Hampshire, England. Emigrated with parents to Newbury, Massachusetts. Harvard, A.B., 1671; A.M., 1674. Ordained minister; left pulpit to establish printing press, 1677. In Court of Assistants, 1684; to England on business, 1688; as special commissioner acted in witchcraft cases at Salem; later repented share in the proceedings and imposed a public penance upon himself. Chief justice of Massachusetts, 1718. "Diary" kept from 1674 to 1729; pamphlet against slavery, "The Selling of Joseph," 1700.

SHAW, HENRY WHEELER (1818–1885), b. Lanesborough, Massachusetts. Entered Hamilton College; left and went West, working way on steamboats and farms and as auctioneer. Settled at Poughkeepsie, New York, 1858. Attracted attention by "An Essa on the Muel, bi Josh Billings," 1860. Published burlesque "Farmer's Allminax," 1870–1880; in second year sold 127,000 copies. Began lecturing, 1863. Contributed to the *New York Weekly*, and to *The Century* under name "Uncle Esek."

SHERMAN, STUART PRATT (1881–1926), b. Anita, Iowa, of New England stock. Williams College, A.B., 1903; Harvard, Ph.D., 1906. Taught at Northwestern University, 1906–1907, and University of Illinois, 1907–1924. Edited literary supplement of the *New York Herald Tribune*, 1924–1926. Essays and reviews largely printed in magazines and collected for book publication. Notable for vigorous championship of traditional standards and lapse in last years to less militant position.

SILL, EDWARD ROWLAND (1841–1887), b. Windsor, Connecticut, of Puritan ancestry. Graduated from Yale, 1861. Earned living variously in California, 1861–1865. Entered and left Harvard Divinity School. Taught school Ohio and California, 1869–1874; in English department of University of California, 1874–1882. Returned to Ohio for remaining four years. Privately printed a few volumes; published others. Contributor to *The Atlantic* in Aldrich's editorship, under pseudonym "Andrew Hedbrook."

SIMMS, WILLIAM GILMORE (1806–1870), b. Charleston, South Carolina; son of Irish merchant. Scant education; apprenticed to druggist; made trip to Mississippi, 1824. Admitted to bar, 1827; published volume of poems. Edited the *Charleston City Gazette*, 1828–1833. Began novel-writing, 1833. Second marriage (1836) brought possession of large plantation. In state legislature, 1844–1846. Edited the *Southern Quarterly Review*. Leader of group who founded *Russell's Magazine*, 1857–1860. Supported Southern cause; contributed to "Pro-Slavery Argument." House burned by Sherman, 1865; fortune lost; exhausted self in attempt to rehabilitate estate.

SINCLAIR, UPTON (1878–   ), b. Baltimore, of Southern family with navy connections. Earned way, writing, through College of City of New York. Graduated, 1897. With Helicon Home colony in New Jersey. Founder of the Intercollegiate Socialist Society and of the American Civil Liberties Union, California. Prolific in plays, novels, and documented protests against social, economic, and political abuses. Has been translated in thirty-four countries, led by Russia, Germany, and Japan. Democratic nominee for governor of California, 1934.

SMITH, JOHN (1579(80)–1631), b. Willoughby, Lincolnshire. Numerous adventures as soldier of fortune in France, the Low Countries, Italy, Austria. Said to have been a slave in Turkey. Returned to England, 1605; entered service of London Company. Leader of settlement at Jamestown, 1607; conducted trading expeditions with Indians; explored Chesapeake Bay. President of the Council, 1608; authority supreme in the colony, 1609, put on self-supporting basis in spite of opposition of company officials and enmity of settlers. Displaced by reorganization of company, 1610. Entered service of Sir Ferdinando Gorges. Explored New England coast, 1614; attempted settlements there, 1615, 1617. Offer to pilot *Mayflower* in 1619 rejected. Last years engaged in production of pamphlets and maps to excite colonization in America.

SMITH, SEBA (1792–1868), b. Buckfield, Maine. Graduated from Bowdoin College, 1818. Edited papers in Portland, Maine, to one of which, the *Daily Courier*, he first contributed his letters from "Major Jack Downing." Two volumes of these published in 1833. The character was borrowed by others. Five other volumes followed in the next thirty years. One of the earliest to use Yankee humor in political satire.

STANSBURY, JOSEPH (1750?–1809), b. England. Came to Philadelphia, 1767, entering business. Loyalist; commissioner of city watch during British occupation; wrote gay Tory verse. "Reconstructed" after war.

STEDMAN, EDMUND CLARENCE (1833–1908), b. Hartford, Connecticut. At Yale; dropped, but later given A.B. and A.M., 1871; LL.D., 1895. Edited the Norwich (Connecticut) *Tribune*, 1852; Winsted *Herald*, 1853–1855. Moved to New York; connected with *Tribune*; war correspondent for *World*, 1861–1863. Private secretary to Attorney General Bates in Washington. Interested in financing Union Pacific Railroad. On New York Stock Exchange, 1865–1900, of which he edited a history, 1905. Wrote poems, essays, criticism. Editor, "Library of American Literature," with E. M. Hutchinson, 1888–1889.

STODDARD, RICHARD HENRY (1825–1903), b. Hingham, Massachusetts; moved to New York, 1835. Common-school education; wide reading; worked in iron foundry. First volume of poems, "Footprints," 1849. Through Hawthorne secured position in New York custom house, 1853–1870; literary editor, *New York World*, 1860–1870; edited *The Aldine*, 1869–1874. Private secretary to George B. McClellan in dock department, 1870–1873. Literary editor, *Mail and Express*, 1880–1893.

STOWE, HARRIET BEECHER (1811–1896), b. Litchfield, Connecticut, seventh child of Lyman Beecher; sister of Henry Ward Beecher. Educated, Litchfield and Hartford, where she became assistant in her sister Catherine's school. Moved to Cincinnati when father became president of Lane Theological Seminary, 1832. Married Professor Calvin Stowe, 1836. Moved to Maine and Massachusetts when Stowe went to professorships at Bowdoin College and Andover Theological Seminary. Lived for a time in Florida. Last years in Hartford. Wrote steadily from early married life. "Minister's Wooing," serial in first year of *The Atlantic*; regular contributor also to *The Independent* and the *Christian Union*. Fame and fortune rested on "Uncle Tom's Cabin," published serially in the *National Era*, then reaching fabulous circulation in book form.

TARKINGTON, (NEWTON) BOOTH (1869–   ), b. Indianapolis. Educated at Phillips Exeter Academy, Purdue University (Indiana), and Princeton, 1893. Planned to paint, but acceptance of story turned him to writing. Indiana legislature, 1902–1903. Pulitzer prize for fiction: for "The Magnificent Ambersons," 1919; "Alice Adams," 1922. Creator of Penrod, the adolescent, a name used by Mark Twain. Several successful plays, original or dramatized from his novels.

TAYLOR, (JAMES) BAYARD (1825–1878), b. Pennsylvania, of English-German ancestry. Ran away from apprenticeship to printer, roaming two years through Europe; this the origin of his travel articles, books, and lectures. Joined staff of *New York Tribune,* 1847, going as correspondent to California with the gold rush. In Europe, 1851–1853; lectured for short time on German literature, Cornell University. Secretary of American Legation to Russia, 1862–1863; minister to Germany, 1877–1878. In addition to travels, wrote many volumes of verse, four novels, and a notable translation of Goethe's "Faust."

THOMAS, AUGUSTUS (1859–1934), b. St. Louis. Educated, public schools. Page in Forty-first Congress; six years a railroad employee; illustrator and special writer for St. Louis, Kansas City, and New York papers; edited the Kansas City *Mirror,* 1889. Member of American Academy of Arts and Letters; president, 1914–1916; president of Society of American Dramatists, 1906–1911. For many years held administrative position for Frohman Theater interests. Plays number nearly three dozen.

THOMPSON, WILLIAM TAPPAN (1812–1882), b. Ravenna, Ohio. Various journalistic adventures in Philadelphia, in Florida, in Atlanta (Georgia). Associated with Longstreet in editing the *States' Rights Sentinel*; volunteer against Seminoles, 1835–1836. Various newspaper connections; founded *Morning News,* 1850, in Savannah. Served in Confederate Army. Fame as humorist, from "Major Jones Letters" to "The Miscellany." Associated with Park Benjamin in publishing, Baltimore. Several plays.

THOREAU, HENRY DAVID (1817–1862), b. Concord, Massachusetts, of French and Scotch extraction; son of pencil maker. Graduated from Harvard, 1837; taught school; private tutor at Staten Island, New York. Abandoned teaching; returned to Concord; lived by making pencils, surveying, carpentering, or day labor. Contributed to *The Dial*; inmate of Emerson's home at various times; resided in a hut on the shore of Walden Pond, 1845–1847. Abolitionist; hailed John Brown as martyr. Two books published in lifetime supplemented to twenty by posthumous printing of his essays, poems, letters, and "Journal."

TIMROD, HENRY (1829–1867), b. Charleston, South Carolina. Studied at University of Georgia; studied law under James Petigru; became private tutor. Contributed to *Russell's Magazine* and the *Southern Literary Messenger.* War correspondent of the Charleston *Mercury*; moved to Columbia, South Carolina, 1864; edited the *South Carolinian.* Property destroyed in burning of the city; last years in ill-health and poverty. Member, Charleston literary coterie with Hayne and Simms.

TRUMBULL, JOHN (1750–1831), b. Watertown, Connecticut. Passed entrance examinations for Yale at age of seven; entered, 1763, graduated, 1767; remained as student and as tutor, 1771–1773. Contributed essay series, "The Meddler" to the *Boston Chronicle*, 1769–1770, "The Correspondent" to the *Connecticut Journal* and the *New Haven Post Boy*. Studied law in office of John Adams, 1773–1774; practiced in Hartford. First canto of "M'Fingal," 1776; this, divided into two, and two more cantos added, 1782. Center of "Hartford Wits"; contributed to "The Anarchiad." State's attorney, 1789; in Connecticut Assembly, 1792, 1800; judge of the superior court, 1801–1807, and of the court of errors, 1808–1819. In Detroit, Michigan, 1825–1831.

TUCKER, NATHANIEL BEVERLEY (1784–1851), b. Matoax, Virginia. Graduated from William and Mary College. Entered the law; practiced in Virginia to 1815. Removed to Missouri; judge in circuit court, 1815–1830; professor of law at William and Mary, 1834. "The Partisan Leader," published under pseudonym in 1836, purported to be historical novel of 1856, forecast Civil War; was suppressed; reissued in 1861 as "A Key to the Disunion Conspiracy."

TYLER, ROYALL (1757–1826), b. Boston. Graduated from Harvard, 1776; studied law under John Adams; aide to General Lincoln in Revolution and in Shays's rebellion. Visited New York, 1787; witnessed his first theatrical performance; wrote "The Contrast," produced by the "American Company" at the John Street Theater, April 16. Moved to Vermont, 1790; judge, 1794, chief justice of the state, 1800. Contributed light verse and literary criticism to Dennie's *Farmer's Museum* and the *Port Folio*. Author of novel, "The Algerine Captive."

WARD, ARTEMUS (Charles Farrar Browne) (1834–1867), b. Waterford, Maine. Compositor at thirteen; later occasional contributor to papers in Boston, Cincinnati, Toledo. Began "Artemus Ward" papers in the Cleveland *Plain Dealer*, 1858, which attracted attention in America and England. On staff of *Vanity Fair*, New York; began lecturing, 1861. First volume, "Artemus Ward, His Book" (1862), sold forty thousand copies. Triumphal tour of Pacific coast, 1863, where he met Samuel Clemens; in England, 1866.

WARD, NATHANIEL (1578–1652), b. Haverhill, Suffolk, son of curate; M.A. at Emmanuel College, Cambridge, 1603. Traveled on Continent; took orders, 1618. Exiled by Laud in 1633 for Puritan views; settled in Massachusetts at Agawam (Ipswich). Joined Cotton in framing first code of laws, the "Body of Liberties," 1641. Wrote the "Simple Cobler of Agawam," 1645; published in London, 1647, and went through four editions. Returned to England; preached before House of Commons against domination of the army. Retired to a living at Shenfield, Essex, 1648.

WARREN, MERCY OTIS (1728–1814), b. Barnstable, Massachusetts; sister of James Otis, wife of James Warren. Brilliant; intimate with Jefferson and John and Abigail Adams. Wrote plays and poems forwarding the Revolution and satirizing Tories; also two tragedies and a history of the Revolution, valuable because of her personal associations.

WESCOTT, GLENWAY (1901–), b. Kewaskum, Wisconsin, of pioneer stock. Educated in high schools of Wisconsin and University of Chicago, where, as president of the poetry club, he decided upon a literary career. Has lived abroad since 1923. His novel "Grandmothers" won the Harper Prize Novel Contest in 1927.

WHARTON, EDITH (NEWBOLD JONES) (1862–), b. New York City, of an old New York family. Traveled much as a child. Educated by tutors; learned French, German, and Italian abroad. After marriage to Edward Wharton, a Boston banker, lived much abroad. Began writing soon after marriage: some verse, but her most notable works are short stories and novels. Since 1906 has lived in France. For war work among craftswomen of France made a Chevalier of the Order of Leopold, and officer of the Legion of Honor. The first woman to be awarded the gold medal of the National Institute of Arts and Letters. Pulitzer prize for "The Age of Innocence," 1920. Her autobiography, "A Backward Glance," was published in 1934.

WHITMAN, WALT (1819–1892), b. Huntington, Long Island. Attended public school in Brooklyn and received experience and discipline in printing shops and school-teaching. Started and carried on a weekly paper in Huntington, 1839; worked variously as compositor and news writer till 1855, largely in and around New York. Took a leisurely trip through the middle states, 1847–1848, down the Ohio and Mississippi rivers to New Orleans, where he did some news-writing; back by way of the Great Lakes and Canada. To the front in 1862 to attend wounded brother; continued as hospital nurse till the end of the war. The strain of the work combined with septic poisoning to undermine his health permanently. Short time as clerk in the Department of the Interior; discharged as the "author of an indecent book." In 1873 a paralytic stroke made him an invalid for the nineteen remaining years of his life, spent almost in poverty in or near Camden, New Jersey.

WHITTIER, JOHN GREENLEAF (1807–1892), b. Haverhill, Massachusetts, of Quaker family. Worked on father's farm; supported self during two years at Haverhill Academy, making slippers, teaching school. Early talent for verse, stimulated by admiration for Robert Burns; contributed to William Lloyd Garrison's *Free Press*; edited the *American Manufacturer*, Boston, 1829; the *New England Review*, Hartford, Connecticut, 1830–1832. Returned to farm; wrote "Justice and Expediency," an antislavery pamphlet. Delegate to antislavery congress in Philadelphia, 1833; in Massachusetts legislature, 1835, 1836. Spokesman of abolitionist crusade; edited the *Pennsylvania Freeman*, Philadelphia, 1838–1840. Settled in Amesbury, Massachusetts, 1840. Contributed to various magazines. Celebrated as antislavery propagandist, 1833–1865; major reputation based on poems of New England, notably "Snow-Bound," 1866. In latter years rivaled Longfellow in popularity.

WIGGLESWORTH, MICHAEL (1631–1705), b. Yorkshire, England. Emigrated with family, 1638. Graduated from Harvard, 1651, where he was tutor, 1652–1654, 1697–1705. Pastor at Malden, 1656, to his death, also serving the town as physician. "Day of Doom" (1662) reached six editions by 1715.

WILLIAMS, ROGER (1607–1684), b. Wales; son of merchant tailor. Educated under patronage of Sir Edward Coke, Charterhouse, and Pembroke College, Cambridge, A.B., 1626. Refused preferment in Church of England. Migrated to Massachusetts, 1631; quarreled with authorities at Boston. Assistant pastor, Plymouth, 1631–1633. In Salem, 1633; questioned king's right to Indians' land; other heresies led to trial by General Court and banishment, 1635. Eluded arrest; fled, 1636, to Manton's Neck; founded Rhode Island on principle of almost complete toleration. Friend to the Indians; learned their language; acted as their counselor in wars. In England, 1643, to obtain charter for Providence, Newport, and Portsmouth; again, in 1652–1654; friendship with Cromwell, Milton. Governor, 1654–1657. Controversy with Cotton over religious toleration.

WILLIS, NATHANIEL PARKER (1806–1867), b. Portland, Maine. Phillips Andover Academy; graduated from Yale, 1827, where he was known as writer of religious verse. First poems in *Youth's Companion,* which his father edited. Edited annuals, *The Legendary* (1828), *The Token* (1829), for S. G. Goodrich. Founded the *American Monthly Magazine,* Boston, 1829; merged it with the New York *Mirror,* 1831. Traveled in Europe and Asia Minor, 1831–1836. Left the *Mirror,* 1839; edited various short-lived papers; again in Europe, 1839, 1845. Established the *Home Journal,* 1846. Most successful writer for periodicals of his time.

WINTHROP, JOHN (1587(8)–1649), b. Suffolk, of well-to-do family. At Cambridge, 1602–1605. Youth one of profound religious introspection. Justice of peace at ancestral manor of Groton; attorney in the Court of Ward and Liveries, 1623; at Inner Temple, 1628. Decided to remove with the Massachusetts Bay Company, 1629; chosen governor in October; led the migration and settlement at Boston, 1630. Governor until 1634; again, in 1637, when he defeated Vane and the Antinomian party. Henceforth the chief power in the colony. Began his "History" as a journal with the voyage in 1630 and continued it almost to his death.

WOOLMAN, JOHN (1720–1772), b. Northampton, New Jersey, of Quaker family. Itinerant preacher from 1746; preached and wrote against slavery as early as 1754; preached to the Indians on the Susquehanna, 1763. Died on a visit to England. "Journal" (1775), edited by Whittier in 1871.

INDEX

NOTE ON THE INDEX. In the effort to make the Index more than a bare topic-finding instrument the titles of the contributions to American literature have been subjected to a rough classification and listed alphabetically in groups. As a classification under only seven heads, in addition to NEWSPAPERS and PERIODICALS, must involve occasional arbitrary judgments, it seems best to state how the terms are used.

AUTOBIOGRAPHY includes also journals and diaries.

LITERARY CRITICISM includes works on the theory and works in the practice of literary criticism.

PHILOSOPHY, the loosest of the terms, is an omnium gatherum for prose exposition on the general theory of life, almost entirely non-philosophical in any technical sense.

PLAYS includes, in addition to all the orthodox forms, burlesques and spectacles.

POETRY perforce includes much verse which is far from poetry.

PROSE NARRATIVE includes fiction long and short, sketches, and some chronicles.

SOCIAL and POLITICAL CRITICISM includes prose exposition concerned with the theory or with the facts of political and social life.

These classifying terms are applied only to works in American literature. The few American titles which elude them, and all foreign literature, appear in the general alphabetical listing. It is the author's hope that there may be some rough bibliographical value for students in the indicated groupings.

PRINTED IN THE UNITED STATES OF AMERICA

Gramley Library
Salem College